How to Price

A Guide to Pricing Techniques and Yield Management

Over the past four decades, business and academic economists, operations researchers, marketing scientists, and consulting firms have increased their interest in and research on pricing and revenue management. This book attempts to introduce the reader to a wide variety of research results on pricing techniques in a unified, systematic way at varying levels of difficulty. The book contains a large number of exercises and solutions and therefore can serve as a main or supplementary course textbook, as well as a reference guide for pricing consultants, managers, industrial engineers, and writers of pricing software applications. Despite a moderate technical orientation, the book is accessible to readers with a limited knowledge in these fields as well as to readers who have had more training in economics. Most pricing models are first demonstrated by numerical and calculus-free examples and then extended for more technically oriented readers.

Oz Shy is a Research Professor at WZB – Social Science Research Center in Berlin, Germany, and a Professor of Economics at the University of Haifa, Israel. He received a BA degree from the Hebrew University of Jerusalem and a PhD from the University of Minnesota. His previous books are *Industrial Organization: Theory and Applications* (1996) and *The Economics of Network Industries* (Cambridge University Press, 2001). Professor Shy has published more than 40 journal and book articles in the areas of industrial organization, network economics, and international trade, and he serves on the editorial boards of *International Journal of Industrial Organization, Journal of Economic Behavior & Organization*, and *Review of Network Economics*. He has taught at the State University of New York, Tel Aviv University, University of Michigan, Stockholm School of Economics, and Swedish School of Economics at Helsinki.

How to Price

A Guide to Pricing Techniques and Yield Management

Oz Shy

WZB – Social Science Research Center, Berlin, Germany
and
University of Haifa, Israel

CAMBRIDGE UNIVERSITY PRESS
Cambridge, New York, Melbourne, Madrid, Cape Town, Singapore, São Paulo, Delhi

Cambridge University Press
32 Avenue of the Americas, New York, NY 10013-2473, USA

www.cambridge.org
Information on this title: www.cambridge.org/9780521887595

First published 2008

Printed in the United States of America

A catalog record for this publication is available from the British Library.

Library of Congress Cataloging in Publication Data

Shy, Oz.
How to price: a guide to pricing techniques and yield management / Oz Shy.
    p. cm.
Includes bibliographical references and index.
ISBN 978-0-521-88759-5 (hardback). – ISBN 978-0-521-71564-5 (pbk.)
1. Pricing – Mathematical models.   I. Title.
HF5416.5.S549   2008
658.8′16–dc

ISBN   978-0-521-88759-5 hardback
ISBN   978-0-521-71564-5 paperback

For Sarah, Daniel, and Tianlai

Contents

Preface   xi

1   Introduction to Pricing Techniques   1
   1.1   Services, Booking Systems, and Consumer Value   2
   1.2   Overview of Pricing Techniques   5
   1.3   Revenue Management and Profit Maximization   9
   1.4   The Role Played by Capacity   10
   1.5   YM, Consumer Welfare, and Antitrust   12
   1.6   Pricing Techniques and the Use of Computers   13
   1.7   The Literature and Presentation Methods   14
   1.8   Notation and Symbols   14

2   Demand and Cost   19
   2.1   Demand Theory and Interpretations   20
   2.2   Discrete Demand Functions   24
   2.3   Linear Demand Functions   26
   2.4   Constant-elasticity Demand Functions   30
   2.5   Aggregating Demand Functions   34
   2.6   Demand and Network Effects   39
   2.7   Demand for Substitutes and Complements   42
   2.8   Consumer Surplus   45
   2.9   Cost of Production   52
   2.10   Exercises   56

3   Basic Pricing Techniques   59
   3.1   Single-market Pricing   60
   3.2   Multiple Markets without Price Discrimination   67
   3.3   Multiple Markets with Price Discrimination   79
   3.4   Pricing under Competition   89
   3.5   Commonly Practiced Pricing Methods   99
   3.6   Regulated Public Utility   104
   3.7   Exercises   110

4   Bundling and Tying   115
4.1   Bundling   117
4.2   Tying   131
4.3   Exercises   145

5   Multipart Tariff   151
5.1   Two-part Tariff with One Type of Consumer   152
5.2   Two-part Tariff with Multiple Consumer Types   159
5.3   Menu of Two-part Tariffs   165
5.4   Multipart Tariff   171
5.5   Regulated Public Utility   176
5.6   Exercises   178

6   Peak-load Pricing   181
6.1   Seasons, Cycles, and Service-cost Definitions   183
6.2   Two Seasons: Fixed-peak Case   185
6.3   Two Seasons: Shifting-peak Case   190
6.4   General Computer Algorithm for Two Seasons   194
6.5   Multi-season Pricing   194
6.6   Season-interdependent Demand Functions   201
6.7   Regulated Public Utility   205
6.8   Demand, Cost, and the Lengths of Seasons   214
6.9   Exercises   223

7   Advance Booking   227
7.1   Two Booking Periods with Two Service Classes   232
7.2   Multiple Periods with Two Service Classes   238
7.3   Multiple Booking Periods and Service Classes   245
7.4   Dynamic Booking with Marginal Operating Cost   248
7.5   Network-based Dynamic Advance Booking   250
7.6   Fixed Class Allocations   254
7.7   Nested Class Allocations   258
7.8   Exercises   262

8   Refund Strategies   265
8.1   Basic Definitions   267
8.2   Consumers, Preferences, and Seller's Profit   270
8.3   Refund Policy under an Exogenously Given Price   274
8.4   Simultaneous Price and Refund Policy Decisions   280
8.5   Multiple Price and Refund Packages   288
8.6   Refund Policy under Moral Hazard   290
8.7   Integrating Refunds within Advance Booking   293
8.8   Exercises   294

9   Overbooking   297
   9.1   Basic Definitions   299
   9.2   Profit-maximizing Overbooking   305
   9.3   Overbooking of Groups   313
   9.4   Exercises   322

10   Quality, Loyalty, Auctions, and Advertising   325
   10.1   Quality Differentiation and Classes   326
   10.2   Damaged Goods   332
   10.3   More on Pricing under Competition   335
   10.4   Auctions   343
   10.5   Advertising Expenditure   352
   10.6   Exercises   355

11   Tariff-choice Biases and Warranties   359
   11.1   Flat-rate Biases   360
   11.2   Choice in Context and Extremeness Aversion   362
   11.3   Other Consumer Choice Biases   366
   11.4   Warranties   369
   11.5   Exercises   375

12   Instructor and Solution Manual   377
   12.1   To the Reader   377
   12.2   Manual for Chapter 2: Demand and Cost   378
   12.3   Manual for Chapter 3: Basic Pricing Techniques   382
   12.4   Manual for Chapter 4: Bundling and Tying   387
   12.5   Manual for Chapter 5: Multipart Tariff   391
   12.6   Manual for Chapter 6: Peak-load Pricing   395
   12.7   Manual for Chapter 7: Advance Booking   402
   12.8   Manual for Chapter 8: Refund Strategies   406
   12.9   Manual for Chapter 9: Overbooking   411
   12.10   Manual for Chapter 10: Quality, Loyalty, Auctions, and
         Advertising   414
   12.11   Manual for Chapter 11: Tariff-choice Biases and Warranties   417

References   421

Index   431

Preface

What This Book Will NOT Teach You

The key to successful profit-maximizing pricing is *knowing your potential customers*. If a firm does not manage to learn the characteristics of all its potential customer types, such as consumers' willingness to pay, the firm will not be able to properly price its products and services.

This book will *not* teach you how to identify the characteristics of your consumers. Although several econometric techniques for identifying these characteristics are described in Chapter 2, a comprehensive analysis of this subject is beyond the scope of this book. The two main reasons for not attempting to include these techniques in this book are (a) consumers' preferences in general, and willingness to pay in particular, vary all the time when new competing products, services, and brands are introduced to the market, which means that (b) the most efficient way of learning about customers is by *trial and error*, or simply experimenting with different tariffs while recording how consumers respond. That is, as this book shows, successful pricing techniques should not only be profitable, they should also induce consumers to *reveal* their characteristics.

What This Book Attempts to Teach You

Revenue and profit are affected by a wide variety of observable and unobservable parameters. Therefore, even if various pricing techniques are well chosen and properly used, there is still no guarantee that the firm will be profitable. However, despite the high degree of uncertainty, if one takes the approach that pricing with some reasoning cannot be inferior (profitwise) to implementing arbitrary pricing strategies, then it is hoped this book will provide you with the right intuition and with a wide variety of tools under which sellers can enhance their profits. During the past 40 years, business and academic economists, operations researchers, marketing scientists, and consulting firms have increased their interest in and research on pricing and revenue management. This book attempts to introduce the reader to a wide variety of their research results in a unified systemic way, but at varying levels of difficulty. Traditionally, the different disciplines manifested different views on pricing techniques; however, recently the attitudes toward pricing in these disciplines have exhibited a sharp convergence that recognizes price discrimination and market segmentation as an important part of the design of profitable pricing techniques. It is hoped that the present book contributes to this convergence process.

Motivation for Writing This Book

Yield and revenue management (or profit management, as it should be called) is commonly taught in business schools, where very often teachers simply combine it with a marketing course. Revenue management is also taught in special courses and seminars for employees of the airline and hotel industries. Most of these special courses tend to be nontechnical. All this means that the analytical work on yield management, which was written mainly by scientists in the field of operations research, cannot be diffused to the general audience. Such a diffusion is not always needed, however, given that large companies tend to rely on software packages and automated reservation systems.

On the other side of the campus, the economics profession has managed over the years to develop a large number of theories on profitable pricing techniques. Most of these techniques are based on price discrimination. Other theories come from extensive research conducted by economists during the 1970s and 1980s on optimal regulation and deregulation of public utilities. Often, the economics approach goes somewhat further than the operations research approach by considering the strategic response of rival firms competing in the same market.

The purpose of this book is to combine the relevant theories from economics (mainly from microeconomics, industrial organization, and regulation) with some operations research, and to make it accessible to students and practitioners who have limited knowledge in these fields. On the other hand, readers who have had more training in economics will easily find more advanced material. Knowledge of calculus is not needed for the major part of this book, because calculus techniques are not very useful for handling discrete data, which a computer can manipulate. However, more mathematically trained readers should be able to find various topics and extensions that are based on calculus. To summarize, this book attempts to introduce the formal analysis of revenue management and pricing techniques by bridging the knowledge gained from economic theory and operations research. This book is also designed as a reference guide for pricing consultants and managers as well as computer programmers who are equipped with the appropriate technical knowledge.

Computer Applications

Professional price practitioners may want to simulate the studied pricing techniques on a computer to ultimately bring these techniques to practical use. For this reason, I have attempted to sketch some algorithms according to which programmers can write simple macros. These macros can be easily written using popular spreadsheet software and thus do not always require sophisticated programming. Of course, some readers may feel more comfortable writing in formal programming languages. The reader is invited to visit the Web site `www.how-to-price.com` to observe how these short macros can be implemented on the Web using the JavaScript language. Clearly, limited space does not allow me to write complete algorithms. But I hope that the logic behind the suggested algorithms would benefit the potential programmer by serving as a benchmark for more sophisticated pricing software. For convenience, the algorithms in this book are written to resemble algorithms in Pascal (a computer programming language designed in 1970 for teaching students structured programming).

To the Instructor

The instructor will find sufficient material to fill at least a one-semester course, if not an entire year. This book uses lots of calculus-free models, so it can be used without calculus if needed. An instructor's manual is provided in Chapter 12, where I also provide abbreviated solutions for all exercises. I urge the instructor to read this manual before writing the course syllabus because for each chapter, I provide some suggestions regarding which topics should suit students with different backgrounds.

Basically, the book can be divided into three parts. Although topics from all chapters are interrelated, Chapters 2 through 5 may be classified as pricing techniques (mostly for static and stationary markets). Chapters 6 through 9 roughly fall under the category of yield and revenue management as they analyze dynamic markets under capacity constraints. Chapters 10 and 11 offer a variety of topics related to both pricing and revenue management.

Each chapter ends with several exercises. These exercises attempt to motivate students to understand and memorize the basic definitions associated with the various theories developed in that chapter. The solution to all these exercises are provided in Chapter 12. Providing all the solutions to students has its pros and cons. However, I have found that students who go over these solutions perform much better on the exams than do students who are not exposed to the solutions. As a result, instead of placing the solution manual on the Internet (as I have done for my other books), I have integrated the solutions into the book itself.

This book is clearly on the technical side. However, most topics in this book are covered at multiple levels of difficulty. Hence, numerical examples should appeal to the less technical reader, whereas the general formulations and computer algorithms should appeal to more technical readers and researchers. Topics from this book can be arranged as a one-semester course for advanced undergraduate and graduate students in economics, as well as for those in some advanced MBA programs that go beyond the purely descriptive case-based method. Students of industrial engineering should also be able to grasp most of the material.

Errors, Typos, and Errata Files

My experience with my first two books (Shy 1996, 2001) has been that it is nearly impossible to publish a completely error-free book. Writing a book very much resembles writing a large piece of software because literally all software packages contain some bugs that the author could not predict. In addition, 80% of the time is devoted to debugging the software after the basic code has been written. I will therefore make an effort to publish all errors known to me on my Web site: www.ozshy.com.

Typesetting and Acknowledgments

This book was typeset by the author using the LaTeX 2_ε document preparation software developed by Leslie Lamport (a special version of Donald Knuth's TeX program) and modified by the LaTeX3 Project Team. For most parts, I used MikTeX, developed by Christian Schenk, as the main compiler.

Staffan Ringbom, Swedish School of Economics at Helsinki and HECER, has offered many suggestions, ideas, and comments that greatly improved the exposition and the content of this book. In addition, Staffan was the first to teach this book in a university environment and to collect some comments directly from students. I also would like to thank the Social Science Research Center Berlin (WZB) for providing me with the best possible research environment, which enabled me to complete this book in only two years.

During the preparation of the manuscript, I was very fortunate to work with Scott Parris of Cambridge University Press, to whom I owe many thanks for managing the project in the most efficient way. Scott has been fond of this project for several years, and his interest in this topic encouraged me to go ahead and write this book. Finally, I thank Barbara Walthall of Aptara, Inc. and the entire Cambridge University Press team for the fast production of this book.

Berlin, Germany (May 2007)
www.ozshy.com

Chapter 1
Introduction to Pricing Techniques

1.1   **Services, Booking Systems, and Consumer Value**   2

    1.1.1   Service definitions

    1.1.2   Dynamic reservation systems

    1.1.3   Consumer value

1.2   **Overview of Pricing Techniques**   5

    1.2.1   Why is price discrimination needed?

    1.2.2   Classifications of market segmentation

    1.2.3   Classifications of price discrimination

1.3   **Revenue Management and Profit Maximization**   9

1.4   **The Role Played by Capacity**   10

    1.4.1   Price-based YM under capacity constraints

    1.4.2   Quantity-based YM versus price-based YM

1.5   **YM, Consumer Welfare, and Antitrust**   12

1.6   **Pricing Techniques and the Use of Computers**   13

1.7   **The Literature and Presentation Methods**   14

1.8   **Notation and Symbols**   14

This book focuses on pricing techniques that enable firms to enhance their profits. This book, however, cannot provide a complete recipe for success in marketing a certain product as this type of recipe, if it existed, would depend on a very large number of factors that cannot be analyzed in a single book. However, what this book does offer is a wide variety of pricing methods by which firms can enhance their revenue and profit. Such pricing strategies constitute part of the field called *yield management*. As explained and discussed in Section 1.3, throughout this book we will be using the term *yield management* (YM) to mean profit management and profit maximization, as opposed to the more commonly used term *revenue management* (RM).

1.1   Services, Booking Systems, and Consumer Value

Before we discuss pricing techniques, we wish to characterize the "output" that firms would like to sell. Therefore, Subsection 1.1.1 defines and characterizes the type of services and goods for which YM turns out to be most useful as a profit-enhancing set of tools. Clearly, this book emphasizes services that constitute around 70% of the gross domestic product of a modern economy. Subsection 1.1.2 identifies dynamic industry characteristics that make YM pricing techniques highly profitable. These characteristics highlight the role of the timing under which the potential consumers approach the sellers for the purpose of booking and purchasing the services sellers provide. Subsection 1.1.3 discusses the difficulty in determining consumer value and willingness to pay for services and products.

1.1.1   Service definitions

YM pricing techniques will not enhance the profit of *every* seller of goods and services. YM pricing techniques are particularly profitable for selling services, for the following reasons:

- *Nonstorability*: Services are time dependent and are therefore nonstorable. This feature is essential as otherwise service providers could transfer unused capacity from one service date to another. For example, airline companies cannot transfer unsold seats from one aircraft to another. Hotel managers cannot "save" vacant rooms for future sales.

- *Advance purchase/booking*: Time of purchase need not be the same as the service delivery time. In this book we demonstrate how reservation systems can be designed to enhance profits from the utilization of a given capacity level. For example, we show how airline companies can exploit consumer heterogeneity with respect to their ability to commit to buying services.

- *No-shows and cancellations*: Consumers who book in advance may not show up and may even cancel their reservation. Service providers should be able to segment the market according to how much refund (if any) is given upon no-shows.

- *Service classes*: The service can be provided in different quality classes. Market segmentation is profitable whenever the difference in price between, say, first and second class exceeds the difference in marginal costs.

The first item on the list is essential for the practice of YM to be profitable. The second item is not essential but definitely helps to generate extra revenue from segmenting the market according to the time reservations are made. The third item on the list also applies to physical products (as opposed to services) because sellers often practice refund policies for goods in the form of monetary refunds and product replacements.

1.1.2　Dynamic reservation systems

As it turns out, the procedure under which consumers buy or reserve a service can be viewed as part of the service itself. Moreover, another characteristic of the type of many of the services analyzed in this book is that consumers make their reservations at different time periods. More precisely, some consumers reserve the service long before the service is scheduled to be delivered. Others make last-minute reservations.

　In the absence of full refunds on purchased services, an early reservation reflects a commitment on the part of the consumer. Service providers can exploit different levels of willingness to commit by offering discounts to those consumers who are willing to make an early commitment, and charge higher prices for a last-minute booking.

　The airline industry was perhaps the first industry to fully computerize reservation systems. It was also the first to systematically discriminate in price according to when bookings are made. During the late 1980s, these computerized reservation systems (CRS) were perfected and became fully dynamic so that capacity allocations could be revised according to which types of reservations were already made in addition to which reservation types would be expected to emerge before the service delivery time.

　This discussion and the analysis provided in this book should help us understand the following observed phenomena, for example:

(a) Why travelers sitting in the same economy class on the same flight pay different airfares. Why people who stay at identical hotel room sizes end up paying different prices.

(b) Why capacity underutilization is often observed, such as empty seats on an aircraft and vacant hotel rooms.

Roughly speaking, the answer to (a) is that profit is enhanced when passengers and consumers pay near their maximum willingness to pay. Therefore, as long as consumers are heterogeneous with respect to their willingness to pay, proper use of YM always results in having people paying different prices for what appears to be an identical service. This is implemented via market segmentation, discussed in Subsection 1.2.2.

　The answer to (b) is that because service providers seek to maximize profit, it may become profitable not to sell the entire capacity but to leave some capacity in case consumers with high willingness to pay show up at the last minute. If they don't, then sellers are left with unused capacity. However, the reader may be wondering at this point whether profit is indeed maximized and may be asking why service providers do not at the last minute sell unused capacity at low prices, thereby avoiding empty seats and vacant rooms. The answer is simple. If consumers observe that a certain service provider sells discounted tickets at the last minute, they may be deterred from making early reservations. Thus, service providers may suffer from a bad reputation if they often practice last-minute discounts. This is known as the *sellers' commitment problem*. That is, in the short run, service providers may find it profitable to sell last-minute unbooked capacity at a lower price just to fill up the entire capacity. However, long-run considerations, such as reputation effect, prevent such practices.

1.1.3   Consumer value

The main point that this book attempts to stress is that sellers earn much higher profit if they set prices according to consumer value as opposed to basing all pricing decisions on unit cost only.   It is not rare to hear managers state that their profits are generated by charging consumers a certain fixed markup above unit cost. In most cases, such cost-based pricing techniques fail to extract a large part of what consumers are actually willing to pay.

In view of this discussion, the "conflict" between buyers and sellers, particularly if the two parties allow bargaining to take place, is manifested in the following two rules:

Rule for sellers: Make an effort to set the price according to buyers' value and not according to cost.

Rule for buyers: Bargain, if you can, for prices closer to marginal cost.

Note that the rule for sellers becomes essential for services produced at near-zero marginal costs, such as those provided on the Internet.

With a few exceptions, throughout this book it is assumed that sellers know the consumers' value and willingness to pay for the services and products they sell. The firms may not know the exact valuation of a specific consumer, but it is assumed that they know the distribution of the willingness to pay among different consumer groups. Clearly, firms should exert a lot of effort to unveil these valuations. For demand functions, the next chapter shows how this can be done by running regressions on data on past sales collected from the market. However, because these data are not always available, firms may resort to market surveys. Market surveys are less reliable because consumers don't always understand the question they are asked, and even if they do, they may understate their willingness to pay.

In cases in which the seller faces competition from other firms selling similar products and services, consumers may base their willingness to pay on the prices charged by the competing firms, that is, by placing a reference value for the product or service. In this situation, the seller must carefully study and compare the features of products and services offered by his or her competitors with the features of the product or service he or she offers. In fact, as often argued in this book, the seller should attempt to differentiate his or her brand from competing brands, by adding more features, including his or her services. Clearly, a lack of features relative to competing brands would necessitate a price reduction. After translating the observed differences between brands into their monetary equivalent, a seller should determine consumer value by

Value of the brand = Reference value

+ "Positive" differentiation values − "Negative" differentiation values.

The above formula relies on the assumption that all consumers agree on the pluses and minuses of each brand, which need not always be the case − for example, in markets where the brands are horizontally differentiated (as opposed to vertically differentiated).

Finally, there are other factors that affect consumers' willingness to pay for a certain brand, including:

Switching costs: If the seller is an established firm with a large number of returning customers, the seller can add to the price the cost consumers would pay to switch to a competing brand. If the seller is a new entrant, the seller may want to reduce the price to subsidize consumer switching costs; see the analysis in Section 3.4.

Essential input: Sellers can augment the price in cases in which the product/service serves as an essential input to goods and services produced by buyers. Some economists refer to this type of action as the "holdup problem."

Location costs: When reference prices are used, the cost of shipping or the location of the service should be reflected in the price, or shared by the parties.

1.2   Overview of Pricing Techniques

YM pricing techniques are not cost based. On the contrary, the key to successful YM is to make different consumers pay different prices for what seem to be identical services. The key to profit-enhancing pricing plans is the ability to engage in price discrimination via what economists call market segmentation. *Price discrimination* prevails if different (groups of) consumers pay different prices for what appears to be the same or a similar service or good. *Market segmentation* prevails whenever firms manage to divide the market into subgroups of consumers in which consumers belonging to different groups end up paying different prices.

1.2.1   Why is price discrimination needed?

An inexperienced reader may wonder why price discrimination is so important and ask why a strategy whereby all consumers are charged the same price is generally not profit maximizing? The answer to this question is that the practice of price discrimination enables service providers to enlarge their customer base and to create new markets. Consider the following example taken from a market for classical orchestra performances. Table 1.1 displays the willingness to pay by students and nonstudents. Suppose that each potential consumer considers buying at most one

	Students	Nonstudents
Max. Price	$5	$10
Number	200	300

Table 1.1: Maximum willingness to pay by students and nonstudents

ticket for a specific concert. As Table 1.1 indicates, each student will not pay more than $5 for a ticket, whereas a nonstudent will not pay more than $10.

First suppose that the concert hall is restricted to offering all tickets at the same price to all consumers. Then, a profit-maximizing single price can be set to a high level of $10, thereby serving nonstudents only. Alternatively, the provider can set a low price of $5, in which case both consumer groups will buy tickets. Ignoring costs, a high price would generate a revenue of $10 \times 300 = \$3000$, whereas a low price would generate a revenue of $5 \times (200 + 300) = \$2500$. Clearly, in this example the concert hall would set the price equal to $10 per ticket and sell only to nonstudents.

Suppose now that the concert hall announces that all consumers who show a valid student ID are entitled to a $5 discount from the price printed on the ticket. Under this policy, nonstudents pay the full price of $10, whereas students end up paying $5 for a ticket. The total revenue is given by $10 \times 300 + \$5 \times 200 = \$4000$, which is greater than $3000, which is the maximal revenue generated by a single uniform pricing strategy.

Three major conclusions can be drawn from this simple example. First, as noted in Varian (1989), the key step to revenue maximization is to avoid average pricing (in our example, prices between, but not equal to, $5 and $10). Second, setting more than one price will increase revenue only if market segmentation is feasible. To make market segmentation feasible, the service provider must possess the physical means for avoiding *arbitrage*. In the present example, it is the student ID card that prevents arbitrage because, if checked, it prevents students from selling discounted tickets to nonstudents. If student cards are not required, all students will buy some extra tickets and sell them to nonstudents for a profit at any price between $5.01 and $9.99. The third conclusion to be drawn from this example is that a *discount* does not mean lower revenue. Here, revenue increases precisely because student cards make it possible to lower the price for low-valuation consumers. In fact, later on we will analyze a similar strategy in which damaging a good (artificially lowering the quality of the service) can also enhance sales revenue.

1.2.2   Classifications of market segmentation

The above discussion was intended to convince the reader that market segmentation is necessary for the success of any price discrimination strategy. Broadly speaking, a market can be segmented along the following dimensions:

- *Consumer identifiable characteristics*: Charging different prices according to age group, profession, affiliation, location, type of delivery, and means of payment.

- *Quality*: Selling high-quality versions of the product/service to high-income buyers, and low-quality versions to low-income buyers. Segmentation of this type is possible only if the desire for higher quality increases with income. Note that firms often reduce quality (damaging the good/service) to keep differential pricing.

- *Bundling and tying*: Bundling refers to volume discounts. Segmentation of this type is possible only if consumers have different demand elasticity with respect to the quantity they purchase. Tying refers to selling packages of different goods at a single price. This market segmentation is profitable when consumer preferences for the different goods are negatively correlated.

- *Delivery time and delay*:   The seller segments the market according to consumers' willingness to pay for how fast the product or service is provided or delivered. This segmentation is feasible provided that those consumers who urgently need the product or service are willing to pay a higher amount than those who don't mind waiting.

- *Components*: Sellers can segment the market by mixing different components and providing a different number of components comprising the system to be used by the buyer. This strategy is commonly observed in the software industry, where a piece of software is sold in standard, pro, and professional versions.

- *Advance booking and refunds*: Sellers can segment the market based on consumers' willingness to commit to showing up at the time the service is scheduled to be delivered. Market segmentation is achieved by charging lower prices either to those who reserve in advance or to those who seek less refund on a no-show. Conversely, those who seek to obtain a full refund on a no-show are charged a higher price.

As this book will make clear, these classifications are not mutually exclusive. To the contrary, many types of the above-listed segmentations are often combined into a single pricing strategy. For example, book publishers tend to sell books with a hard cover during the first year of publication. Then, the same book is printed with a soft cover and sold at a lower price. Thus, consumers' willingness to pay for the first printing (fast delivery) seems to be correlated with the quality of the binding.

1.2.3 Classifications of price discrimination

Traditionally, academic economists (see, for example, Varian 1989) classify price discrimination according to first, second, and third degrees as follows:

- *First degree*: Consumers may be charged different prices so that the price of each unit they buy equals each consumer's maximum willingness to pay.

- *Second degree*: Each consumer faces the same price schedule, but the schedule involves different prices for different amounts of the good purchased. This practice is sometimes referred to as bundling (quantity discounts).

- *Third degree*: The seller segments the market into different consumer groups (with identifiable characteristics) that are charged different per-unit prices. This practice is referred to as market segmentation.

In this book, we will *not* be making much use of these classifications because the goal of this book is to characterize the proper pricing strategy to be able to segment the market, rather than just targeting a specific type of price discrimination taken from the above list. That is, from a practical point of view, the firm should be attempting to ensure that the chosen pricing techniques will indeed lead to the desired market segmentation, and that the resulting segmentation is the most profitable segmentation among all the feasible market segmentations. Moreover, the problem with the above classifications (according to first, second, and third degrees) is that these three classifications are *not* mutually exclusive. For example, second- and third-degree price discrimination can be implemented by, say, offering students different bundles from those offered to customers who cannot present student identification cards. For this reason, we deviate from the traditional classifications and follow the entry on price discrimination in Wikipedia, which suggests the following classifications based on a seller's ability to segment a market:

- *Complete discrimination*: Basically, the same as the first-degree price discrimination described above. Each consumer purchases where the marginal benefit equals the consumer-specific price.

- *Direct segmentation*: The seller segments the market into different consumer groups (with identifiable characteristics).

- *Indirect segmentation*: The seller offers variations of the product based on quality, quantity, delivery time, bundled service, and so on. The proper use of this technique leads to self-selection of consumers according to their nonidentifiable characteristics.

The reader should note that there is a fundamental difference between direct and indirect segmentation. Direct segmentation is clearly more profitable but requires the ability and knowledge to group consumers according to age, gender, geographic location, profession, prior consumption record, and so on. However, if this knowledge is not available (or illegal under nondiscrimination laws), sellers must resort to the less profitable indirect segmentation, which relies on selecting product and service variations instead of directly selecting different consumer groups. Finally, complete segmentation is clearly the most profitable; however, it is unlikely to become feasible (and more likely to be illegal) as it requires the seller to obtain full characterization of each consumer separately.

1.3 Revenue Management and Profit Maximization

Students of economics generally fail to understand why academic and nonacademic business people use the terms *yield* and *revenue management* as the goal of their pricing strategy. This is because economics students are always taught that firms should attempt to maximize profit and that revenue maximization does not imply profit maximization in the presence of strictly positive marginal costs.

However, as it turns out very often, profit-maximizing pricing strategies are sometimes better understood in the context of revenue maximization rather than by attempting to maximize profits even when all production costs are taken into account. In addition, with the ongoing information revolution and the fast penetration of the Internet as the main source of information, yield and revenue management can in many cases lead to profit-maximizing prices, mainly because most costs of producing information are sunk whereas the cost of duplicating information services could be negligible. But even if we ignore information products, there are some industries that operate under significant capacity constraints, such as the airline and hotel industries. In these industries, most costs are sunk and indeed the marginal costs can be ignored as long as the firms operate below their full capacity.

In view of this discussion, this book uses the term *yield management* to mean the utilization of profit-maximizing pricing techniques. Therefore, we will generally avoid mentioning the commonly used term *revenue management*, although recently it seems that the use of RM is gradually replacing the use of YM. Historically, YM was associated with early problems that treated price and capacity as fixed and maximized "yield" or utilization of capital. This book, however, interprets the term *yield* as profit.

To demonstrate why profit maximization differs from revenue maximization, Table 1.2 displays the willingness to pay for a meal by three consumer groups: students, civil servants, and members of parliament. When marginal cost is zero,

	Students	Civil Servants	Parliament Members
Maximal Price:	$5	$8	$10
# Consumers:	200	100	100
Marginal Cost		Profit Levels	
$0	**2000**	1600	1000
$4	400	**800**	600
$7	−800	200	**300**

Table 1.2: The effect of marginal cost on the choice of profit-maximizing price. *Note*: Boldface figures are profit levels under the profit-maximizing price.

profit equals revenue. Under zero marginal cost, profit/revenue is $5(200 + 100 + 100) = 2000 when the price is lowered to $5. Raising the price to $8 and $10 lowers the profit/revenue levels. Now, if the marginal cost equals 4, profit does not equal revenue. Clearly, the revenue-maximizing price has already shown to be $5. However, it can be shown that the profit-maximizing price is $8, yielding a profit of $(8 − 4)(100 + 100) = 800$. As Table 1.2 indicates, any other price generates lower profit levels. Finally, for a high marginal cost, Table 1.2 reveals that the profit-maximizing price is $10, resulting in a profit level of $($10 − $7)100 = 300.

1.4   The Role Played by Capacity

Capacity constraints play a key role in yield management. First, if the service provider (seller) uses various pricing techniques as the sole strategic variable (price-based YM), these prices must depend on the amount of available capacity. This is discussed in Subsection 1.4.1. In contrast, if the seller fixes the prices according to the estimated maximum willingness to pay by the potential consumers, or if prices are fixed by competing sellers, profit can be maximized by allocating different capacities according to the different fare classes (quantity-based YM); see the discussion in Subsection 1.4.2.

1.4.1   Price-based YM under capacity constraints

To see why capacity matters, let us recall our concert hall example displayed in Table 1.1. That example showed that under unlimited capacity, price discrimination via market segmentation between students and nonstudents enhances sales to the entire potential consumer population. Now, suppose that we add a restriction to Table 1.1 whereby no more than 250 people can be seated in one performance. Such a restriction may be imposed by a regulator such as the fire department or could be structural, such as the size of the concert hall itself. Clearly, under this capacity constraint, market segmentation is not profitable as the entire capacity can be filled by high-valuation consumers (nonstudents in the present example). Each consumer is willing to pay $10, so the revenue $10 \times 250 = \$2500$ is maximal.

The above discussion demonstrates that the stock of capacity is crucial for the determination of revenue and profit-maximizing prices. But, clearly capacity constraints can only be temporary because the service operator can always invest and expand her service capacity in the long run. Using the present example, the concert hall can expand or build new halls to accommodate a larger audience. All this leads us to the following conclusions:

(a) Pricing strategy in the short run may differ from pricing in the long run.

(b) A complete short-run and long-run pricing strategy must also include a plan for investing in additional capacity.

The above decisions must be made by any utility company. For example, electricity companies must decide on prices based on how much electricity they can generate as measured by the number of Kw/H (kilowatts per hour) the currently operable generators can produce. However, in the long run, an electricity company can vary its electricity generation capacity by purchasing additional generators or by switching to nuclear technologies, for example. The tight connection between pricing and capacity decisions actually defines the classical peak-load pricing problem to be analyzed in Chapter 6.

1.4.2 Quantity-based YM versus price-based YM

Yield management gained momentum (in fact, was initiated) as a result of the 1978 deregulation of the airline industry in the United States (followed by a similar deregulation in Europe in 1997). Newly emerging airlines, such as People's Express in the United States in the early 1980s, undercut the airfare charged by the established airlines by more than 60%. Established airlines were left with excess capacity (empty seats) on each route served by a new entrant. Consequently, during the 1980s all established airlines began allocating the seating capacity of each flight according to different fare classes. The practice of class allocation is commonly referred to as *quantity-based* YM.

The "art" of conducting proper YM is not so much how to divide the capacity among the different fare classes, but how to restrict the low-fare classes so that passengers with high willingness to pay will continue to buy the high-fare tickets. Such restrictions include advance purchase, nonrefundability, and Saturday night stay, as well as the more visible market segmentation techniques involving the division of service into classes (first class, business class, and economy class).

In this book, we do not make much use of the formal distinction between price-based YM and quantity-based YM, and this is for two reasons. First, price decisions and quantity decisions are related. For example, if an airline reservation system closes the booking of economy-class tickets, this may look like a quantity decision, but actually this decision is equivalent to raising all airfares to match the airfare for business class. Second, the book is organized according to topics (subjects) rather than according to whether price or quantity techniques are used.

Academic economists have always been interested in profit-maximizing pricing techniques, long before the airline industry was deregulated. For this reason, most of the pricing models in this book are taken directly from economic theory. In contrast, a large number of YM theorists have been working mainly on capacity/quantity allocation techniques (quantity-based YM). These operations research techniques are also applied to inventory control problems, commonly referred to as *supply chain management* (SCM). Only recently, have academic economists been combining the choice of price into models in which consumers make advance reservations before the contracted service is scheduled to be delivered.

1.5   YM, Consumer Welfare, and Antitrust

This book is about pricing techniques firms can use to enhance their revenues and profits. At first thought, one might be tempted to say that when profits and revenue are up, consumer welfare is reduced. However, as it turns, out this is not necessarily the case. There are situations under which firms can use certain profit-maximizing pricing techniques that also increase consumer welfare.

In particular, it is now well known (see Varian 1985) that price discrimination could, under certain circumstances, enhance consumer welfare. To see an example, let us return to the example displayed in Table 1.1. Consider two scenarios: (a) If price discrimination is prohibited or simply impossible to implement, we have already shown that the firm should charge a uniform price of $10, thereby servicing only nonstudents and, yielding a revenue of $3000. (b) Suppose now that price discrimination between students and nonstudents becomes feasible. Then, suppose that the firm announces that students are eligible for a $6 discount on a ticket (upon presentation of a valid ID). The resulting revenue level is ($10 − $6)200 + $10 × 300 = $3800 > $3000. Comparing consumer welfare in the absence of price discrimination with the level when price discrimination is implemented, nonstudents are indifferent as they pay the same price. However, students are strictly better off with price discrimination as they are able to purchase a ticket at $4, which is $1 less than their maximum willingness to pay.

The key element in this example is that uniform pricing results in the exclusion of low-valuation consumers from the market. In contrast, price discrimination "invites" the students to enter the market. The entrance of low-valuation consumers constitutes a net gain in social welfare. Thus, a *necessary* condition for price discrimination to enhance social welfare is the inclusion of newly served consumers who are not served when price discrimination is not used.

Unlike textbooks in microeconomics and industrial organization, this book does not analyze social welfare. In rare cases, we will compute social welfare when

YM via price discrimination is used by a regulator (such as in public utility pricing). Further, we will not discuss and analyze the antitrust implications of each pricing technique, mainly because competition bureaus do not have general rules and guidelines to judge pricing techniques directly, unless these techniques reduce competition. Thus, reading antitrust law could be misleading as strict interpretation implies that most of these techniques are simply illegal. Just to take an example, Section 2 of the Clayton Act of 1914 amended by the Robinson-Patman Act of 1936, states that

> It shall be unlawful for any person engaged in commerce, in the course of such commerce, either directly or indirectly, to discriminate in price between different purchasers of commodities of like grade and quality, ... where the effect of such discrimination may be substantially to lessen competition or tend to create a monopoly in any line of commerce, or to injure, destroy, or prevent competition. ...

Thus, Section 2 explicitly states that price discrimination should not be considered illegal unless price discrimination substantially decreases competition.

Finally, perhaps the main reason general rules regarding the use of each pricing strategy studied in this book do not exist is that nowadays most competition courts apply the so-called *rule of reason* as opposed to the *per se rule*. In plain language, this means that each case is judged individually and the only concern of the court is whether the action taken by a firm weakens price competition.

1.6 Pricing Techniques and the Use of Computers

This book tries something new, at least in comparison with standard textbooks on economics and business. This book provides a wide variety of computer algorithms that can provide the core for building the software needed for the computation of profit-maximizing prices. The algorithms are written in a language closely resembling the well-known Pascal programming language that makes it easy to follow the basic logic behind the algorithms. Clearly, the idea of using computers for selecting prices is not novel. In fact, there are many software companies selling services to hotel chains and airlines. Therefore, the only attempt here is to demonstrate how economic theory can be embedded into simple computer algorithms.

As we mentioned earlier in this chapter, computers cannot substitute for human intuition in determining profit-maximizing prices. Most companies still determine prices by intuition combined with trial and error. Moreover, at least at the time of writing this book, computers cannot determine which pricing techniques should be used in each market. Loosely speaking, computers cannot think. All computers can do is process a large number of computations at a much greater speed and with greater accuracy than what humans can do. Because of this feature, computers can be used to verify whether a particular intuition happens to be correct or false.

Having said all that, it should be pointed out that with the increase in speed and reduction in the cost of running computers, there is a growing tendency among researchers to try different methods of explorations with the use of computers (see, for example, Wolfram 2002). Computers can simply search large databases and experiment with different price structures. The simple algorithms in this book can serve as examples of what kinds of "programming loops" are needed for searching for the "right" prices. Price practitioners who use such algorithms should also design additional algorithms that test the results against alternative price mechanisms.

1.7   The Literature and Presentation Methods

As I mentioned before in this introduction, similar to my earlier two books, the presentation in this book is based on two beliefs of mine: First, high-level math is not always needed to present a full argument. For example, a model with two or three states of nature can easily replace a continuous density function. More importantly, my second belief (although many researchers may disagree) is that a simple model is not necessarily less general than a complicated model, or a model that uses high-level math.

For these reasons, and because the presentation level in scientific journals differs substantially from the presentation of this book, I was not able to fully use scientific literature for writing this book. Therefore, this book is not intended to survey the vast literature on yield management. The reason is that to make the models accessible to undergraduate students as well as to general pricing practitioners, I had to design my own models rather than use someone else's. I guess this is the right place to formally apologize to all those researchers whose work is not cited. Clearly, the choice of which paper to cite or not cite is not based on any value judgment, but on convenience and relevance to the simplified version used in this book. Readers seeking a comprehensive reading list of the scientific literature on YM should consult recent books by Talluri and van Ryzin (2004), and Ingold, Yeoman, and McMahon (2001), as well as a literature survey by McGill and van Ryzin (1999). On pricing in general, Monroe (2002), Nagle and Holden (2002), McAfee (2005, Ch. 11), and Winer (2005) provide comprehensive studies of pricing techniques as well as extensive discussions on all aspects related to pricing, including behavioral and psychological approaches.

1.8   Notation and Symbols

The book tries to minimize the use of mathematical symbols. For the sake of completeness, Table 1.3 contains all the symbols used in this book.

Notation is classified into two groups: *parameters*, which are numbers that are treated as exogenous by the agents described in the model, and *variables*, which are endogenously determined. Thus, the purpose of every theoretical model is to define an equilibrium concept that yields a unique solution for these variables for given values of the model's parameters.

For example, production costs and consumers' valuations of products are typically described by parameters (constants), which are estimated in the market by econometricians and are taken exogenously by the theoretical economist. In contrast, quantity produced and quantity consumed are classical examples of variables that are endogenously determined, meaning that they are solved within the model itself.

We now set the rule for assigning notation to parameters and variables. *Parameters are denoted either by **Greek** letters or by **uppercase English** letters. In contrast, variables are denoted by **lowercase English** letters.* Table 1.4 lists the notation used for denoting parameters throughout this book. Finally, Table 1.5 lists the notation used for denoting variables throughout this book.

Symbols

$=$	equal by derivation
$\stackrel{\text{def}}{=}$	equal by definition
$\approx$	approximately equal
$\Longrightarrow$	implies that
$\Longleftrightarrow$	if and only if
Σ	sum [Sigma]
Δ	a change in a variable/parameter [Delta]
$\%\Delta$	percentage change in a variable/parameter
∂	partial derivative
$\in$	is an element of the set
E	expectation operator (expected value of...)
$\times$ or $\cdot$	simple multiplication operators
$!$	factorial, for example, $3! = 1 \times 2 \times 3 = 6$
$\lfloor x \rfloor$	floor of x, for example, $\lfloor 3.16 \rfloor = \lfloor 3.78 \rfloor = 3$
$\lceil x \rceil$	ceiling of x, for example, $\lceil 3.16 \rceil = \lceil 3.78 \rceil = 4$
$func(var)$	is a function of the variable, for example, $f(x)$
$\leftarrow$	assignment operation in a computer algorithm, $x \leftarrow 2$
$\Pr\{\text{event}\}$	probability of an event: $[0, 1]$
$\mathbb{R}$	positive or negative real numbers: $(-\infty, +\infty)$
$\mathbb{R}^+$	nonnegative real numbers: $[0, +\infty)$
$\mathbb{R}^{++}$	strictly positive real numbers: $(0, +\infty)$
$\mathbb{Z}$	integer numbers: $\ldots, -2, -1, 0, 1, 2, \ldots$
$\mathbb{N}^+$	natural numbers: $0, 1, 2, 3, \ldots$
$\mathbb{N}^{++}$	strictly positive natural numbers: $1, 2, 3, \ldots$
$\emptyset$	empty set (a set containing no elements)
$\{,,,\}$	set of elements (order does not matter)
$(,,,)$	vector (order does matter)
LHS, RHS	Right-hand side and left-hand side of an equation

Table 1.3: Symbols.

Parameters

Notation	Type	Interpretation
ϕ	$\mathbb{R}^+$	fixed or sunk production cost [phi]
μ_o	$\mathbb{R}^+$	marginal operating/production cost [mu]
μ_k	$\mathbb{R}^+$	marginal cost of capital/capacity/reservation
K	$\mathbb{R}^+, \mathbb{N}^+$	available capacity level, or amount of capital
F	$\mathbb{N}^+$	number of firms in a given industry
α	$\mathbb{R}^{++}$	demand (shift) parameter [alpha]
β	$\mathbb{R}^+$	demand parameter (slope or exponent) [beta]
π	$[0,1]$	probability $(0 \leq \pi \leq 1)$ [pi]
π^i	$[0,1]$	probability of a booking request for class i, $i \in \mathscr{B}$
π^0	$[0,1]$	probability of not booking $(\pi^0 \stackrel{\text{def}}{=} 1 - \sum_i \pi^i)$
τ	$\mathbb{N}^+$	a particular time period (e.g., $t = \tau$) [tau]
T	$\mathbb{N}^{++}$	number of periods/seasons, or the last period/season
D	$\mathbb{R}^{++}$	duration of a season
ε	$\mathbb{R}^{++}$	a small number [epsilon]
M	$\mathbb{N}^{++}$	# of consumer types, # markets $(\ell = 1, 2, \ldots, M)$
V_ℓ	$\mathbb{R}^+$	consumer ℓ's willingness to pay for a product/service
N	$\mathbb{N}^{++}$	number of consumers $(N_\ell$ of type $\ell)$ $(N_i$ in group $i)$
$U_\ell(\cdot)$	func.	consumer ℓ's utility function (of V_ℓ, p, etc.)
δ	$\mathbb{R}^{++}$	differentiation (or switching) cost [delta]
ψ	$\mathbb{R}^+$	penalty level [psi]
P	$\mathbb{R}^+$	exogenously given price charged by a firm
G	$\mathbb{N}^{++}$	grid (computer algorithms' precision of price change)
B	$\mathbb{N}^+$	maximum allowable booking level, or # block rates
$\mathscr{B}$	set	booking classes, set of goods, set of quality levels, for example, $\mathscr{B} = \{A, B, C, .., i, ..\}$, $i \in \mathscr{B}$, etc.

Table 1.4: General notation for parameters (uppercase English and Greek letters).

Variables

Notation	Type	Interpretation
d_t	0, 1	decision in period t, $d_t = 1$ (accept), $d_t = 0$ (reject)
x	$\mathbb{R}^+$	(expected) revenue of a firm
c	$\mathbb{R}^+$	(expected) total cost borne by a firm
y	$\mathbb{R}$	(expected) profit of a firm ($y \overset{\text{def}}{=} x - c$)
p or f	$\mathbb{R}^+$	endogenously determined price/fee set by a firm
up	$\mathbb{R}^+$	markup on marginal cost ($up \overset{\text{def}}{=} p - \mu$)
q	$\mathbb{R}^+$	quantity produced or quantity demanded
$\bar{q}$	$\mathbb{R}^+$	aggregate industry output ($\bar{q} \overset{\text{def}}{=} \sum_j q_j$)
e	func.	elasticity function [$e(q) \overset{\text{def}}{=} (\Delta q / \Delta p)(p/q)$]
$\check{e}$	func.	arc elasticity function
gcs	$\mathbb{R}^+$	gross consumer surplus
ncs	$\mathbb{R}$	net consumer surplus ($= gcs - $ expenditure)
b	$\mathbb{N}^+$	booking level (number of confirmed reservations)
b_t^i	$\mathbb{N}^+$	period t cumulative booking level for class $i \in \mathscr{B}$
k_t	$\mathbb{N}^+$	period t remaining capacity ($k_t = K - \sum_i b_t^i$)
p^i	$\mathbb{R}^+$	price of a service of class $i \in \mathscr{B}$
p_t	$\mathbb{R}^+$	period t price offer (by a consumer or set by a seller)
r	$\mathbb{R}^+$	refund level ($r \leq p$)
cn	$\mathbb{R}^+$	cancellation fee
n	$\mathbb{R}^+$	number of consumers who buy/book the product/service
s	$\mathbb{R}^+$	number of consumers who show up
ds	$\mathbb{R}^+$	number of consumers who are denied service
g	$\mathbb{N}^+$	number of (booked) consumer groups
a	$\mathbb{R}^+$	advertising expenditure
Indexing variables		
i	$\mathbb{N}^+$	general, product/service types, booking classes & groups
j	$\mathbb{N}^+$	general firms in a given industry
ℓ	$\mathbb{N}^+$	consumer types
t	$\mathbb{N}^+$	time period or season (e.g., $t = 0, 1, 2, \ldots, T$)

Table 1.5: General notation for variables (lowercase English letters) and indexing.

Chapter 2
Demand and Cost

2.1   Demand Theory and Interpretations   20

    2.1.1   Definitions

    2.1.2   Interpreting goods and services

    2.1.3   The elasticity and revenue functions

2.2   Discrete Demand Functions   24

2.3   Linear Demand Functions   26

    2.3.1   Definition

    2.3.2   Estimation of linear demand functions

    2.3.3   Elasticity and revenue for linear demand

2.4   Constant-elasticity Demand Functions   30

    2.4.1   Definition and characterization

    2.4.2   Estimation of constant-elasticity demand functions

    2.4.3   Elasticity and revenue for constant-elasticity demand

2.5   Aggregating Demand Functions   34

    2.5.1   Aggregating single-unit demand functions

    2.5.2   Aggregating continuous demand functions

2.6   Demand and Network Effects   39

2.7   Demand for Substitutes and Complements   42

2.8   Consumer Surplus   45

    2.8.1   Consumer surplus: Discrete demand functions

    2.8.2   Consumer surplus: Continuous demand functions

2.9   Cost of Production   52

2.10   Exercises   56

The key to a successful implementation of any yield management strategy is getting to know the consumers. Large firms invest tremendous amounts of money on research seeking to characterize their own customers as well as potential consumers. In economic theory, the most useful instrument for characterizing consumer behavior is the demand function. A demand function shows the quantity demanded by an individual, a group, or all the consumers in a given market, as a function of market prices, and some other variables.

Knowing the demand structure is a necessary condition for proper selection of profit-maximizing actions by the firm. But it is not a sufficient condition because the firm must also take cost-of-production considerations into account. Therefore, price decision makers within a firm should properly study the structure of the cost of the service or the product sold by their own firms. They should also distinguish among the different types of costs, particularly between costs associated with a marginal expansion of output and costs associated with investing in infrastructure, research and development (R&D), and capacity.

For this reason, we devote an entire chapter to study the most widely used demand and cost structures. Some readers, particularly readers who took micro-economics courses at a second-year undergraduate level, may be familiar with this material. In general, readers can skip this chapter and use it as a reference for the various concepts whenever necessary.

2.1 Demand Theory and Interpretations

In most cases, knowing consumers' demands constitutes the key information on which producers, service providers, and sellers in general base their profit-maximizing pricing and marketing techniques. However, the concepts of demand, products, and services may be given a wide variety of interpretations. In this section, we discuss some of these interpretations as it is important that firms identify the precise type of demand they are facing before they design their pricing mechanisms.

2.1.1 Definitions

DEFINITION 2.1

(a) The **demand function** $q(p)$ *shows the quantity demanded at any given price,* $p \geq 0$, *by a single consumer or a group of consumers.*

(b) The **inverse demand function** $p(q)$ *shows the maximum amount that an individual or a group of individuals is willing to pay at any given consumption level,* $q \geq 0$. *Mathematically, the function $p(q)$ is the inverse of the function* $q(p)$.

Notice that Definition 2.1 is general enough to be applied to different levels of market aggregation in the sense that it can be applied to individuals as well as to different-sized markets. The technique for how to combine individuals' demand functions into a single market demand function will be studied in Section 2.5.

Definition 2.1 is incomplete in the sense that it makes the quantity demanded depend on the price/fee only. However, as the reader may be well aware of, demand is also influenced by a wide variety of other factors, such as prices of other goods and services that consumers may view as substitutes or complements, income levels, time of delivery, bundling and tying with other goods and services, advertising, social conformity and nonconformity, social pressure, network effects, environmental concerns, brand loyalty, and more. Clearly, all these factors are very important, and most of them are incorporated in this book.

2.1.2 Interpreting goods and services

This book analyzes profit-maximizing pricing techniques. For this reason, producers and service providers should fully understand and very often define the nature of the products and services they supply. Furthermore, it is important that sellers understand how these products and services are used by consumers and how consumers perceive the benefit they gain from consuming these goods. For this reason, we now attempt to characterize goods and services according to several criteria.

Frequency of purchase: Flow versus stock goods

The distinction between flow and stock goods is based on the frequency of purchase. Theoretically, pure stock goods are those that can be stored indefinitely. Diamonds, gold, silver, and artworks are good examples. However, often we view mechanical and electrical appliances also as stock goods despite the fact that they tend to be replaced every few years. Flow goods are generally perishable goods for which the quantity demanded is measured by units of consumption during a certain time period. By *perishable*, we mean goods that cannot be stored for a long time, if at all. Therefore, perishable products must be repeatedly purchased. Food items, perhaps, provide the best examples of flow goods. Some food items can be stored for only a week, whereas others (such as boxed food) can be stored for six months or even longer.

Because the majority of pricing models presented in this book apply to services, we should mention that services are generally regarded as highly perishable, which means they are nonstorable. The reason for this is that most services are time dependent, so postponements and delays may result in a partial or total utility loss to consumers. For example, traveling today via ground, air, or sea transportation, or a hotel room for tonight, may be regarded as totally different services from traveling and a hotel room tomorrow. Reading or watching the news today constitute a totally different service from getting tomorrow's news. Of course, this is not always the case as for some services, such as changing the engine oil in your car, postponing the service for a limited time will not matter to you very much. Despite the fact that most services are perishable, not all services are flow goods in the sense that some services, such as a trip to the Galápagos Islands, may be purchased once in a lifetime. In contrast, a bus trip to work is definitely a flow good, as it is repeated on a daily basis. A ski trip can also be repeated on a yearly basis or for some people, can be a once-in-a-lifetime event.

Back to products, in the "new" information economy, information goods consume a large portion of individuals' budgets. We interpret *information goods* in the broad sense of the term to include books, software, encyclopedias, databases, music, and video. We tend to treat these information products as stock goods. Not only can these products be stored for a long period of time, they can also be duplicated without any deterioration if they are stored in digital formats. Of course, storage devices such as magnetic tapes, digital disks, and diskettes, are themselves perishable and therefore require some maintenance or replacement. We should point out that in some sense, information goods can also be viewed as services simply because there is no benefit from storing them. News on current prices in the stock markets, or any other type of news, can be viewed as perishable goods that consumers must purchase repeatedly.

Quantity of purchase and willingness to pay

Generally, there are two major interpretations for demand schedules. The first interpretation involves consumers who increase the number of units purchased when the price drops (holding other parameters affecting demand constant). This interpretation is commonly found in introductory textbooks that are used in university microeconomics courses. With the risk of finding many counterexamples, we can say that this interpretation is more suitable for markets of flow goods, where frequent purchases make the quantity purchased highly sensitive to short-run and small changes in prices. Figure 2.1(left) illustrates a downward-sloping inverse demand function for one individual consumer. Thus, the consumer depicted on Figure 2.1(left) demands $q = 2$ units at the price of $p = \$30$, $q = 3$ units at $p = \$25$, and so on.

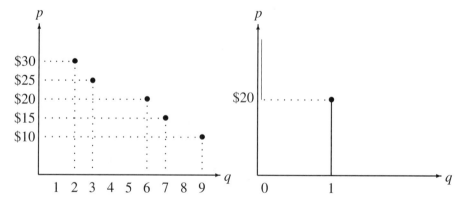

Figure 2.1: Illustration of inverse demand functions by individuals. *Left*: Downward-sloping demand. *Right*: Single-unit demand.

The second interpretation, which will be used extensively in this book, applies to markets composed of a large number of individuals. Each consumer is assumed to buy *at most one unit* of the product/service, and will not buy additional units even when the price drops. Figure 2.1(right) exhibits a demand function where the consumer does not purchase the product ($q = 0$) at prices exceeding \$20 ($p >$ \$20). However, as the price drops to \$20 or below ($p \leq$ \$20), the consumer demands exactly *one unit* ($q = 1$) and does not buy more units, even as the price drops to zero. We should point out that consumers with this type of demand are not homogeneous in the sense that each consumer may have a different level of willingness to pay for a unit of consumption. That is, we could also plot a similar demand function whose maximum willingness to pay is \$40 and not \$20 as for the consumer plotted in Figure 2.1(right). These differences may be generated by differences in income, value of time, and the utility generated from the services of the product or the service. Under this interpretation, the market demand function represents a summation of the individuals whose willingness to pay exceeds the market price. We refer the reader to Section 2.5 for a demonstration of how market demand functions can be derived from groups of individuals whose demand functions are not price sensitive, as illustrated in Figure 2.1(right).

2.1.3 The elasticity and revenue functions

The elasticity function is derived from the demand function and maps the quantity purchased to a very useful number that we call the *elasticity at a point* on the demand. The elasticity measures how fast quantity demanded adjusts to a small change in price. Formally, we define the price elasticity of demand by

$$e(q) \stackrel{\text{def}}{=} \left(\frac{\Delta q}{\Delta p} \right) \left(\frac{p}{q} \right) = \frac{\text{percentage change of } q}{\text{percentage change of } p} = \frac{\%\Delta q}{\%\Delta p}. \tag{2.1}$$

DEFINITION 2.2
At a particular level of consumption q, the demand
- *is called **elastic** if $e(q) < -1$ (or, $|e(q)| > 1$),*
- *is called **inelastic** if $-1 < e(q) < 0$, (or, $|e(q)| < 1$),*
- *and has a **unit elasticity** if $e(q) = -1$ (or, $|e(q)| = 1$).*

The inverse demand function shows the maximum amount a consumer is willing to pay per unit of consumption at a given consumption level q. The *revenue* function shows the amount of revenue collected by a seller at a particular price–quantity combination. Formally, we define the revenue function by

$$x(q) \stackrel{\text{def}}{=} p(q) \cdot q, \tag{2.2}$$

which is the the price multiplied by the corresponding quantity demanded.

Finally, the *marginal revenue* function is the change in revenue resulting from a "slight" increase in quantity demanded. Formally we define the marginal revenue function by $\Delta x/\Delta q$, for "small" increments of q, as given by Δq.

2.2 Discrete Demand Functions

Data on demand are discrete in nature because the number of observations in the form of data points that can be collected is always finite. Therefore, when a researcher plots the raw data, the demand function consists of discrete points in the price–quantity space. We refer to graphs representing the raw data as *discrete* demand functions, and distinguish them from the continuous demand functions we also analyze in this chapter. In fact, in Sections 2.3 and 2.4, we demonstrate how to generate *continuous* linear and constant-elasticity demand functions from discrete demand by estimating the continuous functions directly from the raw data. Although most textbooks in economics use continuous demand functions, this book focuses mainly on discrete demand functions. The reason is that, by construction, computers generally handle computations based on a finite amount of data. This means that the computations based on raw data, or based on data generated by computer reservation systems, must be handled using discrete algebra (as opposed to calculus).

The first two rows of Table 2.1 display the raw data for a discrete demand function. Rows 3–6 in this table display various computations derived directly

p	\$35	\$30	\$25	\$25	\$20	\$20	\$15	\$15	\$10
q	1	2	3	4	5	6	7	8	9
$e(q)$	−7.00	−3.0	n/d	−1.25	n/d	−0.67	n/d	−0.38	n/a
$\check{e}(q)$	−4.33	−2.2	n/d	−1	n/d	−0.54	n/d	−0.29	n/a
$x(q)$	\$35	\$60	\$75	\$100	\$100	\$120	\$105	\$120	90
$\frac{\Delta x(q)}{\Delta q}$	\$25	\$15	\$25	\$0	\$20	−\$15	\$15	−\$30	n/a

Table 2.1: Discrete demand function $\langle p, q \rangle$, and the corresponding price elasticity $e(q)$, arc price elasticity $\check{e}(q)$, total revenue $x(q)$, and marginal revenue $\frac{\Delta x(q)}{\Delta q}$. *Note*: n/d means not defined (division by 0), n/a means data not available.

from the raw data. Figure 2.2 plots the raw data provided by Table 2.1. The third row of Table 2.1 computes the price elasticity defined by (2.1). To demonstrate two examples, we compute the price elasticity at $q = 1$ and $q = 6$ units of consumption to be

$$e(1) = \frac{2-1}{\$30 - \$35} \frac{\$35}{1} = -7 \quad \text{and} \quad e(6) = \frac{7-6}{\$15 - \$20} \frac{\$20}{6} = -0.67. \quad (2.3)$$

Observe that we are unable to compute the price elasticity at $q = 9$, because we have no data on the price that would induce the consumer(s) to buy $q = 10$ units. For this reason, we marked $e(9)$ as n/a in Table 2.1.

Inspecting the elasticity computations given by (2.3) reveals that the elasticity formula is based on the evaluation of the price and the corresponding quan-

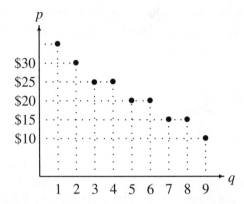

Figure 2.2: Discrete demand function based on data given in Table 2.1.

tity "before" the change takes place. For example, $e(6)$ in (2.3) is evaluated at the pair $\langle p,q \rangle = \langle \$20, 6 \rangle$, although there is no reason why this evaluation should not be made at $\langle p,q \rangle = \langle \$15, 7 \rangle$, which is the demand point "after" the changes $\Delta p = \$15 - \$20$ and $\Delta q = 7 - 6$ take place. The arc elasticity function, denoted by $\breve{e}(q)$, corrects this problem somewhat by evaluating the elasticity at the midpoints $\bar{p} = (\$15 + \$20)/2 = \$17.5$ and $\bar{q} = (6+7)/2 = 6.5$ instead of at the "start" and "end" points of this change. Therefore, redoing the computation (2.3) for the arc elasticity yields

$$\breve{e}(1) = \frac{2-1}{\$30 - \$35} \frac{\$32.5}{0.5} = -4.33 \quad \text{and}$$

$$\breve{e}(6) = \frac{7-6}{\$15 - \$20} \frac{\$17.5}{0.5} = -0.54, \quad (2.4)$$

which is considered to be a more accurate measure of elasticity.

The revenue collected by sellers (which equals consumers' expenditure on this good) and the marginal revenue function are simply defined by

$$x \stackrel{\text{def}}{=} p(q)\,q \quad \text{and} \quad \frac{\Delta x(q)}{\Delta q}. \quad (2.5)$$

For example, using the data in Table 2.1, $\frac{\Delta x(1)}{\Delta q} = x(2) - x(1) = \$60 - \$35 = \$25$, and $\frac{\Delta x(6)}{\Delta q} = x(7) - x(6) = \$105 - \$120 = -\$15$.

Inspecting Table 2.1 reveals that the maximum revenue that can be extracted from consumers is \$120, which is accomplished by setting the price either to $p = \$20$ and selling $q = 6$ units, or to $p = \$15$ and selling $q = 8$ units. Moreover, the price elasticities $e(q)$ and $\breve{e}(q)$ are close to -1 around the revenue-maximizing output levels. This is not a coincidence, and as shown in Sections 2.3 and 2.4, for continuous demand functions, revenue is always maximized at the output level where both elasticities take a value of $e(q) = \check{e}(q) = -1$. Observe that regular and arc elasticities are always equal for continuous demand functions because their evaluation is based on infinitesimal changes.

2.3 Linear Demand Functions

2.3.1 Definition

A linear demand is a special type of the general demand function characterized by Definition 2.1. Its special property is that it is drawn as, or fitted to be represented by, a straight line. Formally, the general formulas for the inverse and the direct demand functions are defined by

$$p(q) \stackrel{\text{def}}{=} \alpha - \beta\, q \quad \text{or} \quad q(p) \stackrel{\text{def}}{=} \frac{\alpha}{\beta} - \frac{1}{\beta}\, p, \tag{2.6}$$

where the parameters α and β may be estimated using econometric techniques, as we briefly demonstrate in Section 2.3.2. Figure 2.3 plots the linear inverse demand function given by the formula on the left-hand side of (2.6). Note that part of the

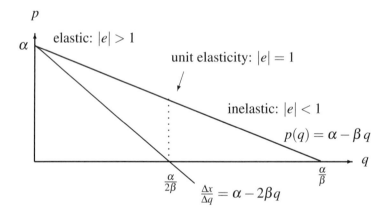

Figure 2.3: Inverse linear demand function.

demand is not drawn in Figure 2.3. That is, for any price exceeding the intercept α, the (inverse) demand becomes vertical at $q = 0$. In other words, the demand coincides with the vertical axis for prices in the range $p > \alpha$.

For the inverse demand function, the parameter $\alpha > 0$ is called the demand intercept, whereas the parameter $\beta \geq 0$ is called the slope of the inverse demand curve. We should mention that in rare cases, $-\beta$ may be found to have a positive slope for some price range. Inverting the inverse demand function formulated on the left-hand side of (2.6) generates the direct demand function on the right-hand side of (2.6), with an intercept α/β and a slope of $-1/\beta$.

2.3.2 Estimation of linear demand functions

Firms can collect data on the demand facing their products and services by experimenting with different prices and recording the quantity demanded at every price. Alternatively, firms can conduct consumer surveys. What is common to both methods is that the data collected are discrete (as opposed to continuous). In other words, observations generally consist of data points that are a collection of the pairs $\langle p, q \rangle$. Table 2.2 provides an example of data points on quantity demanded at various prices.

ℓ (observation no.)	1	2	3	4	5	Mean
p_ℓ (price)	\$30	\$25	\$20	\$15	\$10	\$20.00
q_ℓ (quantity)	2	3	6	7	9	5.40

Table 2.2: Data points for estimating linear demand.

The discrete data on price and quantity observations provided by Table 2.2 may often be hard to use for analyzing pricing techniques. That is, some pricing tactics are easier to configure when the demand is represented by a continuous function. We therefore would like to fit a formula that would approximate the behavior of the consumer whose preferences are represented by the data given in Table 2.2. Figure 2.4 illustrates how a linear regression line can be fit to approximate the linear demand function. In fact, using the data in Table 2.2, regressing q on p yields the direct demand function

$$q = 12.6 - 0.36\,p, \quad \text{or, in an inverted form,} \quad p = 35 - 2.7777\,q. \tag{2.7}$$

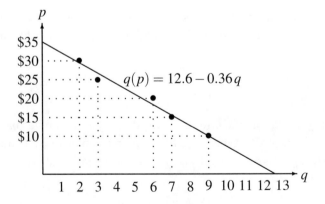

Figure 2.4: Fitting a linear regression line.

Note that regressing q (the dependent variable) on p (an independent variable) is different from regressing p on q. In fact, regressing p on q yields $p =$

$34.63855 - 2.71084\,q$, which is somewhat different from the inverse demand function (2.7) obtained from the estimation of the direct demand function. Unfortunately, there is no easy way to reconcile the two estimation methods. Given that our computations rely on frequent inversions of direct demand functions into inverse demand functions, and the other way around, in this chapter we always estimate the direct demand function equation, and then derive the inverse demand function from the estimated direct demand equation.

The estimated demand function (2.7) is drawn in Figure 2.4. The linear regression yielding the demand schedule (2.7) from the data given in Table 2.2 can be computed on basically any personal computer that runs a popular spreadsheet program, or a commonly used statistical package. Most widely used spreadsheet programs allow users to type in the observed data points then highlight the relevant rows or columns and obtain the intercept and slope of the demand function. In fact, some of these packages even draw the regression line with the data points, just as we did in Figure 2.4. Therefore, there is no need for us to go into detail about how to derive the formulas for obtaining the intercept and the slope. For the sake of completeness, we merely add a few remarks on the regression fitting technique. In general, regression is a statistical technique of fitting a functional relationship among economic variables by cataloging the observed variables, and then using well-known formulas to extract the exogenous parameters of the functional relationship. The most commonly used regression method is known as ordinary least squares (a method that minimizes the sum of squared errors). Let M be the number of observations in hand ($M = 5$ in the example given in Table 2.2). Then, define the mean price (or average price) and mean quantity demanded (or average quantity) by

$$\bar{p} \stackrel{\text{def}}{=} \frac{p_1 + p_2 + \cdots + p_M}{M} = \frac{\sum_{\ell=1}^{M} p_\ell}{M} \quad \text{and} \quad \bar{q} \stackrel{\text{def}}{=} \frac{\sum_{\ell=1}^{M} q_\ell}{M}. \tag{2.8}$$

Under the ordinary least squares method, the slope of the direct demand function $q(p) = \gamma - \delta p$ and its intercept with the horizontal q-axis are obtained from

$$\delta = -\frac{\sum_{\ell=1}^{M} (q_\ell - \bar{q})\,(p_\ell - \bar{p})}{\sum_{\ell=1}^{M} (p_\ell - \bar{p})^2} \quad \text{and} \quad \gamma = \bar{q} + \delta\,\bar{p}. \tag{2.9}$$

Again, it may not be practical to use (2.9) directly to compute that $\delta = 0.36$ and $\gamma = 12.6$ as given in (2.7), because linear regressions can be computed on most spreadsheet programs, statistical packages, and even some freely available Web pages.

2.3.3 Elasticity and revenue for linear demand

The elasticity and revenue functions defined in Section 2.1.3 for the general case can be easily derived for the linear demand function given by (2.6). Using calculus, we obtain

$$e(q) = \frac{\mathrm{d}q(p)}{\mathrm{d}p} \frac{p}{q} = \left(-\frac{1}{\beta} \right) \left(\frac{\alpha - \beta q}{q} \right) = 1 - \frac{\alpha}{\beta q}. \tag{2.10}$$

Therefore, the demand has a unit elasticity at the consumption level $q = \alpha/(2\beta)$. Consequently, according to Definition 2.2, the demand is elastic at output levels $q < \alpha/(2\beta)$ and is inelastic for $q > \alpha/(2\beta)$. The elasticity regions for the linear demand case are illustrated in Figure 2.3.

The total revenue function associated with the linear demand function (2.6) is derived as follows:

$$x(q) = p(q)\, q = \alpha q - \beta q^2. \tag{2.11}$$

Hence, using calculus, the marginal revenue function is given by

$$\frac{\mathrm{d}x(q)}{\mathrm{d}q} = \frac{\mathrm{d}[p(q)\, q]}{\mathrm{d}q} = \alpha - 2\beta q. \tag{2.12}$$

The total and marginal revenue functions (2.11) and (2.12) are drawn in Figure 2.5.

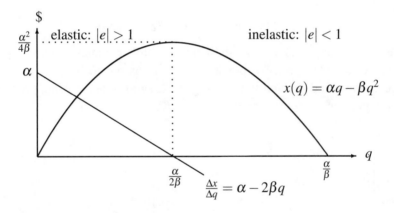

Figure 2.5: Total and marginal revenue functions for linear demand.

Comparing the marginal revenue function (2.12) with the inverse demand function (2.6) reveals that the marginal revenue function has the same intercept α and twice the negative slope of the inverse demand function. This comparison can be easily visualized by comparing Figure 2.3 with Figure 2.5, which illustrates a linear marginal revenue function that intersects the quantity axis at $\alpha/2\beta$, which equals half of α/β (the quantity at the intersection with the demand function). As also shown in Figure 2.5, revenue is maximized when the firm sells $q = \alpha/(2\beta q)$ units where the demand elasticity is $e(\alpha/2\beta) = -1$, or in absolute value $|e(\alpha/2\beta)| = 1$.

Finally, you probably have noticed already that the demand elasticity and the marginal revenue functions are related. That is, Figures 2.3 and 2.5 illustrate that $\Delta x/\Delta q = 0$ when $e(q) = 1$, and $\Delta x/\Delta q > 0$ whenever $|e(q)| > 1$. In fact, as it turns out, we can express the marginal revenue as a function of the elasticity at a point. Formally,

$$\frac{\Delta x}{\Delta q} = \frac{d[p(q)\,q]}{dq} = p + q\,\frac{dp(q)}{dq} = p\left[1 + \frac{q}{p}\,\frac{1}{\frac{dq(p)}{dp}}\right] = p\left[1 + \frac{1}{e(p)}\right]. \quad (2.13)$$

All this means that the revenue earned by a seller increases with sales at the elastic part of the demand curve where $e(q) < -1$, but declines at the inelastic part of the demand curve where $-1 < e(q) \leq 0$. Clearly, this explains why a monopoly would never sell on the inelastic part of the demand curve.

2.4 Constant-elasticity Demand Functions

2.4.1 Definition and characterization

A constant-elasticity demand function and the corresponding inverse function are defined by

$$q(p) \stackrel{\text{def}}{=} \alpha\,p^{-\beta} \quad \text{and} \quad p(q) = \alpha^{\frac{1}{\beta}}\,q^{-\frac{1}{\beta}}, \quad (2.14)$$

where $\alpha > 0$ can be viewed as the demand "shift-parameter" and $\beta \geq 0$ is the absolute value of the price exponent, which turns out to have a very important interpretation to be derived below. Figure 2.6 illustrates two constant-elasticity demand functions.

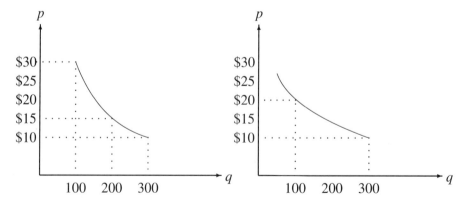

Figure 2.6: Constant-elasticity demand functions. *Left*: Unit elasticity, $e(q) = -1$. *Right*: Elastic demand, $e(q) < -1$.

Both constant-elasticity demand functions are drawn as rectangular hyperbolas, meaning that the curves do not touch the axes. In other words, as the price declines to zero, quantity demanded increases to infinity. Conversely, quantity demanded drops to a level closer to zero as the price increases to infinity.

The demand on the left-hand side of Figure 2.6 has a particular feature where the revenue $x = q(p)\,p$ does not vary with any price–quantity movement on the demand curve. In contrast, the revenue associated with demand on the right-hand side of Figure 2.6 increases when price drops. Clearly, a third graph is missing from Figure 2.6 – showing that revenue drops with a decrease in price – because we will not be analyzing such markets. In Section 2.4.3, we characterize these different cases by computing the demand elasticity associated with each type of demand.

2.4.2 Estimation of constant-elasticity demand functions

Section 2.3.2 demonstrates how observed discrete demand data can be described by a linear demand function. We now demonstrate how a linear regression can also be used to fit a constant-elasticity demand function. The "trick" is to transform the nonlinear constant-elasticity demand into a linear formula. This is accomplished by taking the natural logarithm from both sides of the direct demand function on the left-hand side of (2.14). Hence,

$$\underbrace{\ln q}_{\text{dependent variable}} \quad = \quad \underbrace{\ln \alpha}_{\text{constant}} \quad \underbrace{-\beta}_{\text{slope}} \underbrace{\ln p}_{\text{indept. var.}} . \tag{2.15}$$

The basic idea now is to run an ordinary least squares linear regression by treating $\ln q$ and $\ln p$ as the observed data (instead of q and p), and to estimate the intercept, now given by $\ln \alpha$, and the slope $-\beta$. As before, the reader is advised to use either a spreadsheet program or a statistical package to run linear regressions. However, for the sake of completeness, the log-transformed parameters described by (2.15) are estimated by the following equations

$$-\beta = \frac{\sum_{\ell=1}^{M}(\ln q_\ell - \overline{\ln q})\,(\ln p_\ell - \overline{\ln p})}{\sum_{\ell=1}^{M}(\ln p_\ell - \overline{\ln p})^2} \quad \text{and} \quad \ln \alpha = \overline{\ln p} + \beta\,\overline{\ln q}, \tag{2.16}$$

where the above means (averages) are defined by

$$\overline{\ln p} \stackrel{\text{def}}{=} \frac{\sum_{\ell=1}^{M} \ln p_\ell}{M} \quad \text{and} \quad \overline{\ln q} \stackrel{\text{def}}{=} \frac{\sum_{\ell=1}^{M} \ln q_\ell}{M}. \tag{2.17}$$

Thus, the averages defined by (2.17) sum up the logarithms of the observed data which clearly differ from the averages of the unmodified raw data defined by (2.8).

Let us now rework the example given by Table 2.2, but instead of fitting a linear demand, we now fit a constant-elasticity demand. The original data as well as the natural log of these observations are displayed in Table 2.3. Regressing the logarithmic transformation of the constant-elasticity demand function defined by (2.15) on the logarithmic data displayed in Table 2.3 obtains $\ln \alpha = 5.4801$ and $\beta = 1.345$. Therefore, $\alpha = e^{5.4801} = 239.8723$ (here, $e = 2.718281828$ is the base of the natural log, not to be confused with the elasticity function). Hence, the direct

ℓ (observation no.)	1	2	3	4	5	Mean
p_ℓ (price)	$30	$25	$20	$15	$10	$20.00
$\ln p_\ell$ (log price)	3.40	3.22	3.00	2.71	2.30	2.93
q_ℓ (quantity)	2	3	6	7	9	5.40
$\ln q_\ell$ (quantity)	0.69	1.10	1.79	1.95	2.20	1.55
Estimated $q_\ell(p_\ell)$	2.47	3.16	4.27	6.28	10.84	5.40

Table 2.3: Data points for estimating constant-elasticity demand.

and associated inverse estimated constant-elasticity demand functions based on the observations in Table 2.3 are given by

$$q(p) = 239.87\, p^{-1.345} \quad \text{or, in an inverted form,} \quad p(q) = 58.82\, q^{-0.743}. \quad (2.18)$$

Again, note that the inverse demand function on the right-hand side of (2.18) is not an estimated function but a function derived from the estimated direct demand equation. As we remarked on the linear case, regressing $\ln q$ on $\ln p$ and inverting it need not yield the same result as regressing $\ln p$ on $\ln q$. Therefore, for the purpose of this chapter, we always estimate the direct demand function first, and then invert it, taking into consideration the possible error. Furthermore, note that there are some alternative methods for estimating constant-elasticity demand functions that depend on the specification of the error term.

The estimated quantity levels for each price observation are written on the bottom row of Table 2.3. For example, the *observed* quantity demanded at the price $p = \$30$ was $q = 2$, but the *estimated* constant-elasticity demand function (2.18) predicts $q = 2.47$. Notice that the sampled average quantity demanded and the estimated average are the same, $\bar{q} = 5.4$.

Figure 2.7 plots the inverse demand function from the formula displayed on the right-hand side of (2.18). This formula yields $p(2) = \$35.13 > \$30$, $p(3) = \$25.99 > \$25$, $p(6) = \$15.52 < \$20$, $p(7) = \$13.84 < \$15$, and $p(9) = \$11.48 > \$10$. Figure 2.7 also compares the constant-elasticity estimated demand given by (2.18) to the estimated linear demand given by (2.7) on the same graph. A deeper comparison between the two fitted functions would require the use of a regression analysis tool such as the measure of correlation, known as R^2, and the p–value. These are beyond the scope of this book but can be found in any econometrics textbook as well as on some Web sites.

2.4.3 Elasticity and revenue for constant-elasticity demand

Although constant-elasticity demand functions are more difficult to draw compared with linear demand functions, they have some useful features that make revenue and

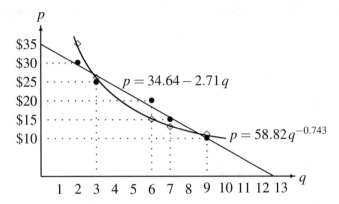

Figure 2.7: Fitting a constant-elasticity demand versus linear fitting. • are observed data points, ◇ are estimated constant-elasticity points.

elasticity computations much easier. We first would like to establish that constant-elasticity demand functions indeed have constant elasticity. Using calculus and Definition 2.2, we have

$$e(q) = \frac{dq(p)}{dp}\frac{p}{q} = -\alpha \beta p^{-\beta-1}\frac{p}{\alpha p^{-\beta}} = -\beta. \qquad (2.19)$$

Amazing, isn't it? What (2.19) shows is that the price elasticity of a constant-demand function is constant and is equal to the exponent of the price. Thus, one can easily find the elasticity by just looking at the exponent of the direct demand function (2.14), without resorting to any computation.

Another "attractive" feature of the constant-elasticity function is the simplicity of the resulting revenue function. More precisely, the revenue function is given by

$$x(p) \stackrel{def}{=} pq(p) = p\alpha p^{-\beta} = \alpha p^{1-\beta}. \qquad (2.20)$$

Notice that for convenience only, we choose to express the revenue as a function of price rather than of quantity. Without even having to compute the marginal revenue function (which will require us to reformulate (2.20) as a function of quantity instead of price), we can simply observe directly from (2.20) that a reduction in price will raise revenue only if $\beta = |e(q)| > 1$, that is, if the demand is elastic. This case is illustrated in Figure 2.6(right). Otherwise, if the demand is inelastic so that $\beta = |e(q)| < 1$, revenue falls when the price falls. A case of particular interest to economists is the unit-elasticity demand function illustrated in Figure 2.6(left). Substituting $\beta = 1$ into (2.14) and (2.20) yields

$$q(p) = \frac{\alpha}{p}, \quad p(q) = \frac{1}{q}, \quad \text{and} \quad x(p) = \alpha. \qquad (2.21)$$

That is, a constant unit-elasticity demand function implies that the revenue extracted from consumers is constant and is equal to α. Figure 2.6(left) demonstrates that a fall in price is compensated by an exact proportional increase in quantity demanded. Thus, the revenue equals $9000 at all price levels.

The estimated constant-elasticity demand function drawn in Figure 2.7 has a price elasticity of $|e(p)| = |1.345| > 1$, meaning that the demand is elastic, hence any price reduction would result in higher revenue extracted from consumers. This is in contrast to the linear demand, for which there is always a price level below which the demand becomes inelastic.

2.5 Aggregating Demand Functions

In this section, we learn how to combine individual consumers' demand functions into a single market demand function faced by firms. We distinguish between two representations of demand functions. Section 2.5.1 shows how to aggregate discrete single-unit demand functions. This procedure is most suitable for computers because it involves summations over discrete numbers. Section 2.5.2 shows how to aggregate continuous demand functions, which are represented by algebraic formulas. We also show how to implement this aggregation procedure on a computer.

2.5.1 Aggregating single-unit demand functions

Section 2.1.2 has already proposed two interpretations for demand functions. Under one interpretation, which is extensively used in this book, market demand is viewed as a composition of many consumers, each demanding *at most* one unit. This interpretation does not rule out the possibility that consumers may differ in their willingness to pay for a unit of consumption. In this section, we demonstrate how to combine these individual demand functions into a single market demand function. This procedure is very important because this aggregation generates discrete market demand functions in the form we have already analyzed in Section 2.2. The resulting aggregate market demand becomes handy when one wishes to use a computer to implement profitable pricing techniques.

Figure 2.8 illustrates how different consumer groups (groups combined of individuals with the same willingness to pay) can be aggregated to form an aggregate market demand function. The left-hand side of Figure 2.8 illustrates the demand functions of three representative consumers with different levels of willingness to pay. Each consumer buys at most one unit (at a given time period, say). Formally, they are $N_1 = 200$ consumers, with a maximum willingness to pay of $30; $N_2 = 600$, whose maximum willingness to pay is $20; and $N_3 = 200$, whose maximum willingness to pay is $10. The right-hand side illustrates the aggregate market demand function faced by the firm.

The technique used to aggregate demand functions is known as *horizontal summation* of demand functions. We use this technique in the computer algorithm that follows. The idea is to start with a high price exceeding the maximum willingness

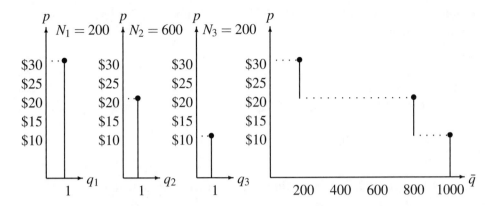

Figure 2.8: Aggregating the single-unit demand functions of three consumer types.

to pay of all consumer types. Then, gradually lowering the price induces more and more consumers to enter the market, where each newly entering consumer purchases one unit. More precisely, at any price $p > \$30$ aggregate demand is $\bar{q} = 0$. At the price range $\$20 < p \leq \$30$, there are exactly $N_1 = 200$ consumers buying a total of $\bar{q} = 200$ units. At the price range $\$10 < p \leq \$20$, there are exactly $N_1 + N_2 = 200 + 600$ consumers buying a total of $\bar{q} = 800$ units. At prices satisfying $p \leq \$10$, $N_1 + N_2 + N_3 = 200 + 600 + 200$ consumers buy a total of $\bar{q} = 1000$ units. Finally, the reader can easily confirm that the maximum revenue that can be extracted from consumers is given by the price–quantity pair $p = \$20$ and $\bar{q} = 800$, yielding a revenue of $y(800) = \$1600$.

Algorithm 2.1 relies on some parameters that the software must input, and some output variables that should be defined. First, the program should input the number of consumer types M. Next, for each consumer type ℓ, the software must input the type's maximum willingness to pay $V[\ell]$ and the number of consumers of this type $N[\ell]$. One can construct a loop such as **Read**(ℓ); $1 \leq \ell \leq M$, until, say, an end of line is reached, assuming that each pair of data points consisting of maximum willingness to pay and the number of consumers of this type ends with an end-of-line character. Hence, the program should define a real-valued array $V[\ell]$ of dimension $M + 1$, and a nonnegative natural numbers array $N[\ell]$ of dimension M. $V[M+1]$ is an ad hoc parameter defined solely for the sake of convenience. Finally, the software must *sort* consumer types according to declining willingness to pay. Formally, Algorithm 2.1 will rely on the assumption that consumers are ordered so that their maximum willingness to pay satisfies $V[1] \geq V[2] \geq \cdots \geq V[M]$.

We now proceed to define the output variables of Algorithm 2.1. Given that there are M consumer types, there are M internal kinks on the market demand curve; see Figure 2.8 for an example of $M = 3$ consumer types. We therefore define an output $(M+1)$-dimensional array $\bar{q}[\ell]$ of nonnegative natural numbers for the aggregate quantity demanded. $\bar{q}[0]$ is an ad hoc variable defined merely for the sake of convenience.

$V[M+1] \leftarrow 0; \bar{q}[0] \leftarrow 0; /*$ Defining ad hoc consumer types `*/`
for $\ell = 1$ **to** M **do**

$\quad \bar{q}[\ell] \leftarrow N[\ell] + \bar{q}[\ell - 1]; /*$ Loop over consumer types `*/`
$\quad$ **writeln** ("At the price range ", $V[\ell+1]$, "$< p \leq$ ", $V[\ell]$, "aggregate quantity demanded is $\bar{q} =$ ", $\bar{q}[\ell]$);

Algorithm 2.1: Aggregating single-unit demand functions.

Algorithm 2.1 is rather straightforward. It runs a loop from the valuation of the highest type to the lowest valuation type, $\ell = 1, 2, \cdots, M$, and for each type it adds the number of consumers of this type $N[\ell]$ to the number of consumers who have higher valuations, given by $\bar{q}[\ell - 1]$. Note that just for the sake of completeness, we could define an additional M-dimensional output array $p[\ell]$ of prices that would correspond to the aggregate demand levels $\bar{q}[\ell]$. However, this is redundant given that we merely assign valuations to prices in the form of $p[\ell] \leftarrow V[\ell]$ for each consumer type $\ell = 1, 2, \ldots, M$.

2.5.2 Aggregating continuous demand functions

Using software for symbolic algebra, computers can also handle formulas. Continuous demand functions can be constructed by fitting these functions using discrete observed data points, as we have already demonstrated in Sections 2.3.2 and 2.4.2. Continuous functions can take the form of a linear function (straight lines as in Figure 2.3) or of nonlinear functions (as illustrated in Figure 2.6).

Aggregating linear demand functions

We now demonstrate how to aggregate linear demand functions. The aggregation method for adding the inverse demand functions drawn in Figure 2.9 is commonly called *horizontal summation*. This method involves starting at a price high enough so the quantity demanded is zero then gradually reducing the price and adding quantity demanded from all markets with strictly positive demand. For example, in Figure 2.9, $\bar{q} = q_1 + q_2 = 0 + 0$ for all prices $p \geq \$30$. For all prices $\$20 \leq p < \$30$, $\bar{q} = q_1 + 0$, hence at this price range the aggregate demand function coincides with the demand function of market 1 only. For prices in the range $0 \leq p < \$20$, $\bar{q} = q_1 + q_2$ as illustrated on the right-hand side of Figure 2.9. Thus, the aggregate demand function exhibits a kink each time the price drops below the level that induces consumers in a new market to enter the market and make purchases. If we were to add three demand functions (instead of two), we would have two kinks

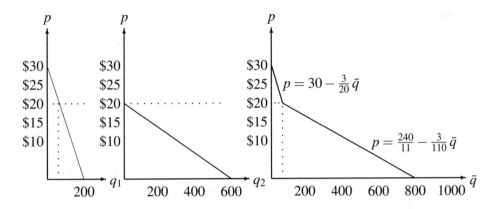

Figure 2.9: Aggregating linear demand functions.

(instead of one). Adding four demand functions would generate three kinks on the aggregate demand curve, and so on.

At this point, the reader should ask whether this horizontal summation method is really needed. That is, why don't we just add the algebraic expressions of the demand functions to obtain the aggregate demand? To answer this question, we formulate the algebraic equations associated with markets 1 and 2 drawn in Figure 2.9 as

$$p_1 = 30 - \frac{3}{20}q_1 \quad \text{and} \quad p_2 = 20 - \frac{1}{30}q_2. \tag{2.22}$$

Inverting the above inverse demand function into the corresponding direct demand functions and summing up the two direct demand functions yield

$$q_1 = \frac{200}{3} - \frac{20}{3}p_1, \quad q_2 = 600 - 30p_2, \quad \text{hence} \quad \bar{q} = 800 - \frac{110}{3}p. \tag{2.23}$$

Inverting the aggregate demand function on the right-hand side of (2.23) yields

$$p = \frac{240}{11} - \frac{3}{110}\bar{q}, \quad \text{or approximately} \quad p = 21.82 - 0.027\bar{q}. \tag{2.24}$$

The demand function (2.24) coincides with the aggregate demand drawn in Figure 2.9 only for the price range $p \le \$20$. But, clearly (2.24) is *not* the aggregate market demand curve for prices in the range $p > \$20$. Thus, the lesson we have just learned is that an algebraic summation of direct demand function obtains the aggregate demand *only* for the price range at which consumers in *all* markets demand strictly positive amounts. This explains why the horizontal summation method is needed. Summing up, the correct way of writing the algebraic expression for the inverse aggregate demand function is

$$p(\bar{q}) = \begin{cases} 0 & \text{if } p > \$30 \\ 30 - \frac{3}{20}\bar{q} & \text{if } \$20 < p \le \$30 \\ \frac{240}{11} - \frac{3}{110}\bar{q} & \text{if } 0 \le p < \$20. \end{cases} \tag{2.25}$$

Aggregating nonlinear continuous demand functions

Once the principle of the horizontal summation method is understood, it can be applied to aggregating all types of demand functions, including nonlinear as well as discontinuous demand functions. This means that there is no need to develop any new tool for aggregating nonlinear continuous functions. This section is included here mainly for the sake of completeness, as no new tools will be developed. Figure 2.10 provides an example of aggregating two constant-elasticity demand functions. The double-arrow lines indicate how horizontal summation is implemented. At any given price, one should simply add the horizonal distance q_1 to q_2 (and other additional markets, if any) to obtain the aggregate demand at a particular price.

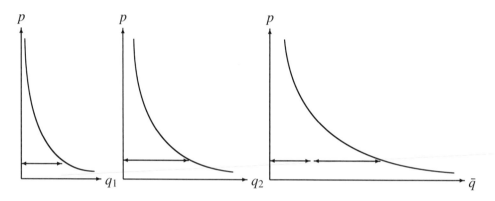

Figure 2.10: Aggregating constant-elasticity demand functions using the *horizonal summation* method.

Algebraically, suppose that we start with M direct constant elasticity demand functions as defined by (2.14). Then, the aggregate demand is found by the simple summation

$$\bar{q} = \alpha_1 \, p^{-\beta_1} + \alpha_2 \, p^{-\beta_2} + \cdots + \alpha_M \, p^{-\beta_M}. \tag{2.26}$$

This summation is valid for all nonnegative prices because constant-elasticity demand functions do not "touch the axes," so there is no danger of summing up negative output levels. Clearly, at this level of generality we cannot invert the aggregate demand function. This should not pose a problem because we can still plot the direct demand function by flipping the axes in Figure 2.10 so that aggregate quantity is measured on the vertical axis instead of the horizontal axis.

One particular case in which we can invert the aggregate demand function is worth examining. Suppose that all price elasticities are estimated to be approximately the same among all consumers. That is, if $\beta = \beta_1 = \cdots = \beta_M$, we can invert the direct aggregate demand (2.26) to obtain the aggregate inverse demand function given by

$$p(\bar{q}) = \left(\frac{\bar{q}}{\alpha_1 + \alpha_2 + \cdots + \alpha_M} \right)^{-\frac{1}{\beta}} = \left(\frac{\bar{q}}{\sum_{\ell=1}^{M} \alpha_\ell} \right)^{-\frac{1}{\beta}}, \tag{2.27}$$

which can be plotted directly on the inverse demand space as illustrated in Figure 2.10.

Computer algorithm for continuous demand

Because we are dealing now with continuous demand functions that are representable by algebraic formulas, it may be more beneficial to use symbolic algebra software to sum up these equations. However, as illustrated earlier for the linear case, when summing up formulas, one must be careful not to add negative output levels. Clearly, this problem can be avoided provided that the formulas are properly defined by the computer program so that the "kinks" are recognized.

If a symbolic algebra software solution is not an option, or if the researcher wishes to plot the aggregate demand function, in which case a continuous demand function must be transformed into a discrete demand, the following algorithm may be useful. Algorithm 2.2 is rather straightforward. It runs a loop on prices using a precision chosen by the user, and adds the quantity demanded (after checking for nonnegativity) from all user-defined (or user-inputted) types of direct demand functions. The software should input the parameter M which is the number of different demand functions. Then, either the user defines or the program inputs (this may be complicated if demand functions are of very different types) an array of M direct demand functions: $\mathtt{Quant}(p)[1]$, $\mathtt{Quant}(p)[2]$, ..., $\mathtt{Quant}(p)[M]$. To make this algorithm more general than the examples illustrated by Figures 2.9 and 2.10, the following algorithm can accommodate an arbitrary number of consumers of each type, where each type can be represented by a different demand function. Formally, the program should input the number of type ℓ consumers having the demand function $\mathtt{Quant}(p)[\ell]$ into $N[\ell]$, where $N[1], \ldots, N[M]$ is an array of nonnegative natural numbers. It should also input the desired price range $p^{\min}$ and $p^{\max}$, where $p^{\max} > p^{\min} \geq 0$, as well as the grid $G \in \mathbb{N}^{++}$, which determines the precision (number of points) for the outputted aggregate demand. Δp will serve as the variable of the price change between data points, determined by the grid parameter G.

2.6   Demand and Network Effects

So far, our analysis was confined to consumers whose demand functions were independent of consumption choices made by other consumers. However, it is often observed that consumers' choices of what and how much to consume (and at what price) are influenced by the choices made by other consumers. There can be two reasons for that. The first is a psychological reason stemming from social pressure either to look like everybody else or to look very different from everyone else. Second, as we demonstrate below, the demand for telecommunication services de-

```
Δp ← (p^max − p^min)/G; /* Defining price intervals            */
p ← p^max /* Setting initial (highest) price                   */
repeat
    q̄ ← 0; /* Loop over demand function types begins          */
    for ℓ = 1 to M do
        if Quant(p)[ℓ] > 0 then
            /* Aggregating nonnegative quantity demanded over
               all types                                       */
            q̄ ← q̄ + N[ℓ] × Quant(p)[ℓ]
    writeln ("At the price p = ", p, "aggregate quantity demanded is q̄ = ",
        q̄); p ← p − Δp; /* Reducing the price                  */
until p < p^min ;
```

Algorithm 2.2: Aggregating predefined continuous demand functions.

pends on how many other consumers have access to the *same* telecommunication channel. This behavior calls for the following definition.

DEFINITION 2.3

*Consumers' behavior is said to exhibit positive **network externalities** (or network effects) if consumers' willingness to pay for the service/product increases when more consumers buy the same or a compatible service/product.*

Clearly, one can also define negative network effects, under which willingness to pay declines when more consumers buy the same or a compatible brand. Negative network externality reflects snob, nonconformist, and vanity behavior; see Shy (2001) for an introduction to network economics. However, in this book we focus mainly on positive network effects which often characterize the demand for telecommunication services.

We now demonstrate how to construct an aggregate demand function for consumers whose behavior exhibits network externalities. We make the following assumptions:

ASSUMPTION 2.1

(a) *Each consumer views him or herself as **small** in the sense that his or her decision whether or not to purchase the service does not influence the aggregate number of purchases $\bar{q}$. Formally, each consumer views $\bar{q}$ as a constant.*

(b) *Consumers have a **perfect foresight** in the sense that at the time of purchase they can correctly anticipate $\bar{q}$, which is the total number of consumers who will be buying the service or a specific brand.*

Assumption 2.1(b) is not without problems, as the reader may ask how can a consumer predict or even know how many consumers will buy the same service? The answer to this question is that perfect foresight should be viewed as an integral part of consumers' rationality in the sense that if the network size is important to them, they will invest in reading consumer magazines and newspapers and may even hire a consulting firm in extreme cases, to try to predict the market size. Another justification for the perfect foresight assumption would be that any other assumption would be even more ad hoc as it may hint that consumers are not optimizing their knowledge before making purchase.

Let us now modify the example given by Figure 2.8 to include network effects on consumer demand. Suppose now that the $N_1 = 200$ type 1 consumers are willing to pay a maximum of $v_1 = \$30 + \alpha \bar{q}$ instead of just $v_1 = \$30$ as previously assumed. This means that a consumer's willingness to pay is composed of a fixed amount plus an extra amount that is a function of the total number of consumers who buy the same service, $\bar{q}$. The parameter $\alpha \geq 0$ measures the intensity of the network size on a consumer's willingness to pay for one unit of consumption. If $\alpha = 0$, $V_1 = \$30$ and we are back to the example in Figure 2.8 with no network effects. For the sake of demonstration, let us take a specific example and assume that $\alpha = 0.1$. Under this configuration, consumers' willingness to pay as a function of the aggregate number of buyers is given by

$$V_1 = \$30 + 0.1\,\bar{q}, \quad V_2 = \$20 + 0.1\,\bar{q}, \quad \text{and} \quad V_3 = \$10 + 0.1\,\bar{q}, \qquad (2.28)$$

where the corresponding numbers of consumers of each type are the same as those in Figure 2.8, thus given by $N_1 = 200$, $N_2 = 600$, and $N_3 = 200$.

We now show that Figure 2.11 is the aggregate demand function for the consumers defined by (2.28). First, we show that the price–quantity pair $(\bar{q}, p) =$

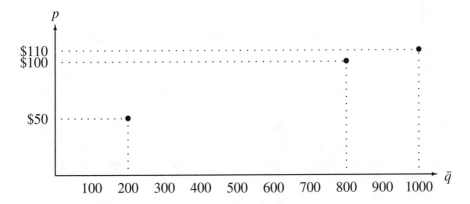

Figure 2.11: Aggregate demand under network effects.

$(200, \$50)$ is indeed on the aggregate demand curve as drawn in Figure 2.8. When $\bar{q} = 200$ consumers buy the service, the willingness to pay of type 1 consumers is $V_1 = \$30 + 0.1 \cdot 200 = \$50$. Hence, type 1 consumers will buy the service at the price $p = \$50$. In addition, to provide complete proof that the pair $(200, \$50)$ is indeed on the demand curve, we must also verify that type 2 and 3 consumers will *not* buy the service (of course, given that they all expect that $\bar{q} = 200$). To see this, observe that $V_2 = \$20 + 0.1 \cdot 200 = \$40 < \$50$ and that $V_1 = \$10 + 0.1 \cdot 200 = \$30 < \$50$, which confirms that only type 1 is willing to pay for the service.

The demand equilibrium point $(200, \$50)$ is considered to be "bad" for sellers because it is generated from self-fulfilling low expectations on the market size. However, as illustrated in Figure 2.8, it is not the only equilibrium demand point. Consider now a more "optimistic" expectation for the market size in which consumer expect that $\bar{q} = 800$ consumers will purchase this service. We now verify that the price–quantity pair $(\bar{q}, p) = (800, \$100)$ is indeed on the aggregate demand curve as drawn in Figure 2.8. Type 1 consumers will purchase the service because $V_1 = \$30 + 0.1 \cdot 800 = \$110 > \$100$. Type 2 consumers will purchase the service because $V_2 = \$20 + 0.1 \cdot 800 = \$100 = \$100$. Type 3 consumers will not purchase because $V_3 = \$10 + 0.1 \cdot 800 = \$90 < \$100$.

Finally, $(\bar{q}, p) = (1000, \$110)$ is on the demand curve because all consumers' willingness to pay is higher or equal to $p = \$110$. This follows from $V_1 = \$30 + 0.1 \cdot 1000 = \$130$, $V_2 = \$20 + 0.1 \cdot 1000 = \$120$, and $V_3 = \$10 + 0.1 \cdot 1000 = \$110$.

Now that we established that Figure 2.8 is indeed the demand function for the consumers whose willingness to pay is characterized by (2.28), we would like to characterize some general properties associated with aggregate demand functions of consumers whose behavior is influenced by network effects.

- Under network effects, aggregate demand may be upward sloping, reflecting higher willingness to pay when the product/service is adopted by more consumers.

- The demand function (in fact, a correspondence for readers with a mathematical background) is not uniquely determined in the sense that at some given prices, there may be several equilibrium quantities. That is, to a given price, there may correspond different levels of quantity demanded associated with different self-fulfilling consumer expectations.

- The demand may be unstable at low levels of quantity demanded, because a slight drop in price may trigger larger adoption levels that would then "convince" more consumers that this market is "hot," thereby further enhancing quantity demanded, and so on.

2.7 Demand for Substitutes and Complements

So far, our analysis focused on stand-alone services and products that are consumed independently of other goods and services. However, in reality, the benefits from products and services also depend on the consumption of other goods. These "other" goods may be produced by the same seller, or by different competing sellers. In this section we analyze the demand for such goods by looking at *systems* of aggregate demand equations.

Let us suppose that consumers choose their consumption levels of two goods, labeled A and B. The market aggregate direct linear demand functions for goods A and B are given by

$$q_A(p_A, p_B) \stackrel{\text{def}}{=} \alpha_A - \beta_A\, p_A + \gamma_A\, p_B, \tag{2.29}$$
$$q_B(p_A, p_B) \stackrel{\text{def}}{=} \alpha_B + \gamma_B\, p_A - \beta_B\, p_B.$$

Thus, the demand for each good also depends on the price of the other good (in fact, on the prices of all other goods in a more general setup). The parameters β_A, β_B, γ_A, and γ_B must be estimated from real-life data, as we demonstrate below. In general, unless network effects are present, one should expect to find that the parameters β_A and β_B (known as the own-price effect parameters) are strictly negative, thereby reflecting downward-sloping demand curves.

The signs of the remaining two parameters, γ_A and γ_B, have the following interpretations:

DEFINITION 2.4
Consumers are said to view goods A and B as

(a) **Substitutes**, *if an increase in the price of B increases the demand for A, and an increase in the price of A increases the demand for B. In the present example,* $\gamma_A > 0$ *and* $\gamma_B > 0$.

(b) **Complements**, *if an increase in the price of B decreases the demand for A (and B), and an increase in the price of A decreases the demand for A (and B). In the present example,* $\gamma_A < 0$ *and* $\gamma_B < 0$.

In fact, for some purposes (for example, see the analysis of peak-load pricing under interdependent demand in Section 6.6) it is more useful to use a system of inverse demand functions rather than a system of direct demand functions. Thus, inverting the system of inverse demand (2.29) obtains the system of inverse demand functions given by

$$p_A(q_A, q_B) = \frac{\alpha_A \beta_B + \alpha_B \gamma_A - \beta_B q_A - \gamma_A q_B}{\beta_A \beta_B - \gamma_A \gamma_B}, \tag{2.30}$$
$$p_A(q_A, q_B) = \frac{\alpha_B \beta_A + \alpha_A \gamma_B - \beta_A q_B - \gamma_B q_A}{\beta_A \beta_B - \gamma_A \gamma_B}.$$

Clearly, it must be assumed (or verified if the demand is estimated from actual data) that $\beta_A \beta_B > \gamma_A \gamma_B$, which means that price is more sensitive to changes in its own purchased quantity than changes in the quantity purchased of the competing brand.

There are two ways to estimate the system of linear demand functions defined in (2.29). If the researcher is an economist seeking to predict long-term market outcomes and trends, or is a regulator seeking to regulate this market, then the demand equations (2.29) should be estimated as a system. The only problem with such estimations is that most spreadsheet programs cannot estimate a system of equations, therefore, a statistical software package may be needed. However, if a single firm would like to compute its profit-maximizing price assuming that the prices set by its rivals are fixed at certain levels, it may be sufficient to use a second, simpler estimation method, which is to estimate one equation at a time. In particular, this may be the only choice if the firm does not have sales data from competitors. Given the scope of this book, for our purposes we demonstrate how the demand for good A can be estimated given the data displayed in Table 2.4.

Observation no.	1	2	3	4	5
q_A (quantity of A)	2	3	6	7	9
p_A (price of A)	$30	$25	$20	$15	$30
p_B (price of B)	$20	$30	$40	$30	$60
$e(q_A, p_B)$	1.00	3.00	-0.67	0.28	1.00
$\breve{e}(q_A, p_B)$	1.00	2.33	-0.54	0.37	1.00
Linear fitting (2.31)	-1.05	3.02	7.09	6.30	8.67
Exponential fitting (2.36)	1.80	3.73	6.85	6.12	8.03

Table 2.4: Data points for estimating multivariate linear demand.

Running this multivariate regression on a spreadsheet yields the regression result

$$q_A(p_A, p_B) = 3.928 - 0.328\, p_A + 0.243\, p_B. \tag{2.31}$$

Because $\gamma_A = 0.243 > 0$, goods A and B are substitutes according to Definition 2.4. Therefore, an increase in the quantity demanded of brand A can be attributed to either a fall in p_A or a rise in p_B. Some values of estimated demand function (2.31), evaluated at the observed prices, are listed in the second to last row of Table 2.4.

One useful tool that should be introduced into the analysis of demand affected by more than one price is the cross-elasticity of demand. Following our definition of own-price elasticity given by (2.1), the cross-elasticity is defined by

$$e(q_A, p_B) \stackrel{\text{def}}{=} \left(\frac{\Delta q_A}{\Delta p_B}\right)\left(\frac{p_B}{q_A}\right) = \frac{\text{percentage change of } q_A}{\text{percentage change of } p_B} = \frac{\%\Delta q_A}{\%\Delta p_B}. \tag{2.32}$$

That is, the cross-elasticity function measures the percentage increase in the demand for brand A given a small increase in the price of B. Just like direct price elasticity, it is a function that must be evaluated at a point on the demand curve

(q_A, p_A, p_B). Table 2.4 provides some computation of the cross-elasticity and the arc cross-elasticity, the analog of (2.4) for discrete observations.

Using calculus and the formula given by (2.32), we can compute the cross-elasticity function for the linear demand function for brand A given by (2.29) to be

$$e(q_A, p_B) = \frac{dq_A}{dp_B} \frac{p_B}{q_A} = \gamma_A \frac{p_B}{q_A}. \tag{2.33}$$

For example, if we apply this derivation to the estimated demand (2.31), we obtain $e(3, \$30) = 2.43$, which is close to the arc cross-elasticity given by $\breve{e}(3, \$30) = 2.33$.

The reader should ask at this point whether we can formulate a constant-elasticity demand function in the presence of substitutes and complements. As we now show, the analog of (2.14) for the two goods is given by

$$q_A(p_A, p_B) \overset{\text{def}}{=} \alpha_A \, p_A^{-\beta_A} \, p_B^{\gamma_A}, \tag{2.34}$$

$$q_B(p_A, p_B) \overset{\text{def}}{=} \alpha_B \, p_A^{\gamma_B} \, p_B^{-\beta_B}.$$

In view of (2.33), the cross-elasticities of demand are easy to spot as the exponents of the relevant prices. Thus, $e(q_A, p_B) = \gamma_A$ and $e(q_B, p_A) = \gamma_B$.

To estimate these demand functions using linear regressions, one can formulate the analog of (2.15) as

$$\underbrace{\ln q_A}_{\text{dependent variable}} = \underbrace{\ln \alpha_A}_{\text{constant}} \underbrace{-\beta_A}_{\text{slope}} \underbrace{\ln p_A}_{\text{var.}A} \underbrace{+\gamma_A}_{\text{slope}} \underbrace{\ln p_B}_{\text{var.}B}. \tag{2.35}$$

Running the linear regression (2.35) on the data given in Table 2.4 yields the parameters $\ln \alpha_A = -0.1919$, hence $\alpha = 0.825$, $-\beta_A = -0.965$, and $\gamma_A = 1.357$. Consequently, the estimated constant-elasticity demand function can be written as

$$q_A(p_A, p_B) = 0.825 \, p_A^{-0.965} \, p_B^{1.357}. \tag{2.36}$$

Some values of estimated demand function (2.36), evaluated at the observed prices, are listed in the bottom row of Table 2.4. Observe that the demand function (2.36) is inelastic with respect to its own price because $|e(q_A, p_A)| = 0.965 < 1$, but it is elastic with respect to the cross price because and $e(q_A, p_B) = 1.357 > 1$.

2.8 Consumer Surplus

In this section, we develop the concept of *consumer surplus* to measure consumers' satisfaction generated from purchasing a certain quantity of a product or a service. Gross consumer surplus is commonly used by economists to approximate the utility generated by consuming at a certain quantity level. Net consumer surplus is then used to measure the utility after consumers have paid for the amount they consume.

Clearly, a higher expenditure on one good reduces utility via a reduction in the consumption of other goods corresponding to the consumers' budget constraints.

There are two advantages to using consumer surplus over utility functions (a theoretical tool widely used in economic theory to measure satisfaction and welfare):

(a) Consumer surplus is measured in dollar terms (or any other currency). Thus, the net consumer surplus is the satisfaction level "minus" the total payments consumers must make to consume this good. Therefore,

(b) Consumer surplus can be aggregated over different consumers and over different markets to measure total aggregate consumer satisfaction in a given market or a variety of markets.

The validity of using consumer surplus as a measure of consumer welfare has been debated in the literature for many years. Willig (1976) provides a justification for using consumer surplus by demonstrating that in most applications, the error with respect to the widely used compensating and equivalent variations is very small.

Sellers should make every effort to learn about consumers' satisfaction because this information can lead to more profitable pricing techniques, such as bundling and tying (Chapter 4) and the implementation of multipart tariffs (Chapter 5). We will be using the following terminology:

DEFINITION 2.5
(a) **Gross consumer surplus** *at a given consumption level q, denoted by $gcs(q)$, is the area formed beneath the demand curve when quantity consumed is increased from zero consumption to the level of q.*
(b) **Net consumer surplus** *at a given consumption level q, denoted by $ncs(q)$, is the gross consumer surplus after subtracting all consumer expenditures involving the purchase of the q units of consumption.*
(c) **Marginal gross (net) consumer surplus** *at a given consumption level q, is the change in gross (net) consumer surplus generated by an increase in consumption by one unit. For calculus users, these values can be computed as $\mathrm{d}gcs(q)/\mathrm{d}q$ and $\mathrm{d}ncs(q)/\mathrm{d}q$, respectively.*

2.8.1 Consumer surplus: Discrete demand functions

Figure 2.12 illustrates how to compute consumer surplus for the two types of demand functions discussed in Section 2.1.2. It should be emphasized that the consumer expenditure that should be used for measuring net consumer surplus may include some fixed fees in addition to pq, which measures the expenditure based on the per-unit price multiplied by the consumption level. For example, consumers often have to pay lump-sum (quantity-independent) fees for entering amusement parks or clubs, or other subscription fees, before they can pay for any additional units of consumption. In fact, Chapters 4 and 5 analyze some pricing methods in which the seller bundles the product into packages and sells them for a fixed price (as opposed to charging a price per unit). When we compute consumer surplus generated from buying such packages, we must subtract these fixed fees from gross consumer surplus to obtain net consumer surplus.

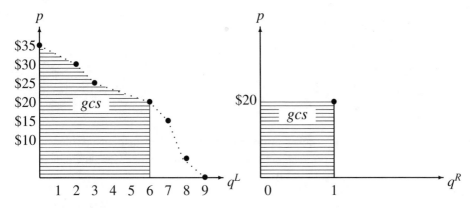

Figure 2.12: Approximating gross consumer surplus *gcs* for two types of discrete demand functions. *Note*: The discrete data points on left are connected by straight lines.

Often, it is more convenient to compute the *changes* in net and gross consumer surplus generated by a price reduction from p_1 to p_2, and the corresponding increase in quantity consumed q_1 and q_2. In this case, we can write

$$\Delta gcs(q_1, q_2) \overset{\text{def}}{=} \frac{(p_1 + p_2)(q_2 - q_1)}{2} \quad \text{and}$$

$$\Delta ncs(q_1, q_2) = \Delta gcs(p_1, p_2) - \Delta \text{expenditure}. \quad (2.37)$$

Thus, the change in gross consumer surplus resulting from a drop in price from p_1 to p_2 and an increase in quantity from q_1 to q_2 is the average price $(p_1 + p_2)/2$ multiplied by the change in the corresponding quantity consumed $q_2 - q_1$. Graphically, the above formula for Δgcs defines an area of a trapezoid, where p_1 and p_2 form the parallel sides of this trapezoid. Next, the net change in consumer surplus defined by (2.37) subtracts the change in consumer expenditure from the change in gross consumer surplus. Note that this expenditure may rise or fall depending on whether the demand is elastic or inelastic at the relevant range.

Table 2.5 displays the computation results of gross and net consumer surplus for the demand functions illustrated by Figure 2.12. The gross consumer surplus in Table 2.5 is computed by adding the changes in gross consumer surplus, where the changes are computed according to the formula (2.37). The initial change in gross consumer surplus is computed by reducing the price from the prohibitive level $p = \$35$ to $p = \$30$, hence increasing quantity demanded from $q^L = 0$ to $q^L = 2$.

p	\$35	\$30	\$25	\$20	\$15	\$10	\$5	\$0
q^L	0	2	3	6	7	7.5	8	9
pq^L	\$0	\$60	\$75	\$120	\$105	\$75	\$40	\$0
Δgcs	n/a	\$65	\$27.5	\$67.5	\$17.5	\$6.25	\$3.75	\$2.5
gcs	\$0	\$65	\$92.5	\$160	\$177.5	\$183.75	\$187.5	\$190
ncs	\$0	\$5	\$17.5	\$40	\$72.5	\$108.75	\$147.5	\$190
q^R	0	0	0	1	1	1	1	1
pq^R	\$0	\$0	\$0	\$20	\$15	\$10	\$5	\$0
gcs	\$0	\$0	\$0	\$20	\$20	\$20	\$20	\$20
ncs	\$0	\$5	\$0	\$0	\$5	\$10	\$15	\$20

Table 2.5: Gross (*gcs*) and net (*ncs*) consumer surplus. *Top*: For the demand illustrated in Figure 2.12(left). *Bottom*: For Figure 2.12(right). *Note*: Computations of *ncs* are limited to single tariffs p only (no fixed fees).

Using (2.37), we have $\Delta gcs(0,2) = \$65$. Next, we reduce the price from $p = \$30$ to $p = \$25$, thereby increasing quantity demanded from $q^L = 2$ to $q^L = 3$. Hence, $\Delta gcs(2,3) = \$27.5$. Therefore, the gross consumer surplus when consumers buy $q^L = 3$ units is $gcs(3) = \Delta gcs(0,2) + \Delta gcs(2,3) = 65 + 27.5 = \$92.5$. Finally, let us further reduce the price from $p = \$25$ to $p = \$20$, thereby increasing quantity demanded from $q^L = 3$ to $q^L = 6$. Using (2.37), $\Delta gcs(3,6) = \$67.5$. Therefore, the gross consumer surplus when consumers buy $q^L = 6$ units is $gcs(6) = \Delta gcs(0,2) + \Delta gcs(2,3) + \Delta gcs(3,6) = 65 + 27.5 + 67.5 = \$160$.

Figure 2.12(left) illustrates a downward-sloping demand curve, which, following Section 2.1.2, can be interpreted as an individual consumer's demand curve, where the individual increases quantity demanded when the price falls, or an aggregated demand curve composed of many consumers, each with either a downward-sloping demand curve or a single-unit demand curve as illustrated on the right part of Figure 2.12. The bottom part of Table 2.5 demonstrates how to compute the consumer surplus for a consumer with a single-unit demand function, as illustrated in Figure 2.12(right). These calculations are rather trivial because this consumer's maximum willingness to pay is $V = \$20$ and the consumer buys at most one unit. Therefore, this consumer will not buy at any price in the range $p > \$20$. If the price drops to $p = \$20$, the consumer buys one unit and gains a gross consumer surplus of $gcs = \$20$ and a net consumer surplus of $ncs = V - pq^R = \$20 - \$20 = \$0$. Next, if the price falls to $p = \$10$, gross consumer surplus does not change because quantity demanded stays at $q^R = 1$, hence $gcs = \$20$. However, because of the price reduction and the perfectly inelastic demand, net consumer surplus increases to $ncs = \$20 - \$10 = \$10$.

```
q[1] ← 0; gcs[1] ← 0; /* High p[1] generates zero demand        */
for ℓ = 2 to M do
    /* Loop over demand observations and Price reductions */
    Δgcs[ℓ] ← (p[ℓ − 1] + p[ℓ])(q[ℓ] − q[ℓ − 1])/2; /* Change in gcs  */
    gcs[ℓ] ← gcs[ℓ − 1] + Δgcs[ℓ]; /* gcs at q[ℓ] units               */
    writeln ("At the price p =", p[ℓ], "quantity demanded is q = ", q[ℓ],
    "gross consumer surplus is gcs =", gcs[ℓ]);
    writeln ("Increasing consumption from ", q[ℓ − 1], "to ", q[ℓ], has
    increased gross consumer surplus by ", Δgcs[ℓ]);
```

Algorithm 2.3: Computing gross consumer surplus for discrete demand.

Algorithm 2.3 computes gross consumer surplus for discrete demand functions. Algorithm 2.3 should input, using the **Read()** command, and store the data points of the discrete demand function based on $M \geq 1$ price–quantity observations. More precisely, the program must input the price $p[\ell]$ and the corresponding quantity demanded $q[\ell]$ for each observation $\ell = 1, \ldots, M$, where $p[\ell]$ and $q[\ell]$ are M-dimensional arrays of real-valued demand observations. It is recommended that the program run some trivial loops verifying nonnegativity as well as some strictly positive demand observation. It is very important that prices be ordered from high to low so that $p[1] > p[2] > \cdots > p[M]$ and that $p[1]$ will be sufficiently high to induce $q[1] = 0$ (zero consumption). In any case, the proposed algorithm assigns $q[1] \leftarrow 0$ as otherwise consumer surplus cannot be computed for discrete demand.

Algorithm 2.3 runs a loop over all observations $\ell = 2, \cdots, M$, and computes the *change* in gross consumer surplus. Then, it adds up this change to the gross consumer surplus computed for previous observation. Thus, the program outputs the results onto the real-valued M-dimensional arrays $\Delta gcs[\ell]$ and $gcs[\ell]$, where the algorithm presets $gcs[1] \leftarrow 0$ and $q[1] \leftarrow 0$ (no consumption).

2.8.2 Consumer surplus: Continuous demand functions

The computations of gross consumer surplus turn out to be much simpler when applied to continuous linear and constant-elasticity demand functions. The left part of Figure 2.13 illustrates how to compute gross consumer surplus for the linear demand function analyzed in Section 2.3. Figure 2.13(right) illustrates how to compute gross consumer surplus for the constant-elasticity demand function analyzed in Section 2.4.

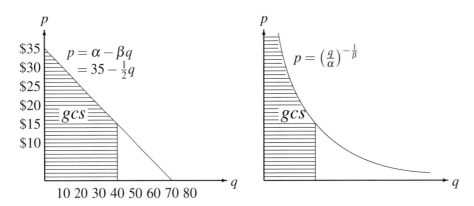

Figure 2.13: Gross consumer surplus. *Left*: Linear demand function. *Right*: Constant-elasticity demand function.

Linear demand function

Figure 2.13(left) is drawn according to $p = 35 - 0.5q$. For this particular linear demand function, the gross consumer surplus evaluated at a consumption level of $q = 40$ units is the area of the trapezoid defined by

$$gcs(40) = \frac{(35+15)(40-0)}{2} = \$1000. \tag{2.38}$$

For the general linear demand case $p = \alpha - \beta q$, the gross consumer surplus at any arbitrary consumption level q is

$$gcs(q) = \frac{(\alpha+p)(q-0)}{2} = \frac{(\alpha+\alpha-\beta q)(q-0)}{2} = \frac{(2\alpha-\beta q)q}{2}. \tag{2.39}$$

Readers who prefer to use calculus can simply integrate the inverse demand function $\int_0^q (\alpha - \beta q)dq$ to obtain (2.39). In fact, the formula derived in (2.39) can be extended to capture the change in consumer surplus generated by increasing consumption from q_1 to q_2 so that

$$\Delta gcs(q_1,q_2) = \frac{(p_1+p_2)(q_2-q_1)}{2} = \frac{(\alpha-\beta q_1+\alpha-\beta q_2)(q_2-q_1)}{2}$$
$$= \frac{(q_2-q_1)[2\alpha-\beta(q_1+q_2)]}{2}. \tag{2.40}$$

If we return to the specific example drawn in Figure 2.13(left) where $p = 35 - 0.5q$, formula (2.40) implies that the change in consumer surplus generated by increasing consumption from $q_1 = 20$ to $q_2 = 40$ is $\Delta gcs(20,40) = \$400$.

Several chapters in this book make heavy use of the consumer surplus concept. For example, a proper characterization of consumer surplus is essential for pricing bundles of products and services containing more than one unit of consumption (see Chapter 4). Therefore, it is often useful to plot consumer surplus as a function of quantity consumed. Figure 2.14 illustrates the gross consumer surplus (2.39) derived from the general demand function $p = \alpha - \beta q$ (also plotted).

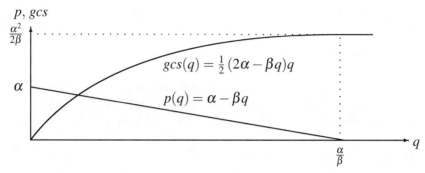

Figure 2.14: Illustration of gross consumer surplus for linear demand. *Note*: Figure is not drawn to scale.

Calculus lovers who wish to characterize the gross consumer surplus function can simply differentiate (2.39) with respect to quantity consumed to obtain

$$\frac{\mathrm{d}gcs(q)}{\mathrm{d}q} = \alpha - \beta q = p(q). \tag{2.41}$$

That is, the *marginal* gross consumer surplus function (see Definition 2.5(c)) is equal to the inverse demand function that equals the price a consumer is willing to pay at a given consumption level. Intuitively, the change in gross consumer surplus associated with a small increase in consumption (the marginal gross consumer surplus) must be equal to the consumer's willingness to pay as captured by the price on the inverse demand function.

Constant-elasticity demand function

Figure 2.13(right) illustrates the inverse demand function derived from the direct constant-elasticity demand function $q = \alpha(q)^{-\beta}$, which was analyzed in Section 2.4. Thus, assuming $\beta > 1$ (elastic demand), the inverse demand function and the corresponding gross consumer surplus are given by

$$p = \left(\frac{q}{\alpha}\right)^{-\frac{1}{\beta}} \quad \text{hence} \quad gcs(q) = \int_{0}^{q} \left(\frac{x}{\alpha}\right)^{-\frac{1}{\beta}} \mathrm{d}x = \frac{\beta q\left(\frac{q}{\alpha}\right)^{-\frac{1}{\beta}}}{\beta - 1}. \tag{2.42}$$

The gross consumer surplus (2.42) evaluated at a given consumption level q is marked by the shaded area in Figure 2.13(right).

2.9 Cost of Production

If this book were to explore the subject of yield (revenue) management only, we would not have to study firms' cost structure. However, because our goal is to study pricing techniques leading to profit maximization, we must take production cost considerations into account. In this section, we will not explore the structure of the cost of production in much detail (as opposed to the extensive description of the demand side in the chapter), so the reader who is interested in more comprehensive analyses of production cost, and more microfoundations of how cost of production relates to the concept of the production function, can find these topics in almost any intermediate microeconomics textbook as well as some industrial organization textbooks.

Perhaps the most difficult decision to make in devising pricing strategies is how to classify the wide variety of costs borne by sellers and producers. Whereas all rules are meant to be broken, this book treats cost according to the following logic:

- Costs that have already been paid, or already contracted, are considered to be sunk. Cost that have not been paid should be considered as fixed if not directly related to output level expansion, and marginal if borne when sales or production is increased by one unit.

- Sunk costs are generally irrelevant for pricing decisions, at least in the short run.

- Standard accounting techniques are generally not suitable for making pricing decisions. Managers should ask their accountants and engineers to issue reports according to whether costs are sunk, fixed, or marginal, or according to some other cost classification discussed in this book.

This "logic" implies that there is a great deal of arbitrariness in how costs are classified. What this book recommends is that in cases in which some costs cannot be attributed to a single classification, the pricing manager should work out different pricing strategies using different options and then evaluate the relative loss resulting from making the wrong choice. The last item on the above list stems from the fact that accounting procedures are not designed to help in making profit-maximizing pricing decisions, because these procedures are generally designed for tax-reporting purposes as well as for stockholders and board members.

Sunk, fixed, and marginal costs are not the only cost classifications used in this book. Fixed costs can be broken into the following subgroups:

Firm's fixed cost: Costs associated with the general operation of a plant (in a case which the seller is also the producer) or a retail firm (if the firm is only a seller).

Market specific: Costs associated with entry and maintaining a presence in different markets.

Clearly, entry fixed costs become sunk after entry is completed and fixed costs are reduced to the general cost of operating in the specific market. The firm's total fixed cost is denoted by ϕ, and market ℓ fixed cost is denoted by ϕ_ℓ for each market $\ell = 1, \ldots, M$.

Marginal costs can be broken into the following two subgroups:

Marginal operating cost: Cost associated with serving one additional customer.

Marginal capacity cost: Cost of increasing capacity that enables the production of one additional unit, or serves one additional consumer.

For example, the marginal operating cost for an electricity company is the additional fuel and transmission costs associated with the production and sale of one additional kilowatt per hour. The marginal capacity cost would be the cost of upgrading production and transmission capacity to generate one additional kilowatt per hour. This distinction becomes important in Chapter 6, where we analyze peak and off-peak pricing, as well as in Chapters 7 and 8, where we analyze airline booking strategies.

From a technical point of view, in what follows we focus our analysis on cost structures confined to constant marginal cost only. Perhaps the simplest representation of a firm's cost structure is given by

$$c(q) = \begin{cases} \phi + \mu q & \text{if } q > 0 \\ 0 & \text{if } q = 0, \end{cases} \qquad (2.43)$$

where $q \geq 0$ is the output level of the firm. The parameter ϕ is called a *fixed* or *sunk* cost that sums up all the firm's costs that are independent of the chosen output level. Formula (2.43) assumes that the firm has the option of going out of service, thereby avoiding paying the fixed cost ϕ. However, as long as some output is produced, the firm must bear the full amount.

The parameter μ is called the *marginal* cost of production and is defined as the change in cost associated with an increase in output by one unit (or infinitesimal change if calculus is used). Formally, for nonnegative output levels $q \geq 0$, we define the marginal and average cost functions by

$$\frac{\Delta c(q)}{\Delta q} = \mu \quad \text{and} \quad \frac{c(q)}{q} = \frac{\phi}{q} + \mu. \qquad (2.44)$$

Unlike the marginal cost, which measures the change in cost when output level slightly increases from a certain level q, the *average* cost measures the production cost per unit of output. Inspecting (2.44) reveals that under the present specification (where the marginal cost μ is constant), the average cost would be equal to the

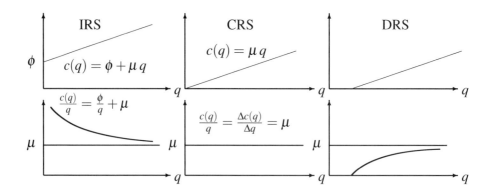

Figure 2.15: *Top*: Total cost curves. *Bottom*: Average and marginal cost curves.

marginal cost if there are no fixed costs, that is, if $\phi = 0$. Figure 2.15 illustrates the marginal cost and three types of average cost functions defined by (2.44): The shapes of the average cost functions drawn in Figure 2.15 lead us to the following definitions.

DEFINITION 2.6
We say that a production technology exhibits (a) **increasing returns to scale** *(IRS) if the cost per unit declines with an increase in the production level, (b)* **constant returns to scale** *(CRS) if the cost per unit is constant and equals the marginal cost, and (c)* **decreasing returns to scale** *(DRS) if the cost per unit increases with the level of output produced.*

In this book, we focus mainly on increasing and constant returns to scale as these cost configurations fit the industries we analyze.

The cost structure defined by (2.43) turns out to be extremely useful when a firm's manager has to decide on the location of production. More precisely, suppose a firm has two plants located in different cities. Let q_1 denote the output level produced in plant 1. q_2 is similarly defined. Suppose both plants operate under increasing returns to scale and that the cost functions of the plants are given by

$$c_1(q_1) = \begin{cases} \phi_1 + \mu_1 q_1 & \text{if } q_1 > 0 \\ 0 & \text{if } q_1 = 0 \end{cases} \quad \text{and}$$

$$c_2(q_2) = \begin{cases} \phi_2 + \mu_2 q_2, & \text{if } q_2 > 0 \\ 0 & \text{if } q_2 = 0, \end{cases} \quad (2.45)$$

where we assume that $\phi_1 > \phi_2 \geq 0$ and $\mu_2 > \mu_1 \geq 0$. That is, plant 1 has a higher fixed cost but a lower marginal cost compared with plant 2. Figure 2.16 illustrates the cost functions of the two plants.

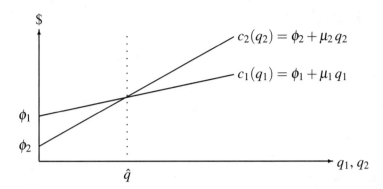

Figure 2.16: Allocating production between two plants under increasing returns.

Because the cost structure (2.45) implies that firms' technologies exhibit increasing returns to scale (provided that $\phi_2 > 0$), the manager will allocate the entire production to a single plant. Figure 2.16 shows that there exists a unique threshold output level $\hat{q}$ for which production at any level satisfying $q < \hat{q}$ is cheaper in plant 2 than in plant 1. If a higher production level is desired, that is, if $q > \hat{q}$, then the entire production should be allocated to plant 1. This is because the higher fixed cost in plant 1 covers a larger production volume, so the lower marginal cost in plant 1 minimizes production cost relative to plant 2. To find the threshold production level, we solve for $\hat{q}$ satisfying $\phi_1 + \mu_1 \hat{q}_1 = \phi_2 + \mu_2 \hat{q}_1$, yielding

$$\hat{q} = \frac{\phi_1 - \phi_2}{\mu_2 - \mu_1}. \tag{2.46}$$

In the outsourcing literature (see, for example, Shy and Stenbacka 2005 and their references), plant 1 is viewed as the "home" firm and plant 2 as the "outsourced" firm. Intuitively, the idea here is that the construction of an in-house production line inflicts a high fixed cost but a lower marginal cost compared with outsourcing. Outsourcing reduces the fixed cost (perhaps eliminates it), but the outsourcing firm must pay a higher price for each additional unit outsourced outside the firm.

2.10   Exercises

1. Fill in the missing parts in Table 2.6 based on the discrete demand analysis in
   Section 2.2.

p	$9.5	$9.0	$8.5	$8.0	$7.5	$7.0	$6.5	$6.0
q	15	16	17	18	19	20	21	22
$e(q)$								
$\breve{e}(q)$								
$x(q)$								
$\frac{\Delta x(q)}{\Delta q}$								

Table 2.6: Data for Exercises 1 and 2.

2. Use a computer to estimate linear and constant-elasticity demand using the raw
   data on demand observations given in the first two lines of Table 2.6.

   (a) Using the procedure described in Section 2.3.2, estimate the parameters γ
   and δ of the direct linear demand function $p(q) = \gamma - \delta q$.

   (b) Formulate the inverse demand function corresponding to the direct demand
   function you estimated in part (a).

   (c) Using the procedure described in Section 2.4.2, estimate the parameters α
   and β of the direct constant-elasticity demand function $q(p) = \alpha p^{-\beta}$.

   (d) What is the value of the elasticity of the constant-elasticity demand function
   you have estimated? Is this function elastic or inelastic?

3. Consider the following direct linear demand function $q(p) = 34 - 2p$.

   (a) Formulate the corresponding inverse demand function $p(q)$ and the revenue
   function $x(q)$.

   (b) This exercise requires the use of calculus. Using the analysis of Section 2.3.3,
   compute the revenue maximizing output level and the corresponding price.

   (c) Compute the resulting revenue level and the price elasticity assuming that a
   single firm sells the revenue-maximizing output level.

4. Consider the example of aggregating single-unit demand functions analyzed in
   Section 2.5.1 and plotted in Figure 2.8. Suppose that a fourth type of new consumers $N_4 = 200$ enters this market (say, because of a large wave of immigration
   into this city). Draw the new aggregate demand function assuming that the maximum willingness to pay of each newly entering consumer is $25.

5. Consider the example of aggregating linear demand functions analyzed in Section 2.5.2 and plotted in Figure 2.9. Suppose that, following an intensive advertising campaign, new consumers enter this market with a group demand function given by $q = 200 - 20q$.

   (a) Redraw the aggregate inverse demand Figure 2.9, taking into consideration the newly added group of consumers.

   (b) Reformulate the algebraic expression (2.25) of the aggregate demand function to account for the newly added group of consumers.

6. Consider consumers whose behavior is influenced by network effects, as analyzed in Section 2.6. Now, let us modify the willingness to pay of type 3 consumers initially defined by (2.28), and assume that $V_3 = \$10 + 0.2\bar{q}$. Thus, the modified type 3 consumers have the lowest basic willingness to pay but are much more sensitive to the network size than type 1 and type 2 consumers. Redraw the aggregate demand function illustrated in Figure 2.11 taking into consideration the above modification. Explain your derivations.

7. Suppose the direct demand for apples (good A) and that for bananas (good B) are given by equation (2.29). Solve the following problems.

   (a) Estimate the parameters α_A, β_A, and γ_B of demand function for apples using the data provided in Table 2.7.

Observation no.	1	2	3	4	5
q_A (quantity of A)	20	30	40	50	60
p_A (price of A)	\$5	\$4	\$2	\$3	\$1
p_B (price of B)	\$5	\$4	\$6	\$7	\$8
$e(q_A, p_B)$					
$\breve{e}(q_A, p_B)$					
Linear fitting (2.29)					
Exponential fitting (2.34)					

Table 2.7: Data points for Exercise 7.

   (b) Estimate the parameters α_A, β_A, and γ_B in the regression equation (2.35), which assumes that direct demand for apples is given by equation (2.34).

   (c) Fill in the missing parts in Table 2.7.

8. Fill in the missing items in Table 2.8 using the derivations of gross and net consumer surplus given in Section 2.8.1 for discrete demand functions. For the last row, in computing *ncs* assume that consumers pay only a per-unit price *p* and do not bear any additional fixed fees.

p	$40	$30	$20	$10	$0
q	0	10	20	40	70
pq					
Δgcs	n/a				
gcs					
ncs					

Table 2.8: Data for Exercise 8.

9. Consider the analysis of consumer surplus given in Section 2.8.2 for linear demand functions. Answer the following questions assuming that the demand function is given by $p = 120 - 2q$.

   (a) Compute gross consumer surplus assuming that consumers buy $q = 40$ units. Formally, compute $gcs(40)$.

   (b) Compute the change in consumer surplus $\Delta gcs(40, 50)$ generated by an increase in consumption level from 40 units to 50 units.

   (c) Compute net consumer surplus assuming that consumers pay a per-unit price of $p = \$40$ and in addition they must pay a (quantity-independent) fixed fee of $f = \$600$.

10. Consider the production cost analysis of Section 2.9. Suppose that production in city 2 is heavily subsidized by the government, say because the government would like to encourage people to move to and settle in city 2. In contrast, production in city 1 is not subsidized. Assume that you have been appointed (congratulations!) the CEO of a company with plants in both cities. The plants' cost functions are given by

$$c_1(q_1) = \begin{cases} 100 + 4q_1 & \text{if } q_1 > 0 \\ 0 & \text{if } q_1 = 0 \end{cases} \quad \text{and} \quad c_2(q_2) = \begin{cases} -50 + 5q_2, & \text{if } q_2 > 0 \\ 0 & \text{if } q_2 = 0. \end{cases}$$

Suppose that you intend to produce q units of output. For each value of q, determine whether the production should be allocated to plant 1 or plant 2.

Chapter 3
Basic Pricing Techniques

3.1   Single-market Pricing   60

3.1.1   Price setting under discrete demand

3.1.2   Quantity setting under continuous linear demand

3.1.3   Price setting under continuous linear demand

3.1.4   Continuous constant-elasticity demand

3.2   Multiple Markets without Price Discrimination   67

3.2.1   Market-specific fixed costs and exclusion of markets

3.2.2   A computer algorithm for market selections

3.2.3   Multiple markets under single-unit demand

3.2.4   Linear demand: Example for two markets

3.2.5   Linear demand: General formulation for two markets

3.2.6   Linear demand: A computer algorithm for multiple markets

3.3   Multiple Markets with Price Discrimination   79

3.3.1   Unlimited capacity: Linear demand

3.3.2   Unlimited capacity: Constant-elasticity demand

3.3.3   Price discrimination under capacity constraint

3.4   Pricing under Competition   89

3.4.1   Switching costs among homogeneous goods

3.4.2   Switching costs among differentiated brands

3.4.3   Continuous demand with differentiated brands

3.5   Commonly Practiced Pricing Methods   99

3.5.1   Breakeven formulas

3.5.2   Cost-plus pricing methods

3.6   Regulated Public Utility   104

3.6.1   Allocating fixed costs across markets while breaking even

3.6.2   Allocating fixed costs: Ramsey pricing

3.7   Exercises   110

This chapter introduces basic pricing techniques. By *basic* we refer to techniques that are limited to simple one-time purchases of a single good only. That is, the simple techniques studied in this chapter do not address more sophisticated markets in which products and services are differentiated by the time of delivery, the length of the booking period, quantity discounts (bundling), and services that are tied with other products and services. In fact, some of basic pricing techniques described in this chapter can also be found in most intermediate college microeconomics textbooks. Clearly, readers must first understand these basic techniques before proceeding to more sophisticated ones analyzed in later chapters.

The basic question that must be addressed before managers select a price is whether competition with other firms prevails, or whether the firm can disregard any potential and existing competition and act as a single-seller monopoly. Most of the algorithms in this book are designed for a single seller simply because the introduction of competition diverts attention from learning the logic behind proper yield management. Clearly, prices should be lowered when a firm observes competition from rival firms. In view of this discussion, we divide this chapter into the analysis of basic monopoly pricing and only then proceed to analyze pricing under competition. The analysis of competition will be brief because there is a large number of market structures that must be considered. The study of market structures defines a subfield of economics called industrial organization and is found in most industrial organization textbooks. A comprehensive analysis of market structure is therefore beyond the scope of this book.

3.1   Single-market Pricing

Suppose that the seller is unable to segment the market into submarkets in which each market serves a different group of consumers. In this case, all the consumers are treated as a single market for which the seller must determine a single price. Recalling our notation given in Tables 1.4 and 1.5, the parameter μ denotes the seller's marginal production cost and ϕ the fixed/sunk cost (see Section 2.9 for precise definitions). The variable p denotes the price to be decided by the seller, and q the associated quantity demanded.

Similar to our analysis in Chapter 2, we divide our examination into discrete and continuous demand functions. A discrete demand analysis is generally more suitable for computer computations. However, using discrete demand may be less intuitive and harder to compute algebraically compared with the continuous demand analysis. Clearly, the two types of demand functions are related, because Sections 2.3.2 and 2.4.2 have already studied the techniques under which continuous demand functions can be used to approximate discrete demand functions.

3.1.1 Price setting under discrete demand

Figure 3.1 illustrates a typical discrete demand function. Suppose that the marginal cost is $\mu = \$20$ and the fixed cost is $\phi = \$10$. Table 3.1 describes the general method how to compute the profit-maximizing price, using the demand data given in Figure 3.1. Table 3.1 shows that the profit-maximizing price is $p = \$30$, yielding a profit of $y(30) = (30 - 20)2 - 10 = \$10$. Notice, however, that the profit-maximizing price may exceed the revenue-maximizing price. In fact, in this example Table 3.1 shows that the revenue-maximizing price is $p = \$20$. Clearly, the revenue-maximizing price cannot be higher than the profit-maximizing price because the latter includes the marginal cost.

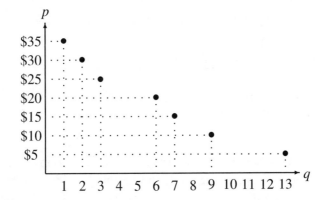

Figure 3.1: Nondiscriminating monopoly facing discrete demand.

p	35	**30**	25	**20**	15	10	5
$q(p)$	1	2	3	6	7	9	13
$x(p) = pq$	35	60	75	**120**	105	90	65
$y(p) = x - \mu q - \phi$	5	**10**	5	-10	-45	-100	-205

Table 3.1: Profit-maximizing and revenue-maximizing prices (boldface) for a single seller facing a discrete demand function. *Note*: Table assumes $\mu = \$20$ and $\phi = \$10$.

We now provide a computer algorithm for selecting the profit-maximizing price and the revenue-maximizing price. Algorithm 3.1 should input (say, using the **Read()** command), and store the discrete demand function based on $M \geq 1$ price–quantity observations. More precisely, the program must input the price $p[\ell]$ and the aggregate quantity demanded $q[\ell]$ for each observation $\ell = 1,\ldots,M$, where $p[\ell]$ and $q[\ell]$ are M-dimensional arrays of real-valued demand observations. It is recommended that the program run some trivial loops verifying nonnegativity as well as some strictly positive demand observations. The program must also input the seller's cost parameters μ (marginal cost) and ϕ (fixed cost).

```
maxy ← 0; maxx ← 0; /* Initialization                              */
for ℓ = 1 to M do
    │  /* Main loop over demand observations                       */
    │  if (p[ℓ] − μ)q[ℓ] − φ ≥ maxy then
    │      │  /* Higher profit found                               */
    │      └  maxy ← (p[ℓ] − μ)q[ℓ] − φ; maxpy ← p[ℓ];
    │  if p[ℓ]q[ℓ] ≥ maxx then
    └      └  maxx ← p[ℓ]q[ℓ]; maxpx ← p[ℓ]; /* Higher revenue found */
writeln ("The revenue-maximizing price is p =", maxpx, "yielding the
revenue level x = ", maxx);
if maxy ≥ 0 then
    │  writeln ("The profit-maximizing price is p =", maxpy, "yielding the
    └  profit level y = ", maxy);
else writeln ("Negative profit. Do NOT operate in this market!")
```

Algorithm 3.1: Computing a monopoly's profit- and revenue-maximizing prices under discrete demand.

Algorithm 3.1 is rather straightforward. It runs a loop on all observations $\ell = 1, 2, \cdots, M$, and computes the profit and revenue levels. Each loop also checks whether the computed levels exceed currently maximized levels stored in nonnegative real variables denoted by $maxpy$ (profit-maximizing price), $maxpx$ (revenue-maximizing price), $maxy$ (maximum profit), and $maxx$ (maximum revenue).

Finally, Algorithm 3.1 could be enhanced to compute what some textbooks call the *short-run profit*. Short-run profit is generally defined as the profit level assuming zero fixed cost. That is, $(p - \mu)q$. In the above algorithm, the maximum short-run profit is simply $maxy + \phi$. If this value is nonnegative, the seller may want to consider the option of staying in business until the fixed cost must be repaid, and only then get out of business (delayed bankruptcy).

3.1.2 Quantity setting under continuous linear demand

One advantage of using a continuous demand function is that it makes it easy to obtain the profit-maximizing quantity produced and the corresponding price using simple algebraic computations (as opposed to having to run loops over all the observed price–quantity combinations, for the case of discrete demand functions). Section 2.3.2 has already demonstrated how a linear function can be used to approximate scattered price and quantity observations.

We now refer the reader back to Section 2.3, where equation (2.6) defines the inverse linear demand function given by $p(q) = \alpha - \beta q$, where the parameters $\alpha, \beta > 0$ are to be estimated by the econometrician. Recalling equations (2.11) and (2.12), the total and marginal revenue functions are given by

$$x(q) = p(q)q = \alpha q - \beta q^2 \quad \text{and} \quad \frac{\mathrm{d}x(q)}{\mathrm{d}q} = \frac{\mathrm{d}[p(q)q]}{\mathrm{d}q} = \alpha - 2\beta q. \qquad (3.1)$$

Let μ denote the marginal production/selling cost, and ϕ the fixed cost. The seller must first verify that the intercept of the inverse demand function exceeds the marginal cost, that is, $\alpha > \mu$. Otherwise, consumers' willingness to pay is below the marginal cost, which means that this product is not profitable even if the fixed cost is not taken into account. We are now ready to describe the procedure for selecting the monopoly's profit-maximizing price assuming that $\alpha > \mu$. As it turns out, it is much simpler to search for the monopoly's profit-maximizing output level first, and only then, using the inverse demand function, determine the profit-maximizing price. The following procedure uses this approach.

Step I: Increase quantity produced until the revenue generated from selling the last unit (the marginal revenue) equals marginal cost. Formally, use (3.1) to solve

$$\frac{\mathrm{d}x(q)}{\mathrm{d}q} = \mu \quad \text{to obtain} \quad q = \frac{\alpha - \mu}{2\beta}. \qquad (3.2)$$

Step II: Compute the "candidate" profit-maximizing price by substituting into the inverse demand function

$$p = \alpha - \beta q \quad \text{to obtain} \quad p = \frac{\alpha + \mu}{2}. \qquad (3.3)$$

Step III: Compute the profit level y by solving

$$y = (p - \mu)q - \phi \quad \text{to obtain} \quad y = \frac{(\alpha - \mu)^2}{4\beta} - \phi. \qquad (3.4)$$

If $y \geq 0$, then p given in (3.3) is the profit-maximizing price. Otherwise, the firm should not sell anything as this market is not profitable.

Note again that even if (3.4) is negative (the seller is making a loss), the seller may want to consider the option of staying in business until the fixed cost has to be repaid, and only then get out of business (delayed bankruptcy).

Figure 3.2 provides a visual interpretation for the above three-step procedure. The "candidate" profit-maximizing output is determined by the intersection of the marginal revenue function with the marginal cost function (lower thick dot). Then, from this point, extending the line upward toward the demand line yields the profit-maximizing price (upper thick dot) because consumers are always on their demand curve. However, note that all these are necessary conditions for profit maximization, which are not sufficient. For this reason, to complete this procedure, *Step III*

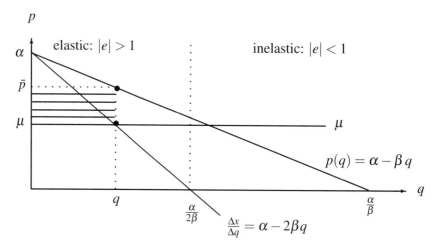

Figure 3.2: Simple monopoly: Profit-maximizing output and price. *Note*: Marked area indicates short-run profit (before the fixed cost ϕ is subtracted).

of this algorithm verifies that the short-run profit, represented by the marked area in Figure 3.2, exceeds the fixed cost parameter ϕ.

Figure 3.2 reveals that a single seller will always choose a price in the region where the demand is elastic (see Definition 2.2). In the elastic region, revenue increases when the price is reduced. In other words, a firm should never sell at a price at which the demand is inelastic. Moreover, as it turns out, the profit-maximizing price and the price elasticity can be linked via the widely used Lerner's index defined by

$$L(p) \stackrel{\text{def}}{=} \frac{p - \mu}{p} = \frac{up}{p} = \frac{1}{|e|}. \tag{3.5}$$

That is, the ratio of the monopoly's markup on marginal cost to the monopoly's price equals the inverse of the demand price elasticity when evaluated at its profit-maximizing levels. Lerner's index is widely used in economics to capture the "monopoly power" of a firm, because under intense competition in homogeneous products prices tend to fall close to marginal cost, thereby reducing Lerner's index to its lowest level, given by $L(\mu) = 0$.

To prove the result stated in (3.5) for the linear demand case, observe that the demand elasticity, defined by (2.1), is

$$e = \left(\frac{dq(p)}{dp} \right) \left(\frac{p}{q} \right) = \left(-\frac{1}{\beta} \right) \left(\frac{\frac{\alpha+\mu}{2}}{\frac{\alpha-\mu}{2\beta}} \right) = -\frac{\alpha + \mu}{\alpha - \mu} < -1, \tag{3.6}$$

where price and quantity are substituted from (3.2) and (3.3). Evaluating Lerner's index, defined on the left-hand side of (3.5), at the profit-maximizing price (3.3) yields

$$L(p) = \frac{\frac{\alpha+\mu}{2} - \mu}{\frac{\alpha+\mu}{2}} = \frac{\alpha-\mu}{\alpha+\mu} = \frac{1}{|e|}. \tag{3.7}$$

3.1.3   Price setting under continuous linear demand

Section 3.1.2 provides the "traditional" way of solving the monopoly's profit-maximization problem as it is commonly described in most textbooks on micro-economics. The commonly used method consisted of first solving for the profit-maximizing output level (by equating marginal revenue to marginal cost), and only then solving for the profit-maximizing price by substituting the desired quantity into the inverse demand function. The purpose of this section is to demonstrate an alternative method for solving the single seller's profit maximization problem by solving directly for the profit-maximizing price.

Starting with the inverse demand function $p(q) = \alpha - \beta q$, the corresponding direct demand function is given by $q(p) = (\alpha - p)/\beta$. Substituting the direct demand function into the profit function (3.4), thereby eliminating the quantity variable q, obtains the profit as a function of price only. Thus, the seller chooses a price p to solve

$$\max_{p} y(p) = (p - \mu)\frac{\alpha - p}{\beta} - \phi. \tag{3.8}$$

The first-order condition for a maximum yields

$$0 = \frac{dy(p)}{dp} = \frac{\alpha + \mu - 2p}{\beta} \implies p = \frac{\alpha + \mu}{2}, \tag{3.9}$$

which is the same price as the price obtained from the "traditional" quantity profit-maximization method given by (3.3). To ensure that the first-order condition (3.9) constitutes a maximum (rather than a minimum), differentiating the first-order condition (3.9) yields $d^2 y(p)/dp^2 = -2/\beta < 0$, which verifies the second-order condition for a maximum.

Finally, the profit-maximizing output level is found by substituting the profit-maximizing price from (3.9) into the direct demand function $q = (\alpha - p)/\beta$ to obtain $q = (\alpha - \mu)/(2\beta)$, which is the same quantity obtained from using the "direct quantity method" and is given by (3.2).

3.1.4   Continuous constant-elasticity demand

The constant-elasticity demand function becomes very handy for solving the simple single-seller profit-maximization problem. We refer the reader back to equation (2.14) in Section 2.4, which defines the direct constant-elasticity demand function given by $q(p) = \alpha p^{-\beta}$, where $\alpha > 0$ and $\beta > 1$ (to ensure elastic demand). Equation (2.19) proves that the elasticity of this demand function is constant and equals $-\beta$. As it turns out, this feature makes it extremely easy to compute the profit-maximizing price for a single seller even without having to compute the profit-maximizing output level first, as we have done for the linear demand case analyzed in the previous section.

The key to fast solving for the profit-maximizing price is to use the relationship between demand price elasticity and the marginal revenue function, which was derived in equation (2.13). Therefore, the marginal revenue function derived from the constant-elasticity demand function can be expressed as

$$\frac{dx(q)}{dq} = p\left(1 + \frac{1}{e}\right) = p\left(1 + \frac{1}{-\beta}\right) = p\left(1 - \frac{1}{\beta}\right). \tag{3.10}$$

As before, let μ denote the marginal production/selling cost, and ϕ the fixed cost. The following three-step procedure describes how the profit-maximizing price can be computed.

Step I: Set the price so that the revenue generated from selling the last unit equals marginal cost. Formally, use (3.10) to solve

$$\frac{dx(q)}{dq} = \mu \quad \text{to obtain} \quad p = \frac{\beta\mu}{\beta - 1}. \tag{3.11}$$

Step II: Compute the "candidate" profit-maximizing quantity by solving

$$q = \alpha p^{-\beta} \quad \text{to obtain} \quad q = \alpha\left(\frac{\beta\mu}{\beta - 1}\right)^{-\beta}. \tag{3.12}$$

Step III: Compute the profit level $y(q)$ by solving

$$y = (p - \mu) - \phi \quad \text{to obtain} \quad y = \alpha\left(\frac{\beta\mu}{\beta - 1}\right)^{1-\beta} - \phi. \tag{3.13}$$

Again, what's neat about the class of constant-elasticity demand functions is that the profit-maximizing price can be obtained via a single calculation given by (3.11). In fact, this equation shows that the profit-maximizing price is proportional to the marginal cost. That is, this price is the marginal cost multiplied by the markup $\beta/(\beta - 1) > 1$. Clearly, this markup increases with no bounds as $\beta \to 1$ (demand approaches unit elasticity) and is not defined for $\beta < 1$, which reflects an inelastic demand.

Finally, using the monopoly's profit-maximizing price (3.11), we can reconfirm Lerner's index for the constant-elasticity demand by

$$L(p) \overset{\text{def}}{=} \frac{p - \mu}{p} = \frac{\frac{\beta\mu}{\beta - 1} - \mu}{\frac{\beta\mu}{\beta - 1}} = \frac{1}{\beta} = \frac{1}{|e|}. \tag{3.14}$$

3.2 Multiple Markets without Price Discrimination

So far, our analysis in this chapter has been confined to a single firm selling in a single market. We now extend our analysis to multiple markets served by a single seller. We assume that the markets cannot be segmented, meaning that the seller must choose a *single price* to prevail in all markets. This section does *not* analyze price discrimination. Price discrimination is analyzed in Section 3.3, in which the seller can select different prices for different markets.

3.2.1 Market-specific fixed costs and exclusion of markets

Our analysis assumes M markets, indexed by $\ell = 1, 2, \ldots M$. The single seller has to determine which markets to serve, and to select a single price to prevail in all served markets. The seller's marginal cost is μ, and the production fixed cost is ϕ. We now extend this cost structure with the following assumption:

ASSUMPTION 3.1
The seller or the producer bears additional market-specific fixed costs, denoted by
$\phi_1, \phi_2, \ldots, \phi_M$.

Assumption 3.1 generalizes the cost structure discussed earlier in Section 2.9 to include market-specific fixed and sunk costs. Thus, $\phi_\ell \geq 0$ should be viewed as the entry and promotion costs associated with operating and maintaining presence in market $\ell = 1, \ldots, M$. Such costs include the establishment of local offices, local promotion and advertising, and the hiring of local staff. All these costs are borne by the firm in addition to the already assumed market-independent fixed cost ϕ associated with the operation of the production facility.

In this section we assume that the seller cannot price discriminate among markets, which means that only one price prevails. Still, our model must specify whether the seller can directly control which markets to operate in, or whether the choice of markets cannot be directly controlled and the seller's actions are limited to selecting a single uniform-across-markets price and then fulfilling all orders from all markets that exhibit positive demand at the selected price. To demonstrate this difference in interpretation, let us look at the aggregate demand illustrated in Figure 3.4 which appears later in this chapter. If the seller sets a price in the range $\$50 < p \leq \$100$, the seller automatically excludes all consumers in market 2, in which case there is no need for the seller to formally announce that market 2 is not served. However, if the seller lowers the price to fall in the range $p < \$50$, the seller must make an explicit decision whether or not to sell in this market.

Clearly, if there are no market-specific fixed costs, then a decision to enter or to exclude a market can be controlled solely via the price. That is, setting a price above $\$50$ automatically excludes all consumers in market 2. In contrast, if there are strictly positive market-specific fixed costs, ϕ_ℓ for each market $\ell =$

$1,\ldots,M$, then we must also assume that no market can be served (hence, consumers cannot buy) unless the seller bears the market-specific fixed cost. To summarize this discussion, non–price discrimination models can have the following two general interpretations:

Explicit exclusion: Regardless of the uniform price set by the seller, the seller controls whether to serve market ℓ by making an explicit decision whether to incur the market-specific fixed cost ϕ_ℓ, for each market $\ell = 1,\ldots,M$.

Implicit exclusion: The seller cannot explicitly control which markets to serve and obviously does not bear any market-specific fixed costs. Exclusion of a certain market is implicitly achieved by setting a price above the maximum willingness to pay of all consumers in a particular market.

The analysis conducted in this chapter relies on the *first* interpretation, which means that the seller can explicitly decide not to serve a certain market by avoiding paying the market-specific fixed cost. However, once the seller selects which markets to operate in, the seller is restricted to setting a single uniform price to prevail in all served markets. There are two reasons for choosing to work with the first interpretation (explicit exclusion), despite the fact that most textbooks in microeconomics implicitly assume the second interpretation:

(a) The first interpretation is the more general one in the sense that it obtains the second interpretation as a special case. That is, if market-specific fixed costs are ruled out by setting $\phi_1 = \phi_2 = \cdots = \phi_M = 0$, the two interpretations become practically the same because the seller has no reason to exclude a market if consumers in this market are willing to pay the uniform-across-markets price set by the seller. Technically speaking, by setting $\phi_1 = \phi_2 = \cdots = \phi_M = 0$, the profit-maximizing price solved under the first interpretation is equal to the price solved under the second interpretation.

(b) Market-specific fixed costs do prevail in many markets. Therefore, it is very important that this book develops general solutions to profit-maximization problems by explicitly taking market-specific fixed costs into account.

Whether or not market-specific fixed costs prevail depends of course on the type of market. If different markets represent different regions or different countries, one may expect to bear a significant fixed cost by opening an outlet to serve a different market. Market-specific fixed costs can be realized even if all markets operate at the same geographic location. For example, products and services may have to be redesigned to appeal to elderly people.

3.2.2 A computer algorithm for market selections

Readers who are not interested in computer applications can skip reading this section and proceed directly to Section 3.2.3. Here, we provide a computer algorithm that selects all possible subsets of markets from a maximum of 2^M markets that can be served by the seller. For example, if there are $M = 3$ markets, the seller can choose to serve the following subgroups of markets: $\{1\}$, $\{2\}$, $\{3\}$, $\{1,2\}$, $\{1,3\}$, $\{2,3\}$, $\{1,2,3\}$ (all markets), and $\emptyset$ (empty set), which indicates not serving any market. Hence, in this example, there are $2^3 = 8$ choices of which markets to serve.

Algorithm 3.2 generates all the 2^M possible selections of markets that the seller can choose to operate in, and writes them into an array of arrays that we call Sel (for selection of markets). We index a selection of the served markets by $i = 0,\ldots,2^M - 1$. Let $\text{Sel}[i,\ell]$ denote an array of arrays of binary variables with dimension $(2^M) \times M$. For example, in the case of $M = 3$ markets, $\text{Sel}[7,2] = 1$ implies that market 2 is served under the seventh possible selection. Also, $\text{Sel}[6,2] = 0$ implies that market 2 is not served under the sixth possible selection, and so on. Thus, a served market is denoted by 1 and an unserved market by 0. Selection $i = 0$ denotes a choice of not serving any market, so $\text{Sel}[0,\ell] = 0$ for all $\ell = 1,\ldots,M$.

```
for ℓ = 1 to M do Sel[0,ℓ] ← 0;
/* Presetting market selection i = 0 (all unserved)        */
for i = 1 to 2^M − 1 do
    for ℓ = 1 to M do Sel[i,ℓ] ← Sel[i−1,ℓ];
    /* Copy selection i−1 to selection i                   */
    Before(1) ← Sel[i,1]; Toggle(Sel[i,1]) ; After(1) ← Sel[i,1];
        /* Market 1 is always toggled on a new selection   */
    for ℓ = 2 to M do
        Before(ℓ) ← Sel[i,ℓ];
        if Before(ℓ−1) = 1 & After(ℓ−1) = 0 then
            Toggle(Sel[i,ℓ]); /* Toggle market ℓ in selection i */
        After(ℓ) ← Sel[i,ℓ]; /* Record the change (if any)     */
```

Algorithm 3.2: Selections of all possible subsets of markets.

Algorithm 3.2 assumes that your program has a predefined binary function called Toggle, which takes the values of $\text{Toggle}(1) = 0$ and $\text{Toggle}(0) = 1$. The changes (toggling) made by this function in market ℓ (if any) are recorded by the difference between the $\text{Before}(\ell)$ and $\text{After}(\ell)$ functions. Thus, the functions Before and After assign to each market $\ell = 1,\ldots,M$ the binary value before and after the market is toggled (if at all), and by comparing the two, we can track whether the market was selected (a change from 0 to 1) or deselected (a change from 1 to 0), or if no change has been made.

Algorithm 3.2 runs as follows. First, the program presets the ad hoc selection $i = 0$ to "all zeros," which means that none of the M markets is served. Then, it is copied to selection $i = 1$, where market $\ell = 1$ is always toggled (in this case, from 0 to 1). No more changes are made for selection $i = 1$ because the program continues to make changes for market ℓ only if market $\ell - 1$ has been toggled from 1 to 0. Now, the selection is advanced to $i = 2$, where selection $i = 1$ is copied and is ready to be modified by the program according to the specified condition.

Selection i	0	1	2	3	4	5	6	7
Market 1	0	1	0	1	0	1	0	1
Market 2	0	0	1	1	0	0	1	1
Market 3	0	0	0	0	1	1	1	1

Table 3.2: Output generated by Algorithm 3.2 for the case of $M = 3$ markets.

Table 3.2 illustrates the output generated by Algorithm 3.2 for the case of $M = 3$ markets. The program presets the ad hoc selection $i = 0$ to all zeros. Then, it is copied to selection $i = 1$. The changes to selection $i = 1$ are made as follows:

$$
\begin{matrix} \text{Market 1} \\ \text{Market 2} \\ \text{Market 3} \end{matrix} \quad (i = 0) \Longrightarrow \begin{pmatrix} 0 \\ 0 \\ 0 \end{pmatrix} \Longrightarrow \begin{pmatrix} 1 \\ 0 \\ 0 \end{pmatrix}.
$$

That is, market 1 is always toggled (from 0 to 1 in this selection $i = 1$). No more modifications are made to selection $i = 1$ because the last change was from 0 to 1 (and not from 1 to 0). Then, selection $i = 1$ is copied to selection $i = 2$. Changes to selection $i = 2$ are made as follows:

$$
\begin{matrix} \text{Market 1} \\ \text{Market 2} \\ \text{Market 3} \end{matrix} \quad (i = 1) \Longrightarrow \begin{pmatrix} 1 \\ 0 \\ 0 \end{pmatrix} \Longrightarrow \begin{pmatrix} 0 \\ 0 \\ 0 \end{pmatrix} \Longrightarrow \begin{pmatrix} 0 \\ 1 \\ 0 \end{pmatrix}.
$$

That is, market 1 is always toggled (from 1 to 0 for the present selection $i = 2$). Then, market 2 is toggled from 0 to 1 because market 1 was changed from 1 to 0. No more modifications are made to selection $i = 2$ because the last change was from 0 to 1 (and not from 1 to 0). The algorithm then copies selection $i = 2$ into selection $i = 3$, toggles market 1 and toggles each market ℓ only if market $\ell - 1$ has been toggled from 1 to 0, and so on.

3.2.3 Multiple markets under single-unit demand

We now demonstrate the technique for computing the profit-maximizing price for multiple markets, where each market is identified by having identical consumers with identical maximum willingness to pay for a single unit that they may buy.

The procedure for aggregating such a demand function has already been studied in Section 2.5.1.

Three-market example

We start our analysis by working on a three-market example, illustrated by Figure 3.3. In this example, market 1 has $N_1 = 200$ consumers who will buy the product/service as long as the price does not exceed \$30. Market 2 has $N_2 = 600$ identical consumers who will not pay more than \$20, and so on.

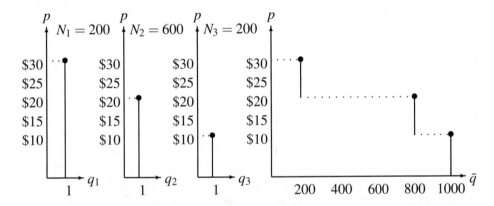

Figure 3.3: Single-unit market demand functions with three markets.

The seller has to set a single price p to prevail in all served markets. In this example, the seller can choose to serve the following subgroups of markets: $\{1\}$, $\{2\}$, $\{3\}$, $\{1,2\}$, $\{1,3\}$, $\{2,3\}$, $\{1,2,3\}$ (all markets), and $\emptyset$ (empty set), which indicates not serving any market. In this example, there are $2^3 = 8$ possible selections of which markets to serve. In the general case of M markets, there are 2^M possibilities to choose from.

Table 3.3 demonstrates how to compute the profit- and revenue-maximizing prices. In this example, the seller bears a marginal cost of $\mu = \$5$; market-specific fixed costs given by $\phi_1 = \$1000$, $\phi_2 = \$5000$, $\phi_3 = 0$; and a production fixed cost of $\phi = \$2000$. This example is rather general as it assumes unequal market-specific fixed costs. For example, the assumption that $\phi_3 = 0$ may be a consequence of the firm's main office being located in the heart of market 3, so no additional costs of maintaining this market are incurred. Figure 3.3 shows that if the seller chooses to operate in markets 1 and 3, the price must not exceed \$10 to induce consumers in market 3 to make a purchase. In this case, with $q_{1,3} = N_1 + N_3 = 400$ customers, the seller's revenue is $x_{1,3} = \$4000$. The resulting profit is then $y_{1,3} = (30 - 5)400 - 1000 - 0 - 2000 = -\$1000$. However, if the seller chooses instead to operate in markets 1 and 2, the price must not exceed \$20 to induce consumers in market 2 to make a purchase. In this case, with

Markets	1	2	3	1&2	1&3	2&3	1&2&3
Price $\$p$	30	20	10	20	10	10	10
Quantity q	200	600	200	800	400	800	1000
Revenue $\$x$	6000	12,000	2000	16,000	4000	8000	10,000
$(p-\mu)q$	5000	9000	1000	12,000	2000	4000	5000
Fixed costs	3000	7000	2000	8000	3000	7000	8000
Profit $\$y$	2000	2000	-1000	4000	-1000	-3000	-3000

Table 3.3: Profit-maximizing price when selling to three markets: Single-unit demand case. Table assumes $\mu = 5$, $\phi_1 = \$1000$, $\phi_2 = \$5000$, $\phi_3 = \$0$, and $\phi = \$2000$.

$q_{1,2} = N_1 + N_2 = 800$ customers, the seller's revenue is $x_{1,2} = \$16,000$. The resulting profit is then $y_{1,2} = (20 - 5)800 - 1000 - 5000 - 2000 = \$4000$, which turns out to be the maximum profit according to Table 3.3.

A computer algorithm for M markets

We now proceed to describe a computer algorithm for selecting the most profitable price when there are M markets, and where each market is composed of homogeneous consumers with identical maximum willingness to pay, as was already illustrated in Figure 3.3 for the example of $M = 3$ markets. The user must run Algorithm 3.2 before running Algorithm 3.3 for the purpose of generating and storing the 2^M possible selections of markets that can be served. Recalling Algorithm 3.2, the results are stored by the array of arrays of binary variables $\text{Sel}[i, \ell]$ of dimension $2^M \times M$, where i is the index of a specific selection of markets, $i = 0, 1, \ldots, 2^M - 1$, and ℓ is a specific market. Market ℓ is served under selection i if $\text{Sel}[i, \ell] = 1$ and is not served if $\text{Sel}[i, \ell] = 0$.

The program should read and store the demand structure of each of the M markets. That is, the program must input (say, using a **Read**() command) the maximum willingness to pay $V[\ell]$ and the number of consumers $N[\ell]$ (each buying one unit) for each market $\ell = 1, \ldots, M$. $V[\ell]$ and $N[\ell]$ are M-dimensional arrays of real and integer values, respectively. It is recommended to run some trivial loops verifying nonnegativity. The program must also input the seller's cost parameters μ (marginal cost), ϕ (fixed cost), and the M-dimensional real-valued array of market-specific fixed costs $\phi[\ell]$ for $\ell = 1, \ldots, M$.

The goal of Algorithm 3.3 is to find the profit- and revenue-maximizing selections of markets out of the 2^M possible selections, and the corresponding prices. These selections are written onto the integer variables maxSy and maxSx, respectively. This algorithm runs a loop over market selections i and computes the profit and revenue generated by each selection. The profit and revenue are stored on $y[i]$ and $x[i]$. The price used for these computations is min$V[i]$, which is the lowest maximum willingness to pay among all consumers in the selected markets. Note that if

---

$\text{max}Sy \leftarrow 1; \text{max}Sx \leftarrow 1; /* \text{ Initialize: } 1^{\text{st}} \text{ selection } */$
for $i = 1$ **to** $2^M - 1$ **do** $\text{min}V[i] \leftarrow 0; y[i] \leftarrow -\phi; x[i] \leftarrow 0;$
for $i = 1$ **to** $2^M - 1$ **do**
   | /* Main loop over market selections i begins $\qquad$ */
   | **for** $\ell = 1$ **to** M **do**
   | | /* Maximum chargeable price for market selection i */
   | | **if** $\text{min}V[i] \cdot \text{Sel}[i,\ell] > V[\ell]$ **then** $\text{min}V[i] \leftarrow V[\ell];$
   | **for** $\ell = 1$ **to** M **do**
   | | /* Add profits from all markets under selection i */
   | | $y[i] \leftarrow y[i] + \{(\text{min}V[i] - \mu) \cdot N[\ell] - \phi[\ell]\} \cdot \text{Sel}[i,\ell];$
   | | $x[i] \leftarrow x[i] + \{\text{min}V[i] \cdot N[\ell]\} \cdot \text{Sel}[i,\ell]; /* \text{ Add revenue } \qquad */$
for $i = 1$ **to** $2^M - 1$ **do**
   | **if** $y[i] > y[\text{max}Sy]$ **then** $\text{max}Sy \leftarrow i; /* i \text{ more profitable } \qquad */$
   | **if** $x[i] > x[\text{max}Sx]$ **then** $\text{max}Sx \leftarrow i; /* i \text{ higher revenue } \qquad */$
writeln ("The profit-maximizing price is $p =$", $V[\text{max}Sy]$, "yielding the profit level $y = $", $y[\text{max}Sy]$, "The following markets are served:");
for $\ell = 1$ **to** M **do** **if** $\text{Sel}[\text{max}Sy, \ell] = 1$ **then** **write** ("market", ℓ);
writeln ("The revenue-maximizing price is $p =$", $V[\text{max}Sx]$, "yielding the revenue level $x = $", $x[\text{max}Sx]$, "The following markets are served:");
for $\ell = 1$ **to** M **do** **if** $\text{Sel}[\text{max}Sy, \ell] = 1$ **then** **write** ("market", ℓ);

Algorithm 3.3: Computing a nondiscriminating monopoly's profit- and revenue-maximizing prices under discrete demand with multiple markets.

the firm raises the price above $\text{min}V[i]$, the firm will exclude some of the markets, thereby contradicting the choice of markets made under market selection i.

The remainder of Algorithm 3.3 consists of a loop for determining the profit- and revenue-maximizing selections of markets. These selections are written onto the integer variables $\text{max}Sy$ and $\text{max}Sx$, respectively. For these selections of markets, the algorithm then writes the corresponding prices, and the list of served markets under these prices.

3.2.4 Linear demand: Example for two markets

We now leave the discrete demand case and proceed to analyze continuous demand functions. First, consider two markets described by the inverse demand functions

$$p_1 = 100 - 0.5q_1 \quad \text{and} \quad p_2 = 50 - 0.1q_2. \tag{3.15}$$

The market-specific fixed cost associated with operating in markets 1 and 2 are $\phi_1 = \phi_2 = \$500$. In addition, the fixed cost associated with the operation of the plant is $\phi = \$1000$. The marginal cost is assumed to be $\mu = \$10$. Figure 3.4 illustrates the two market demand functions as well as the aggregate demand facing this monopoly. We refer the reader to Section 2.5, which explains the procedure for how to construct an aggregate demand function from individual market demand functions.

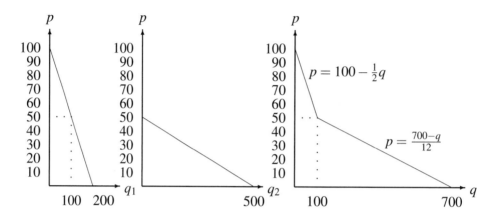

Figure 3.4: Nondiscriminating monopoly selling in two markets.

In this entire section, we assume that the seller is unable to price discriminate between markets. That is, the seller must set a single uniform price p for all markets. In view of Figure 3.4, the seller has four options: First, to sell in both markets, which would require setting a "low" price, $p \leq \$50$; second, to sell in market 1 only, which would enable setting a "high" price in the range $\$50 < p \leq \$100$; third, to sell in market 2 only, which again would require setting a "low" price, $p \leq \$50$; and fourth, not to sell at all.

Selling in both markets

The procedure for finding the profit maximizing price while serving both markets (therefore, setting a price in the range $p \leq \$50$) is as follows:

Step I: Aggregate the two demand functions (3.15) using the procedure described in Section 2.5. This procedure yields the aggregate direct demand function and the corresponding inverse demand function (drawn) given by

$$q = 4(175 - 3p) \quad \text{and} \quad p = \frac{700 - q}{12}. \tag{3.16}$$

Step II: Use the simple monopoly solution described in Section 3.1.2 to solve for the profit-maximizing price and the resulting profit level assuming that there is one described by the aggregate demand function. Therefore, the marginal revenue function $x(q) = (700 - q)q/12$ implies

$$\frac{dx(q)}{dq} = \frac{700 - 2q}{12} = \$10 = \mu, \quad \text{hence} \quad q_{1,2} = 290. \tag{3.17}$$

Substituting (3.17) into (3.16) yields

$$p_{1,2} = \frac{205}{6} \approx \$34.17, \quad \text{hence}$$

$$y_{1,2} = (p - \mu)q - \phi_1 - \phi_2 - \phi = \frac{15025}{3} \approx \$5008.33. \tag{3.18}$$

The subscripts $\{1,2\}$ indicate that both markets are served under this single price.

Selling in market 1 (niche market) only

Inspecting Figure 3.4 reveals that in market 1 there are some consumers whose willingness to pay exceeds that of market 2 consumers. Therefore, the advantage of selling in market 1 only is that the price can be raised to levels $p > \$50$, which exceed the willingness to pay of all market 2 consumers. With the exclusion of market 2, the remaining part of the procedure for selecting the profit-maximizing price is as follows: Using the procedure described in Section 3.1.2, we solve $dx(q_1)/dq_1 = 100 - q_1 = 10 = \mu$ to obtain the desired output level of $q_1 = 90$, and hence a price of $p_1 = 100 - 0.5q_1 = \$55$. The profit generated by serving market 1 only is then given by

$$y_1 = (p_1 - \mu)q_1 - \phi_1 - \phi = \$2550. \tag{3.19}$$

Selling in market 2 only

Similar to the above computations for the case in which only market 1 is served, in market 2 we solve $dx(q_2)/dq_2 = 50 - 0.2q_2 = 10 = \mu$ to obtain the desired output level of $q_2 = 200$, and hence a price of $p_2 = 50 - 0.1q_2 = \$30$. The profit generated by serving market 2 only is then

$$y_2 = (p_2 - \mu)q_2 - \phi_2 - \phi = \$2500. \tag{3.20}$$

Comparing all the options

Because strictly positive profits can be made, we can rule out the option of not serving any market. Comparing the profit when serving both markets (3.18) to the profit when only market 1 is served, and when only market 2 is served, yields $y_{1,2} = \$5008.33 > \$2550 = y_1 > \$2500 = y_2$. Hence, the profit-maximizing price is $p_{1,2} = 205/6 \approx \$34.16$, and the seller should serve both markets.

3.2.5 Linear demand: General formulation for two markets

We now provide the general formulation of the two-market example for general linear demand functions. Let the demand functions for markets 1 and 2 be given by $p_1 = \alpha_1 - \beta_1 q_1$ and $p_2 = \alpha_2 - \beta_2 q_2$, where $\alpha_1 > \mu \geq 0$ and $\alpha_2 > \mu$. We now follow exactly the same steps as in Section 3.2.4 to find the seller's profit-maximizing price.

Using the procedure described in Section 2.5, the aggregate direct demand function and the corresponding inverse demand function are given by

$$q = \frac{\alpha_1\beta_2 + \alpha_2\beta_1 - (\beta_1 + \beta_2)p}{\beta_1\beta_2} \quad \text{and} \quad p = \frac{\alpha_1\beta_2 + \alpha_2\beta_1 - \beta_1\beta_2 q}{\beta_1 + \beta_2}. \quad (3.21)$$

Using the procedure described in Section 3.1.2, we solve

$$\frac{dx(q)}{dq} = \frac{\alpha_1\beta_2 + \alpha_2\beta_1 - 2\beta_1\beta_2 q}{\beta_1 + \beta_2} = \mu, \quad \text{yielding}$$

$$q_{1,2} = \frac{\alpha_1\beta_2 + \alpha_2\beta_1 - (\beta_1 + \beta_2)\mu}{2\beta_1\beta_2}. \quad (3.22)$$

Substituting (3.22) into (3.21) yields

$$p_{1,2} = \frac{\alpha_1\beta_2 + \alpha_2\beta_1 + (\beta_1 + \beta_2)\mu}{2(\beta_1 + \beta_2)} \quad \text{hence} \quad y_{1,2} = (p_{1,2} - \mu)q_{1,2} - \phi_1 - \phi_2 - \phi$$

$$= \frac{[\alpha_1\beta_2 + \alpha_2\beta_1 - \mu(\beta_1 + \beta_2)]^2}{4\beta_1\beta_2(\beta_1 + \beta_2)} - \phi_1 - \phi_2 - \phi. \quad (3.23)$$

We now solve for the profit-maximizing price assuming that only market 1 is served. Thus, solving $dx(q_1)/dq_1 = \alpha_1 - 2\beta_1 q_1 = \mu$ yields a desired output level of $q_1 = (\alpha_1 - \mu)/(2\beta_1)$ and a price of $p_1 = (\alpha_1 + \mu)/2$. The profit generated by serving market 1 only is then

$$y_1 = (p_1 - \mu)q_1 - \phi_1 - \phi = \frac{(\alpha_1 - \mu)^2}{4\beta_1} - \phi_1 - \phi. \quad (3.24)$$

Similarly, when only market 2 is served, solving $dx(q_2)/dq_2 = \alpha_2 - \beta_2 q_2 = \mu$ yields a desired output level of $q_2 = (\alpha_2 - \mu)/(2\beta_2)$, therefore a price of $p_2 = (\alpha_2 + \mu)/2$. The profit generated by serving market 2 only is then

$$y_2 = (p_2 - \mu)q_2 - \phi_2 - \phi = \frac{(\alpha_2 - \mu)^2}{4\beta_2} - \phi_2 - \phi. \quad (3.25)$$

Finally, to be able to select which markets are served, we must compare the profit when serving both markets (3.23) to the profit when only market 1 is served (3.24), and when only market 2 is served (3.24), and then set the price-maximizing price accordingly.

3.2.6 Linear demand: A computer algorithm for multiple markets

Our next generalization extends the previous analysis to any number of markets, each represented by a linear demand function. Our analysis assumes M markets, indexed by $\ell = 1, 2, \ldots M$. Each market is characterized by a downward-sloping inverse linear demand function $p_\ell = \alpha_\ell - \beta_\ell q_\ell$, where $\alpha_\ell, \beta_\ell > 0$ are to be estimated from actual market-specific data, using the procedure studied in Section 2.3.2.

The general principle for selecting the profit-maximizing price is to go over all the $i = 0, 1, \ldots, 2^M - 1$ selections of subsets of markets (including the option of not selling in any market) and then to compare the resulting profit levels. There can be two types of computer algorithms for solving the nondiscriminating monopoly problem selling in multiple markets. One algorithm, which resembles symbolic algebra software, follows exactly the steps described in the previous paragraph. Such an algorithm must read the demand parameters α_ℓ and β_ℓ for all markets $\ell = 1, \ldots, M$, and combine these parameters to construct the aggregate demand function corresponding to the exact choice of markets to be served. The advantage of this type of algorithm is that it computes the exact profit-maximizing price without resorting to an approximation that is sensitive to the precision or grid that must be specified for the loops over price changes. In this section, we take a slightly different approach. For each selection of markets, the proposed algorithm starts from a high price and then gradually decreases the price and computes the profit generated from serving the selected markets. The price reductions depend on the grid, which the user must input into the parameter G. This precision parameter (again, set by the user) determines the degree of accuracy of this computation. Algorithm 3.4 requires first running Algorithm 3.2, which lists and writes all the 2^M possible selections of subsets of M markets onto the array of arrays of binary variables $\mathtt{Sel}[i, \ell]$, where i is the index number of a specific selection of markets and ℓ is a specific market. As before, $\mathtt{Sel}[i, \ell] = 1$ indicates that market ℓ is selected under selection i, whereas $\mathtt{Sel}[i, \ell] = 0$ indicates that market ℓ is excluded. Then, similar to Algorithm 3.3, Algorithm 3.4 computes the profit for each selection of markets by comparing the maximum profit from each selection of markets i. However, because the demand is downward sloping, Algorithm 3.4 must run an additional loop over price p (see the "While" loop) by varying the price (with increments determined by the inputted grid parameter G) and then computing the profit for each price p.

The program should read and store the demand structure of each of M markets. That is, the program must input (say, using a **Read**() command) the inverse demand intercept $\alpha[\ell]$ and the slope $\beta[\ell]$ parameters for each market $\ell = 1, \ldots, M$. It is recommended to run some trivial loops verifying nonnegativity and that $\alpha[\ell] > \mu$ (thereby verifying that the willingness to pay for some consumers in each market exceeds marginal cost), as otherwise market ℓ can be immediately excluded. The program must also input the seller's cost parameters μ (marginal cost), ϕ

$\text{max}y \leftarrow 0; \text{max}x \leftarrow 0; \text{max}Sy \leftarrow 0; \text{max}Sx \leftarrow 0; \text{max}\alpha \leftarrow 0;$
/* Above: Initialization. Below: Highest intercept   */
for $\ell = 1$ **to** M **do if** $\text{max}\alpha < \alpha[\ell]$ **then** $\text{max}\alpha \leftarrow \alpha[\ell];$
for $i = 1$ **to** $2^M - 1$ **do** $\text{max}p[i] \leftarrow \text{max}\alpha; y[i] \leftarrow 0; x[i] \leftarrow 0;$
for $i = 1$ **to** $2^M - 1$ **do**
   /* Main loop over market selections begins   */
   for $\ell = 1$ **to** M **do**
      /* Maximum chargeable price for market selection i */
      if $\text{max}p[i] \cdot \text{Sel}[i,\ell] > \alpha[\ell]$ **then** $\text{max}p[i] \leftarrow \alpha[\ell];$
   $\Delta p \leftarrow \text{max}p[i]/G$ /* Setting price intervals for loops   */
   $x \leftarrow 0; y \leftarrow -\phi; p \leftarrow \text{max}p[i];$ /* Initialize the While loop */
   while $p > 0$ **do**
      for $\ell = 1$ **to** M **do**
         /* Add profit from all selection i's markets   */
         $y \leftarrow y + \{(p - \mu)((\alpha[\ell] - p)/\beta[\ell]) - \phi[\ell]\} \cdot \text{Sel}[i,\ell];$
         $x \leftarrow x + p((\alpha[\ell] - p)/\beta[\ell]) \cdot \text{Sel}[i,\ell];$ /* Add revenue   */
      if $y[i] < y$ **then**
         $y[i] \leftarrow y; p_y[i] \leftarrow p;$ /* Register higher profit for i */
      if $x[i] < x$ **then**
         $x[i] \leftarrow x; p_x[i] \leftarrow p;$ /* Register higher revenue   */
      $p \leftarrow p - \Delta p;$ /* Reduce price for the next While loop */
for $i = 1$ **to** $2^M - 1$ **do**
   if $y[i] > \text{max}y$ **then** $\text{max}Sy \leftarrow i;$ /* i is more profitable   */
   if $x[i] > \text{max}x$ **then** $\text{max}Sx \leftarrow i;$ /* i has higher revenue   */

Algorithm 3.4: Computing profit- and revenue-maximizing prices for a nondiscriminating monopoly selling in multiple markets with linear demand.

(fixed cost), and the M-dimensional array of market-specific fixed costs $\phi[\ell]$ for $\ell = 1, \ldots, M$.

To be able to fit Algorithm 3.4 into a single page, it does not include the short procedure for printing the results obtained by Algorithm 3.4. The printing procedure is described in a separate short procedure given by Algorithm 3.5.

Algorithm 3.4 works as follows: The goal is to write the maximum profit and maximum revenue onto the real variables $\text{max}y \leftarrow 0$ and $\text{max}x \leftarrow 0$. The corresponding profit- and revenue-maximizing prices are written onto p_y and p_x. The main loop runs over all possible selections of markets indexed by i. The last loop compares all the profit and revenue levels $y[i]$ and $x[i]$ and assigns the maximized values to $\text{max}y \leftarrow 0$ and $\text{max}x \leftarrow 0$.

> **writeln** ("The profit-maximizing price is $p =$", p_y, "yielding the profit level $y =$ ", $y[\text{max}Sy]$, "The following markets are served:");
> **for** $\ell = 1$ **to** M **do** **if** $\text{Sel}[\text{max}Sy, \ell] = 1$ **then** **write** ("market", ℓ);
> **writeln** ("The revenue-maximizing price is $p =$", p_x, "yielding the revenue level $x =$ ", $x[\text{max}Sx]$, "The following markets are served:");
> **for** $\ell = 1$ **to** M **do** **if** $\text{Sel}[\text{max}Sx, \ell] = 1$ **then** **write** ("market", ℓ);

Algorithm 3.5: Printing the output of Algorithm 3.4.

The main inner "While" loop runs over all possible prices (given the specified precision) for each selection of markets i. The price starts at the highest demand intercept $\text{max}p[i]$ (which is the highest demand intercept for this specific selection of markets). For each price, the corresponding profit and revenue levels are written onto the real temporary variables y and x. If the price generates higher levels for these, variables are then assigned to the maximum profit and revenue for selection i, $y[i]$ and $x[i]$. The "While" loop ends where the price is reduced by Δp, and the loop continues as long as the price is strictly positive.

3.3 Multiple Markets with Price Discrimination

The ability to price discriminate means that the seller can set different prices in different markets. Setting different prices is possible only if the markets are segmented in the sense that arbitrage (buying at the low-priced market for the purpose of reselling at the high-priced market) is not feasible. The reader is referred to Section 1.2 for extensive discussions of market segmentation and price discrimination. We therefore proceed directly to analyzing pricing techniques. We divide our analysis into situations in which the seller has sufficient capacity to satisfy the demand in all markets, and situations in which capacity is limited.

3.3.1 Unlimited capacity: Linear demand

Two-market example

We start with the two-market example that we analyzed earlier in Section 3.2.4 for the case in which the seller is unable to price discriminate. Recalling the demand functions (3.15),

$$p_1 = 100 - 0.5q_1 \quad \text{and} \quad p_2 = 50 - 0.1q_2. \tag{3.26}$$

Figure 3.5 draws the demand functions (3.26) and the corresponding marginal revenue functions for each market. Section 2.3.3 has already demonstrated how to derive the marginal revenue functions associated with linear demand functions.

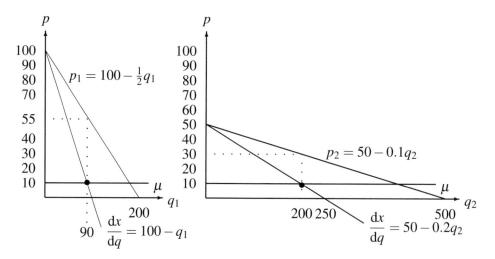

Figure 3.5: Discriminating monopoly selling in two markets.

For the specific demand functions defined by (3.26), the corresponding marginal revenue functions, equated to the marginal cost parameter $\mu = \$10$, are given by

$$\frac{dx_1(q_1)}{dq_1} = 100 - q_1 = 10 \quad \text{and} \quad \frac{dx_2(q_2)}{dq_2} = 50 - 0.2q_2 = 10. \tag{3.27}$$

Solving (3.27) yields $q_1 = 90$. Substituting for q_1 into (3.26) yields $p_1 = \$55$. Similarly, $q_2 = 200$ and $p_2 = \$30$. These candidate equilibrium values are also drawn in Figure 3.5. Therefore, if the seller chooses to serve both markets, total profit is given by

$$y = y_1 + y_2 - \phi = \underbrace{(55 - 10)90 - 500}_{y_1} + \underbrace{(30 - 10)200 - 500}_{y_2} - 1000$$

$$= 3550 + 3500 - 1000 = \$6050. \tag{3.28}$$

Lastly, it is important to also verify that the inclusion of each market separately is profitable, as otherwise profit may rise if some markets are excluded. In the present example, it is easy to confirm that $y_1 \geq 0$ and $y_2 > 0$, where the profit in each market subtracts the market-specific fixed costs ϕ_1 and ϕ_2. In addition, we must also verify that total aggregate profit is nonnegative as it subtracts the fixed cost ϕ.

Unlimited capacity with linear demand: Extension to M markets

We conclude this section on linear demand with price discrimination by extending the two-market analysis to M markets, where each market is characterized by a linear demand function given by $p_\ell = \alpha_\ell - \beta_\ell q_\ell$, for $\ell = 1, 2, \ldots M$. The single seller bears a constant marginal cost of μ, market-specific fixed cost of ϕ_ℓ for $\ell = 1, 2, \ldots M$, and production fixed cost of ϕ. The seller must decide in which markets to operate and the price for each market. To solve this problem, the seller should use the following two-step procedure:

Step I: For each market ℓ, solve

$$\frac{\mathrm{d}x(q_\ell)}{\mathrm{d}q_\ell} = \alpha_\ell - 2\beta_\ell q_\ell = \mu, \quad \text{yielding} \quad q_\ell = \frac{\alpha_\ell - \mu}{2\beta_\ell} \quad \text{and} \quad p_\ell = \frac{\alpha_\ell + \mu}{2}.$$

The price p_ℓ for market ℓ was obtained by substituting q_ℓ into the demand function in market ℓ.

Step II: Compute the profit generated from each market ℓ to obtain

$$y_\ell = (p_\ell - \mu)q_\ell - \phi_\ell = \frac{(\alpha_\ell - \mu)^2}{4\beta_\ell} - \phi_\ell,$$

and choose to serve only the markets for which $y_\ell \geq 0$. Lastly, add all profits generated from all served markets and subtract the production fixed cost ϕ to obtain total profit.

Unlimited capacity with linear demand: Computer algorithm

We now provide a simple computer algorithm for selecting the profit-maximizing price for each market, and for selecting the markets to be served. Algorithm 3.6 assumes that the program already stores the linear demand parameters for each of the M markets. Thus, the program must input the demand intercept $\alpha[\ell]$ and the slope parameter $\beta[\ell]$ for each inverse demand function indexed by $\ell = 1, \ldots, M$. It is recommended to run some trivial loops verifying that $\alpha_\ell > 0$ and that $-\beta_\ell < 0$. The program must also input the seller's cost parameters μ (marginal cost), the market-specific fixed costs $\phi[\ell]$, and the fixed production cost ϕ.

Algorithm 3.6 is rather straightforward. It runs a loop on all markets $\ell = 1, 2, \cdots, M$, and computes the profit level. If the profit from market ℓ (after subtracting the market specific fixed cost $\phi[\ell]$) is nonnegative, it selects market ℓ by assigning 1 to $\mathrm{Sel}[\ell]$, which is an array of binary variables of dimension M. Total output and total profit are added to the aggregate levels represented by the real variables y and q. Finally, note that Algorithm 3.6 also computes the aggregate output level q. This quantity will become very important when we analyze capacity constraints in Section 3.3.3, as this level will have to be compared with the available capacity to check whether the capacity is binding.

3.3.2   Unlimited capacity: Constant-elasticity demand

The procedure for selecting the profit-maximizing price when the seller faces a constant elasticity demand function has already been analyzed in Section 3.1.4 for

```
y ← −ϕ; q ← 0; /* Initialization                                              */
for ℓ = 1 to M do
   │ /* Main loop over markets                                                */
   │ y[ℓ] ← (α[ℓ] − μ)²/(4β[ℓ]) − ϕ[ℓ]; /* Profit from market ℓ              */
   │ Sel[ℓ] ← 0; /* Exclude market ℓ (initialization)                         */
   │ if y[ℓ] ≥ 0 then
   │    │ /* ℓ is profitable, select it, compute p & q                        */
   │    │ Sel[ℓ] ← 1; p[ℓ] ← (α[ℓ] + μ)/2; q[ℓ] ← (α[ℓ] − μ)/(2β[ℓ]);
   │    └ y ← y + y[ℓ]; q ← q + q[ℓ]; /* Add to total                         */
for ℓ = 1 to M do if Sel[ℓ] = 1 then writeln ("Price market", ℓ, " at p =",
p[ℓ], "and sell ", q[ℓ], "units." );
write ("Total quantity sold is q =", q, "total profit is y = ", y);
```

Algorithm 3.6: Computing profit-maximizing prices under price discrimination among M markets with linear demand under unlimited capacity.

the case of a single market. We now extend Section 3.1.4 to multiple markets when there is no capacity constraint.

Unlimited capacity with constant elasticity: Two-market example

Consider two markets with the following constant-elasticity demand functions:

$$q_1 = 1200(p_1)^{-2} \quad \text{and} \quad q_2 = 2400(p_2)^{-3}. \tag{3.29}$$

In Section 2.4.3 we proved that the exponents $e_1 = -2$ and $e_2 = -3$ are the demand elasticities corresponding to these markets. Thus, the demand in market 2 is more elastic than in market 1. As we show below, this implies that the seller can charge a higher price in market 1 compared with market 2.

The single seller bears a marginal cost of $\mu = \$2$, market-specific fixed costs of $\phi_1 = \$100$ and $\phi_2 = \$50$, and a production fixed cost of $\phi = \$30$. As we have shown in Section 3.1.4, the advantage of working with a constant-elasticity demand is that the profit-maximizing price for each market is obtainable in a single calculation. If both markets are served, the seller extracts the price for each market by equating marginal revenue to marginal cost. Hence, recalling the formula for the marginal revenue under constant elasticity demand given by equation (2.13),

$$p_1 \left(1 + \frac{1}{-2} \right) = 2, \quad \text{hence} \quad p_1 = \$4 \quad \text{and} \quad q_1 = 75, \tag{3.30}$$

$$p_2 \left(1 + \frac{1}{-3} \right) = 2, \quad \text{hence} \quad p_2 = \$3 \quad \text{and} \quad q_2 = \frac{800}{9}.$$

Therefore, if the seller chooses to serve both markets, total profit is given by

$$y = y_1 + y_2 - \phi = \underbrace{(4-2)75 - 100}_{y_1} + \underbrace{(3-2)\frac{800}{9} - 50}_{y_2} - 30$$

$$= 50 + \frac{350}{9} - 30 = \frac{530}{9} \approx \$58.88. \quad (3.31)$$

Lastly, it is important to verify that the inclusion of each market separately is profitable, as otherwise it may be profitable to exclude some markets. In the present example, we indeed verify that $y_1 \geq 0$ and $y_2 > 0$, where these market-specific profits already subtract the market-specific fixed costs ϕ_1 and ϕ_2. In addition, we must verify that total profit is nonnegative once the fixed cost ϕ is also taken into account.

The two first-order conditions for profit maximization (3.30) demonstrate why constant-elasticity demand functions are so easy to use for the purpose of selecting the profit-maximizing prices in different markets. In fact, we can show from these conditions that it is sufficient to know only the value of the demand elasticities in each market to be able to tell the profit-maximizing price ratio between any two served markets. Thus, very little information is required to be able to compute the profit-maximizing price ratios. To see this, suppose that you obtain the information that the demand price elasticity in market 1 is a constant given by e_1. Similarly, for market 2, the price elasticity is e_2. Note that we must assume elastic demand, $e_1 < -1$ and $e_2 < -1$, as we have already proved that a monopoly will never charge a price at a point at which the demand is inelastic. Using this information only (yes, even without knowing the value of the marginal cost μ), we can compute that

$$p_1\left(1+\frac{1}{e_1}\right) = \mu = p_2\left(1+\frac{1}{e_2}\right), \quad \text{hence} \quad \frac{p_1}{p_2} = \frac{e_1(e_2+1)}{e_2(e_1+1)}. \quad (3.32)$$

For example, if $e_1 = -2$ and $e_2 = -3$, the profit-maximizing price ratio is $p_1/p_2 = 4/3$, which also reconfirms our earlier computation given in (3.30). Similarly, if $e_1 = -2$ and $e_2 = -4$, the profit-maximizing price ratio is $p_1/p_2 = 3/2$. For this last example, this ratio implies that the seller should set prices so that the price in market 1 is 50% higher than the price in market 2.

Unlimited capacity with constant elasticity: Extension to M markets

We conclude this section on constant-elasticity demand with price discrimination under unlimited capacity by extending the two-market analysis to M markets, where each market $\ell = 1, 2, \ldots M$ is characterized by a constant-elasticity demand function given by $q_\ell = \alpha_\ell p^{-\beta_\ell}$. The single seller bears a constant marginal cost of μ, a market-specific fixed cost of ϕ_ℓ for $\ell = 1, 2, \ldots M$, and a production fixed cost of ϕ. The seller must decide in which market to operate and the price for each served market. To solve this problem, the seller should follow the following two-step procedure:

Step I: For each market ℓ, solve

$$\frac{dx(q_\ell)}{dq_\ell} = p_\ell \left(1 + \frac{1}{\beta_\ell} \right) = \mu \quad \text{yielding}$$

$$p_\ell = \frac{\beta_\ell \mu}{\beta_\ell - 1} \quad \text{and} \quad q_\ell = \alpha_\ell \left(\frac{\beta_\ell \mu}{\beta_\ell - 1} \right)^{-\beta_\ell}.$$

The output level q_ℓ was obtained by substituting p_ℓ into the direct demand function in market ℓ.

Step II: Compute the profit from each market ℓ to obtain

$$y_\ell = (p_\ell - \mu)q_\ell - \phi_\ell = \alpha_\ell \left(\frac{\beta_\ell \mu}{\beta_\ell - 1} \right)^{1-\beta_\ell} - \phi_\ell,$$

and choose to serve only the markets for which $y_\ell \geq 0$. Lastly, add all profits from all served markets and subtract the production fixed cost ϕ to obtain total profit.

3.3.3   Price discrimination under capacity constraint

Our analysis so far in this chapter has implicitly assumed that the seller/producer possesses the capacity of satisfying the entire demand when prices are set at the profit-maximizing level. Clearly, this is not always the case. For example, airlines have a limited seating capacity during high travel seasons. Hotels often face similar limitations on the number of rooms they can rent out. Therefore, in this section we assume that the seller faces a capacity constraint K in the sense that it cannot serve more than K customers (or sell more than K units). Notice that we denote capacity with a capital letter K to indicate that the capacity level is treated as an exogenously given parameter, corresponding to the list of parameters given in Table 1.4. In general, there are two ways of interpreting the capacity level K:

(a) *Capacity has not been paid for:* In this case, the seller must bear a marginal cost, denoted by μ_k for each additional unit of capacity, bringing the total capacity to $\mu_k K$.

(b) *The seller has already paid for it:* Cost of capacity should be regarded as sunk.

Our analysis below captures both situations. If capacity has already been paid for, then the entire cost should be incorporated in the fixed cost parameter ϕ. Otherwise, if capacity has to be purchased for generating higher output levels, capacity cost should be incorporated in the marginal cost parameter μ_k. Generally, managers are advised to experiment with the trade-off between classifying capacity cost as sunk and as the sum of marginal capacity costs to simulate the worst-case scenario.

When capacity is limited, the pricing problem involves a profitable allocation of K units of capacity among the served markets (as opposed to equating the marginal revenue function in each market to the marginal cost). But first, we must check whether the capacity constraint is really binding. In other words, the first stage would be to solve for the profit-maximizing price in each served market assuming unlimited capacity, as we have done in Sections 3.3.1 and 3.3.2. Then, the next stage would be to compute the aggregate quantity demanded, $\bar{q}$ and to check whether $\bar{q} > K$. If this is the case, then we say that the capacity constraint is indeed *binding*. In contrast, if $\bar{q} \leq K$, then capacity is not binding, and the solution assuming unlimited capacity applies.

In this section, we analyze markets with linear demand only. We start with a numerical example for two markets. Then, we provide a general formulation for two markets and conclude with an extension to M markets.

Capacity constraint: Two-market examples

We now solve exactly the same two-market example that we solved in Section 3.3.1, but with an additional assumption that the seller is constrained with K units of capacity. That example was based on demand functions given by $p_1 = 100 - 0.5q_1$ and $p_2 = 50 - 0.1q_2$, as well as on the cost structure given by $\mu = \$10$, $\phi_1 = \phi_2 = \$500$, and $\phi = \$1000$. That section showed that with unlimited capacity, the seller sells $q_1 = 90$ units in market 1, and $q_2 = 200$ in market 2. Thus, for capacity to be binding, we must assume that $K < 290$. We therefore assume now that $K = 150$.

With K units of capacity, the seller must choose prices so that total quantity demanded does not exceed capacity. That is, $\bar{q} = q_1 + q_2 \leq K$. Because we have already shown that without the capacity restriction $\bar{q} = 290 > 150 = K$, we can assume that capacity is binding so that $\bar{q} = q_1 + q_2 = K$. Clearly, when capacity is limited, the seller can price higher than at the point at which marginal revenue equals marginal cost. Higher prices result from the "shortage" generated by the capacity constraint.

When capacity is binding, the seller must ensure that capacity is allocated among the served markets so that the marginal revenue levels are equal across all served markets. In the present example, if both markets are served, that is, $q_1 > 0$ and $q_2 > 0$, the seller must solve the system of two equations with two variables given by

$$\frac{dx_1(q_1)}{dq_1} = 100 - q_1 = 50 - 0.2q_2 = \frac{dx_2(q_2)}{dq_2} \quad \text{and} \quad q_1 + q_2 = K. \quad (3.33)$$

Comparing (3.33) with (3.27) shows the difference between the two optimization methods. Under unlimited capacity, (3.27) equates the marginal revenue in each served market to the marginal cost μ. In contrast, under capacity constraint, (3.33) reveals that the marginal cost μ does not explicitly enter into the optimization's marginal condition as this condition requires that only marginal costs in all served markets will be equalized to a level that may exceed the marginal cost μ, and that in addition total output should be set to equal the given capacity level K.

Solving (3.33) for q_1 and q_2 yields

$$q_1 = \frac{200}{3} \quad \text{and} \quad q_2 = \frac{250}{3}, \quad \text{hence} \quad p_1 = \frac{200}{3} \quad \text{and} \quad p_2 = \frac{125}{3}. \quad (3.34)$$

The prices p_1 and p_2 were obtained by substituting the profit-maximizing output levels q_1 and q_2 into the corresponding market inverse demand functions. Clearly, by construction, total output equals capacity so that $q_1 + q_2 = 150 = K$. The resulting total profit is then given by

$$y_1 = \left(\frac{200}{3} - 10\right)\frac{200}{3} - 500 = \frac{29500}{9} \approx \$3277 > 0, \quad (3.35)$$

$$y_2 = \left(\frac{250}{3} - 10\right)\frac{250}{3} - 500 = \frac{19250}{9} \approx \$2138 > 0.$$

Hence, total profit is given by $y = y_1 + y_2 - 1000 = 13,250/3 \approx \$4416 > 0$. Altogether, because both markets are profitable, and because total profit is also nonnegative, the prices given in (3.34) are indeed the profit-maximizing prices.

The above analysis turned out to be very simple because the capacity constraint was sufficiently large to make it profitable to operate in both markets. However, as we now demonstrate, for a sufficiently low capacity level, the introduction of a capacity constraint may induce the seller to exclude some markets. To demonstrate this possibility, let us "reduce" the amount of available capacity to $K = 40$ (down from $K = 150$). If we attempt to naively solve the two equations (3.33) we obtain $q_1 = 145/3$ and $q_2 = -25/3 < 0$. This means that market 2 should not be served. Indeed, inspecting Figure 3.5 reveals that with only $K = 40$ units of capacity, by selling in market 1 only the seller can charge a much higher price than the price that can be charged if selling also in market 2.

To complete this example with $K = 40$ units of capacity, selling in market 1 only implies that $q_1 = K = 40$, hence, $p_1 = 100 - 0.5 \cdot 40 = \$80$. Therefore, $y = y_1 - \phi = (80 - 10)40 - 500 - 1000 = \$1300$.

Capacity constraint with two markets: General formulation

We now reformulate the above two-market example to generalize it to any linear demand function given by $p_1 = \alpha_1 - \beta_1 q_1$ and $p_2 = \alpha_2 - \beta_2 q_2$, where the parameters α_1, α_2, β_1, and β_2 are nonnegative, to be estimated by the econometrician as demonstrated in Section 2.3.2. To find the profit-maximizing prices and which markets should be served, the manager should follow the following steps:

Step I: Solve the profit-maximization problem assuming unlimited capacity, using the procedure described in Section 3.3.1. Check whether the resulting aggregate quantity demanded $\bar{q}$ exceeds available capacity. If $\bar{q} < K$, then stop, as the capacity level is not binding. Otherwise, proceed to *Step II*.

Step II: Solve for q_1 and q_2 from the following system of equations,

$$\frac{dx_1(q_1)}{dq_1} = \alpha_1 - 2\beta_1 q_1 = \alpha_2 - 2\beta_2 q_2 = \frac{dx_2(q_2)}{dq_2} \quad \text{and} \quad q_1 + q_2 = K, \quad (3.36)$$

to obtain

$$q_1 = \frac{2\beta_2 K + \alpha_1 - \alpha_2}{2(\beta_1 + \beta_2)} \quad \text{and} \quad q_2 = \frac{2\beta_1 K + \alpha_2 - \alpha_1}{2(\beta_1 + \beta_2)}. \quad (3.37)$$

Check for nonnegative quantities. Formally, if either $q_1 < 0$ or $q_2 < 0$, stop here, and proceed directly to *Step IV*.

Step III: If $q_1 \geq 0$ and $q_2 \geq 0$, substitute these quantities into their corresponding inverse demand function to obtain the "candidate" profit-maximizing prices,

$$p_1 = \frac{\alpha_1(\beta_1 + 2\beta_2) + \alpha_2\beta_1 - 2K\beta_1\beta_2}{2(\beta_1 + \beta_2)}, \quad (3.38)$$

$$p_2 = \frac{\alpha_2(2\beta_1 + \beta_2) + \alpha_1\beta_2 - 2K\beta_1\beta_2}{2(\beta_1 + \beta_2)}.$$

Compute the corresponding profit levels $y_1 = (p_1 - \mu)q_1 - \phi_1$ and $y_2 = (p_2 - \mu)q_2 - \phi_2$ using the solutions (3.37) and (3.38). Check for nonnegative profits. Formally, if either $y_1 < 0$ or $y_2 < 0$, stop here, and proceed to *Step IV*. Otherwise, stop here as *you are done!*

Step IV: Allocate the entire capacity to market 1 so that $q_1 = K$. Solve for the price to obtain $p_1 = \alpha_1 - \beta_1 K$ and for the profit $y = y_1 - \phi = (\alpha_1 - \beta_1 K - \mu)K - \phi_1 - \phi$.

Step V: Allocate the entire capacity to market 2 so that $q_2 = K$. Solve for the price to obtain $p_2 = \alpha_2 - \beta_2 K$ and for the profit $y = y_2 - \phi = (\alpha_2 - \beta_2 K - \mu)K - \phi_2 - \phi$.

Step VI: Choose the highest profit between those obtained in *Step IV* and *Step V*. If both are negative, cease operation.

Finally, the above procedure can be modified to compute what some textbooks call the *short-run profit*. Short-run profit is generally defined as the profit level assuming zero fixed cost, so $\phi = 0$. If this value is nonnegative, the seller may want to consider the option of staying in business until the fixed cost has to be repaid, and only then get out of business (delayed bankruptcy).

A few remarks on multiple markets under capacity constraint

To avoid excessive writing, we will only briefly examine how a profit-maximizing single seller should allocate K units of capacity among M markets. If all the M markets are served, the marginal revenue functions in all served markets must be equalized. Hence, the quantity sold in each market, $q_1, \ldots, q_M$, should be solved from the system of M linear equations given by

$$
\begin{aligned}
\alpha_1 - 2\beta_1 q_1 &= \alpha_2 - 2\beta_2 q_2, \\
\alpha_1 - 2\beta_1 q_1 &= \alpha_3 - 2\beta_3 q_3, \\
&\vdots \qquad\qquad \vdots \\
\alpha_1 - 2\beta_1 q_1 &= \alpha_M - 2\beta_M q_M, \\
\text{and} \qquad K &= q_1 + q_2 + \cdots + q_M.
\end{aligned}
\tag{3.39}
$$

The system of M linear equations (3.39) can be solved for the quantity q_ℓ sold in each market ℓ, $\ell = 1, \ldots, M$. The way to solve this system is to use repeated substitution. The first step is to solve for $q_M = K - \sum_{\ell=1}^{M-1} q_\ell$ from the bottom equation and substitute it for q_M in the second-to-the-last equation. Then, solve for q_{M-1} and substitute it into the third equation from the bottom. Working backward all the way up yields the final solution for q_1. To see some examples, note that the solution for $M = 2$ markets is already given by (3.37). For $M = 3$ markets, the solution to (3.39) is

$$
\begin{aligned}
q_1 &= \frac{2K\beta_2\beta_3 + \alpha_1(\beta_2 + \beta_3) - \alpha_2\beta_3 - \alpha_3\beta_2}{2[\beta_1(\beta_2 + \beta_3) + \beta_2\beta_3]}, \\
q_2 &= \frac{2K\beta_1\beta_3 + \alpha_2(\beta_1 + \beta_3) - \alpha_1\beta_3 - \alpha_3\beta_1}{2[\beta_1(\beta_2 + \beta_3) + \beta_2\beta_3]}, \\
q_3 &= \frac{2K\beta_1\beta_2 + \alpha_3(\beta_1 + \beta_2) - \alpha_1\beta_2 - \alpha_2\beta_1}{2[\beta_1(\beta_2 + \beta_3) + \beta_2\beta_3]}.
\end{aligned}
\tag{3.40}
$$

Clearly, by construction, the above market output allocation sums up to $q_1 + q_2 + q_3 = K$. For $M = 4$ markets, the allocation of output to market 1 should be

$$
q_1 = \frac{2K\beta_2\beta_3\beta_4 + \alpha_1[\beta_2(\beta_3 + \beta_4) + \beta_3\beta_4] - \alpha_2\beta_3\beta_4 - \beta_2(\alpha_3\beta_4 + \alpha_4\beta_3)}{2\{\beta_1[\beta_2(\beta_3 + \beta_4) + \beta_3\beta_4] + \beta_2\beta_3\beta_4\}}, \tag{3.41}
$$

and for $M = 5$ markets, the allocation of output to market 1 should be

$$
\begin{aligned}
q_1 = {}& \frac{2K\beta_2\beta_3\beta_4\beta_5 + \alpha_1\{\beta_2[\beta_3(\beta_4 + \beta_5) + \beta_4\beta_5] + \beta_3\beta_4\beta_5\}}{2(\beta_1\{\beta_2[\beta_3(\beta_4 + \beta_5) + \beta_4\beta_5] + \beta_3\beta_4\beta_5\})} \\
& + \frac{-\alpha_2\beta_3\beta_4\beta_5 - \beta_2[\alpha_3\beta_4\beta_5 + \beta_3(\alpha_4\beta_5 + \alpha_5\beta_4)]}{2(\beta_1\{\beta_2[\beta_3(\beta_4 + \beta_5) + \beta_4\beta_5] + \beta_3\beta_4\beta_5\})}.
\end{aligned}
\tag{3.42}
$$

Recall however that the solutions given by (3.37), (3.40), (3.41), and (3.42) may yield negative values for output levels. That is, the repeated substitution method for solving the system of equations (3.39) may yield negative values. In such cases, the markets with "negative output levels" should be excluded one by one, and the resulting reduced systems should be recomputed for the smaller number of markets. In general, the method of allocating K units of capacity to M markets should adhere to the following steps:

Step I: Solve the profit-maximization problem assuming unlimited capacity, using the procedure described in Section 3.3.1. Check whether the resulting aggregate quantity demanded $\bar{q}$ exceeds available capacity. If $\bar{q} < K$, then stop, as the capacity level is not binding. Otherwise, proceed to *Step II*.

Step II: Run Algorithm 3.2, which lists all the $i = 1, \ldots, 2^M$ possible selections of subsets of markets.

Step III: Similar to the system of equations (3.39), solve the system of equations corresponding to *each* selection i of subsets of markets. Check whether the solution yields nonnegative output levels in some of the markets $\ell = 1, \ldots, M$. If negative output is found in some of the markets in selection i, selection i should be ruled out.

Step IV: Compare total profit from each selection of markets i to determine which markets should be served. Substitute the corresponding output levels into the demand function of each selected market to determine the profit-maximizing price to be charged in each selected market.

3.4   Pricing under Competition

In this section we briefly address the issue of competition. Firms' strategic behavior under competition constitutes the core study of industrial organization, which is a field of study in modern economics. For this reason, a comprehensive study of firms' behavior under competition is beyond the scope of this book. Readers who are interested in learning theories of market structures should consult a wide variety of industrial organization textbooks. By *market structure* economists refer to the precise "rules of the game" (yes, just like the game of chess) which describe what actions (such as prices and quantity produced) firms are "allowed" to take when competing with other firms.

There are two alternative approaches that must be considered when setting a price in a market where several competing firms operate.

Myopic rival firms: This approach assumes that rival firms will not respond to price changes made by other firms. Thus, the firm in question views the prices set by its rivals as constants, at least in the short run.

Strategic rival firms: Firms respond to any price changes made by their rivals. Under this approach, economists define various types of equilibria (or market structures). The most commonly used equilibrium concept is the Nash-Bertrand equilibrium, which consists of a vector of prices (one for each firm) under which no firm finds it profitable to deviate from these prices as long as other firms do not deviate.

As mentioned above, strategic behavior of firms has been the main focus of study by economists in the past 30 years and therefore will be given little attention in this book. Instead, in what follows we briefly specify the outcomes that would be generated by industries with myopic and nonmyopic rival firms. Thus, each of the following sections is divided into searching for the price under myopic behavior and how it should affect the decision to price if a firm expects its rivals to react.

Sections 3.4.1 and 3.4.2 analyze firms' price response under discrete demand with switching costs. Section 3.4.3 computes the price response when consumers view the different brands as differentiated.

3.4.1   Switching costs among homogeneous goods

The model presented in this section applies to markets for products and services in which consumers bear a cost of switching from the brand they already use to a competing brand. Switching costs cause consumers to be locked into a certain brand even if competing brands are offered for lower prices. Switching costs may take the following forms: Loyalty programs, such as frequent-flyer programs offered by airlines, and points offered to holders of certain credit cards, all may result in a loss of benefits when switching to competing service providers. Switching costs also prevail when switching between products using different formats or standards, such as storage devices, computer operating systems, and audio and video players. These switching costs also include the cost of learning and training to use products operating on different competing standards. Readers who wish to learn more about switching costs should consult Shapiro and Varian (1999), Shy (2001), and Farrell and Klemperer (2005), and their extensive lists of references.

Myopic rival firms

Consider an industry with F firms indexed by $j = 1, \ldots, F$. Initially, the firms charge prices $P_1, \ldots, P_F$ and serve $N_1 \ldots, N_F$ consumers (each buys one unit of the product/service). Note that N_j and P_j are denoted with capital letters because, following the list of parameters in Table 1.4, we treat the initial consumer allocation among the brands and initial prices as exogenously given parameters. Also, the reader should not confuse the present subscript notation with the meaning of subscripts in earlier sections of this chapter. In earlier sections, the subscripts $\ell = 1, \ldots, M$ denoted different markets (served by a single firm). In contrast, in this section the subscript $j = 1,\ldots,F$ denotes a firm's index number (as now we have competition among several rival firms).

We start with two firms labeled $j = 1,2$. Initially, the firms charge prices P_1 and P_2 and serve N_1 and N_2 consumers, respectively. Suppose now that each consumer must bear a cost of $\$\delta$ when switching from one brand or service provider to another. Thus, if firm 1 would like to attract consumers to switch from brand 2 to brand 1 on their next purchase, firm 1 must undercut firm 2 and set $p_1 < P_2 - \delta$. This price is sufficiently low to "subsidize" consumers for switching from brand 2 to brand 1. Figure 3.6 displays the demand function facing firm 1, assuming that firm 2 holds its price constant at P_2.

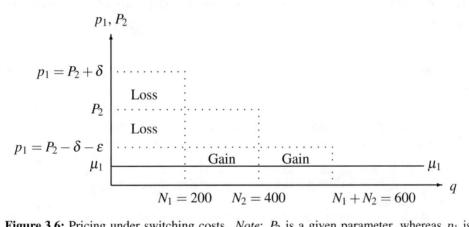

Figure 3.6: Pricing under switching costs. *Note*: P_2 is a given parameter, whereas p_1 is firm 1's choice variable.

Given that firm 2 continues to hold its price at a fixed level P_2, Figure 3.6 reveals that firm 1 has two options to consider.

Undercut: Undercutting firm 2 by setting $p_1 = P_2 - \delta - \varepsilon$, where ε is the smallest currency denomination (say, 1¢). This would induce all firm 2's customers to switch to brand 1, so that firm 1 would sell $q_1 = N_1 + N_2 = 600$ units.

Accommodate: Raising the price up to the level $p_1 = P_2 + \delta$ at which any further raise would induce firm 1's customers to switch to brand 2.

Let μ_1 and ϕ_1 denote the marginal and fixed costs of firm 1. Firm 1 earns a higher profit when it undercuts firm 2 compared with accommodating firm 2 if

$$(P_2 - \delta - \mu_1)(N_1 + N_2) - \phi_1 > (P_2 + \delta - \mu_1)N_1 - \phi_1,$$

$$\text{hence if} \quad \delta < \frac{N_2(P_2 - \mu_1)}{2N_1 + N_2}, \quad (3.43)$$

if we ignore ε, or simply assume that $\varepsilon = 0$. Note that the net gain and loss from undercutting relative to accommodating firm 2 is also illustrated in Figure 3.6. Therefore, undercutting becomes more profitable when the switching cost parameter δ

takes lower values, or when firm 2 charges a higher price, p_2. In the present example in which $N_1 = 200$ and $N_2 = 400$, undercutting is profitable if $\delta < (p_2 - \mu_1)/2$. Moreover, a close inspection of (3.43) also reveals that undercutting is more likely to be realized when the rival firm initially has a high market share (N_2 is large). This result implies that firms with initially large market shares are more vulnerable to undercutting than firms with an initially small market share. Another way of looking at this is to say that firms with low market shares have stronger incentives to undercut firms with initially high market shares.

We now extend the model to F firms. Suppose that each rival firm $j = 2, \ldots, F$ charges a fixed price denoted by P_j. We now compute firm 1's profit-maximizing price, p_1. With no loss of generality, we index the firms according to declining prices so that

$$P_2 \geq P_3 \geq \cdots \geq P_F. \tag{3.44}$$

Also, suppose that the *initial* allocation of consumers among firms is given by $N_1, \ldots, N_F$.

Algorithm 3.7 computes firm 1's profit-maximizing price taking into consideration that setting lower prices would generate further undercutting of rival firms. The program should input the total number of firms into a positive integer vari-

---

if $P[2] > P[F] + \delta$ **then write** ("Inconsistent data. Stop here!");
for $j = 2$ **to** $F - 1$ **do**
     if $p[j] < P[j+1]$ **then write** ("Stop here, and reorder the firms");
$p_1 \leftarrow P[F] + \delta; y_1 \leftarrow (p_1 - \mu_1)N[1] - \phi_1;$ /* Highest price   */
$j \leftarrow 1; n_1 \leftarrow N[1];$ /* Initialization   */
while $(P[j] - \delta > \mu_1)$ & $(j < F)$ **do**
     /* Main loop over all possible undercutting   */
     $j \leftarrow j + 1; n_1 \leftarrow n_1 + N[j];$ /* Undercut firm j */
     while $(P[j] = P[j+1])$ & $(j < F)$ **do**
         /* Handle the case of equal prices $(P[j] = P[j+1])$ */
         $j \leftarrow j + 1; n_1 \leftarrow n_1 + N[j];$ /* Add switching customers */
     if $y_1 < (P[j] - \delta - \mu_1)n_1 - \phi_1$ **then** $p_1 \leftarrow P[j] - \delta;$
         $y_1 \leftarrow (P[j] - \delta - \mu_1)n_1 - \phi_1$; /* Profitable undercutting */
writeln ("The profit maximizing price is $p_1 =$", p_1);
writeln ("Firm 1 serves", n_1, "consumers");
writeln ("Firm 1's profit is $y_1 =$", y_1);
write ("The following firms are being undercut and leave the market:");
for $j = 2$ **to** F **do** **if** $p[1] \leq P[j] - \delta$ **then write** ("firm ", j,", ");

Algorithm 3.7: Undercutting rival firms.

---

able $F \geq 2$ and the price charged by each rival firm into an F-dimensional array of nonnegative real $P[\ell]$, $\ell = 2, 3, \ldots, F$. Note that $p[1]$ need not be assigned an initial value because it is the main choice variable of this algorithm, which is denoted by p_1. Finally, the program should input the switching cost parameter into a nonnegative real parameter δ, as well as firm 1's marginal and fixed cost parameters μ_1 and ϕ_1.

Algorithm 3.7 runs as follows: First, it verifies that the difference between any two prices does not exceed the switching cost parameter δ. Clearly, if the difference in prices exceeds the switching cost, the firm charging the higher price cannot maintain any market share because all of its customers would switch to the cheaper brand. Therefore, such a firm must be excluded from the present analysis. Note that by our assumption regarding the way in which the firms are indexed given in (3.44), it is sufficient to verify that $p_2 - p_F < \delta$. For this reason, Algorithm 3.7 also verifies that the firms are indexed according to (3.44).

Secondly, Algorithm 3.7 initially sets the highest possible price for firm 1 $(p[1] = P[F] + \delta)$ that is consistent with maintaining $N[1]$ customers, and then starts a "While" loop that gradually reduces the price, thereby undercutting more and more firms. Therefore, there are F prices to experiment with, starting with $p_1 = P[F] + \delta$ (keeping the initial $N[1]$ consumers only), then reducing to $p_1 = P[2] - \delta$, thereby serving $N[1] + N[2]$ consumers, and so on. During each loop, the consumers from the firms being undercut are added to the integer-valued variable n_1, which measures firm 1's sales, taking into account all the consumers who switch to firm 1. This loop also compares the resulting profit and chooses the profit-maximizing price. Finally, the second "While loop" is not needed if all rival firms charge strictly different prices, that is, in the case in which (3.44) holds with strict inequalities so that $P[2] > P[3] > \cdots > P[F]$.

We now demonstrate how Algorithm 3.7 works for the case of $F = 3$ firms. There are three values for p_1 that should be compared. The first is no undercutting, in which case the maximum price that firm 1 can set is $p_1 = P[3] + \delta$. The resulting profit is therefore $y_1 = (P[3] + \delta - \mu_1)N[1] - \phi_1$. The second possibility is to undercut firm 2 only by setting $p_1 = P[3] - \delta$, thereby earning $y_1 = (P[2] - \delta - \mu_1)(N[1] + N[2]) - \phi_1$. Note, however, that if firms 2 and 3 charge equal prices $(P[2] = P[3])$, then the "inner While loop" advances the index j to $j = 3$ and computes the profit $y_1 = (P[3] - \delta - \mu)(N[1] + N[2] + N[3]) - \phi_1$, which is the profit generated by undercutting firm 2 and firm 3 at the same time.

Retaliation of rival firms

Our analysis has so far relied on the assumption that only firm 1 is active, whereas all other firms behave myopically in the sense that they don't reduce their prices to avoid being undercut by firm 1. Using a two-firm example, we now demonstrate what would be the outcome if both firms 1 and 2 are free to choose their prices.

There could be several game-theoretic solutions for this type of problem. The solution advocated by the author of this book is to use the so-called *undercut-proof equilibrium* (see Shy 2001, 2002). The undercut-proof equilibrium is defined as follows:

DEFINITION 3.1
For a given initial allocation of consumers between the firms, N_1 and N_2, the **undercut-proof equilibrium** *is the pair of prices (p_1^U, p_2^U) satisfying:*

(a) For a given p_2^U, firm 1 chooses the highest price p_1^U subject to

$$y_2^U = (p_2^U - \mu_2)N_2 - \phi_2 \geq (p_1 - \delta - \mu_2)(N_1 + N_2) - \phi_2.$$

(b) For a given p_1^U, firm 2 chooses the highest price p_2^U subject to

$$y_1^U = (p_1^U - \mu_1)N_1 - \phi_1 \geq (p_2 - \delta - \mu_1)(N_1 + N_2) - \phi_1.$$

The first part states that, in an undercut-proof equilibrium, firm 1 sets the highest price it can, but not too high as to prevent firm 2 from undercutting p_1^U and grabbing firm 1's N_1 customers. More precisely, firm 1 sets p_1^U as high as possible, but not so high that firm 2's equilibrium profit level is not lower than firm 2's profit level when it undercuts firm 1 by setting $\tilde{p}_2 < p_1^U - \delta$ and sells to all the $N_1 + N_2$ consumers.

In equilibrium, the above two inequalities hold as equalities that can be solved for the unique equilibrium prices

$$p_1^U = \frac{(N_1)^2(\delta + \mu_2) + N_1N_2(3\delta + \mu_2)(N_2)^2(2\delta + \mu_1)}{(N_1)^2 + N_1N_2 + (N_2)^2}, \qquad (3.45)$$

$$p_2^U = \frac{(N_1)^2(2\delta + \mu_2) + N_1N_2(3\delta + \mu_1) + (N_2)^2(\delta + \mu_1)}{(N_1)^2 + N_1N_2 + (N_2)^2}.$$

This solution to the undercut-proof equilibrium may generate negative prices, in which case a solution may be found by looking for a price at which one firm can undercut the other firm by leaving it with no customers and therefore with no profit.

We conclude this section on retaliation with a numerical example. Suppose that the initial allocation of consumers is $N_1 = 200$, $N_2 = 400$, $\delta = \$10$, and firms' marginal costs are $\mu_1 = \mu_2 = \$50$. Substituting these values into the undercut-proof equilibrium prices (3.45) obtains the undercut-proof equilibrium prices $p_1^U = 500/7 \approx \$71.42$, and $p_2^U = 470/7 \approx \$67.14$. Observe that in an undercut-proof equilibrium (under equal marginal costs), the firm with the lower market share charges a higher price, so $p_1^U > p_2^U$. The interpretation of this result is that the firm with the higher market share (firm 2 in the present example) has more to fear from being undercut by the small firm, and to prevent this undercutting from being profitable to its rival, it must maintain a lower market price.

The undercut-proof equilibrium derived in this section can be extended in two ways. First, as in the next section, it can incorporate different quality brands, so that consumers' willingness to pay varies between the brands. Second, it can incorporate asymmetric switching costs rather easily by assuming that the cost of switching from brand 1 to brand 2 is $\delta_{1,2}$ whereas the cost of switching from brand 2 to brand 1 is $\delta_{2,1}$, where the two switching costs need not be equal.

3.4.2 Switching costs among differentiated brands

Our analysis in Section 3.4.1 was conducted under the assumption that consumers view all brands as having equal quality and the only reason consumers don't switch brands is that they wish to avoid bearing the switching costs. We now extend Section 3.4.1 to incorporate brands with different qualities.

Myopic rival firms

Suppose that consumers' maximum willingness to pay (net benefit) varies among the different brands. Denote the maximum willingness to pay for the brand sold by firm 1 by V_1. Similarly, V_2 denotes a consumer's maximum willingness to pay for brand 2. Note that if $V_1 > V_2$ we can say that brand 1 is of a higher quality than brand 2, and of course the other way around. We now explore the implications of quality differences on firm 1's ability to undercut firm 2. Let the price set by firm 2 be given as P_2. If firm 1 undercuts firm 2, it must set its price so that

$$V_1 - p_1 - \delta > V_2 - P_2 \quad \text{or} \quad p_1 < p_2 - \delta + V_1 - V_2. \tag{3.46}$$

That is, firm 1 can charge a premium if its brand is of a higher quality than the quality of brand 2. In this case, undercutting can be achieved at a higher price, reflecting brand 1's quality advantage. In contrast, if brand 2 is of a higher quality than brand 1, that is, $V_1 < V_2$, then firm 1 needs to further reduce its price to be able to undercut firm 2.

Figure 3.7 displays the price range under which firm 1 can undercut firm 2, when brand 1 is of a higher quality than brand 2, $V_1 > V_2$, and when it is of a lower quality, $V_1 < V_2$. Comparing the top part of Figure 3.7 to the bottom part reveals

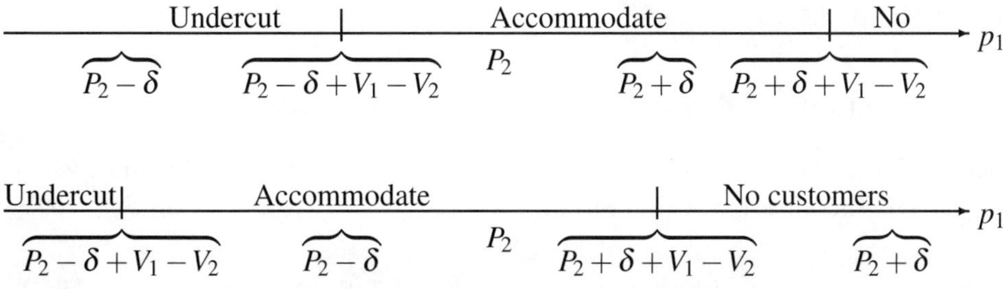

Figure 3.7: Undercutting when brands are differentiated by quality. *Top*: Brand 1 is of a higher quality. *Bottom*: Brand 1 is of a lower quality.

that when firm 1 has a quality advantage, it can undercut firm 2 at a higher price compared with the case in which firm 1 produces the lower-quality product/service. Finally, although we do not show it here, it is clear that Algorithm 3.7 can be slightly modified to accommodate quality differences when searching for firm 1's profit-maximizing price.

Retaliation by rival firms

Suppose now that firm 2 is allowed to retaliate, so p_2 is no longer treated as constant but as a strategic instrument set by firm 2. Under quality differences, Definition 3.1 should be modified as follows:

$$(p_2 - \mu_2)N_2 - \phi_2 \geq (p_1 - \delta + V_2 - V_1 - \mu_2)(N_1 + N_2) - \phi_2, \qquad (3.47)$$
$$(p_1 - \mu_1)N_1 - \phi_1 \geq (p_2 - \delta + V_1 - V_2 - \mu_1)(N_1 + N_2) - \phi_1.$$

That is, when firm 2 undercuts firm 1, it can add the quality difference $V_2 - V_1$ to the undercutting price to reflect its quality advantage or disadvantage. Similarly, when firm 1 undercuts firm 2, it can add the quality difference $V_1 - V_2$ to its undercutting price.

Solving (3.47) for the equality case, the extension of (3.45) to brands differentiated by quality is given by

$$p_1^U = \frac{(N_1)^2(V_1 - V_2 + \delta + \mu_2) + N_1 N_2(V_1 - V_2 + 3\delta + \mu_2)(N_2)^2(2\delta + \mu_1)}{(N_1)^2 + N_1 N_2 + (N_2)^2},$$

$$(3.48)$$

$$p_2^U = \frac{(N_1)^2(2\delta + \mu_2) + N_1 N_2(V_2 - V_1 + 3\delta + \mu_1) + (N_2)^2(V_2 - V_1 + \delta + \mu_1)}{(N_1)^2 + N_1 N_2 + (N_2)^2}.$$

Clearly, substituting $V_1 = V_2$ into (3.48) obtains (3.45). Similar to the the basic solution (3.45), the solution to the undercut-proof equilibrium for differentiated brands (3.48) may also generate negative prices, in which case a solution may be found by looking for a price at which one firm (perhaps the one producing the higher quality) can undercut the other firm by leaving it with no customers, and hence zero profit.

3.4.3   Continuous demand with differentiated brands

Section 2.7 analyzes continuous demand functions for differentiated brands, which for the two-brand case, take the form of

$$q_1(p_1, p_2) \stackrel{\text{def}}{=} \alpha_1 - \beta_1 p_1 + \gamma_1 p_2, \qquad (3.49)$$
$$q_2(p_1, p_2) \stackrel{\text{def}}{=} \alpha_2 + \gamma_2 p_1 - \beta_2 p_2,$$

where $\beta_1 > 0$ and $\beta_2 > 0$ so that quantity demanded for each brand declines with the brand's own price. In addition, we must assume that $\beta_1 > |\gamma_1|$ and $\beta_2 > |\gamma_2|$ so that the "own-price effect" would always dominate the rival's price effect. Definition 2.4 has already established the general properties of the demand structure given by (3.49) by classifying $\gamma_1 > 0$ and $\gamma_2 > 0$ as substitutes, and $\gamma_1 < 0$ and $\gamma_2 < 0$ as complements.

Myopic rival firms

Suppose that the price set by firm 2 is fixed at the level P_2 and that firm 2 has no intention of changing it, regardless of what price is chosen by firm 1. In what follows, we construct what is commonly referred to as firm 1's *best-response function* by using one simple calculus computation.

Let μ_1 and ϕ_1 denote the marginal and fixed costs of firm 1. Using (3.49), the profit function of firm 1 is given by

$$y_1 = (p_1 - \mu_1)q_1 - \phi_1 = (p_1 - \mu_1)(\alpha_1 - \beta_1 p_1 + \gamma_1 p_2) - \phi_1. \qquad (3.50)$$

Readers who know a little bit of calculus can solve for the first-order condition $0 = \partial y_1/\partial p_1 = -2\beta_1 p_1 + \alpha_1 + \beta_1 \mu_1 + \gamma_1 p_2$ and the second-order condition, for a maximum $\partial^2 y_1/\partial(p_1)^2 = -2\beta_1 < 0$. From the first-order condition, we obtain firm 1's best-response function given by

$$p_1(P_2) = \frac{\alpha_1 + \beta_1 \mu_1 + \gamma_1 P_2}{2\beta_1}. \qquad (3.51)$$

Figure 3.8 displays firm 1's best-response function for the case in which brands 2 is a substitute for brand 1 ($\gamma_1 > 0$) and the case in which brand 2 complements brand 1 ($\gamma_1 < 0$).

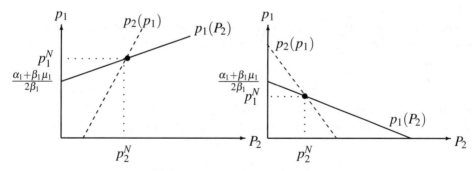

Figure 3.8: Firm 1's price best-response function (solid lines).
Left: Substitute brands ($\gamma_1 > 0$). *Right*: Complements ($\gamma_1 < 0$).

The left side of Figure 3.8 shows that if brand 2 is a substitute for brand 1, firm 1 will raise its price in response to a price increase by firm 2. The right side shows that firm 1 will lower its price in response to a price increase by firm 2, if brand 2 complements brand 1. This is because consumers tend to buy complement brands as bundles, so an increase in the price of one component of a bundle will cause a reduction in the price of a complement component, to keep the demand for both brands from falling sharply. Figure 3.8 also shows that firm 1's best-response function shifts upward with an increase in the demand intercept α_1 and the marginal-cost parameter μ_1. This is because a shift in demand and/or an increase in marginal cost induces firm 1 to raise its price for every given price set by firm 2.

Retaliation by rival firms

Now suppose that firm 2 can also adjust its price in response to price changes made by firm 1. Let μ_2 and ϕ_2 denote the marginal and fixed costs of firm 2. Using (3.49), the profit function of firm 2 is given by

$$y_2 = (p_2 - \mu_2)q_2 - \phi_2 = (p_2 - \mu_2)(\alpha_2 + \gamma_2 p_1 - \beta_2 p_2) - \phi_2. \qquad (3.52)$$

The first-order condition is given by $0 = \partial y_2/\partial p_2 = -2\beta_2 p_2 + \alpha_2 + \beta_2 \mu_2 + \gamma_2 p_1$, and the second-order condition for a maximum is $\partial^2 y_2/\partial(p_2)^2 = -2\beta_2 < 0$. From the first-order condition, we obtain firm 2's best-response function, given by

$$p_2(p_1) = \frac{\alpha_2 + \beta_2 \mu_2 + \gamma_2 p_1}{2\beta_2}. \qquad (3.53)$$

The best-response function (3.53) is drawn in Figure 3.8 using dashed lines. Note that the axes are "flipped" for equation (3.53) in the sense that the dependent variable p_2 is plotted on the horizontal axis, whereas the independent variable p_1 is on the vertical axis.

The last step for computing p_1 and p_2 is to define an equilibrium concept that would serve as a prediction for which prices are likely to be realized once firms stop responding to price changes made by rival firms. We make the following definition:

DEFINITION 3.2
*A pair of prices (p_1^N, p_2^N) is called a **Nash-Bertrand equilibrium** if p_1^N is firm 1's best response to p_2^N, and p_2^N is firm 2's best response to p_1^N.*

In other words, the pair of prices must be on the best-response function of each active firm. The Nash-Bertrand equilibrium pair of prices (p_1^N, p_2^N) is plotted in Figure 3.8 as the intersection of the two best-response functions. To obtain a numerical solution, solving (3.51) and (3.53) yields the equilibrium price pair

$$p_1^N = \frac{\alpha_2 \gamma_1 + \beta_2(2\alpha_1 + 2\beta_1 \mu_1 + \gamma_1 \mu_2)}{4\beta_1 \beta_2 - \gamma_1 \gamma_2}, \qquad (3.54)$$

$$p_2^N = \frac{\alpha_1 \gamma_2 + \beta_1(2\alpha_2 + 2\beta_2 \mu_2 + \gamma_2 \mu_1)}{4\beta_1 \beta_2 - \gamma_1 \gamma_2}. \qquad (3.55)$$

Extension to multiple firms

Consider a market for differentiated brands with $F \geq 2$ firms, each producing a different brand indexed by $j = 1, \ldots, F$. The aggregate consumer demand function for each brand, given by (3.49) for the two-brand case, is now generalized to

$$q_j(p_1, \ldots, p_F) \overset{\text{def}}{=} \alpha_j - \beta_j p_j + \sum_{\substack{i=1 \\ i \neq j}}^{F} \gamma_j^i p_i, \quad j = 1, \ldots, F, \qquad (3.56)$$

where $\alpha_j > 0$, $\beta_j > 0$. In addition, the "own-price effect" parameter must also satisfy $\beta_j > \sum_{i \neq j} |\gamma_j^i|$, so it is greater than the sum of all "cross-price effects." Thus, the demand for brand j is negatively related to p_j, but is also affected by the prices of all other brands p_i for all brands $i \neq j$, via the parameters γ_j^i. These parameters can be estimated using the procedure described in Section 2.7 using time series observations on prices of all existing brands.

Let μ_j and ϕ_j denote the marginal and fixed costs of each firm j, $j = 1, \ldots, F$. Using (3.56), the profit function of a representative firm j is then given by

$$y_j = (p_j - \mu_j)q_j - \phi_j = (p_j - \mu_j)\left(\alpha_j - \beta_j p_j + \sum_{\substack{i=1 \\ i \neq j}}^{F} \gamma_j^i p_i\right) - \phi_j. \qquad (3.57)$$

The first-order condition for a maximum is given by $0 = \partial y_j / \partial p_j = -2\beta_j p_j + \alpha_j + \beta_j \mu_j + \sum_{i \neq j} \gamma_j^i p_i$, and the second-order condition for a maximum is $\partial^2 y_j / \partial (p_j)^2 = -2\beta_j < 0$. From the first-order condition, we obtain the best-response function for each firm j, $j = 1, \ldots, F$,

$$p_j(p_i | i \neq j) = \left(\alpha_j + \beta_j \mu_j + \sum_{\substack{i=1 \\ i \neq j}}^{F} \gamma_j^i p_i\right) \Big/ (2\beta_2). \qquad (3.58)$$

The best-response functions listed in (3.58) constitute a system of F linear equations that can be solved for the Nash-Bertrand equilibrium prices $p_1^N, \ldots, p_F^N$, using repeated substitution or some other method.

3.5   Commonly Practiced Pricing Methods

So far, our analysis in this chapter has been confined to the study of pricing techniques by profit-maximizing firms (mostly monopolies), in which the presentation reflected the standard economics approach. In reality, professional pricing practitioners often use different terminology in specifying their pricing strategies.

3.5.1   Breakeven formulas

Breakeven formulas are commonly used by managers in charge of pricing policies of their firms. Breakeven formulas provide the manager with some rough approximations on how much output the firm should sell to break even. Some formulas also indicate by how much sales should be increased to compensate for a price reduction and leave the firm at the same level of profit that it earned before the reduction in price.

The first breakeven formula that we introduce computes the minimum output level, denoted by $q^b(p)$, that ensures that the seller does not have a loss, for every given price level. Formally, q^b solves $(p - \mu)q^b - \phi = 0$. Hence,

$$q^b(p) = \frac{\phi}{p - \mu}. \tag{3.59}$$

Therefore, the minimum output level that insures no losses to the seller is the ratio of the fixed cost divided by the marginal profit.

Next, we consider the following question that comes up each time a seller considers a price reduction (say, by declaring a "sale"). If the price is reduced by a certain amount, by how much should quantity demanded rise to leave the firm with the same or higher profit than it earned before the reduction took place? Formally, denoting by subscript $t = 1$ the period before price reduction takes place, and by subscript $t = 2$ the period after the price is reduced, we search for q_2 that solves $(p_1 - \mu)q_1 - \phi = (p_2 - \mu)q_2 - \phi$.

Let $\Delta q \stackrel{\text{def}}{=} q_2 - q_1$ and $\Delta p \stackrel{\text{def}}{=} p_2 - p_1$ denote the change in quantity and price, respectively. Note that $\Delta p < 0$ if the price is reduced. Substituting $p_1 + \Delta p$ for p_2 and $q_1 + \Delta p$ for q_2 yields $(p_1 - \mu)q_1 - \phi = (p_1 + \Delta p - \mu)(q_1 + \Delta q) - \phi$. Therefore,

$$\Delta q = -\frac{q_1 \Delta p}{p_1 + \Delta p - \mu} = -\frac{q_1 \Delta p}{p_2 - \mu}. \tag{3.60}$$

Thus, if $\Delta p < 0$ (corresponding to a price reduction), it must be $\Delta q > 0$, which means that quantity sold must grow to compensate for the price reduction. Formula (3.60) provides the exact amount by which the quantity sold must be increased. This formula shows that Δq is larger if the initial quantity sold q_1 is higher, because the per-unit loss stemming from the price reduction is multiplied by higher quantity levels. Formula (3.60) also shows that this amount should be higher when the postreduction price gets closer to the marginal cost. Figure 3.9 provides a visual interpretation for the formula given in (3.60). The distance between price and marginal cost measures the marginal profit. When multiplied by quantity, one can obtain the net profit of fixed cost. Therefore, the area marked as "Loss" measures the reduction in profit associated with the decline in price. The area marked as "Gain" measures the increase in profit stemming from the increase in quantity sold. By setting Gain = Loss, one can compute the corresponding Δq that matches the level computed by formula (3.60).

Often, it is more useful to express formula (3.60) in terms of rates of change, rather than in units of quantity sold. Hence,

$$\frac{\Delta q}{q_1} = -\frac{\Delta p}{p_1 + \Delta p - \mu} = -\frac{\Delta p}{p_2 - \mu}. \tag{3.61}$$

Thus, the rate of increase in quantity demanded needed for maintaining constant profit after a price is reduced is the (negative) ratio of the price change divided by

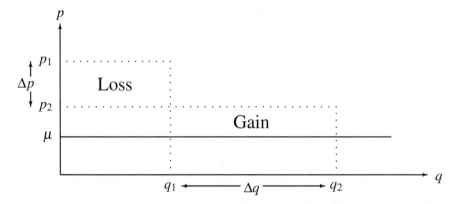

Figure 3.9: An illustration of the breakeven quantity change formula.

the marginal profit. Clearly, the ratio given in (3.61) should be multiplied by 100 to express this rate in percentage terms.

Table 3.4 demonstrates the use of the above formulas for a market consisting of 10 consumers: each formula has a demand function like the one drawn in Figure 3.1 (hence, all quantities are multiplied by 10). Suppose now that the seller is contemplating reducing the price by exactly $5, hence $\Delta p = -5$.

		$35	$30	$25	$20	$15	$10	$5
	p_1	$35	$30	$25	$20	$15	$10	$5
	q_1	10	20	30	60	70	90	130
eq.(3.59):	q^b	3.33	4	5	6.66	10	20	$+\infty$
eq.(3.60):	Δq	2	5	10	30	70	$+\infty$	n/a
eq.(3.61):	$\frac{\Delta q}{q_1} \cdot 100$	20%	25%	33%	55%	100%	$+\infty$	n/a

Table 3.4: Examples for using the breakeven formulas. *Note*: Computations rely on a marginal cost of $\mu = \$5$ and a fixed cost of $100. The last two rows correspond to a price change of $\Delta p = -\$5$.

Table 3.4 displays the computations for breakeven quantities defined by (3.59) and the breakeven quantity changes defined by (3.60) and (3.61), assuming that the seller bears a marginal cost of $\mu = \$5$ and a fixed cost of $\phi = \$100$.

Table 3.4 confirms our earlier observation that when a seller bears a fixed cost, a lower price must be compensated by a higher quantity sold, q^b, to maintain non-negative profit. Any further price reduction must be followed by larger and larger levels of quantity sold to maintain the profit earned before the reduction in price. Table 3.4 also shows that as long as fixed costs must be borne, there is no finite output level that can yield nonnegative profit when the price equals marginal cost. Clearly, if the price is reduced to marginal cost, quantity sold should rise by an infinite amount to maintain the same profit as before the reduction took place.

3.5.2 Cost-plus pricing methods

Managers often tend to be risk averse in the sense that they select a price that covers *average total cost* and perhaps add some markup above average total cost to "ensure" nonnegative profits. Formally, managers often set a price consisting of the following components:

$$p \stackrel{\text{def}}{=} \mu + \frac{\phi}{q} + up, \tag{3.62}$$

where μ is the constant marginal-cost parameter, ϕ is the fixed cost, q is the output produced (predicted sales level), and up is the desired markup. It should be emphasized that the markup up in (3.62) is a markup above all costs (marginal and fixed costs!) as opposed to the ordinary definition of a markup, which is the difference between price and marginal cost, $p - \mu$. This particular definition of up is used *only* in this section.

The pricing technique defined by (3.62) is called *cost plus* because it attempts to secure the firm against a loss by imbedding marginal and fixed costs into the price consumers pay. The term *plus* refers to the markup up, which may ensure some strictly positive profit. Clearly, if the firm sets $up = 0$, the firm breaks even because the price exactly equals the average total cost. The fixed cost component is spread out over the q units that the firm sells to its customers. Thus, if the only goal of the firm is to to break even, the manager can keep the price low by charging a low markup, or even a zero markup. However, if the firm is a profit maximizer, just like the firm we analyzed in earlier sections, the manager may want to compute what should be the markup level that would correspond to the profit-maximizing price.

Cost plus and linear demand

We now compute the markup level up that would generate the profit-maximizing price. For the linear demand case, $p = \alpha - \beta q$, we recall the solution to the "ordinary" monopoly profit-maximization problem given in Section 3.1.2,

$$p = \frac{\alpha + \mu}{2}, \quad q = \frac{\alpha - \mu}{2\beta}, \quad \text{and} \quad y = \frac{(\alpha - \mu)^2}{4\beta} - \phi. \tag{3.63}$$

Because we know that the profit level (3.63) is the "best" that the monopoly can achieve, we now show how this profit level can be duplicated by a proper application of the cost-plus method. To "properly" set the profit-maximizing markup up, we equate (3.62) to the inverse demand function so that

$$p = \alpha - \beta q = \mu + \frac{\phi}{q} + up. \tag{3.64}$$

Substituting the profit-maximizing output level from (3.63) into (3.64), the profit-maximizing markup is then given by

$$up = \max\left\{\frac{\alpha - \mu}{2} - \frac{2\beta\phi}{\alpha - \mu}, 0\right\}. \tag{3.65}$$

Note that the markup specified in (3.65) does not guarantee that the firm earns a positive profit. For example, if the fixed cost ϕ is high and/or the demand intercept α is low, the firm should cease operation in the long run. However, what (3.65) does tell us is that if the firm is able to earn a positive profit, the markup (3.65) is consistent with the profit-maximizing price computed in Section 3.1.2.

For example, let us assume a linear demand function given by $p = 120 - 2q$, so $\alpha = 120$ and $\beta = 2$. Also assume that $\mu = \$30$ and $\phi = \$500$. Then, (3.63) implies that the monopoly's price is $p = \$75$, and (3.65) implies that the corresponding added markup $up = 205/9 \approx \$22.77$. Again, note that this markup is over total average cost (and not over marginal cost only, which is the common definition of a markup). That is, in this example, (3.63) implies that the profit-maximizing output is $q = 45/2$ units. Therefore, the average fixed cost is $\phi/q = 500/(45/2) = 200/9 \approx \$22.22$. Now, if we add up all the components in (3.62) we obtain $\mu + \phi/q + up = 30 + 200/9 + 205/9 = \$75$, which is the profit-maximizing price.

Cost-plus and constant-elasticity demand

For the constant-elasticity demand case, $q = \alpha p^{-\beta}$, we recall the solution to the "ordinary" monopoly profit-maximization problem given in Section 3.1.4, which yields

$$p = \frac{\beta\mu}{\beta - 1}, \quad q = \alpha\left(\frac{\beta\mu}{\beta - 1}\right)^{-\beta}, \quad \text{and} \quad y = \alpha\left(\frac{\beta\mu}{\beta - 1}\right)^{1-\beta} - \phi. \tag{3.66}$$

Because we know that the profit level (3.66) is the "best" that the monopoly can achieve, we now show how this profit level can be duplicated by proper application of the cost-plus method. To "properly" set the profit-maximizing markup up, we equate (3.62) to the price (3.66) so that

$$p = \frac{\beta\mu}{\beta - 1} = \mu + \frac{\phi}{q} + up. \tag{3.67}$$

Substituting the profit-maximizing output level from (3.66) into (3.67), the profit-maximizing markup is then given by

$$up = \frac{\mu}{\beta - 1} - \frac{\phi\left(\frac{\beta\mu}{\beta - 1}\right)^{\beta}}{\alpha}. \tag{3.68}$$

Note again that the markup specified in (3.68) does not guarantee that the firm earns a positive profit. However, what (3.68) does tell us is that if the firm is able to earn a positive profit, the markup (3.68) is consistent with the profit-maximizing price computed in Section 3.1.4.

For example, let us assume that $q = 72,000p^{-2}$, so $\alpha = 72,000$ and $\beta = 2$. Also assume that $\mu = \$30$ and that $\phi = \$500$. Then, (3.66) implies that the monopoly's price is $p = \$60$, and (3.68) implies that the added markup (above average total cost) $up = \$5$. Equation (3.66) also implies that the monopoly's output level is $q = 20$. Hence, the average fixed cost is $\phi/q = 500/20 = \$25$. Now, if we add up all the components in (3.62), we obtain $\mu + \phi/q + up = 30 + 25 + 5 = \$60$, which is the profit-maximizing price.

3.6 Regulated Public Utility

Regulators use different pricing methods as they take consumer welfare into consideration in addition to firms' profits. In this section, we analyze some of these methods. Regulated firms are discussed in Section 5.5 in the context of two-part tariffs, and in Section 6.7 in the context of peak-load pricing. Section 5.5, in particular, contains some discussions on the objectives facing the regulator while deciding on the socially optimal pricing structure.

3.6.1 Allocating fixed costs across markets while breaking even

The problem examined in this section is how to price markets characterized by different demand functions given that the firm incurs a high fixed production cost and given that the firm's objective is to break even (as opposed to maximizing profit). Note that Section 3.2 has already provided the general solution for the profit-maximization problem with no price discrimination, and that Section 3.3 provided the same with price discrimination. These two sections clearly characterize the profit-maximizing prices in the presence of common fixed costs, so no further analysis is needed. For this reason, we now focus only on a firm that attempts to break even.

There are several reasons why a firm's objective would be to break even rather than to maximize profit. First, some regulated public utilities and nonprofit organizations operate precisely under the objective of breaking even. A full investigation of public utilities is beyond the scope of this book. Readers who are interested in regulated public utilities should consult several books, such as Crew and Kleindorfer (1979), Sharkey (1982), Brown and Sibley (1986), Sherman (1989), and Viscusi, Vernon, and Harrington (1995). Also, for more recent books that analyze "regulated competition" (mainly in the telecommunications industry) readers should consult Mitchell and Vogelsang (1991) and Laffont and Tirole (2001). A second reason why the firm may want to break even (instead of maximizing profit) is that a firm may be a subdivision or a unit of a larger conglomerate that supplies parts or other services to its headquarters. In this case, the goal of this subdivision would be merely to ensure that it does not incur any loss while maintaining an efficient production pattern.

Because in this section we do not consider profit maximization as the objective of the firm, one should define an alternative objective according to which prices are selected. The most commonly used objective used by regulators is to maximize social welfare subject to ensuring that the seller or service provider breaks even. However, because this book rarely addresses issues of social welfare, we will be investigating some alternative objectives that vary by the restrictions imposed on the firm in question. Therefore, we begin by first imposing a restriction on the seller to charge equal prices in all markets, so all consumers must equally "share" the fixed cost incurred by this firm. Then, we conclude by showing why "equal sharing" of the firm's fixed cost is inefficient according to a certain criterion.

Two markets with a uniform fee: An example

Consider a single firm serving two markets with the linear demand functions given by

$$p_1 = 80 - q_1 \text{ and } p_2 = 60 - 2q_2, \text{ or } q_1 = 80 - p_1 \text{ and } q_2 = \frac{60 - p_2}{2}. \qquad (3.69)$$

The firm bears a constant marginal cost of $\mu = \$40$ and a fixed cost of $\phi = \$350$. The regulator of this firm requires that (a) the firm break even so that total revenue exactly equal total cost and (b) there is a uniform charge; that is, all the consumers (or actually all units sold) are equally priced, and hence the fixed cost ϕ is equally imbedded into the price of this service/product.

Formally, the firm is allowed to set a surcharge fee f, which must be uniform across markets; the sole purpose of this fee is to pay for the fixed cost of $\phi = \$350$ incurred by this firm. By imbedding this fee (surcharge) into the price, the price can be written as

$$p = \mu + f = \$40 + f, \quad \text{where} \quad f \cdot q_1 + f \cdot q_2 = \phi = \$350. \qquad (3.70)$$

The first part states that the "breakeven" price equals the sum of the marginal cost and the fee, and the second part states that the proceeds from this per-unit fee, which is levied equally in both markets, must exactly cover the fixed cost $\phi = \$350$.

We now demonstrate how to compute the fee f satisfying (3.70). Substituting the direct demand functions (3.69) into (3.70) yields

$$f(80 - 40 - f) + f\frac{60 - 40 - f}{2} = 350, \quad \text{hence} \quad f = \$10. \qquad (3.71)$$

Therefore, the unit price, quantity sold in each market, and aggregate output are given by

$$p = 40 + 10 = \$50, \quad q_1 = 80 - 50 = 30, \quad q_2 = \frac{60 - 50}{2} = 5,$$

$$\text{hence} \quad \bar{q} = q_1 + q_2 = 35. \quad (3.72)$$

Because the firm breaks even and therefore earns exactly zero profit, by construction, the price (3.72) covers exactly the marginal cost $\mu = \$40$ and the average fixed cost, so $f \cdot q_1 + f \cdot q_2 = 10 \cdot 35 = \$350 = \phi$.

Two markets with a uniform fee: General formulation

We now merely repeat the above computations using a general formulation for inverse linear demand functions given by

$$p_1 = \alpha_1 - \beta_1 q_1 \quad \text{and} \quad p_2 = \alpha_2 - \beta_2 q_2, \quad \text{or in a direct form,}$$

$$q_1 = \frac{\alpha_1 - p_1}{\beta_1} \quad \text{and} \quad q_2 \frac{\alpha_2 - p_2}{\beta_2}. \quad (3.73)$$

To compute the fee f, substituting the direct demand functions (3.73) into (3.70) yields

$$f \frac{\alpha_1 - p_1}{\beta_1} + f \frac{\alpha_2 - p_2}{\beta_2} = f \frac{\alpha_1 - \mu - f}{\beta_1} + f \frac{\alpha_2 - \mu - f}{\beta_2} = \phi. \quad (3.74)$$

From equation (3.74) we can obtain an explicit solution for f. This solution may consist of two roots, where one of the roots is the desired nonnegative fee under which the firm breaks even, in the sense that under this fee, all costs are covered by the combined revenue collected in both markets.

The inefficiency of the uniform fee

It is often claimed that consumers in all markets should equally bear the same surcharge fee intended to pay for the firm's fixed cost ϕ. We now show that such a statement is generally incorrect. That is, when markets consist of different consumer groups represented by different demand functions, and if the seller can price discriminate among consumer types by offering a group-specific fee that excludes all consumers outside the group, then it is generally inefficient to charge consumers of different types the same ϕ for the purpose of paying for the firm's market-independent fixed cost. But before we proceed to the formal example, we need to ask, What do we mean by "inefficiency?" Ideally, we would like to construct a social welfare function and show that social welfare can be enhanced by imposing different fees on different markets so that $f_1 \neq f_2$. However, in this section we wish to simplify the computation and therefore choose a different efficiency criterion.

An alternative efficiency objective could be profit maximization. However, by assumption, the firms analyzed in this section have an objective of breaking even, hence by this assumption profit cannot be enhanced. Instead, social welfare can be approximated by the quantity sold to consumers. That is, instead of using the "true" measure of social welfare, we only look at aggregate quantity sold to consumers to approximate social welfare. In view of this discussion, we now demonstrate how consumption could be increased by deviating from the uniform charge of $f = \$10$ computed above.

We look for market-specific fees f_1 and f_2 that would cover the fixed costs so that $f_1 \cdot q_1 + f_2 \cdot q_2 = \phi = \$350$. Substituting the demand (3.69) into this constraint yields

$$f_1 (80 - 40 - f_1) + f_2 \frac{60 - 40 - f_2}{2} = 350, \quad \text{yielding}$$

$$f_1(f_2) = 20 - \frac{\sqrt{100 + 20f_2 - (f_2)^2}}{\sqrt{2}}. \quad (3.75)$$

Equation (3.75) provides all the market-specific fee pairs f_1 and f_2 that are consistent with having the firm breaking even. One can verify that the uniform fee that we solved for above, $f = f_1 = f_2 = \$10$, indeed constitutes one solution for (3.75). Let us deviate from this solution by lowering the market 2 fee to $f_2 = \$2$. Then, (3.75) implies that $f_1 = 20 - 2/\sqrt{17} \approx \$11.75$. Substituting these fees into $p_1 = 40 + f_1$ and $p_2 = 40 + f_2$, and then into the demand functions (3.69) yields $q_1 = 2\sqrt{17} + 20 \approx 28.25$, and $q_2 = 9$. Therefore, total output is enhanced to $\bar{q} = q_1 + q_2 = 37.25 > 35$. That is, output level under the proposed nonuniform fees exceeds the output level under the uniform fee of $f = \$10$.

To conclude, what we have just shown is that price discrimination not only can be used to enhance profit but can also be welfare improving, even when the firm maintains constant (zero in our case) profit. The basic principle is to lower the fee in the market with the more elastic demand to boost quantity. The larger sales in this market would then lower the per-unit-of-output fee because the fixed cost is divided by a larger number of units. Thus, instead of having all consumers paying a uniform price of $p = \$50$ under a uniform fee of $f = \$10$, by setting different fees, consumers in market 1 end up paying a slightly higher price equal to $p_1 = 40 + 11.75 = \$51.75$, whereas consumers in market 2 pay only $p_2 = 40 + 2 = \$42$.

3.6.2 Allocating fixed costs: Ramsey pricing

Regulators of public utilities are often required to set prices above marginal cost to compensate the provider of the public utility for the high fixed cost of investing in infrastructure, paying for loans on these investments, and the high maintenance cost for preventing the depreciation of this infrastructure. One way of doing that is to impose a two-part tariff, which is analyzed later in this book (see Section 5.5).

However, if the regulator is restricted to setting only a one-part tariff, which means a per-unit price, and if the seller can price discriminate among the different consumer groups, say, by age, income, or profession, then the pricing scheme analyzed in this section is known to pass certain criteria of efficiency. Technically speaking, the procedure studied in this section maximizes social welfare subject to the constraint that the firm breaks even, meaning that no subsidy at the expense of taxpayers is needed. The prices generated by the implementation of this objective are known as *Ramsey prices*, based on Ramsey (1927), which analyzed a similar problem related to the financing of a government's budget via taxation. This approach has been applied to public monopolies by Boiteux (1971) and Baumol and Bradford (1970).

Suppose that the regulated public utility bears a fixed cost of $1062.50 and a marginal cost of $\mu = \$10$. The firm can price discriminate between two markets characterized by the demand functions given by

$$p_1 = 80 - 2q_1 \text{ and } p_2 = 40 - \frac{q}{2}, \text{ or } q_1 = \frac{80 - p_1}{2} \text{ and } q_2 = 2(40 - p_2). \quad (3.76)$$

The regulator's problem is to determine the prices p_1 and p_2 for each consumer group so as to maximize social welfare while ensuring that the firm breaks even. Without providing a proof, the solution for this problem in the spirit of Ramsey should satisfy the following two conditions:

$$\frac{L(p_1)}{L(p_2)} \overset{\text{def}}{=} \frac{\dfrac{p_1 - \mu}{p_1}}{\dfrac{p_2 - \mu}{p_2}} = \frac{e_2(q_2(p_2))}{e_1(q_1(p_1))}$$

$$\text{and} \quad (p_1 - \mu)q_1(p_1) + (p_2 - \mu)q_2(p_2) = \phi. \quad (3.77)$$

The two ratios on the left-hand side of (3.77) are the ratio of the markups corresponding to Lerner's indexes defined by (3.5). The right-hand side is a ratio of demand price elasticities, as defined in Section 2.1.3. This condition states that Ramsey prices should be set so that the markup in market 1 divided by the markup in market 2 equals the price elasticity in market 2 divided by the price elasticity in market 1. This condition implies that when Ramsey prices are properly set, the markup is higher in the market where the demand is less elastic. The last condition in (3.77) states that the firm should break even, that is, make zero profit.

The two conditions given in (3.77) can be solved for the Ramsey prices p_1 and p_2. Applying the formula for the elasticity of linear demand given by (2.10) for the assumed demand structure (3.76), the first condition in (3.77) can be stated as

$$\frac{\dfrac{80 - 2q_1 - 10}{80 - 2q_1}}{\dfrac{40 - 0.5q_2 - 10}{40 - 0.5q_2}} = \frac{1 - \dfrac{40}{0.5q_2}}{1 - \dfrac{80}{2q_1}}. \quad (3.78)$$

Also, the first (breakeven) condition in (3.77) is given by

$$(p_1 - 10)q_1 + (p_2 - 10)q_2 = (80 - 2q_1 - 10)q_1 + (40 - \frac{q_2}{2} - 10)q_2 = 625. \quad (3.79)$$

Solving (3.78) yields $q_1 = 7q_2/12$. Substituting this for q_1 in (3.79) yields $q_2^R = 30$. Therefore,

$$q_1^R = 17.5 \text{ and } q_2^R = 30, \quad \text{hence} \quad p_1^R(17.5) = \$45 \text{ and } p_2^R(30) = \$25. \quad (3.80)$$

Figure 3.10 illustrates the Ramsey prices and how they relate to price elasticities in the two markets. Using the formula given by (2.10), the price elasticities in these markets are given by

$$e_1(17.5) = 1 - \frac{\alpha_1}{\beta_1 \cdot 17.5} = \frac{9}{7} \approx -1.28, \text{ and}$$

$$e_2(30) = 1 - \frac{\alpha_2}{\beta_2 \cdot 30} = \frac{5}{3} \approx -1.66. \quad (3.81)$$

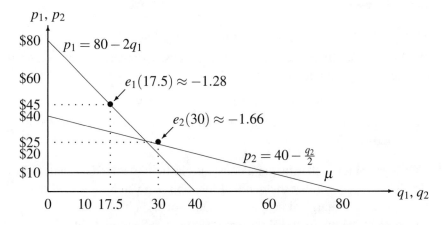

Figure 3.10: An illustration of Ramsey prices.

Thus, as illustrated in Figure 3.10, the markup in market 1 (with the less elastic demand, $|e_1(20 = 1.28|)$ is higher than in market 2 (with the more elastic demand, $|e_2(20 = 1.66|)$.

3.7   Exercises

1. Consider a single seller bearing a marginal cost of $\mu = \$20$ and a fixed/sunk cost of \$30. Similar to the analysis of Section 3.1.1, fill in the missing items in Table 3.5. Indicate on the table the profit-maximizing price and the revenue-maximizing price.

p	70	60	50	40	30	20	10
$q(p)$	1	2	3	4	5	6	7
$x(p) = pq$							
$y(p) = x - \mu q - \phi$							

Table 3.5: Data for Exercise 1.

2. Consider a single seller facing a linear demand as analyzed in Section 3.1.2. Suppose that the inverse demand function is given by $p = 100 - 0.5q$ and that the seller's marginal cost is $\mu = \$20$. Solve the following problems corresponding to the three-step algorithm described in Section 3.1.2.

   (a) Write down the marginal revenue as a function of output.

   (b) Equate marginal revenue to marginal cost to obtain the candidate profit-maximizing output level.

   (c) Compute the candidate profit-maximizing price.

   (d) Compute for what values of the fixed-cost parameter ϕ the monopoly makes strictly positive profit.

3. Consider a single seller facing a constant-elasticity demand as analyzed in Section 3.1.4. Suppose that the demand function is given by $q(p) = 3600p^{-2}$ and that the seller's marginal cost is $\mu = \$30$. Solve the following problems corresponding to the three-step algorithm described in Section 3.1.4.

   (a) Write down the marginal revenue as a function of price.

   (b) Equate marginal revenue to marginal cost to obtain the candidate profit-maximizing price.

   (c) Compute the candidate profit-maximizing output level.

   (d) Compute the values of the fixed cost parameter ϕ under which the monopoly makes strictly positive profit.

4. Continuing from Exercise 3, suppose now that

   (a) Intensive advertising has made this product highly popular among teenagers, thereby shifting the demand to a higher level, given by $q(p) = 7200p^{-2}$. Solve all the problems in Exercise 3 assuming the new demand structure.

   (b) Is there any difference between the price you found in Exercise 3 and the price you solved for in this exercise? Conclude how a change in the demand's shift parameter affects the monopoly's price under constant-elasticity demand.

   (c) Solve for the profit-maximizing price assuming only demand functions given by $q(p) = 3600p^{-3}$ and $q(p) = 3600p^{-4}$. Explain how the change in elasticity affects the profit-maximizing price.

5. Consider the nondiscriminating firm selling a good in possibly three markets for a single price, as analyzed in Section 3.2.3. Fill in the missing parts in Table 3.6 assuming that the seller bears a marginal cost of $\mu = \$10$; market-specific fixed costs are $\phi_1 = \$2000$, $\phi_2 = \$1000$, and $\phi_3 = \$1000$; and $\phi = \$2000$. Which markets should be served, and what should be the profit-maximizing price and the resulting profit level?

Markets	1	2	3	1&2	1&3	2&3	1&2&3
Price $\$p$	30	20	10	20	10	10	10
Quantity q	200	600	200	800	400	800	1000
$(p-\mu)q$							
Fixed costs							
Profit $\$y$							

Table 3.6: Data for Exercise 5.

6. Consider a nondiscriminating single firm selling in two markets with linear demand by setting a single uniform price, as analyzed in Section 3.2.4. Assuming the same demand and cost configurations as in Section 3.2.4, work through all the steps to determine the profit-maximizing price assuming that the marginal cost is now given by $\mu = \$30$ instead of $\mu = \$10$.

7. Consider a price-discriminating firm selling in two markets with linear demand, as analyzed in Section 3.3.1. Suppose that the inverse demand functions in markets 1 and 2 are given by $p_1 = 100 - q_1$ and $p_2 = 50 - 0.5q_2$. The seller bears a constant marginal cost of $\mu = \$2$ and a fixed cost of $\phi = \$1200$. The market-specific fixed costs are $\phi_1 = \phi_2 = \$1200$. Compute the profit-maximizing prices p_1 and p_2 assuming that the seller can price discriminate. Find out which markets should be served by this seller, and compute total profit.

8. Consider a single firm selling in two markets with constant-elasticity demand, as analyzed in Section 3.3.2. Suppose that the demand functions in markets 1 and 2 are given by $q_1 = 3600(p_1)^{-2}$ and $q_2 = 3600(p_2)^{-4}$. The seller bears a constant marginal cost of $\mu = \$3$ and a fixed cost of $\phi = \$100$. The market-specific fixed costs are $\phi_1 = \$100$ and $\phi_2 = \$15$. Compute the profit-maximizing prices p_1 and p_2 assuming that the seller can price discriminate. Find out which markets should be served by this seller, and compute total profit.

9. Consider a single firm selling in two markets under a capacity constraint, as analyzed in Section 3.3.3. The market demand curves are given by $p_1 = 120 - 0.25q_1$ and $p_2 = 240 - 0.5q_2$. The firm bears a marginal cost of $\mu = \$10$, and market-specific fixed and production fixed costs given by $\phi_1 = \phi_2 = \phi = \$10,000$.

   (a) Compute the profit-maximizing prices assuming that capacity is unlimited. Indicate which markets should be served.

   (b) Now suppose that the firm is restricted by a capacity not to produce more than $K = 240$ units. Compute the profit-maximizing prices and indicate which markets are profitable to serve.

10. Consider the three-firm industry studied in Section 3.4.1 in which consumers bear switching costs by changing brands. Firms 2 and 3 are myopic in the sense that they fix their prices at $p_2 = \$40$ and $p_3 = \$20$, respectively. Initially, consumers are allocated among the brands so that firm 1 has $N_1 = 100$ consumers, firm 2 sells to $N_2 = 200$ consumers, and firm 3 to $N_3 = 300$ consumers. Firm 1 bears a marginal cost of $\mu_1 = \$10$ and a fixed cost of ϕ_1 (there is no need to specify a value for ϕ_1 for this problem). Answer the following questions:

   (a) Suppose that firm 1 has decided to undercut firm 2 only, without undercutting firm 3. Compute the maximum value of the switching cost parameter under which firm 1 earns a higher profit under this action compared with not undercutting any firm.

   (b) Find the maximum value of δ that would make it more profitable for firm 1 to undercut firms 2 and 3 at the same time, rather than undercut firm 2 only.

   (c) Find the maximum value of δ that would make it more profitable for firm 1 to undercut firms 2 and 3 at the same time, rather than not undercutting any rival firm.

   (d) From the above results, conclude what action should be taken by firm 1 for every possible value of the switching cost parameter δ.

11. Fill in the missing parts in Table 3.7 according to the breakeven formulas defined in Section 3.5.1. For these computations, assume that the seller contem-
plates reducing the price by \$5 (that is, $\Delta p = -5$) and that the seller bears a
marginal cost of $\mu = \$20$ and a fixed cost of $\phi = \$100$.

p_1	70	60	55	40	30	20	10
q_1	10	20	30	40	50	60	70
q^b							
Δq							
$\frac{\Delta q}{q_1} \cdot 100$							

Table 3.7: Data for Exercise 11.

12. Consider a regulated firm selling in two markets with the objective of maintaining zero profit (breaking even). The firm bears a constant marginal cost of
$\mu = \$30$ and a fixed cost of $\phi = \$550$. The inverse linear demand functions
are given by $p_1 = 120 - q_1$ and $p_2 = 60 - q_2$. The seller's strategy is to set
prices that are uniform across markets so that $p = \mu + f = 30 + f$, where f is
the surcharge needed to cover the fixed cost, so $f(q_1 + q_2) = \phi = \$550$.

(a) Compute the value of f satisfying this constraint, the quantity demanded in
each market q_1 and q_2, and aggregate output $\bar{q}$.

(b) Suppose now that the regulator allows the firm to set market-specific fees
f_1 and f_2 as long as the firm continues to maintain zero profit. That is,
$f_1 \cdot q_1 + f_2 \cdot q_2 = \phi = \$550$. Find a pair of fees f_1 and f_2 that satisfies
this constraint but yields a higher aggregate output level than the aggregate
output level you solved for in part (a).

13. Consider a regulated public utility bearing a large fixed cost, $\phi = \$1600$, but
no marginal cost, $\mu = 0$. The firm sells in two markets, characterized by the
demand functions (3.76). Using the procedure studied in Section 3.6.2, compute
the Ramsey price, quantity sold, and price elasticity in each market.

Chapter 4

Bundling and Tying

4.1   Bundling   117

4.1.1   Single-package bundling with identical consumers

4.1.2   Single-package bundling with two consumer types

4.1.3   A computer algorithm for multiple types

4.1.4   Multi-package bundling

4.2   Tying   131

4.2.1   Pure tying: Theory and examples

4.2.2   Pure tying versus no tying: Computer algorithms

4.2.3   Mixed tying

4.2.4   Multi-package tying

4.3   Exercises   145

Bundling and tying are widely used instruments for implementing price discrimination. Market segmentation is therefore accomplished by offering consumers a variety of packages to choose from. When bundling is used, by choosing different packages, consumers implicity reveal their willingness to pay for different quantity levels of the same good. That is, consumers with a high preference for large quantities will choose large bundles, whereas consumers with a low preference for large quantities will choose small bundles, or simply buy one unit, if available. Similarly, when tying is used, consumers implicitly reveal their preferences for some other types of goods, which are tied to the sale of the original good. Both the bundling and tying pricing techniques constitute special cases of nonlinear pricing under which the price of each unit may vary with the total number of units purchased.

The terms *bundling* and *tying* are used interchangeably both in the academic literature and by pricing experts. In this book, however, we draw a sharp distinction between these two marketing instruments. We will be using the following terminology:

DEFINITION 4.1

(a) *We say that a seller practices **bundling** if the firm sells packages containing at least two units of the same product or service.*

(b) *We say that a seller practices **tying** if the firm sells packages containing at least two different products or services.*

Basically, the easiest way to remember the distinction made by Definition 4.1 is to associate bundling with the sale of different quantities of the same good, whereas tying refers to the sale of different (related or unrelated) goods that are "packed" into a single package. Bundling is widely observed in large warehouses where the seller, for example, tapes five packages of toothpaste together and prices the entire package instead of each unit separately. The practice of bundling often takes the form of subscriptions, for example, by selling a ticket for 10 health club visits or 10 entries to a swimming pool, and a wide variety transportation passes, such as daily, weekly, monthly, or yearly passes that allow the holders of these passes to take unlimited rides on public transportation such as buses and subways.

In some cases it is difficult to distinguish between bundling and tying. For example, when a movie theater sells a ticket for 10 shows, the bundling interpretation would regard it as selling 10 movies for an average price less than the price of a single feature. However, if the variety of movies is limited, one may regard this action as as attempt to sell the less-popular movies together with the more popular ones, thereby increasing the demand for "bad" movies.

Our analysis in this chapter is self-contained and does not follow any particular paper from the scientific literature. Most of the literature in economics journals is about tying (although following our earlier discussion, the term *bundling* is used in place of *tying*). We will not review this literature here. Instead, we list a few important papers on this topic. Burstein (1960) provides an early analysis of tying. Adams and Yellen (1976) introduce a graphical analysis of consumer choice under tying. Other literature includes Schmalensee (1982, 1984), Dansby and Cecilia (1984), Lewbel (1985), Pierce and Winter (1996), and Venkatesh and Kamakura (2003). Literature that deviates from the monopoly market structure includes Anderson and Leruth (1993), Pierce and Winter (1996), Chen (1997a), Liao and Tauman (2002), and Vaubourg (2006).

Several analytical papers, such as McAfee, McMillan, and Whinston (1989); Carbajo, de Meza, and Seidmann (1990); Whinston (1990); Seidmann (1991); and Horn and Shy (1996), tackle the issue of leveraging associated with tied sales, in which the question analyzed is whether a monopoly in one market can enhance its monopoly in another market by tying the sale of the two goods in the two different markets. This line of research went even further by investigating whether the tying firm can foreclose on its rivals in competing markets. This problem may arise in particular in newly regulated telecommunications markets where, for example, a local provider of telephone services can tie in the sale of Internet services to drive competing Internet providers out of this market. Nalebuff (2004) investigated a related issue, arguing that the practice of tying can serve as an entry barrier in the tied good market.

Similar to our analysis of a price-discriminating monopoly in Section 3.3, finding the profit-maximizing bundle also requires the knowledge of the demand by each type of consumer. More precisely, the profit-maximizing bundle(s) cannot be found by knowing the market aggregate demand function alone, because packages must be designed and priced to be purchased by some types of consumers, but not all consumer types. That is, profit-maximizing bundling should result in having different consumer types choosing different packages, thereby paying different prices.

4.1 Bundling

Definition 4.1(a) has already provided a formal characterization of bundling. Most sellers do not use the term *bundling*. Instead, sellers use a marketing gimmick and advertise bundling as a "quantity discount," which basically means that the price of a package containing several units of the same good is lower than the sum of the prices if the goods were purchased separately. Of course we will *not* be using the term *quantity discount* here. In fact, our goal in this chapter is to demonstrate that bundling actually increases consumer expenditure and the surplus the seller can extract from consumers, rather than lowering them.

The basic principle behind bundling is to offer consumers packages containing several units of the same product/service. Thus, the seller must select a package price, denoted by $p^b(q)$, which is the price for a bundle containing q units of the good. The consumer then weighs the consumer surplus generated by buying the entire package against the alternatives. In case there is no alternative, that is, if the seller provides a take-it-or-leave-it offer to buy the package, the consumer will buy this package only if the gross consumer surplus is not lower than the price of the bundle. Formally, a consumer prefers to purchase a package containing q units of the good over not purchasing it at all if

$$gcs(q) \geq p^b(q), \quad \text{or equivalently} \quad ncs(q, p^b) \geq 0, \tag{4.1}$$

where $gcs(q)$ is the gross consumer surplus evaluated at q units of consumption, and $ncs(q, p^b)$ is the net consumer surplus from buying a size q bundle at the price $p^b(q)$; both are characterized in Definition 2.5.

Often, sellers find it profitable to sell a variety of alternative packages and even sell each unit separately in addition to offering a particular package. To be able to distinguish among these alternatives, we will be using the following terminology:

DEFINITION 4.2

The seller practices

(a) **Single-package bundling** *(or simply bundling) if only one package containing at least two units of the good is offered for sale.*

(b) **Multiple bundling** *if more than one package is offered for sale, and at least one package contains at least two units.*

4.1.1   Single-package bundling with identical consumers

Single consumer

Consider a single consumer type with only one consumer, so $N = 1$. The consumer is represented by the demand function illustrated by Figure 4.1. Figure 4.1(left) illustrates the profit (net of fixed costs) made when the consumer is offered a bundle containing $q = 7$ units of the good for a price of $p^b(7) = gcs(7) = \$177.50$. In contrast, Figure 4.1(right) displays the profit from selling single units only for a price of $p = \$20$ each, which corresponds to the familiar, simple solution to the monopoly pricing problem analyzed in Section 3.1.1. The shaded areas in both figures equal the profit made before the fixed cost ϕ is subtracted. Comparing these areas reveals why bundling can be more profitable than selling each unit separately.

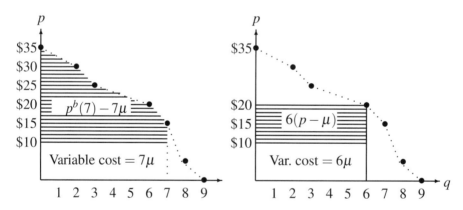

Figure 4.1: Profit made from single-package bundling (*left*) versus profit from selling each unit separately (*right*), assuming a single consumer type.

Table 4.1 displays the computation results of gross and net consumer surplus for the demand function illustrated in Figure 4.1, assuming a marginal cost of $\mu = \$10$ and a fixed cost of $\phi = \$50$. The middle section of Table 4.1 assumes that the seller offers only one package containing $q = 7$ units. From (4.1) we can infer that the seller would charge a package price of $p^b(7) = gcs(7) = \$177.5$. Readers who wish to learn how the gross consumer surplus was computed to be $gcs(7) = \$177.5$ are referred to Table 2.5 which used the same demand data as Table 4.1.

p	$35	$30	$25	$20	$15	$10	$5
q	0	2	3	6	7	7.5	8
$p^b(q)$	$0	$65	$92.5	$160	$177.5	$183.75	$187.5
μq	$0	$20	$30.0	$60	$70.0	$75.00	$80.0
$p^b(q) - \mu q$	$0	$45	−$62.5	$100	$107.5	$108.75	$107.5
$y^b(q)$	−$50	−$5	−$12.5	$50	$57.5	$58.75	$57.5
pq	$0	$60	$75	$120	$105	$75	$40
$(p-\mu)q$	$0	$40	$45	$60	$35	$0	−$40
y	−$50	−$10	−$5	$10	−$15	−$50	−$90

Table 4.1: *Middle*: Computations of the profit-maximizing bundle. *Bottom*: Profit levels in the absence of bundling. *Note*: Computations rely on a marginal cost of $\mu = \$10$, a fixed cost of $\phi = \$50$, one consumer $N = 1$, and bundle prices $p^b(q) = gcs(q)$, where $gcs(q)$ is computed by (2.37).

The bottom section of Table 4.1 indicates that the simple monopoly profit-maximizing price is $p = \$20$, under which the monopoly sells $q = 6$ units only. Comparing the profit levels reveals that bundling enhances profit by more than a factor of five, from $y = \$10$ to $y^b(7) = \$57.5$. The difference is also illustrated in Figure 4.1 (before the fixed cost is subtracted). Thus, by giving the consumer a take-it-or-leave-it offer of a package containing $q = 7$ units with no other alternatives, the seller extracts the entire consumer surplus generated from selling $q = 7$ units. In contrast, as illustrated in Figure 4.1(right), the monopoly cannot extract the entire consumer surplus when selling single units for a per-unit price.

Finally, the reader may observe that the profit-maximizing bundle size falls approximately where the marginal cost $\mu = \$10$ intersects the demand function (at $q = 7$ units of output). The economics literature refers to this outcome as (almost) *perfect price discrimination* because the revenue extracted by the seller equals a hypothetical situation in which the monopoly can charge a different price for each unit sold. It should be noted that the output level $q = 7$ is very close to the output level that maximizes social welfare (again, where marginal cost intersects with the demand curve); in the present case, the entire surplus is allocated to the seller (and none to the buyer).

Single consumer type with many consumers

For the sake of illustration, the above computations were confined to a single consumer only. That illustration was needed because the choice of whether to purchase a bundle must be analyzed at the individual consumer's level by comparing the individual's gross consumer surplus with the price of the package. It will now be shown that the extension from one consumer to many consumers is rather trivial after the profit-maximizing bundle is selected for a single consumer.

To see this, suppose that there are $N = 150$ consumers of the same type, each represented by the demand function illustrated by Figure 4.1 and also on the top section of Table 4.1. Table 4.1 shows that the profit-maximizing bundle contains $q = 7$ units and is sold for a package price of $p^b(7) = \$177.5$. With $N = 150$ consumers, we can write the total profit directly as

$$y^b = N[p^b(q) - \mu q] - \phi = 150[177.5 - 10 \cdot 7] - 50 = \$16{,}075. \qquad (4.2)$$

In contrast, the profit when each unit is sold separately is $y = N(p - \mu) - \phi = 150(20 - 10) - 50 = \$1450$, which shows again that bundling can be much more profitable than selling each unit separately.

Algorithm 4.1 suggests a short computer program for selecting the most profitable bundle. This program should input (say, using the **Read**() command), and store the discrete demand function based on $M \geq 2$ price-quantity observations. More precisely, the program must input the price $p[\ell]$ and the quantity demanded $q[\ell]$ for each demand observation $\ell = 1, \ldots, M$, where $p[\ell]$ and $q[\ell]$ are arrays of dimension M of real-valued demand observations. The program must also input the seller's cost parameters μ (marginal cost), ϕ (fixed cost), and N, which is the number of consumers with the above demand function.

$\text{max}y^b \leftarrow 0;$ /* Initializing output variable   */
for $\ell = 1$ **to** M **do**
   /* Main loop over demand observations   */
   if $N(gcs[\ell] - \mu q[\ell]) - \phi \geq \text{max}y^b$ **then**
      /* If higher profit found, store new values   */
      $\text{max}y^b \leftarrow N(gcs[\ell] - \mu q[\ell]) - \phi;$ $\text{max}qy^b \leftarrow q[\ell];$ $\text{max}py^b \leftarrow gcs[\ell];$
   if $\text{max}y^b \geq 0$ **then**
      writeln ("The profit-maximizing bundle contains $q =$", $\text{max}qy^b$, "units, and priced at $p^b =$", $\text{max}py^b$, "The resulting total profit is $y^b =$ ", $\text{max}y^b$);
      /* Optional: Run Algorithm 3.1 and compare profits   */
      write ("The profit gain from selling a bundle instead of individual units only is:", $\text{max}y^b - \text{max}y$)
   else write ("Negative profit. Do NOT operate in this market!")

Algorithm 4.1: Computing the profit-maximizing bundle for a single consumer type with discrete demand.

After inputting the above data, the user must run Algorithm 2.3 to compute the gross consumer surplus for the inputted discrete demand function, and write the results onto the real-valued M-dimensional array $gcs[\ell]$, $\ell = 1,\ldots,M$, which should also be stored on the system.

Algorithm 4.1 is rather straightforward. It runs a loop over all observations $\ell = 1, 2, \cdots, M$, and computes the profit level, which is the difference between the bundle's price (equal to the gross consumer surplus, $gcs[\ell]$) and the variable cost, $\mu q[\ell]$. Each loop also checks whether the computed profit level exceeds the already-stored value of the maximized profit, $\text{max}y^b$. If the computed level exceeds $\text{max}y^b$, the newly computed level replaces the previously stored value of $\text{max}y^b$.

Using the same data, Algorithm 4.1 can also be used simultaneously with Algorithm 3.1, which computes the simple monopoly profit-maximizing price per unit. Therefore, the two algorithms can be easily integrated to perform a comparison between the profit when the firm bundles, $\text{max}y^b$, and the profit when the firm does not bundle, $\text{max}y$.

Single consumer type: Continuous demand approximation

The computation of gross consumer surplus is greatly simplified if a continuous linear demand function is used instead of the discrete demand function illustrated in Figure 4.1. In fact, equation (2.39) derives the gross consumer surplus for the general linear demand function $p = \alpha - \beta q$ to be

$$gcs(q) = \frac{(\alpha + p)(q - 0)}{2} = \frac{(\alpha + \alpha - \beta q)(q - 0)}{2} = \frac{(2\alpha - \beta q)q}{2}. \quad (4.3)$$

Therefore, for a quick (but less accurate) selection of the profit-maximizing bundle, the seller can fit a linear curve to the discrete demand function, and then compute the price by using (4.3) and the known cost parameters.

Using the regression technique described in Section 2.3.2, a linear fitting of the demand function illustrated by Figure 4.1 and on the top section of Table 4.1 yields $p = 36.93 - 3.66q$. Thus, the estimated coefficients of this linear demand approximation are $\alpha = 36.93$ and $\beta = 3.66$. The fitted demand curve is illustrated in Figure 4.2. This demand intersects marginal cost at $p = 36.93 - 3.66q = \mu = 10$, hence at $q = 7.36$ units.

Figure 4.2 shows that profit, defined as $y = p^b(q) - \mu q - \phi$, is maximized when the firm sells a bundle with q units, where q solves $\mu = \alpha - \beta q$, hence $q = 7.36$ for the present example. Clearly, this is only an approximation because if this good is indivisible, this result hints that the profit-maximizing bundle should consist of either $q = 7$ or $q = 8$ units. Finally, the price of this bundle can be easily found by computing the gross consumer surplus (4.3). Hence,

$$p^b(7.36) = gcs(7.36) = \frac{(2 \cdot 36.93 - 3.66 \cdot 7.36)7.36}{2} = \$172.67. \quad (4.4)$$

The resulting profit is then

$$y^b(7.36) = p^b(7.36) - 7.36\mu - \phi = 172.67 - 7.36 \cdot 10 - 50 = \$49.07. \quad (4.5)$$

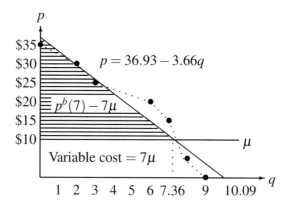

Figure 4.2: Profit-maximizing single-package bundling using a linear demand approximation for single consumer type.

Comparing the bundle's price and profit from the linear demand approximation (4.4) and (4.5) with the profit computed directly from the discrete data given in Table 4.1 yields the magnitude of the error generated by the linear approximation. That is, Table 4.1 indicates that the profit-maximizing bundle has $q = 7$ units, priced at $p^b = \$177.5$, and earns a profit level $y^b = \$57.5$. The analysis under the linear demand approximation suggests a profit-maximizing bundle of $q = 7.36$ units, a price of $p^b = \$172.67$, and a resulting profit of $y^b = \$49.07 < \$57.5$.

Finally, as with the discrete demand case, the linear demand approximation can be extended to $N \geq 2$ consumers of the same type by multiplying revenue and variable cost by N. For the present example, with N consumers, the profit becomes $y^b = N(p^b - \mu q) - \phi = N(172.67 - 7.36 \cdot 10) - 50 = 99.07N - 50$.

The example provided by Figure 4.2 is now generalized to any linear demand function given by $p = \alpha - \beta q$, where $\alpha > \mu$ and $\beta > 0$. This generalization also proves our assertion above that with a single consumer type, the profit-maximizing bundle is determined at the point where the inverse demand function intersects with the marginal cost. Formally, the seller chooses a bundle with q units to solve

$$\max_{q} y^b = N \left[gcs(q) - \mu q \right] - \phi = N \left[\frac{(2\alpha - \beta q)q}{2} - \mu q \right] - \phi, \qquad (4.6)$$

where $gcs(q)$ was substituted from (4.3). The first-order condition for selecting the profit-maximizing bundle implies that

$$\frac{dgcs(q)}{dq} = \alpha - \beta q = \mu, \quad \text{hence} \quad q^b = \frac{\alpha - \mu}{\beta}. \qquad (4.7)$$

This condition proves that the profit-maximizing bundle size is determined by intersection of the demand with the marginal cost. Moreover, recall from equation

(2.41) that the inverse demand function is equal to the *marginal* gross consumer surplus function. Thus, the seller selects the number of units in the bundle by equating the *marginal* gross consumer surplus to the marginal production cost. Figure 4.3 illustrates the procedure for selecting the profit-maximizing bundle size. The seller maximizes the distance between the gross consumer surplus curve $gcs(q)$ and the total variable cost line μq. Condition (4.7) implies that the bundle size that maximizes this distance is found by equating the inverse demand to the marginal cost μ, thereby obtaining the profit-maximizing bundle size $q^b = (\alpha - \mu)/\beta$.

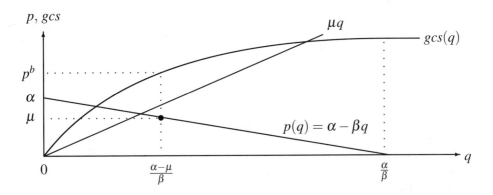

Figure 4.3: Profit-maximizing single-package bundling for a single consumer type with a continuous linear demand function. *Note:* Figure is not drawn to scale.

The last step is to compute the bundle's price and the profit level generated by selling bundles with q^b units. Substituting q^b from (4.7) into the gross consumer surplus function (4.3) and also into the profit function (4.6) obtains the bundle's price and the corresponding profit level:

$$p^b = gcs(q^b) = \frac{\alpha^2 - \mu^2}{2\beta} \quad \text{and} \quad y^b = \frac{N(\alpha - \mu)^2}{2\beta} - \phi. \tag{4.8}$$

Clearly, the seller must verify that the fixed cost ϕ is sufficiently low so that no loss is made, that is, $y^b \geq 0$. Otherwise, the firm may sell in the short run, but should not sell once the fixed cost has to be repaid.

4.1.2 Single-package bundling with two consumer types

The analysis of single-package bundling with two consumer types is confined to continuous linear demand functions. Section 2.3.2 has already shown how discrete demand data can be fitted to obtain a linear demand representation. We start with a numerical example of two groups of consumers using specific linear demand functions, and then proceed to a more general formulation.

Numerical example: One consumer of each type

Suppose first that there is only one consumer of each type, so that $N_1 = N_2 = 1$. The inverse demand function of each type is assumed to be given by

$$p_1 = \alpha_1 - \beta_1 q_1 = 8 - 2q_1 \quad \text{and} \quad p_2 = \alpha_2 - \beta_2 q_2 = 4 - \frac{1}{2} q_2, \qquad (4.9)$$

and are also illustrated in Figure 4.4. Substituting the demand parameters from (4.9) into (4.3) yields the gross consumer surplus of each consumer type as a function of the bundle size q. Hence,

$$gcs_1(q) = q(8-q) \quad \text{and} \quad gcs_2(q) = \frac{q(16-q)}{4}. \qquad (4.10)$$

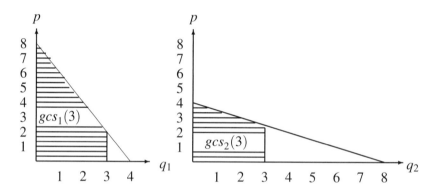

Figure 4.4: Single-package bundling with two consumer types. Shaded areas capture gross consumer surplus from consuming three units: $gcs_1(3) = \$15$ and $gcs_2(3) = \$9.75$.

Table 4.2 displays the gross consumer surplus of each consumer type for all possible bundle sizes $q = 1, \ldots, 7$. Note that (4.9) implies that no consumer would be willing to pay a strictly positive price for any bundle containing $q = 8$ units or more.

The top part of Table 4.2 computes the gross consumer surplus and the profit, assuming that only the type 1 consumer is served. Formally, the price is set to $p^b(q) = gcs_1(q)$, implying a profit of $y_1(q) = gcs_1(q) - \mu q - \phi$. The section below computes the price $p^b(q) = gcs_2(q)$ and the profit y_2, assuming that only the type 2 consumer is served. The section above the bottom row of the table computes the profit, assuming that both consumer types are served. In this case, price must be set to $p^b(q) = \min\{gcs_1(q), gcs_2(q)\}$ to induce both consumer types to purchase a bundle with q units. The profit from serving both types is then computed by $y_{1,2} = 2\min\{gcs_1(q), gcs_2(q)\} - 2\mu q - \phi$, where we multiply by 2 because both consumers are served.

q (bundle size)	1	2	3	4	5	6	7
$gcs_1(q)$	\$7.00	\$12	**\$15.00**	\$16	\$0.00	\$0	\$0.00
$y_1(q)$	\$5.00	\$8	**\$9.00**	\$8	\$0.00	\$0	\$0.00
$gcs_2(q)$	\$3.75	\$7	\$9.75	\$12	\$13.75	\$15	\$15.75
$y_2(q)$	\$1.75	\$3	\$3.75	\$4	\$3.75	\$3	\$1.75
$\min\{gcs_1, gcs_2\}$	\$3.75	\$7	\$9.75	\$12	\$0.00	\$0	\$0.00
$y_{1,2}(q)$	\$3.50	\$6	\$7.50	\$8	<0	<0	<0
$\max\{y_1, y_2, y_{1,2}\}$	\$5.00	\$8	**\$9.00**	\$8	\$3.75	\$3	\$1.75

Table 4.2: Computations of the profit-maximizing bundle with two consumer types. *Note*: Computations rely on a marginal cost of $\mu = \$2$, a fixed cost of $\phi = \$0$ (zero), and one consumer of each type, $N_1 = N_2 = 1$.

The last row in Table 4.2 determines the maximum profit associated with each bundle size q. For example, if the firm sells a bundle with $q = 2$ units, profit is maximized at $y_1 = \$8$, where the price is set to $p^b(2) = gcs_1(2) = \$12 > \$7 = gcs_2(2)$. Hence, the type 2 consumer does not buy at this price. Comparing all the profit levels on the bottom row of Table 4.2 reveals that the profit-maximizing bundle size has $q = 3$ units. This bundle is priced at $p^b(3) = gcs_1(3) = \$15 > \$9.75 = gcs_2(3)$ (see also Figure 4.4), hence only the type 1 consumer buys it, and the firm earns a profit of $y(3) = \$9$.

To conclude this example, observe from Table 4.2 that for small bundles, where $q = 1, 2, 3$, the firm maximizes profit by selecting a price that excludes the type 2 consumer. If the firm sells $q = 4$ units in a bundle, it is indifferent as to whether to price high at $p^b(4) = gcs_1(4) = \$16$ so only type 1 buys or to price sufficiently low at $p^b(4) = gcs_2(4) = \$12$ so both consumer types buy. In either case, the seller earns $y_1(4) = y_{1,2}(4) = \$8$. Bundles of sizes larger than $q \geq 5$ units are priced at $p^b(q) = gcs_2(q)$ (so the type 1 consumer is excluded) because the willingness to pay by the type 1 consumer falls below marginal cost at these quantity levels.

Numerical example: Multiple consumers of each type

The calculation results exhibited in Table 4.2 are based on two consumer types, defined by the demand functions (4.9), and $N_1 = N_2 = 1$ (one consumer per type). We now extend this example to multiple consumers of each type. Formally, suppose that there are $N_1 = 2$ type 1 consumers and $N_2 = 5$ type 2 consumers. Table 4.3 modifies Table 4.2 by recalculating the profit levels for each size q bundle for multiple consumers of each type. The recalculated profit levels in Table 4.3 are based on $y_1(q) = 2[gcs_1(q) - \mu q] - \phi$, $y_2(q) = 5[gcs_2(q) - \mu q] - \phi$, and $y_{1,2}(q) = (2 + 5)[p(q) - \mu q] - \phi$, where $p(q) = \min\{gcs_1(q), gcs_2(q)\}$.

q (bundle size)	1	2	3	4	5	6	7
$gcs_1(q)$	$7.00	$12	$15.00	$16	$0.00	$0	$0.00
$y_1(q)$	$10.00	$16	$18.00	$16	$0.00	$0	$0.00
$gcs_2(q)$	$3.75	$7	$9.75	$12	$13.75	$15	$15.75
$y_2(q)$	$8.75	$15	$18.75	$20	$18.75	$15	$8.75
$\min\{gcs_1, gcs_2\}$	$3.75	$7	$9.75	$12	$0.00	$0	$0.00
$y_{1,2}(q)$	$12.25	$21	$26.25	$28	< 0	< 0	< 0
$\max\{y_1, y_2, y_{1,2}\}$	$12.25	$21	$26.25	$28	$18.75	$15	$8.75

Table 4.3: Extending Table 4.2 to multiple consumers, $N_1 = 2$ and $N_2 = 5$.

The computations exhibited in Table 4.3 reveal that the profit-maximizing bundle has $q = 4$ units. However, unlike the case in which $N_1 = N_2 = 1$, here the seller lowers the price to $p^b(4) = gcs_2(4) = \$12$ so that all the $2+5$ consumers are served. This should come as no surprise considering our assumption that there are $N_2 = 5$ type 2 consumers that the seller does not find it profitable to exclude.

General formulation for two consumer types

We now provide the general formulation for how to pick the profit-maximizing bundle when there are two consumer types. This formulation also serves as a preparation for Section 4.1.3, which incorporates more than two consumer types. With only $M = 2$ consumer types, and N_1 type 1 consumers and N_2 type 2 consumers, using (4.3), for each consumer type $\ell = 1, 2$ we define

$$ p_\ell^b(q) \stackrel{\text{def}}{=} gcs_\ell(q) = \frac{(2\alpha_\ell - \beta_\ell q)q}{2} \quad \text{and} \quad p_{1,2}^b(q) \stackrel{\text{def}}{=} \min\left\{p_1^b, p_2^b\right\}. \quad (4.11) $$

Thus, $p_1(q)$ is the maximum willingness to pay for a size q bundle by a type 1 consumer, and $p_2(q)$ by a type 2 consumer. The price $p_{1,2}^b(q)$ is the highest price that would still induce both consumer types to buy a size q bundle.

The method for selecting the profit-maximizing bundle size involves the comparison of three profit levels:

$$ y_\ell(q) = N_\ell[p_\ell^b(q) - \mu q] - \phi \quad \text{and} \quad y_{1,2}(q) = (N_1 + N_2)[p_{1,2}^b(q) - \mu q] - \phi, \quad (4.12) $$

where $\ell = 1, 2$. That is, for a given bundle size of q units, the profit from selling to type 1 consumers, $y_1(q)$, should be compared to the profit $y_2(q)$ (selling to type 2 consumers only), and to the profit $y_{1,2}(q)$ (selling to both types). Clearly, some of these comparisons are redundant because if $p_1^b > p_2^b$, then $p_2^b = p_{1,2}$, and the other way around, if $p_1^b < p_2^b$, then $p_1^b = p_{1,2}^b$. However, extra comparisons won't use too much extra computer time, so one can still do with these extra comparisons to prevent logical mistakes in the program.

The above comparisons should be performed for all admissible bundle sizes $q = 1, 2, \ldots, q^{\text{max}}$, where q^{max} is the largest quantity beyond which no consumer is willing to pay a strictly positive price, that is, the highest integer q for which a bundle of size $q + 1$ would be associated with a zero price for each consumer type. For each bundle size q, the above comparison should yield a price $p^b(q)$, the corresponding profit level $y(q)$, and the number of consumers who purchase at this price. The final decision on the bundle size should involve the comparison of $y(1), y(2), \ldots, y(q^{\text{max}})$ to determine the profit-maximizing bundle size.

4.1.3   A computer algorithm for multiple types

This section describes an algorithm for computing the profit-maximizing bundle size for the case in which there are M types of consumers, each with $N[\ell]$ consumers, $\ell = 1, \ldots, M$. Algorithm 4.3 (to be described later) assumes that each consumer is characterized by a downward-sloping demand curve $p = \alpha[\ell] - \beta[\ell]q$. The computer program described below should input and store (say, using the **Read()** command), the demand parameters onto two M-dimensional real-valued arrays, $\alpha[\ell]$ and $\beta[\ell]$, for each type of demand function $\ell = 1, \ldots, M$, as well as the number of consumers of each type, to be stored on the integer-valued M-dimensional array $N[\ell]$. The program should also input the seller's cost parameters μ (marginal cost) and ϕ (fixed cost).

For each size q bundle, Algorithm 4.3 calls a procedure, given by Algorithm 4.2, that computes the profit-maximizing price for a bundle with q units.

```
Procedure ComputePrice(q);
for ℓ = 1 to M do
    gcs[ℓ] ← (2α[ℓ] − β[ℓ]q)/2 /* Type ℓ's gcs size q bundle   */
    yᵗᵉᵐᵖ ← N[ℓ](gcs[ℓ] − μq) − φ; /* Profit from type ℓ        */
    for ℓℓ = 1 to M do
        /* Find other types who also buy when price= gcs[ℓ] */
        gcs[ℓℓ] ← (2α[ℓℓ] − β[ℓℓ]q)/2; /* Compute gcs[ℓℓ]       */
        if (ℓℓ ≠ ℓ) and (gcs[ℓℓ] ≥ gcs[ℓ]) then
            /* Type ℓℓ buys at this price, add to profit    */
            yᵗᵉᵐᵖ ← yᵗᵉᵐᵖ + N[ℓℓ](gcs[ℓ] − μq);
    if y[q] < yᵗᵉᵐᵖ then y[q] ← yᵗᵉᵐᵖ; p[q] ← gcs[ℓ];
    /* More profitable bundle size found                    */
```

Algorithm 4.2: Computing the profit-maximizing price $p[q]$ and the corresponding profit level $y[q]$ for a given bundle size q.

For a given size q bundle, the procedure given by Algorithm 4.2 runs a loop over all the $\ell = 1, \ldots, M$ consumer types to compute the profit-maximizing price for a given size q bundle. This internal loop compares the gross consumer surplus $gcs[\ell]$ (candidate price) of a type ℓ consumer with the gross consumer surplus of all other types, indexed by $\ell\ell$. If $gcs[\ell\ell] \geq gcs[\ell]$, then the profit from the $N[\ell\ell]$ consumers is added to the profit. Otherwise, if $gcs[\ell\ell] < gcs[\ell]$, the $N[\ell\ell]$ consumers are excluded from the market because the price exceeds their willingness to pay (their gross consumer surplus).

Algorithm 4.3 states the main computer program. The first part of Algorithm 4.3 computes the largest possible bundle size $q^{\max}$, by running a loop over the $\ell = 1, \ldots, M$ types of demand functions and computing the quantity demanded at a zero price, which is given by $\alpha[\ell]/\beta[\ell]$. The "floor" operator $\lfloor x \rfloor$ rounds this quantity to the highest integer not exceeding the value of this intercept.

$y^b \leftarrow 0; q^b \leftarrow 0;$ /* Initializing output variables   */
$q^{\max} \leftarrow 1$/* Computing largest possible bundle size   */
for $\ell = 1$ **to** M **do**
    /* Loop over all consumer types   */
    if $q^{\max} < \lfloor \alpha[\ell]/\beta[\ell] \rfloor$ **then** $q^{\max} \leftarrow \lfloor \alpha[\ell]/\beta[\ell] \rfloor$;
for $q = 1$ **to** $q^{\max}$ **do** $y[q] \leftarrow 0;$ /* Initialization   */
for $q = 1$ **to** $q^{\max}$ **do**
    /* Main loop over all possible bundle sizes   */
    Call **Procedure** *ComputePrice*(q) ;
    if $y^b < y[q]$ **then** $y^b \leftarrow y[q]; p^b \leftarrow p[q]; q^b \leftarrow q;$
    /* Size q bundle yields higher profit   */
if $y^b \geq \phi$ **then**
    writeln ("The profit-maximizing bundle contains $q^b =$", q^b, "units, and
    priced at $p^b =$", p^b, "The resulting total profit is $y^b =$", y^b);
else write ("Negative profit. Do NOT operate in this market!")

Algorithm 4.3: Computing the profit-maximizing bundle for multiple consumer types with linear demand.

The main loop runs over all possible bundle sizes, $q = 1, 2, \ldots, q^{\max}$. For each bundle size q, the program calls the procedure *ComputePrice*(q) given by Algorithm 4.2, which computes the profit-maximizing price and the corresponding profit level, and outputs these levels onto the $q^{\max}$-dimensional real-valued arrays $p[q]$ and $y[q]$. The last operation in the loop over bundle size q updates the profit y^b, the price p^b, and the profit-maximizing bundle size q^b in the event the last run on q yields a higher profit.

4.1.4 Multi-package bundling

So far, our analysis has been confined to single-package bundling, which means that the seller was restricted to offering a single package containing the same q units to all consumers of all types. In this section, we relax this assumption and allow the seller to sell multiple packages. That is, different packages that contain different amounts of the same good.

We will not provide any general algorithm for selecting the profit-maximizing number and types of packages. Instead, we simply demonstrate the potential profit gain from offering multiple packages by focusing on the numerical example based on the demand functions (4.9) that are illustrated in Figure 4.4.

Inspection of Figure 4.4 reveals that the two consumer types are very different in the sense that type 1 gains "most" of the consumer surplus from the consumption of the first few units. In contrast, the type 2 consumer gains "more" surplus from the consumption of a larger amount. This observation should hint at the possibility that the seller may be able to extract a higher surplus by offering two different packages, rather than a single package. That is, the seller should design one package with a small number of units targeted to type 1 consumers, and a second package with more units targeted to type 2 consumers. We label the first package A, which contains q_A units and is sold for a price p_A. We label the second package B, which has q_B units and is sold for a price p_B.

The mere introduction of two different packages does not guarantee that both packages will be demanded by consumers. Therefore, the following three conditions must be satisfied to have both packages sold simultaneously in the same market.

- A type 1 consumer prefers buying package A over package B, whereas a type 2 consumer prefers buying package B over package A. Formally,

$$ncs_1(q_A, p_A) = gcs_1(q_A) - p_A \quad \geq \quad gcs_1(q_B) - p_B = ncs_1(q_B, p_B),$$
$$\text{and} \tag{4.13}$$
$$ncs_2(q_B, p_B) = gcs_2(q_B) - p_B \quad \geq \quad gcs_2(q_A) - p_A = ncs_2(q_A, p_A).$$

- Both consumer types prefer buying over not buying. Formally, $gcs_1(q_A) - p_A \geq 0$ and $gcs_2(q_B) - p_B \geq 0$.

- The seller earns a higher profit by selling two different packages ($q_A \neq q_B$) than by selling a single package, where $q_A = q_B$.

The first condition implies that a "proper" selection of which bundles to offer for sale would induce all consumers to reveal their type by choosing a specific bundle. More precisely, the seller has no way of knowing and has no legal right to ask consumers directly whether they are of type 1 or type 2. However, a clever design of the two bundles would implicitly reveal consumers' types by the actual choice they make. In the economics literature, the offers made by the seller that result in different types choosing different bundles are referred to as a *preference revealing mechanism*. In other words, by selecting the "right" quantities to be included in the two bundles, the seller can segment the market between the two consumer types, by making type 1 consumers choose bundle A and type 2 choose bundle B.

Suppose now that there is one consumer of each type ($N_1 = N_2 = 1$) with the demand functions described by (4.9), which are also illustrated by Figure 4.4. Recall from Table 4.2, if the seller is restricted to selling only one bundle, the seller would offer for sale a bundle with $q = 3$ units for the price $p^b(3) = \$15$. Now, consider instead the following two bundles:

Bundle $\langle q_A, p_A \rangle = \langle 3, \$13 \rangle$: With $q_A = 3$ units and priced at $p_A = \$13$.

Bundle $\langle q_B, p_B \rangle = \langle 6, \$15 \rangle$: With $q_B = 6$ units and priced at $p_B = \$15$.

Before we compute the profit resulting from the sale of these two bundles, we must verify that they indeed segment the market between the two consumer types according to (4.13). If condition (4.13) does not hold, the market is not segmented, in which case there is no need for the seller to offer two different packages. Using the gross consumer surpluses for the two consumer types given by (4.10) and Figure 4.4, we compute the net consumer surpluses

$$ncs_1(3, \$13) = \$15 - \$13 \quad \geq \quad \$16 - \$15 = ncs_1(6, \$15),$$

$$\text{and} \tag{4.14}$$

$$ncs_2(6, \$15) = \$15 - \$15 \quad \geq \quad \$9.75 - \$13 = ncs_2(3, \$13),$$

which confirm the condition given by (4.13). Therefore, because $ncs_1(3, \$13) \geq 0$ and $ncs_2(6, \$15) \geq 0$, a type 1 consumer buys bundle A whereas a type 2 consumer buys bundle B. Notice that the computation on the upper row of (4.14) where $gcs_1(6) = \$16$ does not follow directly from the consumer surplus formulas (4.10) because, as Figure 4.4 shows, the demand by a type 1 consumer intersects the quantity axis at $q = 4$. Hence, in this case, the consumer surplus should be computed as if this bundle has only $q = 4$ units rather than $q = 6$ units. That is, $gcs_1(6) = gcs_1(4) = \$16$.

We now compute the profit generated from selling the above two bundles. The profit from a type 1 and a type 2 consumer (not including fixed costs) are $y_1 = p_A^b - 3\mu = 13 - 3 \cdot 2 = \$7$, and $y_2 = p_B^b - 6\mu = 15 - 6 \cdot 2 = \$3$. With $N_1 = N_2 = 1$ consumer of each type, total profit is given by

$$y^b(\langle 3, \$13 \rangle, \langle 6, \$15 \rangle) = y_1 + y_2 - \phi = \$10 - \phi > y(\langle 3, \$15 \rangle) = \$9 - \phi, \tag{4.15}$$

which is the maximum profit that can be generated by offering only the bundle $\langle 3, \$15 \rangle$ for sale, as computed earlier in Table 4.2.

Finally, note that despite the fact that bundles $\langle q_A, p_A^b \rangle = \langle 3, \$13 \rangle$ and $\langle q_B, p_B^b \rangle = \langle 6, \$15 \rangle$ indeed generate a higher profit than that obtained from selling only the single bundle $\langle q, p^b \rangle = \langle 3, \$15 \rangle$ computed on Table 4.2, these bundles still do not maximize profit in the sense that one can still find different bundles that generate an even higher profit. The reader is referred to Exercise 4 at the end of this chapter for the computation of such a profit-enhancing bundle.

4.2 Tying

Tying refers to the sale of packages containing different products and/or services (see Definition 4.1). This is in contrast to bundling, in which packages contain several units of the *same* product or service. Tying is practiced in a wide variety of industries. For example, most cable TV operators offer packages containing a variety of channels without giving subscribers the option of buying each channel separately. This practice hints that tying enhances sellers' profit compared with selling each good separately.

Another example of tying are travel agencies that provide organized tours containing accommodations, transportation, and sightseeing in a single package. The last example refers to the practice of tying of related services. However, tying is also observed for unrelated goods – for example, a bookstore tying a T-shirt (or a cup of coffee) with a purchase of a certain book.

For the purpose of this book, the following definition classifies different methods of tying:

DEFINITION 4.3
The seller is said to be practicing
(a) **No tying (NT)** *if each good is sold separately from all other goods.*
(b) **Pure tying (PT)** *(or, more simply, tying) if only one package containing all goods is offered for sale. Goods cannot be purchased separately.*
(c) **Mixed tying (MT)** *if all goods are offered for sale in a single package, and in addition, each good can be purchased separately.*
(d) **Multi-package tying (MPT)** *if more than one package is offered for sale and at least two packages contain two or more different goods.*

Figure 4.5 illustrates how different types of consumers choose what to buy under no tying, pure tying and mixed tying, when there are only two goods, labeled A and B. Good A could, for example, denote a music CD played by the Austrian Symphony Orchestra, whereas good B could be a CD by the Beatles. We assume that each consumer demands at most one CD of each group.

Under no tying, consumers, who buy at most one unit of each good, are offered good A for a price p_A and good B for a price p_B. A type ℓ consumer, $\ell = 1, \ldots, M$, will buy a unit of A if the price does not exceed the consumer's valuation for good A,

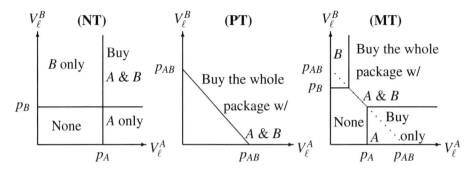

Figure 4.5: Consumer choice under no tying, pure tying, and mixed tying.
Left: No tying. *Middle*: Pure tying. *Right*: Mixed tying.

formally if $V_\ell^A \geq p_A$. Similarly, a type ℓ will purchase a unit of B if $V_\ell^B \geq p_B$. Figure 4.5(left) displays the four regions under which the valuations V_ℓ^A and V_ℓ^B of type ℓ consumers may be realized and the corresponding buy–not-buy decisions.

Under pure tying, consumers are offered one package containing both goods for a price p_{AB}. Clearly, a type ℓ consumer will buy one package if the price does not exceed the consumer's sum of valuations for both goods, formally if $V_\ell^A + V_\ell^B \geq p_{AB}$. Figure 4.5(middle) displays the two regions under which a type ℓ consumer benefits from buying or not buying the package.

Under mixed tying, consumers are offered one package containing both goods for a price p_{AB}, and in addition, good A for the price p_A and good B for the price p_B. Figure 4.5(right) displays the four regions under which a type ℓ consumer benefits from buying or not buying the entire package, or one of the goods. A type ℓ consumer will not buy anything if $V_\ell^A < p_A$, $V_\ell^B < p_B$, and $V_\ell^A + V_\ell^B < p_{AB}$. A type ℓ consumer will buy only good A if

$$V_\ell^A \geq p_A \quad \text{and} \quad V_\ell^B < p_{AB} - p_A. \tag{4.16}$$

The last term in (4.16) follows from the requirement that for given prices the consumer should prefer consuming good A only over the entire package, so that $V_\ell^A - p_A > V_\ell^A + V_\ell^B - p_{AB}$. Note that the difference $p_{AB} - p_A$ represents the implicit price of good B to a consumer already prepared to buy good A. The reader should be able to figure out why the region marked as "Buy A only" in Figure 4.5(right) corresponds exactly to the restrictions given in (4.16) by noting that the displayed price line of a package, p_{AB}, has a slope of -1 (that is, $45°$ if measured from the inside). Next, by symmetry, a type ℓ consumer will buy only good B if

$$V_\ell^B \geq p_B \quad \text{and} \quad V_\ell^A < p_{AB} - p_B. \tag{4.17}$$

Finally, a type ℓ consumer will purchase the whole package if

$$V_\ell^A \geq p_{AB} - p_B \quad \text{and} \quad V_\ell^B \geq p_{AB} - p_A, \tag{4.18}$$

which follows directly from the requirement that

$$V_\ell^A + V_\ell^A - p_{AB} \geq \max\left\{V_\ell^A - p_A, V_\ell^B - p_B\right\}.$$

The classifications made by Definition 4.3 imply that the difference between mixed tying and multi-package tying is that mixed tying offers consumers a choice between two extreme types of packages: They can either buy one package containing all goods tied in a single basket or can purchase each good separately. In contrast, multi-package tying offers consumers a wider variety of packages, in which packages may contain only a subset of all the goods offered by the seller (in contrast to packages offered under pure and mixed tying, which contain all goods).

Definition 4.3 implicitly assumes that packages contain at most one unit of each good. That is, no package contains two or more units of the same good. However, in principle, sellers should experiment with combining tying with bundling, whereby some goods may be offered in large quantities in addition to being tied to different products and services. We rule out this possibility by assuming that consumers have a single-unit demand for each good, as illustrated in Figure 4.6. Thus, the consumer buys at most one unit as long as the price does not exceed a certain valuation level, denoted by V, which reflects the consumer's maximum willingness to pay.

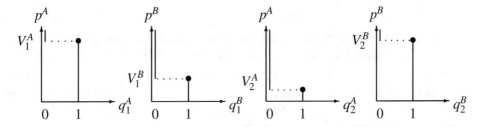

Figure 4.6: Pure tying: Negatively correlated unit demand functions.

4.2.1 Pure tying: Theory and examples

Consider a seller who offers for sale more than one good. By goods, we refer to products or services, or both. The seller has only two options: (a) Offer all the goods in a single package, for a package price, or (b) Sell each good separately at a per-unit price. We now demonstrate the potential gain from tying in a series of examples by varying the number of consumer types and the number of goods that the seller can combine into a single package.

Two consumers and two goods

Consider two goods indexed by $i = A, B$ and two consumers indexed by $\ell = 1, 2$. Each consumer buys at most one unit of good A, good B, or both. Figure 4.6

displays an example of consumers with negatively correlated single-unit demand schedules. Negatively correlated demand schedules mean that consumer 1's willingness to pay for good A exceeds her willingness to pay for good B, whereas the reverse holds for consumer 2. Formally, Figure 4.6 shows that $V_1^A > V_1^B$ whereas $V_2^A < V_2^B$.

Demand schedules like the ones illustrated in Figure 4.6 can be displayed more efficiently in a table such as Table 4.6. Using the example displayed in Table 4.4(right), we now compute and compare the profit levels when there is no tying with profit levels when the seller practices pure tying, assuming marginal costs of $\mu_A = \mu_B = \$1$ and a fixed cost of $\phi \geq 0$.

Consumer Type	A	B
Type 1	V_1^A	V_1^B
Type 2	V_2^B	V_2^B

Consumer Type	A	B
Type 1	$9	$3
Type 2	$2	$8

Table 4.4: Pure tying: Consumers' maximum willingness to pay for products/services A and B. *Left*: General notation. *Right*: Specific numerical example.

No tying: When there is no tying, the seller must price each good separately. Inspecting the first column of Table 4.4(right) reveals that only one consumer will buy good A if $p_A = \$9$, whereas two consumers will buy it if $p_A = \$2$. The profit made from good A when setting $p_A = \$9$ is $y_A = 9 - 1 = \$8$. The profit made from good A when setting $p_A = \$2$ is $y_A = 2(2 - 1) = \$2$. Hence, $p_A = \$9$ is the profit-maximizing price.

Inspecting the second column of Table 4.4(right) reveals that only one consumer will buy good B if $p_B = \$8$, whereas two consumers will buy it if $p_B = \$3$. The profit made from good B when setting $p_B = \$8$ is $y_B = 8 - 1 = \$7$. The profit made from good B when setting $p_B = \$3$ is $y_B = 2(3 - 1) = \$4$. Hence, $p_B = \$8$ is the profit-maximizing price. Summing up, the profit made from selling goods A and B separately (untied) is

$$y^{NT} = y_A + y_B - \phi = \$7 + \$8 - \phi = \$15 - \phi. \tag{4.19}$$

Pure tying: Now suppose that the seller offers the customers a single package containing one unit of good A and one unit of good B, for a price of p_{AB}. Inspecting each row of Table 4.4(right) reveals that consumer 1 will not pay more than $p_{AB} = 9 + 3 = \$12$ for the package, whereas consumer 2 will not pay more than $p_{AB} = 2 + 8 = \$10$ for this package. Therefore, $y^{PT}(12) = 12 - 2 \cdot 1 - \phi = \$10 - \phi$, whereas $y^{PT}(10) = 2(10 - 2 \cdot 1) - \phi = \$16 - \phi$. Thus, the profit-maximizing price of the tied goods is $p_{AB} = 9 + 3 = \$12$ and the profit is

$$y^{PT}(10) = 2(10 - 2 \cdot 1) - \phi = \$16 - \phi > \$15 - \phi = y^{NT}. \tag{4.20}$$

Therefore, pure tying can enhance the seller's profit beyond the level made when each good is sold separately.

Two consumer types with multiple consumers and two goods

The above example assume that there are only two consumers (one of each type). Table 4.5 modifies Table 4.4 by adding more consumers so that there may be more than one consumer of each type. Table 4.5(right) assumes a market with a total of $N = 1000$ potential consumers composed of $N_1 = 200$ type 1 consumers and $N_2 = 800$ type 2 consumers. We now repeat the previous profit calculations, taking into account the multiple consumers of each type.

Consumer Type	A	B	#		Type	A	B	#
Type 1	V_1^A	V_1^B	N_1		Type 1	\$9	\$3	200
Type 2	V_2^B	V_2^B	N_2		Type 2	\$2	\$8	800

Table 4.5: Pure tying with multiple consumers per type. *Left*: General notation. *Right*: Numerical example.

No tying: The profit made from good A when setting $p_A = \$9$ is $y_A = 200(9 - 1) = \$1600$. The profit made from good A when setting $p_A = \$2$ is $y_A = 1000(2 - 1) = \$1000$. Hence, $p_A = \$9$ is the profit-maximizing price. The profit made from good B when setting $p_B = \$8$ is $y_B = 800(8 - 1) = \$5600$. The profit made from good B when setting $p_B = \$3$ is $y_B = 1000(3 - 1) = \$2000$. Hence, $p_B = \$8$ is the profit-maximizing price.

Summing up, the profit made from selling untied goods A and B separately is

$$y^{NT} = y_A + y_B - \phi = \$1600 + \$5600 - \phi = \$7200 - \phi. \tag{4.21}$$

Pure tying: When the package price is set at $p_{AB} = \$12$, $y^{PT}(12) = 200(12 - 2 \cdot 1) - \phi = \$2000 - \phi$, whereas $y^{PT}(10) = 1000(10 - 2 \cdot 1) - \phi = \$8000 - \phi$ if $p_{AB} = \$10$. Thus, the profit-maximizing price of the tied goods is $p_{AB} = 2 + 8 = \$10$ and the profit is

$$y^{PT}(10) = 1000(10 - 2 \cdot 1) - \phi = \$8000 - \phi > \$7200 - \phi = y^{NT}. \tag{4.22}$$

As before, we obtain the result that pure tying can enhance the seller's profit beyond the level attained if each good is sold separately.

General formulation for two consumer types and two goods

For readers who are interested in a general formulation of the two consumer types and two goods tying problems, we now rewrite the above computations using general notation. This writing method also serves as a logical introduction to the general computer algorithm described in Section 4.2.2. Suppose there are N_1 type 1 consumers whose maximum willingness to pay for goods A and B is V_1^A and V_1^B, respectively. For type 2 consumers, N_2, V_2^A, and V_2^B are similarly defined. Let μ_A and μ_B denote the marginal cost of producing and delivering goods A and B, respectively, and ϕ denote the seller's fixed cost.

No tying: Consider the market for one good i (i stands for either good A or good B). If the willingness to pay for good i by type 1 consumers exceeds that of type 2 consumers, that is, $V_1^i > V_2^i$, then setting the price of good i to $p_i = V_1^i$ would result in N_1 purchases, whereas setting $p_i = V_2^i$ would generate $N_1 + N_2$ purchases. Formally, the profit from selling good i as a function of the price of good i is

$$y_i = \begin{cases} N_1(V_1^i - \mu_i) & \text{if } p_i = V_1^i \ \& \ V_1^i > V_2^i \\ (N_1 + N_2)(V_2^i - \mu_i) & \text{if } p_i = V_2^i \ \& \ V_1^i \geq V_2^i. \end{cases}$$

Comparing the above two profit levels yields

$$y_i =$$

$$\begin{cases} N_1(V_1^i - \mu_i) & \text{if } N_1(V_1^i - V_2^i) > N_2(V_2^i - \mu_i) \ \& \ V_1^i > V_2^i \\ (N_1 + N_2)(V_2^i - \mu_i) & \text{if } N_1(V_1^i - V_2^i) \leq N_2(V_2^i - \mu_i) \ \& \ V_1^i \geq V_2^i. \end{cases} \quad (4.23)$$

The "long" condition in (4.23) compares the profit generated by the extra markup $V_1^i - V_2^i$ that the seller can charge type 1 consumers beyond the willingness to pay of type 2 consumers with the reduction in profit from not selling to type 2 consumers, $N_2(V_2^i - \mu_i)$.

Clearly, by symmetry, the polar case in which the willingness to pay for good i by type 2 consumers exceeds that of type 1 consumers, that is, $V_2^i \geq V_1^i$, implies that (4.23) becomes

$$y_i =$$

$$\begin{cases} N_2(V_2^i - \mu_i) & \text{if } N_2(V_2^i - V_1^i) > N_1(V_1^i - \mu_i) \ \& \ V_2^i > V_1^i \\ (N_1 + N_2)(V_1^i - \mu_i) & \text{if } N_2(V_2^i - V_1^i) \leq N_1(V_1^i - \mu_i) \ \& \ V_2^i \geq V_1^i. \end{cases} \quad (4.24)$$

To summarize both cases, the total profit to the seller when selling single units only is given by

$$y^{NT} = y_A + y_B - \phi, \text{ where } y_i \text{ is given by } \begin{cases} (4.23) \text{ if } V_1^i \geq V_2^i \\ (4.24) \text{ if } V_1^i < V_2^i. \end{cases} \quad (4.25)$$

Pure tying: The seller must determine a single price, p_{AB}, for a package containing one unit of A and one unit of B. A type 1 consumer will buy the package if $p_{AB} \leq V_1^A + V_1^B$. Similarly, a type 2 will buy if $p_{AB} \leq V_2^A + V_2^B$. The method for selecting the profit-maximizing price for this package is very similar to the method of selecting the price for a single good. The decision of how to price this package depends also on the types' relative willingness to pay for this package, that is, on whether $V_1^A + V_1^B > V_2^A + V_2^B$, or the other way around. This ordering determines which type of consumer should become a candidate for exclusion. Exclusion is accomplished by setting a price above a type's willingness to pay but below that of the other type, taking into consideration that the marginal cost of the package is $\mu_A + \mu_B$.

If the willingness to pay of type 1 consumers exceeds that of type 2 consumers, that is, $V_1^A + V_1^B > V_2^A + V_2^B$, then setting the price $p_{AB} = V_1^A + V_1^B$ would result in N_1 purchases, whereas setting $p_{AB} = V_2^A + V_2^B$ would generate $N_1 + N_2$ purchases.

Formally, if $V_1^A + V_1^B > V_2^A + V_2^B$, the profit from selling the tied goods in a single package as a function of its price is

$$y^{PT} = \begin{cases} N_1(V_1^A + V_1^B - \mu_A - \mu_B) & \text{if } p_{AB} = V_1^A + V_1^B \\ (N_1 + N_2)(V_2^A + V_2^B - \mu_A - \mu_B) & \text{if } p_{AB} = V_2^A + V_2^B. \end{cases}$$

Similarly, if $V_2^A + V_2^B > V_1^A + V_1^B$, the profit from selling the tied goods in a single package as a function of its price is

$$y^{PT} = \begin{cases} N_2(V_2^A + V_2^B - \mu_A - \mu_B) & \text{if } p_{AB} = V_2^A + V_2^B \\ (N_1 + N_2)(V_1^A + V_1^B - \mu_A - \mu_B) & \text{if } p_{AB} = V_1^A + V_1^B. \end{cases}$$

Comparing the above two profit levels for the case in which $V_1^A + V_1^B > V_2^A + V_2^B$ yields

$$y^{PT} =$$

$$\begin{cases} N_1(V_1^A + V_1^B - \mu_A - \mu_B) - \phi & \text{if } \frac{N_1(V_1^A + V_1^B - V_2^A - V_2^B)}{N_2(V_2^A + V_2^B - \mu_A - \mu_B)} > 1 \\[4mm] (N_1 + N_2)(V_2^A + V_2^B - \mu_A - \mu_B) - \phi & \text{if } \frac{N_1(V_1^A + V_1^B - V_2^A - V_2^B)}{N_2(V_2^A + V_2^B - \mu_A - \mu_B)} \leq 1. \end{cases} \tag{4.26}$$

The condition in (4.26) has the same interpretation as the condition in (4.23). It compares the profit generated by the extra markup, $V_1^A + V_1^B - V_2^A - V_2^B$, the seller can charge type 1 consumers beyond the willingness to pay of type 2 consumers with the reduction in profit from not selling to type 2 consumers, $N_2(V_2^A + V_2^B - \mu_A - \mu_B)$. Next, comparing the above two profit levels for the case in which $V_2^A +$

$V_2^B \geq V_1^A + V_1^B$ yields

$$y^{PT} =$$

$$
\begin{cases}
N_2(V_2^A + V_2^B - \mu_A - \mu_B) - \phi & \text{if } \frac{N_2(V_2^A + V_2^B - V_1^A - V_1^B)}{N_1(V_1^A + V_1^B - \mu_A - \mu_B)} > 1 \\[2em]
(N_1 + N_2)(V_1^A + V_1^B - \mu_A - \mu_B) - \phi & \text{if } \frac{N_2(V_2^A + V_2^B - V_1^A - V_1^B)}{N_1(V_1^A + V_1^B - \mu_A - \mu_B)} \leq 1.
\end{cases}
$$

(4.27)

Finally, the total profit from practicing pure tying is

$$
y^{PT} \text{ is given by }
\begin{cases}
(4.26) \text{ if } V_1^A + V_1^B > V_2^A + V_2^B \\
(4.27) \text{ if } V_2^A + V_2^B \geq V_1^A + V_1^B.
\end{cases}
$$

(4.28)

Therefore, for the seller to determine whether pure tying is more profitable than no tying, the profit levels (4.28) must be compared with (4.25).

Three consumer types and three goods

Before we proceed to Section 4.2.2, which describes a computer algorithm for the case of multiple consumers, multiple consumer types, and multiple goods, we provide a short numerical example of how to compute the profitability from tying (if any) in the case of three goods and three consumer types, with multiple consumers of each type.

Consider a single cable TV operator capable of offering three channels: CNN, BBC, and HIS(tory). Table 4.6 displays the maximum willingness to pay of each consumer type for each channel, the number of consumers of each type, and the marginal cost that the cable TV operator must pay to content providers for each subscribing viewer. The cable TV operator licenses the three channels from their producers for a per-viewer fee. The operator must pay to CNN an amount of $\mu_C = \$1$ for every viewer subscribed to this channel. Table 4.6 indicates that BBC is provided for free, whereas the HIS(tory) content provider must be paid $\mu_H = \$1$ by the operator for every viewer subscribed to this channel.

Consumer Type	CNN	BBC	HIS	# Subscribers
Type 1	$6	$2	$3	$N_1 = 100$
Type 2	$6	$2	$2	$N_2 = 200$
Type 3	$2	$6	$3	$N_3 = 100$
Marginal Cost	$\mu_C = \$1$	$\mu_B = \$0$	$\mu_H = \$1$	

Table 4.6: Pure tying by a cable TV provider: Three consumer types and three channels.

No tying: Each channel is sold separately to potential viewers. Inspecting Table 4.6 reveals that the profit from selling CNN at the price $p_C = \$6$ is $y_C(6) = 300(6-1) = \$1500$. When the price is lowered to $p_C = \$2$, $y_C(2) = 400(2-1) = \$400 < \$1500$.

Table 4.6 also reveals that the profit from selling BBC at the price $p_B = \$6$ is $y_B(6) = 100(6-0) = \$600$. When the price is lowered to $p_B = \$2$, $y_B(2) = 400(2-0) = \$800 > \$600$.

The profit from selling HIS at the price $p_H = \$3$ is $y_H(3) = 200(3-1) = \$400$. When the price is lowered to $p_H = \$2$, $y_H(2) = 400(2-1) = \$400$.

Summing up, the maximum total profit that can be generated without tying is

$$y^{NT} = y_C + y_B + y_H - \phi = 1500 + 800 + 400 - \phi = \$2700 - \phi. \qquad (4.29)$$

Pure tying: Suppose now that the cable TV operator allows viewers to purchase one package containing all three channels for a price of p^{PT} and offers no separate channels. Inspecting Table 4.6 reveals that type 1 and type 3 consumers will not pay more than \$11 for this package, and that type 2 will not pay more than \$10.

If the seller sets $p_{CBH} = \$11$, the profit is $y^{PT}(11) = (100 + 100)(11 - 2) - \phi = \$1800 - \phi$. If the seller lowers the price to $p_{CBH} = \$10$, the profit is $y^{PT}(10) = 400(10 - 2) - \phi = \$3200 - \phi$. Hence,

$$y^{PT} = \$3200 - \phi > \$2700 - \phi = y^{NT}, \qquad (4.30)$$

which shows that practicing pure tying is profit enhancing for this cable TV operator.

4.2.2 Pure tying versus no tying: Computer algorithms

Algorithm 4.4 computes the profit-maximizing prices and the corresponding profit levels when all goods are sold separately (no tying). Then, Algorithm 4.5 computes the package price and profit for the case in which all goods are sold in a single package (pure tying). These two programs should input (say, using the **Read()** command) the following parameters: $M \geq 2$, which is the number of consumer types; $N[\ell]$, the number of consumers of each type $\ell = 1, \ldots, M$; and the set of goods, $\mathcal{B}$. For example, Table 4.6 displays an example of three goods where $\mathcal{B} = \{\text{CNN}, \text{BBC}, \text{HIS}\}$. Then, the program must input consumers' valuations (maximum willingness to pay) for each good and store them onto the array $V[\ell, i]$, where ℓ is the consumer type and $i \in \mathcal{B}$ is the name of a good. The program should also input the seller's unit costs of producing each good $\mu[i]$, $i \in \mathcal{B}$, and the fixed cost ϕ.

Before running Algorithm 4.4, the program should run Algorithm 3.2, which generates all the 2^M possible selections (subsets) of consumer types. The present algorithm uses these selections by searching for the highest price under the constraint that all the consumers in a particular selection will be willing to pay. Then,

```
yNT ← −φ; /* Subtracting fixed cost from total profit    */
for i ∈ ℬ do
    /* Loop over all goods i                              */
    pNT[i] ← 0; yNT[i] ← 0; /* Initial price & profit good i   */
    for j = 1 to 2^M − 1 do
        /* Loop over consumer type selections j           */
        p[j,i] ← V[1,i]; y[j] ← 0; /* Initial price and profit   */
        for ℓ = 2 to M do
            /* Finding max possible price under selection j */
            if p[j,i]·Sel[j,ℓ] > V[ℓ,i] then p[j,i] ← V[ℓ,i]; /* Reduce
                price if type ℓ is excluded from selection j */
        for ℓ = 1 to M do
            /* Profits from all types under selection j      */
            y[j] ← y[j] + {(p[j,i] − μ[i])N[ℓ]}·Sel[j,ℓ];
        if yNT[i] < y[j] then yNT[i] ← y[j]; pNT[i] ← p[j,i]; /* Higher
            profit for good i found in selection j          */
    yNT ← yNT + yNT[i]; /* Add profits from all goods i       */
writeln ("Total profit made under no tying yNT =", yNT);
for i ∈ ℬ do
    write ("The price of good", i, "is pi =", p[i]);
    writeln ("The profit from selling good", i, is yi =", yNT[i]);
```

Algorithm 4.4: Computing profits under no tying with multiple consumer types and multiple goods.

the profits from all selections are compared to find the most profitable selection of consumer types. Algorithm 3.2 writes these subsets onto an array of arrays that we call Sel (for selection of consumer types). The selection of the served consumer types is indexed by $j = 0, \ldots, 2^M − 1$ (not i, in contrast to Algorithm 3.2). Thus, $Sel[j, \ell]$ is an array of arrays of binary variables with dimension $(2^M) \times M$. For example, in the case of $M = 3$ consumer types, $Sel[7, 2] = 1$ implies that type 2 consumers are served under the seventh possible selection. Also, $Sel[6, 2] = 0$ implies that type 2 consumers are not served under the sixth possible selection, and so on.

As for output variables, $p^{NT}[i]$ and $y^{NT}[i]$, $i \in \mathcal{B}$ store the profit-maximizing prices when goods are sold separately (no tying), and the profit made from the sale of each good i. Algorithm 4.4 can be explained as follows: It runs a loop over all goods $i \in \mathcal{B}$ to compute the profit-maximizing price $p^{NT}[i]$. Then, it runs an inner loop over all possible selections of subsets of consumer types indexed by $j = 1, \ldots, 2^M − 1$. For each selection of consumer types j, the program determines the maximum price for which all the consumer types in selection j would find it beneficial to purchase. That is, when this loop ends, the price is set so that $p[j,i] \leq V[\ell,i]$ for every consumer type ℓ belonging to selection j. The next loop over consumer types ℓ adds up the profit earned from each type in selection j by multiplying the marginal profit by the number of consumers $N[\ell]$, and storing on $y[j]$.

Finally, before advancing the counter of type selection j, the program checks whether the profit generated by selling to selection j is higher than $y^{NT}[i]$, which is the highest profit on good i so far. If it is higher, $p[i]$ and $y^{NT}[i]$ are updated. Before the outer loop on good i ends, the program adds the profit made from the separate sale of good i, $y^{NT}[i]$, to the total profit y^{NT} earned from all goods combined.

Algorithm 4.5 computes the profit-maximizing price and the corresponding profit when the seller offers all goods in a single package (pure tying). Then, this profit is compared with the profit under no tying already computed by Algorithm 4.4.

$p^{PT} \leftarrow 0; y^{PT} \leftarrow -\phi; \mu \leftarrow 0;$ /* Initialization   */
for $i \in \mathscr{B}$ **do** $\mu \leftarrow \mu + \mu[i];$ /* Production cost of a package   */
for $\ell = 1$ **to** M **do**
     $V[\ell] \leftarrow 0;$ /* Computing type ℓ's willingness to pay   */
     for $i \in \mathscr{B}$ **do** $V[\ell] \leftarrow V[\ell] + V[\ell,i];$ /* for the whole package   */
for $j = 1$ **to** $2^M - 1$ **do**
     /* Loop over subsets of consumer type selections j */
     $p[j] \leftarrow V[1]; y[j] \leftarrow 0;$ /* Initial price & profit for j */
     for $\ell = 1$ **to** M **do**
         /* Finding max possible price for selection j */
         if $p[j] \cdot \text{Sel}[j,\ell] > V[\ell]$ **then** $p[j] \leftarrow V[\ell];$ /* Reduce price if
            type ℓ is excluded from selection j */
     for $\ell = 1$ **to** M **do**
         /* Add profits from all types under selection j */
         $y[j] \leftarrow y[j] + \{(p[j] - \mu)N[\ell]\} \cdot \text{Sel}[j,\ell];$
     if $y^{PT} < y[j]$ **then** $y^{PT} \leftarrow y[j]; p^{PT} \leftarrow p[j];$ /* Selection j yields
         higher profit. Select package price $p[j]$ */
writeln ("Total profit made under pure tying is $y^{PT} =$", y^{PT}), ("The package price is $p^{PT} =$", p^{PT});
write ("The profit gain (loss if negative) from pure tying over no tying is", $y^{PT} - y^{NT}$); /* Comparing with Algorithm 4.4   */

Algorithm 4.5: Computing profits under pure tying with multiple consumer types and multiple goods.

Algorithm 4.5 works as follows: It adds up all the unit costs of all goods to obtain the unit cost of producing one whole package, so $\mu = \sum_{i \in \mathcal{B}} \mu_i$. Then, it adds up the willingness to pay for each good to obtain consumer type ℓ's willingness to pay for the tied package, so that $V[\ell] = \sum_{i \in \mathcal{B}} V[\ell, i]$ for each consumer type $\ell = 1, \ldots, M$.

After this preparation, Algorithm 4.5 runs over all the 2^M possible selections of consumer types and finds the highest price $p[j]$ that all consumers in a selection j would be willing to pay for the package. Then, the profit from selection j $y[j]$ is compared with the maximum profit y^{PT} already found, and the algorithm updates y^{PT} if necessary.

4.2.3   Mixed tying

Following Definition 4.3(c), under mixed tying the seller offers for sale one package containing all goods, and in addition the seller offers for sale each good separately. Consumers then have to decide whether to purchase the package containing all goods, or whether to buy some or all the goods separately. We will not develop a complete theory of mixed tying and will not provide a computer algorithm for how to design the pricing structure under mixed tying. Instead, we illustrate the rationale behind the potential gains from mixed tying relative to pure tying and no tying with the example exhibited in Table 4.7.

Consumer Type	CNN	BBC	# Subscribers
Type 1	$11	$2	$N_1 = 100$
Type 2	$9	$9	$N_2 = 200$
Type 3	$2	$11	$N_3 = 100$
Marginal Cost	$\mu_C = \$1$	$\mu_B = \$1$	

Table 4.7: Mixed tying by a cable TV provider.

No tying: Suppose now that the cable TV operator allows viewers to subscribe to each channel separately and does not offer any subscription packages. Setting a high price for CNN, $p_C = \$11$ results in 100 subscribers, hence a profit of $y_C = (11 - 1)100 = \$1000$. Setting a lower price, $p_C = \$9$ would bring 300 subscribers, hence a profit of $y_C = (9 - 1)300 = \$2400$. Setting an even lower price, $p_C = \$2$ would bring 400 subscribers, hence a profit of $y_C = (2 - 1)400 = \$400$. Therefore, $p_C = \$9$ is profit maximizing. Similarly, BBC subscriptions should also be sold for $p_B = \$9$. Altogether, total profit under no tying is $y^{NT} = 2400 + 2400 - \phi = \$4800 - \phi$.

Pure tying: Suppose now that the cable TV operator allows viewers to purchase one package containing both channels and offers no separate channels. Inspecting Table 4.7 reveals that setting a high package price, $p_{CB} = \$18$ would bring 200 subscribers, hence a profit of $y^{PT}(18) = (18 - 2)200 - \phi = \$3200 - \phi$. Setting a low price, $p_{CB} = \$13$ results in 400 subscribers, hence a profit of $y^{PT}(13) = (13 - 2)400 - \phi = \$4400 - \phi$. Therefore, $p_{CBH} = \$13$ is the profit-maximizing price.

Mixed tying: Suppose now that the cable TV operator allows viewers to either purchase one package containing the two channels or to subscribe to each channel separately. More precisely, viewers can now subscribe to a "news" package containing CNN and BBC for a price of $p_{CB} = \$18$, or to subscribe to CNN for $p_C = \$11$ and/or to BBC for $p_B = \$11$. Inspecting Table 4.7 reveals that all 200 type 2 consumers will subscribe to the "news" package whereas the 100 type 1 consumers will subscribe only to CNN and all 100 type 3 consumers will subscribe only to BBC. Hence, total profit under mixed tying is

$$y^{MT} = (18 - 2)200 + (11 - 1)100 + (11 - 1)100 - \phi = \$5200 - \phi$$
$$> y^{NT} = \$4800 - \phi > y^{PT} = \$4400 - \phi. \quad (4.31)$$

Hence, for the industry displayed in Table 4.7, mixed tying yields a higher profit than either pure tying or no tying.

4.2.4   Multi-package tying

Following Definition 4.3(d), the seller may offer for sale any combination of packages that may contain a subset of all goods. We will not develop a complete theory of multi-package tying and will not provide a computer algorithm for how to profitably construct such packages. Instead, we illustrate the rationale behind the potential gains from mixed tying, relative to pure tying and no tying, with the following example.

Consider a single cable TV operator capable of offering four channels: CNN, BBC, HIS(tory), and MOV(ies). Table 4.8 displays the maximum willingness to pay of each consumer type for each channel, the number of consumers, and the marginal cost the cable TV operator must pay to content providers for each subscribing viewer. Therefore, the cable TV operator licenses the four channels from the corresponding content providers for a per-viewer fee listed on the bottom row of Table 4.8.

No tying: We now determine the profit-maximizing price of CNN when sold separately. Because the per-viewer cost is $\mu_C = \$2$, the operator is restricted to setting either $p_C = \$4$ or $p_C = \$5$ (setting $p_C = \$1$ would generate a loss). Inspecting the

Consumer Type	CNN	BBC	HIS	MOV	#
Type 1	\$5	\$4	\$1	\$1	$N_1 = 100$
Type 2	\$4	\$5	\$1	\$1	$N_2 = 100$
Type 3	\$1	\$1	\$5	\$4	$N_3 = 100$
Type 4	\$1	\$1	\$4	\$5	$N_4 = 100$
Marginal Cost	$\mu_C = \$2$	$\mu_B = \$2$	$\mu_H = \$2$	$\mu_M = \$2$	

Table 4.8: Multi-package tying by a cable TV provider: Four consumer types and four TV channels.

CNN column of Table 4.8 implies that setting $p_C = \$4$ brings 200 subscribers, thus earning a profit of $y_A = (4-2)200 = \$400$. Setting $p_C = \$5$ would bring 100 subscribers to CNN and a profit of $y_A = (5-2)100 = \$300$. Hence, $p_C = \$4$ is profit maximizing. By the symmetry among channels displayed in Table 4.8, we conclude that all other channels should be priced at $p_B = p_H = p_M = \$4$. Altogether, total profit under no tying is $y^{NT} = 400 \cdot 4 - \phi = \$1600 - \phi$.

Pure tying: Suppose that all channels are sold in a single package. Summing up each row in Table 4.8 reveals that all four consumer types have the same maximum willingness to pay for the entire package. Therefore, only one price should be examined. Setting $p_{CBHM} = \$11$ attracts all consumers to subscribe. Hence, the profit generated under pure tying is $y^{PT} = (11 - 4 \cdot 2)400 - \phi = \$1200 - \phi$. Notice that $y^{PT} < y^{NT}$, hence pure tying is not profitable compared to selling each channel separately.

Multi-package tying: Consider the following marketing strategy: grouping all the "news" channels into one package labeled *CB*, the "entertainment" channels into a second package labeled *HM*, and setting the packages' prices at $p_{CB} = p_{HM} = \$9$. Table 4.8 implies that at these prices, all type 1 and 2 consumers will subscribe to package *CB* only and all types 3 and 4 consumers will subscribe to package *HM* only. In this case, total profit is given by $y^{MPT} = (9-2-2)(100+100) + (9-2-2)(100+100) - \phi = \$2000 - \phi$.

We have shown that multi-package tying can enhance profit levels beyond the profit that can be generated by pure tying or no tying. Formally, for the broadcasting industry described by Table 4.8, we managed to show that $y^{MPT} > y^{NT} > y^{PT}$. As demonstrated in Table 4.8, multi-package tying is profitable when consumer preferences can be grouped, in the sense that all consumers within a group share a high willingness to pay for some goods and also a low willingness to pay for all other goods. In addition, it is necessary to have some negatively correlated preferences among consumers within a group for the goods in which they share a high willingness to pay. In the present example, type 1 and 2 consumers have high preferences for CNN and BBC, but their preferences are negatively correlated between these two channels.

4.3 Exercises

1. Congratulations! You have been appointed the vice president for pricing and marketing at CHEWME, a leading manufacturer of sugarless chewing gum. As a new VP, you are contemplating whether sticks should be sold separately or in a single package containing several sticks bundled together. Your research department has just completed a market survey concluding that there is only one consumer ($N = 1$), whose demand data are summarized in Table 4.9. The marginal cost of producing each stick is $\mu = 10\text{¢}$, and the fixed cost is $\phi = 20\text{¢}$. Using the analysis in Section 4.1.1, answer the following questions. *Hint*: Compare with Table 4.1.

p	40¢	30¢	20¢	10¢	0¢
q	0	2	3	6	7
$p^b(q)$					
μq					
$p^b(q) - \mu q$					
$y^b(q)$					
pq					
$(p - \mu)q$					
y					

Table 4.9: Data for Exercise 1.

(a) Fill in the missing items in the middle section of Table 4.9. Conclude which bundle maximizes CHEWME's profit. *Hint*: For discrete demand data, $gcs(q)$ can be computed directly from the formula given by (2.37).

(b) Suppose now that your decision is not to bundle, hence to sell each stick separately. Fill in the missing items in the bottom section of Table 4.9. What is the profit-maximizing price per stick?

(c) How would your result change if the marketing department informed you that there were $N = 150$ consumers of the type described by the top section of Table 4.9? For this question assume that the fixed cost is given by $\phi = 5000\text{¢}$.

2. In the market where your firm is selling, the demand function by each individual is approximated by a linear function given by $p = 120 - 0.5q$. The marginal production cost is $\mu = \$40$. Solve the following problems.

   (a) Similar to Figure 4.2, draw the demand curve and compute which bundle maximizes your firm's profit, and what the price should be for this bundle.

   (b) Suppose now that there are $N = 5$ consumers with the same demand function. Compute the profit level, assuming that the fixed cost is $\phi = \$30,000$.

3. Suppose that your CHEWME firm (again, a leader in the production of chewing gum) sells to two types of consumers. The inverse demand function of a type 1 consumer is $p = 8 - 2q$ and of a type 2 consumer, $p = 4 - q$. Solve the following problems.

   (a) Write down the gross consumer surplus of each consumer type as a function of the bundle size q. *Hint*: The general formulation of $gcs_1(q)$ and $gcs_2(q)$ for linear demand functions is given by (4.3). A specific example is given in (4.10).

   (b) Fill in the missing parts in Table 4.10 assuming that there are $N_1 = 2$ type 1 consumers, there are $N_2 = 6$ type 2 consumers, the marginal production cost is $\mu = 2\cent$, and there are no fixed costs, $\phi = 0$. *Hint*: Compare with Table 4.3.

q (bundle size)	1	2	3	4
$gcs_1(q)$				
$y_1(q)$				
$gcs_2(q)$				
$y_2(q)$				
$\min\{gcs_1, gcs_2\}$				
$y_{1,2}(q)$				
$\max\{y_1, y_2, y_{1,2}\}$				

Table 4.10: Data for Exercise 3.

   (c) Conclude what the size of the bundle should be (number of units in the bundle) to maximize the seller's profit. Also find the profit-maximizing price of this bundle and the number of consumers who buy it.

4. The analysis of multi-package bundling in Section 4.1.4 demonstrates the possible gains from offering two bundles for sale (rather than only one) when there is more than one type of consumer. Suppose again that there is one consumer of each type characterized by the two demand functions (4.9). Find two bundles

$\langle q_A, p_A^b \rangle$ and $\langle q_B, p_B^b \rangle$ (or modify the ones given in Section 4.1.4) that also satisfy condition (4.13) but generate a higher profit than the profit level computed in (4.15). *Hint*: Notice that equation (4.14) implies that more surplus can be extracted from one type of consumer.

5. Congratulations! You have been appointed the general manager of the PARADISE Hotel, which is the only hotel on Paradise Island, located somewhere in the Pacific Ocean. This hotel also owns the only restaurant in town that serves breakfast. As the hotel manager, your first responsibility is to decide whether to include breakfast in the standard hotel rate or to charge extra for breakfast. Table 4.11 shows the willingness to pay of type 1 and type 2 hotel guests for hotel room (R) and for breakfast (B), as well as the expected number of guests of each type and the hotel's marginal cost of providing each service.

Guest Type	Hotel Room (R)	Breakfast (B)	Expected # guests
Type 1	$100	$5	200
Type 2	$60	$10	800
Marginal Cost	$\mu_R = \$40$	$\mu_B = \$2$	

Table 4.11: Data for Exercise 5.

Solve the following problems using the single-package pure-tying analysis of Section 4.2.1, assuming that there are no fixed costs, so $\phi = 0$.

(a) Compute the hotel's profit-maximizing room rate p_R, breakfast price p_B, and resulting profit y^{NT}, given that both services are sold separately (untied).

(b) Suppose now that the hotel rents a room together with breakfast. Compute the package's profit-maximizing price p_{RB} and the corresponding profit level y^{PT}. Conclude whether the hotel should tie the two services in a single package or sell them separately.

(c) Solve part (a) assuming that the expected number of type 2 guests falls from 800 to $N_2 = 200$ guests, whereas the expected number of type 1 guests remains $N_1 = 200$.

(d) Solve part (b) under the modification made in part (c).

6. Suppose now that the PARADISE Hotel, described in Exercise 5, has invested in building a state-of-the-art gym containing a swimming pool and a sauna. The problem facing the manager is whether to tie breakfast and a visit to the gym with the room rental (pure tying) or whether to sell the three services separately (no tying). The guests' willingness to pay for each service and the hotel's marginal cost of providing each service are given in Table 4.12. Solve the following problems assuming that there are no fixed costs, so $\phi = 0$.

Type	Room (R)	Breakfast (B)	Gym (G)	# Guests
Type 1	$100	$5	$10	200
Type 2	$60	$10	$10	800
Marginal Cost	$\mu_R = \$40$	$\mu_B = \$2$	$\mu_G = \$0$	

Table 4.12: Data for Exercise 6.

(a) Compute the hotel's profit-maximizing room rate p_R, breakfast price p_B, gym entrance fee p_G, and resulting profit y^{NT}, given that each service is sold separately (no tying).

(b) Suppose now that the hotel sells all three services in one package (pure tying). Compute the package's profit-maximizing price p_{RBG} and the corresponding profit level y^{PT}. Conclude whether the hotel should tie the three services in a single package or sell them separately.

7. Suppose now that the PARADISE Hotel offers room rentals and dinner only, and that the guests' willingness to pay is given by Table 4.13 below.

Guest Type	Hotel Room (R)	Dinner (D)	Expected # Guests
Type 1	$50	$0	100
Type 2	$40	$40	100
Type 3	$0	$50	100
Marginal Cost	$\mu_R = \$10$	$\mu_D = \$10$	

Table 4.13: Data for Exercise 7.

Solve the following problems using the analysis of mixed tying given in Section 4.2.3. Assume that there are no fixed costs, so $\phi = 0$.

(a) Compute the hotel's profit-maximizing room rate p_R, dinner price p_D, and resulting profit y^{NT}, given that both services are sold separately (no tying).

(b) Suppose now that the hotel rents a room together with dinner (pure tying). Compute the package's profit-maximizing price p_{RD} and the corresponding profit level y^{PT}. Conclude whether the hotel should tie the two services in a single package or sell them separately.

(c) Can a mixed tying marketing strategy enhance the hotel's profit beyond the profit levels achievable under no tying and pure tying? Prove your answer by writing down the precise packages to be offered and the corresponding prices.

8. Consider a cable TV operator facing viewers and unit costs described in Table 4.14.

Consumer Type	CNN	BBC	HIS	# Subscribers
Type 1	\$11	\$2	\$3	$N_1 = 100$
Type 2	\$11	\$2	\$6	$N_2 = 100$
Type 3	\$2	\$11	\$3	$N_3 = 100$
Type 4	\$2	\$11	\$6	$N_4 = 100$
Marginal Cost	$\mu_C = \$1$	$\mu_B = \$1$	$\mu_H = \$1$	

Table 4.14: Data for Exercise 8.

Solve the following problems using the analysis of multi-package tying given in Section 4.2.4. Assume there are no fixed costs, so $\phi = 0$.

(a) Compute the operator's profit-maximizing subscription rates p_C, p_B, and p_H and the resulting profit y^{NT}, given that each channel is sold separately (no tying).

(b) Compute the profit-maximizing subscription rate p_{CBH} and the corresponding profit level y^{PT}, assuming that the operator offers only subscriptions for a single package composed of all three channels (pure tying).

(c) Can you find alternative packages that would generate a higher profit than that achieved by pure tying and no tying?

Chapter 5

Multipart Tariff

5.1   Two-part Tariff with One Type of Consumer   152

5.1.1   Single consumer type with linear demand: An example

5.1.2   Single type with linear demand: General formulation

5.1.3   One consumer with discrete demand

5.1.4   Discrete demand with many consumers: Computer algorithm

5.2   Two-part Tariff with Multiple Consumer Types   159

5.2.1   Two consumer types: An example

5.2.2   Computer algorithm for multiple consumer types

5.3   Menu of Two-part Tariffs   165

5.3.1   Menu of two two-part tariffs

5.3.2   Menu of multiple two-part tariffs

5.4   Multipart Tariff   171

5.4.1   Example and general formulation

5.4.2   Multipart versus a menu of two parts: Equivalence results

5.5   Regulated Public Utility   176

5.6   Exercises   178

Multipart tariffs constitute another widely practiced technique of nonlinear pricing, under which the price of each unit may vary with the total number of units purchased. To some degree, multipart tariffs can be viewed as an enhancement of the bundling marketing strategy analyzed earlier in Section 4.1. By an enhancement we mean that instead of limiting the pricing strategy to a fixed price for a certain number of goods bundled together in a single package, multipart tariffs consist of a fixed fee and per-unit prices that may vary with the amount consumed.

Multipart tariffs in general, and two-part tariffs in particular, are widely used. Here is a list of examples with which the reader should be familiar:

- Phone companies generally charge a fixed monthly fee for maintaining a line connection and in addition charge for each minute of each phone call.

- Credit card companies charge merchants and often consumers fixed annual fees in additional to per-transaction fees.

- Membership discount retailers, such as shopping clubs, require paying an annual membership fee before consumers are allowed to enter the store (and then pay separately for each item they actually buy).

- Bars and nightclubs tend to collect a "cover" charge in addition to charging for each drink separately.

- Amusement parks tend to charge an entrance fee in addition to charging for each ride separately.

- Cellular phone operators in the United States offer consumers a menu of different tariffs. For example, consumers get to choose from paying $30 for the first 300 minutes plus 40¢ for each additional minute, paying $50 for 600 minutes and 20¢ for each additional minute, or paying $60 for the first 1000 minutes and 10¢ for each additional minute.

In the literature, Coase (1946) and Gabor (1955) provide early analyses of profit-maximizing two-part tariff structures. Oi (1971) is considered to be a pioneering paper on two-part tariffs. Littlechild (1975) and Mitchell (1978) extend the analysis to capture consumption externalities (such as in telecommunications). Schmalensee (1981) provides a comprehensive analysis of profit-maximizing two-part tariffs for multiple consumer types, whereas Feldstein (1972), Ng and Weisser (1974), and Willig (1978) focus mainly on tariffs that enhance social welfare. Social welfare maximization as the main objective of a regulator of a public utility is studied in Section 5.5, which also lists some textbooks on the regulation of public utilities.

5.1   Two-part Tariff with One Type of Consumer

A two-part tariff, as the term indicates, consists of two parts: a fixed (entry) fee and a per-unit (usage) price. The fixed fee, denoted by f, can be interpreted as the price for purchasing the "right to enter" and buy some units of the good or service for an additional per-unit price, denoted by p. To demonstrate it using the above examples, an entrance fee to an amusement park that must be paid to get into the park is the fixed part, and this fixed fee is required to be able to purchase and pay for each ride. Similarly, membership fees (either for retail stores or for credit cards) can be viewed as the fixed fees, which are required for obtaining the right to start purchasing and paying on a per-unit basis.

Figure 5.1 illustrates how the revenue (which equals consumer expenditure) extracted from a consumer varies with the consumption level q. Figure 5.1 shows that to buy the first unit, the consumer must spend an amount of f that would then

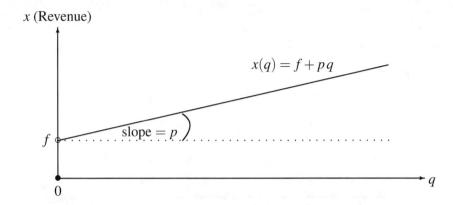

Figure 5.1: Consumer expenditure (firm's revenue) under a two-part tariff as a function of quantity purchased. *Notation*: f = fixed "entry" fee, p = per-unit (usage) price, and q = quantity purchased.

allow the consumer to purchase each unit at the price of p. Total outlay would then add up to $x(q) = f + pq$ for all $q > 0$. Clearly, the consumer has the option of not buying at all and avoiding paying the fixed fee, in which case consumer expenditure collapses to $x(0) = 0$.

5.1.1   Single consumer type with linear demand: An example

Consider a market for cellular phone calls with N consumers all having identical continuous linear demand functions given by

$$p = 40 - \frac{1}{10}q, \tag{5.1}$$

where q is the number of phone calls demanded and p is the price per call. Note that q could be measured in call units or in minutes per month; in this case, the corresponding price p should also be the price per minute. The demand function (5.1) is plotted in Figure 5.2. In Figure 5.2, each consumer buys 400 minutes of phone calls when the price is set at $p = 0\cancel{c}$, whereas no phone calls are demanded when the price is set at $p = 40\cancel{c}$ or above it.

Suppose that there is a single cell-phone operator facing N consumers and each is characterized by the inverse demand function (5.1). The operator bears a marginal cost of $\mu = 10\cancel{c}$ per minute and a fixed cost of ϕ. The per-minute cost may stem from having to pay other phone companies, such as fixed-line operators, who transmit part of each call on their lines (commonly referred to as a termination fee). The fixed cost consists of compensations to the suppliers of the infrastructure for their investment in antennas, transmitters, computers, and so forth. In what follows, we first analyze the implementation of a two-part tariff and compute the profit

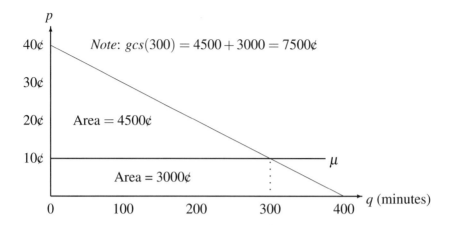

Figure 5.2: An example of a profit-maximizing two-part tariff for a single seller facing a single consumer type with a continuous linear demand function.

generated from using this pricing strategy. Then, we compare the profit generated from a two-part tariff to the profit generated from other pricing strategies that we analyzed in previous chapters, that is, pure bundling and simple monopoly pricing.

Two-part tariff: The operator should choose a fixed fee f, and a per-unit price p, that would extract maximum surplus from each consumer while leaving the consumer with a nonnegative net consumer surplus. For this, we need to recall equation (2.39), which derives the gross consumer surplus for the general linear demand function $p = \alpha - \beta q$. Thus,

$$gcs(q) = \frac{(\alpha + p)(q - 0)}{2} = \frac{(\alpha + \alpha - \beta q)(q - 0)}{2} = \frac{(2\alpha - \beta q)q}{2}. \qquad (5.2)$$

In the present example, (5.1) implies that $\alpha = 40$ and $\beta = -1/10$. A profit-maximizing two-part tariff can be designed using the following three steps:

Step I: Set the per-unit price to equal marginal cost, that is, $p^{2p} = \mu$.

Step II: From the demand function, compute the quantity demanded at this price $q^{2p}(p^{2p})$, assuming that there is no fixed fee, that is, $f = 0$.

Step III: Set the fixed fee as high as possible under the constraint that each consumer must gain a nonnegative net consumer surplus so that

$$ncs(q^{2p}) = gcs(q^{2p}) - q^{2p} \cdot p^{2p} - f \geq 0. \qquad (5.3)$$

That is, in *Step III* the firm raises its fixed fee component of the price to the maximum level beyond which any level would generate a negative net consumer surplus (see Definition 2.5).

Starting with *Step I*, we set the per-unit price at $p^{2p} = \mu = 10\cancel{c}$. Proceeding to *Stage II*, substituting into the inverse demand function (5.1), or simply by looking at Figure 5.2, yields a quantity demanded of $q^{2p}(10\cancel{c}) = 300$ phone calls. Finally, moving to *Step III*, substituting $q^{2p}(10\cancel{c}) = 300$ into (5.2), yields a gross consumer surplus of $gcs(300) = (2 \cdot 40 - 300/10)300/2 = 7500$. Therefore, what is left is to compute the highest fixed fee f that solves

$$ncs(300, 4500, 10) = 7500 - 300 \cdot 10 - f \geq 0, \quad \text{yielding} \quad f^{2p} = 4500\cancel{c}. \quad (5.4)$$

Finally, the profit of this cell-phone operator under the two-part tariff $f^{2p} = 4500\cancel{c}$ and $p^{2p} = 10\cancel{c}$ can be computed as

$$y^{2p} = N\left[f + (p^{2p} - \mu)q^{2p}\right] - \phi = 4,500N - \phi, \quad (5.5)$$

where N is the number of consumes having the demand function (5.1) and ϕ is the operator's fixed cost.

Bundling: Section 4.1.1 analyzes single-package bundling. We now compute the maximum profit that can be generated by using pure bundling rather than a two-part tariff. The seller's problem now is to bundle q^b phone calls in a single package and offer it to consumers on a take-it-or-leave-it basis. Section 4.1.1 has shown that for the continuous linear demand case, the bundle size is determined at the point where the inverse demand function intersects the marginal cost μ (see Figure 4.2). Therefore, in view of Figure 5.2, the profit-maximizing bundle size is $q^b = 300$ phone calls. Hence, the maximum price that can be charged for this bundle is $p^b = gcs(300) = (2 \cdot 40 - 300/10)300/2 = 7500\cancel{c}$. Thus, the profit from bundling is given by

$$y^b = N\left[7500 - 300\mu\right] - \phi = 4500N - \phi = y^{2p}, \quad (5.6)$$

which is the maximum profit that can be obtained under the two-part tariff. Therefore, for the case of identical consumers with a common demand function, a two-part tariff is not more profitable than single-package bundling. In fact, what we have demonstrated here is that the profit-maximizing bundling strategy can be duplicated (that is, yields the same profit level) by an appropriate two-part tariff scheme.

Simple monopoly pricing: We now demonstrate the profit gain via the use of a two-part tariff relative to the monopoly profit obtainable when the seller is restricted to levying only a per-unit price (also called linear pricing). Section 3.1.2, equations (3.2), (3.3), and (3.4) have shown that the monopoly profit-maximizing price is $p^m = (\alpha + \mu)/2 = (40 + 10)/2 = 25\cancel{c}$. Therefore, at this price consumers make $q^m = (\alpha - \mu)/(2\beta) = (40 - 10)/(2/10) = 150$ phone calls, and the seller earns

$$y^m = N\left[(p^m - \mu)q^m\right] - \phi = 2250N - \phi < y^{2p}. \quad (5.7)$$

In fact, if the seller's fixed cost is ignored by setting $\phi = 0$, the single seller earns twice the amount of profit when using a two-part tariff compared with using simple monopoly pricing. Formally, if $\phi = 0$, $y^m = y^{2p}/2$.

5.1.2 Single type with linear demand: General formulation

This short section generalizes the example analyzed in Section 5.1.1 to any inverse linear demand function given by $p = \alpha - \beta q$. As before, we must assume that $\alpha > \mu$, meaning that a consumer's willingness to pay for the first unit exceeds the marginal cost of producing this good/service. Assuming the opposite, $\alpha \leq \mu$ would imply that the provision of this service is never profitable.

To compute the profit-maximizing two-part tariff, we merely follow the three steps listed in Section 5.1.1.

Step I: Set the per-unit price to equal marginal cost, that is, $p^{2p} = \mu$.

Step II: From the demand function, compute the quantity demanded at this price $q^{2p}(p^{2p})$ assuming that there is no fixed fee, that is, $f = 0$, to obtain

$$q^{2p}(\mu) = \frac{\alpha - \mu}{\beta}. \tag{5.8}$$

Step III: Set the fixed fee as high as possible under the constraint that each consumer must gain a nonnegative net consumer surplus so that $ncs(q^{2p}) = gcs(q^{2p}) - q^{2p} \cdot p^{2p} - f \geq 0$. This obtains

$$f^{2p} = gcs(q^{2p}) - q^{2p} \cdot p^{2p} = \frac{(\alpha^2 - \mu^2)}{2\beta} - \frac{\alpha - \mu}{\beta}\mu = \frac{(\alpha - \mu)^2}{2\beta}. \tag{5.9}$$

Note that the above algorithm holds only for identical consumers. If there is more than one consumer type, the profit-maximizing two-part tariff may involve setting the usage price above marginal cost (see, for example, Table 5.4 in Section 5.3). Finally, the seller must verify that the resulting profit y^{2p} is nonnegative by computing

$$y^{2p} = N\left[f + (p^{2p} - \mu)q^{2p}\right] - \phi = \frac{(\alpha - \mu)^2 N}{2\beta} - \phi. \tag{5.10}$$

5.1.3 One consumer with discrete demand

Section 5.1.1 has demonstrated that the profit-maximizing bundling strategy can be duplicated by an appropriate two-part tariff scheme, if all consumers are of the same type (that is, have identical demand functions). For this reason, the discrete demand analysis of this section follows very closely the analysis of bundling conducted in Section 4.1.1 by using the exact same example.

Consider a single consumer type with only one consumer, so $N = 1$. The consumer is represented by the demand function illustrated by Figure 5.3. Table 5.1 displays the computation results of gross and net consumer surplus for the demand function illustrated in Figure 5.3, and the seller's profit assuming a marginal cost of $\mu = \$10$ and a fixed cost of $\phi = \$50$.

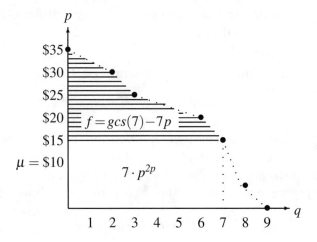

Figure 5.3: Fixed fee under a two-part tariff for a single consumer type. *Note*: Surplus is computed for the case in which $p^{2p} = \$15$.

p	$\$35$	$\$30$	$\$25$	$\$20$	$\$15$	$\$10$	$\$5$
q	0	2	3	6	7	7.5	8
$gcs(q)$	$\$0$	$\$65$	$\$92.5$	$\$160$	$\$177.5$	$\$183.75$	$\$187.5$
pq	$\$0$	$\$60$	$\$75.0$	$\$120$	$\$105.0$	$\$75.00$	$\$40.0$
$f = gcs - pq$	$\$0$	$\$5$	$\$17.5$	$\$40$	$\$72.5$	$\$108.75$	$\$147.5$
μq	$\$0$	$\$20$	$\$30.0$	$\$60$	$\$70.0$	$\$75.00$	$\$80.0$
y^{2p}	$-\$50$	$-\$5$	$-\$12.5$	$\$50$	$\$57.5$	$\$58.75$	$\$57.5$

Table 5.1: Two-part tariff: Single consumer type with discrete demand. *Note*: Computations rely on a marginal cost of $\mu = \$10$, a fixed cost of $\phi = \$50$, one consumer $N = 1$, where $gcs(q)$ is computed by (2.37).

Recall that *Step I* from the previous section indicates that the per-unit price should be set to equal marginal cost μ. However, assuming that the good in question is indivisible so the consumer must purchase whole units, Figure 5.3 shows that setting $p = \mu = \$10$ would induce the consumer to buy only six units and that the same quantity demanded is obtainable also by setting $p = \$15 > \mu$, which is a higher price.

Table 5.1 computes the gross consumer surplus $gcs(q)$ for each quantity demanded q. Readers who wish to learn about these computations are referred to Table 2.5, which uses the same demand data. Similar to *Step III* for the continuous demand case, the fixed fee f is computed by the constraint that consumers do not buy products and services unless they gain nonnegative net consumer surplus, that is, $ncs(q) = gcs(q) - pq - f \geq 0$, which is listed on the fifth row in Table 5.1. Table 5.1 clearly shows that the profit-maximizing two-part tariff involves setting the fixed fee to $f^{2p} = \$72.5$ and the per-unit price to $p^{2p} = \$15$.

5.1.4   Discrete demand with many consumers: Computer algorithm

The three-step procedure underlined in an earlier section of this chapter for a single consumer is also valid for the case in which there are $N \geq 2$ consumers of the same type. The only difference is that the profit function must be slightly modified to take into account that there are N buyers (instead of one buyer only). Therefore, if f^{2p} and p^{2p} constitute the profit-maximizing two-part tariff for a single representative consumer, the profit generated from selling to N consumers of this type is given by

$$y^{2p} = N\left[f + (p^{2p} - \mu)q^{2p}\right] - \phi, \tag{5.11}$$

where q^{2p} is an individual's quantity demanded at the price p^{2p}.

Algorithm 5.1 suggests a short computer program for selecting the most profitable two-part tariff using discrete demand data of N identical consumers. This program should input (say, using the **Read()** command) and store the discrete demand function based on $M \geq 2$ price–quantity observations of a representative consumer. More precisely, the program must input the price $p[\ell]$ and the quantity demanded $q[\ell]$ for each demand observation $\ell = 1, \ldots, M$, where $p[\ell]$ and $q[\ell]$ are M-dimensional arrays of real-valued demand observations. The program must also input the seller's cost parameters μ (marginal cost), ϕ (fixed cost), and N, which is the number of consumers with the above demand function.

After inputting the above data, the user must run Algorithm 2.3 to compute the gross consumer surplus for the inputted discrete demand function, and write the results onto the real-valued M-dimensional array $gcs[\ell]$, $\ell = 1, \ldots, M$, which should also be stored on the system. Note that Algorithm 2.3 requires that the inputted price observations be nonincreasing in the sense that $p[1] \geq p[2] \geq \cdots \geq p[M]$, as displayed in Figure 5.3, for example.

Algorithm 5.1 is rather straightforward. It runs a loop over all demand observations $\ell = 1, 2, \cdots, M$, and computes the maximum obtainable profit level when selling $q[\ell]$ units, which is the difference between the gross consumer surplus, $gcs[\ell]$ and the variable cost, $\mu q[\ell]$. Each loop also checks whether this profit level exceeds the already-stored value of the maximized profit $\text{max}y^{2p}$. If the computed level exceeds $\text{max}y^{2p}$, the newly computed level replaces the previously stored value of $\text{max}y^{2p}$. Note that this procedure is identical to the one used in Algorithm 4.1, because we have already established that when all consumers have the same demand function, the maximum obtainable profit under pure bundling is equal to the maximum profit obtainable under a two-part tariff. When a more profitable sales level $q[\ell]$ is found, the program assigns the price $p[\ell]$ to $\text{max}py^{2p}$ and the part of consumer surplus not extracted by the usage fee $gcs[\ell] - p[\ell]q[\ell]$ to the fixed entry fee $\text{max}fy^{2p}$.

maxy$^{2p} \leftarrow 0$; /* Initializing output variable   */
for $\ell = 1$ **to** M **do**
> /* Main loop over demand observations   */
> **if** $N(gcs[\ell] - \mu q[\ell]) - \phi \geq$ maxy^{2p} **then**
> > /* If higher profit found, store new values   */
> > maxy$^{2p} \leftarrow N(gcs[\ell] - \mu q[\ell]) - \phi$; maxqy$^{2p} \leftarrow q[\ell]$; maxpy$^{2p} \leftarrow p[\ell]$;
> > maxfy$^{2p} \leftarrow gcs[q] - p[\ell] \cdot q[\ell]$;

if maxy$^{2p} \geq 0$ **then**
> **writeln** ("The profit-maximizing two-part tariff is the fixed fee $f^{2p} =$",
> maxfy^{2p}, "usage price $p^{2p} =$", maxpy^{2p}, "The resulting quantity sold is
> $q =$", maxqy^{2p}, "units, and the total profit is $y^{2p} =$ ", maxy^{2p});
> /* Optional: Run Algorithm 3.1 and compare profits   */
> **write** ("The profit gain from using a two-part tariff instead of a per-unit
> price only is:", maxy$^{2p} -$ maxy)
else write ("Negative profit. Do NOT operate in this market!")

Algorithm 5.1: Computing the profit-maximizing two-part tariff for a single consumer type with discrete demand.

Using the same data, Algorithm 5.1 can also be used simultaneously with Algorithm 4.1, which computes the profit-maximizing bundle, and also Algorithm 3.1, which computes the simple monopoly profit-maximizing price per unit. Thus, all three algorithms can be easily integrated to perform a comparison between the maximum obtainable profit under a two-part tariff, maxy^{2p}, and the simple monopoly profit when the firm is restricted to charging only a price per unit, maxy.

5.2   Two-part Tariff with Multiple Consumer Types

Our analysis so far has focused on one consumer type in the sense that all consumers have had identical demand functions. This section analyzes the problem of setting a *single* two-part tariff when there are two types of consumers, each of which has a different demand function.

5.2.1   Two consumer types: An example

The example developed below starts out with only two consumers and then generalizes to capture multiple consumers of each type.

One consumer of each type

Suppose first that there is only one consumer of each type, so $N_1 = N_2 = 1$. The inverse demand function of each type is assumed to be given by

$$p_1 = \alpha_1 - \beta_1 q_1 = 8 - 2q_1 \quad \text{and} \quad p_2 = \alpha_2 - \beta_2 q_2 = 4 - \frac{1}{2}q_2 \qquad (5.12)$$

and are also illustrated in Figure 5.4. The direct demand functions corresponding to the inverse demand functions (5.12) are given by

$$q_1 = \frac{\alpha_1 - p_1}{\beta_1} = \frac{8 - p_1}{2} \quad \text{and} \quad q_2 = \frac{\alpha_2 - p_2}{\beta_2} = 2(4 - p_2). \qquad (5.13)$$

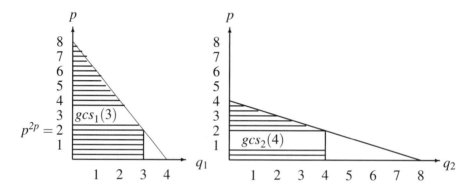

Figure 5.4: Single two-part tariff with two consumer types. Shaded areas capture gross consumer surplus: $gcs_1(3) = \$15$ and $gcs_2(4) = \$12$ when the usage price is set to $p^{2p} = \$2$.

Substituting the demand parameters from (5.12) into (5.2) yields the gross consumer surplus of each consumer type as a function of consumption q. Hence,

$$gcs_1(q) = q(8 - q) \quad \text{and} \quad gcs_2(q) = \frac{q(16 - q)}{4}. \qquad (5.14)$$

Table 5.2 displays the gross consumer surpluses $gcs(q_1)$ and $gcs(q_2)$ for consumer types 1 and 2. The gross consumer surpluses $gcs(q_1)$ and $gcs(q_2)$ are preceded by the computations of the consumption levels q_1 and q_2 associated with prices in the range $p = \$1, \ldots, \$7$, using the direct demand functions (5.13). Then, the fixed fees of the two-part tariffs are computed by subtracting consumer expenditure from their gross consumer surpluses, so $f_1 = gcs(q_1) - pq_1$ and $f_2 = gcs(q_2) - pq_2$. Thus, fixed fees are set to their highest levels that would leave each consumer indifferent between buying and not buying. Clearly, the seller is restricted to setting only one

p	$1	$2	$3	$4	$5	$6	$7
q_1	3.50	3	2.50	2	1.50	1	0.50
$gcs_1(q)$	$15.75	$15	$13.75	$12	$9.75	$7	$3.75
f_1	$12.25	$9	$6.25	$4	$2.25	$1	$0.25
$y_1(f_1,p)$	$8.75	$9	$8.75	$8	$6.75	$5	$2.75
q_2	6.00	4	2.00	0	0.00	0	0.00
$gcs_2(q)$	$15.00	$12	$7.00	$0	$0.00	$0	$0.00
f_2	$9.00	$4	$1.00	$0	$0.00	$0	$0.00
$y_2(f_2,p)$	$3.00	$4	$3.00	$0	$0.00	$0	$0.00
$\min\{f_1,f_2\}$	$9.00	$4	$1.00	$0	$0.00	$0	$0.00
$y_{1,2}(q)$	$8.50	$8	$6.50	$4	$4.50	$4	$2.50
$\max\{y_1,y_2,y_{1,2}\}$	$8.75	$9	$8.75	$8	$6.75	$5	$2.75

Table 5.2: Computations of the profit-maximizing two-part tariff with two consumer types. *Note*: Computations rely on a marginal cost of $\mu = \$2$, a fixed cost of $\phi = \$0$ (zero), and one consumer of each type, $N_1 = N_2 = 1$.

of these fixed fees, either f_1 or f_2 but not both. Lastly, the profit levels $y_1(f_1,p)$ and $y_2(f_2,p)$ corresponding to the above computed fixed fees are computed from

$$y_1(f_1,p) = N_1[f_1 + (p-\mu)q_1] - \phi = N_1[gcs(q_1) - \mu q_1], \quad (5.15)$$
$$y_2(f_2,p) = N_2[f_2 + (p-\mu)q_2] - \phi = N_2[gcs(q_2) - \mu q_2].$$

Clearly, the profit levels (5.15) are not obtainable simultaneously because the seller is restricted to choosing either f_1 or f_2, but not both.

Table 5.2 was constructed for the purpose of computing the profit-maximizing two-part tariff assuming that the seller is restricted to setting *only one* tariff for all consumers. The restriction to a single tariff for all consumers may imply that there could be situations in which the seller sets fees sufficiently high so that one type of consumer would choose not to buy this service. For this firm to sell to both types of consumers, it must ensure that its two-part tariff leaves each consumer type with a nonnegative net consumer surplus. For this reason, Table 5.2 computes $\min\{f_1,f_2\}$, which is the maximum fixed fee that can be charged if the firm sells to all types of consumers. In this case, the firm earns a profit of $y_{1,2} = 2\min\{f_1,f_2\} + 2(p-\mu)q - \phi$, where we multiply by $2 = N_1 + N_2$ because both consumers are served.

The last row in Table 5.2 determines the maximum profit associated with each usage price p. For example, if the firm sets $p = \$2$, profit is maximized at $y_1 = \$9$, where the fixed fee is set to $f = f_1 = \$9$, in which case $ncs_1(3) = 15 - 9 - 2 \cdot 3 = 0$, whereas $ncs_2(4) = 12 - 9 - 2 \cdot 4 < 0$. Hence, type 2 consumers do not buy at this tariff. Comparing all the profit levels on the bottom row of Table 5.2 reveals that the profit-maximizing two-part tariff is $f^{2p} = \$9$ and $p^{2p} = \$2$. As discussed above, only type 1 consumers buy (see also Figure 5.4), and the firm earns a profit of $y(9, 2) = \$9$.

Multiple consumers of each type

The calculation results exhibited in Table 5.2 are based on two consumer types, defined by the demand functions (5.12) and $N_1 = N_2 = 1$ (one consumer per type). We now extend this example to multiple consumers of each type. Formally, suppose that there are $N_1 = 2$ type 1 consumers and $N_2 = 5$ type 2 consumers. Table 5.3 modifies Table 5.2 by recalculating the profit levels for each quantity demanded associated with the price p appearing on the top of this table. The recalculated profit levels in Table 5.3 are based on $y_1(q) = 2[f_1 + (p - \mu)q] - \phi$, $y_2(q) = 5[f_2 + (p - \mu)q] - \phi$, and $y_{1,2}(q) \overset{\text{def}}{=} (2 + 5)[f_{1,2} + (p - \mu)(q_1 + q_2)] - \phi$, where $f_{1,2} = \min\{f_1, f_2\}$.

p	$1	$2	$3	$4	$5	$6	$7
q_1	3.50	3	2.50	2	1.50	1	0.50
$gcs_1(q)$	$15.75	$15	$13.75	$12	$9.75	$7	$3.75
f_1	$12.25	$9	$6.25	$4	$2.25	$1	$0.25
$y_1(f_1, p)$	$17.50	$18	$17.50	$16	$13.50	$10	$5.50
q_2	6.00	4	2.00	0	0.00	0	0.00
$gcs_2(q)$	$15.00	$12	$7.00	$0	$0.00	$0	$0.00
f_2	$9.00	$4	$1.00	$0	$0.00	$0	$0.00
$y_2(f_2, p)$	$15.00	$20	$15.00	$0	$0.00	$0	$0
$\min\{f_1, f_2\}$	$9.00	$4	$1.00	$0	$0.00	$0	$0.00
$y_{1,2}(q)$	$26.00	$28	$22.00	$8	$9.00	$8	$5.00
$\max\{y_1, y_2, y_{1,2}\}$	$26.00	$28	$22.00	$16	$13.50	$10	$5.50

Table 5.3: Extending Table 5.2 to multiple consumers, $N_1 = 2$ and $N_2 = 5$.

The computations exhibited in Table 5.3 reveal that the profit-maximizing usage price is $p^{2p} = \$2$, where each type 1 consumer buys $q_1 = 3$ units and each type 2 consumer buys $q_2 = 4$ units. However, unlike the case in which $N_1 = N_2 = 1$, here the seller lowers the fixed fee to $f^{2p} = \$4 = \min\{\$9, \$4\}$ so that all the $2 + 5$ consumers are served (both have a nonnegative gross consumer surplus). This should come as no surprise because our assumption that there are "many" type 2 consumers, $N_2 = 5$, implies that excluding them is not profitable for this seller.

5.2.2 Computer algorithm for multiple consumer types

This section describes an algorithm for computing the profit-maximizing two-part tariff for the case in which there are M types of consumers, each with $N[\ell]$ consumers, $\ell = 1, \ldots, M$.

Procedure *ComputeFixedFee*(p);
for $\ell = 1$ **to** M **do**
  /* Type ℓ's quantity demanded and gcs at price p */
  $q[\ell] \leftarrow (\alpha[\ell] - p)/\beta[\ell]$; $q^{\text{temp}} \leftarrow q[\ell]$; $gcs[\ell] \leftarrow (2\alpha[\ell] - \beta[\ell]q[\ell])/2$;
  $y^{\text{temp}} \leftarrow N[\ell](gcs[\ell] - \mu q[\ell]) - \phi$; /* Profit from type ℓ */
  $f^{\text{temp}} \leftarrow gcs[\ell] - p \cdot q[\ell]$ /* Set fixed fee to extract all
      surplus from type ℓ consumers   */
  for $\ell\ell = 1$ **to** M **do**
    /* Find all types $\ell\ell \neq \ell$ with $gcs[\ell\ell] \geq gcs[\ell]$ */
    /* First, compute $q[\ell\ell]$ and $gcs[\ell\ell]$ */
    $q[\ell\ell] \leftarrow (\alpha[\ell\ell] - p)/\beta[\ell\ell]$; $gcs[\ell\ell] \leftarrow (2\alpha[\ell\ell] - \beta[\ell\ell]q[\ell\ell])/2$;
    if $(\ell\ell \neq \ell)$ and $(gcs[\ell\ell] - f^{\text{temp}} - p \cdot q[\ell\ell] \geq 0))$ **then**
      /* Type $\ell\ell$ also buys, add to profit y, and q */
      $y^{\text{temp}} \leftarrow y^{\text{temp}} + N[\ell\ell](gcs[\ell] - \mu q[\ell\ell])$; $q^{\text{temp}} \leftarrow q^{\text{temp}} + q[\ell\ell]$;

  if $y < y^{\text{temp}}$ **then**
    $y \leftarrow y^{\text{temp}}$; $qq \leftarrow q^{\text{temp}}$; $f \leftarrow f^{\text{temp}}$;
    /* More profitable fixed fee found   */

Algorithm 5.2: Computing the profit-maximizing fixed fee f corresponding to a given price p.

Algorithm 5.3 assumes that each consumer is characterized by a downward-sloping linear demand function $p = \alpha[\ell] - \beta[\ell]q$. The computer program described below should input and store (say, using the **Read**() command), the demand parameters onto two M-dimensional real-valued arrays, $\alpha[\ell]$ and $\beta[\ell]$, for each type of demand function $\ell = 1, \ldots, M$, as well as the number of consumers of each type, to be stored on the integer-valued M-dimensional array $N[\ell]$. The program should also input the seller's cost parameters μ (marginal cost) and ϕ (fixed cost). Next, the program should input the grid parameter $G \in \mathbb{N}^{++}$, which determines the price increments (precision) to be used in the main loop over prices. For each price p, Algorithm 5.3 calls a procedure, given by Algorithm 5.2, which computes the profit-maximizing fixed fee $f^{2p}(p)$ for a given price p.

Algorithm 5.3 describes the main computer program that computes the highest possible fixed fee f, by running a loop over all possible usage prices and computing the usage price that maximizes profit. The first loop over consumer types ℓ

```
y^{2p} ← 0; q^{2p} ← 0; /* Initializing output variables        */
p^{max} ← 0/* Computing highest possible price                 */
for ℓ = 1 to M do
   │  /* Loop over all consumer types                          */
   │  if p^{max} < α[ℓ] then p^{max} ← α[ℓ]; /* Demand intercept  */
p ← p^{max}; Δp ← p^{max}/G; /* Price increments (precision)    */
while p ≥ 0 do
   │  f ← 0; y ← 0; qq ← 0; /* Main loop over prices            */
   │  Call Procedure ComputeFixedFee(p); /* Algorithm 5.2       */
   │  if y^{2p} < y then y^{2p} ← y; p^{2p} ← p; q^{2p} ← qq; f^{2p} ← f;
   │  /* Fixed fee f yields higher profit                       */
   │  p ← p − Δp; /* Reduce price before repeating this loop    */
if y^{2p} ≥ φ then
   │  writeln ("The profit-maximizing two-part tariff is composed of a fixed
   │  fee f^{2p} =", f^{2p}, "and a usage price p^{2p} =", p^{2p});
   │  write ("The firm sells q^{2p} =", q^{2p}, "units, and the resulting total profit is
   │  y^{2p} =", y^{2p});
else write ("Negative profit. Do NOT operate in this market!")
```

Algorithm 5.3: Computing the profit-maximizing two-part tariff for multiple consumer types with linear demand.

determines the maximum possible price p^{max} beyond which no consumer will be demanding the service. Clearly, $p^{max} = \max_\ell \alpha[\ell]$, which is the highest demand intercept with the price axis. For a given price p, the procedure given by Algorithm 5.2 runs a loop over all the $\ell = 1, \ldots, M$ consumer types to compute the maximum surplus that can be extracted by adjusting the fixed fee f. For each type ℓ, the program sets the fixed fee to extract all the surplus, so $f = gcs_\ell - p \cdot q_\ell$. Then, the internal loop checks which other types of consumers also buy the service under f by checking whether $ncs_{\ell\ell} = gcs_{\ell\ell} - p \cdot q_{\ell\ell} \geq 0$. If this is the case, the profit from the $N[\ell\ell]$ consumers is added to the total profit. Otherwise, the $N[\ell\ell]$ consumers are excluded from the market at this particular fixed fee f and the given price p.

The main loop runs over prices starting from p^{max} and ending with $p = 0$. For each price p, the program calls the procedure *ComputeFixedFee(p)* given by Algorithm 5.2, which computes the profit-maximizing fixed fee f, corresponding profit y, and sales level qq. Algorithm 5.3 updates the profit y^{2p}, the quantity sold, q^{2p}, and the fixed fee f^{2p} in the event that Algorithm 5.2 finds that the price p generates a higher profit.

5.3 Menu of Two-part Tariffs

The analysis in Sections 5.1 and 5.2 is restricted to a single two-part tariff that is offered to all consumers on a take-it-or-leave-it basis. Clearly, when there is only one type of consumer (consumers having the same demand functions), we have shown that a single two-part tariff is sufficient for extracting the entire consumer surplus. However, when there are several types of consumers, such as those already analyzed in Section 5.2.1, a single two-part tariff (a single pair of f and p) offered to all consumer types generally cannot extract all consumer surpluses. This suggests that profit can be enhanced if the seller can carefully design and offer consumers a menu containing several two-part tariffs to choose from.

The major difficulty faced by pricing experts in implementing a menu of two-part tariffs is the design of multiple two-part tariffs that would be *incentive compatible*. Incentive compatibility means that the tariffs should be designed so that different consumer types choose different tariffs from the menu offered by the seller. If a firm fails to design an incentive compatible menu of tariffs, most or all consumer types will choose the same tariff, in which case, the firm may make a higher profit by offering only a single two-part tariff. We will give a more formal presentation of incentive compatibility later in this section when we analyze a specific example of how to construct a menu of two incentive compatible two-part tariffs.

5.3.1 Menu of two two-part tariffs

The above discussion hints that sellers can increase the amount of surplus extracted from consumers by offering a menu of two-part tariffs when consumers have different demand functions. For example, the seller can offer all consumers a choice from a menu of two two-part tariffs labeled as $\langle f_A, p_A \rangle$ and $\langle f_B, p_B \rangle$. Clearly, the introduction of this menu makes sense only if either $f_A < f_B$ and $p_A > p_B$, or $f_A > f_B$ and $p_A < p_B$. Otherwise, if $f_A \leq f_B$ and $p_A \leq p_B$, all consumers would choose plan A over plan B simply because plan A is cheaper at all levels of consumption.

Figure 5.5 illustrates how consumer expenditure varies with the quantity purchased q under the two-part tariff plans A and B. Figure 5.5 clearly shows that consumers who end up purchasing less than $\hat{q}$ units would spend less by choosing tariff A whereas consumers who end up purchasing an amount larger than $q > \hat{q}$ would spend less under tariff B. In fact, the threshold quantity level $\hat{q}$ can be computed directly by equating $f_A + p_A\hat{q} = f_B + p_B\hat{q}$, yielding

$$\hat{q} = \frac{f_B - f_A}{p_A - p_B}. \tag{5.16}$$

For the expression given by (5.16) to be meaningful, we assume that $f_A < f_B$ and $p_A > p_B$, which was also assumed for the construction of Figure 5.5.

Our analysis does not provide any general algorithm for how to select the profit-maximizing number of two-part tariffs to be included in the menu that is offered to

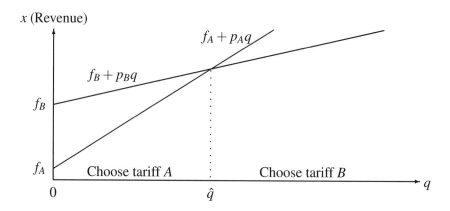

Figure 5.5: Purchased quantity and consumer choice between two two-part tariffs.

consumers. Instead, we simply demonstrate the potential profit gain from offering a menu of two-part tariffs by focusing on a numerical example.

Suppose first that there is only one consumer of each type, so $N_1 = N_2 = 1$. The inverse demand function of each type is assumed to be given by

$$p_1 = \alpha_1 - \beta_1 q_1 = 9 - 4q_1 \quad \text{and} \quad p_2 = \alpha_2 - \beta_2 q_2 = 5 - \frac{1}{2}q_2, \tag{5.17}$$

and is also illustrated in Figure 5.6.

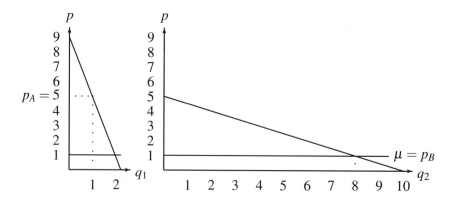

Figure 5.6: Menu of two-part tariffs with two consumer types. Gross consumer surpluses are $gcs_1(1) = \$3.5$ and $gcs_2(8) = \$16$.

Inspection of Figure 5.6 reveals that the two consumer types are very different in the sense that type 1 gains "most" of the consumer surplus from the consumption of the first few units. In contract, type 2 consumer gains "more" surplus from the consumption of a larger amount. This observation should hint at the possibility that the seller may be able to extract a higher surplus by offering consumers a choice from a menu of two different two-part tariffs, rather than a single two-part tariff. More specifically, the seller should design one tariff with a relatively high per-unit usage price targeted for type 1 consumers, and a second tariff with a lower per-unit price targeted for type 2 consumers. We label the tariffs included in this menu as tariff A and tariff B.

The mere introduction of two different tariffs does not guarantee that each tariff will be chosen by some consumers. Therefore, the following two conditions must be satisfied to have some consumers choosing tariff A and some choosing tariff B:

Incentive compatibility: A type 1 consumer prefers tariff A over tariff B, whereas a type 2 consumer prefers tariff B over tariff A. Formally, the following two conditions must be simultaneously satisfied:

$$ncs_1(q_A; f_A, p_A) = gcs_1(q_A) - f_A - p_A q_A \tag{5.18a}$$
$$\geq gcs_1(q_B) - f_B - p_B q_B = ncs_1(q_B; f_B, p_B),$$
$$ncs_2(q_B; f_B, p_B) = gcs_2(q_B) - f_B - p_B q_B \tag{5.18b}$$
$$\geq gcs_2(q_A) - f_A - p_A q_A = ncs_2(q_A; f_A, p_A).$$

Participation: Both consumer types prefer buying over not buying. Formally,
$$gcs_1(q_A) - f_A - p_A q_A \geq 0 \text{ and } gcs_2(q_B) - f_B - p_B q_B \geq 0.$$

The first condition implies that a "proper" selection of which tariffs to offer should induce all consumers to reveal their type by choosing a specific tariff. More precisely, before consumers purchase, the seller has no way of knowing and has no legal right to ask consumers directly whether they are of type 1 or type 2. However, a clever design of the two tariffs would cause consumers to reveal implicitly their type by the actual choice they make. In the economics literature, tariff designs that result in having different consumer types choosing different tariffs are referred to as preference-revealing mechanisms. In other words, by selecting the "right" tariffs, the seller can segment the market between the two consumer types, by making type 1 consumers choose tariff A and type 2 consumers choose tariff B.

Table 5.4 replicates the exact computations performed in Table 5.2 but for the demand functions given by (5.17). Table 5.4 displays the gross consumer surplus $gcs(q_1)$ and $gcs(q_2)$ for consumer types 1 and 2 assuming that the seller's marginal cost is $\mu = \$1$ and there is no fixed cost, $\phi = \$0$.

Suppose that the seller is restricted to setting only a single two-part tariff. Table 5.4 clearly shows that the profit-maximizing tariff is

$$\langle f^{2p}, p^{2p} \rangle = \langle \$6.125, \$2 \rangle. \tag{5.19}$$

A type 1 consumer buys at this tariff because $ncs_1(1.75) = \$9.625 - \$6.125 - \$2 \cdot 1.75 \geq 0$. Similarly, the net surplus of a type 2 consumer is $ncs_2(6) = \$21 - \$6.125 - \$2 \cdot 6 \geq 0$. The resulting profit is

$$y(\$6.125, \$2) = 2 \cdot \$6.125 + (\$2 - \$1)(1.75 + 6) = \$20. \tag{5.20}$$

p	$1	$2	$3	$4	$5	$6	$7
q_1	2	1.750	1.50	1.25	1.0	0.75	0.50
$gcs_1(q)$	$10	$9.625	$9.00	$8.13	$7.0	$5.63	$4.00
f_1	$8	$6.125	$4.50	$3.13	$2.0	$1.13	$0.50
$y_1(f_1,p)$	$8	$7.875	$7.50	$6.88	$6.0	$4.88	$3.50
q_2	8	6.000	4.00	2.00	0.0	0.00	0.00
$gcs_2(q)$	$24	$21.000	$16.00	$9.00	$0.0	$0.00	$0.00
f_2	$16	$9.000	$4.00	$1.00	$0.0	$0.00	$0.00
$y_2(f_2,p)$	$16	$15.000	$12.00	$7.00	$0.0	$0.00	$0.00
$\min\{f_1,f_2\}$	$8	$6.125	$4.00	$1.00	$0.0	$0.00	$0.00
$y_{1,2}(q)$	$16	$20.000	$19.00	$11.75	$4.0	$3.75	$3.00
$\max\{y_1,y_2,y_{1,2}\}$	$16	$20.000	$19.00	$11.75	$6.0	$4.88	$3.50

Table 5.4: Computations of the profit-maximizing menu of two-part tariffs with two consumer types defined by (5.17). *Note*: Computations rely on a marginal cost of $\mu = \$1$, a fixed cost of $\phi = \$0$ (zero), and one consumer of each type, $N_1 = N_2 = 1$.

Note that this particular result is interesting because it demonstrates that sellers may profitably set the usage price to exceed marginal cost when there is more than one type of consumer. This happens because under marginal cost pricing, the seller cannot capture all the surplus from all consumers via the fixed fee.

    We now proceed to our main investigation, which is the offering of a menu of two-part tariffs. Therefore, instead of setting the two-part tariff (5.19), consider now the following menu of two-part tariffs:

Plan A: Two-part tariff $\langle f_A, p_A \rangle = \langle \$1, \$5 \rangle$.

Plan B: Two-part tariff $\langle f_B, p_B \rangle = \langle \$16, \$1 \rangle$.

Before we compute the profit resulting from the offering of this menu of two tariffs, we must verify that these two tariffs indeed segment the market between the two consumer types according to (5.18a) and (5.18b). If even one of these conditions does not hold, the market cannot be segmented, in which case there is no need for the seller to offer two different tariff plans. The computation results listed in Table 5.4 reveal that under plan A, a type 1 consumer buys $q_1 = 1$ unit and gains a gross surplus of $gcs_1(1) = \$7$. A type 2 consumer buys $q_2 = 0$ and hence gains a gross surplus of $gcs_2(0) = \$0$. Table 5.4 also reveals that under plan B, a type 1 consumer buys nothing because $gcs_1(2) = \$10 < \$16 = f_B$. A type 2 consumer buys $q_2 = 8$ and gains a gross surplus of $gcs_2(4) = \$16$. Hence,

$$ncs_1(1;\$1,\$5) = \$7 - \$1 - \$5 \cdot 1 \geq \$10 - \$16 - \$1 \cdot 2 = ncs_1(2;\$16,\$1)$$

and

$$ncs_2(8;\$1,\$16) = \$24 - \$16 - \$1 \cdot 8 \geq \$0 - \$1 - \$5 \cdot 0 = ncs_2(0;\$1,\$5),$$

which confirms the incentive compatibility conditions given by (5.18a) and (5.18b). Because $ncs_1(1;\$1,\$5) \geq 0$ and $ncs_2(8;\$16,\$1) \geq 0$, we can conclude that a type 1 consumer chooses tariff plan A, whereas a type 2 consumer chooses tariff plan B.

We now compute the profit generated from offering plans A and B simultaneously. The profits from a type 1 and a type 2 consumer (not including fixed costs) are $y_1 = \$1 + (\$5 - \$1)1 = \$5$ and $y_2 = \$16 + (\$1 - \$1)8 = \$16$. With $N_1 = N_2 = 1$ consumer of each type, total profit is given by

$$
\begin{aligned}
y(\langle\$1,\$5\rangle,\langle\$16,\$1\rangle) &= y_1 + y_2 - \phi & (5.21) \\
&= \$21 - \phi > y(\langle 6.125,\$2\rangle) = \$20 - \phi,
\end{aligned}
$$

which is the maximum profit that can be generated by offering a single uniform two-part tariff.

Finally, observe that for the system of demand functions plotted in Figure 5.6, to be able to implement a two-part tariff system successfully, the different types must have very different demand functions. For example, implementing a menu of two different tariffs for the consumers depicted in Figure 5.4 yields a lower profit than does setting a single two-part tariff, simply because the two types demand functions are not sufficiently diverse.

5.3.2 Menu of multiple two-part tariffs

Our analysis so far has been confined to a menu of two two-part tariffs. However, menus of three or four two-part tariffs are also commonly observed. For example, cell-phone operators tend to offer these menus to segment the market among a wide variety of consumer types according to willingness to pay, income, and location.

A menu of $B \geq 2$ two-part tariffs is defined as a collection of B pairs, $\langle f_1, p_1\rangle$, $\langle f_2, p_2\rangle$, until $\langle f_B, p_B\rangle$, satisfying

$$f_1 < f_2 < \cdots < f_B \quad \text{and} \quad p_1 > p_2 > \cdots > p_B \geq \mu, \qquad (5.22)$$

where μ is the marginal production cost. Figure 5.7 extends Figure 5.5 from a menu of two tariffs to a menu of three tariffs and illustrates how consumer expenditure varies with the quantity purchased q across the three different two-part tariff plans. All the plans drawn in Figure 5.7 satisfy the monotonicity assumptions given by (5.22). That is, $f_1 < f_2 < f_3$ and $p_1 > p_2 > p_3$. However, despite this, the menu given on the right is not very useful because no consumer will choose tariff plan 2 at any consumption level.

To prevent a situation like the one illustrated on the right side of Figure 5.7, the three plans should satisfy the condition given by

$$\frac{f_2 - f_1}{p_1 - p_2} < \frac{f_3 - f_2}{p_2 - p_3}. \qquad (5.23)$$

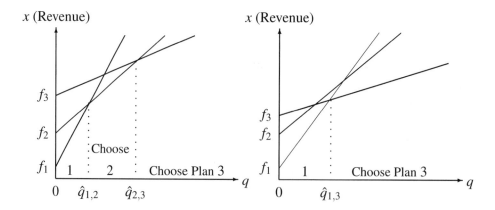

Figure 5.7: *Left*: Implementable menu of three two-part tariffs. *Right*: Poorly adminis-
tered menu of three two-part tariffs.

To prove condition (5.23), observe that the cutoff quantities $\hat{q}_{1,2}$ and $\hat{q}_{2,3}$ plotted in
Figure 5.7 are determined by solving $f_1 + p_1\hat{q}_{1,2} = f_2 + p_2\hat{q}_{1,2}$ and $f_2 + p_2\hat{q}_{2,3} =
f_3 + p_3\hat{q}_{2,3}$, respectively. Hence,

$$\hat{q}_{1,2} = \frac{f_2 - f_1}{p_1 - p_2} < \frac{f_3 - f_2}{p_2 - p_3} = \hat{q}_{2,3}, \tag{5.24}$$

as long as condition (5.23) holds.

We summarize our discussion of menus of multiple two-part tariffs by listing
some guidelines that are necessary (but not sufficient) for making a menu containing B two-part tariffs (5.22) implementable, useful, and profitable.

Menu size: The number of tariffs in the menu should not exceed the number of
consumer types. Formally, $B \leq M$.

Monotone crossing: Similar to condition (5.23),

$$\frac{f_2 - f_1}{p_1 - p_2} < \frac{f_3 - f_2}{p_2 - p_3} < \cdots < \frac{f_B - f_{B-1}}{p_{B-1} - p_B}. \tag{5.25}$$

Incentive compatibility: Each tariff should be adopted by at least one type of consumer. Formally, let plans i and j be on the menu. Then, there must exist
type ℓ consumers for which $ncs_\ell(q_\ell(p_i); f_i, p_i) \geq ncs_\ell(q_\ell(p_j); f_j, p_j)$. That
is, type ℓ consumers prefer plan i over all other plans on this menu.

Participation: For each plan i on the menu, $i = 1, \ldots, B$, there exists a consumer
type ℓ for which $ncs_\ell(q_\ell(p_i); f_i, p_i) \geq 0$.

Relative Profitability: The offering of this menu of two-part tariffs should be more
profitable than offering a single two-part tariff.

Observe that the last requirement ensures that the investment in designing a menu of tariffs pays off. For example, recall that although we are able to demonstrate that a menu of two two-part tariffs is more profitable than a single two-part tariff when the market consists of types of consumers depicted in Figure 5.6, we are not able to do so when the market consists of consumers illustrated by Figure 5.4. Along these lines, it is worthwhile mentioning that Kolay and Shaffer (2003) demonstrate that inducing self-selection among segments of consumers by offering a menu of price–quantity bundles, as studied in Chapter 4, is more profitable to the seller than inducing self-selection by offering a menu of two-part tariffs.

5.4 Multipart Tariff

A multipart tariff is a price schedule with a flat fee and two or more rate steps for the usage price.

5.4.1 Example and general formulation

Table 5.5 provides an example of a multipart tariff provided by a hypothetical phone operator. In reality, as part of a marketing campaign, the phone operator may describe the tariff plan listed in Table 5.5 to its customers as follows: Consumers pay a rate of 6¢ per minute for the first 200 minutes. For the next 100 minutes, they pay 5¢ per minute. Then, for the next 100 minutes, they pay 4¢ per minute. Then, for the next 200 minutes, they pay 3¢ per minute, and 2¢ for each additional minute thereafter.

# Minutes	0 to 200	201 to 300	301 to 400	401 to 600	601+
Rate (per min.)	6¢	5¢	4¢	3¢	2¢

Table 5.5: Example of a multipart tariff for phone calls.

Figure 5.8 illustrates how the rate per minute and consumer expenditure varies with the quantity purchased q according to this tariff plan. The bottom part of Figure 5.8 illustrates how the rate varies with the amount consumed. The top part illustrates total consumer expenditure (labeled x as it equals the revenue of the firm). The computations are as follows: A consumer who makes 300 minutes of phone calls will receive a bill for $17, which is the sum of $200 \cdot 6¢ = \$12$ for the first 200 minutes and $100 \cdot 5¢ = \$5$ for the additional 100 minutes. A consumer who talks 400 minutes on the phone will be billed $21, which is the sum of $17 for the first 300 minutes and $100 \cdot 4¢ = \$4$ for the last 100 minutes. Finally, a consumer who talks 600 minutes on the phone will be billed $27, which is the sum of $21 for the first 400 minutes and $200 \cdot 3¢ = \$6$ for the last 200 minutes.

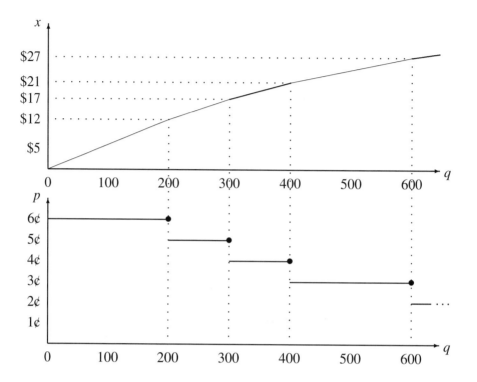

Figure 5.8: Example of a multipart tariff for phone calls. *Note*: For the sake of illustration only, the fixed fee is set at $f = 0$.

Figure 5.8 illustrates why multipart tariffs are often referred to as *block rate tariffs* as the tariffs are indeed divided into blocks that are priced separately. Thus, the total bill consumers end up paying is composed of subpayments for the different quantities according to the predefined blocks. It should be mentioned that the fixed fee is set at $f = 0$ for the sake of illustration only. Most firms that use multipart tariffs do set a fixed fee $f > 0$ in addition to the block rates, in which case the graph drawn on the top part of Figure 5.8 should be shifted uniformly upward by the exact value of f.

We now provide a general definition of a multipart tariff. A multipart tariff consists of a fixed fee, $f^{mp} \geq 0$, and $B \geq 1$ rate steps, with usage prices given by

$$
p^{mp}(q) = \begin{cases} p_1 & \text{if } 0 \leq q \leq \hat{q}_1 \\ p_2 & \text{if } \hat{q}_1 < q \leq \hat{q}_2 \\ \vdots & \quad \vdots \\ p_B & \text{if } q_{B-1} \leq q \leq \hat{q}_B, \end{cases} \tag{5.26}
$$

where $0 < q_1 < q_2 < \cdots < q_B \leq +\infty$. Clearly, $q_B < +\infty$ should be interpreted as if the seller restricts all consumers to buying no more than q_B units (rationing). In contrast, if $q_B = +\infty$, the seller sets B's usage price for all consumption levels exceeding q_{B-1} units. Clearly, if $B = 1$, the multipart tariff collapses to a two-part tariff (a fixed fee and a one usage price). As an example, the general formulation of the six-part tariff ($B = 5$) described in Table 5.5 can be written as

$$f^{mp} = 0 \quad \text{and} \quad p^{mp}(q) = \begin{cases} 6\textcent & \text{if } 0 \leq q \leq 200 \\ 5\textcent & \text{if } 201 \leq q \leq 300 \\ 4\textcent & \text{if } 301 \leq q \leq 400 \\ 3\textcent & \text{if } 401 \leq q \leq 600 \\ 2\textcent & \text{if } q \geq 601. \end{cases} \qquad (5.27)$$

Clearly, the formulation given in (5.27) assumes that the service/product is indivisible in the sense that it is sold for whole units only. However, the general formulation given by (5.26) applies to both cases in which the good is divisible or indivisible.

5.4.2 Multipart versus a menu of two parts: Equivalence results

This section demonstrates that from a technical point of view there is not much difference between offering consumers a multipart tariff and a menu of multiple two-part tariffs. Brown and Sibley (1986) attribute the finding of this link to Faulhaber and Panzar (1977). Here, we demonstrate this link first by constructing a menu of two-part tariffs that is equivalent to the following multipart tariff defined by the fixed fee and quantity-dependent marginal usage prices:

$$f^{mp} = \$2 \quad \text{and} \quad p^{mp}(q) = \begin{cases} 4\textcent & \text{if } 0 \leq q \leq 200 \\ 2\textcent & \text{if } 201 \leq q \leq 300 \\ 1\textcent & \text{if } q \geq 301. \end{cases} \qquad (5.28)$$

Figure 5.9 depicts the revenue (consumer expenditure) generated by the multipart tariff defined by (5.28). Figure 5.9 also demonstrates a geometric methodology for how to convert a multipart tariff (with four parts in the present example) to a menu of multiple two-part tariffs (a menu of three plans in the present case). Clearly, the two-part tariff corresponding to purchase levels up to $q = 200$ units is $\$2 + 4\textcent q$. Figure 5.9 demonstrates that to find the two-part tariff corresponding to purchase levels $200 < q \leq 300$, the line corresponding to $p_B = 2\textcent$ needs to be extended to the left and that the fixed fee f_B is determined at the point where the dashed line intersects the vertical axis, that is, at $f_B = \$6$. Similarly, extending the line corresponding to $p_C = 1\textcent$ leftward determines the third fixed fee, $f_C = \$9$. Altogether, the menu of three two-part tariffs equivalent to the four-part tariff (5.28) is given by

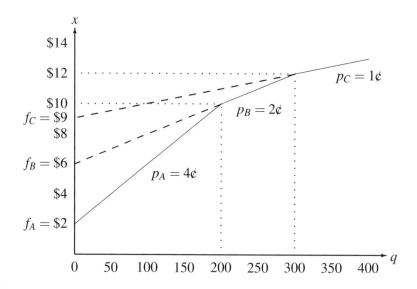

Figure 5.9: Converting a four-part tariff to a menu of three two-part tariffs.

Plan A: Two-part tariff $\langle f_A, p_A \rangle = \langle \$2, 4¢ \rangle$.

Plan B: Two-part tariff $\langle f_B, p_B \rangle = \langle \$6, 2¢ \rangle$.

Plan C: Two-part tariff $\langle f_C, p_C \rangle = \langle \$9, 1¢ \rangle$.

The geometric method for converting a multipart tariff to a menu of two-part tariffs illustrated by Figure 5.9 hints that we should also be looking for an algebraic method for performing the conversion from a multipart tariff to a menu of two-part tariffs. Obviously, an algebraic method is more convenient, more accurate, and easy to implement on computers, which would clearly save time. The recursive algorithm for this conversion is as follows:

Plan A: Set $f_A = f^{mp}$. Hence, $f_A + p_A q = \$2 + 6¢ q$.

Plan B: Set $f_B = f_A + (p_A - p_B)\hat{q}_{A,B} = \$2 + (4¢ - 2¢)200 = \$6$.
      Hence, $f_B + p_B q = \$6 + 2¢ q$.

Plan C: Set $f_C = f_B + (p_B - p_C)\hat{q}_{B,C} = \$6 + (2¢ - 1¢)300 = \$9$.
      Hence, $f_C + p_C q = \$9 + 1¢ q$.

Now that the equivalence between a multipart tariff and a menu of two-part tariffs has been established, there is a question as to why multipart tariffs are needed. Indeed, multipart tariffs are less commonly observed than menus of multiple two-part tariffs, but multipart tariffs are still used by some service providers. From the consumers' point of view, there might be an advantage to accepting a multipart tariff rather than a menu of multiple two-part tariffs if the seller insists that the buyer commit to one specific tariff plan before the consumer knows the exact consumption level (as happens in most cases). In this case, a multipart tariff offers more flexibility in the sense that an unexpected rise in consumption will correspond to a lower rate than a commitment to a specific two-part tariff based on a low expected consumption level. Of course, the two plans are identical even in this respect if the seller allows consumers to choose a specific two-part tariff from the menu, even after the consumer has consumed the service. However, sellers generally insist that consumers commit to a specific tariff before actual consumption.

One disadvantage that a multipart tariff might have relative to a menu of two-part tariffs is that it is somewhat harder to compute, and therefore may irritate some consumers. For example, if a consumer buys $q = 350$ units and is obligated to pay according to the multipart tariff illustrated in Figure 5.9, the bill should include the rather complicated computation given by

$$\$2 + 4\text{¢} \cdot 200 + 2\text{¢} \cdot 100 + 1\text{¢} \cdot 50 = \$12.5.$$

This is somewhat more complicated than computing the equivalent menu of two-part tariffs given by

$$\begin{aligned} \textit{Plan A}: & \quad \$2 + 6\text{¢} \cdot 350 = \$23. \\ \textit{Plan B}: & \quad \$6 + 4\text{¢} \cdot 350 = \$20. \\ \textit{Plan C}: & \quad \$9 + 1\text{¢} \cdot 350 = \$12.5. \end{aligned}$$

We conclude this section with the general formulation of the menu of B two-part tariffs, which is equivalent to the $(B+1)$-part tariff defined by (5.26). Thus, the recursive sequence of fixed fees is given by

$$\begin{aligned} f_1 &= f^{mp}. \\ f_2 &= f_1 + (p_1 - p_2)\hat{q}_1. \\ \vdots \ \ \vdots & \qquad \vdots \\ f_i &= f_{i-1} + (p_{i-1} - p_i)\hat{q}_{i-1}. \\ \vdots \ \ \vdots & \qquad \vdots \\ f_B &= f_{B-1} + (p_{B-1} - p_B)\hat{q}_{B-1}. \end{aligned} \tag{5.29}$$

The general formulation given in (5.29) relies on the assumption that the usage prices listed in (5.26) satisfy $p_1 > p_2 > \cdots > p_B$, which means that larger quantities are discounted in terms of the usage price. The algorithm described by (5.29) may not work if some of these inequality signs are reversed.

Finally, it should be noted that the established equivalence between multipart tariffs and a menu of two-part tariffs also holds with respect to implementation difficulties stemming from the incentive compatibility constraints that we have already discussed in Section 5.3. That is, very often it is hard to find multipart tariffs that would segment the market among consumers so that consumers of different types end up paying different usage rates according to (5.26).

5.5 Regulated Public Utility

Our analysis of multipart tariffs focuses on profit-maximizing firms. However, most of the academic research on multipart tariffs in general and two-part tariffs in particular is confined to regulated firms such as electricity, phone, and gas companies. These types of firms are called public utilities. Until very recently, these public utilities were not allowed to set their own tariffs. Instead, states established regulatory commissions that determined the exact rates that consumers were charged. Readers who wish to learn more about the wide variety of regulated tariffs commonly practiced by public utilities can consult some classic books by Brown and Sibley (1986), Crew and Kleindorfer (1986), and Wilson (1993).

There are two (related) major differences between a monopoly firm and a regulated public utility with respect to the setting of two-part tariffs.

(a) A monopoly firm attempts to extract maximum surplus from consumers. In contrast, the regulator seeks to maximize social welfare, which, for the case of a single firm, is commonly defined as

$$W(q_1,\ldots,q_M) \stackrel{\text{def}}{=} \sum_{\ell=1}^{M} gcs_\ell(q_\ell) + \pi\left(\sum_{\ell=1}^{M} q_\ell\right). \tag{5.30}$$

Thus, for most purposes, social welfare is defined as the sum of consumers' gross surpluses and the profit made by the regulated firm (which is a function of total output sold to consumers).

(b) The regulator must ensure that total consumer spending covers not only variable costs but also the fixed cost ϕ borne by these public utilities. In contrast, the objective of an unregulated monopoly is to extract maximum surplus from consumers.

(c) A regulator may consider giving a subsidy (or a tax break) to a public utility. However, our analysis here is confined to a firm that always breaks even, so a subsidy is not needed.

Note that utility suppliers often bear extremely high fixed costs that may involve repaying for their investments in infrastructure. These investments are essential for the purpose of transmitting these utilities directly to consumers' homes. In addition, fixed costs never cease, even after all loans are repaid, because of the need for continuous maintenance of these infrastructures.

As it turns out, both a regulator who seeks economic efficiency and a single seller seeking to maximize profit only find the two-part tariff extremely useful because the fixed part f^{2p} can be set so that consumers pay their share in the large fixed costs borne by firms, ϕ, whereas the per-unit usage fee p^{2p} can be set to cover the variable cost associated with the marginal cost μ. In fact, if all consumers are of the same type, both the regulator and the single seller can set the two-part tariff at certain levels that maximize social welfare. The only difference is the amount of surplus extracted from consumers. Whereas the regulator seeks to use the fixed fee to pay for firms' fixed costs only, a monopoly firm attempts to extract maximum surplus from consumers.

If all N consumers are of the same type (sharing identical demand functions) the socially optimal two-part tariff, that is, a tariff that maximizes (5.30), is

$$f^{2p} = \frac{\phi}{N} \quad \text{and} \quad p^{2p} = \mu. \tag{5.31}$$

Under this tariff, each consumer pays an equal share of the fixed cost ϕ. The resulting consumption levels are identical to levels consumed under a two-part tariff set by a profit-maximizing firm given by (5.8).

Suppose now that there are M types of consumers, each having a different demand function. A natural extension of the two-part tariff designed for a single consumer type (5.31) to multiple consumer types would be to set the socially optimal two-part tariff to

$$f^{2p} = \frac{\phi}{\sum_{\ell=1}^{M} N_\ell} \quad \text{and} \quad p^{2p} = \mu. \tag{5.32}$$

Here, the fixed cost is also equally divided among all the consumers, hence the firm also breaks even.

Our analysis could end here if the tariff (5.32) would be a feasible solution to all possible configurations of consumer types. However, as it turns out, the proposed socially optimal two-part tariff (5.32) is not feasible if some consumers have low demand in the sense that their derived gross consumer surplus is lower than the sum of their expenditure. Formally, if under this tariff, a type ℓ consumer realizes that $gcs_\ell(q_\ell^{2p}) < f^{2p} + p^{2p} q_\ell^{2p}$, the consumer will not buy this service.

To demonstrate this case, suppose now that there are $N_1 = 600$ type 1 consumers and $N_2 = 400$ type 2 consumers. Further, suppose that the demand functions of the two types are given by (5.12), which are also plotted in Figure 5.4. Finally, assume that the firm's marginal cost is $\mu = \$2$ and that the firm bears a fixed cost of $\$5000$. Because there are $N_1 + N_2 = 600 + 400 = 1000$ consumers, the candidate socially optimal two-part tariff should take the form of

$$f^{2p} = \frac{\phi}{\sum_{\ell=1}^{M} N_\ell} = \frac{\$5000}{600 + 400} = \$5 \quad \text{and} \quad p^{2p} = \$2. \tag{5.33}$$

However, inspection of Table 5.2 reveals that no type 2 consumer would be willing to pay a fixed fee exceeding $4 when the usage price is set at $p^{2p} = \$2$. Hence, type 2 consumers will not buy this service. Furthermore, because under the tariff (5.33) only the $N_1 = 600$ consumers buy, the firm is making a loss given by $\pi = 600[\$5 + (\$2 - \$2)3] - \$5000 = -\$2000 < 0$. To break even, the regulator will be forced to raise the fixed fee to $f^{2p} = \phi/N_1 = 5000/600 = \$8.34$. A type 1 consumer will still buy at this fee because Table 5.2 shows that type 1 consumers will buy as long as $p^{2p} = \$2$ and $f^{2p} < \$9$.

Now, will the setting of the fixed fee to equal $f^{2p} = \$8.34$ solve the regulator's problem? The answer depends on the goal of the regulator. If the regulator cannot price discriminate between the two consumer types and is restricted to setting one two-part tariff for all consumers, and if the objective of the regulator is to maximize the social welfare function (5.30), then $f^{2p} = \$8.34$ may be a solution. However, unlike unregulated monopoly firms, regulators are often very sensitive to the exclusion of consumers from various groups of society. For example, in the case of basic phone services, if type 2 consumers happen to be low-income families, regulators may decide to deviate from the objective function (5.30) and even decide to subsidize part of the fixed cost using taxpayers' money.

Finally, if the regulator is able to price discriminate between the consumer types, say on the basis of age, income, or profession, the regulator can simply set different two-part tariffs for different consumer groups. A good design of such a scheme could result in an even higher welfare level compared with the adoption of Ramsey pricing analyzed in Section 3.6.2.

5.6   Exercises

1. In the market in which your firm is selling, the demand function by each individual is approximated by a linear function given by $p = 120 - 0.5q$. The marginal production cost is $\mu = \$40$, and the fixed cost is denoted by ϕ. Solve the following problems.

   (a) Similar to Figure 5.2, draw the demand curve and compute the two-part tariff f^{2p} and p^{2p} that maximizes your firm's profit.

   (b) Suppose now that there are $N = 5$ consumers with the same demand function. Compute the profit level assuming that the fixed cost is $\phi = \$30,000$.

2. As the new VP for pricing of BLABLA, a cell-phone operator, you are in charge of proposing a two-part tariff structure for your customers. Your research department has just completed a market survey concluding that there is only one consumer ($N = 1$), whose demand data are summarized in Table 5.6. The marginal cost of a unit of phone calls is $\mu = 10\cent$ and the fixed cost is $\phi = 20\cent$. Using the analysis in Section 5.1.3, fill in the missing items in the middle section of

Table 5.6. State the two-part tariff that maximizes your firm's profit. *Hint*: Compare with Table 5.1, and note that $gcs(q)$ can be computed directly from (5.2).

p	40¢	30¢	20¢	10¢	0¢
q	0	2	3	6	7
$gcs(q)$					
pq					
$f = gcs(q) - pq$					
μq					
$y^{2p}(q)$					

Table 5.6: Data for Exercise 2.

3. Suppose that your firm sells to two consumers of different types. The inverse demand function of consumer 1 is $p_1 = 2 - 4q_1$. The inverse demand function of consumer 2 is $p_2 = 1 - 0.5q_2$. Solve the following problems.

p	$0	$1	$2
q_1			
$gcs_1(q)$			
f_1			
$y_1(f_1, p)$			
q_2			
$gcs_2(q)$			
f_2			
$y_2(f_2, p)$			
$\min\{f_1, f_2\}$			
$y_{1,2}(q)$			
$\max\{y_1, y_2, y_{1,2}\}$			

Table 5.7: Data for Exercise 3.

(a) Fill in the missing items in Table 5.7, assuming that the firm does not bear any production costs, that is, $\mu = \phi = \$0$.

(b) Suppose that your firm would like to set a *single* two-part tariff to be offered to all consumers. Find the two-part tariff $\langle f^{2p}, p^{2p} \rangle$ that maximizes the firm's profit, and compute the corresponding profit level. *Hint*: There are two solutions to this problem.

(c) Find a menu of *two* two-part tariffs under which the firm makes a higher profit compared with the profit made under a single two-part tariff. Prove your answer by computing the net consumer surplus $ncs(q)$ for each consumer under two tariff plans that you propose.

4. Consider the analysis of offering a menu of multiple two-part tariffs given in Section 5.3.2. Suppose now that the seller offers a menu with four two-part tariffs given by $f_A + p_A q = 10 + 5q$, $f_B + p_B q = 20 + 4q$, $f_C + p_C q = 30 + 3q$, and $f_D + p_D q = 40 + 2q$. Solve the following problems.

(a) Plot the four two-part tariffs where you measure quantity purchased q on the horizontal axis, and consumer expenditure (firm's revenue) on the vertical axis; see Figure 5.7 for an example.

(b) Find which tariff minimizes consumer expenditure for every given quantity purchased q.

(c) Conclude whether this menu obeys or violates the monotone crossing conditions given by (5.25).

5. Using the conversion algorithm described in Section 5.4.2, formulate the menu of two-part tariffs that would be equivalent to the multipart tariff given by (5.27). Label the plans Plan A, B, C, D, and E.

Chapter 6
Peak-load Pricing

6.1   **Seasons, Cycles, and Service-cost Definitions**   **183**

   6.1.1   Seasons and cycles

   6.1.2   Three types of costs

6.2   **Two Seasons: Fixed-peak Case**   **185**

   6.2.1   Winters and summers: An example

   6.2.2   Two seasons: General formulation for the fixed-peak case

6.3   **Two Seasons: Shifting-peak Case**   **190**

   6.3.1   Winters and summers: An example

   6.3.2   Two seasons: General formulation for shifting peak

6.4   **General Computer Algorithm for Two Seasons**   **194**

6.5   **Multi-season Pricing**   **194**

   6.5.1   Multi-season pricing: A three-season example

   6.5.2   Multi-season pricing: Method and computer algorithm

6.6   **Season-interdependent Demand Functions**   **201**

   6.6.1   Winters and summers: An example

   6.6.2   Interdependent demand: General formulation

6.7   **Regulated Public Utility**   **205**

   6.7.1   Winters and summers: An example

   6.7.2   Two seasons: General formulation and computer algorithm

   6.7.3   Multi-season pricing: A three-season example

   6.7.4   Multi-season pricing: General formulation for public utility

6.8   **Demand, Cost, and the Lengths of Seasons**   **214**

   6.8.1   Daytime and nighttime supply of electricity: Examples

   6.8.2   General formulations

6.9   **Exercises**   **223**

Services constitute what economists call *nonstorable goods*. Electricity, telephone, transportation, banking, and most other services are consumed at the time of purchase. This nonstorability characteristic of services may lead to congestion of service systems when the demand for the service is unevenly distributed among different periods or seasons. The demand for telephone services is at the highest level during daytime, during weekdays, and tends to be lower during nights, weekends, and some holidays. The demand for air travel for most places tends to be relatively high during the summer, whereas the demand for transportation to ski resorts is greatly enhanced during the winter. Electricity use follows a daily cycle related partly to the use of appliances and lighting devices. In addition, it also follows a yearly cycle because of climatic changes. Thus, the demand follows several, sometimes overlapping, periodic cycles.

Peak-load pricing techniques are commonly observed in vacation-related services (airline, restaurant, and hotel industries) as well as in utility services (phone and electricity). The utilization of peak-load pricing techniques is profitable in industries with the following main characteristics:

(a) Demand varies significantly among the different seasons.

(b) Services are time-related and perishable in the sense that they cannot be postponed or delivered earlier than the scheduled time of delivery.

(c) Service providers must acquire a significant amount of costly capital.

(d) The acquired capital cannot be easily liquidated and cannot be easily rented out or sold to other firms.

Clearly, the airline industry possesses all of the above-listed characteristics, because traveling in the winter differs from traveling during the summer. In addition, airlines must invest in acquiring expensive aircraft and must precontract gates, parking spots, and other services at various airports. Finally, aircraft cannot be easily liquidated at the price purchased, even if depreciation is deducted from the price of new aircraft. Electricity and phone companies also exhibit the same characteristics because they must also invest in illiquid and costly equipment. In addition, the demand for electricity and phone calls fluctuates according to the hours of the day, and days of the week, and across the different seasons in a given year.

To summarize, the nonstorability of services together with periodic fluctuations in demand makes the peak-load pricing mechanism both profitable and socially efficient. If instead prices were uniform across seasons, the quantity demanded would rise and fall as the seasons changed. To meet demand at peak seasons would then require the installation of capacity, which would be underused during off-peak seasons. Because capacity can be highly costly to buy and maintain, the resulting idleness during off-peak seasons would be highly inefficient. On this basis, peak-load pricing can partially fix this inefficiency by lowering the price during off-peak seasons, thereby reducing the amount of idle capacity.

In solving the peak-load pricing problem, the seller has to make the following two major decisions:

(a) How much capital to invest in, and hence how much production capacity to maintain to be able to meet demand in the peak season.

(b) How to price this service in each season.

There is a vast literature on peak-load pricing, which is surveyed in Crew, Fernando, and Kleindorfer (1995), and in some classic books such as Crew and Kleindorfer (1979, 1986), Brown and Sibley (1986), and Sherman (1989). Boiteux (1960), Steiner (1957), Hirshleifer (1958), and Williamson (1966) are considered to be highly influential papers on peak-load pricing. The survey and the above-mentioned books also discuss additional topics that are not addressed in this book, such as multiple technologies and issues related to uncertainty that may lead to rationing and outage costs.

6.1   Seasons, Cycles, and Service-cost Definitions

To maintain service capacity, the provider must invest in building some capital stock. Investment in service capacity allows the firm to provide service over time. The way costs are defined plays a crucial role in successful and profitable implementation of peak-load pricing strategies. Readers are urged to consult Section 6.8, which analyzes various possible cost accounting methods, taking into account the relative duration of each season over a cycle.

6.1.1   Seasons and cycles

We use the general term *season* to represent a certain time interval during which the demand is kept more or less stable. Seasons could be daytime, nighttime, weekdays, weekends, and of course, summer and winter.

Seasons will be indexed by $t = A, B, \ldots, T$ or by $t = 1, 2, \ldots, T$. Let p_t denote the price in season t and q_t denote quantity of service demanded and supplied in each season t. Before we formally begin to write down the firm's cost function, we must further extend our discussion of cycles of seasons. We define a *cycle* as the time interval consisting of one full cycle of all seasons. For example, a cycle called one year consists of four seasons called summer, fall, winter, and spring. Alternatively, if we wish to simplify our pricing strategy, we can divide a cycle of one year into summer and winter only. Table 6.1 provides some additional examples.

Cycle	Seasons ($t = 1, 2, \ldots, T$)
Year	Summer, fall, winter, and spring
Year	Summer and winter
Year/month	Business days and holidays
Day	Morning, afternoon, evening, and night
Day	Daytime and nighttime
Week	Sunday, Monday, $\cdots$, Saturday
Week	Weekdays and weekends

Table 6.1: Examples of cycles consisting of seasons.

6.1.2   Three types of costs

In view of the notation used consistently throughout this book, which is listed in Table 1.4, we assume that the cost function of a service provider can be decomposed into three components:

Sunk and fixed costs: Denoted by ϕ, measures all costs that are independent of the level of service provided or the scale of production.

Marginal capacity cost: Denoted by μ_k, measures the cost of expanding the capacity to be able to provide one additional unit of service throughout one full cycle of all seasons.

Marginal operating cost: Denoted by μ_o, measures the cost of providing one additional unit of service (or serving one additional consumer) that is not related to capacity expansion.

Sunk and fixed costs have already been discussed several times in this book. Examples include company registration fees, marketing surveys, advertising, and all costs of infrastructure that are not directly related to capacity. Of course, one may argue that, for some companies, advertising expenditure tends to increase with the scale of production, in which case advertising should be counted as of part of the operating cost.

Marginal capacity cost is the only difficult component on the above list of service costs. This is because the units in which capital is measured must be adjusted to be consistent with the units at which the demand is stated and also with respect to the lengths of seasons and cycles. Readers are urged to consult Section 6.8, which introduces various possible accounting methods for allocating the cost of capital throughout the duration of seasons and cycles. For an airline, marginal capacity cost is the expenditure per cycle needed for upgrading an aircraft (or a fleet of aircraft) so that it can accommodate one additional passenger seat. Looking at airlines' costs in this way makes sense, especially because nearly half of the airplanes flying today are leased, not owned, by the airlines.

For an electricity company, marginal capacity cost is the expenditure per one cycle of upgrading a generator so it can generate one additional kilowatt of electricity. For a phone operator, marginal capacity cost may include the cost of enhancing the network to be able to accommodate one additional phone call, or an additional phone line.

Marginal operating cost of an airline includes the cost of in-flight services needed for accommodating one additional passenger, such as food, boarding personnel, and entertainment. Marginal operating cost of an electrical power company consists of the additional expenditure on coal, gas, fuel, oil, and labor attributed to increasing electricity output by an additional kilowatt-hour. Marginal operating cost of a telephone company is negligible. However, some economists may count the cost of congestion as part of the operating cost because when the system operates near full capacity, customers are likely to receive busy signals. Congestion cost is most noticeable on the Internet, when the response time could become very long when the network operates near full capacity.

It should be emphasized that the two types of marginal costs defined above differ substantially with respect to their time span (see Section 6.8 for a discussion of problems related to capital cost accounting). More precisely, the marginal capacity cost is configured on a cost basis *adjusted for exactly one full cycle* of all seasons. Thus, if we associate a cycle with one year, an airline that buys aircraft lasting for 10 years should divide the total cost spent on this capital by 10 years and then by the total (daily) capacity of the acquired fleet. An easier way of looking at this is to assume that the purchase of capital is fully financed by commercial banks. Under this interpretation, the yearly cost equals the interest payments made to the bank for this loan, divided by the service capacity of this capital (number of passengers that can be flown on these aircraft). Depreciation cost of capital can also be added. In contrast, the marginal operating cost is the *cost per served customer*, so it does not bear any time dimension. Table 6.2 provides some further examples. Table 6.2 demonstrates the difference between marginal capacity cost μ_k and marginal operating cost μ_o. The marginal operating cost is materialized only when and if a customer is actually being served. In contrast, the marginal capacity cost is based on potential service capacity. In this aspect, this distinction very much resembles the distinction made in Definition 8.4 in the context of refunds on no-shows. Using the airline example, total operating cost is computed by multiplying μ_o by the actual demand level in a particular season. In contrast, total capacity cost is chosen at the procurement stage and cannot vary or fluctuate with the demand across the seasons in a given cycle.

6.2 Two Seasons: Fixed-peak Case

The fixed-peak season analysis applies to markets where the demand level varies significantly between the seasons. The exact measure to determine whether there

Industry	Cycle	μ_k	μ_o
Airline	Year	$\dfrac{\left(\dfrac{\text{Aircraft cost}}{\text{Passenger capacity}}\right)}{\text{Durability (years)}}$	In-flight service cost
Airline	Year	$\dfrac{\text{Yearly interest payments}}{\text{Passenger capacity}}$	In-flight service cost
Hotel	Year	$\dfrac{\left(\dfrac{\text{Construction cost}}{\text{\# Rooms or \# beds}}\right)}{\text{Expected duration (years)}}$	Room cleaning cost
Hotel	Month	$\dfrac{\text{Monthly interest payments}}{\text{\# Rooms or \#beds}}$	Room cleaning cost
Restaurant	Month	$\dfrac{\text{Monthly rent on space}}{\text{\# Tables}}$	Meal cost

Table 6.2: Examples of marginal capacity and marginal operating costs.

is a significant difference in demand between seasons will be discussed later, but it should be noted at this stage that this measure of difference in demand will also depend on the marginal cost parameters μ_k and μ_o.

6.2.1 Winters and summers: An example

Consider a small airline by the name of LUFTPAPA that flies passengers to a sea resort on an island near Greece. The marginal capacity cost is $\mu_k = \$20$ and the marginal operating cost is also $\mu_o = \$20$. The fixed cost is assumed to be $\phi = \$2000$. The demand varies between summer (S) and winter (W), and is given by

$$p_S = \alpha_S - \beta_S q_S = 200 - q_S \quad \text{and} \quad p_W = \alpha_W - \beta_W q_W = 100 - q_W. \quad (6.1)$$

The inverse demand functions defined by (6.1) are drawn in Figure 6.1.

Computing summer and winter airfares

We first recall the formula for the marginal revenue function associated with the inverse demand function $p = \alpha - \beta q$. Thus,

$$MR(q)\frac{\mathrm{d}x(q)}{\mathrm{d}q} = \frac{\mathrm{d}[p(q)q]}{\mathrm{d}q} = \alpha - 2\beta q. \quad (6.2)$$

Therefore, $MR_S = 200 - 2q_S$ and $MR_W = 100 - 2q_W$.

Next, the computations of the profit-maximizing price during each season resemble the steps of price determination by a monopoly seller listed by (3.2) and

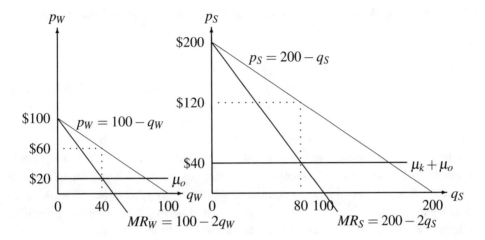

Figure 6.1: Profit-maximizing peak-load pricing for LUFTPAPA Airlines: Fixed-peak case.

(3.3). Here we apply these steps for each season separately. We first assume (and later verify) that summer is the peak season, which means that summer's marginal revenue function should be equated to the sum of capacity and operating marginal costs, whereas winter's marginal revenue function should be equated to the marginal operating cost only. Hence,

$$MR_S(q_S) = 200 - 2q_S \;=\; \$20 + \$20 = \mu_k + \mu_o, \Longrightarrow q_S^{pl} = k^{pl} = 80,$$
$$MR_W(q_W) = 100 - 2q_W \;=\; \$20 = \mu_o, \Longrightarrow q_W^{pl} = 40 < k^{pl}. \qquad (6.3)$$

Thus, the profit-maximizing amount of capacity k that the firm should be investing in is determined by equating the peak season's marginal revenue function to the sum of marginal capacity and marginal operating costs. This procedure implies that LUFTPAPA will be operating at full capacity $q_S^{pl} = k^{pl} = 80$ during the summer, which is the peak season. Equating winter's marginal revenue function to marginal operating cost only, yields the winter's number of passengers, $q_W^{pl} = 40 < k^{pl} = 80$. This verifies that the resulting winter consumption level does not exceed the capacity level, which confirms that summer is indeed the peak season. If it happens that under this procedure $q_W > k$, then either we may have to declare winter the peak season or more likely, we encounter the *shifting-peak* case analyzed in Section 6.3. Finally, substituting the summer and winter numbers of passengers (6.3) into the inverse demand functions (6.1) yields the summer and winter airfares

$$p_S^{pl} = 200 - q_S^{pl} = \$120 \quad \text{and} \quad p_W^{pl} = 100 - q_W^{pl} = \$60. \qquad (6.4)$$

The resulting total profit earned by LUFTPAPA in one cycle (consisting of one summer and one winter season) is

$$y^{pl} = (p_W^{pl} - \mu_o)q_W^{pl} + (p_S^{pl} - \mu_k - \mu_o)q_S^{pl} - \phi$$
$$= (60 - 20)40 + (120 - 20 - 20)80 - 2000 = \$6000. \quad (6.5)$$

The logic behind the method demonstrated above, which is also illustrated in Figure 6.1, is that the seller invests in the last unit of capacity to be able to accommodate the extra seating capacity needed to satisfy the peak-season demand (which happens to be the summer season in the present example). Therefore, the cost of capacity should be attributed to summer passengers only because the winter passengers are served on an underused capacity, and adding an additional passenger during the winter does not require any extra investment in capacity.

Why is peak-load pricing profitable?

The reader may ask why peak-load pricing is more profitable than charging a uniform price across all seasons. To answer this question, we need to recall our analysis of discriminating monopoly selling in two markets with different demand curves (see Section 3.2.4). In view of Figure 6.1, LUFTPAPA Airlines can choose between two uniform prices. It can charge a low price $p < \$100$, thereby serving both summer and winter passengers. Alternatively, it can charge a high price $p \geq \$100$, thereby excluding all winter passengers, thereby resorting to summer operation only.

For any uniform price in the range $0 < p_{S,W} < \$100$, the aggregate direct demand function is $q_{S,W} = 200 - p + 100 - p = 300 - 2p_{S,W}$. Therefore, the aggregate inverse demand function is $p_{S,W} = 150 - q_{S,W}/2$. By the formula given in (6.2), the aggregate marginal revenue function is $MR_{S,W}(q_{S,W}) = 150 - q_{S,W}$. Setting $MR_{S,W}(q_{S,W}) = \mu_k + \mu_o = \$40$ yields $q_{S,W} = 110$ and therefore a price $p_{S,W} = 150 - q_{S,W}/2 = \$95 < \$100$. Hence, both markets are indeed served at this price.

Before we compute the total profit generated by setting $p_{S,W} = \$95$ and serving both markets, we must figure out how much aircraft seating capacity LUFT-PAPA should invest to be able to meet this demand. Because $q_S = 200 - 95 = 105$, whereas $q_W = 100 - 95 = 5$, to be able to accommodate all passengers in each season, LUFTPAPA Airlines must invest in a seating capacity of 105. Therefore, the profit of LUFTPAPA from serving summer and winter passengers under uniform prices across both seasons is

$$y_{S,W} = (p_{S,W} - \mu_o)q_{S,W} - \mu_k q_S - \phi =$$
$$(95 - 20)110 - 20 \cdot 105 - 2000 = \$4,150 < \$6,000 = y^{pl}, \quad (6.6)$$

which is lower than the profit generated under peak-load pricing.

Next, under uniform pricing, the seller also computes the profit when the seller raises the price above $100, in which case, in view of Figure 6.1, only summer passengers will book their flights with the airline. However, the top line in equation (6.3) already provides the solution $q_S = 80$ passengers. The corresponding price $p_S = \$120$ was already computed in (6.4). In this case, the profit is given by

$$y_S = (p_S - \mu_k - \mu_o)q_S - \phi$$
$$= (120 - 20 - 20)80 - 2000 = \$4400 < \$6000 = y^{pl}. \quad (6.7)$$

This concludes the proof showing why peak-load pricing is more profitable than uniform pricing. Clearly, this formal proof was not really needed because one can simply adopt a revealed preference argument to prove it. More precisely, under peak-load pricing, the seller can always choose to set $p_S = p_W$. However, if the firm chooses (as our computations above recommend) to set unequal prices across the seasons so that $p_S \neq p_W$, then it must be enhancing its profit. However, from time to time, such a comparison may be needed if the cost of implementing peak-load pricing is significantly higher than the cost of marketing under a single uniform price.

6.2.2 Two seasons: General formulation for the fixed-peak case

This section extends the two-season airline example of the previous section to general linear demand functions $p_A = \alpha_A - \beta_A q_A$ during season A, and $p_B = \alpha_B - \beta_B q_B$ during season B. The single seller's fixed cost is ϕ, marginal capacity cost is μ_k, and marginal operating cost is μ_o (see Section 6.1 for precise definitions). It must be verified first that either $\alpha_A > \mu_k + \mu_o$ or $\alpha_B > \mu_k + \mu_o$, which is a necessary (but not sufficient) condition for making nonnegative profit. In addition, it must be verified that consumers' willingness to pay exceeds the marginal operating cost so that $\alpha_A > \mu_o$ and $\alpha_B > \mu_o$.

The computation of the profit-maximizing price in each season should follow the following steps:

Step I: Check if A is the peak season by setting $MR_A(q_A) = \alpha_A - 2\beta_A q_A = \mu_k + \mu_o$ to obtain

$$q_A = \frac{\alpha_A - \mu_k - \mu_o}{2\beta_A} \quad \text{and} \quad p_A = \frac{\alpha_A + \mu_k + \mu_o}{2}. \quad (6.8)$$

Similarly, for season B (off-peak season) set $MR_B(q_B) = \alpha_B - 2\beta_B q_B = \mu_o$ to obtain

$$q_B = \frac{\alpha_B - \mu_o}{2\beta_B} \quad \text{and} \quad p_B = \frac{\alpha_B + \mu_o}{2}. \quad (6.9)$$

Now, check if A is indeed the peak season so that $q_B \leq q_A$. If this is the case, then set the capacity level to $k = q_A$ and skip to *Step III*.

Step II: Check if B is the peak season by setting $MR_B(q_B) = \alpha_B - 2\beta_B q_B = \mu_k + \mu_o$ to obtain

$$q_B = \frac{\alpha_B - \mu_k - \mu_o}{2\beta_B} \quad \text{and} \quad p_B = \frac{\alpha_B + \mu_k + \mu_o}{2}. \tag{6.10}$$

Similarly, for season A (off-peak season) set $MR_A(q_A) = \alpha_A - 2\beta_A q_A = \mu_o$ to obtain

$$q_A = \frac{\alpha_A - \mu_o}{2\beta_A} \quad \text{and} \quad p_A = \frac{\alpha_A + \mu_o}{2}. \tag{6.11}$$

Now, check if B is indeed the peak season so that $q_A \leq q_B$. If this is the case, then set the capacity level to $k = q_B$. If this is not the case, *stop here* as you reached the shifting-peak case analyzed in Section 6.3.

Step III: Compute the profit level using the relevant prices and quantities computed in *Step I* or *Step II* above. Thus,

$$y^{pl} = \begin{cases} (p_A^{pl} - \mu_k - \mu_o)q_A^{pl} + (p_B - \mu_o)q_B^{pl} - \phi & \text{if } A \text{ is the peak} \\ (p_A^{pl} - \mu_k)q_A^{pl} + (p_B^{pl} - \mu_k - \mu_o)q_B^{pl} - \phi & \text{if } B \text{ is the peak.} \end{cases} \tag{6.12}$$

Then, verify that the firm does not make a loss by checking whether $y^{pl} \geq 0$. The above algorithm indicates that the marginal cost of capacity (capital) should be attributed to the peak-season consumers only. In particular, the profit function (6.12) indicates that the cost of capital $\mu_k \max q_A, q_B$ should be counted only once, because capital is assumed to be durable for the entire cycle consisting of season A and season B.

6.3 Two Seasons: Shifting-peak Case

The case of shifting peak has been analyzed in Steiner (1957). Bailey and White (1974) pointed out the possibility of peak reversals. Shifting peak occurs when the marginal capacity cost μ_k is relatively high so that it cannot be charged to the peak-season consumers only. In this case, capacity cost should be shared among consumers in all seasons. Another way of looking at this is to realize that a rise in the price of capital raises the cost of maintaining idle capacity during the low season. Hence, for a sufficiently high cost of capital, the seller should adjust seasonal prices so that capacity is fully used in all seasons, in which case the seller sells equal amounts in all seasons. Shifting peak is also likely to occur when there are only small variations in demand across the different seasons. In either case, the algorithm described in Section 6.2 for the fixed-peak case cannot be used. Therefore, the algorithm developed in this section is based on the principle that consumers in all seasons should be charged for the use of capacity, and the key question is how to split this cost of capital among consumers from different seasons. As before, we also need to compute the profit-maximizing amount of investment in capacity.

6.3.1 Winters and summers: An example

Consider LUFTPAPA Airlines, which we analyzed in Section 6.2.1. Suppose that
the summer and winter demand functions are still given by (6.1), but because of
an acquisition of new aircraft the marginal cost of capacity has risen to a level of
$\mu_k = \$140$. Let the marginal operating cost be $\mu_o = \$20$ and the fixed cost be
$\phi = \$1000$.

  Our first task is to compute the profit-maximizing investment in capacity, k. To
do that, we resort to a somewhat unusual procedure of summing up the marginal
revenue functions, which we call *vertical summation*. To perform this summation,
we recall from (6.3) the summer and winter marginal revenue functions $MR_S(q_S) =
200 - 2q_S$ and $MR_W(q_W) = 100 - 2q_W$. The *vertical summation* of marginal rev-
enue as a function of capacity k is given by

$$\sum_{S,W} MR^v(k) =$$

$$\begin{cases} 200 - 2k + 100 - 2k = 300 - 4k & \text{if } 0 < k = q_S = q_W \le 50 \\ 200 - 2k & \text{if } 50 < k = q_S = q_W \le 100 \quad (6.13) \\ 0 & \text{if } k = q_S = q_W > 100. \end{cases}$$

Again, under the shifting-peak case, capacity is fully used in both seasons, so
$q_S = q_W = k$. Figure 6.2 modifies Figure 6.1 to demonstrate how to graphically
construct the vertical summation of the summer and winter marginal revenue functions. Figure 6.2 exhibits a kink at output/capacitly level of $q = k = 50$ as the
marginal revenue in the winter falls below zero at output levels $q > 50$, thus only
the summer marginal revenue is taken into consideration.

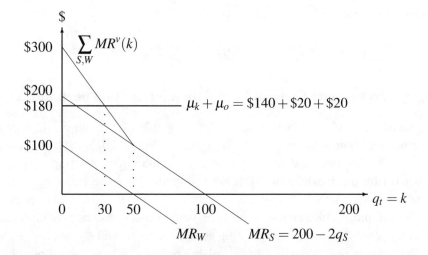

Figure 6.2: Vertical summation of summer and winter marginal revenue functions.

The vertical sum $\sum MR^v(k)$ has the following interpretation: It reflects the additional revenue that can be generated by expanding capacity by one additional seat. Because under the shifting peak case prices are set so that passenger demand reaches full capacity in both seasons, the sum of the two marginal revenue functions reflects the revenue gain from investing in an additional passenger seat. The reader should be aware of the difference between vertical and horizontal summations of marginal revenue and demand functions. For a comparison between vertical and horizontal summations, the reader can refer to Section 2.5, which focuses on horizontal summations.

Figure 6.2 illustrates that the profit-maximizing capacity level is determined by equating the vertical sum of the marginal revenue functions with the sum of marginal capacity and operating costs. Formally, solving

$$\sum_{S,W} MR^v(k) = 300 - 4k = \$140 + \$20 + \$20 = \$180 = \mu_k + 2\mu_o \tag{6.14}$$

yields

$$k^{pl} = q_S^{pl} = q_W^{pl} = 30, \quad p_S^{pl} = 200 - 30 = \$170,$$

$$\text{and } p_W^{pl} = 100 - 30 = \$70. \tag{6.15}$$

Notice that the marginal capacity cost μ_k appears only once, whereas the marginal operating cost appears twice in the profit-maximization condition (6.14). This follows from our assumptions that capital is durable and that the cost of capacity is computed on the basis of an entire cycle (one year in the present example). In contrast, the marginal operating cost applies only for passengers who are actually being served and therefore must be added up across all seasons (winter and summer in the present example). Finally, total profit is given by

$$y^{pl} = (170 - 20)30 + (70 - 20)30 - 140 \cdot 30 - 1000 = \$800. \tag{6.16}$$

6.3.2 Two seasons: General formulation for shifting peak

This section extends the two-season airline example of Section 6.3.1 to general linear demand functions $p_A = \alpha_A - \beta_A q_A$ and $p_B = \alpha_B - \beta_B q_B$. The seller bears a fixed cost of ϕ, marginal capacity cost μ_k, and marginal operating cost μ_o (see Section 6.1 for precise definitions). It must be verified first that either $\alpha_A > \mu_k + \mu_o$ or $\alpha_B > \mu_k + \mu_o$, which is a necessary (but not sufficient) condition for making nonnegative profit. In addition, it must be verfied that consumers' willingness to pay also exceeds the marginal operating cost, so $\alpha_A > \mu_o$ and $\alpha_B > \mu_o$.

The computation of the profit-maximizing price in each season follows the following steps:

Step I: Verify that A is *not* a peak season by setting $MR_A(q_A) = \alpha_A - 2\beta_A q_A = \mu_k + 2\mu_o$ to obtain

$$q_A = \frac{\alpha_A - \mu_k - \mu_o}{2\beta_A} \quad \text{and} \quad p_A = \frac{\alpha_A + \mu_k + \mu_o}{2}. \qquad (6.17)$$

Similarly, for season B, set $MR_B(q_B) = \alpha_B - 2\beta_B q_B = \mu_o$ to obtain

$$q_B = \frac{\alpha_B - \mu_o}{2\beta_B} \quad \text{and} \quad p_B = \frac{\alpha_B + \mu_o}{2}. \qquad (6.18)$$

Now, verify that A is *not* a peak season by confirming that $q_B > q_A$. If this is *not* the case, *stop here* as you have reached the fixed-peak case that was analyzed in Section 6.2.

Step II: Verify that B is *not* a peak season by setting $MR_B(q_B) = \alpha_B - 2\beta_B q_B = \mu_k + \mu_o$ to obtain

$$q_B = \frac{\alpha_B - \mu_k - \mu_o}{2\beta_B} \quad \text{and} \quad p_B = \frac{\alpha_B + \mu_k + \mu_o}{2}. \qquad (6.19)$$

Similarly, for season A, set $MR_A(q_A) = \alpha_A - 2\beta_A q_A = \mu_o$ to obtain

$$q_A = \frac{\alpha_A - \mu_o}{2\beta_A} \quad \text{and} \quad p_A = \frac{\alpha_A + \mu_o}{2}. \qquad (6.20)$$

Now, confirm that B is *not* a peak season by verifying that $q_A > q_B$. If this is *not* the case, *stop here* as you have reached the fixed-peak case that was already analyzed in Section 6.2.

Step III: Sum up vertically the two marginal revenue functions and equate the sum to the sum of marginal capacity and marginal operating costs over a full cycle

$$\sum_{A,B} MR^v(k) = \alpha_A + \alpha_B - 2(\beta_A + \beta_B)k = \mu_k + 2\mu_o, \qquad (6.21)$$

which obtains the desired capacity level

$$k^{pl} = q_A^{pl} = q_B^{pl} = \frac{\alpha_A + \alpha_B - \mu_k - 2\mu_o}{2(\beta_A + \beta_B)}. \qquad (6.22)$$

Step IV: Substitute $k^{pl} = q_A^{pl} = q_B^{pl}$ into each demand function to obtain the price in each season:

$$p_A^{pl} = \frac{\alpha_A(\beta_A + 2\beta_B) + \beta_A(\mu_k + 2\mu_o - \alpha_B)}{2(\beta_A + \beta_B)}, \qquad (6.23)$$

$$p_B^{pl} = \frac{\alpha_B(2\beta_A + \beta_B) + \beta_B(\mu_k + 2\mu_o - \alpha_A)}{2(\beta_A + \beta_B)}.$$

Observe that unlike the prices set under the fixed-peak case given by (6.8)–(6.11), here the marginal capacity cost μ_k directly affects the prices in both seasons, not only the summer price. This is a direct consequence of the outcome that capacity is fully used in all both seasons. The resulting profit is given by

$$y^{pl} = (p_A^{pl} - \mu_o)k^{pl} + (p_B^{pl} - \mu_o)k^{pl} - \mu_k k^{pl} - \phi$$
$$= \frac{(\alpha_A + \alpha_B - \mu_k - 2\mu_o)^2}{4(\beta_A + \beta_B)} - \phi. \quad (6.24)$$

Note that the profit function (6.24) indicates that the cost of capital should be counted only once, $\mu_k k^{pl}$ (as opposed to $2k^{pl}$), because capital is assumed to be durable for the entire cycle consisting of seasons A and B.

6.4 General Computer Algorithm for Two Seasons

This section suggests a computer program for determining the profit-maximizing seasonal prices. The program determines whether these prices should be computed for the fixed-peak case or for the shifting-peak case.

Algorithm 6.1 below assumes two seasons, $t = 1, 2$. Each t is characterized by a downward-sloping linear demand function $p = \alpha[t] - \beta[t]q$. The computer program described below should input and store (say, using the **Read()** command), the demand parameters onto two real-valued arrays, $\alpha[t]$ and $\beta[t]$. The program should also input the seller's cost parameters μ_k (marginal capacity cost), μ_o (marginal operating cost), and ϕ (fixed cost).

Algorithm 6.1 simply follows the algebraic procedures described in Section 6.2.2 (fixed-peak season case) and Section 6.3.2 (shifting-peak case), so a lengthy explanation is not needed. The integer valued variables $peak \in \{0, 1, 2\}$ and $off \in \{0, 1, 2\}$ store which season should be treated as the peak season and which should be the off-peak season. $peak = 0$ is interpreted as shifting peak, in which case $q_1 = q_2 = k$ (demand equals capacity in both seasons). Finally, the season-dependent prices and demand levels are outputted onto two real-valued non-negative arrays, $p[t]$ and $q[t]$, for seasons $t = 1, 2$.

6.5 Multi-season Pricing

Recall that we assume that time is measured in cycles, where each cycle consists of one full cycle of all seasons (see examples in Table 6.2). So far in our analysis, a cycle has consisted of exactly two seasons (such as summer and winter, daytime and nighttime, weekdays and weekends). This section extends the two-season analysis to multiple seasons, indexed by $t = 1, \ldots, T$.

$peak \leftarrow 0; off \leftarrow 0; /* \texttt{Initialization}$ */
if $(\alpha[1] - \mu_k - \mu_o)/(2\beta[1]) \geq (\alpha[2] - \mu_o)/(2\beta[2])$ **then**
$\quad$ $peak \leftarrow 1; off \leftarrow 2; /* \texttt{Season 1 is peak, 2 is off-peak}$ */
if $(\alpha[2] - \mu_k - \mu_o)/(2\beta[2]) \geq (\alpha[1] - \mu_o)/(2\beta[1])$ **then**
$\quad$ $peak \leftarrow 2; off \leftarrow 1; /* \texttt{Season 2 is peak, 1 is off-peak}$ */
if $peak \neq 0$ **then**
$\quad$ $/* \texttt{Fixed-peak case}$ */
$\quad$ $q[peak] \leftarrow (\alpha[peak] - \mu_k - \mu_o)/(2\beta[peak]);$
$\quad$ $p[peak] \leftarrow \alpha[peak] - \beta[peak]q[peak]; q[off] \leftarrow (\alpha[off] - \mu_o)/(2\beta[off]);$
$\quad$ $p[off] \leftarrow \alpha[off] - \beta[off]q[off];$
$\quad$ $y^{pl} \leftarrow (p[peak] - \mu_k - \mu_o)q[peak] + (p[off] - \mu_o)q[off] - \phi;$
$\quad$ **writeln** $(peak,$" is the peak season, and the seller should invest in $k = $",
$\quad$ $q[peak],$ " units of capacity."); **writeln** ("The peak season price should
$\quad$ be set to ", $p[peak],$ "The off-peak season price should be set to ",
$\quad$ $p[off]$); **writeln** ("The peak season demand equals full capacity" ,
$\quad$ $q[peak],$ "The off-peak season demand is ", $q[off]$);
if $peak = 0$ **then**
$\quad$ $/* \texttt{Shifting-peak case}$ */
$\quad$ $k \leftarrow (\alpha[1] + \alpha[2] - \mu_k - 2\mu_o)/(2\beta[1] + 2\beta[2]); p[1] \leftarrow \alpha[1] - \beta[1]k;$
$\quad$ $p[2] \leftarrow \alpha[2] - \beta[2]k; y^{pl} \leftarrow (p[1] - \mu_k - \mu_o)k + (p[2] - \mu_o)k - \phi;$
$\quad$ **writeln** ("Shifting peak case so $q[1] = q[2] = k$. The seller should invest
$\quad$ in $k = $", $k,$ " units of capacity."); **writeln** ("The price in season 1 should
$\quad$ be set to ", $p[1],$ "and in season 2 to ", $p[2]$);
if $y^{pl} \geq 0$ **then writeln** ("The resulting profit is ", y^{pl}); **else write** ("Negative
profit. Do NOT operate in this market!")

Algorithm 6.1: Two seasons: Profit-maximizing peak-load pricing.

6.5.1 Multi-season pricing: A three-season example

Suppose now that each cycle consists of three seasons: fall, winter, and summer, and that LUFTPAPA Airlines operates in all three seasons. Passenger demand in each season and the corresponding marginal revenue functions are given by

$$\begin{array}{llll}
p_S = 200 - q_S & \text{summer} & MR_S = 200 - 2q_S \\
p_W = 100 - q_W & \text{winter} & MR_W = 100 - 2q_W & (6.25) \\
p_F = 200 - 0.5q_F & \text{fall} & MR_F = 200 - q_F.
\end{array}$$

Suppose now that the airline's marginal operating cost is $\mu_o = \$20$. Figure 6.3 depicts the three marginal revenue functions listed in (6.25). Figure 6.3 also plots

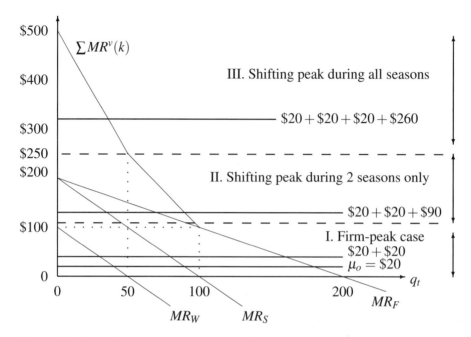

Figure 6.3: Vertical summation of summer, winter, and fall marginal revenue functions and three regions corresponding to the marginal capacity cost μ_k. *Note*: Regions do not necessarily coincide with the kinks of $\sum MR^v$.

the marginal operating cost $\mu_o = \$20$ and two examples of sums of marginal costs $\mu_k + 2\mu_o$ and $\mu_k + 3\mu_o$.

Figure 6.3 turns out to be very useful for locating the quantity thresholds where the *vertical summation* of the marginal revenue functions has a kink. The kinks occur because we do not sum negative values of marginal revenue functions (no seller would find it profitable to expand production in a market where the marginal revenue is negative). Therefore, the *vertical summation* of the marginal revenue functions is given by

$$\sum_{t=F,W,S} MR^v(k) = \begin{cases} 500 - 5k & \text{if } k \le 50 \\ 400 - 3k & \text{if } 50 < k \le 100 \\ 200 - k & \text{if } 100 < k \le 200 \\ 0 & \text{if } k > 200. \end{cases} \quad (6.26)$$

The vertical summation of the three marginal revenue functions is illustrated in Figure 6.3 as a continuous line with three segments and two kinks.

Our analysis in Sections 6.2 and 6.3 has demonstrated that shifting-peak cases occur when the marginal capacity cost is sufficient high relative to both the demand and the marginal operating cost. In this case, the service provider may operate under full capacity in more than one season. That is, capacity is "too expensive" to be left idle in off-peak seasons. Now, with more than two seasons, our first task is to determine which seasons exhibit a shifting peak, or whether we can identify one season with a fixed peak. In what follows, we characterize three possibilities. Figure 6.3 illustrates three regions, divided by dashed lines, corresponding to increasing levels of the exogenously given marginal capacity cost parameter μ_k, which we analyze in this section. It is important to note, as Figure 6.3 clearly illustrates, that the regions analyzed below do not necessarily coincide with the "kinks" of the vertical sum of the marginal revenue functions.

Region I. Three seasons with a fixed peak season

Under a relatively low marginal capacity cost, fall turns out to be the peak season. So, suppose that $\mu_k = \mu_o = \$20$. The sum of $\mu_o + \mu_k$ is plotted in Figure 6.3 as a solid horizontal line in region I. If fall is the peak season, the seller should attribute all marginal costs to Fall passengers only. Hence,

$$MR_F = 200 - q_F = \$20 + \$20 \implies q_F^{pl} = 160 \text{ and } p_F^{pl} = \$120. \tag{6.27}$$

Next, for the low seasons, spring and winter, the seller should attribute the marginal operating cost $\mu_o = \$20$ only so that

$$MR_S = 200 - 2q_S = \$20 \implies q_S^{pl} = 90 \text{ and } p_S^{pl} = \$110. \tag{6.28}$$
$$MR_W = 100 - 2q_W = \$20 \implies q_W^{pl} = 40 \text{ and } p_W^{pl} = \$60.$$

Clearly, because $q_F > \max\{q_S, q_W\}$, fall is the peak season. Finally, total profit is given by

$$y^{pl} = (p_F - \mu_k - \mu_o)q_F + (p_S - \mu_o)q_S + (p_W - \mu_o)q_W - \phi = \$21,100 - \phi. \tag{6.29}$$

Region II. Multiple seasons with shifting peak in two seasons only

Under intermediate values of the marginal capacity cost parameter μ_k, shifting peak may occur between two seasons only, whereas during the third season, the airlines will serve a small number of passengers, leaving some capacity underused. Therefore, suppose now that $\mu_k = \$90$. The sum $2\mu_o + \mu_k$ is plotted as a solid horizontal line in region II of Figure 6.3.

We first check whether fall is a peak season. If fall is the peak season, then similar to (6.27) the seller should solve $MR_F = 200 - q_F = \$20 + \$90$, yielding $q_F = 90$. However, for the off-peak summer season, the seller solves $MR_S = 200 - 2q_S = \$20$, yielding $q_S = 90 = q_F$, which indicates that this is a borderline case between the fixed-peak and the shifting-peak cases. We proceed by computing the prices under the shifting peak case, which, not surprisingly, turn out to be the same as those under the fixed-peak case.

Next, suppose that shifting peak occurs between fall and summer, but not between winter and any other season. In this case, the seller should equate the vertical sum of the fall and summer marginal revenue functions to the sum of capacity and operating costs so that

$$\sum_{F,S} MR^v = 200 - k + 200 - 2k = 400 - 3k = \$20 + \$20 + \$90 = 2\mu_o + \mu_k. \quad (6.30)$$

Therefore,

$$k^{pl} = q_F^{pl} = q_S^{pl} = 90, \Longrightarrow p_F^{pl} = \$155 \quad \text{and} \quad p_S^{pl} = \$110. \quad (6.31)$$

For the remaining off-peak winter season, the seller should solve

$$MR_W = 100 - 2q_W = \$20, \Longrightarrow q_W^{pl} = 40 \quad \text{and} \quad p_W = \$60. \quad (6.32)$$

To verify that winter is indeed an off-peak season, observe that $q_W^{pl} = 40 < 90 = k^{pl}$. Finally, the profit is given by

$$y^{pl} = (p_F - \mu_k - \mu_o)k + (p_S - \mu_o)k + (p_W - \mu_o)q_W - \phi = \$15,750 - \phi. \quad (6.33)$$

Region III. Multiple seasons with shifting peak in all seasons

For sufficiently high values of the marginal capacity cost parameter μ_k, shifting peak occurs among all seasons. Let $\mu_k = \$260$. In this case, the seller resorts to the same method as the one described in Section 6.3.2 for two seasons, which equates the vertical sum of all marginal revenue functions to the sum of all marginal costs. Formally,

$$\sum_{F,W,S} MR^v = 200 - k + 200 - 2k + 100 - 2k = 500 - 5k = 3 \cdot \$20 + \$260$$

$$= 3\mu_o + \mu_k, \quad \text{yielding} \quad k^{pl} = q_F^{pl} = q_S^{pl} = q_W^{pl} = 36. \quad (6.34)$$

It is important to verify that the service level $k^{pl} = 36$ is sufficiently low so that all the season-specific marginal revenue functions drawn in Figure 6.3 take nonnegative values. This is indeed the case because $q_t = k^{pl} = 36 < 50$ for every $t = F, S, W$. Therefore,

$$p_F^{pl} = \$182, \quad p_S^{pl} = \$164, \quad \text{and} \quad p_W^{pl} = \$64. \quad (6.35)$$

Finally, the profit is given by

$$y^{pl} = (p_F - \mu_k - \mu_o)k + (p_S - \mu_o)k + (p_W - \mu_o)k - \phi = \$2,268 - \phi. \quad (6.36)$$

6.5.2 Multi-season pricing: Method and computer algorithm

The three-season example of Section 6.5.1 hints at the method for determining peak-load pricing when there are more than two seasons. This procedure consists of the following steps:

Step I: Equate $MR_t(q_t) = \mu_k + \mu_o$ and solve for q_t, for each season $t = 1, \ldots, T$. Find the highest q_t, and set $\hat{t} = \text{argmax}_{t=1,\ldots,T}\{q_t\}$. If $q_t \le q_{\hat{t}}$ for all $t \ne \hat{t}$, skip to Step V as $\hat{t}$ is the fixed-peak season.

Step II: Equate $MR_t(q_t) = \mu_k + 2\mu_o$ and solve for q_t, for each season $t = 1, \ldots, T$. Find the two highest q_ts, and label them $\hat{t}_1$ and $\hat{t}_2$. If $q_t \le \min\{q_{\hat{t}_1}, q_{\hat{t}_2}\}$ for all $t \ne \hat{t}_1$ and $t \ne \hat{t}_2$, skip to step V as $\hat{t}_1$ and $\hat{t}_2$ are shifting-peak seasons, whereas all others are off-peak seasons.

Step III: Equate $MR_t(q_t) = \mu_k + 3\mu_o$ and solve for q_t, for each season $t = 1, \ldots, T$. Find the three highest q_ts, and label them $\hat{t}_1$, $\hat{t}_2$, and $\hat{t}_3$. If you find that $q_t \le \min\{q_{\hat{t}_1}, q_{\hat{t}_2}, q_{\hat{t}_3}\}$ for all $t \ne \hat{t}_1$, $t \ne \hat{t}_2$, and $t \ne \hat{t}_3$, skip to Step V as $\hat{t}_1$, $\hat{t}_2$, and $\hat{t}_3$ are shifting-peak seasons, whereas all others are off-peak seasons.

Step IV: Repeat the above procedure for $4, 5, \ldots, T$ shifting-peak seasons.

Step V: For each off-peak season t, solve for q_t using $MR_t(q_t) = \mu_o$ (marginal operating cost only), and then find the price from $p_t = \alpha_t - \beta_t q_t$. Next, sum up vertically the marginal revenue functions of all peak seasons, and solve for the profit-maximizing capacity level k from $\sum_{\text{peak}} MR^v(k) = \mu_k + n \cdot \mu_o$, where n is the number of peak seasons. Lastly, compute prices directly from the inverse demand functions so that $p_t = \alpha_t - \beta_t k$.

The above procedure can be put into a computer program such as Algorithm 6.2. This algorithm assumes $T \ge 2$ seasons indexed by $t = 1, \ldots, T$. Each season t is characterized by a downward-sloping linear demand function $p = \alpha[t] - \beta[t]q$. The computer program described below should input and store the number of seasons T and the demand parameters onto two strictly positive real-valued arrays, $\alpha[t]$ and $\beta[t]$. The program should also input the seller's non-negative cost parameters μ_k (marginal capacity cost), μ_o (marginal operating cost), and ϕ (fixed cost). Algorithm 6.2 basically follows the steps listed above. The main idea is to find which seasons should be classified as having a shifting peak by running a loop over i, where the variable $i \in \mathbb{N}^+$ is the number of seasons with a shifting peak. Therefore, $i = 1$ is a fixed-peak case, whereas $i = 2$ is a case in which a shifting peak occurs in two seasons, and so on.

For a given i, the program computes q_t from $MR_t(q_t) = \mu_k + i \cdot \mu_o$ and selects the i seasons with the highest q_t. Clearly, one should write a procedure for this selection, which is not given here. The i indexes of these seasons are stored in the set *peak*$[i]$, which is the candidate set of seasons with a shifting peak. Note

---

$Stop \leftarrow no; y \leftarrow 0; \text{/* Initialization}$ */
for $i = 1$ **to** T **do**
  /* Main loop over the number of shifting-peak seasons */
  if $Stop = no$ **then**
      $n \leftarrow i; Stop \leftarrow yes; q_i \leftarrow (\alpha[i] - \mu_k - i \cdot \mu_o)/(2\beta[i]);$
        $peak[i] \leftarrow \{t : i \text{ highest } q_t\}; \text{/* set has } i \text{ elements}$ */
      for $t \notin peak[i]$ **do**
          $q[t] \leftarrow (\alpha[t] - \mu_o)/(2\beta[t]); \text{/* Off-peak levels}$ */
          for $s \in peak[i]$ **do** **if** $q[t] > q[s]$ **then** $Stop \leftarrow no;$
          /* if off-peak demand exceeds capacity   */

for $t \in peak[n]$ **do** $\alpha_\Sigma \leftarrow \alpha[t]; \beta_\Sigma \leftarrow \beta[t]; \text{/* Sum } MR_t \text{ vertically}$ */
$k \leftarrow (\alpha_\Sigma - \mu_k - n \cdot \mu_o)/(2\beta_\Sigma); \text{/* Capacity level}$ */
writeln ("The peak is shifting across n seasons."); **writeln** ("The service
provider should invest in ", k, "units of capacity");
for $t \in peak[n]$ **do**
  $p[t] \leftarrow \alpha[t] - \beta[t] \cdot k; y \leftarrow y + (p[t] - \mu_o)k; \text{/* Peak prices}$ */
  writeln ("Set peak season", t, "price to $p_t^{pl} =$", $p[t]$)
for $t \notin peak[n]$ **do**
  $p[t] \leftarrow \alpha[t] - \beta[t] \cdot q[t]; y \leftarrow y + (p[t] - \mu_o)q[t];$ **writeln** ("Set off-peak
    season", t, "price to $p_t^{pl} =$", $p[t]$, "and serve $q_t^{pl} =$", $q[t]$,
    customers."); /* Off-peak prices   */
$y \leftarrow y - k \cdot \mu_k - \phi;$ **if** $y \geq 0$ **then writeln** ("The resulting profit is ", y^{pl}); **else**
write ("Negative profit. Do NOT operate in this market!")

Algorithm 6.2: Multiple seasons: Profit-maximizing peak-load pricing.

that the number of sets containing the indexes of peak seasons $peak[i]$ could be
between 1 and T, depending on how early on the loop over i the variable $Stop$ is
assigned with a yes. Then, the program must confirm that the service levels during
off-peak seasons $t \notin peak[i]$ do not exceed capacity k. If this is the case, then the
variable $Stop$ is assigned with a yes and the number of seasons with shifting peak i
is assigned to n, where $n \in \mathbb{N}^+$. After that, only the set $peak[n]$ is used as the set of
indexes of all peak seasons.

After the variable $Stop$ is assigned with a yes, the program constructs the vertical sum of the marginal revenue functions of peak seasons indexed in the set
$peak[n]$, and then computes the prices. Off-peak season prices as well as the profit
are also computed.

6.6 Season-interdependent Demand Functions

Our analysis so far was based on the assumption that the demand for service in each season is independent of how the service is priced in all other seasons. However, in reality, for some consumers the demand functions are interdependent, which means that a reduction in price during one season may cause some consumers to postpone or advance their service demand to the "discounted" season. For example, friends tend to delay long phone conversations to off-peak hours, including late-night hours, weekends, and holidays, because these time periods are heavily discounted. Also, people tend to postpone or advance their nonbusiness trips to travel during discounted off-peak seasons. In both examples, if the service provider charges uniform prices in all seasons, most consumers may demand the service during the peak-season only.

In the literature, there are several formulations that introduce substitution among seasons. Crew and Kleindorfer (1986, Sec. 3.4), following Dansby (1975), allow for nonzero cross-derivatives of a season's demand function with respect to output sold in different seasons. Bergstrom and MacKie-Mason (1991) and Shy (1996, Ch. 13) allow for substitution between seasons in utility-based models.

6.6.1 Winters and summers: An example

To capture consumer substitution across seasons, we slightly modify the example of a small airline, LUFTPAPA. More precisely, we transform the system of independent seasonal demand functions (6.1) into the interdependent inverse demand functions given by

$$p_S = \alpha_S - \beta_S q_S - \gamma_S q_W = 200 - q_S - 0.2 q_W, \tag{6.37}$$
$$p_W = \alpha_W - \beta_W q_W - \gamma_W q_S = 100 - q_W - 0.2 q_S.$$

The system of demand functions formulated in (6.37) implies that winter service and summer service are substitutes to some degree. Here, an increase in the number of passengers who fly over the winter will reduce passengers' willingness to pay in both seasons. The same applies for an increase in the number of passengers who fly over the summer. This is what makes the service in both seasons substitute goods (see Definition 2.4 for the direct demand case).

Next, the seasonal total revenue functions associated with the demand functions (6.37) are

$$x_S(q_S, q_W) = (200 - q_S - 0.2 q_W) q_S, \tag{6.38}$$
$$x_W(q_S, q_W) = (100 - q_W - 0.2 q_S) q_W.$$

Notice that the revenue generated in each season now depends on the level of service provided in all seasons because the seasonal demand functions (6.37) are interdependent. Thus, instead of deriving only two marginal revenue functions, one for each market, we now must derive four marginal revenue functions defined by

$$MR_{SS} \stackrel{\text{def}}{=} \frac{\partial x_S}{\partial q_S} = 200 - 2q_S - 0.2q_W,$$

$$MR_{SW} \stackrel{\text{def}}{=} \frac{\partial x_S}{\partial q_W} = -0.2q_S, \qquad (6.39)$$

$$MR_{WW} \stackrel{\text{def}}{=} \frac{\partial x_W}{\partial q_W} = 100 - 2q_W - 0.2q_S,$$

$$MR_{WS} \stackrel{\text{def}}{=} \frac{\partial x_W}{\partial q_S} = -0.2q_W.$$

The newly defined cross-marginal revenue function MR_{SW} measures the change in revenue during the summer generated by a "small" increase in service level during the winter. Similarly, the cross-marginal revenue function MR_{WS} measures the change in revenue during the winter generated by a "small" increase in service level during the summer.

Interdependent demand airline example: Fixed-peak case

Suppose that LUFTPAPA's cost parameters are now given by $\mu_k = \mu_o = \$20$ and $\phi = \$2000$. We basically follow the same steps as in Section 6.2.2, except that now four marginal revenue functions enter the calculations instead of only two. We first assume (and later verify) that summer is the peak season. In this case, the seller should solve for the summer and winter service levels q_S and q_W using the following two conditions:

$$\begin{aligned} MR_{SS} + MR_{WS} &= 200 - 2q_S - 0.2q_W - 0.2q_W = \$20 + \$20 = \mu_k + \mu_o, \\ MR_{WW} + MR_{SW} &= 100 - 2q_W - 0.2q_S - 0.2q_S = \$20 = \mu_o. \end{aligned} \qquad (6.40)$$

The top equation equates the sum of summer and winter's marginal revenues associated with a small expansion of service during the summer, to the sum of all marginal costs. The bottom condition equates the sum of marginal revenue functions associated with a small increase in the service level during the winter to the marginal operating cost only. Solving (6.40) for service levels q_S and q_W and then substituting these into the inverse demand functions (6.37) yield

$$k^{pl} = q_S^{pl} = 75, \quad q_W^{pl} = 25, \quad p_S^{pl} = \$120, \quad \text{and} \quad p_W^{pl} = \$51. \qquad (6.41)$$

This confirms that summer is indeed the peak season. Comparing the prices (6.41) with the prices computed under independent seasonal demand (6.4) reveals that when demand functions are interdependent, the seller lowers the price during the low season (Winter in the present example). Lowering the off-peak price is done for the purpose of trying to make passengers switch from the peak season to the lower season. Finally, for the sake of completeness, the total profit earned by the seller by using the above peak-load pricing is

$$y^{pl} = (p_S - \mu_k - \mu_o)q_S + (p_W - \mu_o)q_W - \phi = \$4775. \tag{6.42}$$

Interdependent demand airline example: Shifting-peak case

Suppose that LUFTPAPA's cost parameters are now given by $\mu_k = \$160$, $\mu_o = \$20$, and $\phi = \$1000$. We basically follow the same steps as in Section 6.3.2, except that now we have four marginal revenue functions given by (6.39) instead of only two.

To demonstrate that summer is not a peak season, we investigate conditions (6.40) under the new cost structure. Hence,

$$
\begin{aligned}
MR_{SS} + MR_{WS} &= 200 - 2q_S - 0.2q_W - 0.2q_W = \$160 + \$20 = \mu_k + \mu_o, \\
MR_{WW} + MR_{SW} &= 100 - 2q_W - 0.2q_S - 0.2q_S = \$20 = \mu_o,
\end{aligned} \tag{6.43}
$$

yielding $q_S = 25/12 < 475/12 = q_W$. Thus, summer is not a peak season. Clearly, using the same method, we can show that winter is also not a peak season, which implies that the shifting-peak case applies.

Under the shifting-peak case, the airline serves at full capacity in both seasons so that $k = q_S = q_W$. Equating the vertical sum of the four marginal revenue functions at full capacity to the sum of marginal capacity and operating costs yields

$$\sum_{S,W} MR^v(k) = 300 - \frac{24k}{5} = \$160 + \$20 + \$20 = \mu_k + 2\mu_o,$$

$$\text{yielding} \quad k^{pl} = q_S^{pl} = q_W^{pl} = \frac{125}{6}. \tag{6.44}$$

Therefore,

$$p_S^{pl} = 200 - k^{pl} - 0.2k^{pl} = \$175 \quad \text{and} \quad p_W^{pl} = 100 - k^{pl} - 0.2k^{pl} = \$75. \tag{6.45}$$

Finally, for the sake of completeness, the total profit earned by the seller by using the above peak-load pricing is

$$y^{pl} = (p_S - \mu_k - \mu_o)k^{pl} + (p_W - \mu_o)k^{pl} - \phi = \frac{3125}{3} - 1000 = \frac{125}{3}. \tag{6.46}$$

6.6.2 Interdependent demand: General formulation

We now extend the airline example of Section 6.6.1 to general demand functions as specified in (6.37). As explained in Section 2.7 (for the direct demand case), the parameters of this system of inverse demand functions α_S, α_W, β_S, β_W, γ_S, and γ_W can be estimated from past data on seasonal prices and the number of served passengers. It must be verified that the estimated demand parameters satisfy

$\min\{\beta_S, \beta_W\} > \max\{\gamma_S, \gamma_W\}$, which means that a season's price is more sensitive to variations in the service of the same season relative to the variation in the service level during other seasons. Economists often state this condition by saying that the "own" effect is stronger than the substitute effect.

The demand functions (6.37) yield the revenue functions

$$
\begin{aligned}
x_S(q_S, q_W) &= (\alpha_S - \beta_S q_S - \gamma_S q_W) q_S, \\
x_W(q_S, q_W) &= (\alpha_W - \beta_W q_W - \gamma_W q_S) q_W.
\end{aligned}
\qquad (6.47)
$$

The corresponding four marginal revenue functions are therefore given by

$$
\begin{aligned}
MR_{SS} &\overset{\text{def}}{=} \frac{\partial x_S}{\partial q_S} = \alpha_S - 2\beta_S q_S - \gamma_S q_W, \\
MR_{SW} &\overset{\text{def}}{=} \frac{\partial x_S}{\partial q_W} = -\gamma_S q_S, \\
MR_{WW} &\overset{\text{def}}{=} \frac{\partial x_W}{\partial q_W} = \alpha_W - 2\beta_W q_W - \gamma_W q_S, \\
MR_{WS} &\overset{\text{def}}{=} \frac{\partial x_W}{\partial q_S} = -\gamma_W q_W.
\end{aligned}
\qquad (6.48)
$$

Interdependent demand general formulation: Fixed-peak case

Assuming first (and verifying later) that summer is a peak season, the seller determines the amount of service q_S and q_W by solving

$$
\begin{aligned}
MR_{SS} + MR_{WS} &= \alpha_S - 2\beta_S q_S - \gamma_S q_W - \gamma_W q_W = \mu_k + \mu_o, \\
MR_{WW} + MR_{SW} &= a_W - 2\beta_W q_W - \gamma_W q_S - \gamma_S q_S = \mu_o,
\end{aligned}
\qquad (6.49)
$$

yielding the service levels

$$
\begin{aligned}
q_S^{pl} &= \frac{2\alpha_S \beta_W - \alpha_W(\gamma_S + \gamma_W) - 2\beta_W(\mu_k + \mu_o) + (\gamma_S + \gamma_W)\mu_o}{4\beta_S \beta_W - (\gamma_S + \gamma_W)^2}, \\
q_W^{pl} &= \frac{2\alpha_W \beta_S - \alpha_S(\gamma_S + \gamma_W) - 2\beta_S \mu_o + (\gamma_S + \gamma_W)(\mu_k + \mu_o)}{4\beta_S \beta_W - (\gamma_S + \gamma_W)^2}.
\end{aligned}
\qquad (6.50)
$$

At this stage, it should be verified that $k^{pl} = q_S^{pl} > q_W^{pl}$, meaning that summer is indeed a peak season. Finally, the profit-maximizing seasonal prices p_S^{pl} and p_W^{pl} are computed by substituting the service levels (6.50) into the system of inverse demand functions (6.37). The profit is then found by substituting the service levels and prices into the profit function (6.42).

Interdependent demand general formulation: Shifting-peak case

The seller should equate the vertical sum of the four marginal revenue functions at full capacity to the sum of marginal capacity and operating costs so that

$$\sum_{S,W} MR^v(k) = \alpha_S + \alpha_W - 2(\beta_S + \beta_W + \gamma_S + \gamma_W)k = \mu_k + 2\mu_o. \qquad (6.51)$$

Setting $k = q_S = q_W$ yields the desired capacity level

$$k = q_S = q_W = \frac{\alpha_S + \alpha_W - \mu_k - 2\mu_o}{2(\beta_S + \beta_W + \gamma_S + \gamma_W)}. \qquad (6.52)$$

Finally, the profit-maximizing seasonal prices p_S^{pl} and p_W^{pl} are computed by substituting the capacity level from (6.52) into the system of inverse demand functions (6.37). The profit is then found by substituting the service levels and prices into the profit function (6.46).

6.7 Regulated Public Utility

The difference between a regulator of a public utility and a profit-maximizing firm is that a regulator is concerned with consumer welfare and industry profit, whereas a firm seeks to maximize profit only. The regulator often sets prices to maximize a social welfare function, which for the present formulation (with no fixed costs) boils down to maximizing consumer welfare subject to the constraint that the firm break even (hence does not make any loss). The objective of a regulator of a public utility has been discussed earlier in this book (see Sections 3.6.2 and 5.5). Therefore, we confine the analysis of this section to modifying the monopoly seller's algorithm for determining peak-load pricing to an algorithm for regulating public utilities.

The main difference between the algorithms used by a profit-maximizing single seller and those employed by the regulator is that a regulator tends to equate the *prices* to the "relevant" marginal costs, as opposed to a monopoly firm that deviates from marginal cost pricing by equating the *marginal revenue* to the "relevant" marginal cost, thereby restricting its output. However, marginal cost pricing would generate a loss to the seller as marginal cost pricing will not generate any revenue that may be needed to cover the fixed cost ϕ. For this reason, our analysis here is limited to the case in which the fixed costs are either nonexisting or are financed by the taxpayers. It should be noted that if fixed costs were present, the regulator could use two-part tariffs whereby the fixed fees levied on consumers could be used for financing the seller's fixed cost (see Section 5.5). Alternatively, in the presence of fixed costs, the regulator could deviate from marginal cost pricing according to the Ramsey principle as explained in Section 3.6.2.

In view of the above discussion, consider a single service provider with a marginal capacity cost of μ_k, marginal operating cost of μ_o, and no fixed costs so that $\phi = 0$. It is assumed that the reader is familiar with the monopoly seller's analysis of Sections 6.2 and 6.3, or at least with the airline example analyzed in Sections 6.2.1 and 6.3.1 for the fixed-peak and shifting cases, respectively. Thus, the analysis in this section will be rather sketchy because once the monopoly case is understood, the modification to a regulated public utility is rather straightforward.

6.7.1   Winters and summers: An example

We now modify the examples given in Sections 6.2.1 (fixed-peak case) and 6.3.1 (shifting-peak case) to compute the prices set by a regulator of a public utility.

The summer and winter demand functions are given by

$$p_S = \alpha_S - \beta_S q_S = 200 - q_S \quad \text{and} \quad p_W = \alpha_W - \beta_W q_W = 100 - q_W. \qquad (6.53)$$

The inverse demand functions defined by (6.53) are drawn in Figure 6.4.

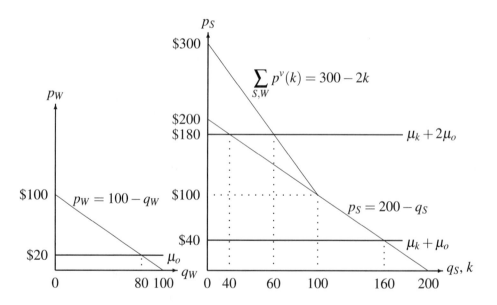

Figure 6.4: Social welfare maximizing peak-load pricing.

We analyze a *fixed-peak case* by assuming a relatively low marginal capacity cost so that $\mu_k = \mu_o = \$20$. A regulator seeking marginal cost pricing should set the summer price to equal the sum of marginal capacity and operating costs so that $p_S^{pl} = \$20 + \$20 = \$40$. At this price, $q_S^{pl} = 160$ customers are served during the summer. During the winter, the regulator sets the winter price to equal the marginal operating cost only so that $p_W^{pl} = \$20$, which implies that $q_W^{pl} = 80$ passengers are served during winter. The reader is urged at this point to compare these results, also drawn in Figure 6.4, with the single seller's peak and off-peak prices drawn in Figure 6.1. Clearly, there is no need to compute profit because under marginal cost pricing, the firm earns zero profit due to our assumption that this service provider does not incur any fixed costs.

We can obtain the *shifting-peak case* by assuming a relatively high marginal capacity cost so that $\mu_k = \$140$ and $\mu_o = \$20$. To see why summer is not a peak season, we set $p_S = \$140 + \$20 = \$160$ and $p_W = \$20$. Under these prices, $q_S = 40 < 80 = q_W$, which proves that summer is not a peak season. Next, under the shifting-peak case, the regulator has to sum up the demand vertically. Formally, the vertical sum of the demand functions (6.53) is

$$\sum_{S,W} p^v(k) = \begin{cases} 300 - 2k & \text{if } 0 < k \le 100 \\ 200 - k & \text{if } 100 < k \le 200 \\ 0 & \text{if } k > 200. \end{cases} \tag{6.54}$$

The vertical summation of demand functions is similar to the vertical summation of marginal revenue functions that we first encountered in (6.13) and Figure 6.2. Note that this procedure is totally different from the one of demand aggregation studied in Section 2.5, which involves horizontal summation of market demand functions.

The vertical summation of the summer and winter demand (6.54) is also plotted in Figure 6.4. The socially optimal investment in capacity is determined by intersecting the vertical sum of demand (6.54) with the sum of marginal capacity and operating costs. Hence, solving $300 - 2k = 20 + 20 + 140$ yields $k^{pl} = 60$. Substituting $q_S = q_W = k^{pl}$ into the demand functions (6.53) yields the socially optimal prices $p_S^{pl} = \$140$ and $p_W^{pl} = \$40$. Again, there is no need to compute profit because at marginal cost pricing, the firm earns zero profit.

6.7.2 Two seasons: General formulation and computer algorithm

The above example is now extended to general linear demand functions $p_A = \alpha_A - \beta_A q_A$ and $p_B = \alpha_B - \beta_B q_B$. We basically modify the single seller's procedure described in Sections 6.2.2 and 6.3.2 to the problem solved by the regulator. The regulated public utility's marginal capacity cost is μ_k, the marginal operating cost is μ_o, and there are no fixed costs, so $\phi = 0$ (see Section 6.1 for precise definitions of these costs). It must be verified first that either $\alpha_A > \mu_k + \mu_o$ or $\alpha_B > \mu_k + \mu_o$, which is a necessary (but not sufficient) condition for making nonnegative profit. In addition, it must be verified that consumers' willingness to pay also exceeds the marginal operating cost, so $\alpha_A > \mu_o$ and $\alpha_B > \mu_o$.

The computation of the socially optimal prices and the investment in capacity should follow the following steps:

Step I: Check if A is the peak season by setting $p_A^{pl} = \alpha_A - \beta_A q_A = \mu_k + \mu_o$ and $p_B^{pl} = \alpha_B - \beta_B q_B = \mu_o$ to obtain

$$q_A^{pl} = \frac{\alpha_A - \mu_k - \mu_o}{\beta_A} \quad \text{and} \quad q_B^{pl} = \frac{\alpha_B - \mu_o}{\beta_B}. \tag{6.55}$$

Now, check if A is indeed the peak season so that $q_B^{pl} \le q_A^{pl}$. If this is the case, then set the capacity level to $k^{pl} = q_A^{pl}$ and *stop here*.

Step II: Check if B is the peak season by setting $p_B^{pl} = \alpha_B - \beta_B q_B = \mu_k + \mu_o$ and $p_A^{pl} = \alpha_A - \beta_A q_A = \mu_o$ to obtain

$$q_B^{pl} = \frac{\alpha_B - \mu_k - \mu_o}{\beta_B} \quad \text{and} \quad q_A^{pl} = \frac{\alpha_A - \mu_o}{\beta_A}. \tag{6.56}$$

Now, check if B is indeed the peak season so that $q_A^{pl} \le q_B^{pl}$. If this is the case, then set the capacity level to $k^{pl} = q_B^{pl}$ and *stop here*. If this is not the case continue to *Step III* as you have reached the *shifting-peak* case.

Step III: Sum up vertically the two demand functions and equate this sum to the sum of marginal capacity and marginal operating costs

$$\sum_{A,B} p^v(k) = \alpha_A + \alpha_B - (\beta_A + \beta_B)k = \mu_k + 2\mu_o, \tag{6.57}$$

which obtains the desired capacity level

$$k^{pl} = q_A^{pl} = q_B^{pl} = \frac{\alpha_A + \alpha_B - \mu_k - 2\mu_o}{\beta_A + \beta_B}. \tag{6.58}$$

Step IV: Substitute $k^{pl} = q_A^{pl} = q_B^{pl}$ into each demand function to obtain the price in each season

$$\begin{aligned} p_A^{pl} &= \frac{\alpha_A \beta_B - \beta_A(\alpha_B - \mu_k - 2\mu_o)}{\beta_A + \beta_B}, \\ p_B^{pl} &= \frac{\alpha_B \beta_A - \beta_B(\alpha_A - \mu_k - 2\mu_o)}{\beta_A + \beta_B}. \end{aligned} \tag{6.59}$$

Using the steps listed above, we now modify Algorithm 6.1, designed for maximizing profit, to an algorithm used by a regulator seeking to maximize social welfare. Note that this algorithm is valid as long as there are no fixed costs, $\phi = 0$. The explanation of Algorithm 6.3 and the variable inputting required for running this program are very much the same as the ones described for Algorithm 6.1 and therefore will not be repeated here.

```
peak ← 0; off ← 0; /* Initialization                                    */
if (α[1] − μ_k − μ_o)/β[1] ≥ (α[2] − μ_o)/β[2] then
  └ peak ← 1; off ← 2; /* Season 1 is peak, 2 is off-peak             */
if (α[2] − μ_k − μ_o)/β[2] ≥ (α[1] − μ_o)/β[1] then
  └ peak ← 2; off ← 1; /* Season 2 is peak, 1 is off-peak             */
if peak ≠ 0 then
  │ /* Fixed-peak case                                                */
  │ p[peak] ← μ_k + μ_o; q[peak] ← (α[peak] − μ_k − μ_o)/β[peak];
  │ p[off] ← μ_o; q[off] ← (α[off] − μ_o)/β[off]; writeln (peak," is the peak
  │ season, and the seller should invest in k^{pl} = ", q[peak], " units of
  │ capacity."); writeln ("The peak season price should be set to ", p[peak],
  │ "The off-peak season price should be set to ", p[off]); writeln ("The
  │ peak season demand equals full capacity, q[peak], "The off-peak season
  └ demand is ", q[off]);
if peak = 0 then
  │ /* Shifting-peak case                                             */
  │ k ← (α[1] + α[2] − μ_k − 2μ_o)/(β[1] + β[2]); p[1] ← α[1] − β[1]k;
  │ p[2] ← α[2] − β[2]k; y^{pl} ← (p[1] − μ_k − μ_o)k + (p[2] − μ_o)k − φ;
  │ writeln ("Shifting peak case so q[1] = q[2] = k^{pl}. The seller should
  │ invest in k^{pl} = ", k, " units of capacity."); writeln ("The price in season 1
  └ should be set to ", p[1], "and in season 2 to ", p[2]);
```

Algorithm 6.3: Two seasons: Welfare-maximizing peak-load pricing.

6.7.3   Multi-season pricing: A three-season example

We now modify the three-season analysis of Section 6.5.1 to apply to a pricing decision made by a welfare-maximizing regulator, instead of by a profit-maximizing service provider. This modification is rather simple as it basically involves changing to marginal cost pricing instead of equating marginal revenues to marginal costs, and therefore will be presented here without extensive discussions. Similar to Section 6.5.1, suppose that the demand functions during summer, winter, and fall are given by

$$p_S = 200 − q_S, \quad p_W = 100 − q_W, \quad \text{and} \quad p_F = 200 − \frac{q_F}{2}. \tag{6.60}$$

Figure 6.5 depicts the three demand functions (6.60). Figure 6.5 also plots the marginal operating cost $\mu_o = \$20$ and two examples of sums of marginal capacity and operating costs.

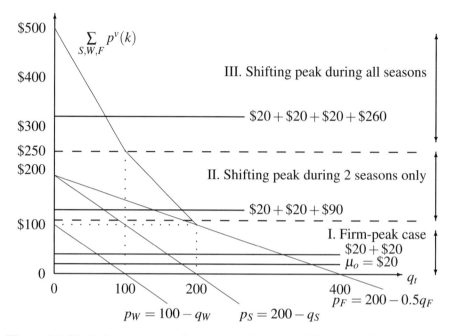

Figure 6.5: Vertical summation of summer, winter, and fall demand functions and three regions corresponding to the marginal capacity cost μ_k. *Note:* Regions do not necessarily coincide with the kinks of $\sum p^v$.

The vertical sum of the three demand functions (6.60) is given by

$$\sum_{S,W,F} p^v(k) = \begin{cases} 500 - \frac{5k}{2} & \text{if } 0 < k \le 100 \\ 400 - \frac{3k}{2} & \text{if } 100 < k \le 200 \\ 200 - \frac{k}{2} & \text{if } 200 < k \le 400 \\ 0 & \text{if } k > 400. \end{cases} \tag{6.61}$$

Figure 6.5 illustrates three regions divided by dashed lines corresponding to increasing levels of the marginal capacity cost parameter μ_k, which we analyze in this section.

Region I. Multiple seasons with a fixed peak

Under a relatively low marginal capacity cost, fall turns out to be the peak season. So, suppose that $\mu_k = \mu_o = \$20$, which is plotted as the bottom horizontal line in Figure 6.5. If fall is the peak season, the seller should attribute all marginal costs to fall passengers. Hence,

$$P_F = 200 - \frac{q_F}{2} = \$20 + \$20 = \$40 \implies q_F^{pl} = 320. \tag{6.62}$$

Next, for the off-peak seasons spring and winter, the seller should attribute the marginal operating cost $\mu_o = \$20$ only so that

$$p_S = 200 - q_S = \$20 \implies q_S^{pl} = 180, \tag{6.63}$$
$$p_W = 100 - q_W = \$20 \implies q_W^{pl} = 80.$$

Clearly, fall is the peak season because $q_F^{pl} > \max\{q_S^{pl}, q_W^{pl}\}$.

Region II. Multiple seasons with shifting peak in two seasons only

Under intermediate values of the marginal capacity cost μ_k, shifting peak may occur between two seasons only, whereas the third season will serve a small number of customers with no shifting peak. Therefore, suppose now that $\mu_k = \$90$. The sum $\mu_o + \mu_k$ is plotted as a solid horizontal line in Region II of Figure 6.5.

We first check whether fall is a peak season. If fall is the peak season, then the seller should solve $p_F = 200 - q_F/2 = \$20 + \$90$, yielding $q_F = 180$. However, during the off-peak summer season, the seller solves $p_S = 200 - q_S = \$20$, yielding $q_S = 180 = q_F$, implying that this is a borderline case between the fixed- and shift-peak cases. We proceed by solving it as a shifting-peak case, which should yield the same result as solving it under the fixed-peak case.

Next, suppose that shifting peak occurs between fall and summer, but not between winter and any other season. In this case, the seller should equate the vertical sum of the fall and winter demand to the sum of capacity and operating costs so that

$$\sum_{F,S} p^v(k) = 200 - \frac{k}{2} + 200 - k = 400 - \frac{3k}{2} = \$20 + \$20 + \$90 = 2\mu_o + \mu_k. \tag{6.64}$$

Therefore,

$$k^{pl} = q_F^{pl} = q_S^{pl} = 180, \quad \text{hence} \quad p_F^{pl} = \$110 \quad \text{and} \quad p_S^{pl} = \$20. \tag{6.65}$$

For the remaining off-peak winter season, the seller should solve

$$p_W = 100 - q_W = \$20 \implies q_W^{pl} = 80. \tag{6.66}$$

To verify that winter is indeed an off-peak season, observe that $q_W^{pl} = 80 < 180 = k^{pl}$.

Region III. Multiple seasons with shifting peak in all seasons

For sufficiently high values of the marginal capacity cost parameter μ_k, shifting peak occurs among all seasons. In this case, the seller equates the vertical sum of all demand functions to the sum of all marginal costs. Formally, if $\mu_k = \$260$ and $\mu_o = \$20$,

$$\sum_{F,W,S} p^v(k) = 200 - \frac{k}{2} + 200 - k + 100 - k = 500 - \frac{5k}{2} = \$20 + \$20 + \$20 + \$260$$

$$= 3\mu_o + \mu_k \implies k^{pl} = q_F^{pl} = q_S^{pl} = q_W^{pl} = 72. \quad (6.67)$$

Therefore,

$$p_F^{pl} = \$164, \quad p_S^{pl} = \$128, \quad \text{and} \quad p_W^{pl} = \$28. \quad (6.68)$$

6.7.4 Multi-season pricing: General formulation for public utility

The three-season example of Section 6.7.3 hints at the method for determining peak-load pricing when there are more than two seasons. This method consists of the following steps:

Step I: Equate $p_t = \alpha_t - \beta_t q_t = \mu_k + \mu_o$ and solve for q_t for each season $t = 1, \ldots, T$. Find the highest q_t, and set $\hat{t} = \text{argmax}_{t=1,\ldots,T}\{q_t\}$. If $q_t \leq q_{\hat{t}}$ for all $t \neq \hat{t}$, skip to Step V as $\hat{t}$ is the fixed-peak season.

Step II: Equate $p_t = \alpha_t - \beta_t q_t = \mu_k + 2\mu_o$ and solve for q_t for each season $t = 1, \ldots, T$. Find the two highest q_ts, and label them $\hat{t}_1$ and $\hat{t}_2$. If $q_t \leq \min\{q_{\hat{t}_1}, q_{\hat{t}_2}\}$ for all $t \neq \hat{t}_1$ and $t \neq \hat{t}_2$, skip to Step V as $\hat{t}_1$ and $\hat{t}_2$ are shifting-peak seasons, whereas all others are off-peak seasons.

Step III: Equate $p_t = \alpha_t - \beta_t q_t = \mu_k + 3\mu_o$ and solve for q_t for each season $t = 1, \ldots, T$. Find the three highest q_ts, and label them $\hat{t}_1$, $\hat{t}_2$, and $\hat{t}_3$. If $q_t \leq \min\{q_{\hat{t}_1}, q_{\hat{t}_2}, q_{\hat{t}_3}\}$ for all $t \neq \hat{t}_1$, $t \neq \hat{t}_2$, and $t \neq \hat{t}_3$, skip to Step V as $\hat{t}_1$, $\hat{t}_2$, and $\hat{t}_3$ are shifting-peak seasons, whereas all others are off-peak seasons.

Step IV: Repeat the above procedure for $4, 5, \ldots, T$ shifting-peak seasons.

Step V: For each off-peak season t, set $p_t = \mu_o$ and extract q_t from $\alpha_t - \beta_t q_t = \mu_o$ (marginal operating cost only). Next, sum up vertically the inverse demand functions of all peak seasons, and solve for the profit-maximizing capacity level k from $\sum_{\text{peak}} p^v(k) = \mu_k + n \cdot \mu_o$, where n is the number of peak seasons. Compute prices directly from the inverse demand functions so that $p_t = \alpha_t - \beta_t k$.

The above procedure can be put into a computer program such as Algorithm 6.4. This algorithm assumes $T \geq 2$ seasons indexed by $t = 1, \ldots, T$. Each season t is characterized by a downward-sloping linear demand function $p = \alpha[t] - \beta[t]q$. The computer program described below should input and store the number of seasons T and the demand parameters onto two strictly positive real-valued arrays, $\alpha[t]$ and $\beta[t]$. The program should also input the seller's nonnegative

```
Stop ← no; /* Initialization                                                  */
for i = 1 to T do
    /* Main loop over the number of shifting-peak seasons */
    if Stop = no then
        n ← i; Stop ← yes; q[i] ← (α[i] − μ_k − i · μ_o)/(β[i]);
            peak[i] ← {t : i highest q_t}; /* set has i elements           */
        for t ∉ peak[i] do
            q[t] ← (α[t] − μ_o)/(β[t]); /* Off-peak levels              */
            for s ∈ peak[i] do  if q_t > q_s then Stop ← no;

for t ∈ peak[n] do  α_Σ ← α[t]; β_Σ ← β[t];
/* Sum up vertically peak demand functions                          */
k ← (α_Σ − μ_k − n · μ_o)/(β_Σ); /* Capacity level                  */
writeln ("The peak is shifting across", n, "seasons."); writeln ("The service
provider should invest in ", k, "units of capacity");
for t ∈ peak[n] do
    p[t] ← α[t] − β[t] · k; /* Peak prices                          */
    writeln ("Set the price in peak season", t, "to p^{pl} =", p[t])
for t ∉ peak[n] do
    p[t] ← μ_o; writeln ("Set the price in off-peak season", t, "to p^{pl} =", p[t],
        "and serve q^{pl} =",q[t], customers."); /* Off-peak           */
```

Algorithm 6.4: Multiple seasons: Profit-maximizing peak-load pricing.

cost parameters μ_k (marginal capacity cost) and μ_o (marginal operating cost). As we discussed earlier, we assume that there are no fixed costs, $\phi = 0$.

Algorithm 6.4 basically follows the steps listed above. The main idea is to find which seasons should be classified as having a shifting peak by running a loop over i, where the variable $i \in \mathbb{N}^+$ is the number of seasons with a shifting peak. Therefore, $i = 1$ is a fixed-peak season case. $i = 2$ is a case in which a shifting peak occurs in two seasons, and so on.

For a given i, the program computes $q[t]$ from $\alpha[t] - \beta[t]q[t] = \mu_k + i \cdot \mu_o$ and selects the i seasons with the highest $q[t]$. Clearly, one should write a procedure for this selection, which is not given here. The i indexes of these seasons are stored in the set $peak[i]$, which is the candidate set of seasons with a shifting peak. Note that the number of sets $peak[i]$ containing the indexes of peak seasons could be between 1 and T, depending on the value of i in the loop over i when the variable $Stop$ is assigned with a yes. Then, the program must confirm that the service levels during off-peak seasons do not exceed capacity k. If this is the case, then the variable $Stop$ is assigned with a yes and the number of seasons with shifting peak i is assigned to the n, where $n \in \mathbb{N}^+$. After that, only the set $peak[n]$ is used as the set of indexes of all peak seasons.

Once the variable *Stop* is assigned with a *yes*, the program constructs the vertical sum of the marginal revenue functions of all peak seasons then computes the prices. Lastly, off-peak season prices as well as the profit are also computed.

6.8   Demand, Cost, and the Lengths of Seasons

Our analysis has so far abstracted from analyzing the precise relationship among the specification of demand functions, the cost of investing in capacity, and the duration of each season. To see why improper specification of these may result in computation errors, consider the LUFTPAPA Airlines example of Sections 6.2.1 and 6.3.1, where q_S and q_W denote the total number of passengers during the summer and winter, respectively. We have shown that if summer is a fixed-peak season, the airline invests in $k = q_S \geq q_W$ units of capacity. However, this result may be falsely interpreted that this airlines maintains a capacity level that enables it to serve q_S passengers at each moment in time. For example, if the airline serves 2 million passengers, our specification implies that this airline has the potential of flying 2 million passengers at the same time on its existing fleet of aircraft. If the average aircraft capacity is 200 passengers, this interpretation implies that LUFTPAPA Airlines must acquire $10,000$ airplanes, which is impossible.

The above-mentioned inconsistency can also be demonstrated by looking at electrical power plants. If consumers of electricity use a few billion of kilowatt-hours of electricity in a given season, this does not imply that the power plant should maintain a capacity of this magnitude at each hour during this season. In this case, what matters is whether the electric company invests in a sufficient amount of capacity that would enable it to supply the flow of electricity demanded at each point in time. These issues have been carefully investigated by Wilson (1972), who reconciled the Steiner (1957) approach, used so far in this book, with Williamson (1966), who proposed a solution to peak-load pricing with seasons of unequal lengths.

A successful implementation of profitable peak-load pricing schemes depends on proper definitions of the duration of service, the lengths of seasons and cycles, and the marginal capacity and operating costs. These definitions must be consistent with respect to their time dimension, as we demonstrate in Table 6.3. Table 6.3 demonstrates that before any analysis of peak-load pricing (in fact, before setting any price) the seller must specify the duration upon which the service is measured. In Table 6.3, electricity is measured in kilowatt-hours, which is the standard measure used by all electric companies. Then, μ_o is the operating cost associated with increasing electricity output by one kilowatt-hour. Notice that services are generally classified as flow goods, which means that once they are consumed, they must be reproduced for additional consumption. Thus, μ_o should also be treated as a

Industry	Electricity	Hotel
Service μ_o (operating)	Kilowatt-hours per kilowatt-hour	Rooms per night per room per night
Cycle μ_k (capacity)	24 hours per kilowatt over 24 hours	365 days per room over 1 year
Season A Season B	Daytime (8 hours) Nighttime (16 hours)	Summer (120 days) Winter (245 days)

Table 6.3: Examples of consistent definitions of durations of service, seasons, cycles, and marginal capacity and operating costs.

"flow cost" in the sense that each additional kilowatt-hour bears an additional cost of μ_o, which includes the cost of extra fuel, depreciation, and labor associated with increasing production on an existing generator. This does not include the cost of buying or leasing a generator, which is a cost of a stock good classified as capacity cost.

Next, after defining the service and the corresponding marginal operating cost, Table 6.3 defines a cycle that is the time interval associated with one full cycle of all seasons. In this chapter, the marginal capacity cost μ_k is defined as the cost of a small increase in capacity (stock of capital) *over one full cycle*. In our electricity example, this is the cost per one day of increasing generation capacity by one kilowatt. Lastly, Table 6.3 defines the seasons embedded in a cycle and the duration of seasons in the same units of time as those that define the service itself. Thus, if service is measured by kilowatt-hours, durations of seasons and cycles must also be measured in terms of hours.

According to Table 6.3, hotel services are measured by the number of guests per night, where we assume that each guest occupies exactly one room. Alternatively, one can simply define the unit of service as a room per night. Under these interpretations, μ_o is the operating cost of accommodating one additional guest (or renting one additional room), which includes the cost of cleaning and meals (if included with room rental). Given that service is measured per one night, a cycle may be defined as one year (365 days), and hence, the cost of one additional guest/room capacity should be measured per one full year. Lastly, the summer and winter seasons should also be measured in terms of days so that the sum of the duration of all seasons equals exactly one year.

6.8.1 Daytime and nighttime supply of electricity: Examples

In this section, we explore the electricity supply example displayed in the middle column of Table 6.3. We analyze the single monopoly problem as well as the problem solved by a regulator of a public utility. The hotel example displayed in the right column of Table 6.3 is solved in Exercise 8 at the end of this chapter.

Monopoly's electricity pricing

Consider a single supplier of electricity who determines the price of kilowatt-hours during daytime p_D and during nighttime p_N. The duration of seasons and the way in which marginal costs are measured are described in the middle column of Table 6.3. Let the demand function during each hour in each season be given by $p_D = 200 - q_D$ and $p_N = 100 - q_N$. It is very important to emphasize again that because q_D and q_N are measured in kilowatt-hours, these two linear demand functions represent the quantity of electricity during each hour of the day or night, respectively. That is, the demand for electricity is a flow.

Because the demand for electricity is a flow measured in kilowatt-hours, the total quantity demanded during daytime is $8q_D$, whereas the total quantity demanded during nighttime is $16q_N$. Suppose now that the marginal costs are $\mu_k = \mu_o = 20\cent$ per kilowatt-hour. In view of Section 6.2, in the fixed-peak season case, if day is the peak season, the profit-maximizing per-hour electricity supply during daytime and nighttime is determined from

$$8MR_D(q_D) = 8(200 - 2q_D) \;=\; 20\cent + 8 \cdot 20\cent = \mu_k + 8\mu_o,$$
$$16MR_W(q_W) = 16(100 - 2q_W) \;=\; 16 \cdot 20\cent = 16\mu_o. \tag{6.69}$$

Therefore,

$$q_D^{pl} = k^{pl} = \frac{355}{4} \approx 88.75 \quad \text{and} \quad q_N^{pl} = 40 < k^{pl}, \tag{6.70}$$

which confirms that daytime is indeed the peak season. Observe that we need to verify only that $q_N^{pl} < q_D^{pl}$ and not that $16q_N^{pl} < 8q_D^{pl}$ because q_D and q_N are flows that any capacity level satisfying $k \geq q_D$ can accommodate each hour. Next, substituting the quantity demanded into the demand functions yields

$$p_D^{pl} = 200 - q_D^{pl} = \frac{445}{4} \approx 111.25\cent \quad \text{and} \quad p_N^{pl} = 100 - q_N^{pl} = 60\cent. \tag{6.71}$$

Hence, total profit over one full cycle (one day) is

$$y^{pl} = 8(p_D^{pl} - \mu_o)k^{pl} + 16(p_N^{pl} - \mu_o)q_N^{pl} - \mu_k k^{pl} - \phi = \frac{177,225}{2} - \phi. \tag{6.72}$$

Let us now explore a shifting-peak example by "raising" the marginal capacity cost to $\mu_k = 880\cent$. In view of Section 6.3, we first prove that daytime is not a peak season. Suppose that daytime is the peak season. Then, the seller determines the capacity level by solving $8MR_D(q_D) = 8(200 - 2q_D) = 880\cent + 8 \cdot 20\cent = \mu_k + 8\mu_o$, yielding $q_D = k = 35$. The nighttime demand is found by solving $16MR_W(q_W) = 16(100 - 2q_W) = 16 \cdot 20\cent = 16\mu_o$, yielding $q_N = 40 > 35 = k$, implying that daytime is not a peak season. Suppose instead that nighttime is the peak season. Then, the seller determines the capacity level by solving $16MR_N(q_N) = 16(100 - 2q_N) = 880¢ + 16 \cdot 20¢ = \mu_k + 16\mu_o$, yielding $q_N = k = 12.5$. In this case, daytime demand is found from $8MR_D(q_D) = 8(200 - 2q_D) = 8 \cdot 20¢ = 8\mu_o$, yielding $q_D = 90 > k$, implying that nighttime is also not a peak season. This proves that a shifting-peak season case prevails.

Under the shifting-peak season case, the profit-maximizing electricity generation capacity is found by equating the vertical sum of the marginal revenue functions to the sum of marginal costs so that

$$\sum_{D,N} MR^v(k) = 8(200 - 2k) + 16(100 - 2k) = 880 + 24 \cdot 20 = \mu_k + 24\mu_o$$

$$\implies k^{pl} = \frac{115}{3} \approx 38.33. \quad (6.73)$$

Observe that the marginal operating costs μ_o (and also marginal capacity cost, μ_k) in (6.73) are measured over a full cycle of 24 hours. Substituting into the inverse demand function yields

$$p_D^{pl} = 200 - k^{pl} = \frac{485}{3} \approx 161.66¢, \quad (6.74)$$

$$p_N^{pl} = 100 - k^{pl} = \frac{185}{3} \approx 61.66¢.$$

Clearly, nighttime electricity turns out to be cheaper than daytime electricity. Finally, total profit under the shifting-peak season case is computed by

$$y^{pl} = 8(p_D^{pl} - \mu_o)k^{pl} + 16(p_N^{pl} - \mu_o)k^{pl} - \mu_k k^{pl} - \phi = \frac{105,800}{3} - \phi. \quad (6.75)$$

Electricity supply by a regulated public utility

Consider the regulator analyzed in Section 6.7, who sets prices that maximize social welfare. Also, assume now that there are no fixed costs, so $\phi = 0$. Let $\mu_k = \mu_o = 20¢$ per kilowatt-hour. If daytime is a fixed-peak season, the regulator equates the daytime price to the sum of all marginal costs and the nighttime price to marginal operating cost only, so

$$8p_D = 8(200 - q_D) = 20¢ + 8 \cdot 20¢ = \mu_k + 8\mu_o,$$
$$16p_W = 16(100 - q_W) = 16 \cdot 20¢ = 16\mu_o. \quad (6.76)$$

Therefore,

$$q_D^{pl} = k^{pl} = \frac{355}{2} \approx 177.5 \quad \text{and} \quad q_N^{pl} = 80 < k^{pl}, \quad (6.77)$$

which confirms that daytime is indeed the peak season.

We now explore a shifting-peak case by "raising" the marginal capacity cost to $\mu_k = 880¢$. We first prove that daytime is not a peak season. If daytime is the peak season, the regulator determines the capacity level by solving $8p_D = 8(200 - q_D) = 880¢ + 8 \cdot 20¢ = \mu_k + 8\mu_o$, yielding $q_D = k = 70$. The nighttime demand is found by solving $16p_W = 16(100 - q_W) = 16 \cdot 20¢ = 16\mu_o$, yielding $q_N = 80 > 70 = k$, implying that daytime is not a peak season. If nighttime is the peak season, the regulator determines the capacity level by solving $16p_N(q_N) = 16(100 - q_N) = 880¢ + 16 \cdot 20¢ = \mu_k + 16\mu_o$, yielding $q_N = k = 75$. In this case, daytime demand is found from $8p_D(q_D) = 8(200 - q_D) = 8 \cdot 20¢ = 8\mu_o$, yielding $q_D = 180 > k$ implying that nighttime is also not a peak season. This proves that a shifting-peak case prevails.

Under the shifting-peak season case, the socially optimal electricity generation capacity is determined by equating the vertical sum of the inverse demand functions to the sum of marginal costs so that

$$\sum_{D,N} p^v(k) = 8(200 - k) + 16(100 - k) = 880 + 24 \cdot 20 = \mu_k + 24\mu_o$$

$$\implies k^{pl} = \frac{230}{3} \approx 76.66. \quad (6.78)$$

Substituting into the inverse demand function yields

$$p_D^{pl} = 200 - k^{pl} = \frac{370}{3} \approx 123.33¢, \quad (6.79)$$

$$p_N^{pl} = 100 - k^{pl} = \frac{70}{3} \approx 23.33¢.$$

Again, we obtain the result that the nighttime price of electricity should be lower than the daytime electricity price.

6.8.2 General formulations

This section extends the previous examples to any number of seasons with an arbitrary duration of each season. Assume that there are $T \geq 2$ seasons in one full cycle, where each season is indexed by i, $i = 1, 2, \ldots, T$. Let D_i denote the *duration* of each season (in terms of minutes, hours, days, weeks, or months), and let q_i denote the quantity demanded for the flow of service generated at each moment in time, corresponding to the duration of season i. For example, in the electricity example in Table 6.3, $D_D = 8$ hours, $D_N = 16$ hours, and the corresponding q_D and q_N are measured in kilowatt-hours, precisely because durations of seasons are also measured in terms of hours.

General formulation for two seasons: Monopoly supplier

Suppose that one cycle consists of two seasons labeled A and B. The duration of seasons A and B are D_A and D_B units of time, respectively. q_A and q_B denote the demand for the service per unit of time during seasons A and B, respectively. The prices for the service (per service unit, per unit of time) are denoted by p_A and p_B. Linear demand functions are assumed so that $p_A = \alpha_A - \beta_A q_A$ and $p_B = \alpha_B - \beta_B q_B$, where α_A, α_B, β_A, and β_B are all strictly positive parameters to be estimated by the econometrician of the firm.

If season A is a peak season, the seller should solve

$$\begin{aligned} D_A MR_A(q_A) = D_A(\alpha_A - 2\beta_A q_A) &= \mu_k + D_A \mu_o, \\ D_B MR_B(q_B) = D_B(\alpha_B - 2\beta_B q_B) &= D_B \mu_o, \end{aligned} \qquad (6.80)$$

yielding

$$k^{pl} = q_A^{pl} = \frac{D_A(\alpha_A - \mu_A) - \mu_k}{2D_A \beta_A} \quad \text{and} \quad q_B^{pl} = \frac{\alpha_B - \mu_o}{2\beta_B}. \qquad (6.81)$$

Clearly, it must be verified at this stage that season A is the peak season by checking whether $q_B^{pl} \le k^{pl}$. Otherwise, one should check whether season B might be the peak season (we do not do it here), or whether a shifting-peak case is encountered. At this stage, one can also investigate how demand in each season is affected by extending the duration of the season. More precisely, (6.81) implies that

$$\frac{dk^{pl}}{dD_A} = \frac{dq_A^{pl}}{dD_A} = \frac{\mu_k}{2\beta_A D_A^2} > 0 \quad \text{and} \quad \frac{dq_B^{pl}}{dD_A} = 0. \qquad (6.82)$$

Thus, an increase in the duration of the peak season results in a higher investment in service capacity, and hence in the flow of service provided during the peak season. In contrast, the off-peak service flow is invariant with respect to changes in the duration of seasons. This is because at each point in time during the off-peak season, consumers are charged proportionally to the flow of marginal operating cost only. In contrast, prolonging the peak season implies that the cost of capacity is spread over a longer period of time, which permits a higher investment in capacity.

To conclude the general formulation of the two-season analysis for a single profit-maximizing seller, the prices are computed by

$$\begin{aligned} p_A^{pl} &= \alpha_A - \beta_A q_A^{pl} = \frac{D_A(\alpha_A + \mu_o) + \mu_k}{2D_A}, \\ p_B^{pl} &= \alpha_B - \beta_B q_B^{pl} = \frac{\alpha_B + \mu_o}{2}. \end{aligned} \qquad (6.83)$$

Clearly, $dp_A^{pl}/dD_A < 0$ implies that the peak-season price drops with an increase in the duration of the peak season because the cost of capital is spread over a longer peak season. The off-peak season price does not vary with the duration of the season because consumers are charged proportionally to the flow of operating cost only. Finally, the profit level for the case in which season A is the fixed peak is computed by substituting (6.81) and (6.83) into

$$y^{pl} = D_A(p_A^{pl} - \mu_o)k^{pl} + D_B(p_B^{pl} - \mu_o)q_B^{pl} - \mu_k k^{pl} - \phi. \qquad (6.84)$$

Note that the terms $(p_i^{pl} - \mu_o)q_i^{pl}$ for $i = A, B$ capture the proceeds from the sale of flows, and therefore must be multiplied by the corresponding duration D_i to obtain the profit from each season. Only then can capacity and fixed costs be subtracted.

Suppose now that the above computations yield that $q_B^{pl} > k^{pl}$, which implies that A is not a peak season. Suppose also, using similar computations, that it turns out that B is also not a peak season. Then, a *shifting-peak* case occurs. Under a shifting-peak season case, the profit-maximizing investment in service capacity is determined by

$$D_A MR_A(k) + D_B MR_B(k) = D_A(\alpha_A - 2\beta_A k) + D_B(\alpha_B - 2\beta_B k)$$
$$= \mu_k + (D_A + D_B)\mu_o. \quad (6.85)$$

Observe that the marginal operating cost on the right-hand side of (6.85) is multiplied by the entire duration of one full cycle, which is equal to $D_A + D_B$. This follows from our assumption that service levels are measured as flows per unit of time, which implies that operating costs are also flows and therefore must be multiplied by the length of time under which the service is consumed. Therefore,

$$k^{pl} = q_A^{pl} = q_B^{pl} = \frac{D_A(\alpha_A - \mu_o) + D_B(\alpha_B - \mu_o) - \mu_k}{2(D_A\beta_A + D_B\beta_B)}. \quad (6.86)$$

Comparing (6.86) with (6.81) reveals that under the shifting-peak case, the duration of all seasons affects the determination of the profit-maximizing capacity level (and not only the duration of the peak season). Substituting (6.86) into the inverse demand functions yields the profit-maximizing price in each season:

$$p_A^{pl} = \frac{\beta_A\mu_k + \beta_A\mu_o(D_A + D_B) + D_A\alpha_A\beta_A + D_B(2\alpha_A\beta_B - \alpha_B\beta_A)}{2(D_A\beta_A + D_B\beta_B)}, \quad (6.87)$$

$$p_B^{pl} = \frac{\beta_B\mu_k + \beta_B\mu_o(D_A + D_B) + D_B\alpha_B\beta_B + D_A(2\alpha_B\beta_A - \alpha_A\beta_B)}{2(D_A\beta_A + D_B\beta_B)}.$$

Thus, under the shifting-peak case, the price in each season is affected by the duration of all seasons. Finally, the monopoly's profit under the shifting-peak case can be computed by substituting (6.86) and (6.87) directly into (6.84).

General formulation for two seasons: Regulated public utility

We slightly modify the above analysis to solve the pricing problem faced by a regulator of a public utility. Thus, instead of equating marginal revenue to the relevant marginal costs as in (6.80), a regulator who maximizes social welfare equates prices to the relevant marginal costs, so for the case in which season A is a peak season,

$$D_A p_A(q_A) = D_A(\alpha_A - \beta_A q_A) = \mu_k + D_A\mu_o,$$
$$D_B p_B(q_B) = D_B(\alpha_B - \beta_B q_B) = D_B\mu_o, \quad (6.88)$$

yielding

$$k^{pl} = q_A^{pl} = \frac{D_A(\alpha_A - \mu_o) - \mu_k}{D_A\beta_A} \quad \text{and} \quad q_B^{pl} = \frac{\alpha_B - \mu_o}{\beta_B}. \tag{6.89}$$

Clearly, at this stage it must be verified that season A is the peak season by checking whether $q_B^{pl} \leq k^{pl}$. Otherwise, one should check whether season B might be the peak season (we do not do it here), or whether a shifting-peak case is encountered. Substituting (6.89) into the inverse demand functions obtains the prices set by a regulator when A is the peak season. Therefore,

$$p_A^{pl} = \alpha_A - \beta_A q_A^{pl} = \mu_o + \frac{\mu_k}{D_A} \quad \text{and} \quad p_B^{pl} = \alpha_B - \beta_B q_B^{pl} = \mu_o. \tag{6.90}$$

Thus, the peak price should be equal to the marginal operating cost plus the cost of capacity divided by the duration of the peak season. The off-peak season price should be equal to the marginal operating cost only, because some capacity remains idle.

Under the shifting-peak case, the socially optimal investment in service capacity is determined by

$$D_A p_A(k) + D_B p_B(k) = D_A(\alpha_A - \beta_A k) + D_B(\alpha_B - \beta_B k)$$
$$= \mu_k + (D_A + D_B)\mu_o. \tag{6.91}$$

Observe again that the marginal operating cost on the right-hand side of (6.91) is multiplied by the duration of one full cycle, which is equal to $D_A + D_B$. Therefore,

$$k^{pl} = q_A^{pl} = q_B^{pl} = \frac{D_A(\alpha_A - \mu_o) + D_B(\alpha_B - \mu_o) - \mu_k}{D_A\beta_A + D_B\beta_B}. \tag{6.92}$$

Comparing (6.92) with (6.89) reveals again that in a shifting-peak case, the duration of all seasons influences the determination of the profit-maximizing capacity level (rather than the duration of the peak season only). Substituting (6.92) into the inverse demand functions yields the socially optimal price in each season:

$$p_A^{pl} = \frac{\beta_A\mu_k + \beta_A\mu_o(D_A + D_B) + D_B(\alpha_A\beta_B - \alpha_B\beta_A)}{D_A\beta_A + D_B\beta_B}, \tag{6.93}$$

$$p_B^{pl} = \frac{\beta_B\mu_k + \beta_B\mu_o(D_A + D_B) + D_A(\alpha_B\beta_A - \alpha_A\beta_B)}{D_A\beta_A + D_B\beta_B}.$$

As with the monopoly shifting-peak case, the price in each season is affected by the duration of all seasons.

General formulation for multiple seasons: Monopoly supplier

Suppose now that the firm sells in T seasons, where the inverse demand function for this service at each unit of time in season i is given by $p_i = \alpha_i - \beta_i q_i$, $i =$

$1, 2, \ldots, T$. The parameters α_i and β_i are all strictly positive and are to be estimated by the econometrician of the firm. The reader is now referred to Section 6.5.2 which describes the general procedure for determining which seasons should be treated as peak seasons and which are off-peak seasons. This procedure should be slightly modified to take into account the more general formulation that assumes that seasons may have different durations. Let D_i denote the duration of season i, $i = 1, 2, \ldots, T$.

Once the peak seasons are identified, let the set *peak* contain all the indexes i, where i is a peak season. The seller then determines the profit-maximizing capacity level k^{pl} by solving

$$\sum_{i \in peak} D_i MR_i(k) = \sum_{i \in peak} D_i(\alpha_i - 2\beta_i k) = \mu_k + \mu_o \sum_{i \in peak} D_i. \qquad (6.94)$$

Observe that the marginal operating cost on the right-hand side of (6.94) is multiplied by the sum of the duration of all peak seasons, which is equal to $\sum_{i \in peak} D_i$. This is because service levels q_i are measured as flows.

For each off-peak season $i \notin peak$, the seller determines service levels q_i by solving

$$D_i MR_i(q_i) = D_i(\alpha_i - 2\beta_i q_i) = D_i \mu_o. \qquad (6.95)$$

The socially optimal prices are then computed by substituting service levels q_i into the inverse demand functions $p_i^{pl} = \alpha_i - \beta_i q_i^{pl}$, where $q_i^{pl} = k^{pl}$ for each $i \in peak$. Total profit is then computed from

$$y^{pl} = \sum_{i \in peak} D_i(p_i^{pl} - \mu_o)k^{pl} + \sum_{i \notin peak} D_i(p_i^{pl} - \mu_o)q_i^{pl} - \mu_k k^{pl} - \phi. \qquad (6.96)$$

General formulation for multiple seasons: Regulated public utility

A regulator who seeks to maximize social welfare equates the vertical sum of demand functions of peak seasons to the sum of marginal and capacity costs. Therefore, the condition for determining the capacity level k^{pl} (6.94) is now modified to

$$\sum_{i \in peak} D_i p_i(k) = \sum_{i \in peak} D_i(\alpha_i - \beta_i k) = \mu_k + \mu_o \sum_{i \in peak} D_i. \qquad (6.97)$$

For the off-peak seasons $i \notin peak$, (6.95) is now modified to

$$D_i p_i(q_i) = D_i(\alpha_i - \beta_i q_i) = D_i \mu_o. \qquad (6.98)$$

Prices are then computed by substituting service levels q_i into the inverse demand functions $p_i^{pl} = \alpha_i - \beta_i q_i^{pl}$, where $q_i^{pl} = k^{pl}$ for each $i \in peak$.

6.9   Exercises

1. Congratulations! You have been appointed the CEO of LUFTMAMA Airlines (a partner of LUFTPAPA Airlines analyzed in Section 6.2.1). The passengers' inverse demand functions facing LUFTMAMA during summer and winter are $p_S = 12 - q_S/2$ and $p_W = 24 - 2q_W$, respectively. There are no fixed costs, so $\phi = 0$, but the marginal capacity cost and the marginal operating costs are given by $\mu_k = \mu_o = \$2$. Solve the following problems:

   (a) Compute the summer and winter airfares, assuming that LUFTMAMA implements a peak-load pricing structure.

   (b) During an election campaign, the transportation minister in your country declares that if her party gets reelected, she will require all airlines to fix their airfares during the entire year, so $p_{S,W} \stackrel{\text{def}}{=} p_S = p_W$. Compute the profit-maximizing season independent price $p_{S,W}$, and compare the resulting profit level to the profit generated by peak-load pricing.

2. Suppose that LUFTMAMA Airlines faces a sharp rise in its marginal cost parameters, so now $\mu_k = \$8$ and $\mu_o = \$4$, whereas $\phi = 0$.

   (a) Prove that winter is not a peak season.

   (b) Prove that summer is not a peak season.

   (c) Using the analysis on shifting peak of Section 6.3, compute the profit-maximizing number of passengers, the seasonal prices, and the resulting profit.

3. AIR VIVALDI operates continuously during all four seasons: fall, winter, spring, and summer. Let q_F, q_W, q_G, and q_S denote the number of passengers in these four seasons, respectively. Passengers' demand in each season is given by

$$p_F = 200 - 0.5q_F, \quad p_W = 100 - q_W,$$

$$p_G = 100 - 0.5q_G, \quad \text{and} \quad p_S = 200 - q_S.$$

   Solve the following problems:

   (a) Derive and plot each season's marginal revenue function.

   (b) Compute and plot the vertical sum of all four marginal revenue functions. *Hint*: Compare with (6.26) and Figure 6.3.

   (c) Suppose that VIVALDI's marginal operating cost is $\mu_o = \$20$, marginal capacity cost is $\mu_k = \$90$, and fixed cost is $\phi = \$10,000$. Compute the profit-maximizing price for each season, and the resulting total profit.

   (d) Solve the previous problem assuming that $\mu_o = \$20$, $\mu_k = \$340$, and $\phi = \$400$.

4. The TwoSeasons Hotel operates continuously during summer and winter. Let q_S and q_W denote the summer and winter number of vacationers, respectively. The inverse demand function is $p_S = 120 - 2q_S - q_W$ during the summer, and $p_W = 120 - 3q_W - q_S$ during the winter. Solve the following problems using the analysis of interdependent demand in Section 6.6.

   (a) Write down the summer and winter total revenue functions, and derive the corresponding four marginal revenue functions.

   (b) Suppose now that the hotel's fixed cost is $\phi = \$1000$ and marginal capacity and operating costs are $\mu_k = \mu_o = \$20$. Using the analysis of interdependent demand given in Section 6.6, compute the hotel's profit-maximizing summer and winter rates and the resulting total profit.

   (c) Solve the previous problem assuming that the hotel's cost parameters are now given by $\phi = \$500$, $\mu_k = \$40$, and $\mu_o = \$20$.

5. Suppose that LuftMama Airlines, described in Exercise 1, has been nationalized and is now being operated as a regulated public utility. Using the analysis of Section 6.7, compute the socially optimal summer and winter airfares as well as the socially optimal seating capacity.

6. Suppose that the company described in Exercise 2 has been nationalized and is now being operated as a regulated public utility. Compute the socially optimal summer and winter airfares as well as the socially optimal seating capacity.

7. Suppose that Air Vivaldi, described in Exercise 3, has been nationalized and is now being operated as a regulated public utility. Compute the socially optimal airfare in each season, as well as the socially optimal seating capacity assuming that $\mu_o = \$20$, $\mu_k = \$100$, and there are no fixed costs, $\phi = 0$.

8. As the new manager of the four-star Schlafen Hotel, you are in charge of setting room rates during the summer season, denoted by p_S, and during the winter season, denoted by p_W. The duration of the summer and winter seasons, also described in Table 6.3, are $D_S = 120$ days and $D_W = 245$ days, respectively. The marginal capacity cost (infrastructure cost of adding one additional room per one year) is $\mu_k = \$24{,}000$. The marginal operating cost (cost of cleaning up a room after it has been occupied for one night) is $\mu_o = \$20$. Finally, the inverse demand functions for rooms are given by

$$p_S = 240 - \frac{q_S}{2} \quad \text{and} \quad p_W = 240 - q_W,$$

where q_S and q_W are the number of rooms demanded during *each* summer night and *each* winter night, respectively. Solve the following problems:

(a) Compute the most profitable room rates during summer nights and winter nights, the investment in room capacity, and the resulting profit level, assuming that the SCHLAFEN Hotel is the only hotel in a 200-mile radius.

(b) Compute the socially optimal room rates during summer and winter nights and the investment in room capacity assuming the hotel is now operated as a regulated public utility.

Chapter 7
Advance Booking

7.1	**Two Booking Periods with Two Service Classes**	**232**
	7.1.1	A numerical example
	7.1.2	General formulation
	7.1.3	Salvage value of capacity
	7.1.4	Dynamic advance booking for a small population
7.2	**Multiple Periods with Two Service Classes**	**238**
	7.2.1	Single capacity unit: Example I
	7.2.2	Single capacity unit: Example II
	7.2.3	Two capacity units example
	7.2.4	Large-capacity example
7.3	**Multiple Booking Periods and Service Classes**	**245**
	7.3.1	General formulation
	7.3.2	Computer algorithm
7.4	**Dynamic Booking with Marginal Operating Cost**	**248**
	7.4.1	Converting prices to marginal profits
	7.4.2	Computer algorithm
7.5	**Network-based Dynamic Advance Booking**	**250**
	7.5.1	A numerical example
	7.5.2	General formulation
7.6	**Fixed Class Allocations**	**254**
	7.6.1	Nonoptimality of fixed class allocations
	7.6.2	How to determine fixed class allocations: An example
	7.6.3	Computer algorithm for fixed class allocations
7.7	**Nested Class Allocations**	**258**
	7.7.1	Nested class allocation versus fixed allocations
	7.7.2	How to determine nested class allocations: An example
	7.7.3	Computer algorithm for nested class allocations
	7.7.4	Protective (theft) nested capacity allocations
7.8	**Exercises**	**262**

Service providers, particularly providers of services related to travel, engage in advance booking that use a wide variety of advance reservation systems. From consumers' perspective, this practice seems to be beneficial for the following two reasons:

- *Value of time and capacity constraint*: Advance reservations save considerable amount of time for consumers as otherwise they would have to travel several times to the theater, airport, train station, or hotel, just to find out that these services may have already been fully booked.

- *Purchase of complementary services*: Travel arrangements almost always consist of a wide variety of complementary services that must be booked from multiple providers (flights, trains, hotels). In addition, travelers must alter their work schedule, which may include asking for vacation time or a leave of absence. Advance reservations ensure the fulfilment of these multiple obligations at the same time.

Whereas both of the above examples demonstrate why advance booking is beneficial to consumers, the purpose of this chapter is to show that advance booking also enhances the profit of service providers. Moreover, this chapter suggests several algorithms under which advance booking becomes the major strategic tool for making YM most profitable. Perhaps the most interesting feature of advance reservation systems is that they can be used to identify and sort consumers according to their willingness to pay without having to formally ask them to reveal their preferences. For example, students who can plan their vacation time according to semester schedules posted by their schools tend to purchase discounted advance-purchase tickets. In contrast, people who travel on business generally cannot plan their business trips in advance and therefore resort to last-minute full-price tickets. In the language of economics, well-designed advance booking mechanisms induce consumers to *reveal their preferences* and their true types by simply observing what type of service classes they book.

The formal analysis in this chapter is presented according to an increasing order of complexity associated with the number of booking periods, the number of booking classes (fare classes), and the amount of capacity. This is because profit-maximizing YM requires the use of dynamic optimization, commonly referred to as *dynamic programming*. The two booking period cases are analyzed in great detail to enable readers to gain the full intuition behind the dynamics of booking strategies. Readers who wish to avoid the entire dynamic programming analysis should skip Sections 7.1 through 7.5 and concentrate on Sections 7.6 and 7.7 only.

The analysis in this chapter assumes that time is discrete and is indexed by $t = 1, 2, \ldots, T, T+1$. Potential consumers are allowed to book during the periods $t = 1, \ldots, T$. Then, the contracted service is delivered in period $T+1$ when no further bookings can be made. The service provider announces a number of booking classes indexed by i, $i \in \mathscr{B} = \{A, B, C, \ldots\}$, and the price for each booking class (fare class) as P^A, P^B, P^C, and so on, where $P^A > P^B > P^C > \ldots$. Thus, class A is the most expensive class, followed by class B, and so on. Lastly, let $P^0 = 0$ denote a zero revenue "obtained" from a consumer who does not make a reservation. That is, for analytical convenience we treat a period when no booking is made as if a consumer requests to be booked at a class for which she has to pay $P^0 = 0$ for the service. Because prices are written in capital letters, they are treated as exogenous parameters of the model developed in this chapter (compare P in Table 1.4 with p in Table 1.5).

We denote by K the amount of service capacity, which equals the maximum possible total number of bookings that can be made in all classes combined. Hence, by the end of period T, the total number of bookings cannot exceed K.

The potential consumer population consists of a fraction, denoted by π^A, of high-valuation consumers who are willing to pay P^A for a class A service, where $0 \le \pi^A \le 1$. Similarly, π^B, π^C, and so on are the fractions of the population willing to pay for class B and class C services, respectively. Lastly, we assume that some part of the population will either not use the reservation system or will not book after contacting the reservation agent. We denote this fraction by π^0. Formally, we define $\pi^0 = 1 - \sum_{i \in \mathscr{B}} \pi^i$ as the fraction of the population who never books this service.

Most of our formal analysis also interprets the fraction π^i as the *probability* that a booking on a certain class will be made. For this interpretation to be valid, we need to distinguish between two types of potential consumer populations as described in the following definition:

DEFINITION 7.1
We say that the potential consumer population is
- **Large** *if the fractions π^i are also the probabilities that a consumer will request a booking on class $i \in \mathscr{B}$, and that these probabilities are independent of the number of bookings that have been made before this booking request.*
- **Small** *if the fractions π^i, $i \in \mathscr{B}$, reflect initial probabilities; however, they must be updated after each booking period to reflect how many bookings of each consumer type have already been made.*

Thus, for a large population, the expected composition of the consumer population remains unchanged during all booking periods and is independent of the number and type of bookings already made. This is not the case for a small population size, for which if many bookings are made for class B, the service provider should expect future bookings to consist of all classes other than class B. In this case, the probability of a consumer requesting a booking on a certain class must be updated after each booking period. Unless stated otherwise, the analysis in this book will be restricted as follows:

ASSUMPTION 7.1

The potential consumer population is large according to Definition 7.1(a).

The reader is referred to Subsection 7.1.4 where our analysis deviates from this assumption.

Before we begin describing the algorithms behind profitable advance booking systems, we must specify the timing under which reservations are made. We make the following assumption:

ASSUMPTION 7.2

In each period t, $t = 1, 2, \ldots, T$, there is at most one consumer who books the service.

Assumption 7.2 is motivated by the fact that a computer system can book at most one person at a time, because before allowing any further reservations to be made, the software must readjust the level of remaining capacity. There are two additional ways to justify the use of this assumption. First, we can assume that time periods are very short. In fact, our T-period dynamic model can easily accommodate short time periods corresponding to a large number of booking periods (higher levels of T). Second, time periods can be adjusted during the 24-hour cycle so that off-peak periods (say, late night) will be made relatively long whereas peak periods will be made very short.

Clearly, if $K \geq T$, the capacity constraint is not binding and the service provider should accept any booking request. Accordingly, we make the following assumption:

ASSUMPTION 7.3

(a) *The total amount of capacity available for booking is smaller than the number of booking periods. Formally, $K < T$.*
(b) *Overbooking is not allowed.*
(c) *Capacity can be costlessly and instantaneously shifted among the various service classes.*

Assumption 7.3(a) makes our problem interesting, as it eliminates the trivial case of excess capacity in which every booking request should be accommodated. Assumption 7.3(b) imposes a restriction on our analysis. Because overbooking is widely observed and is considered an integral part of YM, we devote an entire chapter to the entire analysis of overbooking, which is given in Chapter 9.

Assumption 7.3(c) implies that classes differ mainly according to the amount of extra services given to the customers, or by the restriction levels imposed on their tickets. In some services, however, reallocation of capacity among the different booking classes is costly and time consuming. For example, aircraft seats assigned to first-class passengers are much wider than the seats assigned to economy-class passengers. In this case, a reallocation of aircraft capacity is both costly and time consuming and therefore cannot adhere to an otherwise profit-maximizing book-ing strategy. In this situation, only fixed class allocations of capacity are possible, which we analyze in Section 7.6. However, in many instances, even physical capac-ity can be easily shifted from one class to another. For example, a railway company may replace a regular car with a more luxurious first-class car (or even a sleeper) when it observes a high demand for its first-class tickets. For this reason, most of our analysis will rely on Assumption 7.3(c).

Given that at most one consumer can be booked in each period t, let $P_t \in \{P^0, P^A, P^B, \ldots\}$ denote the price/fare for the booking class requested by a period t consumer. The reader is reminded that $P^0 = 0$ denotes the (non)revenue from a nonbooking consumer. Also, let d_t denote the *decision* rule for whether or not to accommodate a booking request by a period t consumer. This decision can be au-tomated by a computerized reservation system. $d_t = 1$ means that the reservation has been confirmed and one unit of capacity is reserved for the period t booking consumer. In contrast, $d_t = 0$ means that the period t booking request has been denied. Altogether, the period t profit can be written as $d_t(P_t - \mu_o)$, where μ_o is the marginal operating cost of providing an additional unit of service (or the marginal cost of making an additional successful booking). Finally, we assume that the marginal operating cost is zero ($\mu_o = 0$). This assumption is relaxed in Section 7.4, which demonstrates how our basic models can be easily modified to capture marginal profits associated with having strictly positive marginal operating cost.

The earliest condition for accepting or denying a consumer's booking request is attributed to Littlewood (1972). Other scientific literature on the theory of dynamic booking systems includes Lee and Hersh (1993) and Lautenbacher and Stidham (1999); see also Talluri and van Ryzin (2004, Ch. 2). Most of the analysis in this chapter uses dynamic programming. Our main purpose is to develop the logic behind the algorithm for deciding whether and what type of booking offers should be accepted by the service provider in each booking period $t = 1, 2, \ldots, T$. The solution method we use in this book is called *Bellman's principle of optimality* due to Bellman (1957). In general, the key to solving any finite-horizon dynamic optimization is to work the solution backward using backward induction. That is, we start with the last period $t = T$ and work backward period by period until the first booking period $t = 1$. Our analysis in each period t is divided into two parts:

- *Booking decision*: In each booking period t, we determine a decision rule $d_t(P_t) \in \{0, 1\}$, which indicates whether to reject or accept a booking request for the class associated with the price $P_t \in \{P^A, P^B, \ldots\}$. The period t decision rule is determined by maximizing the sum of current profit associated with the requested P_t, and all future value of remaining capacity k_{t+1}.

- *Expected value of capacity*: Given the optimal period t decision rule $d_t(P_t)$, we compute the expected value of period t available capacity, which we denote by $EV(k_t)$.

That is, each booking decision must take into account that accepting a booking in period t will reduce the amount of capacity available for booking in period $t + 1$. Formally, if a booking is accepted, the capacity available for bookings in periods $t + 1$ and on becomes $k_{t+1} = k_t - 1$. In contrast, if a booking is not made or simply denied, the amount of capacity available for booking during period $t + 1$ and on remains the same level given by $k_{t+1} = k_t$. Thus, the trade-off between accepting a current booking request and the effects of a reduction in the amount of capacity available for booking in subsequent periods is evaluated by comparing the period t price offer with the difference between the expected period $t + 1$ value of capacity resulting from a reduction in one unit of capacity. This difference is given by $EV(k_t) - EV(k_t - 1)$ if $d_t(P_t) = 1$.

7.1 Two Booking Periods with Two Service Classes

Let $t = 1, 2, 3$ denote two booking periods ending with period $t = 3$ when the service is scheduled to be delivered. Let there be two booking classes labeled class A and class B. The service provider announces the prices for these classes as P^A and P^B, where $P^A > P^B > 0$. The probabilities of booking a consumer in class A and class B in a given period are given by π^A and π^B, respectively, where $0 \le \pi^i < 1$. The probability of not booking any consumer in a given period is $\pi^0 = 1 - \pi^A - \pi^B$. To close the model, and for the sake of this demonstration only, we assume that the capacity is limited to a single consumer only so that only one booking can be made. Formally, we set $K = 1$. Subsection 7.1.1 starts with a numerical example. Subsection 7.1.2 follows with more formal and general presentations. Subsection 7.1.3 introduces salvage value of capacity into the model.

7.1.1 A numerical example

Suppose that the first-class price is $P^A = \$40$, whereas second class is offered for $P^B = \$10$. The corresponding probabilities of booking a consumer into the two classes in each given period are $\pi^A = 0.1$ and $\pi^B = 0.8$. This means that the probability that no booking is made in a given period is $\pi^0 = 0.1$. Table 7.1 summarizes the data on the potential consumer population.

Because period $t = 2$ is the last booking period, any booking request should be accepted provided that at least one unit of capacity is available. Otherwise, some capacity will remain unused in period 3 when the service is scheduled to be

Class (i)	0	A	B
Proportion (π^i)	0.1	0.1	0.8
Price/fare (P^i)	$0	$40	$10

Table 7.1: Potential consumer population under two service classes.
Note: Class 0 refers to consumers who end up not booking.

delivered. Formally, the period 2 decision rule is given by

$$d_2(P_2) = \begin{cases} 1 & \text{if } k_2 \neq 0 \\ 0 & \text{otherwise,} \end{cases} \tag{7.1}$$

which, again, means that any type of booking request should be accepted provided that capacity is not fully booked. Given the assumed probability distribution, we can now compute the period 2 expected value of capacity. Thus, in view of Table 7.1,

$$\text{EV}_2(k_2) = \begin{cases} (0.1 \times 0) + (0.1 \times 40) + (0.8 \times 10) = \$12 & \text{if } k_2 \neq 0 \\ 0 & \text{if } k_2 = 0. \end{cases} \tag{7.2}$$

Using words, equation (7.2) shows that if some capacity remains unbooked after period $t = 1$ – that is if $k_2 \neq 0$ – then because (7.1) implies that any booking request is accepted during the last period, the expected period $t = 2$ value of capacity is the expected revenue, which equals the sum of the prices offered to each consumer type multiplied by the probability that such consumer type will emerge.

Moving *backward* to period $t = 1$, recall that this simple example assumes that there is only one unit of capacity available for booking in periods $t = 1$ and $t = 2$ combined. That is, if a reservation is accepted in period $t = 1$ so that $d_1 = 1$, no capacity is left for booking in period $t = 2$. In this case, (7.2) implies that the period $t = 2$ value of capacity is $0. Altogether, total value of capacity (profit) would be $P_2 + 0$ if a booking were made in $t = 1$. In contrast, if a booking is not made in period $t = 1$, that is, if $d_1 = 0$, then (7.2) implies the expected profit in period $t = 2$ is $0 + \$12$ (because the profit in $t = 1$ becomes zero). Therefore, a period t booking request should be accepted if $P_1 \geq \text{EV}_2(1) - \text{EV}_2(0) = \$12$. Hence, the period $t = 1$ profit-maximizing decision rule is given by

$$d_1(P_1) = \begin{cases} 1 & \text{if } P_1 \geq 12 \\ 0 & \text{otherwise,} \end{cases} \quad \text{hence, } d_1(P_1) = \begin{cases} 1 & \text{if } P_1 = 40 \\ 0 & \text{if } P_1 = 10. \end{cases} \tag{7.3}$$

That is, in the first period the service provider should accept a booking request for class A only and should deny a booking request for class B. In fact, the sequence of decisions (d_1, d_2) given by (7.1) and (7.3) form the dynamic decision rule under which a profit-maximizing service provider should design its advance booking system.

Let us now compute the profit for some possible realizations of booking requests. Suppose that in period 1 a consumer requests a class B booking, meaning that $P_1 = \$10$, whereas another consumer requests a class B booking in period 2. The decision rule (7.3) implies that $d_1(\$10) = 0$ (booking request denied), whereas $d_2(\$10) = 1$ (accepted). Hence, total realized profit is $y = \$10$.

Perhaps the most interesting feature of this example is that the dynamic decision rule (d_1, d_2) that we found may profitably lead to a sequence of events in which capacity that could have been booked remains unused. This happens when a consumer who wishes to be booked into class B in period $t = 1$ is denied booking and when eventually no one is booked in period $t = 2$ as well. Formally, consider the sequence of booking requests given by $P_1 = \$10$ and $P_2 = \$0$. This sequence of events is realized with probability $\pi^B \times \pi^0 = 0.8 \times 0.1 = 0.08$, which is the probability that a class B booking request is made (and denied) in period $t = 1$ and that no booking is made in period $t = 1$. Because $d_1(\$10) = 0$ and $d_2(\$0) = 0$, the realized profit is $y = \$0$.

Finally, it may be interesting to compute the period $t = 1$ value of capacity since the value provides the key indication as to whether investing in this capacity is profitable for this service provider. The decision rule given in (7.3) and Table 7.1 implies that

$$EV_1(1) = 0.1(40 + 0) + 0.9(0 + 12) = \$14.8. \tag{7.4}$$

Equation (7.4) reflects the maximum amount of money the service provider may want to spend on buying or renting a single unit of capacity.

7.1.2   General formulation

Although specific examples are extremely helpful in demonstrating the logic behind dynamic booking strategies, they often fail to demonstrate some general rules that govern dynamic optimizations. More precisely, general formulations have some advantages over specific examples in that they can condense the optimization rules into a small number of equations that apply to every booking period t. In contrast, analyzing specific examples requires the characterization of T separate equations corresponding to each booking period.

We now formalize our simple two-booking period problem. Using general notation, the booking periods are now labeled $T - 1$ and T (which is the last booking period). The service is then delivered in period $T + 1$. Applying Bellman's principle of optimality to the present problem means that at each point of time t, the seller must choose a booking strategy to maximize the sum of expected value of capacity from period t (inclusive) until period T. The expected sum of future value of capacity is influenced by how much capacity is available for booking in future periods.

Starting with the last booking period, the seller chooses to book ($d_T = 1$) or to deny booking ($d_T = 0$), yielding the profit (revenue in this case) given by $d_T P_T$, where $P_T \in \{P^0, P^A, P^B\}$ is the booking request received in period T. Clearly, if capacity is still available in period T ($k_T \neq 0$), the seller must accept any booking request as otherwise capacity will remain underused during period $T + 1$ when the service is scheduled to be delivered. However, if no capacity is available in period T, then no decision has to be made. All this implies that the expected period T value of capacity before a booking request arrives is

$$
EV_T(k_T) = \begin{cases} (\pi^0 \times 0) + (\pi^A \times P^A) + (\pi^B \times P^B) & \text{if } k_T \neq 0 \\ 0 & \text{if } k_T = 0. \end{cases} \tag{7.5}
$$

The key feature behind (7.5) is that the expected period T value of capacity is influenced by the amount of remaining capacity at the end of period $T - 1$.

Moving backward to period $T - 1$, we have already demonstrated how the period $T - 1$ booking decision affects the period T value of capacity by controlling the amount of remaining unbooked capacity. Therefore, the period $T - 1$ profit-maximizing decision rule is given by

$$
d_{T-1}(P_{T-1}) = \begin{cases} 1 & \text{if } P_{T-1} \geq EV_T(k_{T-1}) - EV_T(k_{T-1} - 1) \\ 0 & \text{otherwise.} \end{cases} \tag{7.6}
$$

That is, a period $T - 1$ booking request should be accepted as long as the operating profit from this booking exceeds the difference between period T value function under k_T units of capacity and its value under a reduced capacity $k_{T-1} - 1$ caused by this booking. Hence, this condition reflects a trade-off between a sure profit in period $T - 1$ and an expected period T difference in the value of capacity associated with leaving one unit of unbooked capacity for period T. Finally, for the sake of completeness, the expected period $t = 1$ value of capacity is given by

$$
\begin{aligned}
EV_{T-1}(1) = {} & \pi^0 EV_2(1) \\
& + \pi^A \left\{ d_{T-1}(P^A)[P^A + EV_2(0)] + [1 - d_{T-1}(P^A)]EV_2(1) \right\} \\
& + \pi^B \left\{ d(P^B)[P^B + EV_2(0)] + [1 - d_{T-1}(P^B)]EV_2(1) \right\}. \tag{7.7}
\end{aligned}
$$

Equation (7.7) reflects the initial value of a single unit of capacity. This value should be considered during the investment stage because it indicates the maximum amount that a service provider should be willing to invest in buying or renting one unit of capacity.

7.1.3 Salvage value of capacity

Our analysis so far has assumed that failing to book the capacity before the service delivery time in period $T + 1$ results in a total loss of this capacity. In practice, some service providers can sell unused capacity at a discount price during the period when the service is delivered. Examples include airlines who sell last-minute discounted and standby tickets, as well as concert halls selling (generally to students) last-minute tickets for empty seats about 30 minutes before performances begin. In view of these observations, in this subsection we investigate the impact of salvage value on service providers' advance booking policies.

Let P^S denote the *salvage value* of capacity. That is, in the event some capacity is left unbooked in period T, the service provider can sell each unit of remaining capacity at the price P^S. We assume that $0 \leq P^S < P^B < P^A$, which means that booking a consumer at any class is more profitable than the salvage value. Consider a service provider with $T = 2$ booking periods and one unit of capacity ($K = 1$), facing the potential consumer population described in Table 7.2.

Class (i)	0	A	B	S
Proportion (π^i)	0.6	0.1	0.3	
Price/fare (P^i)	$0	$40	$10	$6

Table 7.2: Potential consumer population under two fare classes with salvage value of capacity $P^S = \$6$.

Table 7.2 shows that $P^A > P^B > P^S$, meaning that the salvage value is below the price of any booking class. Hence, the service provider should accept any booking request in the last booking period. Formally, $d_2(\$40) = d_2(\$10) = 1$. Therefore, the expected value of capacity in the last booking period is

$$EV_2(k_2) =$$
$$\begin{cases} (0.6 \times 6) + (0.1 \times 40) + (0.3 \times 10) = \$10.6 & \text{if } k_2 \neq 0 \\ 0 & \text{if } k_2 = 0. \end{cases} \quad (7.8)$$

Hence, if no booking is made in period 2 (probability 0.6), the service provider can sell the unbooked capacity for $P^S = 6$ rather than earning nothing from unbooked capacity.

Moving backward, (7.8) implies that the period 1 decision rule should be

$$d_1(P_1) = \begin{cases} 1 & \text{if } P_1 \geq \$10.6 \\ 0 & \text{otherwise} \end{cases} \quad \text{hence} \quad d_1(P_1) = \begin{cases} 1 & \text{if } P_1 = \$40 \\ 0 & \text{if } P_1 = \$10. \end{cases} \quad (7.9)$$

Therefore, because $k_1 = 1$ by assumption, the expected period 1 value of capacity is given by
$$EV_1(1) = (0.6 + 0.3)10.6 + (0.1 \times 40) = \$14.6. \quad (7.10)$$

That is, the first term in (7.10) is the expected value of capacity if no booking is made in period 1. This happens when either no consumer requests a booking (probability 0.6) or a booking for class B is requested (probability 0.3) and denied. The second term is the immediate profit if a class A booking is made with probability 0.1.

Finally, we now ask, What is the effect of having a strictly positive salvage value on the decision regarding which booking requests to accept? To answer this question, let us assume that capacity does not have any salvage value, so $P^S = 0$. Then, (7.8) becomes $EV_2(P_2, k_2) = (0.6 \times \$0) + (0.1 \times \$40) + (0.3 \times \$10) = \$7$ provided that $k_2 \neq 0$. Because now $EV_2(P_2, k_2) < \$10$, the period 1 decision rule (7.9) now changes to $d_1(\$40) = 1$ as well as $d_1(\$10) = 1$. That is, now that capacity does not have any salvage value, the profit-maximizing decision rule in any period is to accept all booking requests, including a booking request for the less profitable class B.

7.1.4 Dynamic advance booking for a small population

This subsection demonstrates how our analysis could be modified to capture a small consumer population, as described by Definition 7.1. When the consumer population is small, the service provider must revise the probability of realizing requests for each booking class by subtracting the consumers who have already been booked from the list of potential customers and the list of potential requests for the booked classes.

Table 7.3 displays a simple example with two service classes, A and B; two booking periods, $t = 1, 2$; one unit of capacity, $K = 1$; and five potential consumers. These five consumers are divided as follows: One consumer is expected not to make any booking ($P^0 = 0$), one consumer is expected to request a booking on class A ($P^A = \$40$), and the remaining three are expected to request class B ($P^0 = \$10$). The resulting period $t = 1$ probabilities of booking on each class i are listed as π_1^i in Table 7.3.

Class (i)	0	A	B	$EV_2(1)$
Price (P^i)	\$0	\$40	\$10	
π_1^i	$\frac{1}{5}$	$\frac{1}{5}$	$\frac{3}{5}$	
π_2^i (given $P_1 = \$0$)	0	$\frac{1}{4}$	$\frac{3}{4}$	$\frac{1}{4}40 + \frac{3}{4}10 = \$17.5$
π_2^i (given $P_1 = \$40$)	$\frac{1}{4}$	0	$\frac{3}{4}$	$\frac{1}{4}0 + \frac{3}{4}10 = \$7.5$
π_2^i (given $P_1 = \$10$)	$\frac{1}{4}$	$\frac{1}{4}$	$\frac{1}{2}$	$\frac{1}{4}40 + \frac{1}{2}10 = \$15$

Table 7.3: Small consumer population: Illustration for five consumers.

The important thing to notice in Table 7.3 is that when the population is small, the probability of booking on each class during period $t = 2$ depends on what type of consumer makes a request in period $t = 1$. Recall that under a large consumer population (assumed throughout this chapter), the probability of booking on each class remains constant during the entire booking process. Here, if no booking is made in period $t = 1$, it means that in period $t = 2$ the service provider knows for certain that either class A or B will be requested. If class A is requested in period $t = 1$, the service provider knows for certain that class A will be requested in period $t = 2$, hence the initial probability $\pi_1^A = 1/5$ drops to $\pi_2^A = 0$. Similarly, if class B is requested in $t = 1$, the number of potential consumers requesting class B falls from three to two. Hence, $\pi_1^B = 3/5$ drops to $\pi_2^B = 1/2$.

Once period $t = 2$ expected values of capacity are computed, we can proceed to our main investigation, which is characterizing the decision rules regarding which booking requests to accept during the two booking periods, $d_1(P_1)$ and $d_2(P_2)$. The logic behind the construction of these decision rules is identical to that given in all previous sections. More precisely, working backward from period $t = 2$, clearly $d_2(\$40) = d_2(\$10) = 1$ as otherwise capacity will remain unused during the period when the service is scheduled to be delivered.

Moving backward to period $t = 1$, the generalized decision rule given by (7.6) implies that a booking request for class A should be accepted because $P_1 = \$40 \geq \mathrm{EV}_2(1) - \mathrm{EV}_2(0) = \$7.5$. Similarly, a period $t = 1$ booking request for class B should be denied because $P_1 = \$10 < \mathrm{EV}_2(1) - \mathrm{EV}_2(0) = \$15$. Therefore,

$$d_1(P_1) = \begin{cases} 1 & \text{if } P_1 = \$40 \\ 0 & \text{otherwise,} \end{cases} \quad \text{and} \quad d_2(P_2) = \begin{cases} 1 & \text{if } P_2 = \$40 \\ 1 & \text{if } P_2 = \$10. \end{cases} \tag{7.11}$$

7.2 Multiple Periods with Two Service Classes

So far, our analysis has been restricted to $T = 2$ booking periods. In this section, we extend the model to any number of booking periods, thus allowing for $T > 2$. Subsection 7.2.1 extends the single-unit capacity example of Subsection 7.1.1. Subsection 7.2.3 analyzes $K = 2$ units of capacity. Finally, Subsection 7.2.4 provides the general formulation for any number of T booking periods, and any level of capacity K.

7.2.1 Single capacity unit: Example I

We now extend the two booking examples analyzed in Subsection 7.1.1 to any number of booking periods indexed by $t = 1, 2, \ldots, T$. Recalling (7.2), the expected value of capacity in the last booking period is

$$\mathrm{EV}_T(k_T) = \begin{cases} (0.1 \times 0) + (0.1 \times 40) + (0.8 \times 10) = \$12 & \text{if } k_T \neq 0 \\ 0 & \text{if } k_T = 0. \end{cases} \tag{7.12}$$

Moving backward to period $T - 1$, recall that the decision rule (7.3) implies that the service provider should accept a booking request $P_{T-1} = P^A = \$40$ so that $d_{T-1}(\$40) = 1$, and deny a booking request $P_{T-1} = P^B = \$10$ so that $d_{T-1}(\$10) =$

0. Hence, the period $T-1$ expected value of capacity is given by

$$EV_{T-1}(k_{T-1}) = \begin{cases} 0.1[40 + EV_T(0)] + 0.9[0 + EV_T(1)] & \text{if } k_{T-1} \neq 0 \\ 0 & \text{if } k_{T-1} = 0 \end{cases}$$

$$= \begin{cases} 0.1(40+0) + 0.9(0+12) = \$14.8 & \text{if } k_{T-1} \neq 0 \\ 0 & \text{if } k_{T-1} = 0. \end{cases} \quad (7.13)$$

That is, the period $T-1$ expected value of unbooked capacity is the sum of two components: first, the price of class A times the probability 0.1 that class A is requested, plus zero (as no capacity is left for booking in a subsequent period); and second, the expected period T value of capacity, which equals \$12 in the event no booking is requested in period $T-1$, multiplied by the sum of two probabilities $(\pi^0 + \pi^B = 0.1 + 0.8)$. These probabilities reflect the two events in which bookings are not made in period $T-1$.

Moving backward to analyze period $T-2$, we can infer directly from (7.13) that a class A booking request will be accepted because $P^A = \$40 > \$14.8$. In contrast, a class B booking request will be denied because $P^B = \$10 < \$14.8$. Formally, $d_{T-2}(40) = 1$, whereas $d_{T-2}(10) = 0$. Therefore, the period $T-2$ expected value of capacity is

$$EV_{T-2}(k_{T-2}) = 0.1[40 + EV_{T-1}(0)] + 0.9[0 + EV_{T-1}(1)]$$
$$= 0.1(40+0) + 0.9(0 + 14.8) = \$17.32 \quad \text{if } k_{T-2} \neq 0. \quad (7.14)$$

Moving backward to analyze period $T-3$, we can infer directly from (7.14) that a class A booking request will be accepted because $P^A = \$40 > \$17.32$. In contrast, a class B booking request will be denied because $P^B = \$10 < \$17.32$. Formally, $d_{T-3}(40) = 1$ whereas $d_{T-3}(10) = 0$. Therefore, the period $T-3$ expected value of capacity is

$$EV_{T-3}(k_{T-3}) = 0.1[40 + EV_{T-2}(0)] + 0.9[0 + EV_{T-2}(1)]$$
$$= 0.1(\$40 + 0) + 0.9(0 + \$17.32) = \$19.59 \quad \text{if } k_{T-3} \neq 0. \quad (7.15)$$

At this stage, the reader should notice a repeating pattern in the expected value of capacity functions given by (7.13), (7.14), and (7.15). In fact, for any period t, $\$10 < EV_{t+1}(1) < \$40$ implies that $d_t(\$40) = 1$, whereas $d_t(\$10) = 0$. Therefore,

$$EV_t(1) = 0.1[40 + 0] + 0.9[0 + EV_{t+1}(1)].$$

Using this pattern, we can easily compute that

$$EV_{T-4}(1) = 0.1 \times 40 + 0.9 \times 19.58 = \$21.63,$$
$$EV_{T-5}(1) = 0.1 \times 40 + 0.9 \times 21.63 = \$23.47,$$
$$\vdots \quad (7.16)$$
$$EV_{T-23}(1) = 0.1 \times 40 + 0.9 \times EV_{T-22}(1) = \$37.52.$$

In fact, it is easy to infer that $EV_t(k_t) \rightarrow \$40$ as t becomes smaller and smaller. To see why, simply solve $EV = 0.1 \times 40 + 0.9 \times EV$ to obtain $EV = \$40$.

Finally, the series of expected value functions listed in (7.16) indicates that the value of capacity declines as time progresses. Intuitively, as the booking advances toward the service delivery time, there is a higher probability that capacity will remain underbooked. This reduces the value of unbooked capacity. In contrast, way back during the early stages of the booking process, there is a small probability that no booking will be made in one of the booking periods. Formally, if there are four booking periods ($T = 4$), the probability that capacity will not be booked in all periods is $(\pi^0)^4 = 0.1^4 = 0.0001$. However, from booking period $t = 2$ (inclusive) forward this probability is reduced to $(\pi^0)^2 = 0.1^2 = 0.01$, and in the last period to $\pi^0 = 0.1$. For this reason, the value of capacity declines over time and reaches its lowest level in period T.

7.2.2 Single capacity unit: Example II

The example analyzed in Subsection 7.2.1 turned out to be very simple (and rather boring) because, except except for the last booking period, it generated the same decision rule in each period, $d_t(40) = 1$ and $d_t(10) = 0$, in every booking period $t = 1, 2, \ldots, T - 1$. Table 7.4 provides an example in which the decision rule changes at some point during the booking process.

Class (i)	0	A	B
Proportion (π^i)	0.6	0.1	0.3
Price/fare (P^i)	\$0	\$40	\$10

Table 7.4: The consumer population under two fare classes and T booking periods.

Comparing Table 7.4 with our first example, displayed in Table 7.1, reveals that in the present example we have increased the probability of no booking from 0.1 to 0.6. This modification will result in a reduction of capacity value in all booking periods, thereby increasing the profitability of accepting booking requests at early stages of the booking process. Table 7.4 implies that the expected value of capacity in the last booking period is

$$EV_T(k_T) = \begin{cases} (0.6 \times 0) + (0.1 \times 40) + (0.3 \times 10) = \$7 & \text{if } k_T \neq 0 \\ 0 & \text{if } k_T = 0. \end{cases} \quad (7.17)$$

Moving backward we now analyze the period $T - 1$ booking decision. In view of (7.17), $d_{T-1}(\$40) = d_{T-1}(\$10) = 1$ because $P^A = \$40 > P^B = \$10 > \$7$. That is, because the expected period T value of capacity is low, the service provider should accept booking requests on classes A and B. Because every booking request is accepted in $T-1$, the period $T-1$ expected value of capacity is

$$
\begin{aligned}
&\mathrm{EV}_{T-1}(k_{T-1}) \\
&\quad = \begin{cases} 0.1(40+0)+0.3(10+0)+0.6(0+7)=\$11.2 & \text{if } k_{T-1}\neq 0 \\ 0 & \text{if } k_{T-1}=0. \end{cases}
\end{aligned} \tag{7.18}
$$

The first two terms correspond to the expected revenue from accepted booking requests. The last term in (7.18) corresponds to expected value of capacity from postponing the booking to a subsequent period.

Moving backward to analyze period $T-2$ booking decision, we can now observe a change in the booking strategy. Comparing (7.18) with (7.17) reveals a sharp fall in the expected value of capacity between booking period $T-1$ and period T. Thus, whereas booking class B in period $T-1$ is profitable, it is not profitable in booking period $T-2$. Formally, $d_{T-2}(P^B)=0$ because $P^B=\$10<\$11.2$. However, $d_{T-2}(P^A)=1$ because $P^A=\$40>\$11.2$.

Moving backward to analyze periods $T-3$, $T-4$, and so on, we will show that the decision to accept booking requests for class A and to deny booking requests for class B is profit maximizing. Formally, we will have to show that $d_t(P^A)=1$ and $d_t(P^B)=0$ for all $t=1,2,\ldots,T-2$. Under this decision rule (to be verified later), the expected value functions are given by

$$
\begin{aligned}
\mathrm{EV}_{T-2}(1) &= 0.1\times 40+0.9\times 11.2 = \$14.08, \\
\mathrm{EV}_{T-3}(1) &= 0.1\times 40+0.9\times 14.08 = \$16.67, \\
&\vdots \\
\mathrm{EV}_{T-25}(1) &= 0.1\times 40+0.9\times \mathrm{EV}_{T-24} = \$37.7.
\end{aligned} \tag{7.19}
$$

Note $\mathrm{EV}_t(k_t)\to\$40$ as t gets smaller and smaller. To see why, simply solve $\mathrm{EV}=0.1\times\$40+0.9\times\mathrm{EV}$ to obtain $\mathrm{EV}=\$40$. Finally, our *guess* that $d_t(P^A)=1$ and $d_t(P^B)=0$ for all $t=1,2,\ldots,T-2$ can be easily verified because (7.19) implies that $P^B=\$10<\mathrm{EV}_t(k_t)<\$40=P^A$ for every $t<T$.

7.2.3 Two capacity units example

We now extend the previous analysis of many periods with a single unit of capacity to many periods with two units of capacity. Subsection 7.2.4 provides the most general formulation conforming to any amount of capacity.

Under $K=2$, because at most only one consumer can be booked in each booking period (Assumption 7.2), the service provider should accept any booking request during period T. Otherwise, some capacity will not be used during period $T+1$ when the service is provided. Formally, $d_T(\$40)=d_T(\$10)=1$. Therefore, Table 7.4 implies that the period T expected value of capacity is given by

$$EV_T(k_T) = \begin{cases} (0.6 \times 0) + (0.1 \times 40) + (0.3 \times 10) = \$7 & \text{if } k_T \neq 0 \\ 0 & \text{if } k_T = 0. \end{cases} \qquad (7.20)$$

Moving backward to booking period $T - 1$, the service provider will accept any booking request at $T - 1$ because $P^B = \$10 > EV_T(2) - EV_T(1) = \$7$. Formally, $d_{T-1}(\$40) = d_{T-1}(\$10) = 1$. Hence, the period $T - 1$ expected value of capacity is

$$EV_{T-1}(k_{T-1}) =$$
$$\begin{cases} (0.1 \times 40) + (0.3 \times 10) + 7 = 2 \times 7 = \$14 & \text{if } k_{T-1} = 2 \\ (0.1 \times 40) + (0.3 \times 10) + 0.6(0+7) = \$11.2 & \text{if } k_{T-1} = 1 \quad (7.21) \\ 0 & \text{if } k_{T-1} = 0. \end{cases}$$

Moving backward to period $T - 2$, (7.21) implies that $\$14 - \$11.2 < \$10 < \$11.2 - 0$. Hence, the period $T - 2$ decision rule, as a function of available capacity, is given by

$$d_{T-2}(\$40) = 1 \quad \text{and} \quad d_{T-2}(\$10) = \begin{cases} 1 & \text{if } k_{T-2} = 2 \\ 0 & \text{if } k_{T-2} \leq 1. \end{cases} \qquad (7.22)$$

Therefore, a booking request for class B should be rejected if only one unit of capacity remains, but should be accepted if two units of capacity are available for booking. In view of decision rule (7.22), the period $T - 2$ expected value of capacity is given by

$$EV_{T-2}(k_{T-2}) =$$
$$\begin{cases} 0.1(40+11.2) + 0.3(10+11.2) + 0.6(0+14) = \$19.88 & \text{if } k_{T-2} = 2 \\ 0.1(40+0) + 0.9(0+11.2) = \$14.08 & \text{if } k_{T-2} = 1 \quad (7.23) \\ 0 & \text{if } k_{T-2} = 0. \end{cases}$$

Moving backward to analyze booking periods $T - 3$, $T - 4$, and so on, we first *guess* from (7.23), and later verify, that for every booking period $t \leq T - 3$,

$$d_t(\$40) = 0 \quad \text{and} \quad d_t(\$10) = \begin{cases} 1 & \text{if } k_{T-2} = 2 \\ 0 & \text{if } k_{T-2} \leq 1. \end{cases} \qquad (7.24)$$

Decision rule (7.24) can be verified for period $t = T - 3$ by observing that $P^B = \$10 > EV_{T-2}(2) - EV_{T-2}(1) = \$19.88 - \$14.08$, whereas $P^B = \$10 < EV_{T-2}(1) -$

$EV_{T-2}(0) = \$14.08 - 0$. Therefore, the period $T - 3$ expected value of capacity is given by

$$EV_{T-3}(k_{T-3}) =$$
$$\begin{cases} 0.1(40+14.08)+0.3(10+14.08)+0.6(0+19.88) = \$24.56 & k_{T-3} = 2 \\ 0.1(40+0)+0.9(0+14.08) = \$16.67 & k_{T-3} = 1 \\ 0 & k_{T-3} = 0. \end{cases}$$
$$(7.25)$$

Moving backward to period $T - 4$, decision rule (7.24) can be verified for period $T - 4$ by observing that $P^B = \$10 > EV_{T-3}(2) - EV_{T-3}(1) = \$24.56 - \$16.67$, whereas $P^B = \$10 < EV_{T-3}(1) - EV_{T-3}(0) = \$16.67 - 0$. Therefore, (7.25) can be generalized to

$$EV_t(k_t) =$$
$$\begin{cases} 0.1[40+EV_{t+1}(1)]+0.3[10+EV_{t+1}(1)]+0.6[0+EV_{t+1}(2)] & \text{if } k_t = 2 \\ 0.1(40+0)+0.9[0+EV_{t+1}(1)] & \text{if } k_t = 1 \\ 0 & \text{if } k_t = 0. \end{cases}$$
$$(7.26)$$

In fact, working backward, the following two equations simultaneously yield that the period $T - 30$ expected value of capacity as a function of available capacity k_{T-30} is given by $EV_{T-30}(2) = \$72.71$ and $EV_{T-30}(1) = \$38.64$. Finally, under decision rule (7.24), $EV_t(2) \to \$80$ and $EV_t(1) \to \$40$ as t gets smaller and smaller. Using words, a larger number of booking periods increases the probability that each unit of capacity will be booked in class A for the price $P^A = \$40$.

7.2.4   Large-capacity example

In this subsection, we further extend the model from two units of capacity to any amount of capacity so that $K \geq 2$. By Assumption 7.3(a), the only interesting cases must satisfy $K < T$, meaning that the number of booking periods must exceed the level of capacity. Otherwise, any booking request should be accepted in each booking period. Using the consumer information given in Table 7.4, in this subsection we still maintain two booking/fare classes denoted by A and B. Section 7.3 further extends the model to include any number of booking classes.

The decision rules and the resulting expected values of capacity during booking periods T and $T - 1$ are already given by (7.20) and (7.21) by replacing $k_t = 2$ with $k_t \geq 2$, for $t = T - 1, T$. Next, period $T - 2$ decision rule (7.22) should be slightly modified to

$$d_{T-2}(\$40) = 1 \quad \text{and} \quad d_{T-2}(\$10) = \begin{cases} 1 & \text{if } k_{T-2} \geq 3 \\ 1 & \text{if } k_{T-2} = 2 \\ 0 & \text{if } k_{T-2} \leq 1. \end{cases} \quad (7.27)$$

Clearly, if $k_{T-2} = 3$, any booking request should be accepted, as this capacity level equals exactly the number of remaining booking periods. Therefore, the period $T - 2$ expected value of capacity is given by

$$\text{EV}_{T-2}(k_{T-2}) =$$
$$\begin{cases} (0.1 \times 40) + (0.3 \times 10) + 14 = 3 \times 7 = \$21 & \text{if } k_{T-2} \geq 3 \\ 0.1(40 + 11.2) + 0.3(10 + 11.2) + 0.6(0 + 14) = \$19.88 & \text{if } k_{T-2} = 2 \\ 0.1(40 + 0) + 0.9(0 + 11.2) = \$14.08 & \text{if } k_{T-2} = 1 \\ 0 & \text{if } k_{T-2} = 0. \end{cases} \quad (7.28)$$

The first line in (7.28) corresponds to excess capacity relative to the number of booking periods in which any booking request is accepted. Other cases are identical to those given by (7.23).

Moving backward to analyze booking periods $T - 3$, $T - 4$, and so on, we can first *guess* from (7.28) and later verify that for every booking period $t \leq T - 3$,

$$d_t(\$40) = 0 \quad \text{and} \quad d_t(\$10) = \begin{cases} 1 & \text{if } k_{T-2} \geq 2 \\ 0 & \text{if } k_{T-2} \leq 1. \end{cases} \quad (7.29)$$

Decision rule (7.29) is verified for period $t = T - 3$ by observing that $P^B = \$10 > \text{EV}_{T-2}(3) - \text{EV}_{T-2}(2) = \$21 - \$19.88$, $P^B = \$10 > \text{EV}_{T-2}(2) - \text{EV}_{T-2}(1) = \$19.88 - \$14.08$, and $P^B = \$10 < \text{EV}_{T-2}(1) - \text{EV}_{T-2}(0) = \$14.08 - 0$. Therefore, the period $T - 3$ expected value of capacity is given by

$$\text{EV}_{T-3}(k_{T-3}) =$$
$$\begin{cases} (0.1 \times 40) + (0.3 \times 10) + 21 = 4 \times 7 = \$28 & k_{T-3} \geq 4 \\ 0.1(40 + 19.88) + 0.3(10 + 19.88) + 0.6(0 + 21) = \$27.55 & k_{T-3} = 3 \\ 0.1(40 + 14.08) + 0.3(10 + 14.08) + 0.6(0 + 19.88) = \$24.56 & k_{T-3} = 2 \\ 0.1(40 + 0) + 0.9(0 + 14.08) = \$16.67 & k_{T-3} = 1 \\ 0 & k_{T-3} = 0. \end{cases}$$
$$(7.30)$$

Moving backward to period $T - 4$, decision rule (7.29) can be verified for period $T - 4$ by observing that $P^B = \$10 > \text{EV}_{T-3}(4) - \text{EV}_{T-3}(3) = \$28 - \$27.55$, $P^B = \$10 > \text{EV}_{T-3}(3) - \text{EV}_{T-3}(2) = \$27.55 - 24.56$, $P^B = \$10 > \text{EV}_{T-3}(2) -$

$EV_{T-3}(1) = \$24.56 - \$16.67$, and $P^B = \$10 < EV_{T-3}(1) - EV_{T-3}(0) = \$16.67 - 0$. In fact, working backward decision rule (7.29) yields $EV_t(K) \to K \times \$40$ as t gets smaller and smaller. Using words, a larger number of booking periods increases the probability that each unit of capacity will be booked in class A for the price $P^A = \$40$. Hence, the total value of capacity converges to $K \times \$40$, which also constitutes the expected profit of this service provider.

Finally, let us compute the profit level for a case in which the service provider books $K = 3$ units of capacity over five booking periods. Suppose that the following sequence of booking requests is realized: $P_{T-4} = \$10$, $P_{T-3} = \$40$, $P_{T-2} = P_{T-1} = \$10$, and $P_T = \$40$. Then, decision rule (7.29) implies that $d_{T-4}(\$10) = 1$ because $k_{T-4} = 3$. Also, $d_{T-3}(\$40) = 1$ because $k_{T-3} = 2$. Next, decision rule (7.22) implies that $d_{T-2}(\$10) = 0$ because $k_{T-2} = 1$. Clearly, $d_{T-1}(\$40) = 1$, whereas $d_T(\$40) = 0$ because $k_T = 0$ (all capacity has been fully booked). Total realized profit is then given by $y = 10 + 40 + 0 + 40 + 0 = \$90$.

7.3 Multiple Booking Periods and Service Classes

This section provides a general exposition of the advance booking problem allowing for any number of booking periods, $t = 1, \ldots, T$; any number of booking classes, $i \in \mathcal{B} = \{A, B, \ldots\}$; and an arbitrary amount of service capacity satisfying $K < T$ by Assumption 7.3(a). Subsection 7.3.1 provides the general formulation of advance booking decisions. Then, Subsection 7.3.2 outlines two computer algorithms that construct and implement the dynamic advance booking model of this section.

7.3.1 General formulation

Let $P^S \geq 0$ denote the salvage value of a unit of capacity; see Section 7.1.3 for further discussion. For example, $P^S = 0$ is a special case in which there is no salvage value for unused capacity. The value of unused capacity during the period when the service is delivered (so that further bookings are possible) is given by

$$EV_{T+1}(k_{T+1}) = P^S \times k_{T+1}, \quad \text{for all capacity levels } k_T \geq 0. \tag{7.31}$$

We now proceed to analyze booking periods T, $T - 1$, and so on. A direct implication of Bellman's principle of optimality is that a period t booking request for a price P_t should be accepted only if the price plus the subsequent period's expected value of the *remaining* capacity exceeds the subsequent period's expected value of capacity if no booking is made in period t. Formally, the profit-maximizing decision rule in each booking period $t \geq T$ is

$$d_t(P_t) = \begin{cases} 1 & \text{if } P_t > EV_{t+1}(k_t) - EV_{t+1}(k_t - 1) \text{ and } k_t > 0 \\ 0 & \text{Otherwise.} \end{cases} \tag{7.32}$$

Note, however, that decision rule (7.32) is incomplete unless we specify how the expected values of capacity $EV_t(k_t)$ are determined.

To determine the value of capacity in each booking period $t \leq T$, we denote by $\mathscr{B}_t(k_t)$ the set of service/fare requests the firm will find profitable to accept in period t. Formally let

$$\mathscr{B}_t(k_t) \stackrel{\text{def}}{=} \left\{ i \in \mathscr{B} \mid P^i > EV_{t+1}(k_t) - EV_{t+1}(k_t - 1) \right\} \text{ for } t \leq T. \tag{7.33}$$

Equation (7.33) follows directly from (7.32), which indicates that a booking request for class i is accepted only if the price exceeds the subsequent period's reduction in the value of capacity associated with the booking of one unit of capacity. Thus, the set $\mathscr{B}_t(k_t)$ is the collection of booking classes that are profitable to book during booking period t. That is, $d_t(P^i) = 1$ for all $i \in \mathscr{B}_t(k_t)$, whereas $d_t(P^i) = 0$ for all $i \notin \mathscr{B}_t(k_t)$.

The booking decisions associated with the accepted booking classes given in (7.33) imply that the resulting expected period t value of capacity is given by

$$EV_t(k_t) = \sum_{i \in \mathscr{B}_t(k_t)} \pi^i \left[P^i + EV_{t+1}(k_t - 1) \right] + \left(1 - \sum_{i \in \mathscr{B}_t(k_t)} \pi^i \right) EV_{t+1}(k_t) \tag{7.34}$$

if $k_t > 0$, whereas $EV_t(k_t) = 0$ if $k_t = 0$. The term on the left in (7.34) measures the expected profit from accepting a booking plus the future expected value of capacity, taking into consideration the resulting reduction in capacity, so $k_{t+1} = k_t - 1$. The term on the right measures the period $t + 1$ value of capacity in the event that no booking is made in period t, so $k_{t+1} = k_t$.

7.3.2 Computer algorithm

In this section, we sketch the basic logic for building and implementing a computer advance reservation system. We present two algorithms. Algorithm 7.1 constructs the advance reservation system based on consumer characteristics and the service/fare classes offered by the service provider. Assuming that the processed data are stored on the computer, Algorithm 7.2 then demonstrates a simple implementation, whereby realized sequential booking requests are logged into the computer, which responds with an acceptance or a denial decision in each booking period.

Algorithm 7.1 relies on some parameters that the software must input and some output variable that should be defined. The number of booking periods T and the amount of capacity K are both nonnegative integer valued. One possible check omitted from Algorithm 7.1 is the verification that $K < T$, as otherwise it is profitable to accept any booking request (see Assumption 7.3(a)).

The software must input the parameters describing the booking classes and the corresponding prices as offered to the public. Let $\mathscr{B}$ be the *set* containing the names of the offered booking classes. One can construct a loop such as **Read**(i); $\mathcal{B} \leftarrow \mathcal{B} \cup \{i\}$, until, say, an end of line is reached. Next, we input the price of each booking class into the real-valued array $P[i]$, and the salvage value of capacity P^S. Finally, we input the probability (frequency) of realizing each possible requested booking class into an array $\pi[i]$ valued on the unit interval $[0, 1]$, as well as $\pi[0]$ (probability of no booking). It may be a good idea to check that $\pi[0] + \sum_{i \in \mathcal{B}} \pi[i] = 1$.

We now proceed to define the output variables of Algorithm 7.1. Let t (booking period) and k (remaining capacity level) be integer valued. Then, let the expected capacity value $EV[t, k]$ define the array of arrays of real variables with a dimension of $T + 1$ by $K + 1$. Finally, the decisions whether to accept or deny a period t booking request as functions of remaining capacity k are written into an array of arrays of arrays $d[t, k, P[i]]$ confined to the binary set $\{0, 1\}$, with a dimension of T by $K + 1$ by the number of elements in the set $\mathcal{B}$.

---

for $k = 0$ **to** K **do** $EV[T + 1, k] \leftarrow P^S \times k;$ /* Salvage value   */
for $t = T$ **downto** 1 **do**
    /* Main backward loop over booking periods   */
    for $k = 0$ **to** K **do**
        /* Loop over remaining capacity k_t */
        forall $i \in \mathcal{B}$ **do**
            /* Loop over booking classes   */
        if $P[i] > EV[t + 1, k] - EV[t + 1, k - 1]$ **then**
            /* If booking P^i is profitable, accept it   */
            $d[t, k, P[i]] \leftarrow 1;$ $EV[t, k] \leftarrow EV[t, k] + \pi[i] \times P[i];$
            /* Updating period t expected capacity value */
        else if then $d[t, k, P[i]] \leftarrow 0;$ /* Deny P^i request   */
    if $EV[t, k] \neq 0$ **then** $EV[t, k] \leftarrow EV[t, k] + EV[t + 1, k - 1];$
    /* Finalizing expected value of remaining capacity */
    if $EV[t, k] = 0$ **then** $EV[t, k] \leftarrow EV[t, k] + EV[t + 1, k];$

Algorithm 7.1: Advance booking: Building the system.

We now turn to the implementation stage assuming that the decision rules $d[t, k, P[i]]$, the corresponding expected values of capacity $EV[t, k]$, and the parameters K and T are all stored on the system after Algorithm 7.1 ends. The advance booking implementation described in Algorithm 7.2 reads a request by one consumer in each booking period t into an array $PP[t]$ of nonnegative reals with a dimension of T. That is, the array $PP[t]$ stores the sequence of class requests. It may be a good idea to check that $PP[t] = P[i]$ for some $i \in \mathcal{B}$, to confirm that the requested price matches a valid booking class. Algorithm 7.2 computes the total

```
k ← K; /* Initializing to full capacity                              */
for t = 0 to T do
    /* Main loop over all booking periods                            */
    read (PP[t]); /* Below check if PP[t] request is accepted */
    if d[t, k, PP[i]] = 1 then
        k ← k − 1; /* Reduce next period's capacity                  */
        y ← y + PP[t]; /* Add price to cumulated profit              */
        write ("Booking request", PP[t], "accepted in period", t, ".");
        writeln (k, "capacity remained.", T − t, "periods remained.");
    writeln ("Total profit made:", y); /* Profit summary             */
```

Algorithm 7.2: Advance booking: Implementation.

profit from all booking requests made using the nonnegative real variable y and lists all the types of bookings made.

7.4 Dynamic Booking with Marginal Operating Cost

Our analysis so far has ignored marginal operating cost by assuming that $\mu_o = 0$. This simplification clearly reduces the amount of writing and therefore serves the purpose of demonstrating the logic behind dynamic optimization with as little algebra as possible. However, the reader may wonder how booking strategies may vary when we look for profit maximization rather than revenue maximization.

7.4.1 Converting prices to marginal profits

In this section, we demonstrate that algorithms developed in the previous sections can be easily modified to accommodate strictly positive marginal operating costs. Consider the following consumer population described in Table 7.5.

Class (i)	0	A	B	C	D	S
Proportion (π^i)	0.2	0.2	0.1	0.2	0.3	
Price/fare (P^i)	$0	$40	$30	$20	$10	$15
Proportion ($\hat{\pi}^i$)	0.7	0.2	0.1	n/a	n/a	
Marginal profit ($\hat{P}^i$)	$0	$15	$5	n/a	n/a	$15

Table 7.5: Potential consumer population under four booking classes with marginal operating cost $\mu_o = \$25$ and salvage value of capacity $P^S = \$15$.
Top: Original price data. *Bottom*: Data modified to marginal profits.

Table 7.5 demonstrates how original raw price data can be modified for the purpose of solving for the profit-maximizing booking strategies instead of revenue-maximizing strategies using the same algorithms described throughout this chapter. Clearly, profit maximization is identical to revenue maximization as long as the marginal cost is $\mu_o = 0$.

With strictly positive marginal cost, we modify the data so that only classes i satisfying $P^i > \mu_o$ are made available for booking. For these classes, we compute the marginal profit by subtracting the marginal operating cost from the price to obtain $\hat{P}^i \stackrel{\text{def}}{=} P^i - \mu_o$. We mark all unprofitable fare classes j satisfying $P^j \le \mu_o$ as not available (n/a). Next, because some booking classes are eliminated when marginal operating cost is subtracted from the price consumers pay, we must adjust the probability that no booking is made in each booking period. More precisely, in the example displayed in Table 7.5, we have eliminated booking classes C and D as we found them unprofitable. This means that any booking request for class C or D will be denied. As a result, the probability that no booking is made in each period increases from π^0 to $\hat{\pi}^0 + \pi^C + \pi^D$. In the present example, $\hat{\pi}^0 = 0.2 + 0.2 + 0.3 = 0.7$.

Finally, Table 7.5 shows that the salvage value of capacity does not change when marginal operating cost is taken into account. This is because in this book we interpret the marginal operating cost parameter μ_o as a cost that the service provider bears only if a consumer is actually being served. This is the reason we stress the word *operating* (as opposed to *marginal capacity cost*, which is denoted by μ_k). Note that the differences between marginal operating cost and marginal capacity cost have already been discussed in great detail in our analysis of peak-load pricing in Chapter 6. For example, in the airline industry, marginal operating cost is the cost associated with boarding one additional passenger on a certain flight, which consists of the cost of meals, entertainment, baggage space, and handling time. In contrast, marginal capacity cost consists of the cost of buying an airplane with one additional seat. Table 7.5 demonstrates that under the marginal operating cost interpretation, the salvage value of capacity remains unchanged with our modification because by not making a booking, the firm saves the marginal operating cost and therefore can count the salvage value of $15 per unit of capacity as part of its net profit. However, if we were to interpret marginal cost as the marginal capacity cost μ_k, then we would have to deduct $\mu_k = \$20$ from the salvage value of $15 to obtain $-\$5$ per unit of capacity.

7.4.2 Computer algorithm

Similar to the algorithm described in Section 7.3.2, the software must input the parameters describing the booking classes and their prices/fares as offered to the public. Let $\mathcal{B}$ be the *set* containing the names of the offered booking classes. One can construct a loop such as **Read**(i); $\mathcal{B} \leftarrow \mathcal{B} \cup \{i\}$ until, say, an end of line is reached. Next, we input the marginal operating cost μ_o and the price of each booking class into the real valued array $P[i]$, as well as the salvage value of capacity P^S. Finally, we input the probability (frequency) of realizing each possible requested booking class into an array $\pi[i]$ valued on the unit interval $[0,1]$, as well as $\pi[0]$ (probability of no booking). It is useful to perform a check that $\pi[0] + \sum_{i \in \mathscr{B}} \pi[i] = 1$. The program suggested in Algorithm 7.3 transforms the above input into the corresponding modified variables, which we denote by $\hat{\mathscr{B}}$ and $\hat{\pi}[0]$.

```
forall i ∈ ℬ do
    /* Main loop over available booking classes        */
    if P[i] > μₒ then
        /* If booking Pⁱ exceeds marginal cost          */
        ℬ̂ ← ℬ̂ ∪ {i}; /* Add i to new set of bookable classes */
    else if then
        π̂⁰ ← π̂⁰ + πⁱ /* Update probability of no booking   */

forall i ∈ ℬ̂ do
    /* Writing:  Loop over adjusted bookable classes    */
    writeln ("Booking price", P[i], "yields marginal profit of", P[i] − μₒ, "is
    requested with probability" π[i]);
    write ("Adjusted probability of no booking is", π̂⁰);
```

Algorithm 7.3: Advance booking: Marginal operating cost.

7.5 Network-based Dynamic Advance Booking

Our analysis so far has assumed that services use specific capacity that is not used by other services provided by the firm. In this section, we relax this assumption and assume that capacity can be used to provide other complementary services. Thus, accepting a booking request for one service may reduce the amount of capacity available for other services. This implies that an advance reservation system must compute the trade-off between the extra revenue generated by an acceptance of a booking request for one service and the potential revenue loss not only from the reduction in capacity of the same service but also from the potential reduction in revenue from complementary services. For earlier scientific literature on network yield management, see Glover, Glover, Lorenzo, and McMillan (1982) and Wang (1983). Additional references are provided in Talluri and van Ryzin (2004, Ch. 3).

To take a specific case, consider an airline serving three cities labeled A, B, and H. Passengers seek to book tickets for traveling from city A to H, H to B, and A to B. These cities and the desired connections are depicted in Figure 7.1.

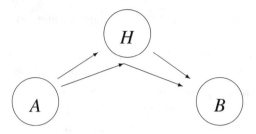

Figure 7.1: Booking airline tickets under a hub-and-spokes network.

For the sake of demonstration only, we ignore return flights and round-trip tickets. The connections displayed in Figure 7.1 are commonly referred to as forming a hub-and-spokes network. City H serves as a hub if there is no direct connection between cities A and B.

Suppose that the airline company does not provide a direct connection between A and B, which means that passengers on the route from A to B have to first board the flight from A to H, and then change to the flight from H to B. The airline allocates K^{AH} units of capacity (number of seats in the present example) for the route AH, and K^{HB} units of capacity for the route HB. Clearly, these capacity allocations serve two types of passengers: passengers who wish to travel to and from the hub city H (A to H and H to B in the present example) and those traveling between non-hub cities (A to B in the present example).

7.5.1 A numerical example

Consider the single-airline three-city example illustrated in Figure 7.1. There are two booking periods labeled $t = 1, 2$. All flights take off during period $t = 3$, after the booking periods end. Suppose that on each flight there is only one unit of capacity. Formally, let $K^{AH} = K^{HB} = 1$. Table 7.6 describes passengers wishing to travel on these three routes.

Route (i)	0	AH	HB	AB
Proportion (π^i)	0.1	0.2	0.2	0.5
Airfare (P^i)	$0	$20	$30	$40

Table 7.6: Passengers on a hub-and-spokes network. *Note*: Route 0 refers to passengers who end up not booking any flight.

The fractions in Table 7.6 refer to the proportion of passengers out of the entire potential passenger population who wish to travel on a certain route. As before, we also interpret these fractions as probabilities of making a booking on a certain route. The airfares on these routes are denoted by P^{AB}, P^{AH}, and P^{HB}. Models of this sort generally assume that $P^{AB} < P^{AH} + P^{HB}$, as otherwise a passenger to or from the hub city would buy a ticket for the route AB and get off (or embark) in city H.

Similar to the previous section, our analysis investigates which type of reservation requests should be accepted and which should be denied by a profit-maximizing airline company, where in each period, at most one passenger makes a booking request. In solving this problem, we follow exactly the same steps as for the single-route booking problem analyzed in Subsection 7.1.1.

Because period $t = 2$ is the last booking period, the airline should accept any booking request provided that capacity remains on the desired route. Hence, the period $t = 2$ decision rule is given by

$$d_2(P_2) = \begin{cases} 1 & \text{if } k_2^{AH} \neq 0 \text{ and } P_2 = \$20 \\ 1 & \text{if } k_2^{HB} \neq 0 \text{ and } P_2 = \$30 \\ 1 & \text{if } k_2^{AH} \neq 0, k_2^{HB} \neq 0, \text{ and } P_2 = \$40 \\ 0 & \text{otherwise.} \end{cases} \tag{7.35}$$

From the probability distribution given in Table 7.6, we can now compute the period $t = 2$ expected value of capacity. Thus,

$$EV_2(k_2^{AH}, k_2^{HB}) =$$
$$\begin{cases} 0.2 \times \$20 = \$4 & \text{if } k_2^{AH} \neq 0 \text{ and } k_2^{HB} = 0 \\ 0.2 \times \$30 = \$6 & \text{if } k_2^{AH} = 0 \text{ and } k_2^{HB} \neq 0 \\ 0.2 \times \$20 + 0.2 \times \$30 + 0.5 \times \$40 = \$30 & \text{if } k_2^{AH} \neq 0 \text{ and } k_2^{HB} \neq 0 \\ 0 & \text{Otherwise.} \end{cases} \tag{7.36}$$

Using words, equation (7.36) shows that if capacity remains unbooked on both routes in period $t = 2$, that is, if $k_2^{AH} \neq 0$ and $k_2^{HB} \neq 0$, then the expected period 2 value of capacity is the expected value of three events corresponding to the three possible booking requests that can be made on the three routes. However, if the capacity on one of the routes is already fully booked, then the expected value of capacity drops to the expected profit from a single route only.

Next, observe that

$$P^{AH} = \$20 < EV_2(1,1) - EV_2(0,1) = \$30 - \$6 < \$40 = P^{AB};$$

however,

$$P^{AB} = \$40 > P^{HB} = \$30 > EV_2(1,1) - EV_2(1,0) = \$30 - \$4.$$

Therefore, the period $t = 1$ decision rule is given by

$$d_1(P_1) = \begin{cases} 0 & \text{if } P_1 = \$20 \\ 1 & \text{if } P_1 = \$30 \\ 1 & \text{if } P_1 = \$40. \end{cases} \tag{7.37}$$

What can we conclude from this model? Perhaps the most interesting aspect of this model is that it can explain why we often observe vacant seats on many commercial flights. To demonstrate this possibility, let us compute the probability that the capacity on route *AH* will not be booked. First, period $t = 1$ decision rule (7.37) states that a booking request on route *AH* should be denied. Such a request is made with probability 0.2. Next, in period 2, route *AH* is not requested if passengers request bookings on route *HB* (probability 0.2), or if no request is made (probability 0.1). Summing up, the probability that capacity on route *AH* will not be booked is $0.2(0.5 + 0.1) = 0.12 = 12\%$.

7.5.2   General formulation

In this subsection, we introduce a more formal description for the backward induction algorithm developed as an example in Subsection 7.5.1. Because period T is assumed to be the last booking period, any booking request should be accommodated provided that the relevant capacity is available. Therefore, the period T expected value of capacity is given by

$$
EV_T(k_T^{AH}, k_T^{HB}) =
\begin{cases}
\pi^{AH} \times P^{AH} & \text{if } k_T^{AH} \neq 0 \text{ and } k_T^{HB} = 0 \\
\pi^{HB} \times P^{HB} & \text{if } k_T^{AH} = 0 \text{ and } k_T^{HB} \neq 0 \\
\pi^{AH} \times P^{AH} + \pi^{HB} \times P^{HB} + \pi^{AB} \times P^{AB} & \text{if } k_T^{AH} \neq 0 \text{ and } k_T^{HB} \neq 0 \\
0 & \text{if } k_T^{AH} = k_T^{HB} = 0.
\end{cases}
\tag{7.38}
$$

Moving *backward*, the period $T - 1$ decision rule can be solved for by comparing the effects of accepting a booking on the period T expected value of capacity (7.38). Hence,

$$
d_{T-1}(P_{T-1}) =
\begin{cases}
1 & \text{if } P_{T-1} = P^{AH} \text{ \& } P^{AH} \geq EV_T(k_{T-1}^{AH}, k_{T-1}^{HB}) - EV_T(k_{T-1}^{AH} - 1, k_{T-1}^{HB}) \\
1 & \text{if } P_{T-1} = P^{HB} \text{ \& } P^{HB} \geq EV_T(k_{T-1}^{AH}, k_{T-1}^{HB}) - EV_T(k_{T-1}^{AH}, k_{T-1}^{HB} - 1) \\
1 & \text{if } P_{T-1} = P^{AB} \text{ \& } P^{AB} \geq EV_T(k_{T-1}^{AH}, k_{T-1}^{HB}) - EV_T(k_{T-1}^{AH} - 1, k_{T-1}^{HB} - 1) \\
0 & \text{otherwise.}
\end{cases}
\tag{7.39}
$$

Period $T - 1$ decision rule (7.39) highlights once again the logic behind Bellman's principle of optimality by demonstrating the trade-off between the currently offered price and the expected reduction in period T value of capacity resulting from accepting a period $T - 1$ booking request.

7.6 Fixed Class Allocations

The dynamic booking strategies studied so far in this chapter clearly present true optimization with respect to profit maximization and the amount of surplus that service providers can extract from heterogeneous consumer groups. These algorithms and some more complicated variants can be programmed into advance reservation systems and booking software.

However, some industries and particular service providers facing a small number of potential consumers may find the dynamic algorithms hard to control and hard to correct in the event that the computer generates "bad" results. Moreover, in some cases it may be useful to implement simple booking plans rather than the dynamic booking strategies described so far in this chapter. Simplicity is especially desirable when some external constraints must be imposed on the entire booking process. Examples for such constraints include allowing for overbooking and realizations of no-shows, which we analyze in Chapter 9. When no-shows and overbooking are taken into consideration, service providers may be induced to limit the bookings of high-risk consumers, or to further segment the market by offering nonrefundable tickets to some consumers (see Chapter 8). For this reason, this section and Section 7.7 describe some commonly practiced booking techniques that are much simpler to implement than the booking strategies that use full dynamic optimization.

Under a fixed class allocation, the service provider allocates the K units of capacity among the booking classes before the bookings process begins. Once the total number of booking requests for a certain class reaches the capacity allocation for that specific class, the class is declared as fully booked and remains closed for all future bookings.

Most importantly, in the short run, fixed class allocations may be the only available method of booking. This happens when capacity cannot be transferred among the classes during the booking process. For example, regular-size hotel rooms cannot be easily transformed into luxurious suites. An aircraft's economy-class seats cannot be instantaneously replaced by the wider first-class seats in the event of a surge in the demand for first-class tickets. For this reason, in this subsection we relax Assumption 7.3(c) and assume that capacity must be allocated among the service classes before the booking process begins. In addition, this allocation cannot be changed until after the service is delivered.

7.6.1 Nonoptimality of fixed class allocations

As mentioned earlier, there are services for which capacity cannot be easily reallocated among the service classes. Clearly, in a situation like this, when Assumption 7.3(c) is reversed, a fixed class allocation is optimal simply because it becomes the only available booking method. Therefore, nonoptimality of the fixed class allocation refers only to services for which Assumption 7.3(c) holds, so capacity can be shifted from one booking class to another during the periods when consumers submit their booking requests.

Table 7.7 provides an example of how $K = 100$ units of capacity are allocated among four booking classes labeled A, B, C, and D.

Class (i)	A	B	C	D
Price/fare (P^i)	P^A	P^B	P^C	P^D
Capacity allocation (K^i)	30	20	10	40

Table 7.7: Fixed allocation of $K = 100$ units of capacity among four service classes.

Suppose that the service provider commits to T booking periods and to the fixed class allocation described in Table 7.7. Clearly, the problem becomes interesting only if $T > K$, as otherwise every booking request should be accepted (see Assumption 7.3(a)).

To demonstrate why under Assumption 7.3(c) the fixed class allocation is not profit maximizing, suppose that by the end of booking period $t = 50$, 30 consumers have already been booked on class A. Then, because $K^A = 30$, class A closes and only booking requests on classes B and lower are accepted during booking periods $t = 51, \ldots, T$. Now, suppose that in some period $51 \le t \le T$ the service provider receives a request for a class A booking. Under the fixed class allocation, this request is turned down and the consumer is booked on a lower class (or not at all). Thus, the fixed class allocation is not profit maximizing because it denies a booking on a more profitable class while capacity is still available. More precisely, fixed class allocations prohibit the updating of booking decisions as the demand materializes. This is in contrast to the dynamic booking algorithms described elsewhere in this chapter in which class A booking requests are given a priority.

7.6.2 How to determine fixed class allocations: An example

In this section, we assume that for some exogenously given reasons, the service provider must commit to a fixed allocation of capacity and has no ability to change it during the booking process. Given this constraint, we now ask how classes should be allocated to maximize the total expected profit of this service provider.

We now demonstrate how to fix the profit-maximizing class allocation, assuming that only two service classes, labeled A and B, are offered to consumers for the prices P^A and P^B, respectively, where $P^A > P^B$. Suppose that there are $T = 3$ booking periods and $K = 2$ units of capacity to be allocated to classes A and B combined. Observe that Assumption 7.3(a) is satisfied because $2 = K < T = 3$. The purpose of the present analysis is to compute the profit-maximizing fixed class allocation K^A and K^B satisfying $K^A + K^B = K$. Table 7.8 shows how expected profit can be computed from all possible realizations of sequential booking requests. To

Booking Periods			Expected Profit: Capacity Allocation $\langle K^A, K^B \rangle$		
$t=1$	$t=2$	$t=3$	$\langle 2,0 \rangle$	$\langle 1,1 \rangle$	$\langle 0,2 \rangle$
A	A	A	$(\pi^A)^3 2P^A$	$(\pi^A)^3 P^A$	0
B	A	A	$(\pi^A)^2 \pi^B 2P^A$	$(\pi^A)^2 \pi^B (P^A + P^B)$	$(\pi^A)^2 \pi^B P^B$
A	B	A	$(\pi^A)^2 \pi^B 2P^A$	$(\pi^A)^2 \pi^B (P^A + P^B)$	$(\pi^A)^2 \pi^B P^B$
A	A	B	$(\pi^A)^2 \pi^B 2P^A$	$(\pi^A)^2 \pi^B (P^A + P^B)$	$(\pi^A)^2 \pi^B P^B$
B	B	B	0	$(\pi^B)^3 P^B$	$(\pi^B)^3 2P^B$
A	B	B	$\pi^A (\pi^B)^2 P^A$	$\pi^A (\pi^B)^2 (P^A + P^B)$	$\pi^A (\pi^B)^2 P^B$
B	A	B	$\pi^A (\pi^B)^2 P^A$	$\pi^A (\pi^B)^2 (P^A + P^B)$	$\pi^A (\pi^B)^2 P^B$
B	B	A	$\pi^A (\pi^B)^2 P^A$	$\pi^A (\pi^B)^2 (P^A + P^B)$	$\pi^A (\pi^B)^2 P^B$
Total expected profit:			$Ey(2,0)$	$Ey(1,1)$	$Ey(0,2)$

Table 7.8: Fixed capacity allocations: Booking requests and the resulting expected profits. *Note*: $Ey(K^A, K^B)$ equals the sum of the column above.

demonstrate how Table 7.8 was constructed, we look at the second row, in which a period $t=1$ consumer requests a class B booking and period $t=2$ and $t=3$ consumers each request a booking for class A. This specific sequence of realizations occurs with probability $(\pi^A)^2 \pi^B$. We now compute the expected profit under the three possible capacity allocations. If $\langle K^A, K^B \rangle = \langle 2,0 \rangle$, the booking request for class B cannot be accommodated because no capacity is allocated for class B. Hence, only the two class A requests are accepted, thereby generating a profit of $2P^A$. Next, if $\langle K^A, K^B \rangle = \langle 1,1 \rangle$, only one class A request can be accepted, thereby generating a profit of $P^A + P^B$. Lastly, if $\langle K^A, K^B \rangle = \langle 0,2 \rangle$, the class A booking request must be denied (no capacity is allocated to class A); thus, the generated profit is P^B.

Summing up, $Ey(K^A, K^B)$ measures the expected profit of each possible fixed class allocation, which is the sum of each column. The service provider should choose the fixed class allocation $\langle K^A, K^B \rangle$ that maximizes $Ey(K^A, K^B)$. Table 7.9 provides three examples of capacity allocations of $K=2$ units between two booking classes.

The most important lesson to be learned from Table 7.9 is that the decision regarding how to allocate capacity must be based on comparisons of expected total profits, not only on the probabilities of realizing a booking request for each class. More precisely, the example provided in the third row of Table 7.9 clearly demonstrates a case in which all capacity should be allocated to class A only, despite the fact that there is a probablility of 50% that class B will be requested in each of the three booking periods.

Booking Data				Capacity Allocation			Profitable
P^A	P^B	π^A	π^B	$\langle 2,0 \rangle$	$\langle 1,1 \rangle$	$\langle 0,2 \rangle$	Choice
$30	$10	0.1	0.9	$8.97	$18.12	$19.71	$\langle 0,2 \rangle$
$20	$10	0.1	0.9	$5.98	$15.41	$19.71	$\langle 1,1 \rangle$
$30	$10	0.5	0.5	$41.25	$35.00	$13.75	$\langle 2,0 \rangle$

Table 7.9: Examples of profit-maximizing fixed class allocations, based on specific data inserted into Table 7.8. Total capacity equals $K = 2$.

7.6.3 Computer algorithm for fixed class allocations

We now sketch a brief computer algorithm for finding the fixed class allocation that maximizes expected profit. The following parameter and variable definitions should be declared at the beginning of the program: $\mathcal{B}$, a finite set of all booking classes, that is, $\mathcal{B} = A, B, \ldots, i, \ldots$; the price vector $P[i]$ for every booking class $i \in \mathcal{B}$; and $\pi[i]$, the corresponding probability that a consumer will submit a request for booking on class $i \in \mathcal{B}$. The auxiliary integer valued vector component $c[i]$ will serve as a counter of how many bookings have been made on class $i, i \in \mathcal{B}$. Finally, the integer-valued parameter K inputs the capacity level, and T inputs the number of booking periods.

The algorithm suggested below also omits two procedures (subroutines) for generating two sets. Formally, the program should add a procedure for constructing the set of all possible allocations of capacity among all booking classes that satisfy

$$\mathcal{K} \overset{\text{def}}{=} \left\{ \langle k[A], k[B], \ldots, k[i], \ldots \rangle \;\middle|\; \sum_{i \in \mathcal{B}} k[i] = K \right\}. \tag{7.40}$$

For example, if A and B are the only booking classes,

$$\mathcal{K} = \{ \langle K, 0 \rangle, \langle K-1, 1 \rangle, \langle K-2, 2 \rangle, \ldots, \langle 0, K \rangle \}.$$

Elements of the set $\mathcal{K}$ are denoted by the vectors $\vec{k} \in \mathcal{K}$ and $\max \vec{k} \in \mathcal{K}$.

The program should also include a procedure for constructing the set of all possible realizations of booking requests according to their arrival period,

$$\mathcal{R} \overset{\text{def}}{=} \{ \langle r[1], r[2], \ldots, r[t], \ldots, r[T] \rangle \mid r[t] \in \mathcal{B} \}, \tag{7.41}$$

where $r[t]$ is the requested class during booking period $t, t = 1, \ldots, T$. An element of the set $\mathcal{R}$ will be denoted by a vector $\vec{r} \in \mathcal{R}$, which lists the realizations of booking requests in the order they are received. For example, Table 7.8 has already shown that if there are only $T = 3$ booking periods,

$$\mathcal{R} = \{ \langle AAA \rangle, \langle BAA \rangle, \langle ABA \rangle, \langle AAB \rangle, \langle BBB \rangle, \langle ABB \rangle, \langle BAB \rangle, \langle BBA \rangle \}.$$

A probability of realizing a specific sequence of booking requests is captured by the variable $\pi r \in [0,1]$ defined by $\pi r = \pi[r[1]] \times \pi[r[2]] \times \cdots \times \pi[r[T]]$, which is the product of probabilities of sequential realizations of booking requests. Finally, real-valued output variables measuring *expected* profits are denoted by y, yk, and yr. All these parameters and variables are now implemented in Algorithm 7.4.

```
for k⃗ ∈ 𝒦 do
    /* Main loop over all possible class allocations        */
    yk ← 0; /* Initializing profit from allocation k⃗         */
    for r⃗ ∈ ℛ do
        /* Loop over all possible booking realizations       */
        yr ← 0; /* Initializing profit from realization r⃗     */
        for i ∈ ℬ do c[i] ← 0/* Initializing counters         */
        for t = 1 to T do πr ← πr × π[r[t]]/* Realization Prob. */
        for t = 1 to T do
            /* Registering feasible booking requests         */
            if c[r[t]] < k[r[t]] then
                /* If requested class r[t] is underbooked     */
                c[r[t]] ← c[r[t]] + 1;   yr ← yr + πr × P[r[t]];
                /* Updating booking counter and exp. profit   */
        yk ← yk + yr; /* Updating class alloc. profit         */
    if maxy < yk then
        /* If class k⃗ is so far the most profitable           */
        maxy ← yk;   maxk⃗ ← k⃗; /* Register solution k⃗          */
for i ∈ ℬ do writeln ("Allocate", maxk⃗[i], "capacity for class", i);
write ("The expected profit from this class allocation is", maxy);
```

Algorithm 7.4: Advance booking: Fixed class allocation. *Note*: The main loops may have to be simplified as they reach high orders for a large number of booking periods.

7.7   Nested Class Allocations

The advantage of the nested class allocation over the fixed class allocation, such as the one described in Table 7.7, is that it can prevent a situation in which booking requests for class A are being denied because the capacity allocated for class A has been fully booked, whereas some capacity allocated for lower classes remains unbooked. A nested booking allocation always allows bookings at higher classes if capacity remains. Of course, this is possible only if capacity can be easily shifted from lower classes to higher classes, as stated in Assumption 7.3(a), which we now must reinstate.

7.7.1   Nested class allocation versus fixed allocations

Table 7.10 provides an example of how $K = 100$ units of capacity are allocated among four booking classes labeled A, B, C, and D. The reader should notice that the initial allocation in Table 7.10 is identical to the fixed allocation displayed in Table 7.7. However, once the booking process begins, the nested allocation is modified each time a booking is made, whereas the fixed allocation remains unaltered until classes are fully booked. The difference between the nested and fixed class allocations becomes clear by comparing the first and the second rows in Table 7.10, which correspond to the initial period 0 allocations before bookings begin. The nested class allocation always assigns all the remaining capacity to class A (100 units in the present example). This holds for all other booking periods where $K_t^A = k_t$ for every t.

t	r_t	k_t	Booking Class (i):	A	B	C	D
			Fixed allocation (K^i):	30	20	10	40
1	C	100	Nested allocation (K_1^i):	100	70	50	40
2	D	99	Nested allocation (K_2^i):	99	69	49	40
3	A	98	Nested allocation (K_3^i):	98	68	48	39
4	B	97	Nested allocation (K_4^i):	97	68	48	39
5	n/a	96	Nested allocation (K_5^i):	96	67	48	39

Table 7.10: Nested class allocation (booking limits) of $K = 100$ units of capacity. *Note*: r_t denotes a realization of a period t booking request.

The third row in Table 7.10 demonstrates a realization of the period $t = 1$ booking request, which happens to be for class C. Upon accepting this request, total period $t = 2$ remaining capacity drops to $k_2 = 100 - 1$. Because all classes higher than class C can use class C capacity allocation, the reservation system subtracts one unit of capacity from classes A, B, and C. Formally, $K_2^A = 99$, $K_2^B = 69$, and $K_2^C = 49$. However, under this algorithm, the service provider does not change the capacity allocation for classes lower than C. This means that $K_2^D = K_1^D = 40$. Thus, the capacity allocation for the lowest class is modified only if a booking request for class D is accepted, as demonstrated in the fourth row of Table 7.10. Similarly, the bottom row demonstrates that accepting a booking request for class B in period $t = 4$ implies that capacity allocations for classes C and D remain unchanged in $t = 5$.

7.7.2   How to determine nested class allocations: An example

We now modify the fixed class allocation example analyzed in Subsection 7.6.2 to nested class allocation. Using the exact same figures, Table 7.8 (fixed capacity allocation) is now replaced with Table 7.11, which displays the expected profit from each possible nested capacity allocation.

Periods			Expected Profit: Nested Allocation of $K=2$ Capacity		
1	2	3	$\langle 2,0 \rangle$	$\langle 2,1 \rangle$	$\langle 2,2 \rangle$
A	A	A	$(\pi^A)^3 2P^A$	$(\pi^A)^3 2P^A$	$(\pi^A)^3 2P^A$
B	A	A	$(\pi^A)^2 \pi^B 2P^A$	$(\pi^A)^2 \pi^B (P^A + P^B)$	$(\pi^A)^2 \pi^B (P^A + P^B)$
A	B	A	$(\pi^A)^2 \pi^B 2P^A$	$(\pi^A)^2 \pi^B (P^A + P^B)$	$(\pi^A)^2 \pi^B (P^A + P^B)$
A	A	B	$(\pi^A)^2 \pi^B 2P^A$	$(\pi^A)^2 \pi^B 2P^A$	$(\pi^A)^2 \pi^B 2P^A$
B	B	B	$(\pi^B)^3 0$	$(\pi^B)^3 P^B$	$(\pi^B)^3 2P^B$
A	B	B	$\pi^A (\pi^B)^2 P^A$	$\pi^A (\pi^B)^2 (P^A + P^B)$	$\pi^A (\pi^B)^2 (P^A + P^B)$
B	A	B	$\pi^A (\pi^B)^2 P^A$	$\pi^A (\pi^B)^2 (P^A + P^B)$	$\pi^A (\pi^B)^2 (P^A + P^B)$
B	B	A	$\pi^A (\pi^B)^2 P^A$	$\pi^A (\pi^B)^2 (P^A + P^B)$	$\pi^A (\pi^B)^2 2P^B$
	Profit:		$Ey(2,0)$	$Ey(2,1)$	$Ey(2,2)$

Table 7.11: Nested capacity allocations: Booking requests and the resulting expected profits. *Note*: $Ey(K^A, K^B)$ is the sum of the columns above.

The columns of Table 7.11 display the expected profit of the three possible nested allocations. The allocation $\langle 2,0 \rangle$ is identical to the fixed allocation in which only class A bookings are allowed. Thus, expected profits are identical to those given by Table 7.8. The nested allocation $\langle 2,1 \rangle$ implies that at most one booking can be made on class B (but two bookings can be made on class A). The third allocation $\langle 2,2 \rangle$ allows up to two bookings to be made on each class (but only two bookings in total because $K=2$).

Comparing the expected profit levels given in Table 7.8 with the profits displayed in Table 7.11 reveals that for some entries, the profits are equal and in some others, the profits are higher under the nested capacity allocation. This leads us to conclude that the nested capacity allocation is more profitable than the fixed capacity allocation. Table 7.12 displays three examples showing how expected profit levels vary with all possible nested capacity allocations, given that total capacity is restricted to $K=2$. Comparing Table 7.12 with Table 7.9 clearly shows that the nested capacity allocation yields a higher expected profit compared with the fixed capacity allocation. Therefore, we can conclude that for *every fixed capacity allocation, there exists a nested capacity allocation that yields a higher expected profit.*

| Booking Data | | | | Capacity Allocation | | | Profitable |
P^A	P^B	π^A	π^B	$\langle 2,0 \rangle$	$\langle 2,1 \rangle$	$\langle 2,2 \rangle$	Choice
$30	$10	0.1	0.9	$8.97	$18.37	$24.00	$\langle 0,2 \rangle$
$20	$10	0.1	0.9	$5.98	$15.52	$22.00	$\langle 0,2 \rangle$
$30	$10	0.5	0.5	$41.25	$41.25	$40.00	$\langle 2,0 \rangle, \langle 2,1 \rangle$

Table 7.12: Examples of profit-maximizing nested class allocations, based on specific data inserted into Table 7.11. Total capacity equals $K = 2$.

7.7.3 Computer algorithm for nested class allocations

As it turns out, Algorithm 7.4 which was constructed for the fixed class allocation, can be easily modified so it accommodates booking requests under nested capacity allocations. The tiny procedure that we add reduces the available capacity for all classes equal to and higher than the class in which a booking request is accepted. A second modification that we need to make is to redefine the set of all feasible fixed allocations $\mathcal{K} = A, B, \ldots$, earlier defined by (7.40), to make it the set of all feasible *nested* class allocations. Formally, let

$$\mathcal{K} \overset{\text{def}}{=} \left\{ \langle k[A], k[B], \ldots \rangle \mid k[A] = K \ \& \ k[i] \geq k[j] \text{ if } P^i \geq P^j \right\}. \tag{7.42}$$

For example, if A and B are the only booking classes,

$$\mathcal{K} = \left\{ \langle K,0 \rangle, \langle K,1 \rangle, \langle K,2 \rangle, \ldots, \langle K,K \rangle \right\}.$$

Algorithm 7.5 shows how Algorithm 7.4 should be modified to be applicable for nested class allocations, by replacing one procedure.

```
if c[r[t]] < k[r[t]] then
    /* If the requested class r[t] is not fully booked      */
    c[r[t]] ← c[r[t]] + 1;   yr ← yr + πr × P[r[t]];
    /* Updating booking counter and exp. profit             */
    for j ∈ ℬ do if P^j ≥ P^r[t] then k[j] ← k[j] − 1 /* Reduce capacity
         for classes higher than class r[t]                 */
```

Algorithm 7.5: Advance booking: Modifying Algorithm 7.4 to nested class allocation.

7.7.4 Protective (theft) nested capacity allocations

The protective class allocation (sometimes referred to as "theft" allocation) differs from the standard nested allocation in that the lower service classes close very early because a booking on any class reduces the capacity allocated for all classes. Recall that under the standard nested class allocation, any booking reduces the allocated capacity only in classes higher than (or equal to) the booked class.

Table 7.13 modifies Table 7.10 from standard to protective nested class allocation. The example assumes $K = 100$ units of capacity allocated among four booking classes labeled A, B, C, and D. Table 7.13 demonstrates that under protective

t	r_t	k_t	Booking Class (i):	A	B	C	D
			Fixed allocation (K^i):	30	20	10	40
1	C	100	Protective nested allocation (K_1^i):	100	70	50	40
2	D	99	Protective nested allocation (K_2^i):	99	69	49	39
3	A	98	Protective nested allocation (K_3^i):	98	68	48	38
4	B	97	Protective nested allocation (K_4^i):	97	67	47	37
5	n/a	96	Protective nested allocation (K_5^i):	96	66	46	36

Table 7.13: Protective (theft) nested class allocation of $K = 100$ units of capacity. *Note*: r_t denotes a realization of period t booking request.

nested capacity allocation, each time a booking request is accepted for any class, the next period's capacity allocation is reduced for all classes (as opposed to a reduction in equal or higher classes under the standard nested capacity allocation). In view of this difference between the protective and standard capacity allocations, Algorithm 7.5 can be easily modified to handle protective capacity allocation by removing the condition "if $P^j \geq P^r[t]$" from the last line. Under this modification, any accepted booking request will result in a subsequent period's reduction in capacity allocated for all classes.

7.8 Exercises

1. Consider our first example given in Subsection 7.1.1 of a service provider who allows only two booking periods and two fare classes. Suppose now that we replace the potential consumer population given in Table 7.1 with the following data:

Class (i)	0	A	B
Proportion (π^i)	0.4	0.1	0.5
Price/fare (P^i)	\$0	\$40	\$10

Table 7.14: Potential consumer population for Exercises 1 and 2.

(a) Using the same steps as in Subsection 7.1.1, derive the decision rules $d_1(P_1)$ and $d_2(P_2)$ and the corresponding period 2 expected value of capacity $EV_2(k_2)$ by working backward from period $t = 2$ to period $t = 1$.

(b) Calculate the firm's actual profit assuming that in period $t = 1$, a consumer requested a booking for class B.

2. This exercise extends Exercise 1 by introducing *salvage value* of capacity. Suppose now that the service operator can sell any unit of unused capacity at a discount price of $P^S = \$5$. Using the same steps as in Subsection 7.1.3, derive the decision rules $d_1(P_1)$ and $d_2(P_2)$ and the corresponding period 2 expected value of capacity EV_2 for a service provider facing the consumer population described in Table 7.14.

3. Consider our analysis of booking a small consumer population analyzed in Subsection 7.1.4. However, instead of assuming that there are five consumers, suppose that there are only three consumers. One consumer is expected not to be booked. Another consumer is expected to request a booking on class A, and the third is expected to request class B.

Construct the equivalent of Table 7.3 for this three-consumer case. Then, construct the service provider's profit-maximizing decision rules, $d_1(P_1)$ and $d_2(P_2)$.

4. Suppose that there is an arbitrary number of booking periods indexed by $t = 1, 2, \ldots, T$, as analyzed in Section 7.2. Consider the following information about the potential consumers given in Table 7.15:

Class (i)	0	A	B
Proportion (π^i)	0.3	0.1	0.6
Price/fare (P^i)	\$0	\$60	\$20

Table 7.15: Potential consumer population for Exercise 4.

(a) Compute the decision rules for periods T, $T-1$, $T-2$, $T-3$, and $T-4$. Clearly, you will also need to compute the expected value of capacity EV_T, EV_{T-1}, EV_{T-2}, and EV_{T-3}.

(b) Suppose that this service provider owns exactly $K = 3$ units of capacity. Compute the firm's profit level assuming the following realizations of booking requests: $P_{T-4} = P_{T-3} = P_{T-2} = \$20$, and $P_{T-1} = P_T = \$60$.

5. Consider the advance booking problem with strictly positive marginal cost as illustrated in Table 7.5. How should the adjusted booking data be modified if the marginal operating cost is $\mu_o = \$19$ instead of $\mu_o = \$25$? To answer this question, simply reconstruct Table 7.5.

6. Consider the airline that serves the three cities illustrated in Figure 7.1. Assume that $K^{AH} = K^{HB} = 1$. Suppose now that we replace the passenger information given in Table 7.6 by the data given in Table 7.16.

Route (i)	0	AH	HB	AB
Proportion (π^i)	0.1	0.1	0.1	0.7
Airfare (P^i)	$0	$20	$30	$40

Table 7.16: Airline bookings: Passenger information for Exercise 6.

(a) Using the same steps as in Subsection 7.5.1, derive the decision rules $d_1(P_1)$ and $d_2(P_2)$ and the corresponding expected value of capacity $EV_1(k_1^{AH}, k_1^{HB})$ and $EV_2(k_2^{AH}, k_2^{HB})$ by working backward from booking period $t = 2$ to period $t = 1$.

(b) Using the derived decision rules $d_1(P_1)$ and $d_2(P_2)$, compute the probability that no capacity will be booked, that is, the probability that both flights will take off with no passengers.

(c) Compute the probability that this airline will book a passenger on route AB.

(d) Compute the probability that this airline will book a passenger on route HB.

7. Consider the fixed class allocation model analyzed in Section 7.6. Compute the profit-maximizing fixed class allocation $\langle K^A, K^B \rangle$ assuming that service classes A and B are sold for $P^A = \$20$ and $P^B = \$10$ and are realized with probabilities $\pi^A = 0.2$ and $\pi^B = 0.8$, respectively. Assume that the service provider allows for three booking periods and there are a total of $K = 2$ units of capacity.

8. Solve the previous exercise assuming that there is only one unit of capacity ($K = 1$). *Hint*: You must first modify Table 7.8 to incorporate the two possible class allocations $\langle K^A, K^B \rangle = \langle 1, 0 \rangle$ and $\langle K^A, K^B \rangle = \langle 0, 1 \rangle$.

9. Consider the nested class allocation analyzed in Section 7.7. Assuming the same initial capacity allocation as in Table 7.10, construct a similar table showing the capacity allocation in each booking period $t = 1, 2, 3, 4$ assuming that the realized sequence of booking requests is given by $r_1 = A$, $r_2 = B$, $r_3 = C$, and $r_4 = D$.

10. Compute the profit-maximizing nested class allocation for the industry described in Exercise 7.

11. Solve the previous exercise assuming that there is only one unit of capacity ($K = 1$). *Hint*: You must first modify Table 7.11 to incorporate the two possible nested class allocations: $\langle 1, 0 \rangle$, and $\langle 1, 1 \rangle$.

Chapter 8
Refund Strategies

8.1 Basic Definitions 267

    8.1.1 Survival probabilities, no-shows, and cancellations

    8.1.2 Service provider's cost structure

    8.1.3 Seller's strategies

8.2 Consumers, Preferences, and Seller's Profit 270

    8.2.1 Preferences and profits under lump-sum refunds

    8.2.2 Preferences and profits under proportional refunds

    8.2.3 Multiple consumer types

8.3 Refund Policy under an Exogenously Given Price 274

    8.3.1 Lump-sum refunds under an exogenously given price

    8.3.2 Proportional refunds under an exogenously given price

8.4 Simultaneous Price and Refund Policy Decisions 280

    8.4.1 Two consumer types

    8.4.2 Multiple consumer types: A computer algorithm

8.5 Multiple Price and Refund Packages 288

8.6 Refund Policy under Moral Hazard 290

    8.6.1 Survival probability under moral hazard

    8.6.2 Refund setting under an exogenously given price

8.7 Integrating Refunds within Advance Booking 293

8.8 Exercises 294

Refunds are widely observed in almost all privately provided services and also to some degree in retail industries. Refunds are heavily used by travel-related service providers. Most noticeably, refunds are heavily used by airlines where cheaper tickets allow for a very small refund (if any) on cancellations and no-shows, whereas full-fare tickets are either fully refundable or are subject to low cancellation penalty rates.

In Chapter 7, we analyze service providers who face consumers who value advance reservation systems because they enable them to guarantee that the service will be available at the contracted delivery time. However, the drawback of the advance reservation system, to both consumers and service providers, is that consumers may either cancel their reservations or simply may not show up at the time when the contracted service is scheduled to be delivered. This will leave some capacity unused, thereby resulting in a loss to service providers. Clearly, this loss can be minimized if service providers do not provide any refund to consumers who either cancel or do not show up.

In this chapter, we show how service providers can enhance their profit and extract higher surplus from consumers by offering refunds to consumers who either cancel their reservations or simply do not show up. For most parts of this chapter, we will not distinguish between a *cancellation* and a *no-show*. However, for the sake of completeness, the following definition clarifies the difference between these two terms.

DEFINITION 8.1
*We say that a consumer with a confirmed reservation **cancels** the reservation if the consumer notifies the service provider some time before the service delivery time that the reservation will not be used. In contrast, a confirmed consumer's **no-show** occurs when the consumer does not show up at the service delivery time, with no prior notice.*

Definition 8.1 is not without problems, as the precise meaning of "some time before" the service delivery time is not clear. For example, should five-minute notification by the consumer be considered as a cancellation? However, this difficulty is overcome by having the service provider specify on each confirmed ticket the precise time frame that would qualify as a cancellation time, usually under the terms and conditions of a sold ticket. Moreover, service providers can create such a distinction by simply offering consumers different refund levels depending on whether the consumer cancels in advance (and how long in advance) and whether the consumer does not show up at the service delivery time. Clearly, all these terms and conditions must be clearly specified at the time when the service is contracted, usually when the reservations are made, or a ticket is issued and paid for.

Consumers who make reservations for products and services differ in their probability of showing up to collect the good or the service at the pre-agreed time of delivery. Agencies and dealers that sell these goods and services can save on unused capacity costs, generated by consumers' cancellations and no-shows, by varying the degree of refunds offered to consumers who cancel or do not show up. In this chapter, we show how the introduction of refunds serves as a price discrimination technique by which service providers attract consumers who are more likely to cancel their reservations. The resulting increase in consumer base increases the total surplus extracted from consumers. In the absence of refunds, service providers may be induced to set the price sufficiently high so consumers who are likely to cancel will not book this service.

Why do consumers have different probabilities of showing up? The best way to think about it is to observe airline passengers. Passengers can be divided into business travelers and leisure travelers. Business travelers are most likely to cancel or change their reservations because their travel arrangements depend on others' schedules and business opportunities. In contrast, students can be sure of their time of travel because they tend to travel during semester breaks and holidays that are not subjected to last-minute changes. All this means is that students are more likely to engage in an advance purchase of discounted nonrefundable tickets, whereas business travelers are less likely to commit in advance, and therefore are more likely to either purchase fully refundable tickets or to postpone their ticket purchase to the last minute.

In the economics literature, there are a few papers analyzing the refundability option as a means for segmenting the market or the demand. Most studies have focused on a single seller. Contributions by Gale and Holmes (1992, 1993) compare a monopolist's advance bookings with socially optimal ones. Gale (1993) analyzes consumers who learn their preferences only after they are offered an advance purchase option. Along this line, Miravete (1996) and more recently Courty and Li (2000) further investigate how consumers who learn their valuation over time can be screened via the introduction of refunds. Courty (2003) investigates resale and rationing strategies of a monopoly that can sell early to uninformed consumers or late to informed consumers. Dana (1998) also investigates market segmentation under advance booking made by price-taking firms. Ringbom and Shy (2004) analyze partial refunds set by price-taking firms. Ringbom and Shy (2005) analyzes refund setting under price competition and service providers' incentives to semicollude on a joint industry-wide refund policy.

8.1 Basic Definitions

We now lay out the basic formulation of the refund models used throughout this chapter. Section 8.1.1 explains consumers' behavior under the possibility of no-show. Section 8.1.2 defines three types of service/production costs and explains how each type of cost is affected by consumers' no-shows. Finally, Section 8.1.3 summarizes the type of sellers' refund strategies analyzed in this chapter.

8.1.1 Survival probabilities, no-shows, and cancellations

Let π denote the probability that a consumer will show up and consume the service at contracted delivery time. We call π the *survival probability*, or the show-up probability, where $0 \leq \pi \leq 1$. Therefore, the probability of a cancellation and a no-show is $1 - \pi$. We make the following assumption:

ASSUMPTION 8.1

Consumers' survival probabilities (probabilities of showing up) are constant and are unaffected by the refund level offered on no-shows and cancellations.

Assumption 8.1 implies that consumers' cancellation decisions are exogenously given in the sense that consumers actually do not make the decision to cancel or not to show up. Instead, cancellations are determined by some external circumstances. Clearly, Assumption 8.1 is too strong as it applies mainly to business-oriented services in which cancellations are caused by a loss of business opportunities (or a gain of some alternative opportunities). However, in many service markets, there is a large number of consumers who are more likely to cancel when promised large refunds. In fact, the introduction of refunds may even induce more consumers who know they are likely to cancel to book this service. Some of these consumers will not even bother to book the service when sold under nonrefundable contracts. When survival probabilities change with the refund policy, we say that consumers exhibit *moral hazard* behavior. Refund policy under moral hazard will be analyzed in Section 8.6.

Let p denote the price of this service, and assume that all consumers must pay for the service when the reservation is made. Also, let r denote the refund level offered to consumers upon cancellation or a no-show. We assume consumers are immediately reimbursed in the sense that they are paid r with "no questions asked" if they cancel or simply do not show up. The following definitions establish some terminology regarding the use of refunds by service providers.

DEFINITION 8.2

A refund policy on cancellations and no-shows is said to consist of
(a) **Lump-sum refunds** *if consumers receive a fixed amount $\$r$, where $0 \le r \le p$.*
(b) **Proportional** *or* **percentage refunds** *if refunds are expressed as the fraction r of the prepaid booking price, where $0 \le r \le 1$. In this case, the amount refunded equals $r \times p$.*
(c) **Fixed cancellation fees**, *if consumers are reimbursed the prepaid price less a pre-agreed fixed cancellation fee cn, where $0 \le cn \le p$.*
(d) **Proportional cancellation fees**, *if consumers receive their money back less a certain fraction cn (percentage) of the prepaid price. In this case, the cancellation fee equals $cn \times p$, where $0 \le cn \le 1$.*

Clearly, Definition 8.2(a) is equivalent to Definition 8.2(c) simply because the seller can set $cn = p - r$. Similarly, Definition 8.2(b) is equivalent to Definition 8.2(d) because the seller is free to set $cn = 1 - r$. For this reason, our analysis in this chapter will focus on refunds, but the reader should bear in mind that all refunds can be expressed in terms of cancellation fees (as we just did).

Observe that cancellation fees are commonly used in service sectors. However, in the mail-order industry, retailers tend to use a different terminology, namely, *shipping and handling (s&h) charges*, instead of cancellation or penalty fees. From a technical viewpoint, both types of fees serve the same purpose, which is to limit the amount of refund given to consumers who would like to cancel a service, or simply return a product. Of course, s&h sounds better than cancellation fees, but this terminology does not translate into any practical difference. For this reason, in this chapter we do not analyze s&h charges separately from other refund types.

The following definition classifies three possible refund levels.

DEFINITION 8.3
We say that the payment for a booking of a service is
- *fully refundable if $r = p$, or ($r = 1$ meaning 100%),*
- *nonrefundable if $r = 0$, or ($r = 0$ meaning 0%),*
- *partially refundable if $0 < r < p$, ($0 < r < 1$, meaning less than 100%).*

Definition 8.3 describes the types of refund levels analyzed in this chapter. Thus, we rule out extreme situations in which sellers set refund levels exceeding the prepaid price, $r > p$, as in reality this kind of consumer "subsidy" generates extreme moral hazard effects in which people book the service just for the sake of obtaining refunds.

8.1.2   Service provider's cost structure

We now discuss the service provider's (production side) cost structure. The fixed and sunk costs, denoted by ϕ, are borne by the service provider (the seller or the producer) independent of the seller's refund policy and consumers' cancellation probabilities, and may even be ignored for most parts of our analysis. However, marginal costs, which constitute the cost of providing an *additional* unit of service, are sensitive to consumers' show-up probabilities in the following way:

DEFINITION 8.4
The cost of providing an additional unit of service is called
- *Marginal operating cost, denoted by μ_o, if this cost is borne only when the consumer actually shows up at the service delivery time.*
- *Marginal capacity cost, denoted by μ_k, if this cost is borne each time a consumer books one unit of service.*

The marginal capacity cost (or booking cost) is a direct consequence of our assumption that overbooking is not allowed. Overbooking is examined in detail in Chapter 9. This means that the service provider must secure exactly one unit of capacity each time a booking is made.

To give some examples that would clarify the distinction between the two types of marginal costs described by Definition 8.4, we discuss some travel-related industries. In the airline industry, the marginal operating cost can be viewed as the price of onboard services provided to passengers, such as meals and entertainment. In the hotel industry, the marginal operating cost consists of the cost of cleaning up the room, changing and washing sheets and towels, electricity and water consumption, and so on. In contrast, marginal capacity cost in the airline industry consists of the cost of expanding seating capacity by one seat (which corresponds to a change in aircraft size divided by the number of flights). In the hotel business, this cost could be the cost of building an additional hotel room divided by 365 days, say.

Clearly, the capacity cost is much harder to estimate as it depends on the cost of capital, which depends on the interest rate. In fact, we have already classified these two types of marginal costs in Chapter 6 where we analyzed peak-load pricing problems. As already mentioned in Section 7.1.3, the real difficulty in estimating marginal capacity cost stems from the fact that some of this capital has salvage value. That is, the cost of booking one additional unit of capacity heavily depends on the alternative use of unused capital in a no-show event. Here, we basically assume that there is no salvage value of capital, and even if there is, it is already imbedded into the parameter μ_k.

8.1.3 Seller's strategies

In this chapter, we demonstrate how to compute profit-maximizing prices and refund levels when service providers face a variety of different consumer types. However, industries may differ in the degree of flexibility of setting price and refund levels. For this reason, we will be conducting our analysis under three types of pricing instruments:

Refund setting only: In this type of industry, prices are fixed either by the regulator or by the manufacturer (as opposed to the provider). Our investigation then focuses on finding the profit-maximizing refund policy for any exogenously given price.

Refund and price setting: The service provider is free to set a booking package consisting of a price and a refund policy.

Multiple price–refund packages: The service provider designs a "menu" of different "packages," thereby segmenting the market so that different types of consumers may buy different packages, each containing a different refund–price combination.

8.2 Consumers, Preferences, and Seller's Profit

We now specify how consumers make a decision whether or not to book the service. Each consumer values the service/product at V. That is, V is a consumer's maximum willingness to pay for the actual delivery of the service or the consumption of the product (whichever applies). In other words, the consumer is willing to pay V conditional on actually showing up and actually consuming the service when the service is delivered. Clearly, if full refunds are not offered, the willingness to pay should be lower as the consumer takes into account the possibilities of no-shows and cancellations.

8.2.1 Preferences and profits under lump-sum refunds

We assume that each consumer maximizes the expected net benefit given by

$$
U(p,r) \stackrel{\text{def}}{=} \begin{cases} \pi V - p + (1-\pi)r & \text{if he or she chooses to book the service} \\ \bar{U} & \text{does not book this service.} \end{cases} \tag{8.1}
$$

Equation 8.1 is commonly referred to as a consumer's (expected) utility function. The term πV is the expected net benefit from consuming the service, taking into account that this benefit is realized with probability π. Because the price is prepaid, the price p must be deducted. In contrast, a refund r is reimbursed to the consumer only in a no-show event, which occurs with probability $1 - \pi$.

For example, suppose a consumer values the actual delivery of a certain service by $V = \$10$ and there is a probability of 50% that the consumer will cancel the reservation. The service provider sets a price $p = \$6$ that must be paid at the time the booking is made. Table 8.1 demonstrates how booking decisions are affected by varying the refund level r according to the utility function (8.1). Table 8.1 shows that the service provider can turn a not-booking decision into a booking decision by increasing the promised refund level even without changing the market price. The threshold refund level $r = \$2$ leaves the consumer indifferent between booking and not booking. In such a case, we will always assume that the consumer chooses to book, simply because the seller can always increase the refund by 1¢, thereby making a booking decision generating a strictly positive utility.

π	V	πV	p	r	$(1-\pi)r$	U	Decision
0.5	10	5	6	0	0.0	-1.0	Not book
0.5	10	5	6	1	0.5	-0.5	Not book
0.5	10	5	6	2	1.0	0.0	Book
0.5	10	5	6	3	1.5	0.5	Book

Table 8.1: Refunds and booking decisions made according to (8.1), assuming a threshold utility level of $\bar{U} = 0$.

The examples listed in Table 8.1 assume a threshold utility level given by $\bar{U} = 0$. The threshold utility level reflects the utility generated from using an alternative service, and could generally take values that differ from $\bar{U} = 0$, as shown in Exercise 1 at the end of this chapter. The threshold utility level is often called "reservation utility" by academic economists; however, we avoid using this terminology to prevent confusion with booking (making reservations) decisions analyzed throughout this book.

We end our discussion of the consumer side with a graphical visualization of booking decisions under refunds. Extracting the refund level r from $\pi V - p + (1 - \pi)r = \bar{U}$, where $\bar{U}$ is the threshold utility level, obtains

$$r = \frac{\bar{U}}{1 - \pi} + \frac{p - \pi V}{1 - \pi}. \tag{8.2}$$

In particular, for the specific utility function (8.1) where $\bar{U} = 0$,

$$r = \frac{p - \pi V}{1 - \pi}, \tag{8.3}$$

which is plotted in Figure 8.1. The area above the dashed line represents refund levels exceeding the price, which are ruled out by assumption. Under the dashed line, all booking offers with a sufficiently high refund and/or a sufficiently low price will be accepted by the consumer. Clearly, holding r constant and increasing p beyond a certain level would change the consumer's decision to not book the service. Finally, Figure 8.1 shows that even with a full refund, the price must not exceed $p = r = V$ to induce the consumer to book this service. Note that $p = r = V$ is also the unique solution to (8.3) after substituting $p = r$.

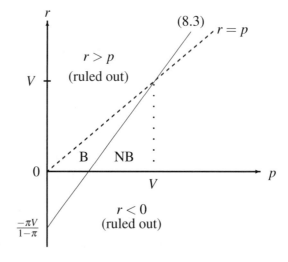

Figure 8.1: Lump-sum refund: Book (B) and no-book (NB) utility decision.

We now define the profit function of a service provider. Suppose that n consumers decide to book the service and prepay the given price of p. Let r be the agreed upon refund level on a no-show. The expected profit of this service provider is given by

$$y \stackrel{\text{def}}{=} n(p - \mu_k) - \pi n \mu_o - (1 - \pi)r - \phi. \tag{8.4}$$

The first term in (8.4) constitutes the sales revenue net of the cost of reserving n units of capacity. The second term is the expected operating cost that depends on the number of actual shows πn. The third term is the expected cost associated with paying refunds to consumers who cancel. The last term is the fixed cost ϕ, which generally does not affect any price decision but should be considered when evaluating the long-run profitability of the firm. For this reason, in a few examples we simply set $\phi = 0$.

8.2.2 Preferences and profits under proportional refunds

Proportional (percentage) refunds are analyzed only in Section 8.3.2, so readers who wish to skip this section as well as Section 8.3.2 can do it without any consequences on the understanding of all other sections in this chapter. Suppose now that instead of giving a lump-sum refund of $\$r$, the service provider commits to a refund that is proportional to the prepaid booking price. So, we now let r be a fraction $0 \le r \le 1$ of the price given to consumers who cancel or do not show. Thus, the refunded amount now becomes $r \times p$. Under proportional refund, the consumers' expected utility function (8.1) becomes

$$U(p,r) \stackrel{\text{def}}{=} \begin{cases} \pi V - p + (1-\pi)rp & \text{if they choose to book the service} \\ 0 & \text{not book this service.} \end{cases} \tag{8.5}$$

We now provide a graphical visualization of booking decisions under proportional refunds. Extracting the refund rate r from $\pi V - p + (1-\pi)rp = 0$ where 0 is the threshold utility level obtains

$$r = \frac{p - \pi V}{(1-\pi)p}, \tag{8.6}$$

which is plotted in Figure 8.2. Similar to Figure 8.1, any combination of price and refund levels above the curve will be accepted and booked by consumers. Any combination below the curve will be rejected as the booking yields an expected utility below the threshold level. Also, Figure 8.2 clearly shows that as long as the service provider charges a price below the expected consumers' benefit πV, consumers will book this service even if no refund is given.

8.2.3 Multiple consumer types

So far, we characterized the preferences of a single individual who has a basic valuation of V for the service, and a survival probability π. We now extend the model to multiple consumer types. Let there be M consumer types, indexed by $\ell = 1, 2, \ldots, M$. When there are only two types, we sometimes index types by $\ell = H, L$ to indicate high and low survival probabilities. There are N_ℓ consumers of

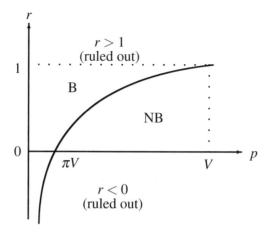

Figure 8.2: Proportional refund: Book (B) and no-book (NB) utility decision.

type ℓ. Each type ℓ consumer is characterized by the survival probability π_ℓ and the valuation V_ℓ.

Because our analysis deals with multiple consumer types, we need to extend the single consumer–type profit function (8.4) to M consumer types. Thus,

$$y \stackrel{\text{def}}{=} \sum_{\ell=1}^{M} [n_\ell(p - \mu_k) - \pi_\ell n_\ell \mu_o - (1 - \pi_\ell)r] - \phi. \qquad (8.7)$$

Similarly, we slightly modify (8.7) from a lump-sum to a proportional refund by replacing r with $r \times p$. Thus,

$$y \stackrel{\text{def}}{=} \sum_{\ell=1}^{M} [n_\ell(p - \mu_k) - \pi_\ell n_\ell \mu_o - (1 - \pi_\ell)rp] - \phi. \qquad (8.8)$$

8.3   Refund Policy under an Exogenously Given Price

Suppose now that the service provider books the service at an exogenously given price denoted by $\bar{p}$, which is set either by the regulator or by the manufacturer under a resale price maintenance (RPM) agreement. For this section *only*, we make the following assumption concerning how consumer types are indexed.

ASSUMPTION 8.2
Consumer types are indexed according to decreasing order of their threshold refund levels (8.3). Formally,

$$\frac{\bar{p} - \pi_1 V_1}{1 - \pi_1} \geq \frac{\bar{p} - \pi_2 V_2}{1 - \pi_2} \geq \ldots \geq \frac{\bar{p} - \pi_M V_M}{1 - \pi_M}.$$

It is very important to stress that Assumption 8.2 is made with no loss of generality whatsoever as it merely requires a re-indexation of consumer types. In other words, Assumption 8.2 is not really an assumption as it only guides us in labeling consumer types to facilitate the profit-maximization algorithms developed in this section.

8.3.1 Lump-sum refunds under an exogenously given price

Under a fixed booking price, this section computes the lump-sum refund level $0 \leq r \leq \bar{p}$ that maximizes the seller's profit.

Two consumer types: An example

Consider a single service provider facing two types of consumers, labeled type $\ell = H$ (high survival probability) and type $\ell = L$ (low survival probability), as described by Table 8.2. All consumers are assumed to make their book–not-book decisions as to maximize the utility function defined by (8.1). In this simple example, there are 500 type H potential consumers with a survival probability of $\pi_H = 0.8$, and a basic valuation for this service given by $V_H = \$10$. Similarly, there are 800 type L consumers with a survival probability of $\pi_L = 0.5$, with a basic valuation of $V_L = \$10$. Thus, the first four columns of Table 8.2 constitute the exogenous data, whereas the remaining three columns are simple computations of expected value of the service, expected number of show-ups of each group, and expected number of no-shows.

Consumers				Some Computations		
ℓ	N_ℓ	π_ℓ	V_ℓ	$\pi_\ell V_\ell$	$\pi_\ell N_\ell$	$(1-\pi_\ell)N_\ell$
H	500	0.8	10	8	400	100
L	800	0.5	10	5	400	400

Seller's Cost		
μ_o	μ_k	ϕ
2	1	1000

Table 8.2: Two-consumer type example.

In what follows, we analyze the possible profit-maximizing refund settings of the service provider with the cost structure given in Table 8.2. Suppose the service price is fixed at the level $\bar{p} = \$6$ and the service provider cannot change this price. Thus, the only strategic variable available to this seller is to set a uniform refund policy for all consumers, r, where $0 \leq r \leq p$. We analyze three refund policies: no refund (NR), where $r = 0$, full refund (FR), where $r = \bar{p} = 6$, and a partial refund (PR), where $0 < r < \bar{p}$.

Under no refund, type L consumers do not book the service because if they do, by (8.1) their utility level would be $U_L = 0.5 \times 10 - 6 < 0$. However, type H consumers book the service because $U_H = 0.8 \times 10 - 6 > 0$. Substituting $\bar{p} = 6$ and the data from Table 8.2 into (8.4) yields the seller's profit level

$$y^{NR} = 500(6-1) - 0.8 \times 500 \times 2 - (1-0.8)0 - 1000 = 700. \qquad (8.9)$$

Now suppose the seller provides a full refund so that $r = 6$. Under this policy, type L consumers book this service because $U_L = 0.5 \times 10 - 6 + (1 - 0.5)6 = 2 > 0$. Type H consumers also book this service because $U_H = 0.8 \times 10 - 6 + (1 - 0.2)6 > 0$. Substituting $r = \bar{p} = 6$ and the data from Table 8.2 into (8.7) yields the seller's profit level

$$y^{FR} = (500 + 800)(6 - 1) - (0.8 \times 500 + 0.5 \times 800)2$$
$$- (0.2 \times 500 + 0.5 \times 800)6 - 1000 = 900. \quad (8.10)$$

Comparing (8.10) with (8.9) shows that in this example giving a full refund yields a higher profit than giving no refund at all. This is not very surprising considering the fact that because the price is fixed, giving refunds substitutes for a price reduction, which is needed to attract the 800 type L consumers to book this service.

Next, we ask whether providing only a partial refund can further increase the seller's profit beyond $y^{FR} = 900$. The answer to this question depends on whether a reduction in the level below $r = 6$ will induce some consumers not to book the service. Thus, we seek to find a refund level r that solves $U_L = 0.5 \times 10 - 6 + (1 - 0.5)r \geq 0$, yielding $r \leq 2$. Hence, a refund level of $r = 2$ is the lowest refund level that would still induce type L consumers to book the service. Notice that $r = 2$ implies that $U_H = 0.8 \times 10 - 6 + (1 - 0.2)2 > 0$, hence, type H consumers would also find it beneficial to book this service. Substituting $r = 2$, $\bar{p} = 6$, and the data from Table 8.2 into (8.7) yields the seller's profit level

$$y^{PR} = (500 + 800)(6 - 1) - (0.8 \times 500 + 0.5 \times 800)2$$
$$- (0.2 \times 500 + 0.5 \times 800)2 - 1000 = 2900 > y^{FR} > y^{NR}. \quad (8.11)$$

It should be pointed out that a partial refund not only increases profit over a full refund, it also has the advantage of reducing moral hazard effects by providing lower incentives for cancellations and no-shows. Moral hazard effects were ruled out by our assumption of fixed show-up probabilities. This assumption is relaxed in Section 8.6 below.

Multiple consumer types: A general algorithm

The two-consumer type analysis conducted so far turned out to be very useful for learning the intuition behind the technique for searching for the profit-maximizing refund level. The above two-consumer type analysis also taught us that we must always take into consideration that the seller may not find it profitable to serve the entire market. That is, under some circumstances, which were carefully characterized in the above analysis, the seller may want to reduce the refund level to exclude consumers with either a low expected valuation and/or a low survival probability.

We now extend the model to M consumer types, which we have already carefully described in Section 8.2.3. Recalling (8.3), given a booking price $\bar{p}$, a type ℓ

consumer will book the service only if

$$r \geq \max \left\{ 0, \frac{\bar{p} - \pi_\ell V_\ell}{1 - \pi_\ell} \right\}, \text{ for each consumer type } \ell = 1, 2, \ldots, M, \qquad (8.12)$$

that is, only if the refund level exceeds the type-specific threshold level described by (8.12). We are now ready to state the complete algorithm for setting refunds, taking into account the possibility of exclusion of some consumer types.

Step I: Check and verify that your data satisfy Assumption 8.2 so that

$$\frac{\bar{p} - \pi_1 V_1}{1 - \pi_1} \geq \frac{\bar{p} - \pi_2 V_2}{1 - \pi_2} \geq \cdots \geq \frac{\bar{p} - \pi_M V_M}{1 - \pi_M}.$$

Step II: Using the threshold refund levels (8.12), set the highest refund level r that would still induce all consumer types to book this service. Substitute r into the profit function (8.7), and record the resulting profit level as y_M (to indicate that all the M consumer types are served).

Step III: Delete the last type from the problem and set the highest refund level that would still induce types $1, \ldots, M-1$ to book the service. Record the profit level as y_{M-1}.

Step IV: Repeat Step III (each time deleting the last type from the problem), and record the resulting profit levels as y_{M-2}, y_{M-3} until y_1.

Step V: Pick the profit-maximizing price–refund pair by comparing the profit levels $y_1, y_2, \ldots, y_M$.

We now implement the above algorithm using the example described in Table 8.3, assuming an exogenously given price of $\bar{p} = 6$. The fifth column of Table 8.3 confirms Assumption 8.2, thus Step I of the above algorithm is now completed.

	Consumers			Some Computations				Seller's Cost		
ℓ	N_ℓ	π_ℓ	V_ℓ	$\frac{\bar{p} - \pi_\ell V_\ell}{1 - \pi_\ell}$	$\pi_\ell N_\ell$	$(1 - \pi_\ell) N_\ell$		μ_o	μ_k	ϕ
1	500	0.8	8	−2	400	100		2	1	1000
2	500	0.5	10	2	250	250				
3	300	0.5	8	4	150	150				

Table 8.3: Three consumer type example.

Moving on to Step II, substituting $\pi_3 = 0.5$ and $V_3 = 8$ into (8.12) yields $r = 4$. Substituting all values into the profit (8.7) obtains $y_3 = 1900$.

Moving on to Step III, substituting $\pi_2 = 0.5$ and $V_2 = 10$ into (8.12) yields $r = 2$. Substituting all values into the profit (8.7) obtains $y_2 = 2000$.

Moving on to Step IV, substituting $\pi_1 = 0.8$ and $V_1 = 8$ into (8.12) yields $r = \max\{0, -2\} = 0$. Substituting all values into the profit (8.7) obtains $y_1 = 700$. Hence, the profit-maximizing refund level is $r = 2$. When this level of refund is offered to consumers, only consumer types 1 and 2 book this service.

Multiple consumer types: A computer algorithm

The computer algorithm described by Algorithm 8.1 should first input the parameters describing consumer types: M (number of consumer types), $N[\ell]$, $\pi[\ell]$, and $V[\ell]$ (each array of a dimension M). The exact nature of these arrays (such as, Real, Integer) are specified in Table 1.4. The program should also input three cost parameters, μ_o, μ_k, and ϕ. Finally, the program should input the price $\bar{p}$. In addition, the program should include some trivial loops to ensure that there are no out-of-range (or negative) parameters and that the ranking given by Assumption 8.2 is obeyed. At this stage, some sorting may be needed to establish the required ranking. Results over the M loops are written onto the refund and profit $M + 1$ dimensional arrays $r[i]$ and $y[i]$, where the final (profit-maximizing) result will be written as $r[0]$ and $y[0]$, respectively. $yy[\ell]$ will record the profit made from type ℓ only (to be added later to the combined profit made from all consumer types who actually book the service).

---

for $\ell = 1$ **to** M **do**
     $r[\ell] \leftarrow \frac{\bar{p} - \pi[\ell] \times V[\ell]}{1 - \pi[\ell]}$; /* Types' threshold refund levels   */
     if $r[\ell] < 0$ **then** $r[\ell] \leftarrow 0$; /* Ensure nonnegative value   */
     $yy[\ell] \leftarrow N[\ell](\bar{p} - \mu_k) - \pi[\ell] \times N[\ell] \times \mu_o - (1 - \pi[\ell])N[\ell] \times r[\ell]$;
     /* Compute the profit made from type ℓ only   */
for $i = M$ **downto** 1 **do**
     /* Bottom-to-top type exclusions: Profits   */
     for $\ell = 1$ **to** i **do** $y[i] \leftarrow y[i] + yy[\ell]$;
     /* Add up profits from all non-excluded types   */
     $y[i] \leftarrow y[i] - \phi$; /* Subtract fixed cost   */
for $\ell = 1$ **to** M **do**
     /* Maximize profit. Write results onto $y[0]$, $r[0]$, $\hat{\ell}$ */
     if $y[0] < y[\ell]$ **then** $y[0] \leftarrow y[\ell]$; $r[0] \leftarrow r[\ell]$; $\hat{\ell} \leftarrow \ell$;
writeln ("The profit-maximizing refund level is ", $r[0]$,".");
writeln ("The resulting profit level is ", $y[0]$, ".");
write ("The following types will book the service: ");
for $\ell = \hat{\ell}$ **to** M **do write** (ℓ, ",");

Algorithm 8.1: Refund setting under an exogenously given price.

8.3.2 Proportional refunds under an exogenously given price

Let us assume again that the service provider books the service for an exogenously given price denoted by $\bar{p}$, which is set either by the regulator or by the manufacturer under an RPM agreement. Under this restriction, this section computes the proportional (percentage) refund rate $0 \le r \le 1$ that maximizes the seller's profit.

As it turns out, as long as the service price is exogenously given, the analysis of proportional refunds is not much different from the analysis of lump-sum refunds described in Section 8.3.1, except that we use the utility function (8.5) instead of (8.1), and the profit function (8.8) instead of (8.7).

Two-consumer type: An example

Consider again the consumers' and the seller's cost structure exhibited in Table 8.2, and suppose that the booking price also remains $\bar{p} = 6$. Because the profit levels under no refund and full refund given by (8.9) and (8.10) remain the same, we will not recompute these profit levels. Instead, we proceed directly to our main question, which is finding the profit-maximizing refund rate. Thus, we seek to find a refund rate r that solves

$$U_L = 0.5 \times 10 - 6 + (1 - 0.5)r \times 6 \ge 0, \quad \text{yielding} \quad r \le \frac{1}{3}.$$

Hence, a refund rate $r = 1/3$ is the lowest refund level that would still induce type L consumers to book the service. Notice that $r = 1/3$ implies that $U_H = 0.8 \times 10 - 6 + (1 - 0.2)(1/3)6 > 0$, hence type H consumers would also find it beneficial to book this service. Substituting $r = 1/3$, $\bar{p} = 6$, and the data from Table 8.2 into (8.8) yields the seller's profit level,

$$y^{PR} = (500 + 800)(6 - 1) - (0.8 \times 500 + 0.5 \times 800)2$$
$$- (0.2 \times 500 + 0.5 \times 800)\frac{1}{3}6 - 1000 = 2900 > y^{FR} > y^{NR}. \quad (8.13)$$

As expected, the profit level (8.13) equals the profit level under the optimal lump-sum refund rate given by (8.11). In fact, this computation was not really needed given our computations in Section 8.3.1 that showed that a lump-sum refund of $2 is profit maximizing. That is, we only need to extract r from $r \times p = 6r = 2$, yielding the refund rate $r = 1/3 \approx 33.3\%$.

Multiple consumer types: A general algorithm

We now extend the model to M consumer types, which we have already carefully described in Section 8.2.3. Recalling (8.6), given a booking price $\bar{p}$, a type ℓ consumer will book the service only if

$$r \ge \max\left\{0, \frac{\bar{p} - \pi V}{(1 - \pi)\bar{p}}\right\} \text{ for each consumer type } \ell = 1, 2, \ldots, M, \quad (8.14)$$

that is, only if the refund level exceeds the type-specific threshold level described by (8.14). Because (8.14) equals the lump-sum threshold (8.12) divided by the price $\bar{p}$, there is no need to restate the complete algorithm for setting the profit-maximizing refund level, developed earlier in Section 8.3.1. In fact, only Step II should be slightly modified as follows:

Step II: Using the threshold refund levels (8.14), set the highest refund rate r that would still induce all consumer types to book this service. Substitute r into the profit function (8.8), and record the resulting profit level as y_M (to indicate that all the M types are served).

All other steps remain unchanged. Therefore, we can conclude that the profit-maximizing refund rate for a seller facing the consumers described by Table 8.3 is $r = 2/\bar{p} = 2/6 = 33.33\%$.

8.4 Simultaneous Price and Refund Policy Decisions

Suppose now that the service provider simultaneously sets the booking price p and the refund policy. We confined our analysis to lump-sum refunds only. Therefore, recalling (8.1), each type ℓ consumer makes a book–not-book decision to maximize a utility function given by

$$U(p,r) \stackrel{\text{def}}{=} \begin{cases} \pi_\ell V_\ell - p + (1 - \pi_\ell)r & \text{if he or she books the service} \\ 0 & \text{does not book this service.} \end{cases} \tag{8.15}$$

On the supply side of this market, recalling (8.7), the service provider chooses a single pair of price and refund levels (p,r) to solve

$$\max_{p,r} y \stackrel{\text{def}}{=} \sum_{\ell=1}^{M} [n_\ell(p - \mu_k) - \pi_\ell n_\ell \mu_o - (1 - \pi_\ell)r] - \phi. \tag{8.16}$$

Thus, $n_\ell = N_\ell$ if type ℓ consumers book the service, whereas $n_\ell = 0$ if they choose not to book. It should be emphasized that in this section the seller chooses one and only one price–refund pair (p,r) that is offered to all consumers, who then each makes a book–not-book decision. The reader is referred to Section 8.5, which analyzes the offering of multiple price–refund packages.

8.4.1 Two consumer types

Suppose there are two types of consumers indexed by $\ell = H, L$. There are N_ℓ consumers with survival probability π_ℓ whose valuation for the service is V_ℓ, for each type $\ell = H, L$.

Two consumer types: Preliminary analysis

From the utility functions (8.15), solving $U(p,r) = 0$ for each type yields all the price–refund pairs (p,r) under which consumers are indifferent between booking and not booking the service. Hence, these pairs are given by

$$r = \frac{p - \pi_H V_H}{1 - \pi_H} \quad \text{and} \quad r = \frac{p - \pi_L V_L}{1 - \pi_L}. \tag{8.17}$$

Some possible consumer indifference curves (8.17) are drawn in Figure 8.3 in the price–refund space. The two far-left and far-right graphs drawn on Figure 8.3, demonstrate cases in which the two indifference curves intersect (a third case, which is not drawn, happens when $r < 0$). The price–refund pair at the intersection point of the curves given by (8.17) can be calculated as

$$p = \frac{(1 - \pi_L)\pi_H V_H + (1 - \pi_H)\pi_L V_L}{\pi_H - \pi_L} \quad \text{and} \quad r = \frac{\pi_H V_H - \pi_L V_L}{\pi_H - \pi_L}. \tag{8.18}$$

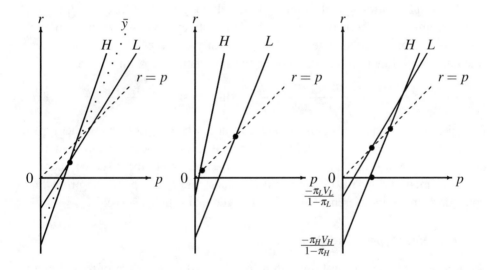

Figure 8.3: Booking decision indifference curves for consumer types H and L, when the seller sets the price and refund simultaneously. *Note*: Dotted line $\bar{y}$ shows one iso-profit line.

To check whether the intersection point (if it exists) is above or below the 45° line where $r = p$, we solve for the following difference:

$$r - p = \frac{\pi_H \pi_L (V_H - V_L)}{\pi_H - \pi_L} \geq 0 \quad \text{if} \quad \text{sign}\,(V_H - V_L) = \text{sign}\,(\pi_H - \pi_L), \tag{8.19}$$

which explains the difference between the intersection points drawn on the far left and on the far right of Figure 8.3.

Turning to the seller side, the set of iso-profit lines in the price–refund space can be derived directly from (8.16) by setting $y = \bar{y}$ to obtain

$$r = \frac{(N_H + N_L)p + \bar{y} + N_H(\mu_k + \pi_H \mu_o) + N_L(\mu_k + \pi_L \mu_o)}{N_H(1 - \pi_H) + N_L(1 - \pi_L)}, \qquad (8.20)$$

which is drawn as a dotted line in Figure 8.3(left) and marked by $\bar{y}$ to indicate a fixed service output level. It is important to note that the iso-profit lines (8.20) are valid only if both consumer types actually book this service. Under this restriction, Figure 8.3 shows that the slope of the iso-profit line falls between the slopes of the types' indifference curves given by (8.17). To confirm that this is indeed the case, the slopes of (8.17) and (8.20) are ranked as follows:

$$\frac{1}{1 - \pi_H} > \frac{N_H + N_L}{N_H(1 - \pi_H) + N_L(1 - \pi_L)} > \frac{1}{1 - \pi_L}, \qquad (8.21)$$

for the case in which $\pi_H > \pi_L$. This ranking confirms the slopes depicted in Figure 8.3(left). Note that if $\pi_H < \pi_L$, we need only the reverse the slopes given by (8.21), but the iso-profit line remains between them.

We must also stress that the ranking of the slopes given by (8.21) is valid only if both consumer types book this service. To demonstrate this point, we now compute the slope of the iso-profit line assuming that only one type ℓ books the service. Then, the profit function (8.16), ignoring the summation sign, implies that

$$r = \frac{N_\ell(p - \mu_k - \pi_\ell \mu_o) - \bar{y}}{N_\ell(1 - \pi_\ell)}, \quad \text{which is sloped} \quad \frac{1}{1 - \pi_\ell}, \qquad (8.22)$$

for type $\ell = H$ or type $\ell = L$, but not both. Hence, when only one consumer type is served, the slope of the iso-profit line coincides with the slope of the type's indifference curve. We can conclude that when only one consumer type is served, there are infinitely many profit-maximizing price–refund pairs because the iso-profit lines coincide with the indifference curves of the type that is being served.

Two consumer types: The algorithm

We now provide the general algorithm for finding the seller's profit-maximizing price and refund levels. First, observe that in Figure 8.3, any movement above and to the left of an indifference curve increases consumers' utility because such a movement is associated with a lower price and a higher refund. Second, a movement in the opposite direction, that is, below and to the right of an iso-profit line, increases the seller's profit because the price increases whereas the refund level declines. Thus, graphically speaking and using Figure 8.3, the seller's profit-maximization problem is to find the price–refund combination that is as far to the right as possible subject to having this combination lying on the relevant indifference curves and the restriction that $r \leq p$ (refunds cannot exceed the booking price by assumption). This suggests the following algorithm for the seller's selection of the price–refund pair, given that there are only two consumer types.

Step I: Check whether the two indifference curves intersect at the quadrant where $0 \leq r \leq p$, that is, below the 45° line as illustrated in Figure 8.3(left). If this is the case, you are done (skip all other steps). Simply substitute the price–refund pair computed by intersecting the two indifference curves given by (8.18) into the profit function (8.16) to obtain

$$y = N_H \pi_H V_H + N_L \pi_L V_L - N_H(\mu_k + \pi_H \mu_o) - N_L(\mu_k + \pi_L \mu_o) - \phi. \quad (8.23)$$

Step II: Compute the profit-maximizing price assuming a full refund ($r = p$). Record the resulting profit level as y^{FR}.

Step III: Compute the profit-maximizing price assuming no refund ($r = 0$). Record the resulting profit level as y^{NR}.

Step IV: Compare the profit level y^{FR} with y^{NR} to determine the profit-maximizing price–refund pair.

Note that both Steps II and III require computing two profit levels: one profit for a "low" price that would induce both types to book and another for a "high" price that would make one consumer type opt out.

Two consumer types: Examples

For the following set of examples, assume a marginal operating cost of $\mu_o = 2$, a marginal capacity cost of $\mu_k = 1$, and a fixed cost of $\phi = 1000$. Suppose there are $N_H = N_L = 1000$ potential consumers of each type. The survival probabilities are $\pi_H = 0.9$ and $\pi_L = 0.5$.

Example I   For the first example, let $V_H = 6$ and $V_L = 8$. Step I requires substituting the data into the intersection point given by (8.18). Hence, $p = 5.75$ and $r = 3.5$. Because $r \leq p$, we are done by substituting into (8.23) to obtain a profit level of $y = 3600$.

Example II   For the second example, let $V_H = 8$ and $V_L = 7$. Step I requires substituting the data into the intersection point given by (8.18). Hence, $p = 8.125$ and $r = 9.25$. Because $r > p$, we know that this is not the solution, and we must proceed with all the remaining steps.

Moving on to Step II for the second example, substituting the consumer data and $r = p$ into (8.17) for a full refund, we obtain $p_H = 8$ and $p_L = 7$ as the maximum prices that each type is willing to pay. Setting $p = 7$ (meaning that both types book this service) and substituting into (8.16) yields $y(7) = 4000$. Setting $p = 8$ (meaning that type L is excluded) and substituting into (8.16) yields $y(8) = 3400$.

Moving on to Step III for the second example, substituting the consumer data and $r = 0$ into (8.17) for no refund, we obtain $p_H = 7.2$ and $p_L = 3.5$ as the maximum prices that each type is willing to pay. Setting $p = 3.5$ (meaning that both types book this service) and substituting into (8.16) yields $y(3.5) = 1200$. Setting $p = 8$ (meaning that type L is excluded) and substituting into (8.16) yields $y(7.2) = 3400$.

Comparing the four profit levels from Steps II and III clearly shows that the solution to the second example is to provide a full refund and to set $p = r = 7$, thereby serving all consumer types and earning a profit of $y^{FR} = 4000$.

Example III   Suppose that $V_H = 8$ and $V_L = 6$. Step I requires substituting the data into the intersection point given by (8.18). Hence, $p = 8.25$ and $r = 10.5$. Because $r > p$, we know that this is not the solution, and we must proceed with all the remaining steps.

Moving on to Step II for the third example, substituting the consumer data and $r = p$ into (8.17) for a full refund, we obtain $p_H = 8$ and $p_L = 6$ as the maximum prices that each type is willing to pay. Setting $p = 6$ (meaning that both types book this service) and substituting into (8.16) yields $y(6) = 2600$. Setting $p = 8$ (meaning that type L is excluded) and substituting into (8.16) yields $y(8) = 3400$.

Moving on to Step III for the third example, substituting the consumer data and $r = 0$ into (8.17) for no refund, we obtain $p_H = 7.2$ and $p_L = 3$ as the maximum prices that each type is willing to pay. Setting $p = 3$ (meaning that both types book this service), and substituting into (8.16) yields $y(3) = 200$. Setting $p = 8$ (meaning that type L is excluded) and substituting into (8.16) yields $y(7.2) = 3400$.

Comparing the four profit levels from Steps II and III clearly shows that any solution to the third example involves serving only type H consumers, thereby earning a profit of $y^{FR}(8) = y^{NR}(7.2) = 3400$.

8.4.2   Multiple consumer types: A computer algorithm

The two-consumer type analysis conducted so far in this section turns out to be very useful for learning the intuition behind the simultaneous setting of profit-maximizing price and refund levels. The two-consumer type analysis is also very useful in demonstrating the extreme linear nature of our refund models, which stems from having to maximize a linear profit function subject to several linear constraints. The constraints are linear because they reflect consumers' indifference curves, which are derived from linear expected utility functions.

The two-consumer type analysis has also taught us that we must always take into consideration that the seller may not find it profitable to serve the entire market. That is, under some circumstances, which were carefully characterized in the above analysis, the seller may want to increase the booking price and/or reduce the refund level, which may exclude consumers with either a low valuation and/or a low survival probability.

From a practical point of view, because all personal computers and even many online JavaScript Web pages are equipped with algorithms for solving linear programming problems, we gear this section toward developing an algorithm that uses built-in linear programming algorithms. We construct such an algorithm, taking into account the possibilities that the profit-maximizing price and refund level may at times be sufficiently high as to exclude consumers with either low valuations or low survival probabilities.

Deriving the general algorithm

The purpose of this algorithm is to choose a pair (p, r) to maximize the profit function (8.16) subject to the following list of constraints:

$$r \geq 0, \quad p \geq 0, \quad r \leq p, \quad \text{and} \quad r \geq \frac{p - \pi_\ell V_\ell}{1 - \pi_\ell}$$

$$\text{for each consumer type } \ell = 1, 2, \ldots, M. \quad (8.24)$$

This profit-maximization problem has $M + 3$ linear constraints and two variables, p and r. The last term in (8.24) is derived from type ℓ's utility function (8.15). Each constraint indicates that the refund level r should be sufficiently high relative to the price p to induce a consumer type ℓ to book this service.

Clearly, this problem can be solved by any elementary linear programming software using, say, the Simplex method. Unfortunately, solving the above problem may not yield the right solution because, as we have learned from the two consumer type examples, in some cases the service provider may find it profitable to raise the price or lower the refund level, which may exclude some consumer types from booking the service. Thus, the reader should not rush to conclude that a single linear programming algorithm always delivers the final solution. For example, let us reformulate our last (third) example where $V_H = 8$ and $V_L = 6$. Substituting all the numerical parameters, the problem reduces to

$$\max_{p,r} y = 200(10p - 3r - 24) - 1000 \quad \text{subject to} \quad r \geq 0, \quad p \geq 0, \quad r \leq p,$$

$$r \geq 2(5p - 36), \quad \text{and} \quad r \geq 2(p - 3). \quad (8.25)$$

The reader who substitutes (8.25) into linear programming software will obtain the solution $p = r = 6$ and $y = 2600$, which is incorrect, as the third example analyzed above shows.

In view of the above example, we now state an algorithm for tackling the possibility of exclusion of some consumer types. The underlying principle of this algorithm is simple. We let the computer determine the profit-maximizing price–refund pair for all possible subsets of the set containing the M consumer types. Then, the computer picks the subset that yields the highest profit level. We now introduce a few more variables for the computer algorithm. Let $\mathcal{M}$ denote the set of all subsets of the set of types $\{1, 2, \ldots, M\}$. $m \in \mathcal{M}$ denotes a subset. The M-dimensional array of binary b denotes whether type ℓ is included so that $b[\ell] = 1$ or excluded in which case $b[\ell] = 0$. Variables with a hat, $\hat{p}$, $\hat{r}$, and $\hat{y}$ (price, refund, and profit), constitute the global solution of this algorithm.

With the above notation, for each subset, this algorithm should have access to an external linear programming procedure that should be able to solve

$$\max_{p,r} y \stackrel{\text{def}}{=} \sum_{\ell=1}^{M} b[\ell] \left\{ N[\ell](p - \mu_k) - \pi[\ell] \times N[\ell] \times \mu_o - (1 - \pi[\ell])r \right\} - \phi$$

$$\text{subject to} \quad r \geq 0, \quad p \geq 0, \quad r \leq p, \quad \text{and} \quad r \geq b[\ell] \times \frac{p - \pi[\ell] \times V[\ell]}{1 - \pi[\ell]}$$

$$\text{for each consumer type } \ell = 1, 2, \ldots, M. \quad (8.26)$$

Notice that the binary variable $b[\ell] \in \{0, 1\}$ "controls" which types are included in the profit-maximization problem and which types are excluded from it.

Algorithm 8.2 formally describes how to compute the profit-maximizing price and refund level as well as which types will book the service as a consequence of implementing it. We should caution that the linear programming procedure may return a range of solutions when it considers only one consumer type, because for one consumer type, the solution is not unique, as we have already noted in equation (8.22). One simple way to avoid dealing with multiple solutions is to insert a small procedure that sets a full refund $r = p$ for the case in which only one consumer type ℓ is considered by the linear programming procedure.

---

for $m \in \mathcal{M}$ **do**
    /* Main loop over all subsets   */
    for $\ell = 1$ **to** M **do**
        if $\ell \in m$ **then** $b[\ell] \leftarrow 1$; **else** $b[\ell] \leftarrow 0$;/* Identify types   */
    Call an external linear-programming procedure to solve (8.26), and to
    write the temporary solution as p, r, and y;
    if $\hat{y} < y$ **then**
        $\hat{p} \leftarrow p$; $\hat{r} \leftarrow r$; $\hat{y} \leftarrow y$; /* Record candidate maximum   */
        for $\ell = 1$ **to** M **do** $\hat{b}[\ell] \leftarrow b[\ell]$;
writeln ("The profit-maximizing p, r, and y are: ", $\hat{p}$,",", $\hat{r}$,",", $\hat{y}$,".");
write ("The following consumer types will choose to book the service:");
for $\ell = 1$ **to** M **do if** $\hat{b}[\ell] = 1$ **then write** (ℓ, ",");

Algorithm 8.2: Simultaneous refund and price setting.

Note that the main loop runs $2^M - 1$ times, which equals the number of *nonempty* subsets in a set of M elements. This should not pose any problem as one generally consider a small number of consumer types. That is, if there are $M = 3$ consumer types, there are $2^3 - 1 = 7$ subsets given by $\{1\}, \{2\}, \{3\}, \{1,2\},$ $\{1,3\}, \{2,3\},$ and $\{1,2,3\}$. If there are $M = 10$ types, the number of nonempty subsets is $2^{10} - 1 = 1023$.

Clearly, some of the loops may be redundant, but for the sake of trying to present the simplest algorithm, there is no point in inserting procedures that would eliminate them. For example, any price–refund pair that induces a consumer type that has a significantly lower valuation or survival probability to book the service should also induce some other types to book the service. Thus, the loop that computes the profit when only this "low" type is served is redundant.

Using the algorithm: Three-consumer type examples

We now demonstrate the operation of the above algorithm with the following three-consumer type example. Assume a marginal operating cost of $\mu_o = 2$, a marginal capacity cost of $\mu_k = 1$, and a fixed cost of $\phi = 1000$. Suppose there are $N_1 = N_2 = N_3 = 1000$ potential consumers of each type. The survival probabilities are $\pi_1 = 0.6$, $\pi_2 = 0.7$, and $\pi_3 = 0.8$. The corresponding valuations are now given by $V_1 = 9$, $V_2 = 7$, and $V_3 = 5$.

There are $2^3 - 1 = 7$ subsets $\{1,2,3\}, \{1,2\}, \{1,3\}, \{2,3\}, \{1\}, \{2\}, \{3\}$ to be investigated. We input each into the linear programming procedure and obtain the following results:

$$\max_{p,r} y_{\{1,2,3\}} = 100(30p - 9r - 82) \quad \text{subject to} \quad r \geq 0, \quad p \geq 0, \quad r \leq p,$$

$$r \geq \frac{5p - 27}{2}, \quad r \geq \frac{10p - 49}{3}, \quad \text{and} \quad r \geq 5(p - 4).$$

The computer solution for this problem is given by $p = 4$, $r = 0$ (no refund), and $y_{\{1,2,3\}} = 3800$.

Next, if only types $\{1,2\}$ are served,

$$\max_{p,r} y_{\{1,2\}} = 100(20p - 7r - 56) \quad \text{subject to} \quad r \geq 0, \quad p \geq 0, \quad r \leq p,$$

$$r \geq \frac{5p - 27}{2}, \quad \text{and} \quad r \geq \frac{10p - 49}{3}.$$

The computer solution for this problem is given by $p = 4.9$, $r = 0$ (no refund), and $y_{\{1,2\}} = 4200$.

Next, if only types $\{1,3\}$ are served,

$$\max_{p,r} y_{\{1,3\}} = 200(10p - 3r - 29) \quad \text{subject to} \quad r \geq 0, \quad p \geq 0, \quad r \leq p,$$

$$r \geq \frac{5p - 27}{2}, \quad \text{and} \quad r \geq 5(p - 4).$$

The computer solution for this problem is given by $p = 4$, $r = 0$ (no refund), and $y_{\{1,3\}} = 2200$.

Next, if only types $\{2,3\}$ are served,

$$\max_{p,r} y_{\{2,3\}} = 200(10p - 3r - 29) \quad \text{subject to} \quad r \geq 0, \quad p \geq 0, \quad r \leq p,$$

$$r \geq \frac{10p - 49}{3}, \quad \text{and} \quad r \geq 5(p - 4).$$

The computer solution for this problem is given by $p = 4$, $r = 0$ (no refund), and $y_{\{2,3\}} = 2000$.

Next, if only type 1 is served, solving $r = (5p - 27)/2$ for, say, $p = r$ yields $p = r = 9$, and $y_{\{1\}} = 2200$.

Next, if only type 2 is served, solving $r = (10p - 49)/3$ for $p = r$ yields $p = r = 7$, and $y_{\{2\}} = 1100$.

Finally, if only type 3 is served, solving $r = 5(p - 4)$ for $p = r$ yields $p = r = 5$, and $y_{\{3\}} = 400$.

Clearly, as we already pointed out, the last two computations were redundant for the present example because when $p = r = 5$, all types find it beneficial to book this service. However, because the cost of computer time is generally low, the present algorithm has an advantage of being extremely simple. Comparing the above profit levels reveals that the profit-maximizing price and refund are given by $p = 4.9$ and $r = 0$ (no refund), thereby earning a profit of $y_{\{1,2\}} = 4200$. Under this policy, type 3 does not book this service.

8.5 Multiple Price and Refund Packages

Our analysis so far has been restricted to offering consumers a single take-it-or-leave-it package. That is, all consumers have had to make a book–not-book decision facing a single booking price bundled with a single refund policy. We now extend our analysis by letting the service provider offer two packages of price–refund pairs. We will not provide a complete analysis of how to choose the profit-maximizing price–refund packages. Instead, we focus on one example that will demonstrate why the introduction of multiple packages may be profit enhancing.

Because of the "linear" nature of our model, dual packages can be more profitable than a single package only if there are at least three consumer types. Assume a marginal operating cost of $\mu_o = 2$, a marginal capacity cost of $\mu_k = 1$, and a fixed cost of $\phi = 1000$. Suppose that there are $N_1 = N_2 = N_3 = 1000$ potential consumers of each type. The survival probabilities are $\pi_1 = 0.6$, $\pi_2 = 0.7$, and $\pi_3 = 0.8$. The corresponding valuations are now given by $V_1 = 9$, $V_2 = 7$, and $V_3 = 5$. Recalling (8.24), the seller is constrained to choosing price–refund packages that satisfy

$$r \geq 0, \quad p \geq 0, \quad r \leq p, \quad \text{and} \quad r \geq \frac{p - \pi_\ell V_\ell}{1 - \pi_\ell}$$

for each participating type $\ell = 1, 2, \ldots, M$. (8.27)

Substituting the above survival probabilities and the valuations into (8.27), the indifference curves of consumer types 1, 2, and 3, respectively, are given by

$$r = 2(5p - 36), \quad r = \frac{10p - 63}{3}, \quad \text{and} \quad r = \frac{5p - 27}{2} \qquad (8.28)$$

and are drawn in Figure 8.4. In Figure 8.4, each type will book any service package that lies on, above, or to the left of the type's indifference curve, and will not book any package that lies strictly below and to the right.

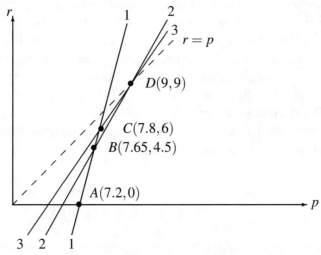

Figure 8.4: Dual price–refund packages with three consumer types. Thick dots, labeled A, B, C, and D, with the (p, r) coordinates, denote potentially profitable packages.

Our main point in this demonstration is to highlight the principle behind the sale of two different packages. This principle can be described as follows:

Threshold utility: If a consumer chooses to book the service, the utility must be equal to or exceed the reservation level (generally normalized to equal $\bar{U} = 0$).

Rational selection: If two packages are sold to different consumers, it must be that a buyer of the first package gains a higher utility compared with buying the second, whereas the buyer of the second package gains a higher utility compared with buying the first.

The threshold utility restriction is not new as it applies to any type of booking, whether it concerns the offering of a single package or several price–refund packages. The second principle is the key to a successful market segmentation and price discrimination, which we already introduced in Chapter 4 when we analyzed successful tying techniques. Loosely speaking, this principle states that two packages cannot be simultaneously sold in the same market when all consumers strictly prefer one package over the other.

The second principle on the above list generates a somewhat difficult task as it constrains the seller to offer packages that are ranked differently by the different consumer types. A close inspection of Figure 8.4 shows that the packages marked A and D segment the market in the sense that type 1 consumers strictly prefer A to D, whereas consumer types 2 and 3 strictly prefer package D to A. Note that strict preference is not essential and that, in general, markets can be segmented even if some consumers are indifferent between packages. The intuition behind this choice of packages is that the seller can offer a very low nonrefundable price to type 1 consumers who show up with a high probability relative to other consumer types. Such a low nonrefundable price will not be profitable when offered to type 2 and 3 consumers because they are very likely to cancel, thereby inflicting a loss of μ_k per booking to the seller. Intuitively, in this example, type 1 consumers resemble leisure travelers who can commit better than business travelers who resemble types 2 and 3. Thus, the seller offers the discount package, A, to leisure travelers and the expensive package, D, to business travelers.

Given that type 1 consumers book package A, and types 2 and 3 book package D, the seller's profit (8.7) is now given by

$$y = N_1(7.2 - \mu_k) - \pi_1 N_1 \mu_o - (1 - \pi_1)4.5 + N_2(9 - \mu_k) - \pi_2 N_2 \mu_o - (1 - \pi_2)9$$
$$+ N_3(9 - \mu_k) - \pi_3 N_3 \mu_o - (1 - \pi_3)9 - \phi = 12,500. \quad (8.29)$$

A natural question to ask at this point is, How much extra profit can be gained by introducing two booking packages instead of the single package that we rigorously analyzed in Section 8.4? To answer this question, we simply compute the profit when only one package (p, r) is offered by the seller. Applying Algorithm 8.2 to the present example yields $y_{\{1,2,3\}} = 9800$, $y_{\{1,2\}} = 6550$, $y_{\{2,3\}} = 7500$, $y_{\{1,3\}} = 4400$. This shows that offering a second package increases the seller's profit by $12,500 - 9800 = 2700$.

8.6 Refund Policy under Moral Hazard

Our analysis so far has been based on Assumption 8.1, which states that the survival probabilities are constant and are not affected by the level of refund. Thus, our analysis clearly has overestimated the profit gains from refunds given on cancellations and no-shows. This is because it ignores two incentives on the part of consumers:

Changing existing survival probabilities: Higher refund levels (or lower cancellation fees) may decrease an individual's survival probability by increasing the incentives to cancel the booking.

Attracting new, "more risky" consumers: Higher refund levels may increase the number of bookings made by new consumers who have low survival probabilities.

These incentives are commonly referred to as the *moral hazard* incentives. These incentives are widely observed in many industries, such as the insurance industry. That is, the first incentive on the above list states that people may be less careful in securing their homes against thieves knowing that their house is fully insured against theft. The second incentive states that the availability of insurance generally attracts more risky people. Another example would be looking at the restaurant sector. The first incentive on the above list states that people tend to eat larger portions in all-you-can-eat restaurants compared with other types of restaurants. The second incentive on this list states that only people with a large appetite go to all-you-can-eat restaurants.

It should be noted that from a purely technical point of view, there is no difference between the two types of moral hazard incentives listed above. The reason is that consumers who are attracted to book a service as a result of the introduction of a generous refund policy can be modeled as existing consumers who have zero survival probability ($\pi = 0$) when refunds are not offered.

8.6.1   Survival probability under moral hazard

Suppose the survival probability varies continuously with the amount of refund given on cancellations and no-shows. Formally, let the survival probability of a type ℓ consumer be a function of the lump-sum refund level and be given by

$$\pi_\ell(r) \stackrel{\text{def}}{=} \frac{\bar{\pi}_\ell}{1 + \gamma \cdot r}, \quad \text{where} \quad 0 \le \bar{\pi}_\ell < 1 \quad \text{and} \quad \gamma \ge 0. \tag{8.30}$$

$\bar{\pi}_\ell = \pi_\ell(r)$ is the survival probability of a type ℓ consumer when no refunds are given. γ is the key parameter because it measures how "sensitive" consumers are with respect to changing the refund level offered by the service provider. For example, setting $\gamma = 0$ brings us back to the model analyzed so far in this chapter in which $\pi_\ell(r) = \bar{\pi}_\ell$ for every r. For all $\gamma > 0$, an increase in the refund level r reduces the survival (show-up) probability. In the limit, $\pi_\ell \to 0$ as $r \to +\infty$. Of course, this limit is purely theoretical as we assumed that the lump-sum refund level cannot exceed the booking price, $r \le p$. The parameter γ can be estimated by econometricians using time series data on varying refund levels and actual rates of show-ups or cancellations. Table 8.4 provides some numerical simulations of (8.30), demon-strating how the initial survival probabilities $\bar{\pi}_\ell$ vary with the refund level r. For example, the second row in Table 8.4 demonstrates how a consumer who shows up with a 90% probability when no refunds are offered ends up showing up with a 75% probability when offered a refund of $2.

$\bar{\pi}_\ell \setminus r$	0.0	0.25	0.50	0.75	1.0	2.0	3.0
0.90	0.90	0.88	0.86	0.84	0.82	0.75	0.69
0.80	0.80	0.78	0.76	0.74	0.73	0.67	0.62
0.70	0.70	0.68	0.67	0.65	0.64	0.58	0.54
0.60	0.60	0.59	0.57	0.56	0.55	0.50	0.46
0.50	0.50	0.49	0.48	0.47	0.45	0.42	0.38
0.40	0.40	0.39	0.38	0.37	0.36	0.33	0.31
0.30	0.30	0.29	0.29	0.28	0.27	0.25	0.23

Table 8.4: Moral hazard effects: How survival probabilities decline with rising refunds. *Note*: Simulations assume a value of $\gamma = 0.1$ in (8.30).

8.6.2 Refund setting under an exogenously given price

To determine the profit-maximizing refund level under an exogenously given price and under moral hazard consumer behavior, we confine the analysis to a subset of Table 8.4 with two consumer types and only two possible refund levels, $r = 0$ or $r = 2$. Taking the two extreme (top and bottom) consumers from Table 8.4, our analysis will be based on the consumer information given in Table 8.5. We assume that the seller's cost structure is given by $\mu_o = 2$, $\mu_k = 1$, and $\phi = 1000$ (same cost as in Table 8.2), and that the exogenously given price is $\bar{p} = 6$.

	Consumers				Some Computations			
ℓ	N_ℓ	$\pi_\ell(0)$	$\pi_\ell(2)$	V_ℓ	$\pi_\ell(0)V_\ell$	$\pi_\ell(2)V_\ell$	$\pi_\ell(0)N_\ell$	$\pi_\ell(2)N_\ell$
H	500	0.9	0.75	10	9.0	7.5	450	375
L	800	0.3	0.25	18	5.4	4.5	240	200

Table 8.5: Two consumer types with moral hazard example.

We first explore the consequences of providing no refund ($r = 0$). In view of the consumers' utility function (8.1) and assuming a threshold utility of $\bar{U} = 0$, type L consumers will not book this service because $U_L = 0.3 \times 18 - 6 + (1 - 0.3)0 < 0$. In contrast, type H will book this service because $U_H = 0.9 \times 10 - 6 + (1 - 0.9)0 \geq 0$. Substituting into the profit function (8.4) yields

$$y^{NR} = 500(6 - 1) - 0.9 \times 500 \times 2 - (1 - 0.9)0 - 1000 = 600. \tag{8.31}$$

Next, suppose the seller promises a lump-sum refund of $r = 2$ on no-shows. Type L consumers will book this service because $U_L = 0.25 \times 18 - 6 + (1 - 0.25)2 \geq 0$. Type H consumers will also book this service because $U_H = 0.75 \times 10 - 6 + (1 - 0.75)2 \geq 0$. Substituting into the profit function (8.4) yields

$$y^{PR} = (500 + 800)(6 - 1) - (0.75 \times 500 + 0.25 \times 800)2$$
$$- [(1 - 0.75)500 + (1 - 0.25)800]2 - 1000 = 2900 > y^{NR}. \quad (8.32)$$

Hence, in this example, providing a refund of $r = 2$ yields a higher profit than providing no refund, despite the fact that refunds reduce consumers' survival probabilities.

From a practical point of view, the above example suggests one method for how to compute the profit-maximizing refund level given that consumers' tendency to cancel or not show intensifies with an increase in the promised refund level. These corrections can be embedded into a computer algorithm by substituting the value of the estimated value of γ into the survival probabilities given by (8.30). The reader is referred to Exercise 10, which provides a good example of how an increase in the refund level leads to an exclusion of type H consumers from the market. In this exercise a high refund leaves the seller serving only the consumers with low survival probabilities.

8.7 Integrating Refunds within Advance Booking

A computer reservation system should integrate all aspects of advance booking, which include the advance booking algorithms analyzed in Chapter 7, the overbooking analyzed in Chapter 9, and the options to give refunds or charge cancellation fees that we analyze in the present chapter.

This short section attempts to suggest one possible way to integrate the advance booking algorithms developed in Chapter 7 with the refund and cancellation fee options analyzed in the present chapter. Note, however, that our comprehensive analysis of advance booking in Chapter 7 lacked an algorithm for selecting profit-maximizing prices. That is, our dynamic booking algorithms were all based on predetermined exogenously given prices (that could vary among booking classes). Because refund decisions are basically part of pricing decisions, there is really no general method to integrate the advance booking algorithms with pricing and refund decisions.

However, because many service providers who are engaged in advance booking may also find it profitable to offer some refunds, we propose the following three-stage methodology for how to integrate these algorithms.

(1) *Pricing and refund determination*: Use the techniques from this chapter as well as Chapter 3 to determine the profit-maximizing price and refund levels.

(2) *Compute the average survival probability*: For consumers your model predicts will book the service, compute the average survival probability by

$$\tilde{\pi} = \frac{\sum_{\ell=1}^{M} (n_\ell \cdot \pi_\ell)}{\sum_{\ell=1}^{M} n_\ell},$$

where $n_\ell = N_\ell$ for participating types, and $n_\ell = 0$ otherwise.

(3) *Modify the advance booking algorithm*: Redefine the class fares so that for each booking class $i \in \mathscr{B}$, $\tilde{p}^i \overset{\text{def}}{=} \tilde{\pi} p^i + (1 - \tilde{\pi})(p^i - r)$.

The third step simply "lowers" the class fare to the expected revenue from each booking, taking into account the possibility of a no-show. The reader should not confuse the survival probabilities $\tilde{\pi}$ and π_ℓ with the probabilities of booking each class i, $i \in \mathscr{B}$.

Finally, the second step may be needed because the advance booking analysis in Chapter 7 was confined to a single price (per class), hence, we basically modeled a single consumer type. In contrast, this chapter allows for multiple types (according to survival probability and willingness to pay). In fact, the gains from giving refunds can be realized only if there are at least two consumer types. Hence, by averaging the survival probabilities of consumers who book the service, we may be able to obtain an approximate value of the average survival probability $\tilde{\pi}$. Obviously, the second step is not needed if the seller already knows the survival probabilities for each booking class.

8.8 Exercises

1. Consider a consumer who can book a service for the price of p and obtain a refund of r in the event the consumer cancels. We now modify the consumer's utility function given by (8.1) to be

$$U(p,r) \overset{\text{def}}{=} \begin{cases} \pi V - p + (1 - \pi)r & \text{if he or she books the service} \\ 3 & \text{does not book this service.} \end{cases}$$

Thus, the consumer now has a threshold utility level of $\bar{U} = 3$. Similar to Table 8.1, fill in the missing entries in Table 8.6.

2. Suppose $V = 10$ and $\pi = 0.5$. Solve the following problems.

   (a) Similar to Figure 8.1, draw the consumer's indifference curve concerning the book–no-book decision for the utility function given in Exercise 1 (with the threshold utility $\bar{U} = 3$).

   (b) Infer the maximum price the consumer will be willing to pay for booking this service, assuming that no refund is given ($r = 0$). Show your calculations.

π	V	πV	p	r	$(1-\pi)r$	U	Decision
0.8	20		13	0			
0.8	20		14	2			
0.9	20		16	9			
0.2	20		4	3			

Table 8.6: Refunds and booking decisions for Exercise 1.

(c) Infer the maximum price a consumer will be willing to pay for booking the service assuming a full refund ($r = p$). Show your calculations.

3. Consider the two-consumer example given by Table 8.2. Similar to our analysis in Section 8.3.1, compute the profit-maximizing refund level assuming that the exogenously given price has been reduced to $\bar{p} = 4$ (instead of $\bar{p} = 6$). Show you calculations.

4. Consider the two-consumer example given by Table 8.2 in Section 8.3.1, but suppose now that the exogenously given price is $\bar{p} = 7$ and that the cost parameters are now given by $\mu_o = 2$, $\mu_k = 3$, and $\phi = 1200$.

(a) Compute the service provider's profit level given that no refunds are offered to consumers.

(b) Compute the profit level given that this seller provides full refunds on no-shows.

(c) Compute the profit-maximizing refund level.

5. Consider the three consumer–type example described by Table 8.3. However, assume that the exogenously given price is now $\bar{p} = 7$. Compute the profit-maximizing lump-sum refund level using the algorithm developed in Section 8.3.1.

6. Consider our analysis of proportional refunds given in Section 8.3.2. Compute the profit-maximizing refund rate $0 \le r \le 1$ under the conditions listed in Exercise 4.

7. Consider the seller's problem of simultaneously setting the price and refund levels when there are only two consumer types, as studied in Section 8.4.1. Assume a marginal operating cost of $\mu_o = 2$, a marginal capacity cost of $\mu_k = 1$, and no fixed costs, so $\phi = 0$. Suppose there are $N_H = N_L = 1000$ potential consumers of each type. The survival probabilities are $\pi_H = 0.9$ and $\pi_L = 0.5$.

Compute the profit-maximizing price and refund level under the following two different cases: (a) $V_H = 5$ and $V_L = 7$ and (b) $V_H = 7$ and $V_L = 6$.

8. Consider the seller's problem of simultaneously setting the price and refund levels with multiple consumer types, studied in Section 8.4.2. Assume a marginal operating cost of $\mu_o = 2$, a marginal capacity cost of $\mu_k = 1$, and no fixed costs, so $\phi = 0$. Suppose there are $N_1 = N_2 = 100$ and $N_3 = 200$ potential consumers of each type. The survival probabilities are $\pi_1 = 0.9$, $\pi_2 = 0.8$, and $\pi_3 = 0.7$. The valuations are now given by $V_1 = 9$, $V_2 = 8$, and $V_3 = 7$. Using the procedure described by Algorithm 8.2, and any basic linear programming software, compute the profit-maximizing price and refund level.

9. Consider the moral hazard model of Section 8.6. Suppose there is only one type of consumer whose survival probabilities are given in the bottom row of Table 8.4. Assume that consumers' basic valuation for the service is $V = 18$ and that the booking price is fixed at the level of $\bar{p} = 6$. Using the bottom row of Table 8.4 and the utility function (8.1), compute the minimum refund level under which the consumers of this type will find it beneficial to book this service. Show your calculations.

10. Consider our moral hazard example with two consumer types displayed in Table 8.5. Suppose now that the service valuation of type H consumers is now $V_H = 7$ (instead of $V_H = 10$). Suppose the service provider is restricted to setting either no refund ($r = 0$) or a lump-sum refund level of $r = 2$. Compute which refund level maximizes the expected profit of this service provider assuming the booking price is $\bar{p} = 6$ and the cost structure is given by $\mu_o = 2$, $\mu_k = 1$, and $\phi = 1000$.

Chapter 9

Overbooking

9.1 Basic Definitions   299

   9.1.1   Show-up probabilities

   9.1.2   Overbooking and probability

9.2 Profit-maximizing Overbooking   305

   9.2.1   Expected cost

   9.2.2   Expected revenue and expected profit

   9.2.3   Simple examples

   9.2.4   Computer algorithm

9.3 Overbooking of Groups   313

   9.3.1   Simple examples

   9.3.2   General formulation

   9.3.3   Computer algorithm

9.4 Exercises   322

We define *overbooking* as a strategy whereby service providers accept and confirm more reservations than the capacity they allocate for providing the service. Thus, the overbooking strategy may result in service denial to some consumers if the number of actual show-ups at the time of service exceeds the allocated capacity. Overbooking should be considered an integral part of the advance booking strategy of service providers. In this chapter, we demonstrate how service providers can increase their profits by using overbooking. Thus, in this chapter, we relax Assumption 7.3, which so far has ruled out the use of the overbooking strategy.

From a practical point of view, the dynamic booking models analyzed in Chapter 7 can be modified to accommodate overbooking by letting the booking capacity K exceed the available capacity level during all booking periods. However, maintaining the same "artificially high" capacity level throughout the entire booking process need not be optimal because it may be more profitable to reduce the amount of overbooking as the reservation period gets closer to the service delivery time. In other words, it may be profitable to allow for a large overbooking level at the beginning of the booking process, but lower levels toward the end, when the service provider can more accurately estimate the final number of reservations made and the expected number of show-ups. Despite this discussion, in this chapter, we do not attempt to integrate overbooking with the dynamic booking models of Chapter 7. Instead, we develop an independent model for computing the profit-maximizing booking levels.

We first must ask why service providers may find it profitable to overbook consumers. The answer to this question is that it is commonly observed that a large number of reservations end up being cancelled by consumers and a somewhat smaller number of consumers simply do not show up at the time of service. Cancellations and no-shows have already been discussed in Chapter 8 where we analyzed refund policies. In fact, the reader is urged to consult Definition 8.1, which makes a clear distinction between cancellations and no-shows. To illustrate this distinction, let us look at the airline industry, for example, in which the data of domestic fights in the United States show that 30–60% of reservations eventually get cancelled, whereas the no-show rate is around 8%. These data clearly indicate that booking up to capacity only will result in a significant amount of unused capacity during the service delivery time (the commonly observed problem of empty seats in the airline industry). The second question we may want to ask is whether consumers can benefit from overbooking. A quick answer to this question would be that overbooking enables more consumers to make reservations.

Overbooking is widely observed in the airline industry. In fact, most readers would recognize the following statement, which is printed on most ordinary airline tickets.

> Airline flights may be overbooked, and there is a slight chance that a seat will not be available on a flight for which a person has a confirmed reservation. If the flight is overbooked, no one will be denied a seat until airline personnel first ask for volunteers willing to give up their reservation in exchange for a payment of the airline's choosing. If there are not enough volunteers, the airline will deny boarding to other persons in accordance with its particular boarding priority. With few exceptions, persons denied boarding involuntarily are entitled to compensation. The complete rules for the payment of compensation and each airline's boarding priorities are available at all airport ticket counters and boarding locations.

In the airline industry, passengers with confirmed reservations who are denied boarding must be offered the choice of a full refund for the ticket or an alternative flight to continue their journey. Furthermore, the carrier should supply meals and refreshments, and accommodation if an overnight stay is required. In addition, since 2005, European Union regulations require airlines to pay denied passengers an amount of € 250 for flights up to 1500 kilometers, € 400 for flights between

1500 and 3500 kilometers, and € 600 for longer flights. In the United States, the mandated payment is limited to 200% of the value of the remaining flight coupons, not exceeding $400.

Overbooking has been analyzed in operational research, transportation, and economics literature; see comprehensive surveys by Belobaba (1987), Rothstein (1985), and McGill and van Ryzin (1999). Other papers include Shlifer and Vardi (1975), Bodily and Pfeifer (1992), and Ringbom and Shy (2002).

9.1 Basic Definitions

A single service provider has the capacity to accommodate a maximum of K customers. This provider decides how many booking requests to accept, which we denote by the decision variable b. Our assumption is that the number of booking requests is sufficiently large in the sense that it far exceeds the capacity level K. For example, K could be measuring the seating capacity available on a certain flight using a certain aircraft type. In this example, b is the number of passenger reservations confirmed by the airline before the time of service.

In many regulated and partially regulated industries, the regulator may limit the number of allowable overbookings. Even when the regulator does not impose any limit, the service provider may want to set a level beyond which no more consumers can be booked to avoid severe reputation effects. We denote this level by B to indicate that the service provider programs the reservation system never to accept booking requests beyond $b = B$. Formally, $b > B$ is ruled out by the booking system. Booking limits are often described in percentage terms relative to capacity. For example, an overbooking limit of 30% would mean that an airline cannot book more than $B = 130$ passengers on a flight served by an aircraft with a seating capacity of $K = 100$.

9.1.1 Show-up probabilities

Let π ($0 < \pi \leq 1$) denote the probability that a consumer with a confirmed reservation actually shows up at the service delivery time. In the professional language, this probability is often referred to as a consumer's *survival probability*. We assume that all consumers have the same show-up probability, and that a consumer's show-up probability is independent of all other consumers. That is, we rule out events such as last-minute *group* cancellations and no-shows, which are analyzed later in Section 9.3. In this chapter, we learn how to compute the expected number of show-ups for each booking level, b. Formally, let the random variable s denote the number of consumers who show up at the service delivery time. Clearly, $s \leq b$, meaning that the number of show-ups cannot exceed the number of bookings. That is, our model does not allow for standby customers, and only customers with confirmed reservations are provided with this service. In fact, because s depends on the number of bookings made, s is a function of b and will often be written as $s(b)$. Also, note that s is a random variable, which also depends on the individual's show-up probability π, hence it can also be written as $s(b; \pi)$.

We start out with simple examples showing how to compute the probability of realizing different numbers of show-ups (different realizations of the random variable s). Suppose that the service provider confirms one reservation only. That is, let $b = 1$. Then, the probability that this booked consumer shows up is $\Pr\{s(1) = 1\} = \pi$, whereas the probability that no consumer shows up is $\Pr\{s(1) = 0\} = 1 - \pi$.

Next, suppose that there are $b = 2$ confirmed reservations. The probability that exactly one consumer shows up is given by

$$\Pr\{s(2) = 1\} = \underbrace{\pi(1 - \pi)}_{1^{st} \text{ arrives, } 2^{nd} \text{ not}} + \underbrace{(1 - \pi)\pi}_{1^{st} \text{ not, } 2^{nd} \text{ arrives}} = 2\pi(1 - \pi).$$

The probability that both consumers show up is then $\Pr\{s(2) = 2\} = \pi^2$.

Suppose now that this service provider books three consumers so that $b = 3$. The probability that no one shows up is $\Pr\{s(3) = 0\} = (1 - \pi)^3$. The probability that exactly one consumer arrives is given by

$$\Pr\{s(3) = 1\} = \underbrace{\pi(1 - \pi)(1 - \pi)}_{1^{st} \text{ yes, } 2^{nd} \text{ no, } 3^{rd} \text{ no}} + \underbrace{(1 - \pi)\pi(1 - \pi)}_{1^{st} \text{ no, } 2^{nd} \text{ yes, } 3^{rd} \text{ no}} + \underbrace{(1 - \pi)(1 - \pi)\pi}_{1^{st} \text{ no, } 2^{nd} \text{ no, } 3^{rd} \text{ yes}}$$

$$= 3\pi(1 - \pi)^2. \tag{9.1}$$

Using the same logic, we can compute the probability that exactly two consumers show up to be

$$\Pr\{s(3) = 2\} = \underbrace{\pi \cdot \pi(1 - \pi)}_{1^{st} \text{ yes, } 2^{nd} \text{ yes, } 3^{rd} \text{ no}} + \underbrace{(1 - \pi)\pi \cdot \pi}_{1^{st} \text{ no, } 2^{nd} \text{ yes, } 3^{rd} \text{ yes}} + \underbrace{\pi(1 - \pi)\pi}_{1^{st} \text{ yes, } 2^{nd} \text{ no, } 3^{rd} \text{ yes}}$$

$$= 3\pi^2(1 - \pi). \tag{9.2}$$

Next, the probability that all three consumers with confirmed reservations show up is $\Pr\{s(3) = 3\} = \pi^3$. Now, if we take for example a survival probability of $\pi = 0.8$, we obtain $\Pr\{s(3) = 0\} = 0.2^3 = 0.008$, $\Pr\{s(3) = 1\} = 3 \times 0.8 \times 0.2^2 = 0.096$, $\Pr\{s(3) = 2\} = 3 \times 0.8^2 \times 0.2 = 0.348$, and $\Pr\{s(3) = 3\} = 0.8^3 = 0.512$. Notice that the sum of all these probabilities is equal to one because they reflect all the possible show-up events given that three consumers are booked for this service.

Finally, it would be interesting to check whether, or under what conditions, the probability that exactly two consumers show up exceeds the probability that exactly one consumer shows up. Formally, the following computation reveals that

$$\Pr\{s(3) = 2\} \geq \Pr\{s(3) = 1\} \iff 3\pi^2(1 - \pi) \geq 3\pi(1 - \pi)^2 \iff \pi \geq \frac{1}{2}.$$

That is, the probability that exactly two consumers show up is higher than the probability that only one consumer shows up if the survival probability exceeds 50%.

Similarly, the probability that three consumers show up exceeds the probability that only two consumers show up if

$$\Pr\{s(3) = 3\} \geq \Pr\{s(3) = 2\} \iff \pi^3 \geq 3\pi^2(1 - \pi) \iff \pi \geq \frac{2}{3}.$$

The above examples demonstrate that it is useful to have a general formula for computing the probability that exactly $\bar{s}$ consumers show up given that b consumers have confirmed reservations for the service. This formula becomes essential for larger values of b, and is given by the following binomial distribution function:

$$\Pr\{s(b) = \bar{s}\} = \frac{b!}{\bar{s}!\,(b - \bar{s})!}\,\pi^{\bar{s}}(1 - \pi)^{b - \bar{s}} \quad \text{for} \quad 0 \leq \bar{s} \leq b. \tag{9.3}$$

The intuition behind the formula given in (9.3) is as follows: The term $\pi^{\bar{s}}$ is the probability that precisely $\bar{s}$ specific people (who we can identify by their names, say) show up. The term $(1 - \pi)^{b - \bar{s}}$ is the probability that precisely $b - \bar{s}$ specific people (who again we can identify by their names) do not show up. The first term, sometimes written as $\binom{b}{\bar{s}}$ and referred to as "b choose $\bar{s}$," computes the number of times that any $\bar{s}$ people can be "pooled" from a group of b consumers. We should note again that the distribution function given by (9.3) relies on the assumption that consumers' actions regarding showing up at the time of service are *independent*. Thus, (9.3) rules out last-minute group cancellations and no-shows, which are analyzed later in Section 9.3.

To practice the use of the formula given by (9.3), let us recompute (9.1), which is the probability that exactly one consumer out of three confirmed reservations will show up. In this case,

$$\Pr\{s(3) = 1\} = \frac{3!}{1!\,(3 - 1)!}\,\pi^1(1 - \pi)^{3-1} = \frac{3!}{1! \cdot 2!}\,\pi^1(1 - \pi)^2 = 3\pi(1 - \pi)^2.$$

Consider now another example that makes use of the binomial distribution. Suppose that an airline confirms 120 reservations on a certain flight. Then, (9.3) implies that the probability that exactly 118 passengers show up for this flight is

$$\Pr\{s(120) = 118\} = \frac{120!}{118! \cdot 2!}\,\pi^{118}(1 - \pi)^2 = 7140 \cdot \pi^{118}(1 - \pi)^2.$$

To take a more specific example, if we assume that the survival probability is $\pi = 0.99$, the above computation implies that $\Pr\{s(120) = 118\} = 0.2180977445$.

We conclude our analysis of the binomial distribution with the computation of the expected number of show-ups. As it turns out, the binomial distribution defined by (9.3) generates a very simple formula for the expected number of show-ups. Without providing a formal proof, we merely state that if the service provider books b consumers, the expected number of show-ups is given by

$$\mathrm{E}s(b) = \sum_{\bar{s}=0}^{b} \Pr\{s(b) = \bar{s}\} \cdot \bar{s} = \pi \cdot b, \tag{9.4}$$

which is the survival probability of each individual multiplied by the number of bookings made by the service provider. For example, if the survival probability is $\pi = 0.8$ and the service provider books $b = 120$ consumers, the expected number of show-ups is $\mathrm{E}s(b) = 0.8 \times 120 = 96$ consumers.

9.1.2 Overbooking and probability

We now make use of our assumption that the service provider has a capacity constraint of admitting no more than K consumers at the time of service. Overbooking is defined as follows:

DEFINITION 9.1
We say that a service provider is engaged in **overbooking** *consumers if the number of confirmed reservations exceeds the service capacity level; that is, if $b \geq K + 1$.*

The reader is urged to consult the notation described in Tables 1.4 and 1.5 to recall that b (lowercase letter) denotes a choice variable, whereas K (capital letter) denotes an exogenously given parameter. Thus, Definition 9.1 identifies which booking levels are regarded as overbooking. The purpose of this chapter is to provide a method for computing the profitable amount of overbooking. A high overbooking level may result in high penalties to be paid to customers who are denied service. Underbooking is likely to result in some unfilled capacity due to no-shows. In this chapter, we weigh this trade-off to find the exact profit-maximizing booking level, b.

A major possible consequence of overbooking is described by the following definition:

DEFINITION 9.2
Suppose that service provider books b consumers. If the number of show-ups exceeds the available capacity level, formally if $s(b) \geq K + 1$, then we say that $ds(b) \stackrel{\text{def}}{=} s(b) - K$ consumers are **denied service***.*

An alternative terminology for denied service that is commonly used in the airline industry is to say that ds passengers are "bumped" from a flight. Note that the number of consumers who are denied service is affected by the number of bookings made, because the number of show-ups $s(b)$ is also a function of the number of bookings, b, made by the service provider.

We now proceed to computing the probabilities of overbooking events. Suppose that the service provider overbooks, so $b \geq K + 1$. The probability that exactly one consumer is denied service is given by

$$\Pr\{ds(b) = 1\} = \Pr\{s(b) = K + 1\}$$

$$= \frac{b!}{(K+1)!\,(b-K-1)!}\,\pi^{K+1}(1-\pi)^{b-K-1}.$$

More generally, the probability that exactly $\overline{ds}$ consumers are denied service given that consumers hold b confirmed reservations is

$$\Pr\{ds(b) = \overline{ds}\} = \Pr\{s(b) = K + \overline{ds}\}$$
$$= \frac{b!}{(K + \overline{ds})! \, (b - K - \overline{ds})!} \, \pi^{K + \overline{ds}}(1 - \pi)^{b - K - \overline{ds}}, \quad (9.5)$$

for all denied service levels satisfying $1 \leq \overline{ds} \leq b - K$.

Let us now practice the use of (9.5) with the following example: Consider an airline that books $b = 104$ passengers on an aircraft with a seating capacity of $K = 100$. We now compute the probabilities that $ds = 1, 2, 3, 4$ consumers are denied service:

$$
\begin{aligned}
\Pr\{ds(104) = 1\} &= \Pr\{s(104) = 101\} = \frac{104!}{101! \cdot 3!} \, \pi^{101}(1 - \pi)^3 \\
&= 182104 \, \pi^{101}(1 - \pi)^3. \\
\Pr\{ds(104) = 2\} &= \Pr\{s(104) = 102\} = \frac{104!}{102! \cdot 2!} \, \pi^{102}(1 - \pi)^2 \\
&= 5356 \, \pi^{102}(1 - \pi)^2. \qquad\qquad (9.6) \\
\Pr\{ds(104) = 3\} &= \Pr\{s(104) = 103\} = \frac{104!}{103! \cdot 1!} \, \pi^{103}(1 - \pi)^1 \\
&= 104 \, \pi^{103}(1 - \pi)^1. \\
\Pr\{ds(104) = 4\} &= \Pr\{s(104) = 104\} = \frac{104!}{104! \cdot 0!} \, \pi^{104}(1 - \pi)^0 = \pi^{104}.
\end{aligned}
$$

A natural question to ask at this point is, What is the probability that *at least* one consumer is denied service? Using the above example, this probability is given by the sum

$$\Pr\{ds(104) \geq 1\} = \Pr\{ds(104) = 1\} + \Pr\{ds(104) = 2\}$$
$$+ \Pr\{ds(104) = 3\} + \Pr\{ds(104) = 4\}.$$

Clearly, the probability that no one is denied service is simply one minus the above probability, that is, $1 - \Pr\{ds(104) \geq 1\}$. More generally, we can write the probability that at least one consumer is denied service when the service provider owns K capacity units and books b consumers, where $b \geq K + 1$, as

$$\Pr\{ds(b) \geq 1\} = \sum_{\overline{ds}=1}^{b-K} \Pr\{ds(b) = \overline{ds}\}. \qquad (9.7)$$

Hence, the probability that no one is denied service is

$$\Pr\{ds(b) = 0\} = 1 - \Pr\{ds(b) \geq 1\} = 1 - \sum_{\overline{ds}=1}^{b-K} \Pr\{ds(b) = \overline{ds}\}. \qquad (9.8)$$

Clearly, we can also express the probabilities that overbooking occurs and does not occur directly as a function of the number of show-ups, $s(b)$. That is, we can rewrite (9.7) as

$$\Pr\{ds(b) \geq 1\} = \Pr\{s(b) \geq K+1\} = \sum_{\bar{s}=K+1}^{b} \Pr\{s(b) = \bar{s}\}$$

$$= \sum_{\bar{s}=K+1}^{b} \frac{b!}{\bar{s}! \, (b-\bar{s})!} \, \pi^{\bar{s}} (1-\pi)^{b-\bar{s}}. \quad (9.9)$$

Similarly, we can rewrite (9.8) as

$$\Pr\{ds(b) = 0\} = \Pr\{s(b) \leq K\} = \sum_{\bar{s}=0}^{K} \Pr\{s(b) = \bar{s}\}$$

$$= \sum_{\bar{s}=0}^{K} \frac{b!}{\bar{s}! \, (b-\bar{s})!} \, \pi^{\bar{s}} (1-\pi)^{b-\bar{s}}. \quad (9.10)$$

That is, the probability computed in (9.7) is identical to (9.9), and the probability computed in (9.8) is identical to (9.10). The probability computed in (9.8) is one minus the probability that at least one consumer is denied service, whereas (9.10) is the sum of probabilities of all possible show-up levels $\bar{s}$ not exceeding the capacity level K. Clearly, both computation methods yield identical results.

We conclude our analysis of service denial with the computation of the expected number of consumers who are denied service. Suppose again that consumers' survival probability is π, service capacity level is K, and b consumers are booked. Clearly, if $b \leq K$, the number of consumers expected to be denied service is $Eds(b) = 0$ because there is no overbooking of consumers. However, if $b \geq K+1$, the number of consumers expected to be denied service is given by

$$Eds(b) = \underbrace{\sum_{\bar{s}=0}^{K} \Pr\{s(b) = \bar{s}\} \cdot 0}_{s(b) \leq K \implies ds(b) = 0} + \underbrace{\sum_{\bar{s}=K+1}^{b} \Pr\{s(b) = \bar{s}\} \, (\bar{s} - K)}_{s(b) \geq K+1 \implies ds(b) = \bar{s} - K}. \quad (9.11)$$

Substituting (9.3) into (9.11) yields the general formula for the expected number of consumers who are denied service given that there are b confirmed reservations for K units of capacity. Therefore,

$$Eds(b) = \begin{cases} 0 & \text{if } b \leq K \\ \displaystyle\sum_{s=K+1}^{b} \frac{b!}{s! \, (b-s)!} \, \pi^{s} (1-\pi)^{b-s} \, (s-K) & \text{if } b \geq K+1. \end{cases} \quad (9.12)$$

That is, the number of consumers expected to be denied service is the sum of the probabilities of all show-up realizations beyond capacity multiplied by the number of consumers who are denied service.

It is important to note that the expected number given by (9.12) cannot be derived directly from the formula for the expected number of show-ups given by (9.4). This follows from the observation that in most cases $\mathrm{E}ds(b) \neq \mathrm{E}[s(b) - K]$, because we must set $ds(b) = 0$ (rather than $ds(b) < 0$) for show-up realizations satisfying $s(b) - K < 0$. Another way of explaining this difference is to observe that the expected number of show-ups (9.4) is independent of the difference $b - K$, whereas the expected number of consumers who are denied service clearly depends on this difference.

9.2 Profit-maximizing Overbooking

The purpose of designing an overbooking plan is to maximize expected profit, taking into consideration that a certain fraction of customers with confirmed reservations will not show up at the time of service. We use the statistical term *expected* because service providers are subjected to random realizations of the number of consumers who show up at the time of service. Moreover, with some probability (which was computed in the previous section), overbooking can be highly costly to service providers when the number of consumers who show up at the time of service exceeds the given capacity level K. Formally, our investigation of the profit-maximizing booking level should take into consideration that a sufficiently high booking level b, where $b \geq K + 1$, and a sufficiently low survival probability π will result in having $ds = s(b) - K$ consumers being denied service.

9.2.1 Expected cost

Service providers bear four types of costs: fixed and sunk costs denoted by ϕ, which are independent of the number of people who book the service and the number of show-ups; per-customer capacity cost, denoted by μ_k; and per-customer operating cost, denoted by μ_o. The reader is referred to Definition 8.4 for a more precise distinction between marginal capacity cost and marginal operating cost. The fourth type of cost borne by service providers is the marginal cost of denying service to a booked consumer. We denote this penalty rate by ψ. The penalty rate ψ consists of a direct payment to a consumer who is denied service and also includes some unobserved reputation and goodwill-related costs that may affect future reservations made by a consumer who is denied service.

In this chapter, we assume that the service provider has already allocated K units of capacity that is capable of serving K customers. Under this assumption, the service provider bears a cost of $\phi + \mu_k K$ independent of the number of bookings. Thus, only the operating cost μ_o and the penalty rate ψ are relevant for determining how total cost increases with an increase in the booking level b. Formally, if $s(b)$ consumers show up, the realized total cost of a service provider who books b

consumers is given by

$$c(s(b)) = \begin{cases} \phi + \mu_k K + \mu_o K + \psi[s(b) - K] & \text{if } s(b) \geq K+1 \\ \phi + \mu_k K + \mu_o s(b) & \text{if } s(b) \leq K. \end{cases} \quad (9.13)$$

That is, in the event of a large number of show-ups so that $s(b) \geq K+1$, the service provider must deny service to $ds = s(b) - K$ confirmed customers and pay a penalty that sums up to $\psi \cdot ds = \psi[s(b) - K]$. Because capacity is fully used, the sum of capacity and operating cost is simply $(\mu_k + \mu_o)K$. The second line in (9.13) reflects the cost when (over- or under-) booking does not result in denied service as the number of show-ups does not exceed capacity. In this case, the firm bears the given capacity cost $\mu_k K$ and the variable operating cost $\mu_o s(b)$ that depends on the realization of the random show-up variable $s(b)$.

We wish to express the total cost function (9.13) in expected terms using the probabilities computed in (9.3), (9.5), (9.9), and (9.10). Thus, if the service provider overbooks, that is, if $b \geq K+1$,

$$c(b) = \underbrace{\phi + \mu_k K}_{\text{fixed costs}} + \underbrace{\sum_{\bar{s}=0}^{K} \Pr\{s(b) = \bar{s}\} \mu_o \bar{s}}_{\text{expected operating cost for } s(b) \leq K}$$

$$+ \underbrace{\sum_{\bar{s}=K+1}^{b} \Pr\{s(b) = \bar{s}\} [\mu_o K + \psi(\bar{s} - K)]}_{\text{expected operating \& penalty costs for } s(b) \geq K+1}. \quad (9.14)$$

The second term is the expected operating cost when there is no service denial when the number of show-ups does not exceed capacity. The last term is the sum of operating cost and penalty incurred when the number of show-ups exceeds capacity so that $\bar{s} - K$ customers must be denied service. In this case, the operating cost equals $\mu_o K$ because the firm cannot accommodate more than K customers.

The expected cost (9.14) is formulated for the case of overbooking, $b \geq K+1$. However, if the service provider does not overbook consumers, that is, if $b \leq K$, the expected total cost given by (9.14) becomes

$$c(b) = \underbrace{\phi + \mu_k K}_{\text{fixed costs}} + \underbrace{\sum_{\bar{s}=0}^{b} \Pr\{s(b) = \bar{s}\} \mu_o \bar{s}}_{\text{expected operating cost for } s(b) \leq b \leq K}. \quad (9.15)$$

Observe that the upper limit of the summation in the second term of (9.14) is K (full capacity), whereas the upper limit of the second term in (9.15) is only $b < K$ (booking below capacity).

Substituting (9.3) into (9.14), the explicit formulation of the expected cost of a service provider that overbooks customers ($b \geq K+1$) is given by

$$c(b) = \phi + \mu_k K + \sum_{s=0}^{K} \frac{b!}{s!\,(b-s)!}\, \pi^s (1-\pi)^{b-s}\, \mu_o s$$

$$+ \sum_{s=K+1}^{b} \frac{b!}{s!\,(b-s)!}\, \pi^s (1-\pi)^{b-s}\, [\mu_o K + \psi(s-K)]. \quad (9.16)$$

The formulation of the expected cost functions under overbooking, given by (9.14) and (9.16), reveal that solving overbooking problems requires the separation of all possible events into two groups. First, when the number of show-ups falls short of capacity, $s(b) \leq K$. Second, when the number of show-ups exceeds capacity, $s(b) \geq K+1$. In the second case, $ds(b) = s(b) - K$ consumers are denied service, in which case the operating cost becomes a constant $\mu_o K$ that is independent of the number of show-ups. This happens because only K consumers can be served.

9.2.2 Expected revenue and expected profit

We now compute a service provider's expected revenue as a function of the number of bookings b. Assume that the service provider offers the service for an exogenously given price denoted by P. Because P is written in a capital letter, it is treated as an exogenous parameter of the model developed in this chapter (compare P in Table 1.4 with p in Table 1.5). Also, assume that $P > \mu_k + \mu_o$, which means that the price exceeds the sum of marginal capacity cost and marginal operating cost. Clearly, the price should be even higher than this sum to cover the fixed cost ϕ. Assuming otherwise implies that the service provider makes a loss on each unit of sales, and hence must shut down.

Similar to our discussion about cost in Section 9.2.1, and because the revenue also depends on the realization of the number of show-ups $s(b)$, we must distinguish between two sets of events, depending on whether the number of show-ups is below capacity or exceeds capacity. Hence, the expected revenue to be collected by a service provider who books b consumers is given by

$$x(b) =$$

$$\begin{cases} \underbrace{\sum_{\bar{s}=0}^{b} \Pr\{s(b) = \bar{s}\}\, P\bar{s}}_{\text{expected revenue for } s(b) \leq b \leq K} & \text{if } b \leq K \\[2em] \underbrace{\sum_{\bar{s}=0}^{K} \Pr\{s(b) = \bar{s}\}\, P\bar{s}}_{\text{expected revenue for } s(b) \leq K} + \underbrace{\sum_{\bar{s}=K+1}^{b} \Pr\{s(b) = \bar{s}\}\, PK}_{\text{expected revenue for } s(b) \geq K+1} & \text{if } b \geq K+1. \end{cases} \quad (9.17)$$

The first term on each row of (9.17) is the revenue generated by show-up levels not exceeding capacity or the booking level (whichever is the lowest). The second term on the bottom row of (9.17) shows that the revenue is constant (PK) when overbooking results in the number of show-ups exceeding the capacity level.

Substituting (9.3) into the second row of (9.17), the explicit formulation of the expected revenue of a service provider that overbooks customers ($b \geq K+1$) is given by

$$x(b) = \sum_{s=0}^{K} \frac{b!}{s!\,(b-s)!}\,\pi^s (1-\pi)^{b-s}\,P s$$

$$+ \sum_{s=K+1}^{b} \frac{b!}{s!\,(b-s)!}\,\pi^s (1-\pi)^{b-s}\,P K. \quad (9.18)$$

We are now ready to state the profit function for a service provider who overbooks his consumers so that $b \geq K+1$. Subtracting (9.14) from the second row in (9.17) yields

$$y(b) \stackrel{\text{def}}{=} x(b) - c(b) = -\underbrace{(\phi + \mu_k K)}_{\text{fixed costs}} + \underbrace{\sum_{\bar{s}=0}^{K} \Pr\{s(b) = \bar{s}\}\,(P - \mu_o)\,\bar{s}}_{\text{expected profit for } s(b) \leq K}$$

$$+ \underbrace{\sum_{\bar{s}=K+1}^{b} \Pr\{s(b) = \bar{s}\}\,[(P - \mu_o)K + \psi(\bar{s} - K)]}_{\text{expected profit for } s(b) \geq K+1}. \quad (9.19)$$

For the case in which there is no overbooking but at least one consumer is booked ($1 \leq b \leq K$), subtracting (9.15) from the first row in (9.17) yields

$$y(b) \stackrel{\text{def}}{=} x(b) - c(b) = -\underbrace{(\phi + \mu_k K)}_{\text{fixed costs}} + \underbrace{\sum_{\bar{s}=0}^{b} \Pr\{s(b) = \bar{s}\}\,(P - \mu_o)\,\bar{s}}_{\text{expected profit for } s(b) \leq b \leq K}. \quad (9.20)$$

Substituting (9.3) into (9.19), we obtain the explicit formulation of the expected profit of an overbooking service provider. Thus, if overbooking is profitable, the service provider chooses a booking level $b \geq K+1$ to solve

$$\max_{K+1 \leq b \leq B} y(b) = -\phi - \mu_k K + \sum_{s=0}^{K} \frac{b!}{s!\,(b-s)!}\,\pi^s (1-\pi)^{b-s}\,(P - \mu_o)s$$

$$+ \sum_{s=K+1}^{b} \frac{b!}{s!\,(b-s)!}\,\pi^s (1-\pi)^{b-s}\,[(P - \mu_o)K + \psi(s - K)], \quad (9.21)$$

where B is the maximum allowable booking level. In the case in which underbooking is profitable, substituting (9.3) into and (9.20), the service provider should also solve

$$\max_{0 \le b \le K} y(b) =$$

$$\begin{cases} 0 & \text{if } b = 0 \\ -\phi - \mu_k K + \sum_{s=0}^{b} \frac{b!}{s!\,(b-s)!}\, \pi^s (1-\pi)^{b-s}\, (P - \mu_o)\, s & \text{if } b \ge 1. \end{cases} \qquad (9.22)$$

The profit-maximization booking level b^* is chosen as the booking level that yields the highest profit level obtained from solving (9.21) and (9.22). However, because of the linear property of the present model, the solution to (9.22) yields either $b^* = 0$ with $y(b^*) = 0$ (no booking at all) or $b^* = K$ (booking exactly to full capacity). This means that to find b^*, we need to compare only the profit levels given by $y(0)$, $y(K)$, and the profit level that solves (9.21).

9.2.3   Simple examples

The following examples demonstrate the logic behind a profitable determination of the overbooking level. These examples are simple in the sense that they do not necessarily require the use of computers, as most of these examples can be solved even without making use of the binomial distribution formula (9.3). In all examples, we continue to assume that the fixed and capacity costs given by $\phi + \mu_k K$ are borne only if the service provider books at least one consumer. Otherwise, if no bookings are made by the service provider ($b = 0$), the firm earns zero profits, so $y(0)$.

How to overbook a single unit of capacity

Suppose that the service provider can accommodate at most one consumer, so $K = 1$. Assume that the regulator restricts overbooking to not exceed 300% of capacity, which translates in the present example to assuming that $B = 3$. We first compute the expected profit levels $y(b)$ for booking levels $b = 0, 1, 2, 3$, assuming a general survival probability π. Then, we proceed with some more specific numerical examples by substituting specific numbers for the parameter π.

If the service provider does not book any consumer, no profit or loss are made as we assumed that $y(0) = 0$. Next, if the firm books at least one consumer, the sum of the fixed and capacity costs is $\phi + \mu_k$ for all booking levels $b \ge 1$. When exactly one booking is made, $b = 1$, the resulting expected profit is given by

$$y(1) = -\underbrace{(\phi + \mu_k)}_{\text{fixed \& capacity costs for } K = 1} + \underbrace{\pi(P - \mu_o)}_{\text{case } s(1)=1}, \qquad (9.23)$$

where the second term is the survival probability multiplied by the profit (net of operating cost) generated by the realization that exactly one consumer shows up. Next, if the firm books two consumers, $b = 2$, expected profit is given by

$$y(2) = -\underbrace{(\phi + \mu_k)}_{\text{fixed costs}} + \underbrace{2\pi(1-\pi)(P-\mu_o)}_{\text{2 cases } s(2)=1} + \underbrace{\pi^2[(P-\mu_o) - \psi(2-1)]}_{\text{case } s(2)=2 \implies d=1}. \qquad (9.24)$$

The second term corresponds to the two possible realizations in which exactly one consumer shows up $s(2) = 1$, which yield an expected profit given by $[\pi(1-\pi) + (1-\pi)\pi](P-\mu_o)$. This profit is the sum of the profit made when the first consumer shows up and the second does not, and the other way around. Readers who still find this argument difficult are referred to Section 9.1.1 for some background calculations. The third term corresponds to the realization in which exactly two consumers show up for the service, which means that one consumer must be denied service.

Finally, if the service provider books to full capacity so that $b = B = 3$, expected profit is given by

$$y(3) = -\underbrace{(\phi + \mu_k)}_{\text{fixed costs}} + \underbrace{3\pi(1-\pi)^2(P-\mu_o)}_{\text{3 cases } s(3)=1}$$

$$+ \underbrace{3\pi^2(1-\pi)[(P-\mu_o) - \psi(2-1)]}_{\text{3 cases } s(3)=2 \implies ds=1} + \underbrace{\pi^3[(P-\mu_o) - \psi(3-1)]}_{\text{case } s(3)=3 \implies d=2}. \quad (9.25)$$

Table 9.1 displays simulation results for the general solution postulated by (9.23), (9.24), and (9.25) for increasing levels of survival probabilities given by $\pi = 0.2, 0.4, 0.6$, and 0.8. All simulations assume parameter values where the fixed cost $\phi = 100$, marginal capacity and operating costs $\mu_k = \mu_o = 5$, price of service $P = 500$, and a penalty rate of denying service to one consumer $\psi = 600$.

π	$y(0)$	$y(1)$	$y(2)$	$y(3)$	b^*	Overbook	$Es(b^*)$	$Eds(b^*)$
0.2	0.00	−6.00	49.20	69.36	3	2	0.4	0.112
0.4	0.00	93.00	115.80	33.48	2	1	0.4	0.160
0.6	0.00	192.00	94.80	−160.08	1	0	0.6	0.000
0.8	0.00	291.00	−13.80	−458.76	1	0	0.8	0.000

Table 9.1: Profit levels and profit-maximizing overbooking levels as functions of survival probabilities under $K = 1$ capacity units. *Note:* Simulations assume $\phi = 100$, $\mu_k = \mu_o = 5$, $P = 500$, and $\psi = 600$.

The results shown in Table 9.1 demonstrate that the profit-maximizing booking level declines with an increase in the survival probability. This happens because a higher show-up probability increases the expected penalty that service providers must pay for denying service. In the present example, the profit-maximizing booking level is $b^* = 3$ for $\pi = 0.2$, but drops to $b^* = 1$ for survival probabilities $\pi \geq 0.6$.

One way of looking at that is to observe that the profit level $y(1)$ increases with π, but $y(3)$ declines with an increase in π.

The last two columns are not essential for solving the overbooking problem, but are presented here for the sake of illustration only and for gaining better intuition. The expected number of show-ups $Es(b^*) = \pi b^*$, see (9.4), is shown to increase with the survival probability π although the profit-maximizing booking level b^* declines with π. In addition, as long as the firm overbooks at least one consumer, the number of consumers expected to be denied service $Eds(b)$, derived in (9.11) and (9.12), also increases with the survival probability as it increases between $\pi = 0.2$ and 0.4. However, it then drops to zero for $\pi \geq 0.6$ because the firm does not overbook any consumer for sufficiently high survival probabilities.

How to overbook two units of capacity

Suppose now that the firm possesses two units of capacity so that $K = 2$. We now compute the profit-maximizing booking levels assuming that the maximum allowable booking level is $B = 4$. The expected profit from booking $b = 2$ consumers is given by

$$y(2) = -\underbrace{(\phi + 2\mu_k)}_{\text{fixed costs}} + \underbrace{2\pi(1-\pi)(P-\mu_o)}_{\text{2 cases } s(2)=1} + \underbrace{\pi^2 \cdot 2(P-\mu_o)}_{\text{case } s(2)=2}. \qquad (9.26)$$

The expected profit from booking $b = 3$ consumers is

$$y(3) = -\underbrace{(\phi + 2\mu_k)}_{\text{fixed costs}} + \underbrace{3\pi(1-\pi)^2(P-\mu_o)}_{\text{3 cases } s(2)=1}$$

$$+ \underbrace{3\pi^2(1-\pi)\cdot 2(P-\mu_o)}_{\text{3 cases } s(2)=2} + \underbrace{\pi^3[2(P-\mu_o) - \psi(3-2)]}_{\text{case } s(3)=3 \Longrightarrow ds=1}. \qquad (9.27)$$

Finally, to compute the expected profit resulting from booking $b = 4$ consumers, it is useful to practice the general formula given by (9.21), which implies that

$$y(4) = -\underbrace{(\phi + 2\mu_k)}_{\text{fixed costs}} \qquad (9.28)$$

$$+ \underbrace{\frac{4!}{1! \cdot 3!}\pi(1-\pi)^3(P-\mu_o)}_{\text{4 cases } s(4)=1} + \underbrace{\frac{4!}{2! \cdot 2!}\pi^2(1-\pi)^2 \cdot 2(P-\mu_o)}_{\text{8 cases } s(4)=2}$$

$$+ \underbrace{\frac{4!}{3! \cdot 1!}\pi^3(1-\pi)[2(P-\mu_o) - \psi(3-2)]}_{\text{4 cases } s(4)=3 \Longrightarrow ds=1} + \underbrace{\pi^4[2(P-\mu_o) - \psi(4-2)]}_{\text{case } s(4)=4 \Longrightarrow ds=2}.$$

Table 9.2 displays simulation results of the general solution postulated by (9.26), (9.27), and (9.28) for increasing levels of survival probability $\pi =$

0.2, 0.4, 0.6, and 0.8. All simulations assume a fixed cost $\phi = 100$, marginal capacity and operating costs $\mu_k = \mu_o = 5$, a service price $P = 500$, and a penalty rate of denying service to one consumer $\psi = 600$. Table 9.2 shows results similar to those in Table 9.1 in the sense that the profitable overbooking level b^* declines with an increase in the survival probability π, the expected number of show-ups $Es(b)$ increases with π, and the expected number of consumers to be denied service $Eds(b)$ also increases as long as the firm overbooks at least one consumer.

π	$y(2)$	$y(3)$	$y(4)$	b^*	Overbook	$Es(b^*)$	$Eds(b^*)$
0.2	88.00	178.24	254.47	4	2	0.8	0.029
0.4	286.00	413.92	457.74	4	2	1.6	0.205
0.6	484.00	544.48	415.74	3	1	1.8	0.216
0.8	682.00	517.36	128.46	2	0	1.6	0.000

Table 9.2: Profit levels and profit-maximizing overbooking levels as functions of survival probabilities under $K = 2$ capacity units. *Note*: Simulations assume $\phi = 100$, $\mu_k = \mu_o = 5$, $P = 500$, and $\psi = 600$.

9.2.4   Computer algorithm

The computer algorithm described by Algorithm 9.1 runs simple loops over the booking levels $b = 0, K, K + 1, \ldots, B$ and compares the resulting profit levels $y(b)$ derived from (9.21) and (9.22). This algorithm should first input (using a **Read()** command, say) the model's parameters describing K (capacity level), B (maximum allowable booking level, where $B \geq K$), ϕ (fixed cost), μ_k (marginal capacity cost), μ_o (marginal operating cost), P (service's sale price), ψ (overbooking penalty rate), and π (survival probability). In addition, the program should include some trivial loops to ensure that there are no out-of-range (or negative) parameter values.

As for variables, the program should define $y[b]$ (expected profit level given that b bookings are made) as an array of real numbers of dimension $B + 1$. The variable b^* outputs the profit-maximizing booking level. Inspecting the expected profit function (9.21) reveals that the "loop" over all possible realizations of the show-up random variable $s(b)$ is decomposed from two sums: the loop over the number of show-ups not exceeding capacity ($s(b) \leq K$) and the loop over show-up realizations exceeding capacity ($s(b) = K + 1, \ldots, b$). Algorithm 9.1 first computes the profit $y[K]$ associated with booking exactly to full capacity ($b = K$). Then, it runs loops over booking levels exceeding capacity $b = K + 1, \ldots, B$. To summarize, Algorithm 9.1 compares the profit levels $y(0)$ to $y(K)$ and to every $y(b)$ for $b \geq K + 1$, because all booking levels satisfying $1 \leq b \leq K - 1$ cannot be profit maximizing in this linear model.

Algorithm 9.2 is a continuation of Algorithm 9.1 and summarizes the results by writing the exact profit-maximizing booking level as well as the corresponding

---

$b^* \leftarrow 0; y[0] \leftarrow 0; \text{/* Initialization} \qquad\qquad\qquad\qquad\qquad\qquad */$
for $b = 1$ **to** B **do** $y[b] \leftarrow -\phi - \mu_k K;$/* Subtracting fixed costs */
for $s = 0$ **to** K **do**
 /* Computing $y[K]$ using (9.22) (booking to capacity) */
 $y[K] \leftarrow y[K] + \frac{K!}{s!(K-s)!} \pi^s (1-\pi)^{K-s} (P - \mu_o) s;$

for $b = K+1$ **to** B **do**
 /* Overbooking main loop computing $y(b)$, $K+1 \le b \le B$ */
 for $s = 0$ **to** K **do**
  /* 1st summation on the RHS of (9.21) */
  $y[b] \leftarrow y[b] + \frac{b!}{s!(b-s)!} \pi^s (1-\pi)^{b-s} (P - \mu_o) s;$
 for $s = K+1$ **to** b **do**
  /* 2nd summation on the RHS of (9.21) */
  $y[b] \leftarrow y[b] + \frac{b!}{s!(b-s)!} \pi^s (1-\pi)^{b-s} [(P - \mu_o)K - \psi(b-K)];$

for $b = K$ **to** B **do**
 /* Finding the profit-maximizing booking level b^* */
 if $y[b] > y[b^*]$ **then** $b^* \leftarrow b;$
if $y[b^*] < 0$ **then** $b^* \leftarrow 0;$ /* Negative profit, no booking */

Algorithm 9.1: Computation of profit-maximizing overbooking.

expected number of show-ups and the number of consumers expected to be denied service. Two additional output variables must be introduced. Es outputs the expected number of show-ups and Eds outputs the number of consumers expected to be denied service.

9.3 Overbooking of Groups

Our analysis so far has been conducted under the key assumption that consumers' survival probabilities are independent in the sense that the event leading to a no-show of one consumer is independent of the event leading to a no-show of any other consumer. However, reservations are often made by groups, which may lead to a cancellation of an entire group. Groups may be large, such as organized tours, conferences, and conventions, or may be as small as two to four people, consisting of family members only. For our purpose, we will be using the term *group* as follows.

DEFINITION 9.3
*We will say that N consumers form a **booking group** if*
(a) All consumers within the group have the same survival probability π, and

---

writeln ("The profit-maximizing refund booking level is ", b^*,".");
$Es \leftarrow \pi b^*$; **writeln** (Es, "consumers are expected to show up.");
writeln ("The resulting expected profit level is ", $y[b^*]$, ".");
if $b^* = 0$ **then write** ("No booking should be made, cease operation.");
if $b^* = K$ **then write** ("Book exactly to full capacity.");
if $b^* \geq K + 1$ **then**
    writeln ("Overbook ", $b^* - K$, "consumers."); $Eds \leftarrow 0$;
    for $s = K + 1$ **to** b^* **do**
        /* Computing $Eds(b^*)$ according to (9.12)   */
        $Eds \leftarrow Eds + \frac{b^*!}{b^*!(b^*-s)!} \pi^s (1 - \pi)^{b^*-s}(s - K)$;
    writeln (Eds, "consumers are expected to be denied service.");

Algorithm 9.2: Overbooking, the expected number of show-ups, and the number of consumers expected to be denied service.

(b) *Within the group, either all the consumers show up together at the time of service or the entire group does not show up. Formally, consumers belonging to the same group are perfectly correlated with respect to their show–no-show decisions.*

A more difficult issue that must be discussed now is how and whether service can be denied to an entire group. Obviously, this policy issue is decided upon by the service provider and should be made known to the group before the booking time. In general, the service provider must make and announce the following policy decisions.

- Can service be denied to any group of any size?

- Can service be denied to a fraction of consumers within a group, or must it be denied to the entire group?

- Can service be denied to any group, or should service be denied on a first-come-first-served basis?

Clearly, the above policy issues should be explicitly stated on the contract or ticket reserved by the group of customers. For the present analysis, we merely state these guidelines in the form of assumptions.

ASSUMPTION 9.1
(a) *Service can be denied to an entire group of confirmed consumers, but cannot be denied to a fraction of consumers within a booked group.*
(b) *Service providers can choose which group is to be denied service so as to maximize their profit.*

Assumption 9.1(a) needs no explanation as most groups are formed on the basis that all group members wish to be served together with their fellow group members. Assumption 9.1(b) is irrelevant for most of our analysis as we restrict our model to handle equal-size groups only. However, this assumption becomes important when groups are of unequal size, because service providers can choose which group to deny service to based on the group's relative size.

Each group attempts to book a service that has a total capacity of K consumers (for all groups together). We make the following assumptions:

ASSUMPTION 9.2
(a) *All groups are of equal size and have N consumers.*
(b) *The size of each booking group is smaller than the service provider's capacity level. Formally, $N \leq K$.*
(c) *All groups have an identical survival probability π.*

Assumption 9.2(a) is a restriction of our analysis, as it rules out booking of groups of unequal sizes. Assumption 9.2(b) restricts our analysis to the more common cases in which a single group cannot consume the entire capacity. For example, this assumption implies that the tour group is smaller than the aircrafts' seating capacity. Assumption 9.2(c) may be justified by the fact that service providers often cannot distinguish among the types of consumers in each of their booking groups, so a common survival probability serves as the best approximation. Of course, this assumption can be tested by looking at real-life rates of group cancellations and comparing them with the rate of individual cancellations.

Clearly if $N = 1$, each group consists of a single consumer, in which case the analysis conducted earlier in Section 9.2 applies. The problem we wish to solve now is to compute the service provider's profit-maximizing number of group bookings. Thus, the difference between the analysis of this section compared with the previous sections is that now we allow groups to be of sizes $N \geq 2$. This means that the booking level, to be decided upon by the service provider, should now take the values of $b = 0, N, 2N, 3N$, and so on, instead of $b = 0, 1, 2, 3, \ldots$ corresponding to a group size of $N = 1$ only.

9.3.1   Simple examples

How to overbook two groups of consumers

Suppose the service provider faces booking requests from two groups, each having N consumers. Thus, this provider has the option of booking $b = 0, N, 2N$ consumers. We continue to assume that $y(0) = 0$, which means that the fixed and capacity costs are not borne if the provider ceases operation. If only one group is booked, there is no overbooking because $b = N \leq K$ by Assumption 9.2(b). Therefore, expected profit is given by

$$y(N) = -\phi - \mu_k K + \pi(P - \mu_o)N, \tag{9.29}$$

which is negative the sum of fixed and capacity costs plus the expected marginal profit multiplied by the group's joint survival probability.

Next, when the service provider books two groups, each of size N, expected profit depends on whether there is an overbooking ($2N \geq K+1$) or underbooking ($2N \leq K$). Therefore, expected profit is given by

$$
\begin{aligned}
y(2N) &= -\phi - \mu_k K \\
&= \begin{cases} \pi^2(P - \mu_o)2N + 2\pi(1 - \pi)(P - \mu_o)N & \text{if } 2N \leq K \\ [\pi^2 + 2\pi(1 - \pi)](P - \mu_o)N - \pi^2 \psi N & \text{if } 2N \geq K+1. \end{cases}
\end{aligned} \tag{9.30}
$$

That is, if $2N \leq K$, the service provider can accommodate the two groups together, and the resulting profit depends on whether both groups show up, one group shows up and the other does not (two cases), or neither. In contrast, if $2N \geq K+1$, the service provider can accommodate at most N consumers and therefore must deny service (and pay a penalty) to one group in the event both groups show up (probability π^2).

The decision whether to book two groups, a single group only, or neither depends on whether $y(2N) \geq \max\{y(N),0\}$, $y(N) \geq \max\{y(2N),0\}$, or $\max\{y(2N),y(N)\} < 0 = y(0)$. Comparing (9.30) with (9.29) implies that $y(2N) \geq y(N)$ whenever $2N \leq K$. That is, when booking two groups does not result in overbooking, booking the two groups yields a higher profit than booking one group only. However, if $2N \geq K+1$,

$$
y(2N) \geq y(N) \iff \psi \leq \psi_{2,1} \stackrel{\text{def}}{=} \frac{(1 - \pi)(P - \mu_o)}{\pi}. \tag{9.31}
$$

Hence, equation (9.31) defines a threshold penalty rate $\psi_{2,1}$ on denying service, such that for every penalty rate lower than the threshold level, booking two groups yields a higher expected profit than booking a single group only.

We conclude the present example with some numerical examples. Consider a service provider with a given capacity of $K = 100$ facing booking requests from two groups of size $N = 60$. Also let $\phi = 5000$ (fixed cost), $\mu_k = \mu_o = 5$ (marginal capacity and operating costs), and $P = 500$ (service's price). Table 9.3 demonstrates how the value of the threshold penalty rate $\psi_{2,1}$ varies with the survival probability parameter π. Table 9.3 demonstrates at a low survival probability of $\pi = 0.2$, booking

$\theta \backslash \pi$	0.2	0.4	0.6	0.8
$\psi_{2,1}$	1980.00	742.50	330.00	123.75
$\psi_{3,2}$	465.88	159.11	60.00	15.47

Table 9.3: Group overbooking: Penalty rate thresholds as functions of survival probabilities *Note*: Simulations assume $K = 100$, $N = 60$, $\phi = 5000$, $\mu_k = \mu_o = 5$, and $P = 500$.

two groups is more profitable than booking one group for a relatively large interval of penalty rates given by $0 \leq \psi \leq 1980$, where the upper bound is almost four
times the service price. However, as the survival probability increases, booking
two groups is more profitable than booking one group only for a smaller interval of
penalty rates. For example, if $\pi = 0.8$, booking two groups is profitable only if the
penalty rate lies on the interval $0 \leq \psi \leq 123.75$, where the upper bound is lower
than a quarter of the price of service.

How to overbook three groups of consumers

Suppose now that the service provider receives booking requests from three different groups, each group with N consumers. If the service provider books all three
groups, expected profit depends on whether there is an overbooking and at what
magnitude, that is, whether $2N \geq K + 1$, $2N < K + 1 \leq 3N$, or $3N \leq K$. Therefore,
taking into consideration these three possibilities, expected profit is given by

$$y(3N) = -\phi - \mu_k K$$
$$= \begin{cases} [\pi^3 3N + 3\pi^2(1-\pi)2N + 3\pi(1-\pi)^2 N](P - \mu_o) & \text{if } 3N \leq K \\ [\pi^3 2N + 3\pi^2(1-\pi)2N + 3\pi(1-\pi)^2 N](P - \mu_o) \\ \quad -\pi^3 \psi N & \text{if } 2N \leq K < 3N \quad (9.32) \\ [\pi^3 N + 3\pi^2(1-\pi)N + 3\pi(1-\pi)^2 N](P - \mu_o) \\ \quad -\psi \pi^3 2N - \psi 3\pi^2(1-\pi)N & \text{if } 2N \geq K + 1. \end{cases}$$

That is, if $3N \leq K$, the service provider can accommodate the three groups and the
profit depends on whether all three groups, two groups, one group, or none show
up. In contrast, if $2N \leq K < 3N$, the service provider can accommodate at most
$2N$ consumers and therefore must deny service (and pay a penalty) to one group in
the event all three booked groups show up (probability π^3). The last case in (9.32)
involves overbooking large groups when only one group can be accommodated. In
this case, the service provider pays a penalty to $2N$ consumers with probability π^3,
and to N consumers with probability $3\pi^2(1 - \pi)$.

The decision whether to book three groups, two groups, a single group only, or
none is determined by comparing the profit levels $y(0) = 0$, $y(1)$, $y(2)$, and $y(3)$.
Comparing (9.32) with (9.30) implies that $y(3N) \geq y(2N)$ whenever $3N \leq K$. That
is, when booking three groups does not result in overbooking, booking all three
groups yields a higher profit than booking two groups, as no penalty will have to

be paid. However, if $3N \geq K + 1$,

$$y(3N) \geq y(2N) \Longleftrightarrow$$

$$\psi \leq \psi_{3,2} \stackrel{\text{def}}{=} \begin{cases} \dfrac{(1-\pi)^2(P-\mu_o)}{\pi(4-3\pi)} & \text{if } 2N > K \\[2mm] \dfrac{(1+\pi-\pi^2)(P-\mu_o)}{\pi(4-3\pi)} & \text{if } 2N \leq K < 3N. \end{cases} \tag{9.33}$$

Table 9.3 has already demonstrated how the value of the threshold penalty rate $\psi_{3,2}$, defined by (9.33), varies with the survival probability parameter π for a particular case in which $2N > K$, so only one group can be accommodated. For this particular case, Table 9.4 displays some examples showing how profit levels vary with the number of booked groups and with the penalty rate, where the penalty rates are chosen to be around the threshold levels computed in Table 9.3. Table 9.4 clearly shows that the profit-maximizing group booking level (weakly) decreases with an increase in the penalty rate ψ, and that this relationship holds uniformly for all survival probability levels.

ψ	$y(0)$	$y(60)$	$y(120)$	$y(180)$	b^*	$b^* - K$	$Es(b^*)$	$Eds(b^*)$
		"High" survival probability: $\pi = 0.8$						
10	0	$18,260$	$22,628$	$22,964$	180	120	144	84.48
100	0	$18,260$	$19,172$	$13,978$	120	60	96	38.40
150	0	$18,260$	$17,252$	8986	60	0	48	0.00
		"Low" survival probability: $\pi = 0.4$						
10	0	6380	$12,548$	$14,137$	180	120	72	24.96
400	0	6380	9668	3193	120	60	48	9.60
800	0	6380	5828	$-11,399$	60	0	24	0.00

Table 9.4: Profits and overbooking of one to three equal-size groups as functions of survival probability. *Note*: Simulations assume $K = 100$, $N = 60$, $\phi = 100$, $\mu_k = \mu_o = 5$, and $P = 500$.

Finally, the last two columns of Table 9.4 compute the expected number of show-ups $Es(b^*)$ and the number of consumers expected to be denied service $Eds(b^*)$. The values for $Es(b^*)$ are based on the simple formulas given by

$$\begin{align} Es(2N) &= \pi^2 2N + 2\pi(1-\pi)N, \tag{9.34} \\ Es(3N) &= \pi^3 3N + 3\pi^2(1-\pi)2N + 3\pi(1-\pi)^2 N. \end{align}$$

The last column of Table 9.4 computes the expected number of consumers (in groups) to be denied service $Eds(b^*)$, based on the formulas given by

$$Eds(2N) = \begin{cases} 0 & \text{if } 2N \leq K \\ \pi^2 N & \text{if } 2N \geq K + 1, \end{cases} \tag{9.35}$$

because at most one group can be denied service, and

$$
\mathrm{E}ds(3N) = \begin{cases} 0 & \text{if } 3N \leq K \\ \pi^3 N & \text{if } 2N \geq K < 3N \\ \pi^3 2N + 3\pi^2(1-\pi)N & \text{if } 2N \geq K+1. \end{cases} \tag{9.36}
$$

The second line in (9.36) is for the case in which at most one group may be denied service, which happens only if all three groups show up. The third line computes for the case in which at most two groups may be denied service.

9.3.2 General formulation

The examples analyzed in Section 9.3.1 were confined to the booking of two and three consumer groups only. We now generalize the above formulation to any number of consumer groups. Recall that the choice variable b denotes the number of confirmed reservations booked by individual consumers. In a similar way, let g denote the number of groups of consumers booked by this service provider. Therefore, $b = gN$. The task of the service provider is to choose the number of groups to book to maximize profit, subject to the constraint that the total number of booked consumers does not exceed the booking limit. Formally, g must be restricted so that $gN \leq B$ (or $g \leq B/N$), where B is the mandated booking limit, what was assumed to exceed capacity, $B > K$.

To be able to separate the computation of profit when the firm overbooks from the profit when the firm does not overbook, let g^K denote the maximum number of groups that can be booked without exceeding the given capacity level K. Formally, define

$$
g^K \stackrel{\text{def}}{=} \max g \quad \text{subject to} \quad gN \leq K. \tag{9.37}
$$

Clearly, if the number of booked groups exceeds capacity, that is, $g \geq g^K + 1$, some groups may be denied service, in which case the service provider must pay large penalties on denying service to groups of consumers. Therefore, if the service provider finds it profitable to overbook groups so that $g \geq g^K + 1$, the profit-maximizing group booking level must solve

$$
\max_g y(gN) = -\phi - \mu_k K + \sum_{i=0}^{g^K} \frac{g!}{i!\,(g-i)!}\, \pi^i (1-\pi)^{g-i}(P-\mu_o)gN
$$

$$
+ \sum_{i=g^K+1}^{g} \frac{g!}{i!\,(g-i)!}\, \pi^i (1-\pi)^{g-i}[(P-\mu_o)g^K N - \psi(i-g^K)N]. \tag{9.38}
$$

The first term is the sum of the fixed and capacity costs. The second term is the expected revenue net of operating cost resulting from all possible show-ups of i groups out of the g^K groups that have confirmed reservations. This sum applies to all possible group show-ups as long as the total show-ups do not exceed capacity.

The third term measures the expected profit in cases of large show-ups in which capacity is exceeded. In this case, the revenue net of operating cost is constant and given by $g^K N(P - \mu_o)$ because all other groups are denied service. Hence, we subtract the penalty from having to deny service to $i - g^K$ groups, given that $i \geq g^K + 1$ groups show up at the time of service. It should be mentioned that the expected profit (9.38) resembles very much the expected profit given by (9.21). The only difference is that (9.38) is formulated for show-ups of groups with N consumers, whereas (9.21) is formulated for show-ups of individuals only. Both formulations should yield identical results if the group size is reduced to $N = 1$.

Consider now the case in which the service provider underbooks so that $g \leq g^K$, and hence $b \leq K$. Because no group is denied service, the service provider's profit-maximization problem is reduced to choosing the number of groups $0 \leq g \leq g^K$ that solves

$$
\max_g y(gN) = -\phi - \mu_k K
$$

$$
+ \begin{cases} 0 & \text{if } g = 0 \\ \sum_{i=0}^{g} \frac{g!}{i! \, (g-i)!} \, \pi^i (1-\pi)^{g-i} (P - \mu_o) i \cdot N & \text{if } 1 \leq g \leq g^K. \end{cases} \tag{9.39}
$$

Again, the expected profit (9.39) resembles (9.22) except that the present formulation is for group booking rather than for individual booking. Because of the linearity of the model, the only two possible solutions to (9.39) are to cease operation ($g = 0$) or to book the maximum number of groups without exceeding capacity ($g = g^K$). Therefore, to find the profit-maximizing group booking level, the service provider need only compare the profits $y(0)$, $y(g^K N)$ with the profit level that solves (9.38).

We conclude this section with the general formulation of the expected number of show-ups and expected number of consumers to be denied service given that the service provider books g groups, each having N consumers. Similar to the expected number of show-ups under individual bookings given by (9.4), we write

$$
Es(gN) = \sum_{i=0}^{g} \frac{g!}{i! \, (g-i)!} \, \pi^i (1-\pi)^{g-i} \cdot i \cdot N, \tag{9.40}
$$

which is the expected number of groups that show up when g groups are booked multiplied by the number of consumers in each group, N. Thus, (9.40) may differ from (9.4) because the expectation operator is implemented on the realization of show-ups of groups rather than show-ups of individuals.

Next, the expected number of consumers to be denied service is calculated by computing the expected number of groups to be denied service, and multiplied by the number of consumers in each group, N. Therefore,

$$E ds(gN) =$$

$$\begin{cases} 0 & \text{if } g \leq g^K \\ \sum_{i=g^K+1}^{g} \frac{g!}{i!(g-i)!} \pi^i (1-\pi)^{g-i} (i-g^K)N & \text{if } g \geq g^K+1. \end{cases} \quad (9.41)$$

The expected number of consumers to be denied service given by (9.41) is some-what different from that of overbooking of individuals given by (9.12), because under group overbooking, a denial of service is likely to result in some underutilization of capacity. That is, in the event the service provider must deny service to some groups, the number of served consumers becomes $g^K N$, which could be strictly below the capacity level K. In other words, because booking and service denial are restricted to "chunks" of consumers in the form of groups, it may happen that capacity will remain underused even if the firm overbooks. To see this, consider the following example: Suppose capacity is $K = 100$, and that each group has $N = 60$ consumers. Even if the firm books two groups so that $b = 120 > 100 = K$, if both groups show up, the firm must deny service to 60 consumers, leading to an underutilization of capacity of 40 consumers. Obviously, this underutilization cannot occur with overbooking of individuals because denying service to individuals still leaves K consumers to be served.

9.3.3 Computer algorithm

The computer algorithm we now derive is a slight modification of Algorithm 9.1 to accommodate booking groups (instead of booking individual consumers). Therefore, the reader is referred to Section 9.2.4 for the list and description of all the parameters that the program should input and the variables that should be defined. In addition to this list, the present algorithm should input N (using a **Read()** command, say), which is the number of consumers in each group. The only new variable that we now introduce is g^B, which is the maximum number of groups (of size N) that can be booked without exceeding the mandated booking limit B. The following algorithm computes this group booking limit by solving $g^B \overset{\text{def}}{=} \max g$, subject to $gN \leq B$.

As with Algorithm 9.1, Algorithm 9.3 first computes $y[g^K N]$, which is the expected profit when $g = g^K$ (booking as close as possible to full capacity without overbooking). Then, it computes the expected profit $y[gN]$ for all booking levels $g^K + 1 \leq g \leq g^B$ associated with overbooking. To summarize, similar to Algorithm 9.1, Algorithm 9.3 compares the profit levels $y(0)$ with $y(g^K N)$ and every $y(gN)$ for $g \geq g^K + 1$ that solve (9.38) because all other group booking levels (satisfying $1 \leq g \leq g^K - 1$) cannot be profit maximizing in this linear model.

Algorithm 9.4 is a continuation of Algorithm 9.3 and summarizes the results by writing the exact profit-maximizing group booking level as well as the corre-

```
g^K ← 0; g^B ← 0; g* ← 0; /* Initialization                                    */
repeat g^K ← g^K + 1 until (g^K + 1)N > K; /* Computing g^K                    */
repeat g^B ← g^B + 1 until (g^B + 1)N > B; /* Computing g^B                    */
for g = 1 to g^B do y[gN] ← −ϕ − μ_k K; /* Fixed costs                        */
for i = 0 to g^K do
    │  /* Computing y[g^K N] using (9.39) (no overbooking)                    */
    │  y[g^K N] ← y[g^K N] + (g^K!)/(i!(g^K−i)!) π^i(1−π)^(g^K−i) (P−μ_o)i·N;
for g = g^K + 1 to g^B do
    │  /* Overbooking loop computing y(gN), g^K+1 ≤ g ≤ g^B                    */
    │  for i = 0 to g^K do
    │      │  /* 1^st summation in (9.38)                                      */
    │      │  y[gN] ← y[gN] + (g!)/(i!(g−i)!) π^i(1−π)^(g−i) (P−μ_o)i·N;
    │  for i = g^K + 1 to g do
    │      │  /* 2^nd summation in (9.38)                                      */
    │      │  y[gN] ← y[gN] + (g!)/(i!(g−i)!) π^i(1−π)^(g−i) [(P−μ_o)g^K − ψ(i−g^K)]N;
for g = g^K to g^B do
    │  /* Finding the profit-maximizing booking level g*                       */
    │  if y[gN] > y[g*N] then g* ← g;
if y[g*N] < 0 then g* ← 0; /* Negative profit, no booking                     */
```

Algorithm 9.3: Computation of profit-maximizing group overbooking.

sponding expected number of show-ups and the number of consumers expected to be denied service.

9.4 Exercises

1. Use the binomial distribution formula given by (9.3) to compute the following probabilities.

   (a) The probability that exactly two consumers show up out of three confirmed reservations, $\Pr\{s(3) = 2\}$. Compare your answer with the result given by (9.2). Show your entire derivation.

   (b) Solve the previous problem assuming that the survival probability is $\pi = 0.8$.

   (c) The probability that exactly 52 passengers will show up for a flight with 55 confirmed reservations, $\Pr\{s(55) = 52\}$.

---

write ("The profitable booking level consists of ", g^*,"groups,");
writeln ("or equivalently, booking ", g^*N,"consumers.");
writeln ("The resulting expected profit level is ", $y[g^*N]$, ".");
if $g^* = 0$ **then write** ("No bookings should be made, cease operation.");
if $g^* = g^K$ **then write** ("Book as close to full capacity as possible.");
if $g^* \geq g^K + 1$ **then**
> **write** ("Overbook ", $g^* - g^K$, "groups.");
> **writeln** ("or equivalently, overbook ", $(g^* - g^K)N$,"consumers.");
> $Es \leftarrow 0$; /* Computing $Es(g^*N)$ according to (9.40)   */
> **for** $i = 0$ **to** g^* **do**
>> $Es \leftarrow Es + \frac{g^*!}{i!(g^*-i)!} \pi^i(1-\pi)^{g^*-i} \cdot i \cdot N$;
>
> **writeln** (Es, "consumers are expected to show up.");
> $Eds \leftarrow 0$; /* Computing $Eds(g^*N)$ according to (9.41)   */
> **for** $i = g^K + 1$ **to** g^B **do**
>> $Eds \leftarrow Eds + \frac{g^*!}{i!(g^*-i)!} \pi^i(1-\pi)^{g^*-i}(i-g^K)N$;
>
> **writeln** (Eds, "consumers are expected to be denied service.");

Algorithm 9.4: Group overbooking, the expected number of show-ups, and the number of consumers expected to be denied service.

(d) Solve the previous problem assuming that the survival probability is $\pi = 0.9$.

(e) Using the formula given by (9.4), compute the expected number of show-ups given that the survival probability is $\pi = 0.7$ and $b = 52$ have been booked.

2. Suppose a service provider books $b = 5$ consumers for a service with a capacity of $K = 3$. Each consumer has an independent survival probability given by $\pi = 0.8$. Using the set of examples given by equation (9.6), do the following calculations and show your derivations.

(a) Compute the probability that exactly one consumer is denied service. Formally, compute $\Pr\{ds(5) = 1\}$.

(b) Compute the probability that exactly two consumers are denied service. Formally, compute $\Pr\{ds(5) = 2\}$.

(c) Compute the probability that at least one consumer is denied service. Formally, compute $\Pr\{ds(5) \geq 1\}$.

(d) Compute the probability that no consumer is denied service, using the method described by equation (9.8).

(e) Compute the probability that no consumer is denied service, using the method described by equation (9.10).

(f) Using equation (9.11), compute the expected number of consumers to be denied service, $Eds(5)$.

3. Suppose you are the CEO of a firm endowed with $K = 3$ units of capacity. The maximum allowable booking level is $B = 4$. That is, your firm has the option of overbooking at most one consumer. In this exercise, you will have to decide how many consumers to book similar to the analysis given in Section 9.2.3. Do the following calculations.

   (a) Formulate the expected profit function $y(3)$ assuming that your firm books exactly $b = 3$ consumers.

   (b) Formulate the expected profit function $y(4)$ assuming that your firm books exactly $b = 4$ consumers.

   (c) Using the above computations, compute the profit-maximizing booking level assuming that the observed parameter values are $\phi = 0$ (fixed cost), $\mu_k = \mu_o = 10$ (marginal capacity and operating cost), $P = 500$ (service's price), $\psi = 3430$ (overbooking penalty rate), and $\pi = 0.5$ (survival probability).

4. You are now in charge of BUMPME, an airline that provides regular service for passengers vacationing on a remote African island. Your airline books only groups of 40 passengers each and operates an aircraft with a seating capacity of 100 passengers. The regulator prohibits the airline from booking more than 200 passengers. Using the analysis of Section 9.3, solve the following problems.

   (a) Formulate the expected profit function $y(80)$ assuming that your firm books exactly $g = 2$ groups.

   (b) Formulate the expected profit function $y(120)$ assuming that your firm books exactly $g = 3$ groups.

   (c) Using your answers to (a) and (b), compute the penalty rate $\widetilde{\psi}$ that would make BUMPME indifferent between booking two and three groups, assuming that the observed parameter values are $\phi = 1000$ (fixed cost), $\mu_k = \mu_o = 10$ (marginal capacity and operating costs), $P = 500$ (service's price), and $\pi = 0.8$ (survival probability). Explain how many groups should be booked if the actual penalty rate is above $\widetilde{\psi}$ and below it.

Chapter 10

Quality, Loyalty, Auctions, and Advertising

10.1 Quality Differentiation and Classes 326

    10.1.1 Preferences for quality: Classifications and assumptions

    10.1.2 Selecting the profit-maximizing quality level

    10.1.3 Computer algorithm for a single-quality choice

    10.1.4 Selecting multiple quality levels

10.2 Damaged Goods 332

10.3 More on Pricing under Competition 335

    10.3.1 Behavior-based pricing

    10.3.2 Price matching

10.4 Auctions 343

    10.4.1 Open English and sealed-bid second-price auctions

    10.4.2 Open Dutch and sealed-bid first-price auctions

    10.4.3 Revenue equivalence under independent valuations

10.5 Advertising Expenditure 352

    10.5.1 Demand functions and advertising

    10.5.2 Profit-maximizing advertising expenditure

10.6 Exercises 355

This chapter analyzes some additional pricing techniques and marketing tactics intended to further enhance sellers' profits. Section 10.1 links pricing decisions to innovation and product design decisions by computing the profit-maximizing quality levels and service classes to be introduced into the market. The underlining assumption in this analysis is that sellers cannot directly price discriminate among the different consumer groups. Therefore, the seller must devise a price scheme under which consumers belonging to different consumer groups choose to purchase different quality levels.

Section 10.2 examines a special case of the above problem by analyzing markets in which the seller may find it profitable to sell a "damaged good" (such as a version containing less features) to consumers with low willingness to pay, to segment the market between consumers with high and low willingness to pay. The interesting feature of this result is that the low-quality product is more costly to produce than the high-quality product. In the case of a service, the low-quality service is more costly to deliver than the original undamaged high-quality service.

Section 10.3.1 analyzes repeatedly purchased services and identifies the conditions under which a firm should provide a discount to its returning "loyal" consumers, and also the conditions for the polar case under which the firm should discount the price for consumers who switch from competing brands. Section 10.3.2 explores the consequences of having sellers commit to matching the prices offered by competing sellers, and demonstrates why this strategy can be profit enhancing. Section 10.4 analyzes auctions. The major advantage of using auctions over price setting is that under auctions, price offers are made by the buyers and not by the seller. Section 10.5 concludes with the analysis of profit-maximizing investment in advertising.

10.1   Quality Differentiation and Classes

As far back as the 19th century, the French economist Dupuit realized that the provision of different qualities of service (different classes) could be profit enhancing. In his words,

> It is not because of the few thousand francs which would have to be spent to put a roof over the third-class carriage ... What the company is trying to do is prevent the passengers who can pay the second-class fare from traveling third class.
> —E. Dupuit (Ekelund 1970)

Differentiating a product or a service according to quality enables the seller to price discriminate between those who have high willingness to pay for the product/service and those who have low willingness to pay. Otherwise, as a direct consequence of the "law of one price," if identical products or services are sold at different prices, no consumer would be willing to pay the high price. By either enhancing the quality of the upper-end product or damaging the quality of the low-end product, the seller can induce consumers with high willingness to pay to buy the upper-end product that is sold at a higher price. This is the essence of market segmentation.

The subject analyzed in this section is of utmost importance to firms racing to innovate new products and services, and for firms upgrading the quality of already-marketed products, because it manifests the tight relationship between engineering-based decisions and marketing decisions. Basically this means that marketing people in charge of pricing decisions should inform product engineers and product designers about consumers' willingness to pay for the different quality levels, whereas engineers should be communicating with the marketing people on the types of product and service quality levels the firm may be able to supply. In fact, the success of such firms depends on proper communication between these two different bodies within the same firm.

Technically speaking, the analysis in this section focuses on pricing tactics the seller should employ when consumers with high willingness to pay cannot be directly distinguished from consumers with low willingness to pay. As we have already discussed in Section 1.2.3, offering consumers a "proper" list of quality-dependent prices can induce different types of consumers to purchase different quality levels, thereby indirectly revealing their type to the seller. By "proper" pricing, we mean that the seller must address the following two major questions:

(a) Which and how many different quality levels should be introduced into the market?

(b) How should the different quality levels be priced so that different consumer types choose to buy different quality levels?

10.1.1 Preferences for quality: Classifications and assumptions

The main variable notation for this section is as follows: The set of all possible quality levels is denoted by $\mathscr{B}$. For example, many software companies sell three versions of the same software, and name these versions "Pro," "Standard," and "Basic." In this example, $\mathscr{B} = \{\text{Pro}, \text{Standard}, \text{Basic}\}$. In general, let the index $i \in \mathscr{B}$ denote a possible quality level, where we often write $i \in \mathscr{B} = \{A, B, C, \ldots, Z\}$, or $i \in \mathscr{B} = \{1, 2, 3, 4\}$, and so forth. The firm's unit production or service-delivery cost of quality i is denoted by μ_i, for every product or service with quality $i \in \mathscr{B}$.

There are M consumer types indexed by ℓ, $\ell = 1, 2, \ldots, M$. In view of Table 1.4, which summarizes the notation used throughout this book, V_ℓ^i denotes a type ℓ consumer's maximum willingness to pay for a quality i product, where $i \in \mathscr{B}$. N_ℓ denotes the number of consumers who are of type ℓ.

The analysis of quality (as opposed to other types of service differentiation) means that all consumers "tend to agree" how to rank the service levels. Therefore, the following assumption is needed for interpreting service differentiation as quality differentiation:

ASSUMPTION 10.1
Services and products with different qualities are **vertically differentiated***. Formally,* $V_\ell^A \geq V_\ell^B \geq \cdots \geq V_\ell^Z$, *for each consumer type* $\ell = 1, \ldots, M$.

Basically, Assumption 10.1 implies all potential consumers, regardless of their type, are willing to pay more for quality A than for quality B, and more for quality B than for quality C, and so on. However, note that Assumption 10.1 does *not* imply that all consumers have equal willingness to pay for each service quality.

The next assumption establishes some correlation between the quality of a product or a service and its unit production cost.

ASSUMPTION 10.2
Higher-quality products (services) are more costly to produce (deliver). Formally, if $V_\ell^A \geq V_\ell^B \geq \cdots \geq V_\ell^Z$ for every consumer type ℓ, then $\mu_A \geq \mu_B \geq \cdots \geq \mu_Z$.

Assumption 10.2 is rather intuitive and applies to most products and services. However, in some cases, such as the ones analyzed in Section 10.2, it may happen that a lower-quality product or service may be more costly to produce.

Finally, the procedure for finding the profit-maximizing quality levels and the corresponding prices is general enough to capture all types of consumer preferences satisfying Assumption 10.1. However, for the sake of completeness and for purposes that are not discussed in this book, occasionally we may want to rank individuals' willingness to pay according to the following criterion:

DEFINITION 10.1
*Consumers are said to be **vertically heterogeneous** if for every given quality i, the willingness to pay of type 1 consumers is higher than that of type 2 consumers, which is higher than that of type 3 consumers, and so on. Formally, $V_1^i \geq V_2^i \geq \cdots \geq V_M^i$, for each quality $i \in \mathcal{B}$.*

Figure 10.1 displays two different consumer configurations according to Definition 10.1, assuming that the product is available in three quality levels, given by $\mathcal{B} = \{L, M, H\}$. Each consumer's willingness to pay is plotted as an upward-sloping function with respect to quality, thereby satisfying Assumption 10.1, which means vertical quality differentiation.

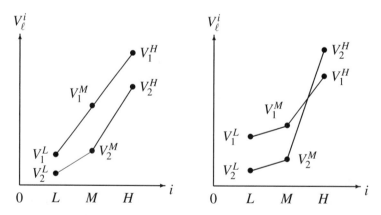

Figure 10.1: Vertically differentiated quality products. *Left*: Vertically heterogeneous consumers. *Right*: Non–vertically heterogeneous consumers.

Figure 10.1(left) illustrates vertically heterogenous consumers by having consumer 1's willingness to pay for all quality levels above those of consumer 2. This is not the case in Figure 10.1(right), where consumer 1 is willing to pay more than consumer 2 for quality levels $i = L, M$ but not for quality $i = H$. Again, the procedure for finding the profit-maximizing quality levels and prices developed and demonstrated in this book is consistent with vertically heterogeneous as well as non–vertically heterogeneous consumers. However, for purposes beyond the scope of the present analysis, in some situations, firms may benefit from sorting out consumer preferences according to Definition 10.1, as illustrated in Figure 10.1.

10.1.2 Selecting the profit-maximizing quality level

Consider a product or a service that can be delivered in one out of three different quality levels indexed by $i = H, M, L$ (high, medium, and low). There are three consumer types indexed by $\ell = 1, 2, 3$. There are $N_1 = 20$ type 1 consumers, $N_2 = 30$ type 2 consumers, and $N_3 = 40$ type 3 consumers. Table 10.1 exhibits the maximum willingness to pay of each consumer type, as well as the unit production cost of each quality. Table 10.1 demonstrates that all consumers are willing to pay more for a quality H product than for quality M or L products, that is, $V_\ell^H \geq V_\ell^M \geq V_\ell^L$. This corresponds to Assumption 10.1, which classifies the qualities H, M, and L as *vertically differentiated* products or services. Table 10.1 also assumes that high-quality products or services are more costly to produce, that is, $\mu_H \geq \mu_M \geq \mu_L$, which corresponds to Assumption 10.2.

i (Quality)	$\ell = 1$	$\ell = 2$	$\ell = 3$	μ_i (Unit Cost)
H (high quality)	$V_1^H = \$8$	$V_2^H = \$6$	$V_3^H = \$4$	$\mu_H = \$3$
M (med quality)	$V_1^M = \$6$	$V_2^M = \$4$	$V_3^M = \$3$	$\mu_M = \$2$
L (low quality)	$V_1^L = \$4$	$V_2^L = \$3$	$V_3^L = \$3$	$\mu_L = \$1$
N_ℓ (# consumers)	$N_1 = 20$	$N_2 = 30$	$N_3 = 40$	

Table 10.1: Willingness to pay and unit cost for three quality levels.

Our analysis is based on the assumption that each consumer buys at most one unit (either quality H, quality M, quality L, or none). The analysis given below demonstrates how the seller selects the profit-maximizing quality level, assuming that the firm is restricted to introducing at most one quality level into the market. The case in which the firm can introduce more than one quality into the market is deferred to Section 10.1.4.

Suppose now that the firm sells only quality H. In view of Table 10.1, setting a high price $p_H = \$8$ would exclude buyer types $\ell = 2$ and $\ell = 3$ from the market, because this price exceeds their maximum willingness to pay. The number of buyers under $p_H = \$8$ is therefore $q_H = 20$. Slightly reducing the price to $p_H = \$6$ would add 30 type $\ell = 2$ consumers, bringing the total demand to $q_H = 20 + 30 = 50$.

Finally, lowering the price to $p_H = \$4$ would induce all consumers to buy the quality H good so that the sales level becomes $q_H = 20 + 30 + 40 = 90$ units. Clearly, the seller cannot enhance profit by any further reduction in price as the entire market is already served under $p_H = \$4$. The profit levels corresponding to the above three prices are therefore given by

$$y_H = \begin{cases} 20(8-3) - \phi = \$100 - \phi & \text{if } p_H = \$8 \\ 50(6-3) - \phi = \$150 - \phi & \text{if } p_H = \$6 \\ 90(4-3) - \phi = \$90 - \phi & \text{if } p_H = \$4, \end{cases} \tag{10.1}$$

where $\phi \geq 0$ is the firm's fixed cost. Next, the profit when only quality M is introduced into the market is

$$y_M = \begin{cases} 20(6-2) - \phi = \$80 - \phi & \text{if } p_M = \$6 \\ 50(4-2) - \phi = \$100 - \phi & \text{if } p_M = \$4 \\ 90(3-2) - \phi = \$90 - \phi & \text{if } p_M = \$3. \end{cases} \tag{10.2}$$

Similarly, the profit when only quality L is introduced into the market is

$$y_L = \begin{cases} 20(4-1) - \phi = \$60 - \phi & \text{if } p_L = \$4 \\ 90(3-1) - \phi = \$180 - \phi & \text{if } p_L = \$3. \end{cases} \tag{10.3}$$

Comparing (10.1), (10.2), and (10.3) reveals that the seller maximizes profit by introducing quality L into the market for the price of $p_L = \$3$, thereby making the product "affordable" to all consumer types. The resulting profit is $y = \$180 - \phi$.

10.1.3   Computer algorithm for a single-quality choice

The examples given above hint at the general method for how to determine the profit-maximizing quality level to be introduced into the market and how to price it. Algorithm 10.1 computes the profit-maximizing quality level, the corresponding price, and the resulting profit level.

The program should input the following parameters: the set $\mathscr{B}$ listing all possible quality levels (such as H, M, and L as in the previous examples) and the number of consumer types M. Consumers' maximum willingness to pay should be input into a nonnegative array of real numbers $V[\ell, i]$ reflecting type ℓ's maximum willingness to pay (valuation) for a quality level i, $i \in \mathscr{B}$ and $\ell = 1, \ldots, M$. The number of consumers of each type should be input into an M-dimensional array of natural numbers $N[\ell]$, $\ell = 1, \ldots, M$. The program should also input the seller's unit costs of producing each quality $\mu[i]$, $i \in \mathscr{B}$, and the fixed cost ϕ.

As for output variables, Algorithm 10.1 stores the profit-maximizing quality choice on $i^{\max}$. For all quality levels, $i \in \mathscr{B}$ (not only for $i^{\max}$), $p^{\max}[i]$ is a nonnegative array of real variables that records the profit-maximizing price when quality

```
ymax ← 0; for i ∈ ℬ do ymax[i] ← 0; /* Initialization            */
for i ∈ ℬ do
   /* Main loop over all possible quality levels            */
   for ℓ = 1 to M do
      p[i] ← V[ℓ,i]; q[i] ← 0; /* Set price for i to equal ℓ's
         valuation, check who else buys at this price        */
      for ℓ = 1 to M do
         if p[i] ≤ V[ℓ,i] then q[i] ← q[i]+N[i]; /* Add buyers   */
         y[i] ← q[i](p[i]−μ[i]); /* Store temporary profit      */
      if ymax[i] < y[i] then
         /* New profit-max price for quality i found           */
         pmax[i] ← p[i]; qmax[i] ← q[i]; ymax[i] ← y[i];
   if ymax < ymax[i] then
      imax ← i; ymax ← ymax[i]; /* New profit-max i found       */
for i ∈ ℬ do ymax[i] ← ymax[i] − φ; /* Subtract fixed cost        */
writeln ("The seller should introduce quality", imax, "Total profit is ymax =",
   ymax[imax], "The number of buyers is", q[imax] );
for i ∈ ℬ do  writeln ("If quality", i, "is selected instead of", imax, "it
   should be priced at", pmax[i], "sales and profit would be", qmax[i], and,
   ymax[i]); /* If other qualities are selected instead        */
```

Algorithm 10.1: Selecting the profit-maximizing quality level.

i is introduced, and $q^{\max}[i]$ and $y^{\max}[i]$ the corresponding sales and profit levels. In addition to writing the profit-maximizing quality level the seller should choose to introduce into the market, the program also writes what should be the price for each other quality level i if the seller chooses to introduce it instead of $i^{\max}$.

10.1.4   Selecting multiple quality levels

Sections 10.1.2 and 10.1.3 restricted the seller's decision to selecting at most one quality level out of multiple quality levels the firm is capable of producing (or delivering, in case of a service). However, often, as this section demonstrates, the firm may be able to further enhance its profit by offering to consumers a variety of quality levels from which to choose. The difficulty with offering multiple quality levels to heterogenous consumers is in computing a price for each quality level so that not all consumers end up buying the same quality level. That is, the "trick" here is to find a vector of prices (price for each quality) so that the market will be segmented in the sense that consumers with relatively high valuations for high-quality goods buy high-quality goods, whereas all other consumers buy goods with lower qualities.

To demonstrate the difficulty in finding the profit-maximizing prices that segment the market among the different consumer types, let us reexamine Table 10.1, in which we have shown that if the seller is restricted to selecting at most one quality level, the profit-maximizing choice would be to introduce quality L into the market and sell it for the price $p_L = \$3$, under which all consumer types would buy it. A closer examination of Table 10.1 reveals that type $\ell = 1$ consumers are willing to pay a high price $p_H = \$8$ for a high-quality good. However, if the seller introduces quality H as a second quality and prices it at $p_H = \$8$, no consumer would choose to buy it. To see this, Table 10.1 implies that the net gain to type 1 consumers from buying H is $V_1^H - p_H = 8 - 8 < 4 - 3 = V_1^L - p_L$, hence they will choose to buy L. For type 2 consumers, $V_2^H - p_H = 6 - 8 < 3 - 3 = 0 = V_2^L - p_L$, and the same for type 3 consumers. Therefore, introducing quality H for the price $p_H = \$8$ will not be successful.

The above discussion hints that the seller must reduce p_H to induce type 1 consumers to purchase quality H instead of L. Formally, the maximum price for H that would induce type 1 consumers to buy H instead of L is determined from $V_1^H - p_H = 8 - p_H \geq V_1^L - p_L = 4 - 3$, yielding $p_H = \$7$. Clearly, type 2 and 3 consumers will choose to buy L because $V_2^H - p_H = 6 - 7 < 0 \leq V_2^L - p_L$ and $V_3^H - p_H = 4 - 7 < 0 \leq V_3^L - p_L$. Therefore, under the prices $p_H = \$7$ and $p_L = \$3$, the market is segmented; however, it remains to check whether this segmentation is more profitable than selling one quality only. In view of Table 10.1, the profit under these prices is

$$y_{H,L} = 20(7 - 3) + (30 + 40)(3 - 1) = \$220 - \phi > \$180 - \phi = y_L, \qquad (10.4)$$

where ϕ is the firm's fixed cost and y_L is the profit when the firm sells quality L only, which was computed in (10.3). Thus, this market segmentation is profit enhancing relative to selling a single quality only.

10.2   Damaged Goods

Perhaps the most interesting pricing technique related to quality classes is that of damaged goods. Here, manufacturers intentionally damage some features of a good or a service to be able to price discriminate among the consumer groups. A proper implementation of this technique may even generate a Pareto improvement, which is a situation in which the seller and all buyers are better off compared with the allocation in which only the original undamaged quality is sold. The most paradoxical consequence of this technique is that the good that is more costly to produce (the damaged good) is sold for a lower price as it has a lower quality. Deneckere and McAfee (1996) and Shapiro and Varian (1999) list a wide variety of industries in which this technique is commonly observed, and Varian (2000) formally analyzes the profits generated from "versioning" information goods. Below, we list only a few real-life examples.

Costly delay: Overnight mail carriers, such as Federal Express and UPS, offer two major classes of service: a premium class that promises delivery before a certain morning hour, generally 8:30 A.M. or 10 A.M., and a standard service promising an afternoon delivery. To encourage the senders to self-select (thereby segmenting the market), overnight carriers will make two trips to the same location rather than deliver the standard packages during the morning hours.

Reduced performance: Intel removed the math coprocessor from its 486DX chip and renamed it 486SX to be able to sell it for a low price of $333 to low-cost consumers, as compared with the $588 it charged for the undamaged version (in 1991 prices).

Delay is also observed in many Internet-provided information services. Real-time information on stock prices is sold for a premium, whereas 20-minute delayed information is often provided for free. What is common to all these examples is that the low-quality version of the good/service bears an additional production/delivery cost associated with damaging, thereby making the low-quality product or service more costly to produce than the high-quality product or service.

Consider the following example: A good (service) is produced (delivered) at a high-quality level, denoted by H, with a unit cost of $\mu_H = \$2$. The seller possesses a technology of damaging the good so it becomes a low-quality product, denoted by L. The cost of damaging is $\mu_D = \$1$. Therefore, the total unit cost of producing good L is $\mu_L = \mu_H + \mu_D$. Table 10.2 displays the product/service unit cost as well as consumers' maximum willingness to pay for the two configurations. Table 10.2 shows that both consumers prefer the H good over the L good as $V_1^H = 10 > 8 = V_1^L$ and $V_2^H = 20 > 9 = V_2^L$. However, type $\ell = 2$ consumers place a much higher value on the original quality relative to type $\ell = 1$ consumers.

i (Quality)	$\ell = 1$	$\ell = 2$	μ_i (Unit Cost)
H (Original)	$V_1^H = \$10$	$V_2^H = \$20$	$\$2$
L (Damaged)	$V_1^L = \$8$	$V_2^L = \$9$	$\$2 + \$1$
N_ℓ (# consumers)	$N_1 = 100$	$N_2 = 100$	

Table 10.2: Maximum willingness for original and quality-damaged product/service.

A profit-maximizing seller with the above-described technology has to make two types of decisions:

Design: Whether or not to introduce a quality-damaged product/service into the market, given that the damaged version requires an additional per-unit cost.

Marketing: How to price the two different qualities when introduced into the market.

In the present example, the seller decides whether to offer quality H (original), L (purposely damaged), or both, and the price of each quality, p_H and p_L, if both qualities are introduced. Clearly, because all consumers prefer H over L and because H is less costly to produce than L, it is not profitable to sell only L (the damaged good) to both consumers. Therefore, the seller is left to consider the following remaining options:

Selling H to type 2 consumers only: This is accomplished by not introducing a damaged version and by setting a sufficiently high price, $p_H = \$20$, under which consumer $\ell = 1$ will not buy. The resulting profit is $y = 100(20 - 2) - \phi = \$1800 - \phi$, where $\phi \geq 0$ is the firm's fixed cost.

Selling H to both consumer types: Again, selling only the original high-quality good but at a much lower price, $p_H = \$10$, to induce consumer $\ell = 1$ to buy. The resulting profit is $y = (100 + 100)(10 - 2) - \phi = \$1600 - \phi$.

Selling H to type 2, and L to type 1 consumers: Introducing the damaged good into the market. Consumer 2 will choose H over L if $V_2^H - p_H \geq V_2^L - p_L$. Thus, the seller must set $p_H \leq V_2^H - V_2^L + p_L = 11 + p_L$. To induce type 1 consumers to buy the damaged good L, the seller should set $p_L = \$8$, which implies that $p_H = 11 + 8 = \$19$. Total profit is therefore $y = 100(19 - 2) + 100(8 - 2 - 1) - \phi = \$22,000 - \phi$.

Clearly, the third option is the profit-maximizing strategy for the example displayed in Table 10.2.

Perhaps the most striking feature of the last pricing scheme (selling H to type 2 and L to type 1) is that no one is worse off compared with the second most profitable strategy (selling only H to type 2 only). Under the first option, consumer 2 pays $p_H = \$20$, thereby excluding all type 1 consumers. However, the introduction of the damaged good L lowers the price of the H good to $p_H = 19$, thereby increasing the welfare of type 2 consumers. In addition, the seller's profit is enhanced to $y = \$22,000 - \phi$ from $y = \$18,000 - \phi$. Type 1 consumers remain indifferent, but it is possible to reduce p_L and p_H by a few cents to make even type 1 consumers strictly better off when the damaged good is introduced.

Figure 10.2 illustrates buyers' decisions on which quality to purchase in the p_L–p_H space. The parallelogram at the center consists of all price pairs p_L and p_H under which the market is segmented in the sense that type $\ell = 1$ consumers choose to purchase L (the damaged good), whereas type $\ell = 2$ consumers choose to buy H (original quality). In this range, $V_1^L - p_L \geq V_1^H - p_H$ and $V_2^H - p_H \geq V_2^L - p_L$.

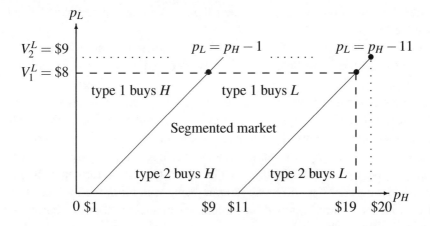

Figure 10.2: Segmenting the market with a "damaged" good. *Note*: The three bullet marks represent candidate profit-maximizing price pairs.

Using Table 10.2, these conditions become $p_L \leq p_H - 1$ and $p_L \geq p_H - 11$, which are the equations for the two solid 45° lines drawn in Figure 10.2. Within each range, profit is increasing in the northeast direction. Consequently, the seller needs to compare the profit generated at the price pairs indicated by the three bullet marks in Figure 10.2. The bullet on the far left reflects the profit-maximizing price pair under the restrictions that both consumer types choose to buy H only. The bullet on the far right indicates the profit-maximizing price pair when type 1 consumers are excluded from the market (because $p_L > V_1^L$ and $p_H > V_1^H$), and, therefore, only the original good H is actually offered for sale. Finally, the middle bullet, which turns out to be the profit-maximizing price pair, indicates the prices leading to market segmentation under which type 1 consumers choose L and type 2 choose H.

10.3 More on Pricing under Competition

Section 3.4 has already analyzed some pricing strategies when the seller is subjected to competition from rival firms, and when consumers bear some cost of switching between service providers. In this section, we expand on the previous analysis by focusing on how sellers compete for consumers who receive offers to switch or to buy at lower prices from competing service providers.

10.3.1 Behavior-based pricing

In today's business environment, service providers have access to technologies that enable them to efficiently implement behavior-based price discrimination based on customers' purchase histories. More precisely, airlines, hotel chains, and phone companies can keep track of their returning "loyal" customers by offering these consumers bonus points, such as frequent-flyer miles that can be viewed as a type of discount.

In contrast, some firms offer discounts to consumers who switch from competing service providers. This behavior is widely observed in the telephone industry, in which cellular and long-distance phone companies provide free new equipment and free minutes that can be viewed as a partial reimbursement for the cost of switching providers. The benefits to those who switch are generally granted on the condition the consumers provide a proof that they have cancelled their service contracts with their former providers. For example, some mobile operators require that switching consumers give up the SIMM cards they obtained from their former mobile operator. In the credit/debit card industry, some banks condition the issuing of a new card with all the "points" earned on the previous card by "forcing" customers to cancel their previous cards.

In view of the above discussion, we define *behavior-based pricing* as a strategy by which firms determine the price of a service based on consumers' purchase history. In particular, we say that a firm provides a *loyalty discount* if consumers who repeat their purchase pay lower prices than consumers who switch from competing service providers. In contrast, we say that a firm levies a *loyalty surcharge* if it charges higher prices to consumers who repeat their purchase than to consumers who switch from competing service providers. The latter case means that the firm subsidizes part or all of consumers' switching costs, an action that is often referred to as *poaching* and that may have some antitrust implications; see Thisse and Vives (1988), Caminal and Matutes (1990), Chen (1997b), Taylor (2003), Gehrig and Stenbacka (2004, 2007), and Caminal and Claici (2007).

Our underlining assumption is that the seller can identify consumers according to their history of purchasing. Moreover, the seller can quote different prices to consumers who have already purchased the same service in the past (loyal consumers) and to consumers who purchased from a competing service provider. Let p_L denote the price quoted to a loyal consumer and p_S the price quote to a consumer who considers switching from a competing service provider. The analysis in this section relies on the following terminology:

DEFINITION 10.2
*We say that a seller offers a **loyalty discount** if $p_L < p_S$. Otherwise, if $p_L > p_S$, we say that the seller charges a **loyalty premium** and engages in poaching, where p_S is the **poaching price**.*

Given the seller's ability to distinguish between returning buyers and switching buyers, the seller can view the two consumer populations as having separate demand functions. Formally, denoting by q_L the number of returning (loyal) consumers and by q_S the number of consumers who switch from a competitor, the seller should be able to obtain estimates for the demand functions given by

$$q_L(p_L, p_S) \overset{\text{def}}{=} \alpha_L - \beta_L p_L + \gamma_L p_S \quad \text{and} \quad q_S(p_L, p_S) \overset{\text{def}}{=} \alpha_S - \beta_S p_S + \gamma_S p_L, \quad (10.5)$$

where β_L, γ_L, β_S, and γ_S are the demand parameters to be estimated by the econometrician of the firm. The parameters β_L and β_S, often called "own-price" parameters, measure the sensitivity of quantity demanded to changes in the price quoted for the specific consumer group. The parameters γ_L and γ_S, often called "cross-price" parameters, measure how an increase in the price quoted to switching consumers affects the demand by loyal consumers, and how a rise in the price quoted to loyal consumers affects the demand by switching consumers, respectively. The parameters γ_L and γ_S can be positive or negative, or zero when cross-demand effects do not exist.

Before computing the profit-maximizing prices, the seller must verify that the estimated parameters satisfy

$$\beta_L > 0, \quad \beta_S > 0, \quad \text{and} \quad 4\beta_L\beta_S > (\gamma_L + \gamma_S)^2. \tag{10.6}$$

The first two inequalities ensure downward-sloping demand functions. The third inequality implies that the demand by each consumer type is more sensitive to changes in the price quoted to this group than the price quoted to the other consumer group. Specifically, the demand by loyal consumers is affected more strongly by the price offer made to loyal consumers than by the price offer made to switching consumers. Similarly, the demand by consumers who switch from a competitor is more sensitive to the price offer made directly to them than by the price offer made to loyal consumers who do not switch. In other words, the third restriction in (10.6) implies that the own-price effects are stronger than the cross-price effects. Also, from a technical perspective as demonstrated below, the third restriction ensures that the seller's profit function is strictly concave with respect to p_L and p_S.

On the seller's cost side, ϕ denotes the fixed cost, whereas μ_L and μ_S denote the cost per unit of service sold to a loyal and switching consumer, respectively. Clearly, this formulation is general in the sense that it permits the analysis of equal unit costs ($\mu_L = \mu_S$) as a special case. However, one can imagine cases in which $\mu_L < \mu_S$ in which the seller may have to modify the product or the service offered to switching consumers to attract them to abandon their loyalty to a competitor. Another interpretation of $\mu_L < \mu_S$ would be that it is more costly to register and train a switching consumer to use the product or service compared with a loyal consumer, who is already familiar with the seller's brand. We proceed with two numerical examples, followed by a general formulation.

An example of a loyalty discount

Consider a special case of the system of demand functions (10.5) given by

$$q_L(p_L, p_S) = 120 - 2p_L + p_S \quad \text{and} \quad q_S(p_L, p_S) = 120 - p_S + p_L. \tag{10.7}$$

This system of demand functions assumes that $\beta_L = 2 > 1 = \beta_S$, meaning that loyal consumers are more price sensitive than switching consumers. This may reflect a situation in which loyal customers face attractive offers from competing sellers, hence a small rise in price would induce them to switch to a competing brand.

Suppose now that the cost of producing the product (or delivering the service) is $\mu_L = \mu_S = \$20$ per unit. The seller has to choose price quotes for loyal and switching consumers to solve

$$\max_{p_L, p_S} y(p_L, p_S) = (p_L - 20)q_L + (p_S - 20)q_S - \phi$$

$$= (p_L - 20)(120 - 2p_L + p_S) + (p_S - 20)(120 - p_S + p_L) - \phi. \quad (10.8)$$

First, it should be verified that this demand system satisfies all the restrictions given in (10.6). Clearly, the own-price parameters are strictly positive. Next, $4\beta_L\beta_S - (\gamma_L + \gamma_S)^2 = 4 \cdot 2 \cdot 1 - (1+1)^2 > 0$, implying that the third restriction holds. Taking the first-order conditions for a maximum profit,

$$0 = \frac{\partial y}{\partial p_L} = -4p_L + 2p_S + 140, \quad \text{and} \quad 0 = \frac{\partial y}{\partial p_S} = 2p_L - 2p_S + 120. \quad (10.9)$$

The second-order conditions for a maximum profit can be verified by computing

$$\frac{\partial^2 y}{\partial p_L^2} = -4 < 0, \quad \frac{\partial^2 y}{\partial p_S^2} = -2 < 0, \quad \text{and}$$

$$\frac{\partial^2 y}{\partial p_L^2}\frac{\partial^2 y}{\partial p_S^2} - \left(\frac{\partial^2 y}{\partial p_L p_S}\right)^2 = (-4)(-2) - 2^2 = 4 > 0. \quad (10.10)$$

The profit-maximizing prices that should be quoted to loyal and switching consumers are found by solving the two first-order conditions (10.9). Hence, $p_L = \$130$ and $p_S = \$190$. Substituting into the demand function (10.7) obtains the number of loyal and switching consumers $q_L = 50$ and $q_S = 60$. Substituting these prices into the profit function (10.8) yields a total profit of $y = \$15,700 - \phi$.

The profit-maximizing prices satisfy $p_S - p_L = \$190 - \$130 = \$60$. Therefore, by Definition 10.2, the seller provides a loyalty discount of $60 to returning customers. This happens because the demand functions (10.7) portray loyal consumers who are much more price sensitive than consumers who switch from competing firms.

An example of a loyalty premium and poaching

Consider now another special case of the system of demand functions (10.5) given by

$$q_L(p_L, p_S) = 120 - p_L + p_S \quad \text{and} \quad q_S(p_L, p_S) = 120 - 2p_S + p_L. \quad (10.11)$$

Comparing (10.11) with (10.7) reveals that in the present example loyal consumers are less price sensitive compared with consumers who switch from competing brands. This situation arises when loyal consumers have high costs of switching to competing brands, for example, if the competing service is less consumer friendly than the currently consumed brand.

The derivation of the profit-maximizing prices p_L and p_S is identical to the previous case as it follows exactly the steps given by (10.8), (10.9), and (10.10). For this reason, we state only the solution that is given by the prices $p_L = \$190$ and $p_S = \$130$, demand levels $q_L = 60$ and $q_S = 50$, and total profit $y = \$15,700 - \phi$. In fact, one could have guessed this particular solution in view of the symmetry between the demand systems (10.11) with (10.7).

Under the demand functions (10.11), the seller subsidizes the cost of consumers switching from a competing brand by reducing the price for these consumers by $p_S - p_L = \$60$. Some literature refers to the lower p_S as a poaching price. Another interpretation that is also consistent with Definition 10.2 is that this seller charges a loyalty premium to returning consumers as, according to (10.11), their demand is less sensitive to price relative to the demand by consumers switching from competing brands.

General formulation

We now briefly repeat the previous derivations using a general notation that allows for arbitrary values for the parameters of the demand functions (10.5). The seller solves

$$
\max_{p_L, p_S} y(p_L, p_S) = (p_L - \mu_L)q_L + (p_S - \mu_S)q_S - \phi
$$
$$
= (p_L - \mu_L)(\alpha_L - \beta_L p_L + \gamma_L p_S)
$$
$$
+ (p_S - \mu_S)(\alpha_S - \beta_S p_S + \gamma_S p_L) - \phi. \quad (10.12)
$$

At this stage, it should be verified that this demand system satisfies all the restrictions given by (10.6). Taking the first-order conditions for a maximum profit,

$$
0 = \frac{\partial y}{\partial p_L} = -2p_L \beta_L + p_S(\gamma_L + \gamma_S) + \alpha_L + \beta_L \mu_L - \gamma_S \mu_S, \quad (10.13)
$$

$$
0 = \frac{\partial y}{\partial p_S} = p_L(\gamma_L + \gamma_S) - 2p_S \beta_S + \alpha_S + \beta_S \mu_S - \gamma_L \mu_L. \quad (10.14)
$$

The second-order conditions imply that the parameters of the model should satisfy

$$
\frac{\partial^2 y}{\partial p_L^2} = -2\beta_L < 0, \quad \frac{\partial^2 y}{\partial p_S^2} = -2\beta_S < 0, \quad \text{and}
$$

$$
\frac{\partial^2 y}{\partial p_L^2} \frac{\partial^2 y}{\partial p_S^2} - \left(\frac{\partial^2 y}{\partial p_L p_S}\right)^2 = (-2\beta_L)(-2\beta_S) - (\gamma_L + \gamma_S)^2 > 0, \quad (10.15)
$$

which explains why (10.6) must be assumed to be able to solve this maximization problem.

Next, solving the two first-order conditions (10.13) yields

$$
p_L = \frac{2\alpha_L\beta_S + (\alpha_S - \gamma_L\mu_L)(\gamma_L + \gamma_S) + 2\beta_L\beta_S\mu_L + \beta_S\mu_S(\gamma_L - \gamma_S)}{4\beta_L\beta_S - (\gamma_L + \gamma_S)^2},
$$

$$
\tag{10.16}
$$

$$
p_S = \frac{2\alpha_S\beta_L + (\alpha_L - \gamma_S\mu_S)(\gamma_L + \gamma_S) + 2\beta_L\beta_S\mu_S + \beta_L\mu_L(\gamma_S - \gamma_L)}{4\beta_L\beta_S - (\gamma_L + \gamma_S)^2}.
$$

Finally, the quantity demanded by each consumer group, q_L and q_S, can be found by substituting the equilibrium prices (10.16) into the demand functions (10.5). The resulting profit is found by substituting the equilibrium prices (10.16) into (10.12).

10.3.2   Price matching

Price matching, often referred to as "meeting (or even beating) the competition," is a statement and a commitment made by a seller to match or to beat price offers made by competing sellers. Of course, such a commitment is generally limited to a certain time period, such as one week. This section demonstrates that stores may find such a commitment to be profit enhancing. It should be noted, however, that in some cases economists may consider meeting or beating the competition to be a violation of antitrust law as it may prevent sellers from being engaged in intensive price competition; see Motta (2004, Ch. 4). Price matching and beating strategies have been analyzed in a number of articles; to state a few, see Salop (1986), Belton (1987), Png and Hirshleifer (1987), Doyle (1988), Logan and Lutter (1989), Corts (1995, 1997), Hviid and Shaffer (1999), and Kaplan (2000).

Consider two adjacent stores labeled A and B that are located in the same shopping mall and sell identical YNOS digital video players (DVD). Each store buys directly from YNOS (the manufacturer) at a cost of $\mu = \$50$ per unit. Let $\phi \geq 0$ denote a store's fixed cost of operation. Each day, 200 potential customers enter this shopping mall with the intention of buying a YNOS DVD. Each consumer has a 50% probability of patronizing store A first (and 50% of patronizing store B first). Figure 10.3 demonstrates the well-known outcome of price competition leading to unit-cost pricing. Figure 10.3 illustrates 200 consumers who are initially equally split between the stores. With 50% probability, each store expects 100 consumers to enter its store first before they proceed to the competing store to request a second price offer for the same YNOS DVD.

Illustration I in Figure 10.3 reflects an initial situation in which both stores quote a price of \$80. Because this price exceeds the unit cost by \$30, each store makes a profit of $y_A(80,80) = y_B(80,80) = 100(80 - 50) - \phi = \$3000 - \phi$.

Because both stores are located in the same shopping mall, consumers can almost costlessly obtain a second price offer from the competing store. Illustration II

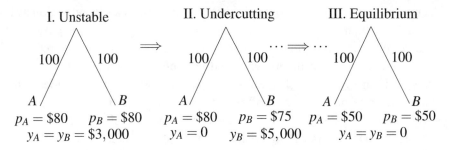

Figure 10.3: Price competition without price matching. *Note*: The fixed cost ϕ should be subtracted from all profits.

shows the gain to store B from undercutting the price of store A by $5. Setting $p_B = \$75$ implies that even consumers who initially go to store A and then get a second offer from store B will not return to store A. Consumers who initially enter store B and then compare their price offer with store A will go back to store B. Hence by undercutting, store B captures the entire market and earns a profit of $y_B(80, 75) = 200(75 - 50) - \phi = \$5000 - \phi$.

Illustration III in Figure 10.3 shows the resulting Nash-Bertrand equilibrium of this price game, where undercutting leads to unit-cost pricing $p_A = p_B = \$50$, and hence to zero or negative profit $y_A(50, 50) = y_B(50, 50) = 0 - \phi$.

Suppose now that each store promises all consumers who enter to obtain a price offer that it will match any price offered by the competing store. Figure 10.4 illustrates the consequences of such a commitment. Under the price-matching commitment, store A (similarly store B) announces an initial price of $p_A = \$80$, which is far above the unit cost of $\mu = \$50$. Store B has two options. It can undercut store A by setting a lower price of $p_B = \$75$ as illustrated by the northeast arrow in Figure 10.4. Consumers who first patronized store A will return to store A, which will match the price of store B by $p'_A = \$75$. Now, with 200 consumers who are initially equally split between the stores, each store ends up selling to 100 consumers. The resulting expected profit levels are therefore $y_A = y_B = 100(75 - 50) - \phi = \$2500 - \phi$.

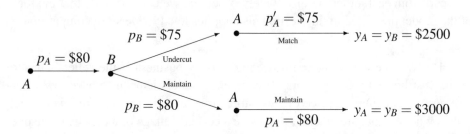

Figure 10.4: Price competition with price matching. *Note*: The fixed cost ϕ should be subtracted from all profits.

In contrast, the southeast arrow in Figure 10.4 illustrates a second option available to store B, which is to maintain the same price as store A so that $p_B = p_A = \$80$. In this case, consumers cannot benefit from visiting more than one store; hence, each store sells to 100 consumers who randomly enter each store. The resulting expected profits are $y_A = y_B = 100(80 - 50) - \phi = \$3000 - \phi$. The key idea here is that under the price-matching commitment by store A, store B *cannot enhance its profit by undercutting* the price of store A because store A will immediately match its price. Thus, the price-matching commitment by store A creates an incentive for store B to maintain a high price. For this reason, the "meeting the competition" price strategy is often regarded as a facilitating practice because it relaxes price competition to some degree.

The above model assumes that the two stores are located near each other, so consumers can costlessly compare prices, and can costlessly return to the first store they entered and demand that the store fulfil its commitment to match a lower price. A natural question to ask at this point is, What happens if the stores are located at different shopping malls, so consumers bear some time and transportation costs in going back and forth between stores? However, such an environment has already been analyzed in Section 3.4.1, which assumed that consumers bear some switching costs in changing suppliers. Application of this model to price matching would require that stores make their price cuts exceed consumers' traveling cost in going back to a store to ask that store to match the price of its rival. Consumers then will have to evaluate the potential gain from traveling to a different store to obtain a lower price, against their loss of value of time. The price level of the product would clearly play a major role in this decision, as consumers are less likely to travel to gain a price reduction of a few cents.

To overcome consumers' transportation costs, stores can offer to beat the competition instead of just matching a price, which would reward consumers who return to a store by reducing the price strictly below that of a competing store. Clearly, because price matching and price-beating announcements made by stores located far apart from each other are also widely observed, we can conclude that the logic of the model presented in this section also applies to citywide store competition.

Finally, price matching could become a risky business if the seller is unsure of the cost borne by competitors. If competing sellers happen to have lower per-unit costs, matching the price of rival stores may turn into a loss. In this respect, sellers who are not sure whether they have a cost advantage or a disadvantage over their rivals should make a meet-or-release commitment that enables the sellers to compensate buyers with a full refund in the event they cannot profitably match the price of a competing seller.

10.4   Auctions

This book analyzes how profit-maximizing firms price their products and services. The pricing techniques suggested in this book rely on firms investigating and forecasting consumer demand. That is, the pricing tactics analyzed in this book require the knowledge of consumers' willingness to pay (valuations) for all products and services and for all quality levels. In this respect, errors in demand estimations translate directly into losses. Moreover, firms often fail to collect the relevant information about consumers' willingness to pay and therefore have no clue on how to price.

In view of the above discussion, the major advantage of using auctions is to let consumers, who obviously know their own willingness to pay much better than the firms, determine the price. In other words, auctions require consumers to make the price offers (or simply to accept a price announcement made by an auctioneer) rather than having sellers make them. In this respect, organizing an auction may turn out to be the best solution because buyers participating in an auction reveal their preferences (willingness to pay) during the bidding process. The general theory of auctions constitutes a major field in economic theory, so a comprehensive analysis of auctions is simply beyond the scope of this book. Readers who wish to study auctions should refer to Krishna (2002) or to Phlips (1988, Ch. 8) for a shorter introduction to this field.

Following the pioneering paper by Vickrey (1961), auctions are generally classified as *open* or *sealed*. The most commonly known *open auctions* are

English: A progressive auction in which bids are announced publicly until no buyer wishes to make any further bid.

Dutch: The seller sets an initial sufficiently high price that exceeds the willingness to pay of all potential buyers. Then, an auctioneer lowers the price until one of the buyers accepts the last price offer.

A sealed-bid auction requires all buyers to place their bids (price offers) in a sealed envelope by a certain deadline. After that, all envelopes are opened and the "winner" is announced. The most commonly known *sealed-bid auctions* are

First-price: The highest bidder "wins" the auction and pays the highest bid.

Second-price: The highest bidder is chosen to be the winner but pays the second-highest bid.

In both sealed-bid auctions, if more than one buyer bids the highest price, the winner is determined by a lottery with equal probability assigned to each buyer with the highest bid.

As it turns out, under some conditions on buyers' valuations, all four types of auctions yield identical outcomes in terms of the final price, the choice of the winner, and the revenue collected by the seller. In particular, the open English auction and the second-price sealed bid auction yield identical outcomes in all respects despite the fact that the English auction is open and requires the presence of all bidders, whereas the other is sealed and does not require active participation on the part of bidders as bidders can simply mail their sealed envelopes from a distance.

In addition to yielding identical outcomes, the open English auction and the sealed-bid second-price auction share two additional common features. First, bidders end up revealing their true willingness to pay during the auction process. Second, bidders' decisions are easy to establish because these decisions are not based on any attempt on the part of bidders to predict the bids made by competing bidders. Technically speaking, in these two auctions, bidders select their value-maximizing bids based on their own valuations only. In contrast, in the open Dutch and the sealed-bid first-price auctions, bidders must form some expectations on the bids made by other participating bidders. For example, a bidder participating in the sealed-bid first-price auction would benefit from knowing whether her bid is likely to be above or below that of the competing bidders. If the buyer bids far above the others, this buyer may benefit from lowering the bid. In contrast, if the buyer bids slightly below the others, this buyer can win the auction by slightly increasing the bid.

The above discussion implies that any analysis of the open Dutch and the sealed-bid first-price auctions requires the imposition of some ad hoc assumptions concerning the distribution of bidders' valuations, and how each bidder perceives this distribution when making the decision on how much to bid. For this reason, Section 10.4.1 starts with the simple open English and sealed-bid second-price auctions. Section 10.4.2 addresses the more complicated auctions that rely on various assumptions concerning how bidders perceive the distribution of willingness to pay of competing bidders.

Suppose there are M potential buyers who bid for a product or a service delivered by a single seller or a firm. Buyer ℓ's maximum willingness to pay (valuation) is V_ℓ, where $V_\ell \geq 0$. Each buyer bids a price p_ℓ^b, where $0 \leq p_\ell^b \leq V_\ell$. If buyer ℓ places the winning bid, the winner will pay p^w. Note that in some auctions (such as the sealed-bid second-price auction), the winner may end up paying a price that is lower than the bid made by the winner. In any event, the payoff to the winner is $V_\ell - p^w$. The payoff to a loser is normalized to equal 0.

10.4.1   Open English and sealed-bid second-price auctions

The open English and the sealed-bid second-price auctions are grouped together not only because they always yield the same outcome, but because they are simple to analyze. The simplicity arises because the participating bidders do not have to form expectations or to forecast the valuations of competing bidders. Table 10.3 displays a sample of three auctions with five participating buyers.

Auction #	V_1	V_2	V_3	V_4	V_5
1	$99	$100	$98	$80	$70
2	$100	$60	$100	$30	$65
3	$20	$20	$20	$100	$20

Table 10.3: Bidders' valuations in three auctions.

Open English auction

Consider auction #1 in Table 10.3. In an English auction, the auctioneer announces ascending prices $1, 2, \ldots$, and so on. When the auctioneer announces $p = \$70$, buyer $\ell = 5$ opts out. Similarly, buyer $\ell = 4$ opts out at $p = \$80$, buyer $\ell = 3$ opts out at $p = \$98$, and finally buyer $\ell = 1$ opts out at $p = \$99$. Consequently, buyer $\ell = 2$ is announced to be the "winner" and pays $p^w = \$99$. The winner's utility from this auction is $V_2 - p^w = 100 - 99 = \$1$. Notice that under the English auction (as well as in some other auctions), the seller can rarely capture the entire surplus from buyers. To see this more clearly, consider auction #3 in Table 10.3. In this auction, bidders 1, 2, 3, and 5 opt out when the auctioneer announces $p = \$20$. The winner, buyer $\ell = 4$ with a maximum willingness to pay of $V_4 = \$100$, ends up paying only $20.

Under auction #2, the auctioneer raises the price until $p^w = \$100$ at which point both remaining buyers opt out at the same time. The auctioneer than flips a coin and determines, say, that buyer $\ell = 3$ is the winner, in which case the winning price is set to $p^w = \$100$ and the winner obtains a utility of $V_3 - p^w = 100 - 100 = 0$. Here, the seller manages to extract the maximum surplus from bidders. Thus, sellers can gain a lot when the two highest bidders have the same valuation.

Sealed-bid second-price auction

Suppose now that buyers are required to submit their bids to the seller in sealed envelopes. When the deadline is reached, the seller opens all the envelopes and announces the winner according to the highest bid. However, the winner is required to pay only the price bid by the second-highest bidder.

The extremely attractive feature of the sealed-bid second-price auction is that *buyers have the incentives to bid their true valuation*. Using the language of game theory, the outcome from each buyer bidding his or her *true* valuation constitutes a *Nash equilibrium*. Technically speaking, there may be some other Nash equilibria; however, from a practical viewpoint, the lesson to be learned here is that it is never a bad idea for a bidder to bid his or her true valuation no matter what bids are made by other bidders. This happens because winners generally do not have to pay the price according to their bid, but according to that of the second-highest bidder. To see this, let us look at auction #1 in Table 10.3. Suppose now that each buyer bids exactly his or her valuation so that $p_1^b = V_1 = \$99$, $p_2^b = V_2 = \$100$, $p_3^b = V_3 = \$98$, $p_4^b = V_4 = \$80$, and $p_5^b = V_5 = \$70$. We first demonstrate that buyer $\ell = 1$ does not have any incentive to change her bid. Clearly, buyer $\ell = 1$ cannot benefit from raising the bid above $V_1 = \$99$, say, to $p_1 = \$100$ because in the event of winning she will be required to pay the bid made by buyer $\ell = 2$, which is $p^w = \$100$, thereby making a loss because $V_1 - p^w = 99 - 100 < 0$. Next, buyer $\ell = 1$ cannot benefit from reducing her bid to $p_1 < \$99$ because this bid does not win anyway, so this buyer is indifferent between bidding $p_1 = \$99$ and $p_1 < \$99$.

Using the above argument, it is easy to show that buyers $\ell = 3, 4$ and $\ell = 5$ cannot benefit from deviating from their valuation-revealing bids. Thus, it remains to analyze buyer $\ell = 2$, who has the highest valuation. Let us examine the winning bid $p_2^b = V_2 = \$100$. The net gain to buyer $\ell = 2$ is $V_2 - p^w = 100 - 99 = \$1$ because the second-highest bid is $p^w = \$99$. Raising the bid, say to $p_2 = \$101$, will not make any difference because buyer $\ell = 2$ will remain the winner and will keep paying $p^w = \$99$ (second highest bid). Also, reducing the bid to $p_2 = \$99$ will reduce the chance of winning by 50% as the seller will flip a coin between buyer 1 and buyer 2, and the winner's price will remain $p^w = \$99$.

Consider now the sealed-bid second-price auction #2 in Table 10.3. Given that all buyers bid their true valuations, the seller would flip a coin to determine whether buyer $\ell = 1$ or $\ell = 3$ should be declared the winner. The chosen winner would pay the second-highest bid, which in this case is \$100 because $p_1^b = p_2^b = \$100$. Thus, the winner, say, buyer 3, gains $V_3 - p^w = 100 - 100 = 0$ surplus. In this case, the seller manages to extract the maximum surplus from the buyer with the highest valuation.

Finally, under auction #3 in Table 10.3, if all buyers bid their true valuations, buyer $\ell = 4$ would be declared the winner after the seller opens all envelopes. Buyer $\ell = 4$'s surplus is then $V_4 - p^w = 100 - 20 = \$80$. Hence, under auction #3 the seller fails to extract most of the surplus from the winning buyer.

Comparing the outcomes of the sealed-bid second-price auction analyzed in this section with the outcomes of the open English auction, the reader should now be convinced that they are identical with respect to the actual bids, the choice of a winner, and the final price paid by the winner. The sealed-bid second-price auction has the advantage that buyers do not have to be present during the auction; for example, buyers can send their bids from overseas. However, the drawback to the seller of buyers not having to be present is that the buyers may be able to collude on placing low bids. In this respect, English auctions may reduce the risk of collusion on the part of buyers, although buyers can always coordinate their bids before entering the auction facility.

We now explain in more detail why buyers participating in sealed-bid second-price auctions bid their true valuations (their maximum willingness to pay). These arguments should also apply to open English auctions. Clearly, buyers do not know whether they have the highest valuation (and thus will win the auction) or not. The following list of arguments proves that bidders cannot benefit from deviating from bidding their true valuations.

(1) The bidder with the highest valuation wins the auction given that all other buyers bid their true (lower) valuations. Hence, increasing the bid beyond the true valuation will not make any difference for the winning buyer.

(2) The bidder with the highest valuation cannot benefit from reducing the bid below the true valuation because the winner pays only the second-highest price bid (and not the highest bid). Hence, reducing the bid will not reduce the price actually paid by the winner but may result in not winning the auction if the reduced bid falls below the valuation of some other bidder.

(3) Bidders with lower valuations cannot benefit from increasing their bids above their true valuations, as in the event they win the auction they will be forced to pay a price above their maximum willingness to pay and end up with negative surplus.

(4) Bidders with lower valuations cannot benefit from reducing their bids below their true valuations because they do not win the auction in any event.

10.4.2 Open Dutch and sealed-bid first-price auctions

In an open Dutch auction, the auctioneer starts with a very high price (above all possible valuations) and gradually reduces the price until a buyer agrees to pay. Under independent valuations, it turns out that this auction generates the same outcome as the sealed-bid first-price auction, in which all buyers place their bids in sealed envelopes and the highest bidder wins and pays the highest bid (as opposed to a sealed-bid second-price auction, which we have already analyzed). Given this equivalence, the analysis below focuses on sealed-bid first-price auctions; however, the reader should bear in mind that the bidding function (10.18) derived below applies to the open Dutch auction as well.

The analytical difficulty with these two auctions is that buyers must form expectations concerning the bids made by all other buyers. Different expectations will result in different bids by all participants. The key assumption here is that buyers' valuations are independent in the sense that each buyer is assumed to "draw" his or her valuations from a distribution and that each draw is statistically independent of draws made by rival buyers. In other words, buyers do not share any common value. Clearly, this assumption is less appealing for financial products, for which actions taken by some buyers (such as buyers who invest in stocks) signal to other buyers the value of the goods.

Suppose there are M potential buyers who bid for a single product or service offered by the seller. Each buyer knows his or her own valuation but does not know the valuations of competing buyers, except that all valuations are drawn uniformly from the interval $[V^L, V^H]$ with equal probability, where $V^H > V^L \geq 0$. Figure 10.5 illustrates the distribution of buyers' valuations and the corresponding probability distribution.

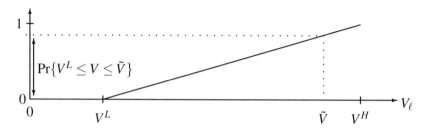

Figure 10.5: Independently distributed buyers' valuations.

The horizontal axis of Figure 10.5 measures buyers' possible valuations, which lie on the interval $V^L \leq V_\ell \leq V^H$. Each buyer knows his or her own valuation for certain, but perceives other buyers' valuations as randomly distributed on this interval with equal probability. The vertical axis measures the probability that a competing buyer ℓ's valuation is in the range of $V^L \leq V_\ell \leq \tilde{V}$. Formally, under the assumed uniform distribution, this probability is given by

$$\Pr\{V^L \leq V \leq \tilde{V}\} = \frac{\tilde{V} - V^L}{V^H - V^L}. \tag{10.17}$$

For example, according to (10.17), the probability that a buyer's valuation is $\tilde{V} = V^H$ or lower is $\Pr\{V^L \leq V \leq V^H\} = (V^H - V^L)/(V^H - V^L) = 1$. Similarly, the probability that a buyer's valuation is $\tilde{V} = V^L$ or lower is $\Pr\{V \leq \tilde{V}^L\} = (V^L - V^L)/(V^H - V^L) = 0$, simply because there are no buyers with valuations below V^L.

The time line for this sealed-bid first-price auction is as follows: First, each buyer ℓ learns his or her own valuation V_ℓ. Then, each buyer places a bid in a sealed envelope knowing only that there are other $M - 1$ competing buyers whose valuations are randomly drawn from the distribution (10.17), who also place their bids in sealed envelopes. Finally, the seller opens all envelopes and awards the product/service to the highest bidder, who has to pay the highest price.

We first postulate and then prove the equilibrium bids for the above-described auction. In this equilibrium, each bidder ℓ with valuation V_ℓ bids

$$p_\ell = \frac{(M-1)V_\ell + V^L}{M}, \quad \text{for each buyer} \quad \ell = 1, 2, \ldots, M. \tag{10.18}$$

In the language of game theory, the M equations in (10.18) constitute a Nash equilibrium. In a Nash equilibrium, no bidder ℓ could benefit from unilaterally deviating from the bid (10.18), given that all other bidders stick to their bids as described by

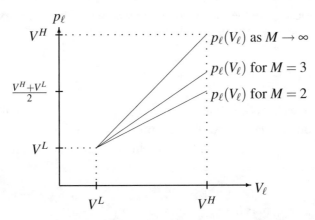

Figure 10.6: Equilibrium bids in sealed-bid first-price auctions as functions of buyers' valuations.

(10.18). The bid functions defined by (10.18) are drawn in Figure 10.6. As in Figure 10.5, the horizontal axis of Figure 10.6 measures buyers' possible valuations on the interval $V^L \leq V_\ell \leq V^H$. The vertical axis measures the bid made by each buyer as a function of the buyer's valuation V_ℓ.

It follows directly from (10.18) or Figure 10.5 that the equilibrium bids have the following properties:

(a) Bids increase monotonically with valuations; that is, a buyer with a higher valuation bids a price higher than that of buyers with low valuations. Formally, $p_\ell \geq p_k$ whenever $V_\ell \geq V_k$, for all buyers $\ell, k = 1, 2, \ldots, M$.

(b) A buyer with the lowest valuation V^L always bids $p = V^L$. All other buyers bid below their valuations so that $p_\ell < V_\ell$ if $V^L < V\ell$.

(c) All bids (except perhaps the lowest bid) increase when the number of buyers increases. Formally, for every valuation V_ℓ, $p_\ell(V_\ell)$ increases with M. In the limit, when the number of buyers gets to be very large, all buyers bid their true valuations. Formally, $p_\ell(V_\ell) \to V_\ell$ as $M \to \infty$.

The reader may wonder why a buyer with the lowest valuation does not bid less than his or her valuation V^L. The reason is that this buyer actually never wins an auction because no other buyer bids below V^L, so there is no benefit from lowering the bid. Next, when the number of buyers increases, each buyer has a lower probability of winning, causing buyers to increase their bids.

We now prove that the M bids given by (10.18) indeed constitute a Nash equilibrium. With no loss of generality, let us concentrate on the actions available to buyer $\ell = 1$, who sets the bid p_1. The probability that buyer $\ell = 1$ wins the auction is

$$\Pr\{p_1 > \max\{p_2, p_3, \ldots, p_M\}\} = \left(\frac{p_1 - p^L}{p^H - p^L}\right)^{M-1}, \qquad (10.19)$$

where p^L and p^H are the bids made by buyers who "draw" the extreme valuations V^L and V^H, respectively, defined by

$$p^L \stackrel{\text{def}}{=} V^L \quad \text{and} \quad p^H \stackrel{\text{def}}{=} \frac{(M-1)V^H + V^L}{M}. \tag{10.20}$$

Buyer $\ell = 1$ seeks to maximize expected surplus, which is the difference between her valuation and her bid (where the bid is also the price to be paid under a first-price auction), multiplied by the probability that she is the winner. Formally, buyer $\ell = 1$ chooses p_1 to solve

$$\max_{p_1} U_1(p_1) = \max_{p_1} (V_1 - p_1) \left(\frac{p_1 - p^L}{p^H - p^L} \right)^{M-1}, \tag{10.21}$$

where p^L and p^H are defined by (10.20). The expected surplus of buyer $\ell = 1$ is strictly concave with respect to p_1. The first-order condition for a maximum surplus is therefore

$$0 = \frac{\mathrm{d}U_1(p_1)}{\mathrm{d}p_1} = \frac{M[M(V_1 - p_1) - V_1 + p^L]}{p_1 - p^L} \left(\frac{p_1 - p^L}{p^H - p^L} \right)^{M-1}. \tag{10.22}$$

Substituting p^L and p^H from (10.20) into (10.22) and solving for p_1 yields $p_1 = [(M-1)V_1 + V^L]/M$, which is exactly the same as the general solution given by (10.18). This concludes the proof that the bids (10.18) indeed constitute a Nash equilibrium.

10.4.3   Revenue equivalence under independent valuations

The objective of the seller is to maximize expected revenue from the sale of products and services via the use of auctions. This means that the seller would choose the auction method that maximizes the expected price to be paid by the winner of the auction. Therefore, a natural question to ask at this point is whether and how the four auctions analyzed in this section differ with respect to the expected revenue earned by the seller. As it turns out, if buyers' valuations are independent and are drawn from the same distribution (like the ones with the uniform distribution depicted in Figure 10.5), all four auctions generate exactly the same expected revenue.

In what follows, we demonstrate how the sealed-bid second-price auction analyzed in Section 10.4.1 and the sealed-bid first-price auction analyzed in Section 10.4.2 yield identical expected revenue to the seller. In fact, this demonstration is sufficient for showing that all four auctions are equivalent with respect to the expected revenue they generate. To simplify the exposition, the following computations assume that $V^L = 0$, which means that all buyers' valuations are uniformly distributed on the interval $[0, V^H]$.

Expected revenue generated by the sealed-bid second-price auction

Section 10.4.1 has shown that under the sealed-bid second-price auction all buyers bid their true valuations. Therefore, because the winner ends up paying the second-highest bid, expected revenue to the seller equals expected value of the second-highest valuation.

The probability that all the M valuations are equal to or below $\tilde{V}$ is $(\tilde{V}/V^H)^M$. Next, the probability that a specific valuation is realized to be exactly the second-highest is $(1 - \tilde{V}/V^H)(\tilde{V}/V^H)^{M-1}$, which is the product of the probability of having one valuation higher than $\tilde{V}$ and the probability that all remaining $M - 1$ valuations are below it. Altogether, the probability that the second-highest valuation does not exceed $\tilde{V}$ is the sum

$$\left(\frac{\tilde{V}}{V^H}\right)^M + M\left(1 - \frac{\tilde{V}}{V^H}\right)\left(\frac{\tilde{V}}{V^H}\right)^{M-1}. \tag{10.23}$$

The first term is the probability that all M buyers bid no higher than $\tilde{V}$. The second term is the probability that one and only one buyer bids higher than the remaining $M - 1$ buyers. The second term is multiplied by M because there are M buyers who may turn out to have the second-highest valuation. Differentiating (10.23) with respect to $\tilde{V}$ yields the density associated with the distribution of the second-highest valuation. Hence,

$$\frac{M(M-1)V^{M-2}(V^H - V)}{(V^H)^M}. \tag{10.24}$$

Therefore, the expected second-highest valuation, which also equals the expected revenue to the seller, is computed by

$$\text{Ex} = \int_0^{V^H} \frac{M(M-1)V^{M-2}(V^H - V)}{(V^H)^M}\, dV = \frac{M-1}{M+1} V^H. \tag{10.25}$$

Thus, the seller's expected revenue increases with the number of buyers participating in this auction. In the limit, when the number of participants becomes very large, the expected revenue to the seller approaches the highest valuation. Formally, $\text{Ex} \to V^H$ as $M \to \infty$. This happens because an increase in the number of participants increases the probability that the buyer with the second-highest valuation "draws" a higher valuation. In the limit, the second-highest valuation will be close to V^H.

Expected revenue generated by the sealed-bid first-price auction

The probability that the highest valuation among M buyers does not exceed $\tilde{V}$ is $(\tilde{V}/V^H)^M$. The density function associated with this probability is given by

$d(V/V^H)^M/dV = MV^{M-1}(V^H)^{-M}$, for $0 \le V \le V^H$. Using the bids of the first-price auction given by (10.18), the expected highest bid, which also equals the expected revenue to the seller, is computed by

$$\mathrm{Ex} = \int_0^{V^H} \left[\frac{MV^{M-1}}{(V^H)^M} \right] \left[\frac{(M-1)V}{M} \right] dV = \frac{M-1}{M+1} V^H. \qquad (10.26)$$

The first term under the integral sign is the valuations' density function. The second term is the bid made by each buyer in a sealed-bid first-price auction.

Comparing (10.25) with (10.26) reveals that the expected seller's revenue under the first- and second-price sealed-bid auctions are the same. This means that the open English ascending and Dutch descending price auctions also generate the same expected seller's revenue as in (10.25) and (10.26). In fact, all four auctions are also "socially optimal" in the sense that the winner is always the buyer with the highest valuation. It should be stressed that these equivalence results may fail to hold when buyers' valuations are not independent. For example, if buyers tend to revise their valuations during an open English auction after the auctioneer raises the price and most buyers agree to pay the higher price, then buyers may share a common value for the auctioned good, which is revealed during the auction process. In this case, the above-mentioned equivalence results may not hold.

10.5   Advertising Expenditure

Pricing techniques often involve large investments in advertising. Advertising is generally defined as a form of providing information about prices, quality, and the location of goods and services. In practice, advertising often lacks some of these features, and instead attempts to convey an image of the type of personalities associated with the advertised good. The economics literature distinguishes between two types of advertising: *persuasive advertising* and *informative advertising*. Persuasive advertising intends to enhance consumer tastes for a certain product, whereas informative advertising carries basic product information such as characteristics, prices, and where to buy it.

Earlier modern authors, such as Kaldor (1950), held the idea that advertising is "manipulative" and reduces competition and therefore reduces welfare for two reasons: First, advertising persuades consumers to believe wrongly that identical products are different because the decision of which brand to purchase depends on consumers' perception of the brand rather than on the actual physical characteristics of the product. Therefore, prices of heavily advertised products may rise far beyond their cost of production. Second, advertising serves as an entry-deterring mechanism because any newly entering firm must extensively advertise to surpass the reputation of the existing firms. Thus, existing firms use advertising as an entry-deterrence strategy and can maintain their dominance while keeping above-normal profit levels.

More-recent authors, such as Telser (1964), Nelson (1970, 1974), and Demsetz (1979), proposed that advertising serves as a tool for transmitting information from producers to consumers about different brands, thereby reducing consumers' cost of obtaining information about where to purchase their most preferred brand.

Nelson (1970) distinguishes between two types of goods: *search goods* and *experience goods*. Consumers can identify the quality and other characteristics of the product before the actual purchase of search goods. Examples include tomatoes or shirts. Consumers cannot learn the quality and other characteristics of experience goods before the actual purchase. Examples include new models of cars and many electrical appliances with unknown durability and failure rates. Note that this distinction is not really clear-cut, because we cannot fully judge the quality of a tomato until we eat it, and we cannot fully judge the quality of a shirt until after the first wash!

10.5.1   Demand functions and advertising

To find out whether advertising enhances the demand for a seller's products and services, the econometrician has to estimate a demand that is a function of both price and advertising expenditure. Clearly, if advertising has only a little effect on the quantity demanded, the firm should not invest in advertising. In contrast, if the demand is greatly enhanced by advertising, the firm may want to take into account a possible trade-off between price reduction and advertising expenditure as both contribute to demand increases.

As it turns out, an extended version of the constant-elasticity demand function analyzed in Section 2.4 is very handy for determining the profit-maximizing expenditure on advertising. Let a denote the firm's expenditure on advertising. The variables q and p denote the quantity demanded and the price set by the firm, respectively. It is assumed that the quantity demanded is enhanced with an increase in advertising expenditure, and declines with price. Formally, a constant-elasticity demand as a function of price and advertising expenditure is defined by

$$q(a,p) \stackrel{\text{def}}{=} \alpha\, a^{e_a} p^{-e_p}, \quad \text{where} \quad 0 < e_a < 1 \quad \text{and} \quad e_p > 0 \qquad (10.27)$$

are the advertising elasticity and the price elasticity, respectively. Formally, in view of the elasticity analysis of Section 2.4.3, the price elasticity is defined and computed by

$$e_p \stackrel{\text{def}}{=} \frac{\partial q(a,p)}{\partial p} \frac{p}{q} = -\alpha\, a^{e_a} e_p\, p^{-e_p - 1} \frac{p}{\alpha\, a^{e_a} p^{-e_p}} = -e_p. \qquad (10.28)$$

Similarly, the advertising elasticity is defined and computed by

$$e_a \stackrel{\text{def}}{=} \frac{\partial q(a,p)}{\partial a} \frac{a}{q} = \alpha\, p^{-e_p} e_a\, a^{e_a - 1} \frac{a}{\alpha\, a^{e_a} p^{-e_p}} = e_a. \qquad (10.29)$$

Before the firm can make a decision on how much to spend on advertising, it must estimate the parameters α, e_a, and e_p of the demand function (10.27). As demonstrated in Section 2.4.2, perhaps the simplest way would be to form a linear regression by taking the natural logarithm of (10.27), yielding

$$\underbrace{\ln q}_{\text{ln quantity}} = \underbrace{\ln \alpha}_{\text{constant}} + \underbrace{e_a}_{\text{elasticity}} \underbrace{\ln a}_{\text{ln advertising}} - \underbrace{e_p}_{\text{elasticity}} \underbrace{\ln p}_{\text{ln price}}. \qquad (10.30)$$

Using past data on prices and advertising expenditure, the econometrician of the firm should be able to estimate the parameter α and the two elasticities e_a and e_p. For the following analysis to be valid, it must be verified that the estimated elasticities e_a and e_p satisfy the restrictions stated in (10.27).

10.5.2 Profit-maximizing advertising expenditure

The constant-elasticity demand function (10.27) turns out to be very useful for computing the profit-maximizing spending on advertising. For this demand function, Dorfman and Steiner (1954) established that a monopoly's profit-maximizing advertising and price levels should be set so that *the ratio of advertising expenditure to revenue equals the (absolute value of the) ratio of the advertising elasticity to price elasticity*. Formally,

$$\frac{a}{pq} = \frac{e_a}{-e_p}. \qquad (10.31)$$

The left side of (10.31) is the ratio of how much the firm should invest in advertising, a, to sales revenue, $x = pq$, made by this firm. The right side is the ratio of the two estimated demand elasticities. Thus, this firm should increase its advertising-to-sales ratio as the demand it faces becomes more elastic with respect to advertising (e_a gets closer to 1), or less elastic with respect to price (e_p gets closer to zero).

We conclude this analysis with a numerical example that demonstrates the usefulness of the formula given by (10.31). Suppose that the estimated advertising elasticity is $e_a = 0.01$, which means that a 1% increase in advertising expenditure would result in a 0.01% increase in quantity demanded. Also suppose that the price elasticity was estimated to be -1.2, which means that a 1% drop in price would result in a 1.2% increase in quantity demanded. We now compute the profit-maximizing expenditure on advertising, assuming that sales revenue is estimated to be around \$120,000. Using the formula (10.31), the above data imply that

$$\frac{a}{\$120,000} = \frac{0.01}{-(-1.2)} \quad \Longrightarrow \quad a = \$1000. \qquad (10.32)$$

10.6 Exercises

1. Congratulations! You have been appointed chief engineer of GIBBERISH, a leading manufacturer of inkjet printers (printers that fire extremely small droplets of ink on paper). Your team of engineers has informed you that the company is able to produce printers of three quality levels: quality F, which is a fast 20 page–per-minute (PPM) printer; quality M, which is a medium-speed 15 PPM printer; and quality S, which is a slow model capable of only 8 PPM.

    Your colleagues at the marketing department have been conducting market surveys to approximate potential buyers' willingness to pay for the different qualities, which are summarized in Table 10.4. Table 10.4 also displays the unit production cost of each printer according to quality. Solve the following problems assuming that there are no fixed costs, $\phi = 0$.

i (Quality)	$\ell = 1$	$\ell = 2$	μ_i (Unit Cost)
F (Fast)	$V_1^F = \$70$	$V_2^F = \$50$	$\mu_F = \$50$
M (Medium)	$V_1^M = \$65$	$V_2^M = \$40$	$\mu_M = \$30$
S (Slow)	$V_1^S = \$40$	$V_2^S = \$30$	$\mu_S = \$10$
N_ℓ (# consumers)	$N_1 = 50$	$N_2 = 40$	

Table 10.4: Data for Exercise 1.

   (a) Compute the profit GIBBERISH earns when it sells quality F only, quality M only, and quality S only.

   (b) Conclude which quality GIBBERISH should introduce into the market, assuming that only one quality can be sold in this market.

   (c) Using the analysis of Section 10.1.4, determine whether GIBBERISH can enhance its profit by introducing more than one model into the market. If your answer is positive, indicate which printer models should be introduced and their profit-maximizing prices. Prove that these prices indeed segment the market in the sense that each model introduced into the market will be demanded by at least one type of consumers.

2. Your company can produce a 20 PPM laser printer at a cost of $50 per unit. In addition, your firm can replace a memory chip on each printer for an additional cost of $10 per unit, which would slow the printer down to 10 PPM (thus raising the unit cost of the damaged printer to $60 per unit). Table 10.5 displays potential consumers' maximum willingness to pay for the two printer configurations. Solve the following problems using the analysis of Section 10.2, assuming that there are no fixed costs, $\phi = 0$.

i (Speed)	$\ell = 1$	$\ell = 2$	μ_i (Unit Cost)
F (Fast)	$V_1^F = \$80$	$V_2^F = \$180$	$\$50$
S (Slow)	$V_1^S = \$80$	$V_2^S = \$90$	$\$50 + \$10$
N_ℓ (# consumers)	$N_1 = 100$	$N_2 = 200$	

Table 10.5: Data for Exercise 2.

(a) Compute the profit-maximizing price of the fast model assuming that the slow printer is not introduced into the market.

(b) Compute the profit-maximizing prices of the fast and slow printers assuming now that the slow (damaged) model is also sold on the market.

(c) Conclude whether the introduction of the slow printer is profit enhancing or profit reducing.

3. This exercise requires the use of calculus. Consider the behavior-based pricing model studied in Section 10.3.1. Let p_L and p_S denote the prices quoted to returning (loyal) consumers and consumers who switch from competing providers, respectively. The quantities (number of consumers) q_L and q_S are similarly defined. Suppose the demand functions of the two consumer groups are

$$q_L(p_L, p_S) = 240 - 3p_L + p_S, \quad \text{and} \quad q_S(p_L, p_S) = 120 - 2p_S + p_L.$$

The seller bears a fixed cost of $\phi = \$7000$ and a per-unit production cost of $\mu = \$20$. Solve the following problems.

(a) Formulate the seller's profit function $y(p_L, p_S)$ and compute the first-order and second-order conditions for a maximum.

(b) Solve for the profit-maximizing prices p_L and p_S and conclude whether this seller provides any loyalty discount to returning customers.

(c) Compute the number of loyal consumers and switching consumers under these prices and the corresponding profit level.

4. Consider separately the three auctions with buyers' valuations displayed in Table 10.3. For each auction, compute the seller's revenue and the net surplus (benefit) of the winning buyer assuming a sealed-bid *third*-price auction, in which the highest bidder wins the auction but has to pay only the third-highest bid.

5. Congratulations! You have been appointed the new CEO of UGLY, Inc., the sole producer of a facial cream that is advertised as making people's skin look 30 years younger. Your first assignment is to determine the advertising budget for next year. The marketing department provides you with three important pieces of information: (1) The company is expected to sell $10 million worth of the

product. (2) It is estimated that a 1% increase in the advertising budget would increase the quantity sold by 0.05%. (3) It is also estimated that a 1% increase in the product's price would reduce quantity sold by 0.2%.

(a) How much money would you allocate for advertising next year?

(b) Now, suppose the marketing department has revised its estimation regarding the demand price elasticity to a 1% increase in price, resulting in a reduction in quantity sold by 0.5%. How much money would you allocate to advertising after getting the revised estimate?

(c) Conclude how a change in the demand price elasticity affects advertising expenditure.

Chapter 11

Tariff-choice Biases and Warranties

11.1 Flat-rate Biases 360

11.2 Choice in Context and Extremeness Aversion 362

11.3 Other Consumer Choice Biases 366

    11.3.1 Odd pricing and the 99¢ fixation

    11.3.2 Price–quality perceptions

    11.3.3 Micropayments and currency denomination

11.4 Warranties 369

    11.4.1 Product replacement warranties

    11.4.2 Money-back guarantee

11.5 Exercises 375

The pricing techniques described throughout this book are based on the presumption that buyers always optimize their selections among the different payment plans and quality classes that are offered by one or more sellers. By optimizing, we mean that buyers operate according to well-defined objectives, such as expenditure minimization, maximization of value versus price, and minimization of expected price in case of uncertainty. Sadly enough for academic economists, consumers do not always behave this way. More precisely, consumers often end up selecting a payment plan, a brand, or a quality level that seems to violate consumers' objective functions as commonly assumed by economists.

The development of profitable marketing and pricing strategies requires an understanding of the manner in which consumers choose among alternatives. This chapter is devoted almost entirely to consumers who seem to be optimizing in ways different from those we have assumed so far in this book. The basic idea is that firms should often take into account what sometimes looks like an irrational behavior on the part of consumers and set their price menus accordingly. In fact, in many instances firms can actually take advantage of certain "odd" consumer behaviors and extract an even higher surplus from these consumers compared with the surplus that can be extracted from consumers who behave according to the way economists want them to behave.

The examination of consumer behavior combines aspects from psychology and economics. That is, the psychology of decision making turns out to be helpful in explaining the observed anomalies on the part of consumers. Along this line, some researchers even argue that consumers often lack the ability to make optimal choices. This is especially true when service providers offer consumers complex packages under which consumers find it difficult to estimate their actual costs. Such complex packages are widely observed in the telephone industry. Consumers' inability to consider all possibilities is known as *bounded rationality*, a term attributed to Simon (1955); see also Kahneman (2003) for recent applications.

The psychological, social, and economic motivations for what appear to be irrational choices on the part of consumers have recently earned a field name in economics called *behavioral economics*. Clearly, this name choice is rather poor because all the major fields that fall under the categories of psychology, sociology, and economics are concerned with modeling human behavior. However, this name serves its purpose as economists nowadays refer to behavioral economics as the study of consumer choice anomalies. A wide variety of these anomalies have been studied over the years; see Thaler (1991, 1992), and in the context of behavioral economics, see Mullainathan and Thaler (2000) and Camerer, Loewenstein, and Rabin (2003). In this chapter, we obviously focus only on some anomalies related to pricing. For more comprehensive discussions and research surveys on consumer perceptions with respect to prices, the reader is referred to Wilkie (1990), Monroe (2002), and Winer (2005).

This chapter ends with the analysis of warranties. Warranties serve two purposes: The first, which is not necessarily related to behavioral economics, serves as insurance to consumers against defects in the products or services they buy. The second is a psychological comfort for which consumers are willing to pay extra.

11.1 Flat-rate Biases

It is widely observed that consumers subscribing to services prefer flat-rate payment plans over paying separately for each unit of consumption, despite the fact that very often flat-rate plans turn out to be more expensive than the sum of all pay-per-use fees and prices under the measured plans. The following list summarizes some of the explanations given in the literature for this anomaly.

Insurance: Risk-averse consumers use the flat-rate option to obtain full insurance against realizations of high demand. According to this view, risk-averse consumers may hedge against an abnormally high bill by paying a flat rate. Thus, pay per use constitutes the riskiest billing plan.

Aversion to being metered: Also known as the taxi meter effect, consumers simply do not like to be monitored with respect to their consumption level.

High expectations: For some services, consumers consistently overestimate their actual use. For example, health-oriented consumers tend to make New Year's resolutions to visit their health clubs more often than they actually do.

Time-inconsistent preferences: Consumers are fully aware of their initially high consumption expectations and the fact that their willingness to pay will diminish over time.

Convenience and confusion: Consumers are often confused when offered a wide variety of payment plans in the form of packages. The flat-rate payment plan is perceived as the simplest plan and is therefore the most convenient. In addition, the flat-rate plan reduces transaction costs.

Option value: People are simply willing to pay extra for the option of using the service at zero marginal usage price.

The anomaly concerning consumers' choice of the flat-rate plan instead of the pay-per-use plan despite the common observation that the latter turns out to be cheaper has been described and analyzed in a variety of papers, including Train, McFadden, and Ben-Akiva (1987); Train, Ben-Akiva, and Atherton (1989); Mitchell and Vogelsang (1991, pp. 176–177); Clay, Sibley, and Srinagesh (1992); Kridel, Lehman, and Weisman (1993); Danielsen, Kamerschen, and Nicolaou (1993); and Miravete (2003). Nunes (2000) reports on surveys showing that people are generally willing to pay a large premium for unlimited access to online shopping, even when neither their current nor their expected usage can justify it. The same paper also presents a different study of health club users in Chicago demonstrating the bias toward a flat-rate membership plan relative to paying for each visit separately. DellaVigna and Malmendier (2006) provide an empirical analysis of the time inconsistency associated with choices in health club membership plans. Lambrecht and Skiera (2006) conduct empirical analyses on the various causes of the flat-rate bias.

Table 11.1 displays some real-life data for three service industries that offer flat-rate subscription and pay-per-use payment plans. The second column of Table 11.1 displays the flat-rate subscription fee f. The third column displays the per-unit price p if a subscription is not made, and the fourth displays the actual observed quantity of the service q used. The fifth column displays the *hypothetical* total expenditure $p \cdot q$ that would be borne had the consumer chosen *not* to subscribe to the flat-rate plan. The sixth column displays the price per use f/q *actually paid*, which equals the flat-rate subscription fee divided by the quantity used.

For the health club market, the three variables f, p, and q are averages for flat-rate subscribers reported by Nunes (2000) and DellaVigna and Malmendier (2006). Nunes (2000) reports on 79 regular club users who averaged $q = 38$ visits per year and paid an annual membership fee of $f = \$610$. Therefore, these users paid an effective price of $f/q = 610/38 \approx \$16.05$ per visit despite the fact that a

Market	f	p	q	$p \cdot q$	f/q
Health club (Y):	$610.00	$10.00	38.00	$380.00	$16.05
Health club (M):	$70.00	$10.00	4.80	$48.00	$14.58
Phone (low q):	$19.85	$0.11	70	$7.70	$0.28
Phone (high q):	$19.85	$0.11	101	$11.11	$0.20
Subscription (M):	$19.95	$6.95	2.42	$16.85	$8.23

Table 11.1: Data on the use of flat rates for three service industries. *Note*: Y stands for yearly membership, M for monthly membership.

one-time guest fee was $10 (an overpayment of 60%). DellaVigna and Malmendier examine more than 7000 members of three New England health clubs. Their data set contains information on the contractual choices and day-to-day attendance of users from 1997 to the early 2000s. As these authors point out, with a monthly average of $q = 4.8$ visits, consumers who subscribed to the monthly flat rate plan ended up paying a price of $f/q = \$70/4.8 \approx \$14.6$ per visit, despite the fact that the pay-per-use plan was obtainable for $10 per visit. That is, consumers "overpaid" 46% more than they could have paid had they chosen not to subscribe to the flat-rate plan.

What conclusions can be drawn from the above findings? Managers in charge of pricing decisions and yield management would clearly benefit from learning how much extra consumers are willing to pay to be on a flat-rate plan instead of the pay-per-use plan. By designing proper tariff schemes, profit-maximizing managers can take advantage of consumers' tariff-choice biases by raising the fixed fee rate proportionally to consumers' willingness to pay for subscribing to flat-rate plans. This means that many service industries should consider introducing flat-rate plans, although in some industries, consumer may "overuse" the service, thereby generating some unnecessarily high costs. For example, it is unlikely that airlines would benefit from selling flat-rate one-year subscriptions to transatlantic flights, although some shorter arrangements are sometimes observed for domestic flights sold to tourists who would like to explore a country in a short time.

11.2   Choice in Context and Extremeness Aversion

Almost all the pricing techniques developed in earlier chapters relied on value maximization, in which consumers are assumed to make purchase decisions based on the difference between the value they derive from a brand and its price, formally written as $V - p$. That is, if, a consumer faces a choice between two brands (or two quality levels of the same brand), labeled A and B, the consumer would then maximize over the set $\{V^A - p_A, V^B - p_B, 0\}$, where 0 is the net benefit generated by the option not to buy. A major implication of this assumption is that consumer choices between two brands, or between two quality classes of the same brand, are independent of the context as defined by the entire set of alternative products and prices facing the consumer. Recall that Sections 10.1 and 10.2 have already demonstrated the possible profit enhancements generated by sellers' introduction of several quality classes into the market when the market consists of heterogenous consumers with diverse preferences regarding quality and extra features. As it turns out, if consumers' selections are affected by the context under which the available choices are presented, it may be profitable to introduce more than one version/quality of the product or service, even in a case in which consumers have identical preferences (in which case the analysis of Section 10.1 would not recommend the introduction of multiple quality classes).

Introducing multiple quality levels into the market often confuses consumers as they find it hard to compute which quality class maximizes their benefit net of price. Firms can exploit consumers' confusion by introducing multiple quality levels and adjusting the price of each version so that consumers will choose the most profitable one. Simonson and Tversky (1992) and Tversky and Simonson (1993) introduce the hypothesis that consumer choice is often influenced by the context under which all choices are presented, as defined by the set of alternative versions being offered. In particular, these authors identify what they call *extremeness aversion*, whereby the attractiveness of an option is enhanced if it is an intermediate option in the choice set and is diminished if the option constitutes an extreme on the choice set. In fact, Shapiro and Varian (1999, p. 72) advise sellers that "if you can't decide how many versions to have, choose three," with the idea that consumers will want to refrain from selecting the high-end and low-end versions of the product.

The above discussion implies very clearly that offering only two versions of a product or a service – say, premium quality and standard quality – tends to irritate consumers, perhaps to a degree that will cause them to reconsider whether they really like the product. More precisely, consumers may refrain from buying the standard-quality good, fearing that later they will have to apologize to family members for being "cheap" as for a few dollars more, they could have enjoyed the good with the higher quality, which probably contains more features. Similarly, consumers may refrain from buying the premium version, fearing that they will end up feeling guilty for overspending. The seller may facilitate consumer choice by offering three versions of the same good to choose from. Consumers then may be tempted to pick the intermediate version as insurance against regretting the purchase of an extreme version.

Simonson and Tversky (1992) report on an experiment conducted on consumers who are willing to buy microwave ovens. Table 11.2 summarizes the subjects' choices. In this experiment, 60 subjects were offered a choice between two microwave ovens: a bargain model for \$110 and a standard model for \$180. The

Model:	Bargain	Standard	Deluxe
Price:	$110	$180	$200
60 subjects:	57%	43%	n/a
60 subjects:	27%	60%	13%

Table 11.2: Subjects' choice between two and among three microwave ovens.

second group, also made up of 60 subjects, had to choose among three ovens: the same bargain and standard models offered to the first group, and an additional "deluxe" model priced at $200. Table 11.2 shows that the introduction of the deluxe model boosted the demand for the standard model despite the low demand for the most expensive deluxe model. This implies that the introduction of a deluxe model makes consumers (at least $60 - 43 = 17\%$ of them) feel that the standard model is a bargain, and also makes the bargain model less attractive. Thus, consumer choice in this case is affected by the context in which the variety of models and the corresponding prices are presented.

If the seller has only one version to offer for sale, the seller need not worry about anything except properly estimating consumers' maximum willingness to pay. However, Sections 10.1 and 10.2 have already demonstrated that introducing a second quality level may be profit enhancing. But if consumer preferences exhibit extremeness aversion, the seller should consider introducing a third version of this product. Consequently, the problem faced by the seller is choosing which additional quality level to introduce and how to price all versions of the good.

Table 11.3 illustrates an example of how to transform the marketing of two quality versions into three versions. Suppose the firm initially sells only two versions: low quality and high quality. If the firm suspects that the preferences of its potential customers exhibit extremeness aversion, it may want to consider introducing a third version.

Initial Production:	n/a	Low Q	High Q	n/a
Unit Cost:	n/a	μ_L	μ_H	n/a
Consumer Valuation:	n/a	V^L	V^H	n/a
1st Configuration:	n/a	Economy	Standard	Deluxe
2nd Configuration:	Economy	Standard	Deluxe	n/a

Table 11.3: Making three versions out of two.

Table 11.3 suggests two possible configurations. The first is to market the low-quality version as "economy" and the high-quality version as "standard." To induce consumers with extremeness aversion to purchase the high-quality version, under this configuration the firm should offer a deluxe version. This case was already shown to be profitable in the microwave oven experiment in Table 11.2, in which the introduction of the deluxe model enhanced the demand for the standard model and only a small fraction of consumers actually bought the deluxe model.

The second configuration in Table 11.3 is intended to attract customers to purchase the low-quality model by introducing a "damaged" version of the product or service, as previously analyzed in Section 10.2. For example, in the case of software, a damaged version can be produced by turning off some features. However, in contrast to Section 10.2, here the introduction of the damaged version is intended to attract most consumers to buy the low-quality version (now labeled "standard") and only a few (or none) to buy the damaged good, which is now labeled "economy."

The following steps should be useful to a seller wishing to determine which of the two product configurations suggested in Table 11.3 is more profitable.

Step I: Compare the maximum possible profit margins $V^L - \mu_L$ and $V^H - \mu_H$, and determine which model has a higher profit potential.

Step II: If $V^L - \mu_L \leq V^H - \mu_H$, then

(a) Label H the standard version and introduce a luxurious model labeled deluxe (first configuration in Table 11.3).

(b) Set the standard model price $p_S = V^H$ and make sure the economy model is priced $p_E > V^L$.

Step III: If $V^L - \mu_L > V^H - \mu_H$, then

(a) Label L the standard version and introduce a damaged version labeled economy (second configuration in Table 11.3).

(b) Set the standard model price $p_S = V^L$ and make sure the deluxe model is priced $p_D > V^H$.

Step I determines which of the two versions has a higher profit margin. If H is chosen (Step II), then H is labeled "standard" and priced by the valuation V^H. The economy version's price is found from $V^H - p_S > V^L - p_E$, which yields $p_E > V^L$ after substituting $p_S = V^H$.

If L is chosen (Step III), then L is labeled "standard" and priced by the valuation V^L. The deluxe version's price is found from $V^L - p_S > V^H - p_D$, which yields $p_D > V^H$ after substituting $p_S = V^L$.

11.3   Other Consumer Choice Biases

Section 11.1 analyzed consumer biases toward flat-rate payment plans. Section 11.2 analyzed consumer biases against high- and low-end versions of products and services in the form of extremeness aversion. This section briefly discusses a few additional biases that are often observed when reviewing consumers' selections among brands, quality levels, and prices.

11.3.1   Odd pricing and the 99¢ fixation

It is widely observed that most retailers in the United States price products and services to end in 99¢. This pricing structure is often referred to as *the 9 fixation*. The scientific literature, such as Basu (1997), Schindler and Kirby (1997), Stiving and Winer (1997), and Thomas and Morwitz (2005), proposed several explanations for this observation.

Rounding illusions: Consumers tend to approximate the prices they pay by a lower integer or a lower decimal number rather than by a higher one. Thus, depending on the level of rounding numbers, consumers may state or report a price of $999.99 as nine-hundred-ninety-nine, or as nine-hundred-ninety, or simply nine-hundred dollars. This means that people tend to underquote a price according to the leading digits of the price. Stores, then, maximize profit by setting the last digits as large as possible, in which case they simply add the relevant sequence of 9s.

Consumers like to receive change: Therefore, if stores take into their pricing consideration the assumption that consumers' utility is enhanced by receiving change, they will maximize profit by handing out the minimum-possible change, which is 1¢. Hence, all prices end with 99¢.

Attractive digits: People find the combinations of 99, 999, 9999, and so on, to be "nice." Thus, consumers are attracted to prices involving many digits of nine. Hence, this "elegant" statement of the price serves as a store-advertising mechanism because after looking at the price itself, consumers are more likely to pay attention to other details and features of the good offered by this seller.

Image of a discount retailer: Discount stores tend to use black-and-white ads to create an image that the store is engaged in significant cost cutting. Similarly, a price of 99¢ may indicate that a store is concerned with all levels of cost cutting and that even a 1¢ cost reduction is being transferred to the consumers in the form of a 1¢ price reduction.

Agency problem and theft: With the absence of on-the-job cameras, owners have no way of ensuring that cashiers collect and transfer the proceeds from all sales. A price of $5.00 means that too many customers will hand over exactly one $5 bill or five $1 bills without waiting for the sale to be rung on the machine. In this case, the cashier can pocket the cash without having to register the transaction. In contrast, a price of $4.99 forces the customer to wait to receive change and the employee to register the transaction to be able to hand out the 1¢ change.

Finally, there is a question regarding the 99¢ pricing structure is only an American phenomenon. As it turns out, although 99¢ prices are perhaps more visible in the United States, more and more stores in other countries are adopting this pricing structure. Thus, it remains to be seen whether the 99¢ component of the price translates into different currencies with different purchasing power. Gabor and Granger (1966) and Gabor (1988, pp. 258–259) report on prices of nylon stockings in England prior to decimalization of the currency. Their striking result is presented on a graph of potential consumers as a function of price and shows that the patterns of no change in potential consumers lie in ranges between prices having the same shilling components, such as 2 shillings and 10 pence, and 2 shillings and 11 pence. Stating it differently, the steepest drops in the buy responses were found when the price changed from 5 shillings and 11 pence to 6 shillings and 0 pence, or any similar changes from 6/11 to 7/−, 7/11 to 8/−, 8/11 to 9/−, and so on. Using Gabor's words, "this price structure has become imprinted on the customers' minds and has found clear expression in their responses."

11.3.2 Price–quality perceptions

It is well known that consumers attach value to the way in which the product is packaged. This is, of course, very strange because packages tend to be thrown away after the consumer starts using the product. For some reason, the quality of the box serves as a signal for the quality of the product. In exactly the same way, consumers perceive the price itself as a signal.

The reader has probably heard many people say "there must be something wrong with this product because it is priced so low." Thus, many consumers believe that within each group of products and services, the quality of the good is somewhat reflected by its price level. This belief on the part of consumers explains why some consumers place a lower bound on the price below which they will reject a price offer in addition to an upper bound beyond which they will also not buy, as they view it as "too expensive." Gabor and Granger (1966) discuss two methods for surveying consumers' reactions to price offers. The first method involves two questions: one asking for the highest price at which the consumer would buy and the second asking for the lowest price. The second method asks consumers to respond to a list of prices for a certain item by stating whether they would buy, whether they would not buy because the price is too high, or whether they would not buy because the price is too low. A reader who cannot rationalize a behavior under which a consumer would refuse to buy a product because it is too cheap should ask himself or herself what he or she would do if she were offered a full-size eight-serving New York cheesecake for a total price of 40¢ (that is, the equivalent of 5¢ per piece). Clearly, some consumers would rightly or wrongly infer that the cake has not been refrigerated properly or that the last date of sale has already passed.

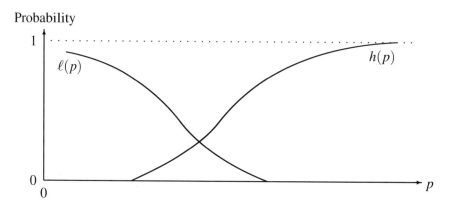

Figure 11.1: Consumer responses to price offers.

Figure 11.1 displays the results from a sample of consumers described in Gabor and Granger (1966). These subjects were asked to respond to price offers of nylon stockings, carpets, and two food items. The horizontal axis indicates the price offers made to the subjects. The figure clearly shows that for sufficiently low prices, there is a high probability that a consumer will reject a price offer on the basis that it is "too cheap." This is reflected by the function $\ell(p)$. As the price offer increases, the function $\ell(p)$ shows that the probability that a consumer would turn it down on the basis that it is too cheap diminishes, whereas the function $h(p)$ shows that the probability that a consumer would turn it down on the basis that it is too expensive increases.

The idea that the price may convey some information about quality is not new and has been analyzed in both the economics and the marketing literature, including Leavitt (1954), Gabor and Granger (1966), Monroe (1971), Wolinksy (1983), Kirmani and Rao (2000), and their references. The basic idea is that a seller can credibly communicate the level of some unobservable quality attributes in a transaction by providing an observable signal in the form of price. This type of signaling is more likely to occur in a transaction involving experience goods, for which the buyer cannot assess the quality before purchase, and credence goods, for which buyers cannot be sure of the quality even after purchase. However, the reader should be warned that if high-quality products are more costly to produce than low-quality products, a high price may not in itself be a signal of high quality, but may only reflect a higher cost of production.

11.3.3   Micropayments and currency denomination

Many consumers are biased toward buying items priced by small currency denom-
inations. The desire for small payments gave rise to the 99¢ stores in the United
States, and more recently, to the €1 stores now widely observed in major European
cities. In addition, the widespread use of the Internet for commerce in general, and
for trade in information goods in particular, as well as the digital convergence of
text, image, audio, and video formats has opened up new ways of transacting in
"small portions" for low prices. For example, instead of buying a full-album CD
for €13, consumers can now purchase one song for 99¢ by downloading it directly
from the Internet. Clearly, this type of "unbundling" was not possible before this
change in technology, as both transportation and data storage costs made it pro-
hibitively costly to market one song at a time.

   Another common way of making the price look smaller is to split the transaction into several currencies. Passengers traveling through European airports may
recall duty-free shops that are willing to accept multiple currencies for small purchases, such as a piece of chocolate or a bottle of whiskey. Travelers generally use
these stores to "get rid" of their unused currencies. Drèze and Nunes (2004) explore how consumers evaluate transactions that involve combined-currency prices,
and prices stated in multiple, relatively new currencies. Some of these new currencies were introduced by loyalty programs and related marketing promotions such
as frequent-flier miles and credit card rewards in the form of points that consumers
accumulate and then spend as they do traditional forms of money. As a result, consumers are increasingly able to pay for goods and services such as airline travel,
hotel stays, and groceries in various combinations of traditional and new currencies. These combined-currency prices are widely visible in the form of prices such
as $39 and 16,000 miles gained from air travel or points gained via financial prod-
ucts such as brand-name credit cards. This pricing technique seems to be lowering
consumers' psychological cost and perceived price associated with a particular purchase.

11.4   Warranties

Warranties provide insurance for consumers that consumers tend to value. In fact,
it is often observed that warranties are priced higher than the expected loss they
insure against. Moreover, stores selling electronic appliances tend to offer their own
supplementary warranties in addition to the warranty supplied by the manufacturer.
Consumers who buy them end up purchasing two warranties for the same product.

   The above discussion implies that consumers tend to value warranties not only
because warranties insure against a loss associated with a defective product or an
improperly delivered service, but also because warranties provide some psychological comfort. Therefore, although the present analysis computes the maximum price

a seller can charge for a warranty on the basis of insurance only, the reader should view this warranty price as a lower bound on this price because many consumers would be willing to pay a higher price for the psychological comfort associated with having a warranty, which is not captured by the following computations. In fact, the analysis of warranties is somewhat related to the analysis of refunds (see Chapter 8) as refunds also provide some psychological comfort in the form of insurance against no-shows. However, the difference between warranties and refunds is that warranties insure against defective products and services, whereas refunds also insure against consumer no-shows (in which case consumers buy "insurance" against their own uncertainty).

The analysis of warranties in this book abstracts from two important aspects. The first is *moral hazard* behavior in which consumers are not careful in operating the product, which could lead to a higher failure rate. The effects of moral hazard can be somewhat mitigated if the warranties state that they do not cover any misuse of the product. The second aspect that is not analyzed in this short presentation is *adverse selection*, which may occur if the seller offers the warranty as an option rather than as a tied-in feature. In this case, it may happen that consumers who are likely to abuse the product will choose to buy the warranty, whereas "responsible" consumers will choose not to buy the warranty. Again, a proper warning by the seller that misuse voids the warranty would help in mitigating this effect.

The analysis below assumes that a seller offers a product for sale that may be either fully functional or totally defective, but nothing in between. The exact condition of each product is not known to the seller or to the potential buyers, but the probability that the product is fully functional is common knowledge. Let π denote the probability that the product in question is fully functional, $0 \leq \pi \leq 1$. Hence, each product is defective with probability $1 - \pi$. There are N potential customers. Consumers' maximum willingness to pay is \$$V > 0$ for a fully functional product and 0 for a defective product. Let μ denote the unit production cost of this product and ϕ the fixed cost. Finally, it must be verified that the expected benefit to a consumer exceeds the marginal production cost, as otherwise this product cannot be profitable. Formally, these parameters should satisfy $\pi V \geq \mu$.

11.4.1   Product replacement warranties

A product replacement warranty is a contract between a seller (or a manufacturer) and a buyer promising the buyer to replace a defective product with a new product. However, buyers should ask themselves what happens if the replacement product also fails, and then what happens if the replacement of the replacement product fails, and so on. For this reason, the analysis of product replacement warranties is conducted under various configurations of replacement possibilities.

Selling without any warranty

The N consumers are fully aware of the fact that the product they buy will be fully functional with probability π only. Hence, the gross expected benefit from buying the profit is πV. Thus, a consumer will buy this product as long as $\pi V - p_0 \geq 0$, hence if $p_0 \leq \pi V$, where the subscript 0 indicates a sale with no warranty. Hence, the profit made by this seller is

$$y_0 = N[p_0 - \mu] - \phi = N[\pi V - \mu] - \phi, \tag{11.1}$$

where the subscript 0 stands for no warranty.

Assuming $V = \$120$ and $\mu = \$60$, the column y_0 in Table 11.4 displays some numerical simulations showing how the profit (11.1) varies with π, which is the probability that the product will be fully functional. The column y_0 clearly shows that profit increases with π, that is, when the product is less likely to fail, simply because consumers are willing to pay a higher price for a more reliable product.

π	y_0	y_1	y_2	y_3	y_∞
0.9	$48N - \phi$	$52.80N - \phi$	$53.28N - \phi$	n/a	$53.33N - \phi$
0.8	$36N - \phi$	$43.20N - \phi$	$44.64N - \phi$	n/a	$45.00N - \phi$
0.7	$24N - \phi$	$31.20N - \phi$	$33.36N - \phi$	n/a	$34.28N - \phi$
0.6	$12N - \phi$	$16.80N - \phi$	$18.72N - \phi$	n/a	$20.00N - \phi$
0.5	$-\phi$	$-\phi$	$-\phi$	n/a	$-\phi$

Table 11.4: Profit levels under no warranty (y_0) and one-time replacement (y_1), two-time replacement (y_2), three-time replacement (y_3), and full-replacement (y_∞) warranties. *Notes*: Table assumes $V = \$120$ and $\mu = \$60$. Entries for y_3 are left for Exercise 2.

One-time replacement warranty

Under a one-time replacement warranty, the seller promises to replace a defective product only once. That is, if the replaced product is also found to be defective, the seller would not replace it.

What is the expected gross benefit to a buyer under the one-time replacement warranty? First, an operating product yields a gross benefit of V. Hence, the expected gross benefit without a warranty is πV. In addition, if the product is found to be defective (with probability $1 - \pi$), it will be replaced with a new product (which may also fail to be operative with probability $1 - \pi$). Therefore, the gross benefit from a replaced product is also πV. Note that the expected gross benefit of πV from a replaced product is conditional on having a defective product on the initial purchase, and this happens with probability $1 - \pi$. Hence, the total expected gross benefit from a product sold with a one-time replacement warranty is

$$\underbrace{\pi V}_{\text{Original purchase}} + \underbrace{(1-\pi)\pi V}_{\text{Replacement}} = (2-\pi)\pi V. \qquad (11.2)$$

What would be the expected cost to the seller (or the manufacturer), given that each unit costs μ to produce? The initial sale costs μ. But the customer will demand a replacement product with probability $(1 - \pi)$. Hence, the total expected production cost borne by the seller or the manufacturer is

$$c_1 = N[\ \underbrace{\mu}_{\text{Original}} + \underbrace{(1-\pi)\mu}_{\text{Replacement}}] - \phi = N(2-\pi)\mu - \phi, \qquad (11.3)$$

where the subscript 1 stands for one-time replacement.

Recall that (11.2) provides consumers' maximum willingness to pay for a product with a one-time replacement warranty. Thus, a monopoly seller should set the price $p_1 = (2 - \pi)\pi V$. Therefore, total profit under a one-time replacement warranty is given by

$$y_1 = Np_1 - c_1 = N(2 - \pi)(\pi V - \mu) - \phi. \qquad (11.4)$$

Column y_1 in Table 11.4 displays some numerical simulations showing how the profit (11.4) varies with π, which is the probability that the product will be fully functional. Column y_1 clearly shows that profit increases with π, that is, when the product is less likely to fail.

Two-time replacement warranty

The total expected gross benefit from a product sold with a two-time replacement warranty is

$$\underbrace{\pi V}_{\text{Original purchase}} + \underbrace{(1-\pi)\pi V}_{\text{1st replacement}} + \underbrace{(1-\pi)^2\pi V}_{\text{2nd replacement}} = (\pi^2 - 3\pi + 3)\pi V. \quad (11.5)$$

That is, the product fails twice with probability $(1 - \pi)^2$. This has to be multiplied by the expected benefit from the second and last replacement πV.

The expected production cost to the seller (or the manufacturer) is

$$c_2 = N[\ \underbrace{\mu}_{\text{Original}} + \underbrace{(1-\pi)\mu}_{\text{1st replacement}} + \underbrace{(1-\pi)^2\mu}_{\text{2nd replacement}}\ ]$$
$$= N(\pi^2 - 3\pi + 3)\mu - \phi, \quad (11.6)$$

where the subscript 2 stands for two-time replacement. The gross benefit (11.5) implies that a monopoly seller would set the price $p_2 = (\pi^2 - 3\pi + 3)\pi V$ for a product tied with a two-time replacement warranty. Therefore, total profit under a two-time replacement warranty is

$$y_2 = Np_2 - c_2 = N(\pi^2 - 3\pi + 3)(\pi V - \mu) - \phi. \tag{11.7}$$

Column y_2 in Table 11.4 displays some numerical simulations showing how the profit (11.7) varies with π, which is the probability that the product will be fully functional. Comparing columns y_1 and y_2 reveals that selling a product tied with a two-time replacement warranty is more profitable than selling one with a one-time replacement warranty (which itself is more profitable than selling without any warranty).

Full-replacement warranty

A full-replacement warranty is a commitment by the seller to replace any defective product with a newly produced one. To compute the total expected cost to the seller/manufacturer of selling a product tied with a full-replacement warranty, note that the initial sale costs μ. Then, the original product fails with probability $(1-\pi)$, in which case production cost increases by a second μ. Similarly, the original and the replacement products both fail with probability $(1-\pi)^2$, in which case the production cost increases by a third μ. Summing up yields

$$c_\infty = N\,[\ \underbrace{\mu}_{\text{Original}} + \underbrace{(1-\pi)\mu}_{\text{1st replacement}} + \underbrace{(1-\pi)^2\mu}_{\text{2nd replacement}} + \underbrace{(1-\pi)^3\mu}_{\text{3rd replacement}} + \cdots\,] - \phi$$

$$= N\frac{\mu}{\pi} - \phi, \quad (11.8)$$

where the subscript ∞ stands for an infinite product replacement warranty. Because $0 < \pi < 1$, to prove (11.8) it sufficient to show that

$$\text{LHS} \overset{\text{def}}{=} 1 + (1-\pi) + (1-\pi)^2 + (1-\pi)^3 + \cdots = \frac{1}{\pi}. \tag{11.9}$$

To establish formula (11.9), notice that it can be written as

$$\text{LHS} = 1 + (1-\pi)\overbrace{[1 + (1-\pi) + (1-\pi)^2 + (1-\pi)^3 + \cdots]}^{\text{LHS}}$$
$$= 1 + (1-\pi)\text{LHS}.$$

Therefore,

$$\text{LHS} = \frac{1}{1 - (1-\pi)} = \frac{1}{\pi},$$

which completes the proof of general formula (11.9) and hence (11.8).

Back to warranties, because under the full-replacement warranty buyers are 100% insured against defects, a monopoly seller can raise the price to consumers' maximum willingness to pay, that is, $p = V$. Therefore, the seller's total profit when supplying a full-replacement warranty is

$$y_\infty = Np_\infty - c_\infty = N\left(V - \frac{\mu}{\pi}\right) - \phi. \qquad (11.10)$$

Table 11.4 shows that the seller maximizes profit when the product is tied with a full-replacement warranty. Thus, by insuring buyers against defective products, the seller can enhance the revenue earned more than the expected increase in the cost associated with warranties that promise more replacements in case the replacement products are also found to be defective. Table 11.4 confirms that this holds true for every given product reliability probability π.

11.4.2 Money-back guarantee

A money-back guarantee is a contract between a seller (or a manufacturer) and a buyer promising the buyer a full refund for the amount paid if the purchased product is found to be defective. Unlike a product replacement warranty, once a refund is provided, the seller ends his or her obligation to the customer, whereas under a product replacement warranty, the seller's obligation may still continue through a replacement warranty on the replaced product.

The gross benefit to a consumer who buys a product tied with a money-back guarantee is composed of the net expected benefit from the product, πV, less the price, but plus the expected refund $(1 - \pi)p$, which is the probability of buying a defective product multiplied by the refunded price. Summing up these components yields

$$\underbrace{\pi V}_{\text{Expected gross benefit}} \quad - \quad p \quad + \quad \underbrace{(1 - \pi)p}_{\text{Refund}} \quad = \quad \pi(V - p). \qquad (11.11)$$

The net benefit (11.11) can be deduced directly by interpreting a money-back guarantee as the consumer paying the price conditional on getting a fully functional product. Under this interpretation, the "expected price paid" by the consumer is πp.

The expected cost per sale is composed of two parts: the unit production cost μ and the expected refund $(1 - \pi)p$ to be paid to the consumer in the event the product is found to be defective. With N consumers, expected total cost is given by

$$c_{mb} = N\left[\underbrace{\mu}_{\text{Unit cost}} + \underbrace{(1 - \pi)p}_{\text{Expected refund}} \right] - \phi, \qquad (11.12)$$

where the subscript mb stands for "money back."

In view of the consumer net benefit function (11.11), a consumer is willing to buy the product with a money-back guarantee as long as $\pi(V - p) \geq 0$, or $p \leq V$. Therefore, a monopoly seller should set the price $p = V$, so that consumers pay a price equal to their gross benefit from a fully functioning product. Hence, the expected total profit of this seller is

$$y_{mb} = Np - N[\mu + (1 - \pi)p] - \phi = NV - N[\mu + (1 - \pi)V] - \phi$$
$$= N(\pi V - \mu) - \phi. \quad (11.13)$$

Comparing (11.13) with (11.1) reveals that the profit earned from selling the product tied with a money-back guarantee is identical to the profit from selling without any warranty. Whereas under no warranty the seller must lower the price to πV to attract the consumer to buy a product that is defective with probability $1 - \pi$, in doing so the seller shifts all the risk to the consumer. In contrast, under a money-back guarantee, the seller bears the entire risk, which explains why the price can be raised to consumers' maximum willingness to pay for a nondefective product. Because the seller and the buyers are assumed to be risk neutral, the transfer of the financial risk exactly offsets the change in price, which leaves the seller with the same profit. It should be noted that this result may not hold for risk-averse sellers and buyers.

The overall recommendation that comes out of our analysis of warranties is that risk-neutral sellers facing risk-neutral buyers should avoid money-back guarantees and instead provide product replacement warranties. However, it should be noted that because money-back guarantees are often observed, they may serve some purpose for the seller after all. One possibility is that sellers in general, and large retail stores in particular, often test new products. To avoid large spending on testing the products before putting them on the shelves, retail stores can use their customer base to test their products by offering them full refunds. Clearly, in this case a money-back guarantee may end up being more profitable than a full-replacement warranty, especially for newly marketed products that have not been tested before.

11.5 Exercises

1. The transportation authority of the City of Berlin (BVG) offers a monthly pass for $f = €67$ (actual data for 2007). A one-way U-Bahn/bus ticket costs $p = €2.10$. Let q denote the monthly number of trips. Mr. Merkel always uses a monthly pass. If Mr. Merkel makes an average of $q = 30$ rides each month, can you tell whether he has a flat-rate bias?

2. Consider a three-time replacement warranty in which the seller commits to replacing a defective product with a new one, replacing the replacement if found to be defective, and replacing the replacement of the replacement, but no more. Using the analysis of Section 11.4.1 solve the following problems.

   (a) Similar to the formulation of price, cost, and profit for the two-time replacement warranty given by (11.5), (11.6), and (11.7), compute the general formulation of price, cost, and profit under the three-time replacement warranty.

(b) Fill in the missing entries for Column y_3 in Table 11.4. Explain how the profit y_3 varies with an increase in the probability that the product is fully functional π.

3. Suppose that the seller offers a "half" money-back guarantee if the product is found to be defective after it is sold to a consumer. More precisely, if the consumer pays a price of $\$p$, the seller promises to refund the consumer with $\$p/2$ in the event the product happens to be defective. Using the analysis of Section 11.4.2 solve the following problems.

(a) Similar to the formulation of price, cost, and profit for the "full" money-back guarantee given by (11.11), (11.12), and (11.13), compute the general formulation of price, cost, and profit for the half money-back guarantee.

(b) Compare the profit you just computed for the half refund guarantee, with the profit earned when the seller offers a full money-back guarantee given by (11.13). Explain the difference (if any).

Chapter 12

Instructor and Solution Manual

12.1 To the Reader

There are two main purposes for adding this extra chapter.

(a) To provide *abbreviated* solutions for all exercises appearing at the end of each chapter.

(b) To provide some suggestions to instructors and to the general reader regarding which topics to emphasize, and to comment on the general logic behind the specific ordering of the topics covered in each chapter.

I emphasize *abbreviated* solutions because I see no need to repeat all the steps developed in the body of each chapter. All I want is to provide the reader with some feedback on whether they can independently solve the kind of problems analyzed in this book. However, students should be required to submit their homework in greater detail than that given in this manual, using all the steps developed in the body of each chapter.

Some instructors may not like the fact that the solutions for all exercises are provided as this will require them to write more exercises for homework and exam purposes. However, I can assure the instructors that even if they do not assign any formal homework, students will learn much better if they can train themselves by looking at the solutions to the problems they are supposed to know how to solve. In fact, in the past, I ended up placing the solutions for all the problem sets that appear in my previous two textbooks on my Web page, www.ozshy.com, simply because I realized that students perform much better in exams after reading the proposed solutions.

As for the book itself, I tried to separate the chapters to make them as independent of each other as possible. This means that the instructor as well as the general reader can choose to teach or study whatever topics he or she wishes without having to follow a long sequence of chapters as a preparation for a certain topic. Regardless, I have tried my best to use consistent notation throughout this book (see Table 1.4).

12.2   Manual for Chapter 2: Demand and Cost

This chapter provides most of the necessary tools for characterizing consumers' demand and firms' cost structures. Some of the material replicates standard second-year microeconomics college courses. Thus, instructors should choose which topics to present (if any). I recommend that the instructor first decide which topics to cover in a course, and then, working backward, determine what background material from this chapter is needed.

Most of the analysis in this book is conducted for discrete (as opposed to continuous) demand functions. There are two reasons for this. First, computers handle mainly discrete numbers with a finite amount of data. The analysis in this book is brought under the assumption that pricing techniques should be optimized with the help of computers. Second, the author of this book thinks that discrete models (as opposed to calculus models) tend to be more intuitive than calculus-based models. For this reason, this chapter devotes a whole section to discrete demand. The other calculus-based material is presented here mainly for the sake of completeness, and for a few calculus-based topics, such as elementary monopoly pricing (Chapter 3) and peak-load pricing (Chapter 6).

Finally, students should be made aware of the fact that the justification for using continuous demand is that such demand functions may approximate the observed data on prices and the quantity demanded. For this reason, it may be beneficial to go over Sections 2.3.2 and 2.4.2, which demonstrate the use of regressions for estimating linear and constant-elasticity demand functions. The instructor may want to assign an exercise that would encourage the students to run a regression and plot the fitted curves using a computer.

Solution to Exercise 2.1. The calculation methods are explained in detail in Section 2.2. Table 12.1 provides the results of these calculations.

p	$9.5	$9.0	$8.5	$8.0	$7.5	$7.0	$6.5	$6.0
q	15	16	17	18	19	20	21	22
$e(q)$	-1.27	-1.13	-1.00	-0.89	-0.79	-0.70	-0.62	n/a
$\breve{e}(q)$	-1.19	-1.06	-0.94	-0.84	-0.74	-0.66	-0.58	n/a
$x(q)$	$142.5	$144	$144.5	$144	$142.5	$140	$136.5	$132
$\frac{\Delta x(q)}{\Delta q}$	$1.5	$0.5	$-$0.5	$-$1.5	$-$2.5	$-$3.5	$-$4.5	n/a

Table 12.1: Results for Exercise 2.1.

Solution to Exercise 2.2. (a) The estimated linear direct demand function is $q(p) = 34 - 2q$. Hence, the intercept with the horizontal axis is $\gamma = 34$, and the absolute value of the slope is $\delta = 2$.

(b) The corresponding direct demand function is $p(q) = 17 - 0.5p$.

(c) Running the linear regression $\ln q = \ln \alpha - \beta \ln p$ on a computer yields $\ln \alpha = 5.50$ and $-\beta = -1.19$. Hence, $q(p) = 244.89 \, p^{-1.19}$.

(d) The price elasticity of a constant-elasticity demand function equals the exponent of the price. Hence, $e(p) = -1.19$. Because $|e(p)| > 1$, the demand is elastic.

Solution to Exercise 2.3. (a) The inverse demand function is given by $p = 17 - 0.5 q$. The revenue function is $x(q) \overset{\text{def}}{=} p(q) q = (34 - q)q/2$.

(b) Using calculus to solve $\max_q x(q)$, the first- and second-order conditions for a maximum are

$$0 = \frac{dp(q)q}{dq} = 17 - q, \quad \text{and} \quad \frac{d^2 p(q)q}{dq^2} = -q < 0,$$

for every output level $q > 0$. Hence, $q = 17$ is the revenue-maximizing output level, and $p = 34 - 17 = \$17$ is the corresponding revenue-maximizing price.

(c) The revenue level evaluated at the revenue-maximizing output is $x(17) = (34 - 17)17/2 = \$144.5$. The price elasticity is

$$e(q) = \frac{dq(p)}{dp} \frac{p}{q} = -2 \frac{17 - 0.5q}{q} = -2 \frac{17 - 0.5 \cdot 17}{17} = -1.$$

As expected, revenue is maximized at the output level associated with a unit price elasticity.

Solution to Exercise 2.4. Horizontally adding the newly entering $N_4 = 200$ consumers to Figure 2.8 yields the new aggregate demand function drawn in Figure 12.1.

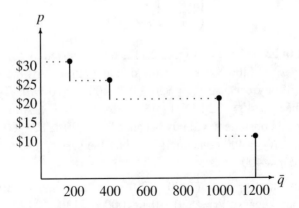

Figure 12.1: Aggregate demand for Exercise 2.4.

Solution to Exercise 2.5. (a) Inverting the demand of the third group of consumers yields $p = 10 - q_3/20$, which is drawn on the left-hand side of Figure 12.2. Horizontally adding this demand curve to Figure 2.9 yields the new aggregate demand function drawn on the right-hand side of Figure 12.2.

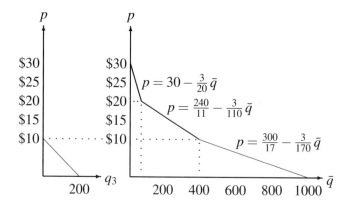

Figure 12.2: Aggregate demand for Exercise 2.5.

(b) The aggregate inverse demand given by (2.25) still holds true for all prices satisfying $p > \$10$. For prices in the range $p \le \$10$, we add $q = 200 - 20q$ to $\bar{q} = 800 - 110p/3$ given by (2.23), yielding a new aggregate demand given by

$$\bar{q}(p) = 1000 - \frac{170}{3} p, \quad \text{hence} \quad p(\bar{q}) = \frac{300}{17} - \frac{3}{170} \bar{q}.$$

Therefore,

$$p(\bar{q}) = \begin{cases} 0 & \text{if } p > \$30 \\ 30 - \frac{3}{20}\bar{q} & \text{if } \$20 < p \le \$30 \\ \frac{240}{11} - \frac{3}{110}\bar{q} & \text{if } \$10 < p \le \$20 \\ \frac{300}{17} - \frac{3}{170}\bar{q} & \text{if } 0 \le p \le \$10. \end{cases}$$

Solution to Exercise 2.6. Figure 2.11 is now replaced by Figure 12.3. We now prove why $(\bar{q}, p) = (400, \$70)$ is on the demand curve. All the $N_2 = 200$ type 1 consumers will buy because $V_1 = \$30 + 0.1 \cdot 400 = \$70 = p$. Type 2 consumers will not buy because $V_2 = \$20 + 0.1 \cdot 400 = \$60 < \$70 = p$. All the $N_3 = 200$ (now modified) type 3 consumers will buy because $V_3 = \$20 + 0.2 \cdot 400 = \$100 > \$70 = p$. Hence, $N_1 + N_3 = 400$ consumers will buy the service under the self-fulfilling expectation of $\bar{q} = 400$.

Next, we prove that $(\bar{q}, p) = (1000, \$120)$ is on the demand curve. Type 1 consumers will buy because $V_1 = \$30 + 0.1 \cdot 1000 = \$130 > \$120 = p$. Type 2 consumers will buy because $V_2 = \$20 + 0.1 \cdot 1000 = \$120 = p$. Finally, type 3 consumers will buy because $V_3 = \$10 + 0.2 \cdot 1000 = \$210 > \$120 = p$.

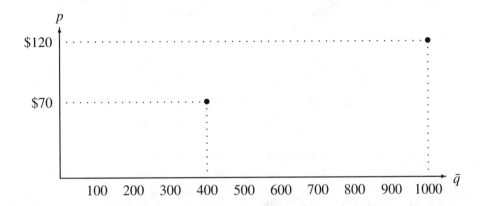

Figure 12.3: Aggregate demand for Exercise 2.6.

Solution to Exercise 2.7. (a) Running the regression $q_A = \alpha_A - \beta_A p_A + \gamma_B p_B$ yields $\alpha_A = 25$, $-\beta_A = -5$, and $\gamma_B = 5$.

(b) Running the linear regression (2.35) yields $\ln \alpha_A = 2.928$, hence $\alpha_A = 18.692$, $-\beta_A = -0.375$, and $\gamma_A = 0.596$.

(c) The results are given in Table 12.2.

Observation No.	1	2	3	4	5
q_A (quantity of A)	20	30	40	50	60
p_A (price of A)	$5	$4	$2	$3	$1
p_B (price of B)	$5	$4	$6	$7	$8
$e(q_A, p_B)$	−2.50	0.66	1.50	1.40	1.00
$\breve{e}(q_A, p_B)$	−1.80	0.71	1.44	1.36	1.00
Linear fitting (2.29)	25.00	25.00	45.00	45.00	60.00
Exponential fitting (2.34)	26.64	25.36	41.89	39.43	64.50

Table 12.2: Results for Exercise 2.7.

Solution to Exercise 2.8. See Table 12.3.

Solution to Exercise 2.9. (a) Given a consumption level $q = 40$, $p = 120 - 2 \cdot 40 = \$40$. Using the same argument leading to (2.39), $gcs(40) = (120 + 40)(40 - 0)/2 = \$3200$.

(b) Given that $q = 50$, $p = 120 - 2 \cdot 50 = \$20$. Using the same argument leading to (2.40), $\Delta gcs(40, 50) = (20 + 40)(50 - 40)/2 = \$300$.

(c) Given that $q = 40$, $p = 120 - 2 \cdot 40 = \$40$. Then, $ncs(40) = gcs(40) - pq - f = 3200 - 40 \cdot 40 - 600 = \$1000$.

p	$40	$30	$20	$10	$0
q	0	10	20	40	70
pq	$0	$300	$400	$400	$0
Δgcs	n/a	$350	$250	$300	$150
gcs	$0	$350	$600	$900	$1050
ncs	$0	$50	$200	$500	$1050

Table 12.3: Results for Exercise 2.8.

Solution to Exercise 2.10. Simple computation reveals that $c_1(q) \leq c_2(2)$ for all output levels satisfying $q \geq 150$. For this output range, the entire production should be allocated to plant 1. Otherwise, if $q < 150$ units, the entire production should be allocated to plant 2.

12.3 Manual for Chapter 3: Basic Pricing Techniques

The single-seller material greatly resembles the material taught in an intermediate microeconomics class. The instructor must confirm that all students are able to solve simple monopoly problems before proceeding to later chapters. The competition part should be somewhat new to most readers who have not taken a course in industrial organization. Instructors who wish to teach a yield management course for a single seller only can simply skip the sections on pricing under competition.

The major part of this chapter (and this book) is devoted to a single seller. It is important to stress to the students the difference between pricing when the seller is able to price discriminate and pricing when the seller cannot segment the market and therefore must charge a uniform price in all markets. Students should understand, by a revealed preference argument, that the ability to price discriminate can only be profit-enhancing because the seller can always choose to charge the same price in all markets, thereby duplicating the profit level when price discrimination is not feasible. However, if the seller selects different prices for the different markets, it means that the seller earns a higher profit compared with the profit level under a uniform price.

This chapter also analyzes some commonly practiced pricing techniques that are generally omitted from standard economics textbooks for the simple reason that these techniques do not always generate maximum profits. Just to mention a few, Section 3.5.1 introduces some breakeven formulas whereas Section 3.5.2 briefly analyzes cost-plus pricing methods.

Perhaps the main novelty of this chapter is the extension of the simple treatment given in most microeconomics textbooks to take into consideration market-specific fixed costs (in addition to the familiar production fixed cost that is commonly assumed). This brings our analysis closer to reality because managers often face decisions on whether to penetrate into new markets and whether to continue serving existing markets. Market-specific fixed costs make our analysis somewhat more tedious in the sense that the procedure for choosing which markets to serve should also include an algorithm by which the firm must consider all possible 2^M selections of subsets of markets out of M available markets. Algorithm 3.2 demonstrates how computers can generate these selections. In the absence of market-specific costs, one can build simpler procedures for pricing in different markets that are based on gradually lowering the price, thereby gradually increasing the number of served markets each time the price falls below the relevant demand intercept. However, as mentioned above, we follow the more general method throughout this chapter by introducing market-specific fixed costs.

Similar to the analysis of Chapter 2, we distinguish between discrete demand functions and continuous (linear and constant-elasticity) demand functions. Readers with no knowledge of calculus can still study the analysis of continuous demand functions by simply taking the formulas for the marginal revenue functions as given. Students with an elementary calculus background can also learn how to derive these formulas. Finally, instructors who plan to skip Chapter 2 can combine the teaching of this chapter with the corresponding demand function analyzed in Chapter 2. In other words, instructors can always provide the background on demand from the relevant section in Chapter 2 before computing the profit-maximizing price.

Solution to Exercise 3.1. Table 12.4 displays the revenue and profit levels associated with each price–quantity pair. The profit-maximizing price is $p = \$50$, yielding a profit of $y = \$60$. The revenue-maximizing price is $p = \$40$, yielding a revenue of $x = \$160$.

p	70	60	**50**	**40**	30	20	10
$q(p)$	1	2	3	4	5	6	7
$x(p) = pq$	70	120	150	**160**	150	120	70
$y(p) = x - \mu q - \phi$	20	50	**60**	50	20	−30	−100

Table 12.4: Results for Exercise 3.1.

Solution to Exercise 3.2. (a) The marginal revenue function is derived by solving $\partial x / \partial q = 100 - q$.

(b) Solving $q = 100 - q = 20$ yields the candidate profit-maximizing output level of $q = 80$ units.

(c) The candidate profit-maximizing price is $p = 100 - 0.5q = \$60$.

(d) The resulting profit level is $y = (p - \mu)q - \phi = \$3200 - \phi$. Hence, the seller makes strictly positive profit as long as $\phi < \$3200$.

Solution to Exercise 3.3. (a) Using the specification (3.10), the marginal revenue function is $p(1 - 1/2) = p/2$.

(b) Solving $p/2 = 30$ yields the candidate profit-maximizing price of $p = \$60$ units.

(c) The candidate profit-maximizing quantity produced is $q = 3600p^{-2} = 1$ unit.

(d) The resulting profit level is $y = (p - \mu)q - \phi = (60 - 30)1 - \phi$. Hence, the seller makes strictly positive profit as long as $\phi < \$30$.

Solution to Exercise 3.4. (a) Repeating the above computations for $q(p) = 7200p^{-2}$ should result in $p = \$60$, $q = 2$, and $y = \$120 - f$.

(b) The profit-maximizing price does not vary with an upward shift in the demand curve because under the constant-elasticity demand function, the price is a function of the elasticity parameter β and the marginal cost μ only. See equation (3.10).

(c) For price elasticity $e = -3$, $p = \$45$. For price elasticity $e = -4$, $p = \$40$. Thus, as expected, price declines as the demand becomes more elastic.

Solution to Exercise 3.5. Table 12.5 clearly reveals that the seller is indifferent between operating in market 2 only and operating in markets 1 and 2. In both cases, the profit-maximizing price is $p = \$20$ and the profit earned is $y = \$3000$.

Markets	1	2	3	1&2	1&3	2&3	1&2&3
Price p	30	20	10	20	10	10	10
Quantity q	200	600	200	800	400	800	1000
$(p - \mu)q$	4000	6000	0	8000	0	0	0
Fixed costs	4000	3000	3000	5000	5000	4000	7000
Profit y	0	3000	-3000	3000	-5000	-4000	-6000

Table 12.5: Results for Exercise 3.5.

Solution to Exercise 3.6. Step I need not be repeated because there is no change in demand. In Step II, we solve $(700 - 2q)/12 = \$30$ obtains $q_{1,2} = 170$ units of output. Substituting into the aggregate demand (3.16) to obtain $p_{1,2} = 265/6 \approx \$44.16$, and $y_{1,2} = 1225/3 \approx \$408.33$.

We now solve for the profit-maximizing price assuming that only market 1 is served by solving $100 - q_1 = 30$ to obtain $q_1 = 70$ units. Substituting into (3.15) yields $p_1 = \$65$. The resulting profit is $y_1 = (p_1 - \mu)q_1 - \phi_1 - \phi = \$950$.

We now solve for the profit-maximizing price assuming that only market 2 is served by solving $50 - 0.2q_2 = 30$ to obtain $q_2 = 100$ units. Substituting into (3.15) yields $p_2 = \$40$. The resulting profit is $y_2 = (p_2 - \mu)q_2 - \phi_2 - \phi = \$400$.

Finally, we compare and find out that $y_1 = \$950 > y_{1,2} = \$408.33 > y_2 = \$400$. Therefore, the profit-maximizing price is $p_1 = \$65$, under which only market 1 is served.

Solution to Exercise 3.7. For market 1, solving $\dfrac{dx(q_1)}{dq_1} = 100 - 2q_1 = 2 = \mu$ yields $q_1 = 49$. Hence, the candidate price for market 1 is $p_1 = 100 - q_1 = \$51$. The resulting profit from market 1 is $y_1 = (51 - 2)49 - 1200 = \$1201 > 0$.

For market 2, solving $\dfrac{dx(q_2)}{dq_2} = 50 - q_2 = 2 = \mu$ yields $q_2 = 48$. Hence, the candidate price for market 2 is $p_2 = 50 - 0.5q_2 = \$26$. The resulting profit from market 2 is $y_2 = (26 - 2)48 - 1200 = -\$48 < 0$. Therefore, market 2 should not be served. Summing up, only market 1 should be served. Total profit is then given by $y = (51 - 2)49 - 1200 - 1200 = \$1 > 0$.

Solution to Exercise 3.8. We solve

$$p_1\left(1 + \frac{1}{-2}\right) = 3, \quad \text{hence} \quad p_1 = \$6 \quad \text{and} \quad q_1 = 100;$$

$$p_2\left(1 + \frac{1}{-4}\right) = 3, \quad \text{hence} \quad p_2 = \$4 \quad \text{and} \quad q_2 = \frac{225}{16}.$$

The resulting profit from market 1 is $y_1 = (6 - 3)100 - 100 = \$200 > 0$. The resulting profit from market 2 is $y_2 = (4 - 3)(225/16) - 15 < 0$. Hence, market 2 should be excluded.

Summing up, only market 1 should be served. Total profit is then given by $y = (6 - 3)100 - 100 - 100 = \$100 > 0$.

Solution to Exercise 3.9. (a) Under unlimited capacity, solving $120 - 2 \cdot 0.25q_1 = 10$ yields $q_1 = 220$. Solving $240 - 2 \cdot 0.5q_2 = 10$ yields $q_2 = 230$. We still have to check whether it is indeed profitable to serve both markets when capacity is unlimited: $p_1 = 120 - 0.25q_1 = \$65$, $p_2 = 240 - 0.5q_2 = \$125$. Hence, $y_1 = (65 - 10)220 - 10,000 = \$2100 > 0$, and $y_2 = (125 - 10)230 - 10,000 = \$16,450 > 0$. In addition, $y = y_1 + y_2 - \phi = \$8550 > 0$.

(b) We first must check whether capacity is binding. In part (a), we found that the quantity produced under unlimited capacity is $\bar{q} = 220 + 230 = 450 > 240 = K$. Thus, we proceed by assuming that capacity will be binding.

Under capacity constraint of $K = 240$, solving $120 - 20.25q_1 = 240 - 20.5q_2$ and $q_1 + q_2 = K = 240$ yields $q_1 = 80$ and $q_2 = 260$. Therefore, $p_1 = 120 - 0.25q_1 = \$100$ and $p_2 = 240 - 0.5q_2 = \$160$. The corresponding profit in market 1 is $y_1 = (100 - 10)80 - 10,000 < 0$. Hence, market 1 should be excluded.

Assigning all the capacity to market 2 yields $q_2 = 240$, $p_1 = 240 - 0.5240 = \$120$. Hence, $y_2 = (120 - 10)240 - 10,000 = \$16,400$. Therefore, total profit is given by $y = y_2 - \phi = \$6400$.

Solution to Exercise 3.10. (a) Undercutting firm 2 only is more profitable than no undercutting if $(40 - \delta - 10)(100 + 200) > (20 + \delta - 10)100$, hence if $\delta < \$20$.

(b) Undercutting firms 2 and 3 is more profitable than undercutting firm 2 only if $(20 - \delta - 10)(100 + 200 + 300) > (40 - \delta - 10)(100 + 200)$, hence $\delta < -\$10$. But because δ cannot be a negative number, we can conclude that undercutting both firms is not profitable.

(c) Undercutting firms 2 and 3 is more profitable than not undercutting any firm if $(20 - \delta - 10)(100 + 200 + 300) > (20 + \delta - 10)100$, hence if $\delta < 50/7 \approx \$7.14$.

(d) Part (b) has shown that undercutting both firms yields lower profit than undercutting firm 2 only. Therefore, part (a) implies that firm 1 should undercut firm 2 only if $\delta < \$20$, and not undercut any firm if $\delta \geq \$20$.

Solution to Exercise 3.11. Table 12.6 displays the computation results using the breakeven formulas.

p_1	70	60	55	40	30	20	10
q_1	10	20	30	40	50	60	70
q^b	2	2.5	3.33	5	10	$+\infty$	n/a
Δq	1.11	2.86	6	13.33	50	n/a	n/a
$\frac{\Delta q}{q_1} \cdot 100$	1.11%	14.28%	20%	33.33%	100%	n/a	n/a

Table 12.6: Results for Exercise 3.11.

Solution to Exercise 3.12. (a) We solve $f(120 - p_1) + f(60 - p_2) = f(120 - 30 - f) + f(60 - 30 - f) = 550$, yielding $f = \$5$. Hence, $p_1 = p_2 = \$35$. Substituting into the direct demand functions yields $q_1 = 120 - 35 = 85$ and $q_2 = 60 - 35 = 25$. Therefore, $\bar{q} = q_1 + q_2 = 110$.

(b) The breakeven constraint is now given by $f_1(120 - 30 - f_1) + f(60 - 30 - f_2) = 550$, which can be solved to obtain $f_1 = 45 - \sqrt{1475 + 30f_2 - (f_2)^2}$. Let us experiment by reducing the fee in market 2 to $f_2 = \$2$. Then, $f_1 = 45 - \sqrt{1531} \approx \$5.87$. Therefore, prices are given by $p_1 = \$35.87$ and $p_2 = \$32$. Hence, the quantities demanded are $q_1 = 120 - 35.87 \approx 84.13$ and $q_2 = 60 - 32 = 28$. Thus, total output is $\bar{q} = 112.13 > 110$, which is the output level under a uniform fee.

Solution to Exercise 3.13. The necessary conditions given by (3.77) imply that

$$\frac{\dfrac{80 - 2q_1 - 0}{80 - 2q_1}}{\dfrac{40 - 0.5q_2 - 0}{40 - 0.5q_2}} = \frac{1 - \dfrac{40}{0.5q_2}}{1 - \dfrac{80}{2q_1}} \quad \text{and}$$

$$(p_1 - 0)q_1 + (p_2 - 0)q_2 = [(80 - 2q_1)]q_1 + \left[40 - \frac{q_2}{2}\right]q_2 = 1600.$$

The first condition implies that $q_1 = q_2/2$. Substituting for q_1 into the second condition yields $q_2^R = 40$, and hence $q_1^R = 20$. Substituting into the demand functions (3.76) yields the Ramsey prices $p_1^R = \$40$ and $p_1^R = \$20$. The demand elasticities are therefore

$$e_1(20) = 1 - \frac{\alpha_1}{\beta_1 \cdot 20} = -1 \quad \text{and} \quad e_2(40) = 1 - \frac{\alpha_2}{\beta_2 \cdot 40} = -1.$$

12.4 Manual for Chapter 4: Bundling and Tying

This chapter is divided into two main sections: bundling and tying. For our purposes, *bundling* refers to the sale of a package containing at least two units of identical products or services. *Tying* refers to the sale of packages containing at least two different products or services. For the entire chapter, it is assumed that each consumer buys at most one unit of each good. The topics of this chapter are presented according to an increased level of difficulty. The bundling analysis starts with a single consumer type with one consumer under pure bundling and then increases the number of consumers; later, the number of consumer types is also increased. The more complicated bundling technique involving multi-package bundling concludes the analysis of bundling. Instructors who wish only to demonstrate the logic behind the profit gains from bundling can confine their teaching to Section 4.1.1, which analyzes a single consumer only. Instructors are urged to review the concept of *gross consumer surplus* analyzed in Section 2.8 before teaching the bundling section.

The analysis of tying in Section 4.2 is conducted independently of the analysis of bundling. Thus, instructors can skip Section 4.1 if they wish to concentrate on teaching about tying only. For a short presentation of tying, teaching Section 4.1.1 would be sufficient for explaining the logic behind tying. The role of negatively correlated preferences should be emphasized to students. For a more complete presentation of tying, the instructor can add Section 4.2.3, which analyzes mixed tying. Both sections are presented according to an increased level of difficulty, so beginning students can learn from numerical examples only. Multi-package tying, presented in Section 4.2.4, can be skipped in a one-semester course on pricing.

p	40¢	30¢	20¢	10¢	0¢
q	0	2	3	6	7
$p^b(q)$	0¢	70¢	95¢	140¢	145¢
μq	0¢	20¢	30¢	60¢	70¢
$p^b(q) - \mu q$	0¢	50¢	65¢	80¢	75¢
$y^b(q)$	0¢	30¢	45¢	60¢	55¢
pq	0¢	60¢	60¢	60¢	0¢
$(p - \mu)q$	0¢	40¢	30¢	0¢	−70¢
y	−20¢	20¢	10¢	−20¢	−90¢

Table 12.7: Results for Exercise 4.1.

Solution to Exercise 4.1. (a) See Table 12.7. Clearly, the profit-maximizing bundle contains $q = 6$ units and is sold for the price of $p^b(6) = 140$¢.

(b) See Table 12.7. Clearly, the profit-maximizing per-unit price is $p = 30$¢, where $q = 2$ units are sold.

(c) With $N = 150$ consumers and a fixed cost of $\phi = 5000$¢, the profit from selling the bundle described in part (a) is $N[p^b(6) - 6\mu] - \phi = 150[140 - 10 \cdot 6] - 5000 = 7000$¢. With no bundling, selling each unit separately for the price $p = 30$¢ derived in part (b) yields a total profit of $N(p - \mu)q - \phi = 150(30 - 10)2 - 5000 = 1000$¢.

Solution to Exercise 4.2. (a) The figure is not drawn here. The most profitable bundle is found by equating the marginal cost to the inverse demand so that $\mu = 40 = 120 - q/2$, yielding a bundle of $q = 160$ units. Substituting $\alpha = 120$, $\beta = 0.5$, and $q = 160$ into the formula for computing gross consumer surplus given by (4.3) yields the profit-maximizing bundle price $p^b(160) = \$12,800$.

(b) The total profit generated by selling the above bundle to $N = 5$ consumers is given by

$$y^b = N(p^b - \mu q) - \phi = 5(12,800 - 40 \cdot 160) - 30,000 = \$2000.$$

Solution to Exercise 4.3. (a) Substituting $\alpha_1 = 8$, $\beta_1 = 2$, $\alpha_2 = 4$, and $\beta_2 = 1$ into (4.3) yields $gcs_1(q) = q(8 - q)$ and $gcs_1(q) = q(8 - q)/2$.

(b) See Table 12.8.

(c) Table 12.8 indicates that the profit-maximizing bundle should contain $q = 3$ units and should be priced at $p^b(3) = gcs_1(3) = 15$¢. Because $gcs_2(3) < 15$¢, only the $N_1 = 2$ consumers buy this bundle.

q (Bundle Size)	1	2	3	4
$gcs_1(q)$	7.0¢	12¢	**15.0¢**	16¢
$y_1(q)$	10.0¢	16¢	**18.0¢**	16¢
$gcs_2(q)$	3.5¢	6¢	7.5¢	8¢
$y_2(q)$	9.0¢	12¢	9.0¢	0¢
$\min\{gcs_1,gcs_2\}$	3.5¢	6¢	7.5¢	8¢
$y_{1,2}(q)$	12.0¢	16¢	12.0¢	0¢
$\max\{y_1,y_2,y_{1,2}\}$	12.0¢	16¢	**18.0¢**	16¢

Table 12.8: Results for Exercise 4.3(b).

Solution to Exercise 4.4. Inspecting equation (4.14) reveals that consumer 1 will continue to prefer bundle A over bundle B, even if the price of A is raised from $p_A = \$13$ to $p_A = \$14$. Therefore, suppose the seller offers two bundles:

Bundle $\langle q_A, p_A \rangle = \langle 3, \$14 \rangle$: With $q_A = 3$ units and priced at $p_A = \$14$.

Bundle $\langle q_B, p_B \rangle = \langle 6, \$15 \rangle$: With $q_B = 6$ units and priced at $p_B = \$15$.

Then, the market is again segmented because

$$ncs_1(3, \$14) = \$15 - \$14 \quad \geq \quad \$16 - \$15 = ncs_1(6, \$15)$$

$$\text{and}$$

$$ncs_2(6, \$15) = \$15 - \$15 \quad \geq \quad \$9.75 - \$13 = ncs_2(3, \$13).$$

The profits from a type 1 and a type 2 consumer (not including fixed costs) are $y_1 = p_A^b - 3\mu = 14 - 3 \cdot 2 = \$8$ and $y_2 = p_B^b - 6\mu = 15 - 6 \cdot 2 = \$3$. With $N_1 = N_2 = 1$ consumer of each type, total profit is given by

$$y^b(\langle 3, \$14 \rangle, \langle 6, \$15 \rangle) = y_1 + y_2 - \phi = \$11 - \phi > \$10 - \phi.$$

Solution to Exercise 4.5. (a) With no tying, pricing R at a high rate so that only type 1 guests book a room, $p_R = \$100$ yields a profit of $y_R = (100 - 40)200 = \$12,000$. Reducing the price so that both types book a room, $p_R = \$60$ yields a profit of $y_R = (60 - 40)1000 = \$20,000$. Therefore, $p_R = \$60$ is the profit-maximizing rate.

Setting a high breakfast price so that only type 2 consumers buy breakfast, $p_B = \$10$, yields a profit of $y_B = (10 - 2)800 = \$6400$. Reducing the price so that both types buy, $p_B = \$5$, yields a profit of $y_B = (5 - 2)1000 = \$3000$. Therefore, $p_B = \$10$ is the profit-maximizing breakfast price.

Adding the profit made from selling these two services separately yields a profit of $y^{NT} = 20,000 + 6400 = \$26,400$.

(b) Selling a room and breakfast in one package for a high price of $p_{RB} = 100+5 = \$105$ results in sales to type 1 consumers only. Hence, $y^{PT} = (105 - 40 - 2)200 = \$12,600$. Reducing the package price to $p_{RB} = 60 + 10 = \$70$ yields $y^{PT} = (70 - 40 - 2)1000 = \$28,000 > \$26,400 = y^{NT}$. Therefore, tying is profitable for this hotel.

(c) Under no tying, setting $p_R = \$100$ yields $y_R = (100 - 40)200 = \$12,000$. Setting $p_R = \$60$ yields $y_R = (60 - 40)400 = \$8000$. Setting $p_B = \$10$ yields $y_B = (10 - 2)200 = \$1600$. Setting $p_B = \$5$ yields $y_B = (5 - 2)400 = \$1200$. Altogether, the maximum profit that can be earned from selling the two services separately is $y^{NT} = 12,000 + 1600 = \$13,600$.

(d) With tying, setting $p_{RB} = \$105$, thereby selling to type 1 only, yields $y^{PT} = (105 - 40 - 2)200 = \$12,600$. Setting $p_{RB} = \$70$, thereby selling to both types, yields $y^{PT} = (70 - 40 - 2)400 = \$11,200$. Therefore, tying is not profitable in this example.

Solution to Exercise 4.6. (a) See Solution 4.5(a) for the computations of p_R, p_B, y_R, y_B, and y^{NT}. Table 4.12 clearly shows that the gym should be priced at $p_G = \$10$, yielding a profit of $y_G = \$10,000$. Altogether, total profit with no tying is $y^{NT} = 20,000 + 6400 + 10,000 = \$36,400$.

(b) Setting a high price for the package, $p_{RBG} = \$115$, attracts only 200 customers, hence yields a profit of $y^{PT} = (115 - 42)200 = \$14,600$. Setting a low price, $p_{RBG} = \$80$, attracts all 1000 customers, hence yields a profit of $y^{PT} = (80 - 42)1000 = \$38,000 > y^{NT}$. Therefore, pure tying is more profitable than no tying.

Solution to Exercise 4.7. (a) Setting a low price for a room, $p_R = \$40$, attracts 200 customers, thereby yielding a profit of $y_R = (40 - 10)200 = \$6000$. Raising the price to $p_R = \$50$ reduces the number of customers to 100, thereby yielding a profit of $y_R = (50 - 10)100 = \$4000$. Therefore, $p_R = \$40$, is the profit-maximizing price for a room. By symmetry, $p_D = \$40$ yielding $y_R = (40 - 10)200 = \$6000$ is also the profit-maximizing price for a dinner. Altogether, the maximum profit under no tying is $y^{NT} = 6000 + 6000 = \$12,000$.

(b) Setting a low price for the package, $p_{RD} = \$50$, attracts 300 customers, thereby yielding a profit of $y^{PT} = (50 - 20)300 = \$9000$. Raising the price to $p_{RD} = \$80$ reduces the number of customers to 100, thereby yielding a profit of $y^{PT} = (80 - 20)100 = \$6,000$. Therefore, $p_{RD} = \$50$ is the profit-maximizing package price. However, observe that $y^{PT} = \$9000 < \$12,000 = y^{NT}$, meaning that pure tying is less profitable than no tying.

(c) Consider the following offers: a package that includes a hotel room and dinner priced at $p_{RD} = \$80$, a room that rents for $p_R = \$50$, and dinner for $p_D = \$50$. Inspecting Table 4.13 reveals that type 2 consumers are better off buying the package, whereas type 1 consumers are better off renting a hotel room only and type 3 consumers are better off buying dinner only. Hence, the total profit under mixed tying is $y^{MT} = (50-10)100 + (50-10)100 + (80-10-10)100 = \$14,000 > y^{NT} > y^{PT}$. Yes, mixed tying is more profitable than pure tying and no tying for the PARADISE Hotel.

Solution to Exercise 4.8. (a) Setting a high price for CNN, $p_C = \$11$, results in 200 subscribers, hence a profit of $y_C = (11-1)200 = \$2000$. Setting a low price, $p_C = \$2$, results in 400 subscribers, hence a profit of $y_C = (2-1)400 = \$400$. Therefore, $p_C = \$11$ is profit maximizing. Similarly, BBC subscriptions should also be sold for $p_B = \$11$.

Setting a high price for HIS, $p_H = \$6$, results in 200 subscribers, hence a profit of $y_H = (6-1)200 = \$1000$. Setting a low price, $p_H = \$3$, results in 400 subscribers, hence a profit of $y_H = (3-1)400 = \$800$. Therefore, $p_H = \$6$ is the profit-maximizing price. Altogether, the total profit under no tying is $y^{NT} = 2000 + 2000 + 1000 = \$5000$.

(b) Setting a high package price, $p_{CBH} = \$19$, results in 200 subscribers, hence a profit of $y^{PT}(19) = (19-3)200 = \$3200$. Setting a low price, $p_{CBH} = \$16$, results in 400 subscribers, hence a profit of $y^{PT}(16) = (16-3)400 = \$5200$. Therefore, $p_{CBH} = \$16$ is the profit-maximizing price.

(c) Suppose now that the cable TV operator makes the following offer: Viewers can subscribe to a "news" package containing CNN and BBC for a price of $p_{CB} = \$13$ and the HIS(tory) channel for $p_H = \$6$. Inspecting Table 4.14 reveals that all 400 consumers will subscribe to the "news" package whereas only 200 will subscribe to the HIS(tory) channel. Hence, total profit under mixed tying is

$$y^{MT} = (13-2)400 + (6-1)200 = \$5400 > y^{PT} = \$5200 > y^{NT} = \$5000.$$

Therefore, for the industry displayed in Table 4.14, multi-package tying is more profitable than either pure tying or no tying.

12.5 Manual for Chapter 5: Multipart Tariff

The multipart tariff serves as a very useful and widely used pricing tool that can enhance sellers' profit far beyond the maximum profit that can be earned by simple monopoly pricing. This tool significantly increases the amount of surplus extracted from consumers. The instructor may want to emphasize the connection between pure bundling studied in Chapter 4 and two-part tariffs analyzed in Section 5.1 when all consumers are of the same type (all have identical demand functions). In fact, because the same profit is obtained under these two pricing strategies, the two-part tariff variables, the fixed entry fee f, and the per-unit usage price p can be computed very easily by first computing the profit-maximizing price of a bundle under pure bundling, p^b, and then finding the fixed fee under a two-part tariff from $f^{2p} = gcs(q^b) - p(q^b)q^b$, where q^b is the bundle's size and $p(q^b)$ is the corresponding price obtained directly from the inverse-demand function. However, it should be emphasized that this connection tends to break when we introduce more than one type of consumer.

Before discussing two-part tariffs, instructors are urged to review the concept of *gross consumer surplus* analyzed in Section 2.8. For a very short demonstration of the logic behind multipart tariffs, the instructor can concentrate on the analysis of two-part tariffs under linear demand functions that appears at the beginning of Section 5.1. The discrete demand case following the linear demand analysis better captures how computers can be used to figure out the most profitable two-part tariff.

Section 5.3 extends the analysis to the offering of more than one two-part tariff. Instructors should emphasize that the major difficulty in implementing a menu of several two-part tariffs stems from the incentive compatibility constraint, which means that the tariffs should be structured taking into consideration that different types of consumers will prefer different tariffs on the menu that is being offered. In some cases, this constraint prevents sellers from offering more than one two-part tariff. Again, the key assumption here is that the seller cannot price discriminate among consumers in the sense that the seller cannot prevent consumers from choosing a specific tariff on the menu. In contrast, if the seller is able to price discriminate among consumer types – for example, by implementing student or senior citizen discounts – the analysis becomes much simpler because it collapses into separate problems of fitting a specifically designed tariff plan to each consumer group.

The purpose of Section 5.4 is to demonstrate that a multipart tariff may not be needed at all, as in most cases, one can design a menu of two-part tariffs that would achieve the same outcome as the multipart tariff. Finally, Section 5.5 is presented here for the sake of completeness only so students can compare the tariff structure set by a regulated public utility and the tariff set by a profit-maximizing monopoly. The point to be emphasized is that when there is only one consumer type, both a regulator and a monopolist set the marginal price to p^{2p} to equal marginal cost μ. The difference between the tariffs is that a monopoly raises the fixed fee to extract the entire consumer surplus, whereas the regulator uses the fixed fee to divide the public utility's fixed cost among the consumers.

Solution to Exercise 5.1. (a) The figure is not drawn here. The most profitable per-unit usage price is found by equating the marginal cost to the inverse demand so that $p^{2p} = \mu = \$40$. At this price, solving $40 = 120 - q/2$ yields $q = 160$ units. Substituting $\alpha = 120$, $\beta = 0.5$, and $q = 160$ into the formula for computing gross consumer surplus given by (5.2) yields $gcs(160) = \$12,800$. Lastly, the fixed fee is found from $f^{2p} = 12,800 - 40 \cdot 160 = \$6400$.

(b) The total profit generated by selling the above bundle to $N = 5$ consumers is given by

$$y^{2p} = N[f + (p - \mu)q] - \phi = 5[6400 - (40 - 40)160] - 30,000 = \$2000.$$

Solution to Exercise 5.2. See Table 12.9. Clearly, the profit-maximizing two-part tariff is $f^{2p} = 80\cent$ and $p^{2p} = 10\cent$. The consumer buys $q = 6$ units.

p	40¢	30¢	20¢	**10¢**	0¢
q	0	2	3	6	7
$gcs(q)$	0¢	70¢	95¢	140¢	145¢
pq	0¢	60¢	60¢	60¢	0¢
$f = gcs(q) - pq$	0¢	10¢	35¢	**80¢**	145¢
μq	0¢	20¢	30¢	60¢	70¢
$y^{2p}(q)$	0¢	30¢	45¢	**60¢**	55¢

Table 12.9: Results for Exercise 5.2.

Solution to Exercise 5.3. (a) See Table 12.10.

p	$0	$1	$2
q_1	0.50	0.25	0
$gcs_1(q)$	$0.50	$0.38	$0
f_1	$0.50	$0.13	$0
$y_1(f_1, p)$	$0.50	$0.38	$0
q_2	2.00	0.00	0
$gcs_2(q)$	$1.00	$0.00	$0
f_2	$1.00	$0.00	$0
$y_2(f_2, p)$	$1.00	$0.00	$0
$\min\{f_1, f_2\}$	$0.50	$0.00	$0
$y_{1,2}(q)$	$1.00	$0.25	$0
$\max\{y_1, y_2, y_{1,2}\}$	$1.00	$0.38	$0

Table 12.10: Results for Exercise 5.3.

(b) Table 12.10 clearly indicates that the maximum obtainable profit is $1.00 when the usage price is set to $p^{2p} = \$0$. If the fixed fee is set to $f^{2p} = \min\{f_1, f_2\} = \$0.50$, both consumers buy the service and the firm earns a profit of $y = 2 \cdot f = 2 \cdot \$0.50 = \$1.00$. Alternatively, the firm can raise the fixed fee to $f^{2p} = \max\{f_1, f_2\} = \$1.00$, thereby excluding consumer 1 and earning a profit of $y = f_1 = \$1.00$ from selling to consumer 2 only.

(c) Consider now the following menu of two-part tariffs:

Plan A: Two-part tariff $\langle f_A, p_A \rangle = \langle \$0.13, \$1 \rangle$.

Plan B: Two-part tariff $\langle f_B, p_B \rangle = \langle \$1, \$0 \rangle$.

By Table 12.10, consumer 1 gains $ncs_1(0.25) = \$0.38 - \$0.13 - \$1 \cdot 0.25 \geq 0$ from adopting plan A. If the same consumer adopts plan B, she gains $ncs_1(0.5) = \$0.50 - \$1 - \$0 \cdot 0.5 < 0$. In contrast, consumer 2 gains $ncs_2(2) = \$1 - \$1 - \$0 \cdot 2 \geq 0$ under plan B and $ncs_2(0) = \$0 - \$0.13 - \$1 \cdot 0 \leq 0$ under plan A.

Solution to Exercise 5.4. (a) The figure is not drawn here. (b) All four tariff plans generate the same revenue at a consumption level of $q = 10$ units; that is, $10 + 5 \cdot 10 = 20 + 4 \cdot 10 = 30 + 3 \cdot 10 = 40 + 2 \cdot 10 = \$60$. Therefore, a cost-minimizing consumer will choose

$$f + pq = \begin{cases} 10 + 5q & \text{for consumption levels } q \leq 10 \\ 40 + 2q & \text{for consumption levels } q > 10. \end{cases}$$

Hence, tariff plans B and C will never be used.

(c) The monotone crossing conditions (5.25) are violated because

$$\frac{f_B - f_A}{p_A - p_B} = \frac{f_C - f_B}{p_B - p_C} = \frac{f_D - f_C}{p_C - p_D} = 10.$$

Solution to Exercise 5.5. Using the procedure described in (5.29), the fixed fee of each two-part tariff that should be on the menu is computed as follows:

$$\begin{aligned} f_A &= \$0 \\ f_B &= \$0 + (6¢ - 5¢)200 = \$2 \\ f_C &= \$2 + (5¢ - 4¢)300 = \$5 \\ f_D &= \$5 + (4¢ - 3¢)400 = \$9 \\ f_E &= \$9 + (3¢ - 2¢)200 = \$15. \end{aligned}$$

Therefore, the menu of five two-part tariffs is

Plan A:	$\$0 + 6¢ \cdot q$
Plan B:	$\$2 + 5¢ \cdot q$
Plan C:	$\$5 + 4¢ \cdot q$
Plan D:	$\$9 + 3¢ \cdot q$
Plan E:	$\$15 + 2¢ \cdot q.$

12.6   Manual for Chapter 6: Peak-load Pricing

The computation of prices is based on the simple monopoly techniques of equating marginal revenue to marginal cost. Therefore, the instructor should review the analysis of a simple monopoly facing a continuous linear demand function given in Section 3.1.2. Furthermore, the computation of prices under the shifting-peak case requires a vertical summation of marginal revenue functions (for the single seller case) and of demand functions (for the regulated public utility case). The instructor is urged to make sure that students can distinguish between vertical summation of demand functions and the more familiar horizontal aggregation of demand functions studied in Section 2.5.

The airline example given in Section 6.2.1 is sufficient for a brief introduction to the concept of peak-load pricing. To get somewhat deeper, the instructor can introduce the problem of a shifting peak using the example given in Section 6.3.1. Section 6.7 on how to set peak-load prices for a regulated public utility is presented here for the sake of completeness.

Instructors who wish to spend more time on peak-load pricing can go beyond two seasons. The three-season example given in Section 6.5.1 is general enough to hint at the procedure for finding which seasons should be classified has having a shifting peak and which seasons should be classified as off-peak seasons. This procedure is further discussed in Section 6.5.2. The instructor may want to point out to the students that the division among the regions under which different seasons are classified as having a shifting peak do not necessarily correspond to the kinks on the vertical summation of the marginal revenue or demand functions. The differences between the locations of the kinks and the dividing lines among the regions are clearly marked in Figure 6.3 and Figure 6.5.

Section 6.6 is for more advanced students who have some experience in using calculus. This section shows how the peak-load pricing model can be modified to capture consumers who can delay or advance their service demand in response to changes in the relative prices among the seasons. Before teaching this section, the instructor should provide a brief introduction to the system of demand equations, perhaps by going over Section 2.7, which also demonstrates how to invert a system of demand equations.

The analysis of peak-load pricing, both for a monopoly firm and for a regulated public utility, relies on the simple optimization procedure of equating marginal revenue or price to the "relevant" marginal cost. However, the major difficulty is in having to decide which type of marginal costs to apply in each season. For this reason, the instructor should spend some time on Section 6.1, which elaborates on how to distinguish between marginal capacity cost and marginal operating costs. In addition, the instructor may want to discuss, at least verbally in class, the problem of matching the lengths of time of each season with the time length under which the marginal capacity cost μ_k is measured. Instructors may want to consult Section 6.8, which attempts to clarify the confusing issues related to the dimension of time in peak-load pricing analyses.

Solution to Exercise 6.1. (a) If summer turns out to be the peak season, the airline should solve

$$MR_S(q_S) = 12 - q_S \quad = \quad \$2 + \$2 = \mu_k + \mu_o, \Longrightarrow q_S^{pl} = k^{pl} = 8,$$

$$MR_W(q_W) = 24 - 4q_W \quad = \quad \$2 = \mu_o, \Longrightarrow q_W^{pl} = \frac{11}{2} < k^{pl}.$$

Therefore, $p_S^{pl} = \$8$ and $p_W^{pl} = \$13$. The profit is then given by

$$y^{pl} = (p_W^{pl} - \mu_o)q_W^{pl} + (p_S^{pl} - \mu_k - \mu_o)q_S^{pl} - \phi$$

$$= (13 - 2)\frac{11}{2} + (8 - 2 - 2)8 - 0 = \$92.5.$$

(b) We first compute the profit under a low price, $p < \$12$, so both markets are served. The aggregate direct demand function is $q_{S,W} = q_S + q_W = 12 - p/2 + 24 - 2p = 36 - 5p/2$. The corresponding inverse demand function is therefore $p_{S,W} = 2(36 - q_{S,W})/5$. Therefore, equating the marginal revenue to marginal cost, $MR_{S,W} = 72/5 - 4q_{S,W}/5 = 2 + 2 = \mu_k + \mu_o$ yields $q_{S,W} = 13$ and $p_{S,W} = 46/5 = \$9.2$.

To compute total profit, we first must calculate how much seating capacity is needed to accommodate the high-season demand. Thus, $q_S = 2(12 - p_S) = 28/5 = 5.6$, and $q_W = (24 - p_W)/2 = 37/5 = 7.4$. Hence, winter is the high season, so the airline must acquire $k = 7.4$ seating capacity. Therefore, the profit under a uniform (low) price is

$$y_{S,W} = (9.2 - 2)5.6 + (9.2 - 2 - 2)7.4 - 0 = \$78.8 < \$92.5 = y^{pl}.$$

Next, we compute the profit generated by setting a uniform high price, $p > \$12$, under which only summer passengers are served. But this case was already computed earlier when we computed $q_S = k = 8$ and $p_S = \$8$. In this case,

$$y_S = (8 - 2 - 2)8 - 0 = \$32 < \$92.5 = y^{pl}.$$

Clearly, uniform pricing is less profitable than peak-load pricing.

Solution to Exercise 6.2. (a) If winter is the peak season, the seller should attribute the entire cost of capital to winter passengers only. Hence, $MR_W = 24 - 4q_W = \$8 + \$4$ yields $q_W = 3$. For the summer (off-peak season), the seller should set $MR_S = 12 - q_S = \$4$ (operating cost only), yielding $q_S = 8$. Because $q_W < q_S$, winter cannot be a peak season.

(b) If summer is the peak season, the seller should set $MR_S = 12 - 4q_S = \$8 + \$4$, yielding $q_S = 0$. Hence, summer cannot be a peak season.

(c) Parts (a) and (b) imply a shifting-peak case. Therefore, equating vertical summation of the marginal revenue functions to the sum of marginal costs yields

$$\sum_{S,W} MR^v(k) = 36 - 5k = \$8 + \$4 + \$4 \Longrightarrow k^{pl} = q_W^{pl} = q_S^{pl} = 4.$$

Substituting into the seasonal inverse demand functions yields $p_W^{pl} = \$16$ and $p_S^{pl} = \$10$. Total profit is therefore

$$y^{pl} = (p_W^{pl} - \mu_o)k^{pl} + (p_S^{pl} - \mu_o)k^{pl} - \mu_k k^{pl} - \phi = \$40.$$

Solution to Exercise 6.3. (a) The marginal revenue functions are given by

$$MR_F = 200 - q_F, \quad MR_W = 100 - 2q_W,$$
$$MR_G = 100 - q_G, \quad \text{and} \quad MR_S = 200 - 2q_S.$$

Figure 12.4 plots all four marginal revenue functions.

(b) Vertically summing up all four marginal revenue functions obtains

$$\sum_{F,W,G,S} MR^v(k) = \begin{cases} 600 - 6k & \text{if } 0 < k \le 50 \\ 500 - 4k & \text{if } 50 < k \le 100 \\ 200 - k & \text{if } 100 < k \le 200 \\ 0 & \text{if } k > 200, \end{cases}$$

which is also plotted in Figure 12.4.

(c) From Figure 12.4, we can first guess (and later verify) that shifting peak occurs during the fall and summer seasons only. Vertically summing up the fall and summer marginal revenue functions and equating that sum to the sum of marginal capacity and operating costs obtains

$$\sum_{F,S} MR^v(k) = 400 - 3k = \$20 + \$20 + \$90 \Longrightarrow k^{pl} = 90.$$

Substituting the capacity level $k^{pl} = q_F^{pl} = q_S^{pl} = 90$ into the fall and summer demand functions yields $p_F^{pl} = \$155$ and $p_S^{pl} = \$110$.

Next, during the off-peak seasons the airline solves $MR_W = 100 - 2q_W = \$20$ and $MR_G = 100 - q_G = \$20$, yielding $q_W^{pl} = 40$ and $q_G^{pl} = 80$. At this stage, it is important

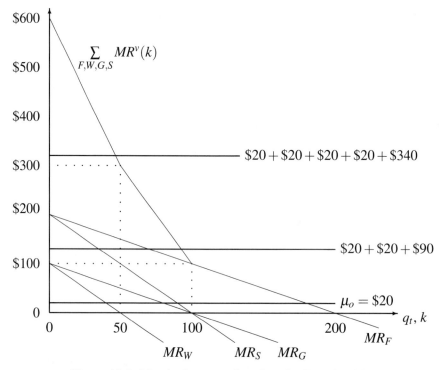

Figure 12.4: Marginal revenue functions for Exercise 6.3.

to verify that the airline operates below capacity during the off-peak seasons by observing that $\max\{q_W^{pl}, q_G^{pl}\} < 90 = k^{pl}$.

Substituting into the winter and spring demand functions yields $p_W^{pl} = p_G^{pl} = \$60$. Finally, the total profit can be computed by

$$y^{pl} = (p_F^{pl} - \mu_k - \mu_o)k^{pl} + (p_S^{pl} - \mu_o)k^{pl} + (p_W^{pl} - \mu_o)q_W^{pl} + (p_G^{pl} - \mu_o)q_G^{pl} - \phi = \$6150.$$

(d) Using Figure 12.4, we can first guess (and later verify) that shifting peak occurs during all seasons. In this case, the airline solves

$$\sum_{F,W,G,S} MR^v(k) = 600 - 6k = \$20 + \$20 + \$20 + \$20 + \$340 \Longrightarrow k^{pl} = 30.$$

Substituting into the four demand functions obtains $p_F^{pl} = \$185$, $p_W^{pl} = \$70$, $p_G^{pl} = \$85$, and $p_S^{pl} = \$170$. Total profit is then given by

$$y^{pl} = (p_F^{pl} - \mu_k - \mu_o)k^{pl} + (p_S^{pl} - \mu_o)k^{pl} + (p_W^{pl} - \mu_o)k^{pl} + (p_G^{pl} - \mu_o)k^{pl} - \phi = \$2300.$$

Solution to Exercise 6.4. (a) The summer revenue function is $x_S(q_S, q_W) = (120 - 2q_S - q_W)q_S$. The winter revenue function is $x_W(q_S, q_W) = (120 - 3q_W - q_W)q_W$. The corresponding four marginal revenue functions are

$$MR_{SS}(q_S, q_W) \stackrel{\text{def}}{=} \frac{\partial x_S}{\partial q_S} = 120 - 4q_S - q_W,$$

$$MR_{SW}(q_S, q_W) \stackrel{\text{def}}{=} \frac{\partial x_S}{\partial q_W} = -q_S,$$

$$MR_{WW}(q_S, q_W) \stackrel{\text{def}}{=} \frac{\partial x_W}{\partial q_W} = 120 - 6q_W - q_S,$$

$$MR_{WS}(q_S, q_W) \stackrel{\text{def}}{=} \frac{\partial x_W}{\partial q_S} = -q_W.$$

(b) We first assume (and later verify) that summer is a peak season. Solving the two equations $MR_{SS}(q_S, q_W) + MR_{WS}(q_S, q_W) = 20 + 20$ and $MR_{WW}(q_S, q_W) + MR_{SW}(q_S, q_W) = 20$ yields $q_S^{pl} = 14$, $q_W^{pl} = 12$. Because $q_S^{pl} > q_W^{pl}$, summer is indeed the peak season. Direct substitution into the inverse demand functions yields the seasons' prices $p_S^{pl} = \$80$ and $p_W^{pl} = \$70$. Finally, total profit is given by $y^{pl} = (p_S^{pl} - \mu_k - \mu_o)q_S^{pl} + (p_W^{pl} - \mu_o)q_W^{pl} - \phi = \$160$.

(c) We first establish that there is no peak season. By way of contradiction, suppose that summer is a peak season. Then, solving $MR_{SS}(q_S, q_W) + MR_{WS}(q_S, q_W) = 40 + 20$ and $MR_{WW}(q_S, q_W) + MR_{SW}(q_S, q_W) = 20$ yields $q_S^{pl} = 8 < q_W^{pl} = 14$, implying that summer is not a peak season. Because the winter demand curve lies below the summer demand curve, we can immediately conclude that winter is also not a peak season.

Under the shifting-peak case, prices are set so that the hotel operates at full capacity in all seasons, $k = q_S = q_W$. To compute the amount of needed capacity, the seller solves

$$\sum_{S,W} MR^v(k) = MR_{SS}(k,k) + MR_{WS}(k,k) + MR_{WW}(k,k) + MR_{SW}(k,k)$$

$$= \$40 + \$20 \implies k^{pl} = q_S^{pl} = q_W^{pl} = 90/7 \approx 12.85.$$

Direct substitution into the inverse demand functions yields the seasons' prices $p_S^{pl} = \$570/7 \approx 81.42$ and $p_W^{pl} = \$480/7 \approx 68.57$. Finally, total profit is given by $y^{pl} = (p_S^{pl} - \mu_k - \mu_o)k^{pl} + (p_W^{pl} - \mu_o)k^{pl} - \phi = \$400$.

Solution to Exercise 6.5. We first assume (and later verify) that summer is the peak season. Solving $p_S = 12 - q_S/2 = \$2 + \$2 = \mu_k + \mu_o$ yields $q_S = 16$. Solving $p_W = 24 - 2q_W = \$2 = \mu_o$ yields $q_W = 11 < 16$. This confirms that summer is the peak season. Therefore, the regulator should set the prices $p_S^{pl} = \$4$, $p_W^{pl} = \$2$, and invest in a seating capacity $k^{pl} = q_S^{pl} = 16$.

Solution to Exercise 6.6. We first demonstrate that summer is not a peak season. Solving $p_S = 12 - q_S/2 = \$8 + \$4 = \mu_k + \mu_o$ yields $q_S = 0$. Next, we demonstrate that winter is not a peak season by solving $p_W = 24 - 2q_W = \$8 + \$4 = \mu_k + \mu_o$, yielding $q_W = 6$. Solving $p_S = 12 - q_S/2 = \$4 = \mu_o$ yields $q_S = 16 > 6$. Therefore, a shifting-peak case prevails.

Equating the vertical sum of the demand functions to the sum of marginal costs

$$\sum_{S,W} D^v(k) = 12 - \frac{k}{2} + 24 - 2k = 36 - \frac{5k}{2} = \$8 + \$4 + \$4 = \mu_k + 2\mu_o$$

$$\implies k^{pl} = 8 \text{ and } p_S^{pl} = p_W^{pl} = \$8.$$

Solution to Exercise 6.7. First we demonstrate that fall is not a peak season. If fall is a peak season, then setting $p_F = \$20 + \$100$ implies that $q_F = 160$. If summer is an off-peak season, then setting $p_S = \$20$ implies that $q_S = 180 > 160$, a contradiction.

Next, we assume (and later verify) that shifting peak occurs between fall and summer, whereas winter and spring are off-peak seasons. Thus, the seller should equate

$$\sum_{F,S} D(k) = 200 - \frac{k}{2} + 200 - k = 400 - \frac{3k}{2} = \$20 + \$20 + \$100$$

to obtain a seating capacity of $k^{pl} = 180$. Substituting into the demand functions yields $p_F^{pl} = \$110$ and $p_S^{pl} = \$20$.

Finally, for the off-peak periods, the seller solves $p_W = 100 - q_W = \$20$ and $p_G = 100 - q_G/2 = \$20$, yielding $q_W^{pl} = 80 < k^{pl}$ and $q_G^{pl} = 160 < k^{pl}$, which confirms that winter and spring are off-peak seasons.

Solution to Exercise 6.8. (a) The manager should first check whether summer is a peak season, in which case the manager should solve

$$\begin{aligned} 120MR_S(q_S) = 120(240 - q_S) &= 24{,}000 + 120 \cdot 20, \\ 245MR_W(q_W) = 245(240 - 2q_W) &= 245 \cdot 20, \end{aligned}$$

yielding $k = q_S = 20$ and $q_W = 110$. Because $q_W > k$, summer is not a peak season.

If winter is a peak season, the manager should solve

$$\begin{aligned} 245MR_W(q_W) = 245(240 - 2q_W) &= 24{,}000 + 120 \cdot 20, \\ 120MR_W(q_W) = 120(240 - q_W) &= 120 \cdot 20, \end{aligned}$$

yielding $k = q_W = 2990/49 \approx 61$ and $q_S = 220$. Because $q_S > k$, winter is not a peak season.

Therefore, a shifting-peak season case occurs, in which case the manager should determine the investment in room capacity according to

$$120MR_S(k) + 245MR_W(k) = 120(240 - k) + 245(240 - 2k)$$
$$= 24,000 + 365 \cdot 20,$$

yielding $k^{pl} = 5630/61 \approx 92.29$. Therefore, the profit-maximizing prices are $p_S^{pl} = 240 - 0.5 \cdot 5630/61 = 11,825/61 \approx \$193.85$ and $p_W^{pl} = 240 - 5630/61 = 9010/61 \approx \$147.7$ (indeed, an expensive hotel, isn't it?).

Finally, the profit level is computed by substituting the above results into

$$y^{pl} = 120(p_S^{pl} - 20)k^{pl} + 245(p_W^{pl} - 20)k^{pl} - 24,000k - \phi$$
$$= \frac{158,484,500}{61} - \phi \approx \$2,598,106.55 - \phi.$$

(b) The regulator should first check whether summer is a peak season, in which case the regulator should solve

$$120p_S(q_S) = 120(240 - \frac{q_S}{2}) = 24,000 + 120 \cdot 20,$$
$$245p_W(q_W) = 245(240 - q_W) = 245 \cdot 20,$$

yielding $k = q_S = 40$ and $q_W = 220$. Because $q_W > k$, summer is not a peak season.

If winter is a peak season, the regulator should solve

$$245p_W(q_W) = 245(240 - q_W) = 24,000 + 120 \cdot 20,$$
$$120p_S(q_S) = 120(240 - \frac{q_S}{2}) = 120 \cdot 20,$$

yielding $k = q_W = 5980/49 \approx 122$ and $q_S = 440$. Because $q_S > k$, winter is not a peak season.

Therefore, a shifting-peak case occurs, in which case the regulator should determine the investment in room capacity according to

$$120p_S(k) + 245p_W(k) = 120\left(240 - \frac{k}{2}\right) + 245(240 - k)$$
$$= 24,000 + 365 \cdot 20,$$

yielding $k^{pl} = 11,260/61 \approx 184.59$. Hence, the socially optimal prices are

$$p_S^{pl} = 240 - 0.5\frac{11,260}{61} = \frac{9010}{61} \approx \$147.7 \text{ and } p_W^{pl} = 240 - \frac{11,260}{61} = \frac{3380}{61} \approx \$55.4.$$

12.7   Manual for Chapter 7: Advance Booking

Business school instructors may view this chapter as the main manifestation of (quantity-based) YM. Thus, if you are using this text in a course on YM, this chapter should not be skipped. All sections on dynamic booking strategies attempt to teach the reader elementary dynamic programming, first by examples then by general formulations. Instructors who feel that this is beyond the capability of their students can skip to Sections 7.6 and 7.7, which analyze elementary and commonly practiced booking mechanisms without resorting to any formal dynamic programming.

Solution to Exercise 7.1. (a) The period 2 decision rule given in (7.1) remains unchanged. However, the expected period 2 value of capacity is now given by

$$EV_2(P_2, k_2) = \begin{cases} (0.4 \times \$0) + (0.1 \times \$40) + (0.5 \times \$10) = \$9 & \text{if } k_2 \neq 0 \\ 0 & \text{if } k_2 = 0. \end{cases}$$

Hence, the expected period 2 value of capacity is lower than the period 1 revenue made from any type of booking. Formally, $EV_2(P_2, k_2) = 9 < \min\{10, 40\} = \min\{P^A, P^B\}$. This means that the service provider should not deny booking to any customer. Formally, the period 1 decision (7.3) now becomes $d_1(\$40) = d_1(\$10) = 1$. Intuitively speaking, it is more profitable to book a consumer in class B, thereby earning \$10, rather than leaving one unit of capacity to period 2, in which its expected value is only \$9.

(b) Given that $P_1 = \$10$, part (a) concluded that $d_1(\$10) = 1$. Because, $k_2 = k_1 - 1 = 0$, no further bookings can be made in period 2. Hence, total profit is $y = \$10$.

Solution to Exercise 7.2. Because the salvage value is lower than the fare on any booking class, that is, $P^S = \$5 < \min\{P^A, P^B\} = \$10$, the service provider should accept any booking request during the last period. Therefore, $d_2(\$40) = d_2(\$10) = 1$. Therefore, the period 2 expected value of capacity is

$$EV_2(P_2, k_2) = \begin{cases} (0.4 \times \$5) + (0.1 \times \$40) + (0.5 \times \$10) = \$11 & \text{if } k_2 \neq 0 \\ 0 & \text{if } k_2 = 0, \end{cases}$$

because in the event no booking is requested (probability 0.4), the service provider sells the capacity at the price of $P^S = \$5$.

Moving backward to period 1, because $\$10 < EV_2(P_2, 1) < \$40$, the period 1 profit-maximizing decision rule is given by

$$d_2(P_2) = \begin{cases} 1 & \text{if } P_2 \geq \$11 \\ 0 & \text{otherwise} \end{cases} \quad \text{hence} \quad d_2(P_2) = \begin{cases} 1 & \text{if } P_2 = \$40 \\ 0 & \text{if } P_2 = \$10. \end{cases}$$

Class (i):	0	A	B	$EV_2(1)$
Price (P^i):	\$0	\$40	\$10	
π_1^i:	$1/3$	$1/3$	$1/3$	
π_2^i (given $P_1 = \$0$):	0	$1/2$	$1/2$	$\frac{1}{2}40 + \frac{1}{2}10 = \$25$
π_2^i (given $P_1 = \$40$):	$1/2$	0	$1/2$	$\frac{1}{2}0 + \frac{1}{2}10 = \$5$
π_2^i (given $P_1 = \$10$):	$1/2$	$1/2$	0	$\frac{1}{2}0 + \frac{1}{2}40 = \$20$

Table 12.11: Computations for Exercise 7.3.

Solution to Exercise 7.3. Under three consumers, the adjusted probabilities and expected period $t = 2$ values of capacity are now given by Table 12.11. Next, the decision rule in the last booking period is clearly $d_2(\$40) = d_2(\$10) = 1$ as otherwise capacity will remain unbooked. Moving backward to period $t = 1$, the generalized decision rule given by (7.6) implies that a booking request for class A should be accepted because $P_1 = \$40 \geq EV_2(1) - EV_2(0) = \$5$. Similarly, a period $t = 1$ booking request for class B should be denied because $P_1 = \$10 < EV_2(1) - EV_2(0) = \$20$. Therefore, decision rule (7.11) applies also to the present case.

Solution to Exercise 7.4. (a) We first compute the expected value of capacity in the last booking period, $t = T$:

$$EV_T(k_T) = (0.3 \times \$0) + (0.1 \times \$60) + (0.6 \times \$20) = \$16,$$

for all $k_T \geq 1$. Clearly, $EV_T(k_T) = 0$ if $k_T = 0$.

Moving backward to period $T - 1$, because $P^A > P^B = 20 > 16 - 0$, $d_{T-1}(\$60) = d_{T-1}(\$20) = 1$ (all booking requests should be accepted in period $T - 1$). Therefore,

$$
\begin{aligned}
EV_{T-1}(k_{T-1}) &= 2 \times 16 = \$32 \text{ for all } k_{T-1} \geq 2, \\
EV_{T-1}(1) &= 0.1(60 + 0) + 0.6(20 + 0) + 0.3 \times 16 = \$22.8.
\end{aligned}
$$

Moving backward to booking period $T - 2$, $d_{T-2}(\$60) = d_{T-2}(\$20) = 1$ for all $k_{T-2} \geq 3$ because the amount of capacity left exceeds the number of remaining booking periods. If $k_{T-2} = 2$, $d_{T-2}(\$60) = d_{T-2}(\$20) = 1$ because $20 > 32 - 22.8$. However, if $k_{T-2} = 1$, $d_{T-2}(\$60) = 1$, whereas $d_{T-2}(\$20) = 0$ because $20 < 22.8 - 0$. Therefore,

$$
\begin{aligned}
EV_{T-2}(k_{T-2}) &= 3 \times 16 = \$48 \text{ for all } k_{T-2} \geq 3, \\
EV_{T-2}(2) &= 0.1(60 + 22.8) + 0.6(20 + 22.8) + 0.3 \times 32 = \$43.56, \\
EV_{T-2}(1) &= 0.1(60 + 0) + 0.9 \times 22.8 = \$26.52.
\end{aligned}
$$

Moving backward to booking period $T - 3$, $d_{T-3}(\$60) = d_{T-2}(\$20) = 1$ for all $k_{T-3} \geq 4$ because the amount of capacity left exceeds the number of remaining booking periods. If $k_{T-3} = 3$, $d_{T-3}(\$60) = d_{T-3}(\$20) = 1$ because $20 > 48 - 43.56$. If $k_{T-3} = 2$, $d_{T-3}(\$60) = d_{T-3}(\$20) = 1$ because $20 > 43.56 - 26.52$. However, if $k_{T-3} = 1$, $d_{T-3}(\$60) = 1$, whereas $d_{T-3}(\$20) = 0$ because $20 < 26.52 - 0$. Therefore,

$$
\begin{aligned}
EV_{T-3}(k_{T-3}) &= 4 \times 16 = \$64 \text{ for all } k_{T-3} \geq 4, \\
EV_{T-3}(3) &= 0.1(60 + 43.56) + 0.6(20 + 43.56) + 0.3 \times 48 = \$62.89, \\
EV_{T-3}(2) &= 0.1(60 + 26.52) + 0.6(20 + 26.52) + 0.3 \times 43.56 = \$49.63, \\
EV_{T-3}(1) &= 0.1(60 + 0) + 0.9 \times 26.52 = \$29.87.
\end{aligned}
$$

Finally, clearly $d_t(\$60) = 1$ for every t. We now can also infer that $d_t(\$20) = 1$ in all booking periods $t \leq T - 4$ provided that $k_t \geq 2$, whereas $d_t(\$20) = 0$ if $k_t \leq 1$.

(b) By part (a), $d_{T-4}(\$20) = 1$ because $k_{T-4} = 3$. Also, $d_{T-3}(\$20) = 1$ because $k_{T-3} = 2$. However, $d_{T-2}(\$20) = 0$ because $k_{T-2} = 1$. Finally, $d_{T-1}(\$60) = 1$, which is feasible because $k_{T-1} = 1$. Clearly, no further bookings can be made because $k_T = 0$. Altogether, the profit level is $y = 20 + 20 + 60 = \$100$.

Solution to Exercise 7.5. Inspecting the upper part of Table 12.12 reveals that only booking class D should be eliminated when a strictly positive marginal cost of $\mu = \$19$ is introduced, because $P^D = \$10 < \$19 = \mu$. Hence, the probability of no booking should be adjusted so that $\hat{\pi}^0 = \pi^0 + \pi^D = 0.2 + 0.3 = 0.5$.

Class (i):	0	A	B	C	D	S
Proportion (π^i):	0.2	0.2	0.1	0.2	0.3	
Price/fare (P^i):	\$0	\$40	\$30	\$20	\$10	\$15
Proportion ($\hat{\pi}^i$):	0.5	0.2	0.1	0.2	n/a	
Marginal profit ($\hat{P}^i$):	\$0	\$21	\$11	\$1	n/a	\$15

Table 12.12: Computations for Exercise 7.5.

Solution to Exercise 7.6. (a) Any booking request is accepted in period 2 provided that the appropriate capacity remains. Therefore, the period 2 value of capital is

$$
EV_2(k_2^{AH}, k_2^{HB}) =
\begin{cases}
0.1 \times \$20 = \$2 & \text{if } k_2^{AH} \neq 0 \text{ and } k_2^{HB} = 0 \\
0.1 \times \$30 = \$3 & \text{if } k_2^{AH} = 0 \text{ and } k_2^{HB} \neq 0 \\
0.1 \times \$20 + 0.1 \times \$30 + 0.7 \times \$40 = \$33 & \text{if } k_2^{AH} \neq 0 \text{ and } k_2^{HB} \neq 0 \\
0 & \text{Otherwise.}
\end{cases}
$$

Next, observe that

$$P^{AH} = \$20 < EV_2(1,1) - EV_2(0,1) = \$33 - \$3 < \$40 = P^{AB},$$

and

$$P^{HB} = \$30 < EV_2(1,1) - EV_2(1,0) = \$33 - \$2 < \$40 = P^{AB}.$$

Therefore, the period 1 decision rule is given by

$$d_1(P_1) = \begin{cases} 0 & \text{if } P_1 = \$20 \\ 0 & \text{if } P_1 = \$30 \\ 1 & \text{if } P_1 = \$40. \end{cases}$$

Hence, in the first booking period, the airline should avoid making reservations on the shorter routes and should reserve the entire capacity for period 2.

(b) No booking is made in period 1 if either no consumer requests to be booked (probability $\pi^0 = 0.1$) or only bookings on routes AH and HB are requested (probabilities $\pi^{AH} = \pi^{HB} = 0.1$). In period 2, the probability that no booking is made is $\pi^0 = 0.1$. Altogether, the probability that all flights leave with no passengers is $(\pi^0 + \pi^{AH} + \pi^{HB})\pi^0 = 0.03 = 3\%$.

(c) The probability that route AB will be booked in one of the booking periods is $\pi^{AB} \times \pi^{AB} = 0.49 = 49\%$.

(d) The above decision rules imply that if a booking on route HB is made, it will be accepted only in the second period. However, such a booking is possible only if route AB is not booked in period 1. Altogether, route HB will be booked with probability $(1 - \pi^{AB})\pi^{HB} = (1 - 0.7)0.1 = 0.03 = 3\%$.

Solution to Exercise 7.7. Substituting the booking information directly into Table 7.8 yields $Ey(2,0) = \$11.84$, $Ey(1,1) = \$19.68$, and $Ey(0,2) = \$18.88$. Hence, the profit-maximizing fixed class allocation is $\langle K^A, K^B \rangle = \langle 1,1 \rangle$.

Solution to Exercise 7.8. With only one unit of capacity, Table 7.8 should be modified. Therefore, the expected profit from each possible class allocation is now given in Table 12.13. Substituting the booking information directly into Table 12.13 yields $Ey(1,0) = \$9.76$ and $Ey(0,1) = \$9.92$. Hence, the profit-maximizing fixed class allocation is $\langle K^A, K^B \rangle = \langle 0,1 \rangle$.

Solution to Exercise 7.9. Under the realization $r_1 = A$, $r_2 = B$, $r_3 = C$, and $r_4 = D$, Table 7.10 should be modified to Table 12.14.

Solution to Exercise 7.10. Substituting the booking information directly into Table 7.11 yields $Ey(2,0) = \$11.84$, $Ey(2,1) = \$20.16$, and $Ey(2,2) = \$24$. Hence, the profit-maximizing fixed class allocation is $\langle K^A, K^B \rangle = \langle 1,1 \rangle$.

| Booking Periods | | | Capacity Allocation $\langle K^A, K^B \rangle$ | |
$t=1$	$t=2$	$t=3$	$\langle 1,0 \rangle$	$\langle 0,1 \rangle$
A	A	A	$(\pi^A)^3 P^A$	0
B	A	A	$(\pi^A)^2 \pi^B P^A$	$(\pi^A)^2 \pi^B P^B$
A	B	A	$(\pi^A)^2 \pi^B P^A$	$(\pi^A)^2 \pi^B P^B$
A	A	B	$(\pi^A)^2 \pi^B P^A$	$(\pi^A)^2 \pi^B P^B$
B	B	B	0	$(\pi^B)^3 P^B$
A	B	B	$\pi^A (\pi^B)^2 P^A$	$\pi^A (\pi^B)^2 P^B$
B	A	B	$\pi^A (\pi^B)^2 P^A$	$\pi^A (\pi^B)^2 P^B$
B	B	A	$\pi^A (\pi^B)^2 P^A$	$\pi^A (\pi^B)^2 P^B$
Total expected profit:			$Ey(1,0)$	$Ey(0,1)$

Table 12.13: Computations for Exercise 7.8.

t	r_t	k_t	Booking Class (i):	A	B	C	D
1	A	100	Nested allocation (K_1^i):	100	70	50	40
1	B	99	Nested allocation (K_2^i):	99	70	50	40
2	C	98	Nested allocation (K_3^i):	98	69	50	40
3	D	97	Nested allocation (K_4^i):	97	68	49	40
4	n/a	96	Nested allocation (K_5^i):	96	67	48	39

Table 12.14: Computations for Exercise 7.9.

Solution to Exercise 7.11. With only one unit of capacity, Table 7.11 should be modified. Therefore, the expected profit from each possible class allocation is now given in Table 12.15. Substituting the booking information directly into Table 12.15 yields $Ey(1,0) = \$9.76$ and $Ey(1,1) = \$12$. Hence, the profit-maximizing nested class allocation is $\langle 1,1 \rangle$.

12.8 Manual for Chapter 8: Refund Strategies

This chapter more or less maintains an increasing level of difficulty, so the instructor should not have any problem finding which topics fit the students' abilities best. Proportional (percentage) refunds are analyzed only in Section 8.3.2, so instructors who wish to skip this section as well as Section 8.2.2 can do so without any effect on the understanding of all other sections in this chapter. Instructors teaching students with low technical ability can focus on refund settings under an exogenously given price, analyzed in Section 8.3. However, it may be worth a try to teach the two consumer-type analyses presented in Section 8.4 as they give a more practical analysis in which sellers choose price and refund levels simultaneously. Propor-

Booking Periods			Nested Allocation $\langle K^A, K^B \rangle$	
$t=1$	$t=2$	$t=3$	$\langle 1,0 \rangle$	$\langle 1,1 \rangle$
A	A	A	$(\pi^A)^3 P^A$	$(\pi^A)^3 P^A$
B	A	A	$(\pi^A)^2 \pi^B P^A$	$(\pi^A)^2 \pi^B P^B$
A	B	A	$(\pi^A)^2 \pi^B P^A$	$(\pi^A)^2 \pi^B P^A$
A	A	B	$(\pi^A)^2 \pi^B P^A$	$(\pi^A)^2 \pi^B P^A$
B	B	B	0	$(\pi^B)^3 P^B$
A	B	B	$\pi^A (\pi^B)^2 P^A$	$\pi^A (\pi^B)^2 P^A$
B	A	B	$\pi^A (\pi^B)^2 P^A$	$\pi^A (\pi^B)^2 P^B$
B	B	A	$\pi^A (\pi^B)^2 P^A$	$\pi^A (\pi^B)^2 P^B$
Total expected profit:			$\mathrm{E}y(1,0)$	$\mathrm{E}y(0,1)$

Table 12.15: Computations for Exercise 7.11.

tional (percentage) refunds are ignored in some parts of this chapter. Instructors who are short on time can simply skip all topics related to proportional refunds.

Solution to Exercise 8.1. The solution is given in Table 12.16.

π	V	πV	p	r	$(1-\pi)r$	U	Decision
0.8	20	16	13	0	0.0	3.0	Book
0.8	20	16	14	2	0.4	2.4	No book
0.9	20	18	16	9	0.9	2.9	No book
0.2	20	4	4	3	2.4	2.4	No book

Table 12.16: Results for Exercise 8.1.

Solution to Exercise 8.2. (a) Substituting $U = 3$, $V = 10$, and $\pi = 0.5$ into equation (8.2) yields $r = 2p - 4$, which is drawn in Figure 12.5.

(b) Substituting $r = 0$ into $r \geq 2p - 4$ yields $p \leq 2$, which is also drawn in Figure 12.5.

(c) Substituting $r = p$ into $r \geq 2p - 4$ yields $p \leq 4$, which is also drawn in Figure 12.5.

Solution to Exercise 8.3. The profit-maximizing refund level is $r = 0$ (no refund). To prove this statement, it is sufficient to show that both types of consumers will book the service, even under zero refund. Substituting $\bar{p} = 4$ and Table 8.2 into utility function (8.1) yields $U_L = 0.5 \times 10 - 4 > 0$ and $U_H = 0.8 \times 10 - 4 > 0$.

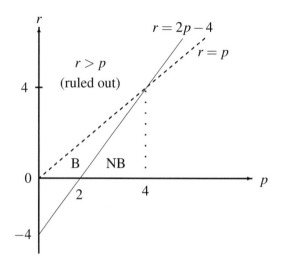

Figure 12.5: Results for Exercise 8.2.

Solution to Exercise 8.4. (a) Under no refund, type L consumers do not book the service because $U_L = 0.5 \times 10 - 7 < 0$. Type H consumers do book the service because $U_H = 0.8 \times 10 - 7 > 0$. Substituting $r = 0$, $\bar{p} = 7$, and the data from Table 8.2 (modified to the new cost structure) into (8.4) yields the seller's profit level,

$$y^{NR} = 500(7 - 3) - 0.8 \times 500 \times 2 - (1 - 0.8)0 - 1200 = 0.$$

(b) Both types book the service because $U_L = 0.5 \times 10 - 7 + (1 - 0.5)7 > 0$, and $U_H = 0.8 \times 10 - 7 + (1 - 0.8)7 > 0$. Substituting into (8.4) yields a loss given by

$$y^{FR} = (500 + 800)(7 - 3) - (0.8 \times 500 + 0.5 \times 800) \times 2$$
$$- (0.2 \times 500 + 0.5 \times 800)7 - 1200 = -1100 < 0.$$

(c) We compute the minimum refund level that would induce type L consumers to book the service. Thus, we look for the minimum level of r satisfying $U_L = 0.5 \times 10 - 7 + (1 - 0.5)r = 0$, yielding a partial refund level of $r = 4$. Under this refund level, the profit (8.4) is now given by

$$y^{PR} = (500 + 800)(7 - 3) - (0.8 \times 500 + 0.5 \times 800) \times 2$$
$$- (0.2 \times 500 + 0.5 \times 800)4 - 1200 = 1600.$$

Solution to Exercise 8.5. The third and fifth columns of Table 8.3 confirm Assumption 8.2, thus step I of the above algorithm is now complete.

Moving on to step II, substituting $\pi_3 = 0.5$ and $V_3 = 8$ into (8.12) yields $r = 6$. Substituting all values into the profit (8.7) obtains $y_3 = 900$.

Moving on to step III, substituting $\pi_2 = 0.5$ and $V_2 = 10$ into (8.12) yields $r = 4$. Substituting all values into the profit (8.7) obtains $y_2 = 2300$.

Moving on to step IV, substituting $\pi_1 = 0.8$ and $V_3 = 8$ into (8.12) yields $r = \max\{0, -2\} = 0$. Substituting all values into the profit (8.7) obtains $y_1 = 1200$. Hence, the profit-maximizing refund level is $r = 4$. When this level of refund is offered to consumers, only consumer types 1 and 2 book this service.

Solution to Exercise 8.6. We compute the minimum refund rate that would induce type L consumers to book the service. Thus, we look for the minimum level of r satisfying $U_L = 0.5 \times 10 - 7 + (1 - 0.5)r \times 6 = 0$, yielding a partial refund rate of $r = 2/3 \approx 66.6\%$. Under this refund level, the profit (8.4) is now given by

$$y^{PR} = (500 + 800)(7 - 3) - (0.8 \times 500 + 0.5 \times 800) \times 2$$

$$- (0.2 \times 500 + 0.5 \times 800)\frac{2}{3}6 - 1200 = 1600.$$

Clearly, this computation was not needed as we know from the solution to Exercise 6 that the profit-maximizing lump-sum refund is $4. Hence, we only need to solve $r \times p = 6r = 4$, yielding $r = 2/3$.

Solution to Exercise 8.7. (a) Step I requires substituting the data into the intersection point given by (8.18). Hence, $p = 4.75$ and $r = 2.5$. Because $r \le p$, we are done by substituting into (8.23) to obtain a profit level of $y = 3200$.

(b) Step I requires substituting the data into the intersection point given by (8.18). Hence, $p = 7.125$ and $r = 8.25$. Because $r > p$, we know that this is not the solution, and we must proceed with all the remaining steps.

Moving on to step II for the second example, substituting the consumer data and $r = p$ into (8.17), we obtain $p_H = 7$ and $p_L = 6$ as the maximum prices that each type is willing to pay. Setting $p = 6$ (meaning that both types book this service) and substituting into (8.16) yields $y(6) = 3600$. Setting $p = 7$ (meaning that type L is excluded) and substituting into (8.16) yields $y(7) = 3500$.

Moving on to step III for the second example, substituting the consumer data and $r = 0$ into (8.17), we obtain $p_H = 6.3$ and $p_L = 3.6$ as the maximum prices that each type is willing to pay. Setting $p = 3.6$ (meaning that both types book this service) and substituting into (8.16) yields $y(3.6) = 2400$. Setting $p = 6.3$ (meaning that type L is excluded) and substituting into (8.16) yields $y(6.3) = 3500$.

Comparing the four profit levels from steps II and III clearly implies that the solution to the second example is to provide a full refund and setting $p = r = 6$, thereby serving all consumer types and earning a profit of $y^{FR} = 3600$.

Solution to Exercise 8.8. There are $2^3 - 1 = 7$ subsets, $\{1,2,3\}, \{1,2\}, \{1,3\}, \{2,3\}, \{1\}, \{2\},$ and $\{3\}$, to be investigated. We input each into the linear programming procedure and obtain the following results:

$$\max_{p,r} y_{\{1,2,3\}} = 10[40p - 3(r - 34)] \quad \text{subject to} \quad r \geq 0, \quad p \geq 0, \quad r \leq p,$$

$$r \geq 10p - 81, \quad r \geq 5p - 32, \quad \text{and} \quad \frac{10p - 49}{3}.$$

The computer solution to this problem is given by $p = r = 7$ (full refund) and $y_{\{1,2,3\}} = 1150$.

Next, if only types $\{1,2\}$ are served,

$$\max_{p,r} y_{\{1,2\}} = 10(20p - 3r - 54) \quad \text{subject to} \quad r \geq 0, \quad p \geq 0, \quad r \leq p,$$

$$r \geq 10p - 81, \quad \text{and} \quad r \geq 5p - 32.$$

The computer solution to this problem is given by $p = r = 8$ (full refund) and $y_{\{1,2\}} = 820$.

Next, if only types $\{1,3\}$ are served,

$$\max_{p,r} y_{\{1,3\}} = 10(30p - 7r - 76) \quad \text{subject to} \quad r \geq 0, \quad p \geq 0, \quad r \leq p,$$

$$r \geq 10p - 81, \quad \text{and} \quad \frac{10p - 49}{3}.$$

The computer solution to this problem is given by $p = r = 7$ (full refund) and $y_{\{1,3\}} = 850$.

Next, if only types $\{2,3\}$ are served,

$$\max_{p,r} y_{\{2,3\}} = 20(15p - 4r - 37) \quad \text{subject to} \quad r \geq 0, \quad p \geq 0, \quad r \leq p,$$

$$r \geq 5p - 32, \quad \text{and} \quad \frac{10p - 49}{3}.$$

The computer solution for this problem is given by $p = r = 7$ (full refund) and $y_{\{2,3\}} = 800$.

Next, if only type 1 is served, solving $r = 10p - 81$ for, say, $p = r$ yields $p = r = 9$ and $y_{\{1\}} = 530$.

Next, if only type 2 is served, solving $r = 5p - 32$ for $p = r$ yields $p = r = 8$ and $y_{\{2\}} = 380$.

Finally, if only type 3 is served, solving $r = (10p - 49)/3$ for $p = r$ yields $p = r = 7$ and $y_{\{3\}} = 500$.

Comparing the above profit levels reveals that the profit-maximizing price and refund are given by $p = r = 7$ (full refund), thereby earning a profit of $y_{\{1,2,3\}} = 1150$. Under this policy, all consumer types are served.

Solution to Exercise 8.9. The utility function (8.1) implies that for every refund level r, $U(r) = \pi \times 18 - 6 + (1 - \pi)r$. Substituting the values of π from the bottom row of Table 8.4 into this utility function yields $U(0) = -0.3$, $U(0.25) = -0.26$, $U(0.5) = -0.21$, $U(75) = -0.16$, $U(1) = -0.09$, $U(2) = 0.25$, and $U(3) = 0.69$. Hence, any refund level of $r = 2$ and above will induce the consumers to book this service.

Solution to Exercise 8.10. Suppose the seller sets $r = 0$. In view of the consumers' utility function (8.2), type L consumers will not book this service because $U_L = 0.3 \times 18 - 6 + (1 - 0.3)0 < 0$. In contrast, type H will book this service because $U_H = 0.9 \times 7 - 6 + (1 - 0.9)0 \geq 0$. Substituting into the profit function (8.4) yields $y^{NR} = 500(6 - 1) - 0.9 \times 500 \times 2 - (1 - 0.9)0 - 1000 = 600$.

Next, suppose the seller sets $r = 2$ on no-shows. Type L consumers will book this service because $U_L = 0.25 \times 18 - 6 + (1 - 0.25)2 \geq 0$. Type H consumers will not book this service because $U_H = 0.75 \times 7 - 6 + (1 - 0.75)2 < 0$. Substituting into the profit function (8.4) yields $y^{PR} = 800(6 - 1) - 0.75 \times 2 - (1 - 0.75)500 \times 2 - 1000 = 1400 > y^{NR}$. Hence, providing a refund of $r = 2$ yields a higher profit than providing no refund. However, what is interesting here is that a high refund level leads to an exclusion of type H consumers, who are more likely to show up for the service.

12.9 Manual for Chapter 9: Overbooking

The purpose of this chapter is to provide the necessary tools needed for computing the profit-maximizing overbooking levels. In addition, this chapter explains why the overbooking strategy may be profitable to service providers, despite the penalty they may incur if that service is denied to some booked customers. Section 9.1 provides all the necessary definitions and tools and therefore must be taught first. Subsection 9.1.1 provides all the necessary background for computing show up probabilities based on the binomial distribution. Section 9.2 computes the expected cost, expected revenue, and resulting expected profit for given booking levels. Section 9.3 extends the model of booking individuals to the booking of groups of consumers, and therefore can be skipped in short course.

The analysis in this chapter may be "too difficult" for some undergraduate students. In this case, the instructor can briefly cover the basic definitions and proceed directly to Section 9.2.3, which contains some basic examples that are sufficient to deliver the logic behind the solution to the overbooking problem. Section 9.2.3

provides basic examples for how to book one or two units of capacity that do not require the use of the general binomial distribution formula.

Perhaps the key issue that the instructor may want to stress in class is that over-booking may generate profit functions that do not strictly increase with the number of consumers (or groups) who show up at the time of service. This happens for two reasons: First, the revenue is bounded by the service capacity level so an increase in the number of show-ups beyond capacity does not enhance the revenue. Second, the penalty that service providers must pay consumers who are denied service becomes effective only if the number of show-ups exceeds capacity. Otherwise, an increase in the number of show-ups does not have any effect on the cost associated with this penalty.

Solution to Exercise 9.1. (a)

$$\Pr\{s(3) = 2\} = \frac{3!}{2!\,(3-2)!}\,\pi^2(1-\pi)^{3-2} = \frac{3!}{2!\cdot 1!}\,\pi^2(1-\pi) = 3\pi^2(1-\pi).$$

(b) Substituting $\pi = 0.8$ into the above expression yields $\Pr\{s(3) = 2\} = 48/125 = 0.384$.

(c)

$$\Pr\{s(55) = 52\} = \frac{55!}{52!\,(55-52)!}\,\pi^{52}(1-\pi)^{55-52}$$

$$= \frac{55!}{52!\cdot 3!}\,\pi^{52}(1-\pi)^3 = 26235\,\pi^{52}(1-\pi)^3.$$

(d) Substituting $\pi = 0.9$ into the above expression yields $\Pr\{s(55) = 52\} = 0.1095195269$.

(e) The expected number of show-ups is $Eb = \pi \cdot b = 0.7 \times 52 = 36.4$ consumers.

Solution to Exercise 9.2. (a) $\Pr\{ds(5) = 1\} = \Pr\{s(5) = 4\}$

$$= \frac{5!}{4!\cdot 1!}\,\pi^4(1-\pi)^1 = 5\pi^4(1-\pi) = \frac{256}{625} = 0.4096.$$

(b) $\Pr\{ds(5) = 2\} = \Pr\{s(5) = 5\} = \frac{5!}{5!\cdot 0!}\,\pi^5(1-\pi)^0 = \pi^5 = 0.32768.$

(c) $\Pr\{ds(5) \geq 1\} = 0.4096 + 0.32768 = 0.73728.$

(d) $\Pr\{ds(5) = 0\} = 1 - 0.73728 = 0.26272.$

(e) $\Pr\{ds(5) = 0\}$

$$= \Pr\{s(5) = 0\} + \Pr\{s(5) = 1\} + \Pr\{s(5) = 2\} + \Pr\{s(5) = 3\}$$
$$= 0.00032 + 0.0064 + 0.0512 + 0.2048 = 0.26272.$$

(f) $\mathrm{E}ds(5) = \underbrace{\dfrac{5!}{4! \cdot 1!}\, 0.8^4(4-3)}_{ds(5)=1} + \underbrace{0.8^5(5-3)}_{ds(5)=2} = 1.06496.$

Solution to Exercise 9.3. (a) There is no overbooking, hence

$$y(3) = \underbrace{3\pi(1-\pi)^2(P-\mu_o)}_{3 \text{ cases } s(2)=1} + \underbrace{3\pi^2(1-\pi)\cdot 2(P-\mu_o)}_{3 \text{ cases } s(2)=2}$$

$$+ \underbrace{\pi^3 \cdot 3(P-\mu_o)}_{\text{case } s(3)=3} - \underbrace{(\phi + 3\mu_k)}_{\text{fixed costs}}.$$

The reader is encouraged to compare the above profit level with (9.27), which provides the profit level under $K = 2$ and to observe the differences associated with an increase in one unit of capacity.

(b) Here, the firm overbooks one consumer. Hence,

$$y(4) = \underbrace{\dfrac{4!}{1! \cdot 3!}\, \pi(1-\pi)^3(P-\mu_o)}_{4 \text{ cases } s(4)=1} + \underbrace{\dfrac{4!}{2! \cdot 2!}\, \pi^2(1-\pi)^2 \cdot 2(P-\mu_o)}_{8 \text{ cases } s(4)=2}$$

$$+ \underbrace{\dfrac{4!}{3! \cdot 1!}\, \pi^3(1-\pi)\cdot 3(P-\mu_o)}_{4 \text{ cases } s(4)=3} + \underbrace{\pi^4[2(P-\mu_o) - \psi(4-3)]}_{\text{case } s(4)=4} - \underbrace{(\phi + 3\mu_k)}_{\text{fixed costs}}.$$

The reader is encouraged again to compare these profit levels with (9.28), which provides the profit level under $K = 2$, and to observe the differences associated with an increase in one unit of capacity.

(c) Substituting $\mu_k = \mu_o = 10$, $p = 500$, $\psi = 3430$, and $\pi = 0.5$ into the above yields $y(3) = y(4) = 705$. Hence, the firm is indifferent between overbooking one consumer and booking exactly to full capacity.

Solution to Exercise 9.4. (a) Expected profit when two groups are booked is given by $y(80) = -\phi - \mu_k \cdot 100 + [\pi^2 80 + 2\pi(1-\pi)40]\,(P - \mu_o)$.

(b) Expected profit when three groups are booked is

$$y(120) = -\phi - \mu_k \cdot 100$$
$$+ [\pi^3 80 + 3\pi^2(1-\pi)80 + 3\pi(1-\pi)^2 40]\,(P - \mu_o) - \pi^3 \psi \cdot 40.$$

In this example, with probability π^3, 120 passengers (three groups) show up, in which case 40 booked consumers are denied service.

(c) Solving $y(80) = y(120)$ yields

$$\widetilde{\psi} = \dfrac{4P\pi(1-\pi) + \pi^2(4\mu_o + 3) - 4\pi(\mu_o + 1) + 1}{\pi^2} = \dfrac{7833}{16} \approx 489.56.$$

Thus, BUMPME should book two groups if $\psi > \widetilde{\psi}$, and three groups if $\psi \le \widetilde{\psi}$.

12.10   Manual for Chapter 10:
Quality, Loyalty, Auctions, and Advertising

This chapter collects some additional pricing techniques that were not included in previous chapters. Section 10.1 ties pricing decisions to product design and engineering decisions. It demonstrates how product design should be influenced by the pricing technique being used and by the ability or inability to price discriminate among the different consumer groups with respect to quality levels. This section can be taught together with Chapter 3 (basic pricing technique); however, the major innovation here is that the design of the product/service is endogenous, whereas in Chapter 3, quality levels are assumed to be exogenously given.

Section 10.1 on sellers' choice of quality and classes can be taught using the simple examples described in Section 10.1.2. Then, the instructor can go back to Section 10.1.1 to introduce the general notation, assumptions, and some useful classification of consumers' valuations. Section 10.2 on damaged goods constitutes a natural extension of the analysis of quality given in Section 10.1. Section 10.2 can be taught at all levels as it uses numerical examples only.

Section 10.3 on pricing under competition extends the basic analysis of Section 3.4. Section 10.3.1 analyzes price discrimination and market segmentation based on consumers' purchase history. This section and the exercise question uses some calculus, which means that the section can be taught only if students have some experience in solving optimization problems using calculus. In contrast, Section 10.3.2 on price matching uses logical arguments only and therefore can be taught at any level.

Section 10.4 provides a brief introduction to auctions. Instructors who wish to devote only one lecture to auctions can concentrate on Section 10.4.1, which analyzes open English and sealed-bid second-price auctions. The analysis of open Dutch and sealed-bid first-price auctions given in Sections 10.4.2 and 10.4.3 are by far more advanced than the previous sections (basically, they can be considered graduate level).

Finally, Section 10.5, which computes the profit-maximizing expenditure on advertising, contains one simple formula and hence can be taught at all levels.

Solution to Exercise 10.1. (a) In view of Table 10.4, the profit from selling the fast printer is

$$y_F = \begin{cases} 50(70-50) = \$1000 & \text{if } p_F = \$70 \\ 90(50-50) = \$0 & \text{if } p_F = \$50. \end{cases}$$

Next, the profit when only model M is introduced into the market is

$$y_M = \begin{cases} 50(65-30) = \$1750 & \text{if } p_M = \$65 \\ 90(40-30) = \$900 & \text{if } p_M = \$40. \end{cases}$$

Similarly, the profit from selling the slow printer S is

$$y_S = \begin{cases} 50(40-10) = \$1500 & \text{if } p_S = \$40 \\ 90(30-10) = \$1800 & \text{if } p_S = \$30. \end{cases}$$

(b) The above computations reveal that the seller maximizes profit by introducing the slow printer only for the price of $p_S = \$30$. Under this low price, all consumer types buy the printer. Hence, the profit earned by GIBBERISH is $y = \$1800$.

(c) Consider the introduction of two printer models, the medium-speed printer M and the slow model S, priced at $p_M = \$55$ and $p_S = \$30$, respectively. First, it must be established that both models are demanded by some consumers in this market. In view of Table 10.4, type 2 consumers will not buy the medium-speed printer because the price exceeds their valuations. However, they will buy the slow model because $V_2^S = \$30 = p_M$. Next, type 1 consumers will prefer the medium-speed printer over the slow printer because $V_1^M - p_M = 65 - 55 = 10 \geq 40 - 30 = V_1^S - p_S$.

Second, it should be determined whether introducing both models is more profitable than selling the slow model only. This is indeed the case, as the profit under the prices $p_M = \$55$ and $p_S = \$30$ is

$$y_{M,S} = 50(55-30) + 40(30-10) = \$2050 > \$1800 = y_S.$$

Solution to Exercise 10.2. (a) There are two pricing options for selling the fast original model only. First, selling at a high price, $p_F^H = \$180$, so only type $\ell = 2$ consumers buy it. At this price, type $\ell = 1$ consumers do not buy it because $V_1^F = 80 < 180 = p_F^H$ (the price exceeds their valuation). The resulting profit is therefore $y_F^H = 200(180-50) = \$26,000$.

Second, the firm can lower the price to $p_F^L = \$80$, thereby serving both consumer types. The resulting profit is therefore $y_F^L = (100+200)(80-50) = \$9000$.

Clearly, $p_F^H = \$180$ is the profit-maximizing price when only the original fast model is sold.

(b) Suppose now that the slow (damaged) model is introduced at an extra per-unit cost of $\$10$. Type $\ell = 1$ consumers would buy the slow model if $V_1^S - p_S \geq V_1^F - p_F$, hence, in view of Table 10.5, if $p_S \leq p_F$. Similarly, type $\ell = 2$ consumers would buy the fast model if $V_2^S - p_S \leq V_2^F - p_F$, hence if $p_S \geq p_F - 90$ or $p_F \leq p_S + 90$. These two equations determine the range of prices that segment the market between the two consumer types.

Table 10.5 implies that the highest price type 1 consumers are willing to pay for the slow model is $p_S = \$80$. Therefore, $p_F = 80+90 = \$170$. The resulting total profit is therefore

$$y_{F,S} = 200(170-50) + 100(80-60) = \$26,000.$$

(c) Because $y_F^H = y_{F,S} = \$26,000$, the seller earns the same profit whether or not the slow model (damaged good) is introduced into the market.

Solution to Exercise 10.3. (a) The profit-maximization problem is given by

$$\max_{p_L, p_S} y(p_L, p_S) = (p_L - 20)(240 - 3p_L + p_S) + (p_S - 20)(120 - 2p_S + p_L) - \phi.$$

The first-order conditions for a maximum are

$$0 = \frac{\partial y}{\partial p_L} = -6p_L + 2p_S + 280, \quad \text{and} \quad 0 = \frac{\partial y}{\partial p_S} = 2p_L - 4p_S + 140.$$

The second-order conditions for a maximum can be verified by computing

$$\frac{\partial^2 y}{\partial p_L^2} = -6 < 0, \quad \frac{\partial^2 y}{\partial p_S^2} = -4 < 0, \quad \text{and}$$

$$\frac{\partial^2 y}{\partial p_L^2}\frac{\partial^2 y}{\partial p_S^2} - \left(\frac{\partial^2 y}{\partial p_L p_S}\right)^2 = (-6)(-4) - 2^2 > 0.$$

(b) Solving the two first-order conditions yields $p_L = p_S = \$70$. Therefore, this seller does not provide any loyalty discount and also does not charge any premium to returning customers.

(c) Substituting $p_L = p_S = \$70$ into the above demand and profit functions yields $q_L = 100$, $q_S = 50$, and $y(70, 70) = \$500$.

Solution to Exercise 10.4. Using the same arguments as the ones made at the end of Section 10.4.2 for the sealed-bid second-price auction, it can be established that bidding true valuations, $p_\ell = V_\ell$ also constitutes a Nash equilibrium for the sealed-bid third-price auction.

Buyer $\ell = 2$ clearly wins auction #1 and pays only $98, which is the third-highest bid, $p_3 = V_3 = \$98$. Hence, the net benefit to the winner is $V_2 - V_3 = \$100 - \$98 = \$2$.

The seller flips a coin to determine whether buyer $\ell = 1$ or $\ell = 3$ wins auction #2. The winner then pays the third-highest bid, which is $65. Hence, the net benefit to the winner is $100 - 65 = \$35$.

Buyer $\ell = 4$ wins auction #3 and pays only $20, which is the third-highest bid. Hence, the net benefit to the winner is $V_4 - V_1 = \$100 - \$20 = \$80$.

Solution to Exercise 10.5. (a) Because

$$e_a = \frac{\%\Delta q}{\%\Delta a} = 0.05 \quad \text{and} \quad e_p = \frac{\%\Delta q}{\%\Delta p} = -0.2,$$

by the Dorfman-Steiner formula (10.31), the profit-maximizing ratio of advertising expenditure to sales revenue is given by

$$\frac{a}{pq} = \frac{a}{\$10\,\text{million}} = \frac{1}{4} = \frac{0.05}{-(-0.2)} = \frac{e_a}{-e_p}.$$

Hence, $a = \$2.5$ million.

(b) Now, $e_p = -0.5$. Therefore, $a = 10 \times 0.05/0.5 = \$1$ million.

(c) When the demand becomes more price elastic, the firm reduces the ratio of advertising expenditure to revenue.

12.11 Manual for Chapter 11: Tariff-choice Biases and Warranties

This last chapter introduces the student to some deviations from "rational" behavior on the part of consumers. In other words, frequently it is observed that consumers optimize differently from what economists expect them to do. This chapter briefly discusses some other factors that may affect consumers' decisions that are generally not addressed by conventional microeconomic theory. The presentation is mostly descriptive and therefore can be taught at any level.

The chapter ends with the analysis of the potential profit gain from supplying warranties with the sale of products. This topic may seem to be unrelated to the "behavioral topics" introduced earlier in this chapter; however, because warranties also function as a psychological comforter for buyers, the students can be told that the extra charge for including a warranty as computed in this chapter should serve as a lower bound on how much extra a seller can actually charge for supplying a warranty.

Solution to Exercise 11.1. Mr. Merkel ends up paying €67 for 30 rides. Therefore, effectively, the price per ride is $f/q =$ €67/30 = €2.33, whereas a single ride costs only €2.10 if paid separately for each ride. Hence, by purchasing the monthly pass, Mr. Merkel reveals that he has a flat-rate bias.

Another way of reaching the same conclusion is to realize that had Mr. Merkel chosen the pay-per-use plan, his monthly bill would be $p \cdot q = 2.10 \cdot 30 =$ €63, which is lower than the monthly pass that costs €67.

Solution to Exercise 11.2. (a) The total expected gross benefit from a product sold with a three-time replacement warranty is

$$\underbrace{\pi V}_{\text{Original purchase}} + \underbrace{(1-\pi)\pi V}_{\text{1st replacement}} + \underbrace{(1-\pi)^2\pi V}_{\text{2nd replacement}} + \underbrace{(1-\pi)^3\pi V}_{\text{3rd replacement}}$$

$$= (2-\pi)(\pi^2 - 2\pi + 2)\pi V.$$

The expected production cost to the seller (or the manufacturer) is

$$c_3 = N\left[\underbrace{\mu}_{\text{Original}} + \underbrace{(1-\pi)\mu}_{\text{1st replacement}} + \underbrace{(1-\pi)^2\mu}_{\text{2nd replacement}} + \underbrace{(1-\pi)^3\mu}_{\text{3rd replacement}}\right]$$

$$= N(2-\pi)(\pi^2 - 2\pi + 2)\mu - \phi.$$

A monopoly seller would set the price $p_3 = (2-\pi)(\pi^2 - 2\pi + 2)\pi V$. Therefore, the total profit under a three-time replacement warranty is

$$y_3 = Np_3 - c_3 = N(2-\pi)(\pi^2 - 2\pi + 2)(\pi V - \mu) - \phi.$$

(b) Substituting $V = \$120$ and $\mu = \$60$ into y_3 computed in part (a) yields $y_3(0.9) = \$53.33$, $y_3(0.8) = \$44.93$, $y_3(0.7) = \$34$, $y_3(0.6) = \$19.49$, and $y_3(0.5) = 0$. Thus, profit increases when the product becomes more reliable (an increase in the probability π).

Solution to Exercise 11.3. (a) Expected net benefit under this "half" money-back guarantee is

$$\underbrace{\pi V}_{\text{Expected gross benefit}} - p + \underbrace{(1-\pi)\frac{p}{2}}_{\text{Refund}} = \pi V - \frac{(1+\pi)p}{2}.$$

The expected cost per sale is composed of two parts: the unit production cost μ and the expected refund $(1-\pi)p/2$. With N consumers, expected total cost is given by

$$c_{hmb} = N\left[\underbrace{\mu}_{\text{Unit cost}} + \underbrace{(1-\pi)\frac{p}{2}}_{\text{Expected refund}}\right] - \phi,$$

where the subscript hmb stands for "half money-back guarantee."

In view of the above computed net benefit function, a consumer is willing to buy the product with this half money-back guarantee as long as

$$\pi V - \frac{(1+\pi)p}{2} \geq 0 \quad \text{or} \quad p \leq \frac{2\pi V}{1+\pi}.$$

Hence, the monopoly's expected profit is

$$y_{hmb} = Np - c_{hmb} = N(\pi V - \mu) - \phi.$$

(b) Comparing this profit level with (11.13) and (11.1) reveals that the profit from the half money-back guarantee is the same as under a full money-back guarantee, which is the same as under no warranty of any type. This happens because the seller and the buyers are risk neutral, so a reduction in the risk taken by the seller (from the need to refund p to only $p/2$) results in an offsetting reduction in price, which makes the seller indifferent to all types of money-back guarantees and the no-warranty option.

References

A

Adams, W., and J. Yellen. 1976. "Commodity Bundling and the Burden of Monopoly." *Quarterly Journal of Economics* 90: 475–498.

Anderson, S., and L. Leruth. 1993. "Why Firms May Prefer Not to Price Discriminate via Mixed Bundling." *International Journal of Industrial Organization* 11: 49–61.

B

Bailey, E., and L. White. 1974. "Reversals in Peak and Off-peak Prices." *Bell Journal of Economics* 5: 75–92.

Basu, K. 1997. "Why Are So Many Goods Priced to End in Nine? And Why This Practice Hurts the Producers." *Economics Letters* 54: 41–44.

Baumol, W., and D. Bradford. 1970. "Optimal Departures from Marginal Cost Pricing." *American Economic Review* 60: 265–283.

Belobaba, P. 1987. "Airline Yield Management – An Overview of Seat Inventory Control." *Transportation Science* 21: 63–73.

Bellman, R. 1957. *Applied Dynamic Programming*. Princeton, N.J.: Princeton University Press.

Belton, T. 1987. A Model of Duopoly and Meeting and Beating the Competition. *International Journal of Industrial Organization* 5: 399–417.

Bergstrom, T., and J. MacKie-Mason. 1991. "Some Simple Analytics of Peak-load Pricing." *Rand Journal of Economics* 22: 241–249.

Bodily, S., and P. Pfeifer. 1992. "Overbooking Decision Rules." *Omega* 20: 129–133.

Boiteux, M. 1960. "Peak-load Pricing." *Journal of Business* 33: 257–179.

Boiteux, M. 1971. "On the Management of Public Monopolies Subject to Budgetary Constraints." *Journal of Economic Theory* 3: 219–240.

Brown, S., and D. Sibley. 1986. *Public Utility Pricing*. Cambridge: Cambridge University Press.

Burstein, M. 1960. "The Economics of Tie-in Sales." *Review of Economics and Statistics* 42: 68–73.

C

Camerer, C., G. Loewenstein, and M. Rabin. 2003. *Advances in Behavioral Economics.* Princeton, N.J.: Princeton University Press.

Caminal, R., and A. Claici. 2007. "Are Loyalty-rewarding Pricing Schemes Anti-competitive?" *International Journal of Industrial Organization* 25: 657–674.

Caminal, R., and C. Matutes. 1990. "Endogenous Switching Costs in a Duopoly Model." *International Journal of Industrial Organization* 8: 353–373.

Carbajo, J., D. de Meza, and D. Seidmann. 1990. "A Strategic Motivation for Commodity Bundling." *Journal of Industrial Economics* 38: 283–298.

Chen, Y. 1997a. "Equilibrium Product Bundling." *Journal of Business* 70: 85–103.

Chen, Y. 1997b. "Paying Customers to Switch." *Journal of Economics & Management Strategy* 6: 877–897.

Clay, K., D. Sibley, and P. Srinagesh. 1992. "Ex Post vs. Ex Ante Pricing: Optional Calling Plans and Tapered Tariff." *Journal of Regulatory Economics* 4: 115–138.

Coase, R. 1946. "The Marginal Cost Controversy." *Economica* 13: 169–189.

Corts, K. 1995. "On the Robustness of the Argument That Price-Matching Is Anti-competitive." *Economics Letters* 47: 417–421.

Corts, K. 1997. "On the Competitive Effects of Price-matching Policies." *International Journal of Industrial Organization* 15: 283–299.

Courty, P. 2003. "Ticket Pricing Under Demand Uncertainty." *Journal of Law & Economics* 46: 627–652.

Courty, P., and H. Li. 2000. "Sequential Screening." *Review of Economic Studies* 67: 697–717.

Crew, M., C. Fernando, and P. Kleindorfer. 1995. "The Theory of Peak-load Pricing: A Survey." *Journal of Regulatory Economics* 8: 215–248.

Crew, M., and P. Kleindorfer. 1979. *Public Utility Economics.* New York: St. Martin's Press.

Crew, M., and P. Kleindorfer. 1986. *The Economics of Public Utility Regulation.* Cambridge, Mass.: MIT Press.

D

Dana, J. 1998. "Advanced Purchase Discounts and Price Discrimination in Competitive Markets." *Journal of Political Economy* 106: 395–422.

Danielsen, A., D. Kamerschen, and C. Nicolaou. 1993. "Local Measured Service and the Attributes of a Sound Rate Structure." *Journal of Economics & Finance*, 17: 85–103.

Dansby, R. 1975. "Peak Load Pricing with Time Varying Demands." Bell Labs, Unpublished.

Dansby, R., and C. Cecilia. 1984. "Commodity Bundling." *American Economic Review* 74: 377–381.

DellaVigna S., and U. Malmendier. 2006. "Paying Not to Go to the Gym." *American Economic Review* 96: 694–719.

Demsetz, H. 1979. "Accounting for Advertising as a Barrier to Entry." *Journal of Business* 52: 345–360.

Deneckere, R., and P. McAfee. 1996. "Damaged Goods." *Journal of Economics and Management Strategy* 5: 149–174.

Dorfman, R., and P. Steiner. 1954. "Optimal Advertising and Optimal Quality." *American Economic Review* 44: 826–836.

Doyle, C. 1988. "Different Selling Strategies in Bertrand Oligopoly." *Economics Letters* 28: 387–390.

Drèze, X., and J. Nunes. 2004. "Using Combined-currency Prices to Lower Consumers' Perceived Cost." *Journal of Marketing Research* 41: 59–72.

E

Ekelund, R. 1970. "Price Discrimination and Product Differentiation in Economic Theory: An Early Analysis." *Quarterly Journal of Economics* 84: 268–278.

F

Farrell J., and P. Klemperer. 2005. "Lock-in and Compatibility." In M. Armstrong and R. Porter (eds.), *Handbook of Industrial Organization*, vol. 3. Amsterdam: Elsevier.

Faulhaber, G., and J. Panzar. 1977. "Optimal Two-part Tariffs with Self-selection." Bell Laboratories Discussion Paper No. 74.

Feldstein, M. 1972. "Equity and Efficiency in Public Pricing." *Quarterly Journal of Economics* 86: 175–187.

G

Gabor, A. 1955. "A Note on Block Tariffs." *Review of Economic Studies* 23: 32–41.

Gabor, A. 1988. *Pricing: Concepts and Methods for Effective Marketing*, 2nd ed. Cambridge: Gower Publishing Ltd.

Gabor, A., and W. Granger. 1966. "Price as an Indicator of Quality: Report on an Enquiry." *Economica* 33: 43–70.

Gale, I. 1993. "Price Dispersion in a Market with Advance-purchases." *Review of Industrial Organization* 8: 451–464.

Gale, I., and T. Holmes. 1992. "The Efficiency of Advance-purchase Discounts in the Presence of Aggregate Demand Uncertainty." *International Journal of Industrial Organization* 10: 413–437.

Gale, I., and T. Holmes. 1993. "Advance-purchase Discounts and Monopoly Allocation of Capacity." *American Economic Review* 83: 135–146.

Gehrig, T., and R. Stenbacka. 2004. "Differentiation-induced Switching Costs and Poaching." *Journal of Economics & Management Strategy* 13: 635–655.

Gehrig, T., and R. Stenbacka. 2007. "Information Sharing and Lending Market Competition with Switching Costs and Poaching." *European Economic Review* 51: 77–99.

Glover, F., R. Glover, J. Lorenzo, and C. McMillan. 1982. "The Passenger Mix Problem in the Scheduled Airlines." *Interfaces* 12: 73–79.

H

Hanson, W., and K. Martin. 1990. "Optimal Bundle Pricing." *Management Science* 36: 155–174.

Hirshleifer, J. 1958. "Peak-loads and Efficient Pricing: A Comment." *Quarterly Journal of Economics* 72: 451–462.

Horn, H., and O. Shy. 1996. "Bundling and International Market Segmentation." *International Economic Review* 37: 51–69.

Hviid, M., and G. Shaffer. 1999. "Hassle Costs: The Achilles' Heel of Price-matching Guarantees." *Journal of Economics and Management Strategy* 8: 489–521.

I

Ingold, A., I. Yeoman, and U. McMahon. 2001. *Yield Management: Strategies for the Service Industries*, 2nd ed. New York: Continuum International Publishing Group.

K

Kahneman, D. 2003. "Maps of Bounded Rationality: Psychology for Behavioral Economics." *American Economic Review* 93: 1449–1475.

Kaldor, N. 1950. "The Economic Aspects of Advertising." *Review of Economic Studies* 18: 1–27.

Kaplan, T. 2000. "Effective Price-matching: A Comment." *International Journal of Industrial Organization* 18: 1291–1294.

Kirmani, A., and A. Rao. 2000. "No Pain, No Gain: A Critical Review of the Literature on Signaling Unobservable Product Quality." *Journal of Marketing* 64: 66–79.

Kolay, S., and G. Shaffer. 2003. "Bundling and Menus of Two-part Tariffs." *Journal of Industrial Economics* 51: 383–403.

Kridel, D., D. Lehman, and D. Weisman. 1993. "Option Value, Telecommunications Demand, and Policy." *Information Economics & Policy* 5: 125–144.

Krishna, V. 2002. *Auction Theory*. San Diego, Calif.: Academic Press.

L

Laffont, J., and J. Tirole. 2001. *Competition in Telecommunications.* Cambridge, Mass.: MIT Press.

Lambrecht, A., and B. Skiera. 2006. "Paying Too Much and Being Happy about It: Existence, Causes and Consequences of Tariff-choice Biases." *Journal of Marketing Research* 43: 212–223.

Lautenbacher, C., and S. Stidham. 1999. "The Underlying Markov Decision Process in the Single-leg Airline Yield Management Problem." *Transportation Science* 34: 136–146.

Leavitt, H. 1954. "A Note on Some Experimental Findings about the Meanings of Price." *Journal of Business* 27: 205–210.

Lee, T., and M. Hersh. 1993. "A Model for Dynamic Airline Seat Inventory Control with Multiple Seat Bookings." *Transportation Science* 27: 252–265.

Lewbel, A. 1985. "Bundling of Substitutes or Complements." *International Journal of Industrial Organization* 3: 101–107.

Liao, C., and Y. Tauman. 2002. "The Role of Bundling in Price Competition." *International Journal of Industrial Organization* 20: 365–389.

Littlechild, S. 1975. "Two-part Tariffs and Consumption Externalities." *Bell Journal of Economics* 6: 661–670.

Littlewood, K. 1972. "Forecasting and Control of Passenger Bookings." In *Proceedings of the Twelfth Annual AGIFORS Symposium.* Nathanya, Israel.

Logan, J., and R. Lutter. 1989. "Guaranteed Lowest Prices: Do They Facilitate Collusion?" *Economics Letters* 31: 189–192.

M

McAfee, P. 2005. *Competitive Solutions: The Strategist's Toolkit.* Princeton, N.J.: Princeton University Press.

McAfee, P., J. McMillan, and M. Whinston. 1989. "Multiproduct Monopoly, Commodity Bundling, and Correlation of Values." *Quarterly Journal of Economics* 114: 371–384.

McGill, J., and G. van Ryzin. 1999. "Revenue Management: Research Overview and Prospects." *Transportation Science* 33: 233–256.

Miravete, E. 1996. "Screening Consumers through Alternative Pricing Mechanisms." *Journal of Regulatory Economics* 9: 111–132.

Mitchell, B. 1978. "Optimal Pricing of Local Telephone Service." *American Economic Review* 68: 517–537.

Mitchell, B., and I. Vogelsang. 1991. *Telecommunication Pricing.* Cambridge: Cambridge University Press.

Monroe, K. 1971. "The Information Content of Prices: A Preliminary Model for Estimating Buyer Response." *Marketing Science* 17: B519–B532.

Monroe, K. 2002. *Pricing: Making Profitable Decisions.* New York: McGraw-Hill/Irwin.

Motta, M. 2004. *Competition Policy.* Cambridge: Cambridge University Press.

Mullainathan, S., and R. Thaler. 2000. "Behavioral Economics." National Bureau of Economic Research Working Paper No. 7948.

N

Nagle, T., and R. Holden. 2002. *The Strategy and Tactics of Pricing: A Guide to Profitable Decision Making*, 3rd ed. Upper Saddle River, N.J.: Prentice Hall.

Nalebuff, B. 2004. "Bundling as an Entry Barrier." *Quarterly Journal of Economics* 119: 159–187.

Nelson, P. 1970. "Information and Consumer Behavior." *Journal of Political Economy* 78: 311–329.

Nelson, P. 1974. "Advertising as Information." *Journal of Political Economy* 82: 729–754.

Ng, Y., and W. Weisser. 1974. "Optimal Pricing with a Budget Constraint – The Case of the Two-part Tariff." *Review of Economic Studies* 41: 337–345.

Nunes, J. 2000. "A Cognitive Model of People's Usage Estimations." *Journal of Marketing Research* 37: 397–426.

O

Oi, W. 1971. "A Disneyland Dilemma: Two-part Tariffs for a Mickey Mouse Monopoly." *Quarterly Journal of Economics* 85: 77–96.

P

Phlips, L. 1988. *The Economics of Imperfect Information.* Cambridge: Cambridge University Press.

Pierce, B., and H. Winter. 1996. "Pure vs. Mixed Commodity Bundling." *Review of Industrial Organization* 11: 811–821.

Png, I., and D. Hirshleifer. 1987. "Price Discrimination through Offers to Match Price." *Journal of Business* 60: 365–383.

R

Ramsey, F. 1927. "A Contribution to the Theory of Taxation." *Economic Journal* 37: 47–61.

Ringbom, S., and O. Shy. 2002. "The 'Adjustable-curtain' Strategy: Overbooking of Multiclass Service." *Journal of Economics* 77: 73–90.

Ringbom, S., and O. Shy. 2004. "Advance Booking, Cancellations, and Partial Refunds." *Economics Bulletin* 13: 1–7.

Ringbom, S., and O. Shy. 2005. "Refunds and Collusion." Available for downloading from www.ozshy.com.

Rothstein, M. 1985. "O.R. and the Airline Overbooking Problem." *Operations Research* 33: 237–248.

S

Salop, S. 1986. "Practices That (Credibly) Facilitate Oligopoly Co-ordination." In J. Stiglitz and F. Mathewson (eds.), *New Developments in the Analysis of Market Structure.* Cambridge, Mass.: MIT Press.

Schindler, R., and P. Kirby. 1997. "Patterns of Rightmost Digits Used in Advertised Prices: Implications for Nine-ending Effects." *Journal of Consumer Research* 24: 192–201.

Schmalensee, R. 1981. "Monopolistic Two-part Pricing Arrangements." *Bell Journal of Economics* 12: 445–466.

Schmalensee, R. 1982. "Commodity Bundling by Single-product Monopolies." *Journal of Law and Economics* 25: 67–71.

Schmalensee, R. 1984. "Gaussian Demand and Community Bundling." *Journal of Business* 57: S211–S230.

Seidmann, D. 1991. "Bundling as a Facilitating Device: A Reinterpretation of Leverage Theory." *Economica* 58: 491–499.

Shapiro, C., and H. Varian. 1999. *Information Rules: A Strategic Guide to the Network Economy.* Boston: Harvard Business School Press.

Sharkey, W. 1982. *The Theory of Natural Monopoly.* Cambridge: Cambridge University Press.

Sherman, R. 1989. *The Regulation of Monopoly.* Cambridge: Cambridge University Press.

Shlifer, R., and Y. Vardi. 1975. "An Airline Overbooking Policy." *Transportation Science* 9: 101–114.

Shy, O. 1996. *Industrial Organization: Theory and Applications.* Cambridge, Mass.: MIT Press.

Shy, O. 2001. *The Economics of Network Industries.* Cambridge: Cambridge University Press.

Shy, O. 2002. "A Quick-and-easy Method for Estimating Switching Costs." *International Journal of Industrial Organization* 20: 71–87.

Shy, O., and R. Stenbacka. 2005. "Partial Outsourcing, Monitoring Cost, and Market Structure." *Canadian Journal of Economics* 38: 1173-1190.

Simon, H. 1955. "A Behavioral Model of Rational Choice." *Quarterly Journal of Economics* 69: 99–118.

Simonson, I., and A. Tversky. 1992. "Choice in Context: Tradeoff Contrast, and Extremeness Aversion." *Journal of Marketing Research* 29: 231–295.

Steiner, P. 1957. "Peak-loads and Efficient Pricing." *Quarterly Journal of Economics* 71: 585–610.

Stiving, M., and R. Winer. 1997. "An Empirical Analysis of Price Endings with Scanner Data." *Journal of Consumer Research* 24: 57–67.

T

Talluri, K., and G. van Ryzin. 2004. *The Theory and Practice of Revenue Management.* Boston: Kluwer Academic Publishers.

Taylor, C. 2003. "Supplier Surfing: Competition and Consumer Behavior in Subscription Markets." *RAND Journal of Economics* 34: 223–246.

Telser, L. 1964. "Advertising and Competition." *Journal of Political Economy* 72: 537–562.

Thaler, R. 1991. *Quasi Rational Economics.* New York: Russell Sage Foundation.

Thaler, R. 1992. *The Winner's Curse: Paradoxes and Anomalies of Economic Life.* Princeton, N.J.: Princeton University Press.

Thisse, J., and X. Vives. 1988. "On the Strategic Choice of Spatial Price Policy." *American Economic Review* 78: 122–137.

Thomas, M., and V. Morwitz. 2005. "Penny Wise and Pound Foolish: The Left-digit Effect in Price Cognition." *Journal of Consumer Research* 32: 54–64.

Train, K., M. Ben-Akiva, and T. Atherton. 1989. "Consumption Patterns and Self-selecting Tariffs." *Review of Economics & Statistics* 71: 62–73.

Train, K., D. McFadden, and M. Ben-Akiva. 1987. "The Demand for Local Telephone Service: A Fully Discrete Model of Residential Calling Patterns and Service Choices." *Rand Journal of Economics* 18: 109–123.

Tversky, A., and I. Simonson. 1993. "Context-dependent Preferences." *Management Science* 39: 1179–1189.

V

Varian, H. 1985. "Price Discrimination and Social Welfare." *American Economic Review* 75: 870–875.

Varian, H. 1989. "Price Discrimination." In R. Schmalensee and R. Willig (eds.), *Handbook of Industrial Organization.* Amsterdam: North-Holland.

Varian, H. 2000. "Versioning Information Goods." In B. Kahin and H. Varian (eds.), *Internet Publishing and Beyond.* Cambridge, Mass.: MIT Press.

Vaubourg, A. 2006. "Differentiation and Discrimination in a Duopoly with Two Bundles." *International Journal of Industrial Organization* 24: 753–762.

Venkatesh, R., and W. Kamakura. 2003. "Optimal Bundling and Pricing under a Monopoly: Contrasting Complements and Substitutes from Independently Valued Products." *Journal of Business* 76: 211–231.

Vickrey, W. 1961. "Counterspeculation, Auctions, and Competitive Sealed Tenders." *Journal of Finance* 16: 8–37.

Viscusi, K., J. Vernon, and J. Harrington. 1995. *Economics of Regulation and Antitrust.* Cambridge, Mass.: MIT Press.

W

Wang, K. 1983. "Optimum Seat Allocation for Multi-leg Flights. In *Proceedings of the Twenty-Third AGIFORS Symposium*. Memphis, Tenn.

Whinston, M. 1990. "Tying, Foreclosure, and Exclusion." *American Economic Review* 80: 837–859.

Wikipedia, the Free Encyclopedia. http://www.wikipedia.org.

Wilkie, W. 1990. *Consumer Behavior,* 2nd ed. New York: John Wiley & Sons.

Williamson, O. 1966. "Peak-load Pricing and Optimal Capacity under Indivisibility Constraints." *American Economic Review* 56: 810–827.

Willig, R. 1976. "Consumer's Surplus without Apology." *American Economic Review* 66: 589–597.

Willig, R. 1978. "Pareto-superior Nonlinear Outlay Schedule." *Bell Journal of Economics* 9: 56–69.

Wilson, G. 1972. "The Theory of Peak-load Pricing: A Final Note." *Bell Journal of Economics and Management Science* 3: 307–310.

Wilson, R. 1993. *Nonlinear Pricing*. Oxford: Oxford University Press.

Winer, R. 2005. *Pricing*. Cambridge, Mass.: Marketing Science Institute.

Wolfram, S. 2002. *A New Kind of Science*. Champaign, Ill.: Wolfram Media.

Wolinsky, A. 1983. "Prices as Signals of Product Quality." *Review of Economic Studies* 50: 647–658.

Index

Accounting, 52
Advance booking, *see* Booking
Advance reservation, *see* Booking
Adverse selection, 370
Advertising, 352
Airline industry, 11, 186, 191, 201, 250
Antitrust, 12, 13
    Clayton Act, 13
    per-se rule, 13
    price discrimination, 13
    Robinson-Patman Act, 13
    rule-of-reason, 13
Arbitrage, 6, 79
Auction, 343

Backward induction, 231
Bellman's principle, *see* Principle of optimality
Best-response function, 97–99
Binomial distribution, *see* Distribution
Booking, 2
    computer, 3, 246, 293
    fixed class allocation, 254
    group, 313
    limit, 299, 319
    nested class allocation, 258
    network, 250
    refund, 265
    show-up, 299
        expected, 301
Bounded rationality, 360
Breakeven, 104
    formula, 99
Bumped, *see* Service, denied
Bundling, 7, 8, 117, 118
    multiple, 129

Cable TV, 138, 142, 143
Cancellation, 266
    fee, 268
    probability, *see* Probability, survival

Capacity constraint, 10, 81, 84, 228, 299, 302
Commitment
    buyer, 2
    seller, 4
Complements, 43, 96
Consumer surplus, 45
    gross, 46, 117, 124, 129, 154, 160, 167
        marginal, 46
    net, 46, 117, 129, 154, 156, 167
        marginal, 46
Cost, 53
    average, 53
    fixed, 52, 53, 184, 269
        market-specific, 67
        sharing, 104
    marginal, 52, 53, 231, 248
        capacity, 53, 84, 184, 269, 305
        operating, 53, 184, 269, 305
    operating, 248
    overbooking, 305
    plus, 102
    sunk, 52, 53, 184, 269
CRS (computer reservations system), *see* Booking

Damaged good, 7
Decision rule, 231
Delay, *see* Delivery time
Delivery time, 7, 266
Demand
    aggregate, 34, 74, 76
        vertical, 207
    correlation, 134
    elastic, 23
    elasticity, 23, 24, 28
        arc, 25
        constant, 30, 45, 51, 65, 82
        cross-, 44
    function, 20, 45
    inelastic, 23

inverse, 20, 23, 26
linear, 26, 50, 62, 73, 76
  differentiated brands, 43, 96
  network effects, 39
  single-unit, 23, 34, 48, 133
Differentiation
  vertical, 327
Discount, 6
  quantity, 117
Distribution
  binomial, 301
    expected value, 301
  uniform, 348
Dynamic programming, *see* Principle of optimality

Elasticity, *see* Demand
Equilibrium
  Nash, 345, 348
  Nash-Bertrand, 90, 98, 99, 341
  Undercut-proof, 94
Experience goods, 353
Externality
  network, 39, 40

Flow goods, 21, 214

Group
  booking, 313

Hotels, 147
Hub-and-spokes network, 251

Incentive compatibility, 167
Incentive compatible, 165
Indifference curves, *see* Utility function
Industrial organization, 60, 89
Information goods, 22, 369
Iso-profit curves, *see* Profit

JavaScript, 285

Lerner's index, 64, 66, 108
Leverage, 116
Linear programming, 285
Lock-in, 90
Loyalty, 336

Mail order, 268

Marginal cost, *see* Cost
Marginal revenue, *see* Revenue
Market segmentation, 5, 7, 8, 79, 270
  bundling, 130, 167
  exclusion, 68, 86
  refund, 290
Money-back guarantee, 2, 374
Moral hazard
  refund, 268, 291
  warranties, 370
Myopic behavior, 89, 95

Network externalities, *see* Externality
No-show, 2, 254, 266, 298
  probability, *see* Probability, survival
Nonlinear pricing, 115, 151
Nonprofit organization, 104
Nonstorable good, 182

Outsourcing, 55
Overbooking, 230, 297
  group, 313
  limit, 299

Pareto
  improvement, 332
Peak-load pricing, 11, 182
  shifting peak, 190
Perfect foresight, 40
Population
  large, 229
  small, 229
Preferences
  revelation, 130, 167, 228, 343, 344
Price
  matching, 340
  undercutting, 91, 341
Price discrimination, 5, 12, 79
  antitrust, 13
  behavior-based, 336
  bundling, 115
  classification, 8
  perfect, 119
  refund, 266, 290
Principle of optimality, 231, 245, 253
Probability
  defective product, 370
  survival, 267, 299
    average, 294

moral hazard, 291
Profit
    iso curves, 281
    marginal, 101, 248
    short-run, 62, 87
Public utility, *see* Regulated firm

Quality, 95, 326, 363, 367
    damaged, 332

Ramsey prices, 108
Reaction function, *see* Best-response function
Refund, 2, 265, 374
    lump-sum, 268
    partial, 269
    proportional, 268, 279
Regression, 27, 28, 31, 32
Regulated firm, 104
    multipart tariff, 176
    peak-load pricing, 205
    Ramsey prices, 107
Resale price maintenance (RPM), 274
Reservation, *see* Booking
Reservation price, *see* Willingness to pay
Retaliation, 93, 96
Revealed preference, *see* Preferences
Revealed preference argument, 189, 382
Revelation, *see* Preferences
Revenue, 23
    constant-elasticity, 33
    linear demand, 29
    marginal, 23, 29, 186
        vertical summation, 191, 196
Revenue management, 9
RM, *see* Revenue management
Robinson-Patman Act, *see* Antitrust

Salvage value, 236, 245, 263
SCM, *see* Supply chain management
Scrap value, *see* Salvage value
Search goods, 353
Seasons, 183
Service, 2
    class, 3
    complementary, 228
    denied, 302
        expected, 304
Shifting peak, *see* Peak-load pricing

Shipping and handling (s&h) charges, 268
Show-up probability, *see* Probability, survival
Signaling, 368
Simplex method, *see* Linear programming
Stock goods, 21, 183
Substitutes, 43, 96
Supply chain management, 12
Survival probability, *see* Probability
Switching costs, 90, 336, 339, 342

Tariff
    blocks, 172
    multipart, 151, 171
    two-part, 152
        menu, 165
Telecommunication, 39
Tying, 7
    mixed, 131, 142
    multi-package, 131, 143
    pure, 131

Undercutting, *see* Price
Unit elasticity, 23
Utility function, 46
    iso curves, 281
    refund, 271, 273
    threshold, 271, 273

Value
    of service/product, 4, 270
    of time, 228
Volume discount, *see* Bundling

Warranties, 369
Welfare
    consumer, 12
    social, 12, 105, 106, 119, 176, 177
Willingness to pay, 4, 23, 34, 70, 95, 133, 270, 344, 370

Yield management, 9
    price-based, 10
    quantity-based, 10, 11
YM, *see* Yield management